CARL A. DAUTEN
Executive Vice Chancellor
and Professor of Finance
Washington University

MERLE T. WELSHANS
Union Electric Company
Vice President — Finance

Introduction to Capital Markets

Principles of Finance

Fourth Edition

Published by

F13　SOUTH-WESTERN PUBLISHING CO.

CINCINNATI　WEST CHICAGO, ILL.　DALLAS　PELHAM MANOR, N.Y.
PALO ALTO, CALIF.　BRIGHTON, ENGLAND

Preface

Principles of Finance is intended for the first course in finance. It is a survey of the whole field of finance, both private and public. Emphasis is placed on current problems in the field as well as on basic principles developed from past experience. Financial institutions and the instruments and procedures used for loans and investments to meet the demand for funds in the capital markets are described and discussed, and loan and investment practices are analyzed. The same is true of institutions, instruments, and procedures for providing the supply of funds in the capital markets. A book of this nature provides the necessary background for courses in business finance, financial management, monetary theory, banking problems, public finance, agricultural finance, security markets, and related courses. It is especially appropriate for the student who is taking only one course in the field of finance.

Principles of Finance is organized around four major topics. The first is the monetary and credit system of the United States. The second is meeting the demand for funds in the business sector of the economy; and the third is meeting the demand for funds in other sectors of the economy. The fourth topic deals with monetary and credit policies and problems.

The second and third sections, which are concerned with meeting the demand for funds, are organized by major types of financing. Consideration is given to business financing, both short-term and long-term; agricultural financing; foreign-trade financing; consumer financing; and government financing. The plan of organization by types of financing rather than by types of financial institutions was adopted for several reasons. For one, it shows the alternatives that may be available to a businessman, a farmer, a consumer, or a governmental unit having a demand for money. This arrangement has been used, too, because it helps to show how specialized institutions and procedures have been developed to meet new demands for financing. Furthermore, it provides a meaningful basis for analyzing trends and current problems in the various fields of financing. The expanded loan activities of commercial banks, for example, and the problems confronting bankers can be understood only when their activities in short-term business lending, real estate financing, consumer lending, and other areas of financing are studied, field by field, in relation to the activities of competing agencies in each field.

At one time, commercial banks handled most of the short-term business financing, and this was their major type of financing. Today other institutions have developed to such a degree that a study of banking alone no longer provides an adequate picture of short-term business financing, to say nothing of the other areas of finance. Nor can banking be clearly understood without a knowledge of the workings of other financial institutions. This is true, in part, because most banks today are engaged in many types of financing. Furthermore, fluctuations in the volume of bank credit and in the velocity of money can be understood only if the loan practices and procedures and the factors affecting the volume of financing of these other agencies are understood.

The approach in *Principles of Finance* is thus appropriate for a first course in finance for any student and for the student who will take only one course in the field. Moreover, it is uniquely suited for students in schools of business. It provides the same comprehensive approach to finance as is given in the first course in such other business fields as marketing, personnel, production, and accounting. *Principles of Finance* provides the background that all citizens, and especially prospective businessmen, need for understanding the financial structure of the economy in which they will live and work and the capital markets in which they will seek funds for business operations.

The authors have benefited greatly from discussions with and from helpful comments of their colleagues at Washington University and elsewhere. Especially significant have been the contributions of John W. Bowyer, Jr., Charles Gilliland, Jr., Elmer Lotshaw, Arthur W. Mason, Jr., Robert J. Oppitz, R. Miller Upton, Lloyd M. Valentine, and Arthur G. Vieth.

Carl A. Dauten / Merle T. Welshans

Contents

PART TWO   MEETING THE BUSINESS DEMAND FOR FUNDS

PART THREE   MEETING THE DEMAND FOR FUNDS IN OTHER SECTORS OF THE ECONOMY

A. Financing Special Areas

B. Financing the Consumer

C. Financing Government

PART FOUR   MONETARY AND CREDIT POLICIES AND PROBLEMS

PART 1

THE MONETARY AND CREDIT SYSTEM

1 | Nature and Role of Finance in Our Economy

Finance is so important in a free-enterprise economy that our system is frequently referred to as finance capitalism. Finance deals with the principles, institutions, instruments, and procedures involved in making payments of all types in our economy. These payments include those for goods and services which are bought for cash and those that are bought on credit and paid for later. It also includes payments when intangible claims to wealth, such as stocks and bonds, are purchased. Finance is also concerned with making available for investment in business and government money that has been saved.

A highly developed financial system is at the very heart of an economy such as ours. Large-scale production and a high degree of specialization of labor can function only if an effective system exists for paying for goods and services, whether they are needed in production or are offered for sale. Business can obtain the money it needs to buy such capital goods as machinery and equipment only if the necessary institutions, instruments, and procedures have been established for making savings available for such investment. Similarly, the federal government and other governmental units can carry out their wide range of activities on the domestic and international scene only if efficient means exist for raising money, for making payments, and for borrowing.

A free-enterprise economy can function effectively only if the price system is instrumental in determining which goods shall be produced and sold. The producer who can make and sell a product at a price that yields him a volume of sales large enough to cover all costs and to make enough profit to attract capital for his business stays in business and grows; the producer who cannot stands still or is forced out of business. In short, our economy could not function as it does without an effective financial system.

BASIC REQUIREMENTS OF AN EFFECTIVE FINANCIAL SYSTEM

A workable financial system needs an efficient monetary system, facilities for creating capital by channeling savings into investment, and markets in which to buy and sell claims to wealth to facilitate the investment process.

The financial system must provide an efficient medium for exchanging goods and services. A basic feature of such a system is a unit in which to measure prices, that is, a unit of account, such as the dollar in our economy or the pound sterling in the British economy. This unit of account must be universally accepted in the economy if exchange is to function smoothly. It must also be a reasonably stable unit if it is to be used widely. There must be convenient means for making payments for goods and services purchased, whether the purchase is a pack of chewing gum or a complete business worth millions of dollars. This means that the monetary system must operate with monetary institutions, instruments, and procedures geared to the needs of the economy.

A second essential feature in a highly developed economy is a financial system that makes possible the creation of capital on a scale large enough to meet the demands of the economy. Capital creation takes place whenever production facilities are used to produce buildings, machinery, or other equipment to be used in the production of goods for consumer or producer use. In a simple economy, such as that on a largely self-sufficient, one-man farm, this process, in part at least, takes place directly. The farmer creates capital when he takes time during the winter months to build a new barn or to fashion a new ax handle. In a highly developed economy, this process takes place when some individuals, businesses, or governmental units do not spend all of their current income. They save some of it and make the savings available to others who use them to buy buildings, machinery, or equipment. This indirect process of capital creation can work only if the proper legal instruments and financial institutions exist so that savers are willing to transfer the ownership of their savings to businesses and other institutions having a demand for them.

A third essential feature in the financial system of a highly developed economy is that it provides markets and procedures for the transfer of claims to wealth, such as promissory notes and shares of ownership in a business, and for the conversion of such claims into cash. Such markets and procedures facilitate the process of capital creation since savings will be made available for investment in sufficient sums by a large group of investors only when the saver can quickly and easily convert his claim into cash when he has a need or desire to do so. For example, several million individuals are willing to invest billions of dollars in the American Telephone and Telegraph Company because the facilities of the New York Stock Exchange make it possible to sell their shares of ownership to other investors easily and quickly.

FUNCTIONS OF FINANCE

In our economy, in order to meet the basic requirements of an effective financial system, the government and private financial institutions of many kinds have developed instruments and procedures to perform the following financial functions:

1. Creation of money.
2. Transferring money.
3. Accumulation of savings in financial institutions.
4. Lending and investing money.
5. Marketing of claims to wealth arising out of the lending and investing process.

6. Other activities that facilitate the lending and investing process.

Creation of Money

One of the most significant functions of the financial system is that of creating the money used as a medium of exchange and in the savings-investment process. This money creation function is carried on by agencies of the federal government and also by the banking system.

Transferring Money

Another function performed by some financial institutions is that of transferring money. When money is put into a checking account at a commercial bank, it can easily be used to make payments by writing checks. Many types of financial institutions carry on the other functions of finance, but in the United States only commercial banks are allowed by law to handle checking accounts.

Accumulation of Savings in Financial Institutions

A function performed by many different types of financial institutions is the accumulation or gathering together of individual savings. For example, a commercial bank handles the accounts of many businesses and individuals, many of them small. When all are accumulated in one place, however, they are available in amounts much larger than any individual depositor could supply. From time to time banks and other financial institutions conduct advertising campaigns and other promotional activities to secure savings deposits.

A part of this function of the gathering together or accumulation of savings is that of acting as a custodian of the savings and cash balances of the public. Most individuals, businesses, and organizations do not want to take the risks involved in having large amounts of cash on hand. They, therefore, put them into a bank or other financial institution for safekeeping.

Lending and Investing Money

Another basic function of financial institutions is the lending and investing function. The money that has been put into these institutions may be loaned to businesses, farmers, consumers, institutions, and governmental units. It may be loaned for different purposes, such as to buy buildings or equipment, or to pay current bills. This money may also be loaned for varying time periods. Some financial institutions make loans of almost all types to all groups of borrowers; others specialize in only one or perhaps several types since procedures are different in different types of lending. Some financial institutions invest all or part of the savings that have been put into them in shares of ownership in a business or in debt obligations of businesses or other institutions.

Marketing of Claims to Wealth

Savings may be placed with financial institutions that invest them, or they may be invested directly. For example, a business may want to sell shares of ownership to the general public. It could do so directly, but the process of finding individuals interested in investing funds in that business might be difficult and time-consuming. A type of financial institution (the investment bank) has been developed to sell these shares of ownership, or shares of stock as they are called. This function is essentially a merchandising function. This function is also involved at times in other fields of financing.

Facilitating the Lending and Investing Process

In the process of lending and of selling securities, several types of institutions serve as facilitating agencies. For example, if shares of stock are to be sold to the general public, it is desirable to have a ready market in which such stocks can be resold later if the investor no longer wants to hold them. The several stock exchanges serve this purpose. If lending is to be done effectively, it is desirable to have readily available up-to-date information on the applicants for loans. Various types of credit-checking agencies have been developed to meet this need.

THE DEVELOPMENT OF THE MONETARY SYSTEM

Our monetary system developed to meet the changing needs of the economy. Adequate records to trace the early developments of the system do not exist, but these can be inferred from such evidence as is available and practices that are still in use in the more primitive economies in our world.

Barter

Primitive economies consisted largely of self-sufficient units or groups that lived by means of hunting, fishing, and simple agriculture. There was little need or occasion to exchange goods or services. Even in such economies, however, some trade took place.

As economies became more developed and some men specialized, to a degree at least, in herding sheep, others in raising grain, others as goldsmiths and silversmiths, and the like, the process of exchange became more important. To help facilitate such exchanges of goods for goods, or *barter* as it is known, tables of relative values were developed from past experience. For example, the table might show the number of furs, measures of grain, amount of cloth, and the like equal to one animal, such as a sheep or cow.

This arrangement helped facilitate exchanges, but the process still had many serious drawbacks. For example, if a man had a cow he wanted to trade for some nuts and some furs, he would need to find someone who had an excess of both of these items to trade. The need for a simpler means of exchange led to the development of money.

Early Development of Money

Money is anything that is generally accepted as a means of paying for goods and services and of discharging debts. The record of the early development of money is very sketchy. In all probability traders found that some items, such as furs and grain, were traded more frequently than other items. Therefore, they could afford to accept these items in exchange even when they did not have an immediate need for them since they could always trade them for goods they wanted. They probably also found it convenient to figure the value of goods less frequently traded in terms of these more frequently traded items because the system gave them a familiar yardstick with which to value them.

This development took place in much this same way in some American prisoner of war camps in Germany during World War II. Cigarettes were used as a general medium of exchange of goods and services since they could always be traded for other goods. Values of all types of goods were also quoted in cigarettes even when there was no intention of exchanging them.

Records in early economies show many items that were useful for food or clothing which were used as a general medium of exchange and, to some degree at least, probably also as a unit for measuring value. Included were grain, salt, skins, spices, tea, seeds, and cattle. Some early economies made use of such commodities as beads, ivory, the plumage of birds, gold, and silver for which there was a general demand for ornamentation. Some items that were useful as tools or in making tools, such as animal claws, fishhooks, shark teeth, and stone discs, were also used. All of these items were generally accepted in exchange because there was a demand for them since they could be used for further exchange or as food, clothing, tools, or ornamentation.

These items were accepted by traders as long as they felt certain that they could use them again in future trading. This meant that the supply of the item had to be limited in relation to the desires of individuals in the economy to have the item. In early economies this was generally true of such items as grains, cattle, and tools. Items of ornamentation could likewise be used as a general medium of exchange only if there was an unfilled demand for them. For example, the American Indians valued wampum beads as a decoration and were not able to get enough of them to meet the desires of everyone. Therefore, such beads could serve as a general medium of exchange.

The Use of Precious Metals as Money

When commodities were used as a medium of exchange, goods could be valued in terms of the item used as money and could be exchanged for it. This process, however, was still clumsy and time-consuming. For example, if furs were used, they were bulky and difficult to carry around. Furthermore, arguments could rise over the quality of the furs. It was also necessary to make a trade of goods equal to one, two, three, or more furs since furs lost their value when cut into pieces.

The transition from the use of such commodities as money to the use of precious metals was probably a gradual one, but the advantages of precious metals eventually led to their general usage. Gold and silver were in great demand for ornamentation due to their durability, malleability, and beauty. The supply of these metals was limited enough so that they had great value, which made them easy to carry around as money. They could also be refined into the pure metal rather easily so that their quality was rather uniform. Various quantities could also be weighed out so that exchanges of varying values could be made. In time, coins with a certain weight of metal in them were developed. Since an unscrupulous trader could cover baser metals with gold or silver or put in short weight, however, this process of coinage needed regulation if coins were to be generally acceptable. For that reason coining money and determining the value thereof has been a governmental function since the earliest days.

Paper Money

Each of the commodities used as money served as a medium of exchange because of its intrinsic value. Its value as a commodity made it useful for money purposes. Even in early days, however, things were used at times that had value only as money. For example, large stones that were too big to be moved were used as money in some of the islands in the Pacific. They were useful, potentially at least, for making building blocks or grinding wheels, but they were not used in this way. Their value as money arose out of their general acceptance as wealth.

Since early modern times, governments have issued money in the form of paper. Gold and silver coins are cumbersome to carry around when large transactions are to be made. To facilitate exchange, governments issued paper money to represent certain quantities of gold or silver that were kept on deposit by the government to back such paper. The paper was generally accepted as a medium of exchange because the persons accepting it knew they could get the precious metal when and if they wanted it. Banks also issued paper money backed by precious metals. This was done at first without specific authorization by governmental authorities; but as time went on, governments regulated the issuance of paper money by the banks. Such paper money backed by gold or silver, or *representative paper money* as it is called, circulated freely. As long as individuals felt certain they could exchange it for the precious metal behind it, there was no inclination to do so.

The general acceptance of paper money as a medium of exchange, with no intention of redeeming it for the precious metal behind it, made possible the issuance of paper money with no such backing. From time to time, money was issued based only on the general credit of the government and on the legal provision that such money was acceptable to pay taxes and to fulfill contracts calling for payment in lawful money.

Banks also issued paper money without metallic backing. As such issues were brought under regulation, the banks were required to have some metallic backing for their paper money and to have some form of collateral, such as government bonds, for the remainder of the face value of the money they issued. The privilege of private banks to issue paper money of any type became more and more restricted in all countries and has been abolished in recent years. The only banks that issue any significant amounts of paper money today are central banks, which are owned or controlled by the national government of the country.

Checks

The process of making exchange more and more convenient did not cease with the widespread use of paper money. Today most transactions for any but small amounts are made by means of checks drawn on banks. Funds that an individual or a business has on deposit in a bank are transferred by means of an order to the bank to pay the amount of money stated on its face to a designated person. Most claims between banks as a result of the use of checks are settled by bookkeeping transactions rather than by actual transfer of funds.

Recent Developments

In recent years facilities have been developed for transferring funds in a matter of minutes by wire service. This may be done through Western Union by giving a check to the sending office. The receiving office in turn gives a check to the recipient of the funds. Some banks also have facilities for transferring funds to other banks by wire.

In the last few years procedures have been developed that simplify the process of exchange still further. The federal government found that most employees in the area of Washington, D. C., in which most government offices are located, deposited or cashed their paychecks in one or two banks in the area. This created peak work loads and poor service at the banks each payday. To eliminate this difficulty, some agencies now send an order to the bank to make funds available to the persons listed in the amounts shown and to withdraw the sum total of such funds from the government account. The employees, upon proper identification, can obtain the money due them at the bank. Those who have checking accounts at the bank may have their money credited directly to their accounts. This system eliminates the writing, distributing, cashing, and depositing of many checks, thus simplifying the process of exchange still further. It is being adopted in other sections of the United States for handling payroll accounts.

Plans have also been worked out whereby consumers can charge goods bought at a group of stores under a single charge plan and pay for them once a month at the local bank. A member store sends copies of its sales slips to the bank, and the bank credits the store's accounts with the amount of the sales less a service charge by the bank. The bank is repaid when the consumers pay the bank for their bills. The majority of such credit card banks are linked in a nationwide interchange which allows credit cards to be used in many parts of the country. Such interchanges are continuing to expand and are dominated by the two leading plans, BankAmericard and Master Charge. Thus, bookkeeping entries are replacing the use of checks in many transactions.

The next step in the payment mechanism will probably be one in which credit to a payee's account is made at the same time the payor's account is charged. These transfers will be made by means of a computer-directed communications network. This network would include commercial banks and possibly also other depository institutions which would be linked to point-of-sale terminals in retail establishments and to computers in businesses. Credit cards would be used to activate electronic payment transfers and the use of checks and paper currency would be reduced significantly.

PRESENT-DAY PROCESSES OF EXCHANGE AND OF TRANSFERRING SAVINGS TO INVESTORS

The present-day processes of exchanging goods and services developed to meet the changing needs of the economy as we progressed from a simple nomadic culture to our modern way of economic life. Payments for most transactions are made by means of checks drawn on bank deposits, but currency is still used for many day-to-day transactions.

Individuals

An individual builds up a claim for funds against his employer as he performs services for him. On payday he presents his paycheck to his bank and may ask for part of it in cash to pay for day-to-day purchases and deposit the balance in his checking account. His bank then has a claim against the employer's bank for funds equal to the face amount of the check. The employee writes checks to pay bills for merchandise bought on charge accounts, for utilities, and for professional services. The recipients of these checks then have a claim against the funds on deposit at the employee's bank. They use these claims in turn to make further payments for goods and services, and so on, in a circular process. Thus, the cash withdrawn for minor day-to-day purchases and the checks drawn against the bank-deposit account serve as the means of exchange.

The pocket money and the funds an individual keeps in his checking account serve not only as a means of exchange, but they also serve as a cushion between the receipt of funds and the making of payments. Income may be received weekly, biweekly, monthly, or at even longer intervals of time. Some payments must be made daily, others less frequently. Goods bought on charge accounts and bills for services are usually paid once a month. Some bills are paid only once or twice a year, as for example, property taxes. An individual generally builds up sufficient funds in his checking account to handle his regular monthly payments and also the payments to be made at longer intervals. He may also build up funds to act as a cushion against unforeseen payments, such as unexpected doctor bills, or to tide him over periods in which he may be unable to earn money.

The funds an individual has on hand and in his checking account, therefore, can be divided into two parts. The active balances are used to handle his regular transactions. Funds in excess of the active balances are used for the purpose of cushioning expected and unexpected imbalances between receipts and disbursements.

From time to time an individual may want to make a purchase that requires a payment larger than the funds he has on deposit in his checking account. He may do this by using a revolving credit account at a retail store in which payments are geared to the amount of credit being used or he may do so through a bank credit card plan. At times he may have exhausted such sources or he may need larger sums of money, as for example, when he decides to buy a new automobile. He now has the problem of obtaining a loan from someone who has excess money that he is willing to lend. He could get a loan from an individual directly, but in our economy the demand for such funds is so great that institutions have been developed to facilitate this process of borrowing money.

On the other hand, an individual may find that he has more funds in his checking account than he needs to handle his ordinary transactions and to provide what he feels is a reasonable cushion for emergencies. He then has the problem of using such funds in a profitable manner. He may invest them directly in a business, or he may loan them to a businessman or a consumer who has need for extra funds. In our economy, however, he will probably put them into a savings account at a bank or one of the many other financial institutions that have been developed to invest funds.

Financial Intermediaries

The process by which savings are accumulated in financial institutions and, in turn, lent or invested by them is referred to as intermediation by financial institutions. In the decade of the 1970's the great bulk of all funds flowing into the credit markets was supplied by financial intermediaries. The role of financial intermediaries has been increasing significantly since the early 1920's. In the 1920's somewhat over half of the net increase in the financial assets of households was in the form of securities purchased directly in the credit markets, but by the 1970's such purchases accounted for only a very small amount of the financial savings of households. The remainder of the savings of households, except for net additions to the holdings of currency, flowed through financial intermediaries.

The role of intermediaries has grown because they offer savers the kind of investment opportunities they are interested in. The notes, bonds, and shares of stock offered by most of those seeking long-term funds are not the assets which most of the public is willing to purchase and hold. Financial intermediaries offer such qualities desired by savers as safety of principal, liquidity, convenience, and availability in small denominations—one or more of which are often lacking in market instruments. Financial institutions have offered these qualities in increasingly diversified forms to meet the varying needs of savers and have done so at attractive rates of return. Small savers also have a preference for financial institutions because of the relatively high cost involved in making small transactions for securities and also because it is more difficult to effect transactions in such markets than it is to put funds into a financial institution. The development of government guarantees and insurance and the governmental supervision of such institutions has made them more attractive to small savers. The small saver is also attracted to financial institutions because he has a multitude of choices among institutions, each of which is competing for his funds. This has led to a variety of services and conveniences for the saver as well as an attractive rate of return.

This increase in intermediation is not without its problems. In years of strong demand for credit and strong restraint on the money supply, such as occurred in 1966, 1969, and 1973-74, the percentage of funds moving through financial institutions to the credit markets has decreased significantly. Such rapid shifts of sources of funds create difficulties in the economy since they impede the flow of funds to such sectors as housing which rely heavily on funds from financial intermediaries.

Businesses, Institutions, and Government Units

Businesses, institutions, and governmental units, like individuals, use checking accounts to handle transactions and to cushion any imbalance between receipts and disbursements. They also at times borrow funds and at other times invest excess funds. Like individuals, they usually perform these activities in our economy through financial institutions. They are more likely, however, to invest directly in financial instruments, such as securities, than are individuals.

Since the funds that are saved and invested give rise to economic activity, the total volume of investment is an important economic variable. Since investment cannot take place unless funds are available, the supply of available savings is also of major significance. The relationship between the available supply of savings and the demand for them for investment funds is one of the most important factors in determining the status of economic activity.

THE PLAN OF STUDY

The subject matter of this book includes the functions of finance and the principles, institutions, instruments, and procedures developed to carry on these functions.

PART 1 deals with the monetary and credit system in the United States economy. The development of the use of money and present-day methods for making payments have been considered briefly in this chapter. The remainder of this part deals with the monetary system of the United States and with the role of commercial banks and the Federal Reserve System in providing money and credit to meet the needs of the economy. The last chapter in this first part summarizes the various factors which lead to the expansion and contraction of the money supply.

PART 2 considers the institutions, instruments, procedures, practices, and principles for meeting the demands for funds in the business sector of the economy. The first chapter analyzes the nature of business financing, both short-term and long-term. Section A of Part 2 deals with short-term business financing. First the organization and the operation of commercial banks are presented in some detail because these banks are the major suppliers of short-term business funds. The practices and procedures of other institutions supplying such funds are also considered. The next chapter in this part considers facilitating agencies and some whose major function is in merchandising.

The last chapter in Section A considers the policies which businesses may follow in short-term financing and analyzes the various factors involved in arriving at policy decisions.

Section B of Part 2 is concerned with long-term business financing. The various sources of long-term funds are explored in the first two chapters; next, merchandising and facilitating agencies in this area of financing. The last chapter is concerned with policy decisions on the extent and type of long-term financing.

PART 3 is concerned with meeting the demand for funds in other sectors of the economy.

Section A of Part 3 covers the institutions and procedures developed to supply short-term and long-term funds in specialized areas. The first to be considered is the financing of agriculture and the second, the financing of international trade and foreign investment.

Section B of Part 3 deals with the financing of the consumer, both for short-term and long-term needs. The first chapter develops the role of consumer financing in the economy. The following chapters cover the development, practices, procedures, and problems of institutions that provide short-term and intermediate-term consumer credit, as well as long-term credit to finance the purchase of residential real estate.

Section C of Part 3 deals with the financing of governmental needs. The first chapter considers the financing of state and local governments and the second, the federal government.

PART 4 analyzes the policies and problems in the broad area of monetary and financial policy. The first chapter considers the role of the Federal Reserve System in this area. The second chapter deals with the relationship of the Treasury and its powers and policies to the supply of money and credit in the capital markets. The relationships of monetary policies to interest rates and the money market, to the price level, to business fluctuations, and to international financial equilibrium are explored in turn. The last chapter considers recent monetary and credit policies in the light of their effects on the economy at large.

QUESTIONS

1. Discuss the role of finance in the American economy.
2. Describe the features that are basic in the financial structure of a highly developed economy.
3. Outline and discuss the functions of finance.
4. Discuss the use of barter as a method of exchange, and show how experience with it probably led to the development of money.
5. Which characteristics did the items used as money in early times have in common? Why did these characteristics make them suitable for use as money?
6. Discuss the qualities of a good unit of account in a monetary system.
7. Discuss the probable development of precious metals as money.
8. Describe the development of paper money. Why was it accepted in exchange in place of coins?
9. Discuss the use of checks and bookkeeping transactions as a means of exchange.
10. Describe the role of currency and checking accounts as a cushion to meet imbalances between receipts and disbursements of funds.
11. Describe the adjustments that have to be made when cash receipts and disbursements do not balance for a period of time.
12. What effect, if any, is the increased use and development of electronic data-processing equipment likely to have on the process of exchange?

SUGGESTED READINGS

BRILL, DANIEL H., and ANN P. ULREY. "The Role of Financial Intermediaries in U. S. Capital Markets." *Federal Reserve Bulletin* (January, 1967), pp. 18-31.

BURNS, A. R. *Money and Monetary Policy in Early Times.* New York: Alfred A. Knopf, Inc., 1927.

"Credit-Card and Check-Credit Plans at Commercial Banks." *Federal Reserve Bulletin* (September, 1973), pp. 646-653.

GROSECLOSE, ELGIN. *Money and Man, A Survey of Monetary Experience.* New York: Frederick Ungar Publishing Company, 1961.

KLISE, EUGENE S. *Money and Banking,* 5th ed. Cincinnati: South-Western Publishing Co., 1972. Chapter 1.

Money: Master or Servant? Federal Reserve Bank of New York, 1955, pp. 1-18.

The Story of American Banking. New York: Banking Education Committee, The American Bankers Association, 1963.

Two Faces of Debt. Federal Reserve Bank of Chicago, 1972.

Monetary System of the United States

The nature of money and its development were discussed in Chapter 1. The essential role of a monetary system in the operation and development of financial institutions to supply credit to business, agriculture, consumers, and the government was also explained. In this chapter, the nature and functions of money are developed more fully, and the nature of the monetary system of the United States is also described and analyzed. Consideration is also given to the monetary standard on which the system is based and to the types of money currently in use to meet the needs of the economy.

THE NATURE OF AND FUNCTIONS OF MONEY

Functions of Money

In the discussion of its early development, money was defined as anything which is generally accepted as a means of paying for goods and services and of discharging debts. This function of money is generally referred to as that of serving as a *medium of exchange*. This is the basic function of money in any economy, but money also serves other functions. It serves as a store of purchasing power and as a standard of value.

Money may be held as a *store of purchasing power* which can be drawn on at will. This may be done shortly after it is received or after it has been held for a period of time. While money is held, it becomes a liquid asset for its owner and gives him flexibility in his decision to spend or to invest. But he pays for this flexibility since he foregoes the potential return he could earn by investing his money or the satisfaction he could receive from spending it for goods or services. Money can perform its function as a store of purchasing power only if its value is relatively stable or is increasing.

The function of serving as a store of purchasing power can also be performed by an asset other than money if it can be converted into money quickly and without significant loss of value. This is the case with time deposits held in commercial banks and in mutual savings banks and with savings and loan shares and savings certificates. Such liquid assets reduce the need for holding money itself as a store of purchasing power.

The third function of money—that of a *standard of value*—refers to the fact that prices are expressed in terms of the monetary unit and that contracts for deferred payments are also expressed in this way. Prices and debts are usually expressed in terms of dollars without any statement as to the type of money to be used. The relationship of money as a standard by which to judge the value of goods is a circular one. The value of money may be stated in terms of the goods it will buy, and a change in prices generally reflects a change in the value of money. If money is to perform its function as a standard of value, it is essential that the value of the monetary unit be relatively stable.

Definition of the Money Supply

In a simple economy in which metallic coins were used, it was easy to define money, since only one form of generally accepted medium of exchange was in use. As the forms of payments have been multiplied to meet the needs of the economy, defining money has become more complex; and differences of opinion have developed on the items that should be included. One of the most common definitions of money includes currency and coin in the hands of the public, demand deposits held by the nonbank public in commercial banks, and foreign demand deposit balances at federal reserve banks. It excludes deposits of one bank in another bank since such funds are not currently available for spending; checks and other items in the process of collection and federal reserve float are excluded to avoid double counting. United States government deposits are also excluded even though they are available for immediate use. This is because of difficulties in accounting and double-counting and also because the levels of such deposits have little bearing on the rate of spending by the federal government. The federal reserve refers to this traditional measure of the money supply as the M_1 measure.

A second definition of the money supply, the M_2 measure, also includes time deposits and savings deposits held by the public in commercial banks except negotiable time certificates of deposit issued in denominations of $100,000 or more by the largest banks in the country. They are excluded because they are really not time or savings deposits but money market instruments issued by the banks to attract funds.

A third measure of the money supply, M_3, includes all of the items in the M_1 and M_2 series and also deposits of mutual savings banks and savings and loan shares and savings certificates. Although deposits of mutual savings banks, savings and loan shares, savings certificates, and time and savings deposits at commercial banks cannot generally be used for making actual transactions, they can be converted with ease into currency or demand deposits with little or no risk of loss. They are therefore almost as readily available for spending as demand deposits. In two states, Massachusetts and New Hampshire, funds in such savings accounts can be withdrawn by use of Negotiable Orders of Withdrawal (NOWs) which are checklike instruments. This makes such savings accounts a form of money just as demand deposits are at commercial banks.

DEVELOPMENT OF MONETARY STANDARDS

In any monetary system it is necessary to have a *monetary standard* which states the unit of value and the value of the various types of money in use. In early economies there was no need for a monetary standard since there was usually only one or, at the most, two or three types of money. Such money had intrinsic value because it was demanded to meet some need or for use in adornment or decoration; it therefore had value as a commodity, which gave it value as money. Later when governments began to develop coins on which kings placed their seals to guarantee the weight and the quality of the metal, the unit of account came to be the basic coin that was minted by the government. In more modern times, governments developed the monetary system further to help facilitate commerce. The basic money unit of the country was established by law, and the weight and fineness of the precious metal in such a coin was stipulated. Any other money in use had its value expressed in terms of the standard money. Thus, monetary standards were developed, some based on gold, some on silver, and some on both metals. In recent years the standard in most countries has been paper money issued by the government.

Not only have different monetary standards been used at different times and in different places, but also there has been little agreement as to the best type of money standard. At the outbreak of World War I in 1914, gold was generally used, but the gold standard was largely abandoned during the war and has never been fully restored.

MONETARY STANDARDS

In this section the characteristics of the major types of standards will be considered; first, the various forms of gold standards; and then in turn silver standards, bimetallic standards, and paper money standards.

Gold-Coin Standard

The earliest gold standards were based on gold coins and for that reason were known as *gold-coin standards*. The monetary unit was defined in terms of a coin containing a certain amount of gold of prescribed purity or fineness,[1] and all other types of money were kept at a parity with gold. Gold that was presented

---

[1] Gold coins are not pure gold since gold is too soft. They are an alloy of gold and baser metals, frequently 90 percent gold and 10 percent baser metals. Such coins are referred to as nine-tenths fine.

to the mint was minted into coins at little or no cost to the suppliers of the metal. It was also legal to melt down at will gold coins in any quantity. These provisions were necessary to keep the monetary value of gold and its value as metal the same.

All other types of money that were in use, either coins or paper, were freely convertible into gold at its face value at the option of the holder. In this way the value of all types of money in use was stabilized in terms of the standard gold money since they could be exchanged for gold money at will. Under the gold-coin standard, free export and import of gold was also allowed. This kept the value of domestic gold in line with world gold prices. It also had a tendency to keep domestic prices in line with prices in other countries on a gold standard since prices in all gold countries were based on the price of gold that was determined by international supply and demand.

Most nations dropped the gold standard during World War I, but they planned to return to it in the postwar period. Many found, however, that they did not have sufficient gold or they feared the loss of gold if it became freely available, and therefore some of these nations adopted a gold-bullion standard.

Gold-Bullion Standard

Under a *gold-bullion standard* gold is not coined, and gold coins are not allowed to circulate. The government or central bank still buys gold at a set price in unlimited quantities. The gold, however, is kept by the government or central bank, and other forms of money not convertible into gold are issued to pay for it. In addition to stopping the coinage of gold when a gold-bullion standard is set up, other forms of money are no longer converted into gold or gold coin in any amount requested by the holder. It is possible, however, to get gold bars of a specified weight that are usually worth several thousand dollars. For example, England, in the period following World War I, was on a gold-bullion standard and used bars worth somewhat over $7,500 each.

This use of gold bars having a large value cuts down the demand for gold. Less gold is demanded because gold coins no longer circulate and are not available for hoarding. Gold is available only to those having sufficient money to buy one or more

gold bars. Since gold bars are available, however, for use in industry, to pay for goods bought from foreign countries, or for hoarding if the purchaser prefers to hold gold bars rather than other forms of money or other assets, the value of gold for money and as a commodity in the arts remains about the same.

In some countries, especially the United States in 1933, a modification of the gold-bullion standard, known as the *limited gold-bullion standard*, was adopted. Under the limited gold-bullion standard gold is under the control of the government and may be dealt in only under government regulations. All gold must be turned in to the Treasury or central bank, and gold bars are available only when a permit is issued for their use in foreign exchange.

Under a limited gold-bullion standard, the price of gold as a money metal and its price for nonmonetary uses need not be the same. Persons who desire gold but cannot get it under the regulations may pay a price above the official price. If the official price is below the world price, gold will be demanded for foreign exchange and may be smuggled out of the country instead of being turned over to the government or central bank as required by law.

These modifications of the gold standard have given central banks and governments more freedom in monetary management. The gold holdings of the government or central bank are generally larger under the limited than under a full gold-bullion standard, thus making ordinary changes in the gold supply less significance since there is less danger of reducing the g supply to a level so low that a loss of confidence in mo would result. Under a limited gold-bullion standard, the p bilities of a serious reduction in the gold supply are fewer under a gold-bullion standard since hoarding gold is illegal. However, a nation will still lose gold if it regularly up more claims against it from foreign nations than met from foreign exchange arising out of the sale of g services abroad.

The concentration of gold in the hands of the gove central bank and the decreased demand for gold al possible to issue a larger amount of money on the sam This gives the monetary authorities more flexibility

the money supply and thus makes internal monetary management easier. Problems will still arise, however, if the balance of payments to foreign countries is not kept in reasonable balance over a period of time.

Gold-Exchange Standard

Some countries which have felt that their gold supply was too limited for a gold-bullion or limited gold-bullion standard have tied their currency to gold by basing it on the currency of another nation that has one of those standards. Such an arrangement is referred to as a *gold-exchange standard*. Under this standard the money of a country is redeemable not in gold but in the currency of a foreign country that is based on a fixed amount of gold. Part or all of the monetary reserves of the country may be kept in the form of claims against the money of the foreign country to which its currency is tied.

Some of the nations in the British Empire have used this system to tie their money to the British pound. For a time the Philippines were on a gold-exchange standard based on the American dollar. Their monetary unit, the peso, was not directly redeemable in gold but in United States dollars to which the Filipino government had a claim because it had deposits in American banks. Indirectly, it was possible to get gold for the peso by first getting dollars and then converting the dollars into gold. Thus, the value of the peso was kept on a parity with the dollar and with gold.

Operation of the Gold Standard

When a nation is operating on a gold standard, the flow of gold into or out of a country changes the money supply. As gold flows into a country, the money supply and the basis for credit expansion are increased; when it flows out, they are reduced. This tends to correct imbalances in trade. As gold flows in, for example, the money supply is expanded, prices tend to rise; and therefore a smaller quantity of goods is sold and the gold inflow is stopped.

The gold standard, when in full operation, also tends to promote stability in exchange rates between currencies of different countries that are on the gold standard. This is true because exchange rates are all fixed in terms of gold. The gold standard

also tends to equalize prices for goods in all the countries on this standard. If prices are low in a country, purchases in that country are increased and gold flows in to pay for them. This flow leads to higher prices and a new equilibrium.

If these advantages of a gold standard are to be achieved, certain rules must be followed. Each country must have a supply of gold which is of such a size that changes in the gold supply will lead to significant changes in the supply of money. Trade between nations must be in reasonable balance so that minor fluctuations can be smoothed out by changes in the general price level caused by changes in the gold supply. The economies must be stable so that political factors do not lead to shifts of gold out of a country. Competition must exist to such a degree that changes in the money supply will affect prices and through prices, economic activity. Also, trade between nations must be reasonably free, or the needed adjustments cannot take place.

The automatic features of the gold standard have much to commend them. The conditions outlined above do not exist in most parts of the world today, however; and, as a result, the gold standard has been abandoned in most countries.

Silver Standard

The monetary standard can be based upon silver as the standard metal. Most of the early monetary systems were based upon silver, but such a standard has been used very little since the middle of the nineteenth century. The steps needed to set up a silver standard and to keep it in operation are the same as those described for a gold standard. Modifications of the silver standard, such as a silver-bullion standard, are possible; but these have been used little because silver standards existed primarily in a period in history when governments did little to manage their monetary systems.

Bimetallic Standard

A *bimetallic standard* is one based upon two metals—in practice, silver and gold. Such standards were widely used in the nineteenth century. The American monetary system before 1900 was based on bimetallism, and controversies over the monetary role of silver have been some of the most bitter in our history. Under the bimetallic standard, the unit of value is kept constant in terms of both gold and silver. This means unlimited coinage of both metals at a nominal charge, the right to demand either gold or silver coins for other types of money and to melt them down if desired, and the free import and export of gold and silver. The basic money unit, such as the dollar in America, must be stated in terms of prescribed weights of both metals.

If such a system is set up and the government or central bank freely coins both metals and makes both available in any quantities desired, the relative prices of the two metals tend to remain fixed at their monetary value. They will not be worth less because the metals can be taken to the mint and coined at the prescribed weights and fineness of metal. They cannot be worth more in the market so long as they are available from the government or central bank in exchange for other types of money. It may not be possible to maintain this ideal relationship as will be seen in the discussion below of the disadvantages of a bimetallic standard.

Several advantages have been claimed for a bimetallic standard. While some nations were on a gold standard, some on silver, and some on both, the proponents of bimetallism claimed that it would tend to stabilize prices of goods bought and sold in foreign trade since the value of gold and silver would be stabilized. Some proponents also claimed that it would tend to stabilize all prices since the value of gold and silver together would be likely to be more stable than the value of either gold or silver.

These contentions have some merit, but the advantages were not gained in actual practice because one of the metals usually disappeared from circulation in a country. This could not happen if all countries on bimetallism used the same ratio between gold and silver in their money units and if this ratio were also in line with the overall supply and demand relationships for the two metals for nonmonetary as well as monetary uses. Suppose that 15 to 1 was the correct relationship of the metals to keep both in circulation; that is, that the silver dollar had 15 times as much metal in it as did the gold dollar, and that the market value of the two metals was also in a relationship of 15 to 1. If a country adopted a monetary ratio of 14 to 1, it would find itself actually on a silver standard because gold would be worth 15 times as much as silver for nonmonetary uses and only 14 times as much for monetary uses and therefore would not be minted. If, on the other hand, the ratio were set at 16 to 1, silver would not be minted since its value for nonmonetary uses would be one fifteenth that of gold and for monetary purposes only one sixteenth.

When one of the metals is undervalued as money, it will not remain in circulation, while the metal that is relatively overvalued will circulate. This is an example of the operation of *Gresham's Law*, which states that when several types of money exist in an economy, the one which is most overvalued as money in relationship to the others will circulate while the other types will disappear from circulation. It is often expressed less formally by saying that *bad* money drives *good* money out of circulation.

Inconvertible Paper Standard

Governments have from time to time, and especially in more recent years, set up monetary systems based upon paper money as the standard. This type of standard is usually referred to as an *inconvertible paper standard*. Under systems of this type, all kinds of money in circulation are kept equal in value by having them interchangeable on request to the central bank or government. No attempt is made to keep the value of the paper in any set relationship to any metal. At times the government has stores of metal on hand as a backing for the paper money, or it continues to purchase metal for monetary reserves; but it does not redeem paper money in metal.

At present, paper standards are used in some cases because a country is short of metals and in other cases because it is felt that a metallic base for the monetary system is unnecessary. In the past, however, paper standards have been associated with extreme cases of inflation. This has been due in large part to the issuance of large quantities of paper money to meet emergency needs during wars or severe, protracted depressions.

Since paper money standards have been used in emergency periods, some have drawn the conclusion that they are undesirable and should be avoided if at all possible. This does not necessarily follow, since the past record of paper standards shows that they were introduced when other monetary standards had already deteriorated or broken down completely. Today no monetary standard is allowed to work without management by governmental or central bank authorities. The success of any standard in use today thus depends on the efficiency with which it is managed. There is still some difference of opinion among economists as to which type of standard can be managed most effectively, one based on metals or an inconvertible paper standard. Some advocate a return to a gold-coin or gold-bullion standard whenever the international financial situation is stable enough to warrant it because they feel that such a system can be more effective in promoting economic progress than any managed monetary standard.

Commodity Standard

Some authorities have advocated a *commodity standard* in which the monetary unit is based on a fixed quantity of a group of commodities in the same manner that the gold standard is based on a fixed quantity of gold. The commodities could be such basic ones as wheat, corn, cotton, coffee, sugar, petroleum, coal, pig iron, and tin. The monetary authority would exchange a unit of money for the package of commodities or some multiple of it, and likewise it would exchange those commodities for a unit of money. This plan is advocated in part because it is believed that it would tend to stabilize the economy. As business declined, the monetary authority would buy commodities and so cushion the decline. It would sell them in prosperous times, thus reducing the degree of inflation. Its advocates believe that if most nations adopted such a standard, it would stabilize exchange rates and prices in various countries just as the gold standard would tend to do if it were working automatically.

But the plan has serious shortcomings. It would be hard to agree on the package of commodities initially. To change the package as one or more of the commodities became less significant would be almost impossible politically. For example, if the demand for zinc in industry had declined because other materials were replacing it, zinc would tend to decline in price. In such a case, the amount of zinc in the package of commodities should also be reduced to reflect its changed importance in the economy.

Since this would decrease demand for zinc even further, zinc producers would be likely to exert political pressure to prevent the change. Another shortcoming is that the monetary authority would be swamped with commodities if price trends were downward, or it would have its stocks depleted if price trends were upward. The stock of commodities held in storage could also become quite large if it were increased as the money supply was increased to take care of the needs of an expanding economy. It would have to be increased or a way found to issue money without backing, and this action would defeat the whole plan.

TYPES OF MONEY

Early monetary systems used the standard money to meet the needs of the economy for a medium of exchange. Under a gold standard, silver standard, or bimetallic standard, coins that were circulated had their full monetary value of metal in them. Such coins are known as *full-bodied money* because their value as a commodity is as great as their value as money.

In order to facilitate the process of exchange as time went on, governments issued paper money for hand-to-hand circulation while keeping the full monetary value of such money in gold or silver on deposit in their vaults. It was much easier to carry or hold a large sum of money in bills than in gold coins or silver coins. This plan was also more economical since gold and silver coins are worn down in use. When gold or silver was brought to the government, the holders accepted gold or silver certificates of equal value in exchange, and the metal was stored either as bullion or as minted coins. Such paper money with full metallic backing is known as *representative full-bodied money*.

At the present time in the United States neither full-bodied money nor representative full-bodied money is in circulation. The money we use is *credit money*, that is, money which has a greater value than the value of the material out of which it is made. This includes coins, paper money, and demand deposits.

The use of coins with less metal in them than their value as money developed from the experience with full-bodied money. In earlier times governments issued coins, including those to be used for small transactions, with the full value of metal in them.

When the market prices of metals for nonmonetary uses increased, the coins were often melted down for metal. To prevent this, *token coins* were made with less than their full weight of metal.

Silver certificates backed by silver coins or bullion in the hands of the Treasury were issued for many years. These silver certificates were *representative token money* during most of the period of their existence since the silver used as backing was not equal to the value of the money at current prices of silver.

Governments have from time to time issued paper money without any backing in metal. This money is backed by the credit of the government and is in effect a government promissory note. It is often referred to as *fiat money*.

As commercial banks developed, they too issued paper money or bank notes, at first largely without regulation but as time went on, under more and more stringent regulation. These were promissory notes of the bank or bank credit money. As central banks developed, they also issued such credit money and have in most countries become the only banks with this privilege. These forms of money are at times referred to as *fiduciary money*.

The most widely used form of money in modern times is not currency of any kind but demand deposits in commercial banks that are transferred by means of checks. Checks have replaced currency to such an extent that most authorities have classified demand deposits subject to transfer by checks as a form of money.

These various types of money may be summarized as follows:

    A. Full-bodied money.

    B. Representative full-bodied money.

    C. Credit money.

        1. Token coins.

        2. Representative token money.

        3. Government promissory notes.

        4. Commercial bank promissory notes.

        5. Central bank promissory notes.

    D. Demand deposits subject to transfer by checks.

AMERICAN EXPERIENCE WITH MONETARY STANDARDS

The first monetary act, which was passed under the new constitution in 1792, provided for a bimetallic standard. The dollar,
which was set up as the unit of value, was defined as 371.25 grains
of pure silver or 24.75 grains of pure gold. Thus, the metal in
the silver dollar was 15 times the weight of the metal in the gold
dollar, or there was a ratio of 15 to 1 between the metals at the
mint. Provision was made for gold coins in denominations of
$2.50, $5, and $10, and for silver coins in denominations of $1,
50¢, 25¢, 10¢, and 5¢. All of these coins contained silver equal to
their full face value, the 10¢ piece one tenth as much as the silver
dollar, and so on. Provision was also made for one-cent copper
coins and for half-cent copper coins.

From 1792 to 1834

Prior to 1792 many foreign coins circulated in the United
States, but it was hoped that the provision for minting gold and
silver would provide enough American coins to meet the demands
of the economy. Until American coins were produced in sufficient
quantities, however, provision was made for the use of foreign
coins. Spanish dollars weighing 415 grains of silver nine-tenths
fine, which gave them a silver content of 373.5 grains,[2] were to
be accepted as full *legal tender*, that is, they had the legal power to
be used to discharge debts, and creditors could not insist on payment in any other type of money if the debt was stated in dollars.
All lighter Spanish dollars and all other foreign coins were to be
accepted only for their actual value in metal. These provisions
were unrealistic, since to carry them out meant weighing coins at
every transaction. Most foreign coins were light due to long
periods of use, while the American coins were of full weight. The
result was that American coins were kept on hand and foreign
coins were circulated. Therefore, the early bimetallic standard
resulted in a monetary system making almost exclusive use of

---

[2] The American silver dollar had 371.25 grains of silver.

foreign coins. This is again an example of the operation of Gresham's Law.

Another problem was that the market ratio between silver and gold, which was about 15 to 1 in 1792, changed somewhat in later years to about 15.5 to 1, and France adopted this ratio. As a result, little gold was brought to the mint because it was found to be worth more in the general market than it was at the mint; consequently, the few gold coins that were minted soon disappeared from circulation.

Even though the government issued no paper money, the First and Second Banks of the United States, which were chartered by the federal government, were given permission to do so; and the various states also chartered state banks with the power to issue bank notes. Even though these notes were supposed to be redeemable in specie, in actual practice they often were not kept at a parity in value with metal coins. Our first monetary system therefore consisted of a gold and silver standard with a varied collection of foreign coins of light weights, many types of paper money of varying values issued by state banks, and the notes of the First and Second Banks during their periods of existence.

From 1834 to the Civil War

In 1834 Congress acted in an effort to remedy the situation. The Congressional committee recommendation was for a ratio between gold and silver of 15.6 to 1, which was about in line with the current market ratio. Congress, however, chose to make the ratio 16 to 1. As a result, silver was undervalued at the mint. Consequently, practically no silver was presented for coinage, but gold did start to come into the mint. Silver coins also were melted down since they had more silver in them than their monetary value. Thus, not only silver dollars but also small silver coins disappeared from circulation. To fill the gap, banks issued paper money in small denominations for use as change. Not only was this inconvenient to use, but bank paper money was not of uniform or stable value, and the supply was not large enough to meet the needs of the economy. Therefore, in 1853 Congress provided for fractional silver coins, which did not have their full weight in silver, thus making silver coins token coins.

From the Civil War to World War I

During the Civil War, the United States went on an inconvertible paper standard. To finance the Civil War, Congress authorized issuance of $450 million of irredeemable paper money known as *greenbacks*; $430 million was issued. These notes were made full legal tender, but they were not redeemable in gold or silver. The money supply was about doubled between 1860 and 1865, and wholesale prices more than doubled. Banks refused to redeem their notes in metal, and coins of all types disappeared from circulation.

At the end of the Civil War, there was no immediate return to a metallic standard. Congress provided for the redemption of paper money in metals by 1879. In effect, the country was placed on a gold standard at that time since provision was made for coining no silver dollars but only gold dollars at the prewar gold content, that is, 23.22 grains of gold. The supply of paper money was also restricted since no additional greenbacks were issued, state bank notes were taxed out of existence, and national bank notes could be issued only with specified government bonds as backing. By 1879 prices dropped to less than 50 percent of 1865 levels.

In 1879 the dollar was made convertible into gold, and the country was for all practical purposes on a gold standard. Even before 1879, however, there was strong agitation again to do something for silver, and some of the silver debates in the period to 1900 were among the most bitter in our history. The demand for the use of silver for monetary purposes came from two sources: the silver producers and the groups that were affected unfavorably by declining price levels and, therefore, wanted to increase the money supply as a means of raising prices.

As a result of the silver movement, Congress passed the Bland-Allison Act in 1878. It directed the Secretary of the Treasury to buy from $2 million to $4 million of silver a month to be coined into silver dollars. In 1890 the Sherman Act went further and called for the purchase of 4 million ounces of silver a month. These purchases were not large enough to raise the market price of silver to the mint value, that is $1.29 an ounce. The Sherman Silver Purchase Act was repealed in 1893 because the Treasury found it almost impossible to keep gold reserves since the paper money issued to pay for the silver was turned in for gold. In 1896 William Jennings Bryan ran for president on a platform of returning to bimetallism at a 16 to 1 ratio. His defeat in 1896 and again in 1900 settled the silver issue for the time being, but it came back again in later years.

In 1900 the Gold Standard Act was passed, clearly putting the United States on a gold standard. Most major nations of the world had money systems based on gold, and it appeared as if gold had become established as the monetary base.

From World War I to the Present

During World War I, which began in 1914, most nations left the gold standard as they resorted to inflationary methods of war finance. They planned to return to gold after the war, and many of them did so. The United States did not redeem currency in gold during the war period but restored full convertibility in 1919 at the prewar gold content of 23.22 grains. Gradually other nations returned to gold, and by 1928 the important commercial nations were again on gold, but most were on gold-bullion or gold-exchange standards.

The great depression that began in 1929 again caused most countries to abandon gold, a few in 1929 and 1930 and most of the remaining countries, except for the United States, in 1931 and 1932. In 1933 the United States also abandoned gold under the new Democratic Administration due to the adoption of a policy to reverse the downward trend of prices during the depression.

Legislation that was enacted in May, 1933, gave the President a grant of broad powers over the monetary system. This included the power to fix the gold value of the dollar but not to reduce it by over 50 percent, to fix the silver value of the dollar and re-establish bimetallism if he saw fit, and to accept up to $200 million in silver at a price not to exceed 50 cents an ounce in payment of debts by foreign governments. The Treasury bought gold on order of the President at increasing prices until in January, 1934, it was paying almost $35 an ounce.

At the end of January, 1934, Congress passed the Gold Reserve Act of 1934, which provided for a modified gold standard. The President was given the power to fix the gold value of the dollar at not less than 50 nor more than 60 percent of its former value. This meant that he could fix the dollar between 11.61 and 13.93 grains of gold, which amounted to a price range for gold of between $34.45 and $41.34 an ounce. Acting under this authority, the President set the dollar at 13.71 grains of gold or $35 for a troy ounce of gold of 480 grains. All gold was ordered turned into the Treasury, and no more gold was to be coined. Gold reserves were held in the form of gold bars, and the Treasury laid down regulations under which gold could be held, transported, imported, or exported.

The changing of the gold content of the dollar created a problem since many mortgage and bond contracts had been written in terms of gold coins of the weight and fineness current at the time such contracts were executed. Congress passed a resolution which made all future gold clauses void and provided that such obligations in existing contracts could be settled by any coin or currency which was legal tender, and all coins and currency were designated as such. The Supreme Court held in a split decision that the gold clause resolution was constitutional.

The Gold Reserve Act placed the United States on a limited gold-bullion standard. Gold was available from the Treasury under regulation for use in settling foreign balances but not for private holding. The value of the dollar in terms of gold was later fixed by Congress at 1/35 of an ounce, with the provision that this ratio could not be changed except by an act of Congress.

Near the end of World War II the United States became a part of an international monetary system developed at the Bretton Woods monetary conference by joining the International Monetary Fund. Parity rates for the currency of each member nation were defined in terms of gold. They were to be altered only to correct fundamental disequilibrium problems in the balance of payments of a country. The United States chose to meet its obligation to maintain its currency at the fixed rate through purchases and sales of gold at $35 an ounce.

In 1968 the International Monetary Fund approved the issuance of Special Drawing Rights (SDR's) which are a form of reserve asset or paper gold, as they are at times called. They are account entries in the books of the International Monetary Fund which are separate from all other accounts and are divided among the members in accordance with their quotas in the fund. The SDR's can be used to meet balance-of-payments deficits with other countries. Countries which hold SDR's receive interest on them at a rate set by the Board of Governors of the Fund and each country must pay a charge to the Fund for its allocations of SDR's.

Even though the United States adopted a limited gold-bullion standard in 1934, programs to aid silver continued. Some silver was accepted in payment of war debts, and silver was bought and added to our monetary reserves under the provisions of the 1933 monetary legislation. Pressure existed to do more for silver, however, and Congress passed the Silver Purchase Act in June, 1934. The Act directed the Secretary of the Treasury to buy silver until the silver stocks were equal to one fourth of the combined silver and gold stocks or until silver increased in price to $1.29 an ounce, its former monetary value under bimetallism. Large amounts of silver were bought under this program. In 1939 Congress directed that the buying price should be 71.11 cents for all newly mined domestic silver, and in 1946 it fixed a minimum buying and selling price of 90.5 cents an ounce. Thus, even though the United States was on a limited gold-bullion standard, monetary reserves were kept in both gold and silver.

In the post-World War II period the demand for silver for industrial uses increased markedly while the supply went up only slightly. The Treasury sold silver at 91 cents per ounce until November, 1961, and then suspended sales because its stocks were being depleted at a rapid rate. In November, 1961, the Treasury started withdrawing $5 and $10 silver certificates from circulation to be replaced by federal reserve notes. In June, 1963, Congress repealed the law that required the Treasury to purchase silver at 90.5 cents an ounce and authorized the issuance of $1 and $2 federal reserve notes to replace $1 and $2 silver certificates. This therefore relieved the Treasury of all responsibility for issuing paper money.

From July, 1963, to July, 1967, the Treasury sold silver for $1.29 an ounce; and after July, 1967, it sold only limited amounts at current market prices which rose well above $1.29. The Coinage Act of 1965 eliminated the use of silver in dimes and quarters and cut the silver content of half dollars from 90 percent to 40 percent. In May, 1967, the Treasury banned the melting, treatment, and export of silver coins and discontinued the sale of silver to all except domestic concerns using the metal in their business. In June, 1967, Congress passed legislation which provided that after June 24, 1968, silver certificates would no longer be redeemable in silver but would continue to be legal tender.

In the period after the early 1950's the dollar became a major component of the international currency of the world along with gold. Problems arose because the dollar became overvalued based on the fixed conversion rate between gold and the dollar at $35 an ounce and many currencies became undervalued. In August, 1971, the Treasury suspended the convertibility of the dollar into gold and dollar prices of most major foreign currencies rose. In December of 1971, agreement was reached by a group of ten major trading countries to appreciate the value of their currencies against the dollar by about 12 percent. As part of this agreement, known as the Smithsonian Agreement, the United States also agreed to raise the official dollar price of gold from $35 to $38 an ounce. Although there was still a sizeable deficit in the balance of payments for 1972, the dollar was devalued again in February, 1973, by 10 percent and the official price of gold raised from $38 an ounce to $42.22 per ounce.

In the fall of 1973 Congress amended the Gold Reserve Act of 1934 so as to permit private citizens to hold gold when the President finds that such action would not adversely affect the U.S. international monetary position. The President set January 1, 1975, as the date on which private citizens could hold gold either in the form of coins or of bullion.

THE PRESENT MONETARY SYSTEM OF THE UNITED STATES

The monetary system of the United States since August 15, 1972, is based on a dollar standard. Gold is worth $42.22 an ounce for monetary purposes, but this is only an accounting measure since the dollar is not convertible into gold. The gold stocks of the country are held by the Treasury, and at the end of December, 1973, amounted to $11.6 billion.[3] Gold certificates are issued

---

[3] *Federal Reserve Bulletin*, February, 1974, p. A15.

Table 2-1

KINDS OF UNITED STATES CURRENCY OUTSTANDING AND IN CIRCULATION

(Condensed from Circulation Statement of United States Money, issued by Treasury Department. In millions of dollars.)

Kind of Currency	Total, Out-standing Dec. 31, 1973	Held in the Treasury				Currency in Circulation [1]		
		As Security Against Gold Certificates	Treasury Cash	For F.R. Banks and Agents	Held by F.R. Banks and Agents	1974 Jan. 31	1973 Dec. 31	1973 Jan. 31
Gold	11,567	(11,460)	107					
Gold certificates	(11,460)			[2]11,459	1			
Federal Reserve notes	68,161		159		5,465	61,529	64,130	56,428
Treasury currency—Total	8,716		78		312	8,351	8,368	7,884
Dollars	767		5		27	736	733	675
Fractional coin	7,338		71		284	7,006	7,026	6,599
United States notes	323		1			321	321	320
In process of retirement [3]	288					288	288	290
Total—Jan. 31, 1971	[4]87,460	(11,460)	344	11,459	5,778	69,880		
Dec. 31, 1973	[4]88,443	(11,460)	317	11,459	4,170		72,497	
Jan. 31, 1973	[4]80,683	(10,303)	372	10,302	5,697			64,312

[1] Outside Treasury and F.R. Banks. Includes any paper currency held outside the United States and currency and coin held by banks.

[2] Consists of credits payable in gold certificates, the Gold Certificate Fund—Board of Governors, FRS.

[3] Redeemable from the general fund of the Treasury.

[4] Does not include all items shown, as gold certificates are secured by gold. Duplications are shown in parentheses.

Note.—Prepared from Statement of United States Currency and Coin and other data furnished by the Treasury. For explanation of currency reserves and security features, see the Circulation Statement or the Aug. 1961 Bulletin, p. 936.

SOURCE: *Federal Reserve Bulletin*, February, 1974, p. A15.

against this gold and are held by the federal reserve banks and their agents.

Federal reserve notes issued by the federal reserve banks are obligations of the United States and also a first lien on all the assets of the federal reserve bank that issues them. They are secured by deposit with the federal reserve of gold certificates, eligible commercial paper, or direct obligations of the United States government. On December 31, 1973, over $64.1 billion in federal reserve notes were in circulation.[4]

At the end of 1973 there were still $767 million in the form of dollars in the money supply and $7,338 million in the form of fractional coins. United States notes or greenbacks are still part of our money supply; and on December 31, 1973, there were $323 million of these outstanding.[5]

Data on each of these types of money and on the amounts of each held by the Treasury, federal reserve banks and agents, and in circulation are shown in Table 2-1.

The average balance of demand deposits held by the public in December, 1973, was $215.5 billion; and the average of currency in circulation was $62.6 billion, making a total money supply of $278.1 billion. Time and savings deposits at commercial banks, excluding negotiable time certificates of deposit of $100,000 or more during this same month were $297.7 billion and deposits at mutual savings banks and savings capital at savings and loan associations totalled $321.7 billion.[6]

QUESTIONS

1. Describe the functions of money. Why must the value of money be relatively stable if it is to perform each of these functions?
2. Define money as it exists in the United States today. Explain why each of the following was or was not included in your definition:
   a. Currency in banks.
   b. Deposits of the federal government in commercial banks.
   c. Time deposits in commercial banks.
   d. Savings and loan shares.
3. Briefly trace the development of monetary standards.

---

[4] *Ibid.*
[5] *Ibid.*
[6] *Ibid.*, p. 16.

4. Describe the operation of the gold-coin standard.
5. Describe the operation of the gold-bullion standard and the limited gold-bullion standard.
6. How does shifting from the gold-coin standard to a gold-bullion standard affect monetary management?
7. What is the gold-exchange standard? Why has it been used?
8. Describe the bimetallic standard. What are its advantages over a single-metal standard? Its disadvantages?
9. What is an inconvertible paper standard? Why has it often been associated with inflation?
10. Describe the operation of a commodity standard. What problems would arise if such a standard were adopted?
11. Briefly trace American experience with monetary standards before World War I and from World War I to the present.
12. Describe our present monetary system.

SUGGESTED READINGS

BURKE, WILLIAM, and YVONNE LEVY. *Silver: End of An Era*. Federal Reserve Bank of San Francisco, 1973.

DEWEY, D. R. *Financial History of the United States*, 12th ed. New York: Longmans, Green & Company, 1934.

HALL, CHARLES W. "Defining Money: Problems and Issues." *Economic Review*, Federal Reserve Bank of Cleveland, October, 1971, pp. 3-12.

KLISE, EUGENE S. *Money and Banking*, 5th ed. Cincinnati: South-Western Publishing Co., 1972. Chapters 2, 3, and 4.

LAUGHLIN, J. L. *The History of Bimetallism in the United States*. New York: D. Appleton & Co., 1892.

"Revision of the Money Stock Measures and Member Bank Reserves and Deposits." *Federal Reserve Bulletin* (February, 1973), pp. 61-79.

3 | Commercial Banking

The importance of the nation's banking system to the processes of a modern industrial economy can hardly be exaggerated. The banking system is an integral part of the monetary system, accumulating and lending idle funds, facilitating the transfer of money, and providing for its safekeeping. As an indication of the importance of the banking system to business, more than $150 billion was outstanding in loans to business by the banks of the United States at midyear 1973. The banking system also provides part of the long-term financing required by industry, by commerce, and by the farmer. It plays an important part, too, in financing the construction of the nation's millions of homes; and it is an important source for personal loans.

It is necessary to distinguish between commercial banks and the many other types of bank organizations, such as savings banks and investment banks. Briefly, *commercial banks* may be described as those banking institutions that provide "checking deposit" facilities. Although the modern commercial bank performs many functions and services that are provided by other banking and nonbanking establishments, the checking account gives to the commercial banking system its unique significance.

In this chapter the development, the functions, and the organization of commercial banks are described, followed by a discussion of bank failures and insurance of bank deposits.

DEVELOPMENT OF BANKING IN THE UNITED STATES

The structure of the modern commercial banking system is the result of historical forces as well as of modern-day banking requirements. Banking, like most forms of economic activity, is more subject to the forces of tradition than to those of innovation. Yet, despite the great influence of early banking practices and legislation on present-day banking, the evolution of commercial banks to meet the requirements of the modern industrial economy has been effective and successful. Nor may we assume that the present structure of commercial banking has achieved permanence. To meet the requirements of a dynamic economy, changes are constantly taking place with respect to banking practices, regulation, and legislation. An understanding of banking in the United States today, therefore, requires an understanding of the development of banking in the economic history of the country.

Banking in America Before the Civil War

Early banking in the United States developed under circumstances that explain much of the apparent confusion and difficulty that accompanied such development. The population lived for the most part on farms; families were self-sufficient; and transportation and communications were poor. The friction between proponents of a strong central government as opposed to state government existed in the early years of our history as it does today. Much controversy raged over the power to charter and regulate banks. The country had little experience in money and financial management.

Early Chartered Banks. During the colonial period, banking took the form of small unincorporated banks that were established to ease the shortage of capital in businesses. Their operations consisted largely in the issue of their own notes. Outside of the larger towns, deposit banking was of minor significance. It was not until 1782 that the first incorporated bank was created along modern lines. The Bank of North America was established in Philadelphia then by Robert Morris to assist in the financing of the Revolutionary War. This bank set a good example for successful banking. Its notes served as a circulating monetary medium, it loaned liberally to the United States government, and it redeemed its own notes in specie upon demand. Two years later the Bank of Massachusetts and the Bank of New York were established. These three incorporated banks constituted the total of such banks until 1790.

The First Bank of the United States. Alexander Hamilton, the first Secretary of the Treasury of the United States, had for several years harbored the idea of a federally chartered bank that would adequately support the rapidly growing economy and would give financial assistance to the government during its crises. His recommendations were submitted to the House of Representatives of the United States in 1790, and in 1791 a 20-year charter was issued to the First Bank of the United States. Although this bank served the nation effectively in the issuance of notes, in the transfer of funds from region to region, in providing useful service to the government, and in curbing the excessive note issues of state banks by presenting such notes periodically for redemption, strong opposition existed to the renewal of its charter; and it ceased operations in 1811. The antagonism of state banking interests was an important cause of the failure of the Bank to have its charter renewed.

Following the expiration of the charter of the First Bank of the United States, the number of state banks increased rapidly, as did the volume of their note issues. Most of the state banks ceased redeeming their notes in gold and silver, and the abuses of banking privileges were extensive.

The Second Bank of the United States. The Second Bank of the United States was chartered primarily to restore order to the chaotic banking situation that had developed after the First Bank of the United States ceased operations. Like the First Bank of the United States, it received a 20-year charter. It began operations in 1816 and, after a short period of mismanagement, set upon a course of reconstruction of sound banking practices. It ably served individuals, businesses, and the government by accepting deposits, making loans, issuing notes, and restraining the note-issuing practices of state banks by presenting periodically the notes of such banks for redemption. The Second Bank of the United States also played a most important and efficient role as fiscal agent for the government.

In 1833 President Andrew Jackson and many of his associates embarked upon such a vigorous campaign against the Second Bank of the United States that it became apparent that its charter would not be renewed upon expiration in 1836. Not until 1863 was another bank in the United States to receive a federal charter.

State Banks from 1836 to the Civil War. Following expiration of the Second Bank's charter, the excesses that had plagued the period 1811-16 again came into play. This period is characterized as one of "wildcat" banking. Although many state banks operated on a conservative and very sound basis, the majority of them engaged in risky banking practices through excessive note issues, lack of adequate bank capital, and insufficient reserves against their notes and deposits.

Because the notes of even the well-established banks were· often of inferior quality, it was easy for skillful counterfeiters to increase the denomination of notes. Also, because of the poor communications that existed between various sections of the country, it was quite often difficult for a banker to be certain of the nature of the notes presented to him. Skillfully prepared counterfeit notes frequently circulated with greater freedom than did the legitimate notes of weak and little-known banks.

In spite of the many abuses of state banks during this period, New York, Massachusetts, and Louisiana originated banking legislation of a highly commendable nature, much of which provided the basis for the establishment of the National Banking System in 1863.

Banking in America from the Civil War to the Present

In 1863 the National Banking Act again made it possible for banks to receive federal charters. So many amendments were submitted for the improvement of the National Banking Act of 1863 that it was repealed in its entirety in 1864. The National Banking Act of June 3, 1864, represented a complete revision of the Act of 1863. This legislation provided the basis for our present national banking laws.

As for the First Bank and the Second Bank of the United States, the reasons for federal interest in the banking system were to provide for a sound banking system and to curb the excesses of the state banks. Probably an important additional purpose of this legislation was to provide for the financing of the Civil War. Secretary of the Treasury Salmon P. Chase and others believed that government bonds could be sold to these nationally chartered banks, which could in turn issue their own notes based in part on the government bonds so purchased.

Through the National Banking Act, various steps were taken to promote safe banking practices. Among other things, minimum capital requirements were established for banks with federal charters, loans were regulated with respect to safety and liquidity, a system of supervision and examination was instituted, and minimum reserve requirements against notes and deposits were established. These reform measures, in general, were constructive; but, in some instances, they have been regarded as altogther too restrictive, as in the case of forbidding loans against real estate. Much of the criticism of the national banking system, in fact, was derived from the inflexibility of its limitations, many of which were either modified or eliminated in 1913 with the establishment of the Federal Reserve System.

The National Banking Act did not establish a system of central banks; it only made possible the chartering of banks by the federal government. The Federal Reserve Act of 1913 brought to the American economy a system of central banks. The Federal Reserve System was designed to eliminate many of the weaknesses that had persisted under the National Banking Act and to increase the effectiveness of commercial banking in general. It brought with it not only strong central domination of banking practices but also many services to commercial banks. The influence of the Federal Reserve System is described in Chapter 4.

The changing character of the economy and the demands placed on the banks and other financial institutions of the nation require a constant evolution. The *Hunt Commission*, a special governmental task force created as a result of a recommendation by the President in his 1970 Economic Report, was charged with the responsibility of recommending changes in the existing structure of banking and other financial institutions. The recommendations of the Commission have been debated intensely. Among the more controversial features of its report were support for statewide branch banking in all states, mandatory membership in the Federal Reserve System for all insured banks, and a restructuring of the federal bank regulatory agencies. These technical aspects of banking are described in this and later chapters.

FUNCTIONS OF COMMERCIAL BANKS

The basic functions of the modern commercial bank are (1) the acceptance of deposits and (2) the granting of loans to business borrowers and to others. In accepting deposits, the commercial bank provides an alternative to the hoarding of funds for future use on the part of the public. Individuals and businesses seldom wish to spend their money as it becomes available; and without the depositary facilities of the bank, such funds may lie idle. Having accumulated deposits, the commercial bank puts them to use through loans to persons and businesses having immediate use for them. The result of the pooling of funds by the commercial banks is a more effective utilization of funds.

Corollary to the acceptance of deposits by commercial banks are the functions of (3) safekeeping for depositors, (4) the efficient and economical transfer of claims to deposits through check-writing procedures, and (5) the record of transactions provided the depositor through the regular bookkeeping and reporting procedures of the bank.

In the granting of business loans, the commercial bank accomplishes a desirable objective of (6) selection of risks. The banker's refusal to finance an ill-conceived venture is in the interest of the bank in protecting its assets, but it may also be in the interest of the prospective operators of the new venture, preventing them from engaging in an activity that will result in loss to them. Furthermore, the careful apportionment of loan funds to those businesses with the best apparent chances of success makes possible the development of the nation's resources to the greatest possible advantage.

ESTABLISHMENT AND ORGANIZATION OF THE COMMERCIAL BANK

In organizing a bank, the first decision to be made is whether the charter application will be made to a state or to the federal government. Many factors enter into this decision. In some states the requirements for bank operation may be considerably less restrictive than those of the federal government. If it is the intention of the bankers to affiliate their bank with the Federal Reserve System, however, or to carry bank deposit insurance provided by the Federal Deposit Insurance Corporation, some of the advantages that would otherwise accrue to a bank through a state charter may be eliminated since both the Federal Reserve System and the Federal Deposit Insurance Corporation insist upon the right to, supervise and examine all participating banks. Many states, on the other hand, have banking laws that are quite as restrictive as are those of the federal government. The prestige of a charter from the federal government may also be an important factor in the determination of a choice of national bank versus state bank status.

Application for Charter

Assuming that a national bank is to be organized, a formal application must be submitted to the Comptroller of the Currency in the United States Treasury Department by the persons desiring to establish the new bank. A complete examination is made of the proposal. The examination includes not only the possibilities for success of the new venture and the need for such banking facilities in the community but also an investigation into the background and qualifications of the persons who will operate the bank. If the report of the examiners is favorable, the venture is permitted to issue its stock to subscribers and cash may be paid into the organization. When the appropriate amount of cash has been paid in and the minimum paid-in surplus established, a certificate of authority to commence business is issued.

Minimum Capital Requirements

One of the requirements of banks with federal charters relates to the amount of capital. If the bank under consideration is to be established in a community having a population of less than 6,000, a minimum capital of $50,000 is required. In cities of more than 6,000 and less than 50,000 population, $100,000 is the minimum capital requirement. In cities of more than 50,000 population, at least $200,000 is required.

National banks are required to begin operations with paid-in surplus of at least 20 percent of the capital stock, to be obtained, of course, through the sale of stock at a premium. (Further, national banks must add not less than one tenth of their net profits to surplus until the surplus is equal to the common stock.) The initial paid-in surplus is to provide for the costs of organization and early losses that may be realized. The organizers of the bank must then decide whether funds secured from the sale of capital stock are to be used to purchase land, buildings, or equipment, or whether such facilities will be leased and the capital funds invested directly in earning assets. The *earning assets* of a bank include all of its investments that provide an income, such as promissory notes, government bonds, and real estate mortgages.

Bank Deposits

Up to this point, the activities of the bank in question differ but little from those of an industrial enterprise. It is here, however, that we diverge from the pattern of industrial operations. Earnings on bank capital alone are hardly sufficient to provide a satisfactory profit to the stockholders; in fact, it would be impossible to operate on a satisfactory basis with no other funds to invest. To increase the earning assets of a bank, other persons and businesses are invited to become customers of the bank and to deposit their funds with the bank. As such deposits are presented to the bank, both the assets and the liabilities of the bank are increased. On *checking-account* or *demand deposits* no interest is paid, and the money earned on the reinvestment of these deposits serves to defray the expenses of bank operations and to provide a net return to the stockholders of the bank.

On *time* or *savings deposits*, which are not legally subject to immediate withdrawal, the depositors may receive a return on their deposits. In the case of either demand deposits or time deposits, however, the specific identity of the items deposited is lost. A claim exists only to a certain amount of money. The bank, therefore, is free to invest the depositor's money and to shift such investments from one form to another within the limits permitted by regulation. The more money a bank attracts from depositors, the larger the possible volume of earning assets the bank will have and, of course, the larger the earnings to the stockholders, other things remaining the same.

Relationship of Deposits to Capital

Although a large volume of deposits makes possible greater earnings for the stockholders of the bank, the larger the volume of deposits in relation to the capital contribution of the stockholders, the smaller the margin of safety for depositors. While the initial function of bank capital is to provide for the buildings and equipment necessary for operations, it serves also as a cushion for possible bank losses. The depositors of a bank, in fact, are creditors and hence have a claim prior to that of the stockholders in case of liquidation. The depositors of a bank lose nothing until the entire stockholder contribution and accumulation is exhausted, at which time the bank is rendered insolvent.

When the deposits of a bank are high in relation to capital funds, it may be said that the stockholders are assuming a small proportion of the risk of the bank and the depositors a large share of the risk. When the deposits of a bank are low relative to its capital funds, the bank will probably be in a poor position to pay satisfactory dividends to the stockholders unless the assets of the bank provide an unusually high yield.

For many years the Federal Deposit Insurance Corporation recommended a ratio of deposits to capital funds of no more than 10 to 1.[1] However, few banks were able to qualify with respect to this recommended ratio. The principal reason for the failure of many banks to maintain such a ratio was the tremendous monetary expansion during and following World War II, which resulted in a corresponding expansion of deposits in the banking

---

[1] The deposits to capital ratio of 10 to 1, for which there appears to be little scientific basis, was in use long before the Federal Deposit Insurance Corporation came into existence. This organization is described later in the chapter.

system. In an effort to maintain a favorable relationship between deposits and capital funds, many banks sold additional stock. Other banks established a policy of retaining a substantial part of their earnings in their surplus account in order to boost the ratio. In recent years the deposits to capital ratio of most commercial banks has been greatly strengthened.

The composition of a bank's earning assets is more important than the simple relationship between the volume of deposits and its capital funds. For example, if the bulk of a bank's deposits and capital is invested in government bonds, high-grade municipal securities, and government guaranteed real estate mortgages, the high ratio between total deposits and capital funds is not so serious as would be the case if the bank had the bulk of its funds invested in less secure assets. By the same token, if a bank has most of its earning assets invested in extremely safe securities, the yield from such investments will be rather modest; and a high ratio between total deposits and capital funds will be necessary in order to avail the stockholders of a competitive rate of return on their investment. For regulatory purposes, authorities now place primary emphasis on a careful examination of the quality of bank assets rather than on a simple application of ratios.

Nonearning Bank Assets

Not all of a bank's funds are available for profitable investment. A bank will maintain a certain amount of vault cash to meet the day-to-day cash transactions, deposits with other banks, and legal reserves as established by regulatory authorities.[2] These funds provide no interest return for the bank.

Concentration in Banking Control

Concentration in banking control has taken a number of forms as banks, like other businesses, have increased their scope and volume of operations to accommodate the growing economy. Yet, commercial banks in the United States are typically single-unit organizations, each bank having its own board of directors and stockholders, exercising no control over branch offices, and

---

[2] The individual classes of bank assets are described in greater detail in Chapter 8.

in turn being responsible to no parent organization. At year end 1973, of the 14,000 commercial banks in the United States, approximately 4,800 operated branch offices. The laws of some states, in fact, prevent the operation of branch banking. Other states permit the operation of branch offices only within limited areas, and still others permit branch operation on a statewide scale. Although the number of banks that operate branches is only about 34 percent, the importance of branch banking has grown rapidly in several states. For example, at the end of 1951, branches accounted for only 26 percent of all bank offices. At year end 1972, branches accounted for 56 percent of all bank offices. The change in the number of banks and branches by states since 1960 is shown in Chart 3-1. A description of various forms that nonindependent banking takes will permit some general conclusions regarding its advantages or disadvantages relative to independently owned and operated banks.

In contrast with banking in the United States, the branch banking system is predominant in Canada and Britain. Canada, for example, has only 10 chartered banks, which in turn operate over 3,000 branch offices; England has approximately 13 incorporated banks, of which 5 account for most of the deposits of that nation. These incorporated banks operate more than 8,000 branches throughout that country.

Branch Banking. *Branch banks* are those banking offices that are controlled by a single parent bank. One board of directors and one group of stockholders control the home office and the branches. Some of our branch banking systems are very small, involving perhaps only two, three, or four branches. Others are quite large, extending over an entire state and having many branches.

As to the merits of branch banking, one of the most important is that branch banking systems are less likely to fail than are independent unit banks. In a branch banking system, more adequate diversification of investments can be made, and the temporary reverses of a single community are not so likely to cause complete failure of the entire banking chain. This would be true primarily of those branch systems that operate over wide geographical areas rather than in a single metropolitan area. The

Chart 3-1

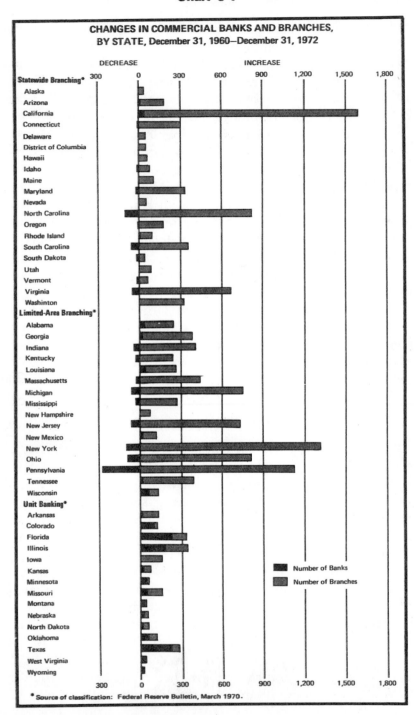

CHANGES IN COMMERCIAL BANKS AND BRANCHES, BY STATE, December 31, 1960—December 31, 1972

* Source of classification: Federal Reserve Bulletin, March 1970.

SOURCE: Federal Deposit Insurance Corporation.

independent bank cannot rely on other banks to offset local economic reverses.

It is on this score that the branch banking operations appear to have their strongest argument, for the record of bank failures in the United States has been one of which the banking system as a whole cannot be proud; but there have been few failures in those systems of banks that have engaged in branch banking practices. Opponents of this form of banking have pointed out, however, that failure of a system of banks, although less frequent, is far more serious.

The record of bank failures in both Canada and England is far superior to the record in the United States in spite of the fact that those countries have also been subject to extreme economic pressures.

In addition to the matter of safety, a system of branch banks may provide more adequate banking service to the local community than the independently owned bank because it has the resources of its other branches on which it may draw. The independently owned unit bank, of course, may have access to larger banks for assistance when requests are made for loans beyond the capacity of the bank.

Other advantages that have been claimed for branch banking systems are the greater convenience to customers that results from the quick placement of branches in newly developed centers of population, the greater uniformity of interest rates throughout the area of branch banking activities due to the mobility of funds from branch to branch, and the operational advantages of bigness in business activity. For example, it may be possible to achieve economies through the large-scale purchase of bank supplies, through the establishment of elaborate operating systems, through the extensive training of personnel, and through the employment of more competent management.

Among the objections that are raised to branch banking are the fear of concentration in control of banking operations, the lack of sincere interest in community affairs of branch managers who may be transferred to other areas, the possibility of loan delays while obtaining approval from main offices, and the possible withdrawal of funds from small towns and rural areas for the benefit of larger cities.

These objections lack substance in the light of experience both in this country and in Canada. Although branch banking does result in some degree of concentration of control, competition remains intense in branch banking areas. With respect to delays in loan approvals, most branch bank managers have the authority to approve practically all loan applications coming to them and can facilitate approval of most of the remaining applications by telephone. Since branch managers establish a successful record of operations through cooperation with and service to the communities which they serve, it is doubtful that lack of interest in local affairs would exist. Finally, the flow of funds from rural areas to the cities is contrary to normal expectations; typically, the higher interest rates prevailing in rural areas result in a flow of funds from the cities to these areas.

Group Banking. *Group banking* involves the use of the holding-company device, whereby two or more individual banks are controlled through a company that holds the voting control of the individual banks. The policies of banks thus controlled by such a holding company are determined by the parent company and coordinated for the purposes of that organization. The holding company itself may or may not engage in direct banking activities, and the banks that are controlled by the holding company may operate branches.

Little control was exercised over bank holding companies until the depression years of the early 1930's. Bank holding companies did not come within the jurisdiction of either state or federal control unless they also engaged directly in banking operations. The Banking Act of 1933 and the Securities Acts of 1933 and 1934 imposed limited control on bank holding companies, but it remained for the Bank Holding Company Act of 1956 to establish clear control of such operations. This Act defined a *bank holding company* as one which directly or indirectly owns, controls, or holds the power to vote 25 percent or more of the voting shares of each of two or more banks. The Bank Holding Company Act Amendments of 1966 established uniform standards for the evaluation of the legality of bank holding company acquisitions. But it remained for the Bank Holding Company Amendments of 1970 to provide the base for modern-day bank operations. These amendments provide that banks can make acquisitions of companies having activities "closely related to banking." Such closely related activities include mortgage, finance, credit card, or factoring subsidiaries. They can have industrial bank or industrial loan company subsidiaries. They can have subsidiaries that service loans, conduct fiduciary activities, or lease personal property. They can have subsidiaries that make equity or debt investments in corporations designed to promote community welfare. They can have subsidiaries that provide bookkeeping or data processing services or that furnish economic or financial information. They can have insurance agency subsidiaries and can underwrite credit life and credit accident and health insurance. And they can have subsidiaries that act as investment or financial advisors to mutual funds and mortgage or real estate investment trusts. As of year-end 1973, there were 18,471 banking offices in holding company groups, constituting 45.7 percent of all banking offices. These banking offices represented 3,097 banks and 14,170 bank branches. The assets of these holding company groups represented 67.4 percent of total commercial bank assets.

Chain Banking. The third general classification, that of *chain banking,* refers to an arrangement whereby two or more banks are brought under the direction and control of a group other than a holding company. This may be accomplished by several banks being owned by the same individual or group of individuals or through having the same members on the board of directors of each of the banks. Such organizations are generally built around one of the larger banks in an area or community. The principal bank is generally referred to as a "key bank," since it sets a pattern for general banking operations in the area or community.

BANK FAILURES AND DEPOSIT INSURANCE

Like all forms of business enterprise, the commercial bank is subject to failure when improper management or unfortunate economic conditions prevail for a long enough period of time. Furthermore, the commercial bank must enjoy the complete confidence of the public. Commercial banks secure their profits largely through the investment of funds that have been deposited with them for safekeeping. These invested funds are necessarily unavailable for a period of time; and immediate withdrawal demand on the part of a large number of depositors, because of a lack of confidence or other reasons, inevitably would lead a commercial bank to insolvency unless help were forthcoming from other quarters. It is necessary, therefore, for the sound and continued operation of a bank that its customers retain confidence in the bank.

The failure of one bank in a community may precipitate the loss of confidence in other banks in the same area, giving rise to panic and demands for withdrawals. Bank failures not only present a hardship to individual depositors but also materially affect business within the community. The smooth flow of business intercourse is interrupted by bank failures through the loss of confidence on the part of the bankers themselves in their ability to meet withdrawals. Few new business loans may be made, and many existing loans may be called or renewal refused.

Whatever the causes of bank failures, until recently the rate of failures in the United States was as high as, or higher than, that in any other highly industrialized country of the world. This had been an intolerable situation for the simple reason that a smoothly operating and highly efficient system of commercial banks is essential to the development of our industrial potential.

Early State Plans for Insurance of Bank Notes and Deposits

Although the federal system of deposit insurance is relatively new, state plans of insurance date back for more than a century. New York in 1829 adopted a plan by which it was to afford protection to both the notes issued by banks in that state and the deposits of the bank customers. The initiation of bank insurance by New York was followed by the establishment of insurance systems by Vermont, Indiana, Michigan, Ohio, and Iowa. The plans of insurance in these states varied from an assessment arrangement, in which participating banks were assessed to take care of the liabilities of a failed bank at the time such failures developed, to the establishment of an initial insurance or "safety" fund. In other states, these two plans were combined, providing for both an initial insurance fund and assessments contingent upon the demand for additional funds to meet liabilities of participating banks that failed.

These early insurance plans were developed primarily to insure the notes issued by the banks of that period; and in a few of the states that attempted such insurance, no provision whatsoever was made for the protection of deposits. Because bank notes played a dominant role as the circulating medium of that period, it is easy to understand the primary concern for insurance of these notes. These early state plans came to an end shortly after the passage of the National Banking Act. In 1865 a prohibitive tax was placed on state bank notes by the federal government, which ended their issuance. The notes of national banks were guaranteed by the federal government, and the need for further insurance was eliminated.

It was not until 1907 that another state insurance plan was to be provided. In that year Oklahoma, followed in later years by Kansas, Nebraska, Texas, Mississippi, South Dakota, North Dakota, and Washington, established bank insurance plans for the protection of depositors. These plans differed in detail but generally provided for the establishment of a guarantee fund to meet the liabilities of participating failed banks. In some of the states, the participating banks were permitted to retain their proportionate contribution, while in other states such funds were collected and invested by an administrative agency of the state. The state deposit insurance plans of that period were stimulated by the financial losses encountered during the panic of 1907.

Failure of State Plans of Deposit Protection

All of these various state plans of deposit insurance failed. Among the reasons for their failure is the fact that supervision of the plans was generally faulty. Also, generally distressed conditions caused more bank failures than had been anticipated, which created an undue strain on the rather meager resources of the insurance plans. Finally, in most of the states that established deposit insurance plans, there was economic dependence primarily upon one agricultural crop with little diversification to offset the risk resulting from a poor year or two for that crop.

Following the stock market crash in 1929 and the accompanying large number of bank failures, there again developed an insistent demand for some form of deposit insurance. This demand followed each such period of major bank failures. A total of 150 bills for guaranty or insurance were introduced in Congress from 1886 to 1933. The proponents of a federal system of deposit insurance finally exercised considerable influence. They contended that in spite of the failure of the state plans of deposit insurance, a plan established on a national basis would prove successful as a result of the diversification which it would entail—diversification that would permit one or more sectors of the economy or geographical areas to experience difficulty, while the system of deposit insurance would remain sound.

The proponents also argued that, if established on a federal basis under very strict supervision and with liberal provision for the accumulation of a reserve from which losses could be met, the chances of success on the part of the deposit insurance fund would be considerably enhanced. Also, they alleged that many of the difficulties which the commercial banks of the country faced resulted from the intense competition between national banks and state banks. A federal system of deposit insurance that would permit participation by both state banks and national banks would tend to eliminate much of this competition and provide a sounder basis for banking operations.

The Federal Deposit Insurance Corporation

The forcefulness of the arguments by the proponents of a national plan of deposit insurance and the intense demand of the general public for such protection caused the Congress to adopt a temporary form of deposit insurance to become effective in 1934. The plan, which resulted from the Steagall Amendment to the Glass Bill of 1933, received the support of a large majority in both houses of Congress. This first plan of federal deposit insurance provided protection of deposits up to $2,500 for each depositor. It continued in effect until 1935, during which time the various interested parties in Congress managed to reach agreement on the form of operation of a permanent plan of deposit insurance. The permanent plan provided for the establishment of a corporation to be known as the Federal Deposit Insurance Corporation. The stock was to be held jointly by the United States Treasury and the federal reserve banks.

Sources of Capital. The Secretary of the Treasury subscribed to $150 million of stock of the Federal Deposit Insurance Corporation (hereafter referred to as the FDIC), and each federal reserve bank was required to subscribe for an amount equal to one half of its surplus on January 1, 1933. The total stock purchased by the Treasury and the federal reserve banks was approximately $290 million. This stock did not provide for voting privileges nor for the payment of dividends. For the purpose of meeting emergency financial claims against it, the FDIC was authorized to issue debentures in an amount aggregating not more than three times the sum of its paid-in capital stock plus the amount received as assessments from insured banks. All capital stock of the FDIC has now been retired. Although part of the original stock of the FDIC was purchased by the federal reserve banks, the Corporation is not a part of the Federal Reserve System. The FDIC has its own board of directors of three members. One of these is the Comptroller of the Currency of the United States Department of the Treasury, and the other two are appointed by the President with the advice and consent of the Senate. The term of office is six years.

Deposit Protection. Until 1950 the maximum amount of deposit insurance afforded each account under the permanent plan of deposit insurance was $5,000. In 1950 the maximum was increased to $10,000, in 1966 to $15,000, in 1969 to $20,000, and in 1974 to $40,000. The costs of such deposit insurance are borne by the member banks of the insurance system.

Although membership in the FDIC is necessary for all banks holding national charters and for member banks of the Federal Reserve System, membership is available for state banks that are not members of the Federal Reserve System. On December 31, 1973, 98 percent of the nation's banks were insured by the FDIC. To protect depositors in state banks from having insurance withdrawn arbitrarily without notice to the depositors, it is provided that although the insured status of a bank is terminated when it ceases to be a member bank of the insurance system, for two years thereafter the bank remains liable for assessments and retains the insurance on insured deposits held by it when it ceased to be a member bank. Deposits received by such a bank after its insured status has been terminated are, of course, not protected under this provision.

The FDIC serves not only to minimize and eliminate the hardships resulting from bank failures, but it serves also to establish sound banking practices and to minimize the chance of such losses developing in the first place. It is empowered, among other things, to pass on applications for deposit insurance, to examine and supervise the general operations of member banks, and to make loans to insured banks or facilitate mergers or consolidations of banks when such actions are in the interest of the depositors.

Evaluation of the Federal Deposit Insurance Corporation. The FDIC has served a very useful purpose. Having minimized the hardships of loss on the part of the depositors in the banks that have failed during the history of the FDIC, the Corporation has also contributed to the present high degree of public confidence in the banking system in general. Such confidence is an essential factor in the successful operation of any banking system.

Among the criticisms of the present system of deposit insurance may be included the claims that the premium paid by the banks is too high, that the FDIC could not withstand the financial pressure resulting from a major depression, and the fact that a large part of the average bank's assets today are either direct or indirect obligations of the federal government anyway. With respect to the first and third points, only future events will determine whether the FDIC is accumulating too great a volume of reserves to meet periods of economic distress on the part of the banks. It is doubtful, however, whether the FDIC could withstand the financial pressure of an economic depression similar to that of the early thirties. It has been suggested that the support given to the banking system by the FDIC during the course of a depression may actually prevent economic conditions in general from deteriorating as much as would otherwise be the case. There is little doubt that the depression of the early thirties was made all the more burdensome by the accompanying failure of many banks.

Loss Experience of the Federal Deposit Insurance Corporation. From the beginning of deposit insurance on January 1, 1934, to December 31, 1973, the FDIC made disbursements to protect depositors in 499 insured banks. Disbursements for the protection of depositors totaled $988 million.[3] The FDIC in turn has recovered approximately 92 percent of its disbursements through the liquidation of assets taken over from closed banks, leaving a net estimated loss of 8 percent on its disbursements.

QUESTIONS

1. Discuss the relationship of commercial banking to the processes of a modern industrialized economy.
2. How vital a role did commercial banking play in the development of the United States economy? Has its importance decreased or increased with industrialization?
3. Describe the principal functions of commercial banks.
4. Why do regulatory authorities insist on certain minimum capital requirements on the part of banks before they may begin banking operations?
5. What are the sources of capital for a bank? Why would the bank wish to increase its capital after operations had begun and its initial capital requirements had been met?
6. Increasing emphasis by regulatory authorities in recent years has been placed on the risk ratio rather than on the deposits to capital ratio of banks. Explain the reasons for this change in attitude.
7. To what extent is concentration in banking control in the United States increasing? Do you anticipate a degree of concentration comparable to that of Canada and Britain during the twentieth century?
8. Compare the relative merits of independent unit banking as opposed to branch banking.
9. Distinguish between branch, group, and chain banking.
10. What are the principal causes of bank failures? Have bank failures been unusual in the history of United States commercial banking? Are bank failures frequent at the present time?
11. Discuss the development of deposit insurance in commercial banking in the United States.

---

[3] *Annual Reports* of the Federal Deposit Insurance Corporation, supplemented by correspondence with FDIC.

12. Evaluate the significance of the Federal Deposit Insurance Corporation to commercial banking in the United States.

SUGGESTED READINGS

BARGER, HAROLD. *Money, Banking, and Public Policy,* 2d ed. Chicago: Rand McNally & Company, 1968. Chapter 11.

CARSON, DEANE (ed.). *Money and Finance: Readings in Theory, Policy, and Institutions.* New York: John Wiley & Sons, Inc., 1966. Chapter 2.

DEWEY, D. R. *Financial History of the United States,* 12th ed. New York: Longmans, Green & Company, 1934.

HAMMOND, BRAY. *Banks and Politics in America from the Revolution to the Civil War.* Princeton, New Jersey: Princeton University Press, 1957.

HUTCHINSON, HARRY D. *Money, Banking, and the United States Economy,* 2d ed. New York: Meredith Corporation, 1971. Chapter 2.

KLEIN, JOHN J. *Money and the Economy,* 2d ed. New York: Harcourt Brace Jovanovich, Inc., 1970. Chapter 3.

KLISE, EUGENE S. *Money and Banking,* 5th ed. Cincinnati: South-Western Publishing Co., 1972. Chapters 6 and 8.

LYON, ROGER A. *Investment Portfolio Management in the Commercial Bank.* New Brunswick, New Jersey: Rutgers University Press, 1960. Chapter 3.

SMITH, HARLAN M. *The Essentials of Money and Banking.* New York: Random House, 1968. Chapters 2 and 3.

The Bank Holding Company—Its History and Significance in Modern America. Washington: Association of Registered Bank Holding Companies, 1973.

4 | The Federal Reserve System

The Federal Reserve Act of 1913 was the culmination of a long series of bills, proposals, and public debates arising from dissatisfaction with the National Banking Act. Although the National Banking Act resulted in substantial improvement in banking practices, certain weaknesses persisted; and new problems developed as the economy expanded.

WEAKNESSES OF THE BANKING SYSTEM

One of the principal weaknesses of the banking system late in the nineteenth century appeared to be the inappropriate arrangement for the holding of reserves. A large part of the reserve balances of banks was held in the form of deposits with the large city banks, in particular with the large New York City banks. During periods of economic stress, the position of these large city banks was precarious because they had the problem of meeting deposit withdrawals not only by their own customers but also by their correspondent banks. The frequent inability of the large banks to meet such deposit withdrawal demands resulted in extreme hardship for their correspondent banks whose reserves they held.

Another weakness of the banking system under the National Banking Act was the inflexibility of the note issue system. In an effort to provide the nation with a sound national currency, no provision had been made for the expansion or contraction of national bank notes with variations in business activity. The volume of national bank notes was governed not by the needs of business but rather by the availability and price of government bonds.

The National Banking Act provided that national banks could issue their own notes only against deposit with the Treasury of United States government bonds. Note issues were limited to 90 percent of the par value (as stated on the face of the bond) or the market value of the bonds, whichever was lower. When bonds sold at prices considerably above their par value, it meant that the advantage of purchasing bonds for the issue of notes was eliminated. For example, if a $1,000 par value bond were available for purchase at a price of $1,150, the banks would not be inclined to make such a purchase since a maximum of $900 in notes could be issued against the bond (90 percent of par value in this case). The interest that the banker could earn from the use of the $900 in notes would not be great enough to offset the premium price of the bond. When government bonds sold at par or at a discount, on the other hand, the prospective earning power of the note issues would be quite attractive and encourage purchase of bonds for note issue purposes. The volume of national bank notes, therefore, depended on the government bond market rather than the seasonal or cyclical needs of the nation for currency.

In addition to the foregoing two weaknesses of banking under the National Banking Act, the collection of out-of-town checks continued to be a cumbersome process. The Federal Reserve System has contributed much to the improvement of the check clearance and collection process.

CENTRAL BANKING

In the last analysis, the financial system of the United States during this period appeared to suffer not so much from the shortcomings of the National Banking Act as it did from the lack of an effective banking structure. Yet throughout the welter of proposals and counterproposals that preceded the enactment of the Federal Reserve Act ran a single theme: that of opposition to a strong central banking system. Although the nation had experienced central banking under the First and Second Banks of the United States, the national banking system itself did not provide for any form of central banking. The opening of the vast western frontiers along with the local autonomy of the southern areas presented an atmosphere of distrust of centralized financial control. This distrust was made all the more pointed by the fact that during the years immediately preceding enactment of the Federal Reserve Act, an era of trust-busting under President Theodore Roosevelt was experienced, and many of the practices of the large corporate combinations were being made public through legislative commissions and investigations.

Although the United States was one of the last major industrial nations to adopt a system of central banking, many financial and political leaders had long recognized the advantages of such a system. These proponents of central banking were given immense assistance by the dissatisfactions arising out of the panic of 1907. It must be acknowledged, however, that the central banking system adopted by the United States was, in fact, a compromise between the system of independently owned unit banks in existence in this country and the central banking systems of such countries as Canada, Great Britain, Spain, and Germany. This compromise took the form of a series of central banks, each representing a specific region of the United States and hence being more responsive to the particular financial problems of that region.

In many respects, a central bank resembles the commercial bank with regard to services performed. A central bank lends money to its members; it is required to hold reserves; it is given the responsibility of creating credit, generally through bank notes and deposits; and it has stockholders and a board of directors as well as other characteristics of the commercial bank. In contrast with the commercial bank, a central bank does not necessarily operate for a profit, but it has a primary responsibility for influencing the cost, the availability, and the supply of money. It facilitates the operations of the commercial banks in their relationships with the business community and with the government.

THE FEDERAL RESERVE SYSTEM

Under the authority of the Federal Reserve Act, twelve federal reserve districts were established. Each federal reserve district is served by a federal reserve bank, and the activities of the twelve banks are in turn coordinated by a Board of Governors in Washington, D. C. The members of the Board of Governors are also members of the Federal Open Market Committee. The Federal Advisory Council provides advice and general information to the Board of Governors. The organizational structure of the Federal Reserve System is shown in Chart 4-1.

The Federal Reserve System did not supplant the system that existed under the National Banking Act but rather was superimposed upon it. Certain provisions of the National Banking Act, however, were modified to permit greater flexibility of operations.

Federal Reserve Membership

The Federal Reserve Act provided that all national banks were to become members of the Federal Reserve System. In addition, state chartered banks, as well as trust companies, were permitted to join the system upon the presentation of evidence of a satisfactory financial condition. It was provided further that all member banks would be required to purchase capital stock of the federal reserve bank of their district up to a maximum of 6 percent of their paid-in capital and surplus. It has been necessary, however, for the banks to pay in only 3 percent; the remainder is subject to call at the discretion of the Federal Reserve System. Member banks are limited to a maximum of 6 percent dividends on the stock of the federal reserve banks that they hold. The federal reserve banks, therefore, are private institutions owned by the many member banks of the Federal Reserve System.

State chartered banks and trust companies are permitted to withdraw from membership with the Federal Reserve System six months after written notice has been submitted to the federal reserve bank of their district. In such cases, the stock originally purchased by the withdrawing member is canceled and a refund is made for all money paid in.

Chart 4–1

FEDERAL RESERVE SYSTEM

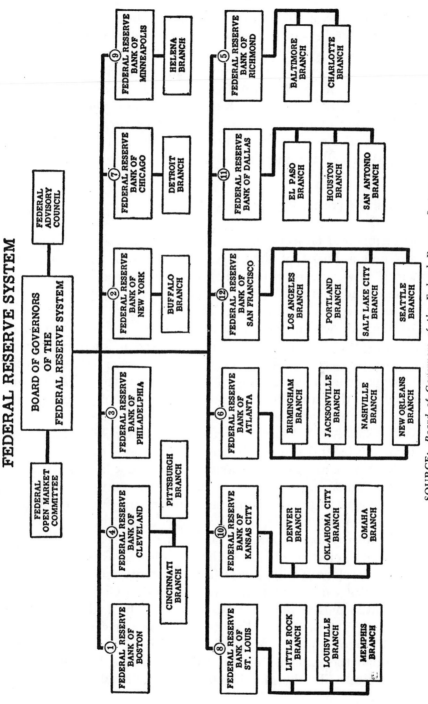

SOURCE: *Board of Governors of the Federal Reserve System.*

As of the close of 1973, of the nation's 14,100 commercial banks 5,717 were members of the Federal Reserve System. Of this number, approximately 4,600 were national banks. Compared with the 98 percent of all commercial banks that carried insurance under the provisions of the Federal Deposit Insurance Corporation as of the end of 1973, the Federal Reserve System's coverage included only 41 percent of all commercial banks. However, member banks of the Federal Reserve System hold approximately 78 percent of the deposits of all commercial banks.

Structure of the Federal Reserve Banks

Directors and Officers. Each federal reserve bank has corporate officers and a board of directors. The selection of officers and directors, however, is unlike that of other corporations. As in the case of member banks, each federal reserve bank has its own board of directors. These nine directors must be residents of the district in which they serve. The directors serve terms of three years, the appointments being staggered in such a way that three directors are appointed each year. In order to assure that the various economic elements of the federal reserve districts are represented, the nine members of the board of directors are divided into three groups: Class A, Class B, and Class C.

Both Class A and Class B directors are elected by the member banks of the federal reserve district. The Class A directors represent member banks of the district, while the Class B directors represent nonbanking interests. These nonbanking interests are commerce, agriculture, and industry. There is a further subdivision of Class A and Class B directors to represent the small banks, the medium-sized banks, and the large banks. Each of these groups is permitted to elect one Class A director and one Class B director. We have, therefore, a wide diversification of interests on the board of directors of each federal reserve bank. The Class C directors are appointed by the Board of Governors of the Federal Reserve System, and it is provided that these persons may not be stockholders, directors, or employees of existing banks.

Although the majority of the directors of the federal reserve banks are elected by the member banks of each district, the three members of each board appointed by the Board of Governors are in a strategic position relative to the other board members. One member appointed by the Board of Governors is designated chairman of the board of directors and a second member is appointed deputy chairman. Despite the precautions taken in establishing the method by which board members are chosen to represent diverse interests of the economy, there is seldom a conflict of interest among board members. Little interest is usually shown by member banks in the election of members for the board of directors.

Each federal reserve bank also has a president and first vice-president who are appointed by the board of directors with the approval of the Board of Governors. A federal reserve bank may have several additional vice-presidents. The president is responsible for the execution of the policies established by the board of directors and for general administration of the affairs of the federal reserve bank. All other officers and personnel of the federal reserve bank are subject to the authority of the president.

Federal Reserve Branch Banks. In addition to the twelve federal reserve banks, 24 branch banks have been established. These branch banks are located, for the most part, in geographical areas not conveniently served by the federal reserve banks themselves; hence, the geographically large western federal reserve districts have a majority of the federal reserve branch banks. The San Francisco district has four, the Dallas district has three, and the Atlanta district has four branch banks. The New York federal reserve district, on the other hand, has only one branch bank, while the Boston district has no branches. The federal reserve districts and the cities in which federal reserve banks and their branches are located are shown in Chart 4-1.

The Board of Governors

The Board of Governors of the Federal Reserve System, previously known as the Federal Reserve Board, is composed of seven members. Each member is appointed for a term of fourteen years. The purpose of the fourteen-year term undoubtedly was to make possible as little partisan political pressure on the Board as possible. This Board need not be bipartisan in nature, nor is there any specific provision with respect to the qualifications a member must have. All members are appointed by the President of the United States with the advice and consent of the Senate, one member being designated as the chairman and another as the vice-chairman.

The primary purpose of the Board of Governors is to give direction and coordination to the activities of the twelve federal reserve banks under its jurisdiction. The Board of Governors is also responsible for passing upon the applications of state-chartered banks applying for membership in the system and for recommending the removal of officers or directors of member banks because of infraction of rules established by the Federal Reserve System and other regulatory authorities. The Board of Governors must approve changes in the level of the rediscount rates of the federal reserve banks, and it implements many of the credit control devices that have come into existence in recent decades.

The Federal Open Market Committee

As early as 1922 efforts were made to coordinate the timing of purchases and sales of securities by the federal reserve banks in order to achieve desirable credit objectives. The Banking Act of 1933 formalized the early committees that had been established to coordinate these activities by the creation of the Federal Open Market Committee. This Committee, with the additional powers granted to it by the Banking Act of 1935, now has full control over all open market operations of the federal reserve banks.

The Federal Advisory Council

In an effort to keep the members of the Board of Governors in close contact with local business conditions, the Federal Advisory Council was created. This organization meets at least four times a year to consult with and to advise the members of the Board of Governors in matters relating to general business conditions, banking operations, and general questions of policy.

FUNCTIONS OF THE FEDERAL RESERVE SYSTEM

The primary responsibility of a central bank is to influence the cost, the availability, and the supply of money. By exercising such influence on the monetary system of the United States, the Federal Reserve System performs its most unique and important function— the promotion of economic stability. The functions of the Federal Reserve System that relate directly to the control of the cost, the availability, and the supply of money are the establishment of reserve requirements for member banks, loans and discounts to member banks, and open market operations. In addition, the Federal Reserve System exercises selective controls, such as the regulation of credit available for the purpose of purchasing listed stocks and the payment of interest on time deposits of member banks. The Federal Reserve System has also at times exercised control over consumer credit. These responsibilities involve policy decisions. Other functions of the System, such as collection of checks and issuance of currency, are regarded as services or chores.

In the remainder of this chapter we shall divide the functions of the Federal Reserve System into those that relate directly to member banks and those that relate to the economy in general. Two of the policy functions relate directly to member bank activities; the other two policy functions are implemented through other channels as well as through commercial banks. The policy functions are described in greater detail in Part Four in connection with the discussion of monetary policies and problems.

The functions to be discussed are as follows:

Bank-Related Functions
  Issuance of Currency
  Bank Reserves
  Loans and Discounts
  Clearance and Collection of Checks
  Supervision and Regulation

General Functions
  Open Market Operations
  Selective Credit Controls
  Government Fiscal Agent
  Reports, Publications, and Research

BANK-RELATED FUNCTIONS OF THE FEDERAL RESERVE SYSTEM

Issuance of Currency

The federal reserve banks are the main source of currency in the United States. Individuals usually receive paper money and coin by making withdrawals from a bank or from the sale of merchandise or services. In either case the bank must provide such money, either directly or through the intermediary of the purchaser of goods or services. Although the flow of currency from the banks to the public is usually matched by a flow of currency deposits, at times the demand for currency by the public may exceed the bank's available supply. At such times member banks depend upon the federal reserve banks for replenishment of their supply. As currency is ordered from a federal reserve bank, the reserves of the bank ordering the currency are charged. Nonmember banks usually obtain their currency from member banks.

The federal reserve banks maintain large stores of paper money and coin on hand at all times to meet the demands of member banks. Approximately 88 percent of all currency in circulation is represented by federal reserve notes, the remainder being made up of United States Treasury paper money and coin. Federal reserve notes are the obligations of both the United States government and of the issuing federal reserve banks, and they are backed by specified collateral, such as notes and government bonds.

As additional coin is required by the federal reserve banks for distribution to member banks, it is received from the mints, and the deposit balances of the Treasury with the federal reserve banks are credited. The cost of issuing federal reserve currency, as well as all transportation costs involved in the shipment of paper money and coin to or from the federal reserve banks, is borne by the federal reserve banks.

The issuance of currency by the federal reserve banks, therefore, eliminated one of the major weaknesses of banking under the National Banking Act prior to the establishment of the Federal Reserve System, that of an inflexible monetary system. As the demand for additional currency is now made by the public and by the banks of the nation, the federal reserve banks increase the flow of such currency from their reservoir of funds. Such increased demands for currency usually accompany an expansion in general business activity. As the economy contracts and the large additional supplies of currency are no longer required, the unnecessary currency is shipped back to the federal reserve banks.

Bank Reserves

One of the basic measures provided by the Federal Reserve Act was the institution of a more appropriate system of maintaining reserves by the banks of the nation. The shortcomings of the system of holding reserves as permitted under the National Banking Act had been recognized, and it was apparent that a remedy would have to be provided before substantial progress could be made toward stabilizing the banking system of the country. To accomplish this, member banks were to keep on reserve with the federal reserve bank of their district a specified percentage of the volume of deposits of the bank.

Although all member banks were subject to the same minimum reserve requirements on time and savings deposits, the member banks were divided into three groups for purposes of determining reserve ratios on demand or checking deposits. These three groups were based on the division established earlier by the National Banking Act: central reserve city banks, reserve city banks, and country banks. The importance of cities as national or regional money centers provided the basis for their classification. Under the provisions of the Federal Reserve Act, a part of the minimum reserves was permitted to be held as cash in the member bank's own vault. This provision was changed in 1917 by an act of Congress that required all legal reserves against time and demand deposits to be kept with the federal reserve banks. This requirement was modified in late 1959; and since November, 1960, all vault cash has been considered as part of a bank's legal reserves.

Although the Board of Governors has the power to alter the legal reserve requirements, Congress establishes the range within which these changes can be made. At the present time, it is provided by law that the range of required reserves for reserve city banks may be from 10 to 22 percent;[1] for country banks, from

---

[1] Authority of the Board of Governors to classify or reclassify cities as central reserve cities was terminated effective July 28, 1962. Banks are now classed as either reserve city banks or country banks.

Table 4-1

RESERVE REQUIREMENTS ON DEPOSITS OF MEMBER BANKS

(Deposit intervals are in millions of dollars. Requirements are in percent of deposits.)

| | NET DEMAND [1] | | | | | TIME | | |
| | | | | | | | OTHER TIME | |
EFFECTIVE DATE	0–2	2–10	10–100	100–400	OVER 400	SAV- INGS	0–5	OVER 5
1972—Nov. 9	8	10	12	16½	17½	3	3	5
Nov. 16	......	......	......	13	......	......	......	......
1973—July 19	......	10½	12½	13½	18	......	......	......
In effect Sept. 30, 1974	8	10½	12½	13½	18	3	3	5

[1] Effective November 9, 1972, reserve city banks were redefined to include those with more than $400 million of net demand deposits. Other banks maintain reserves at ratios based on demand deposit levels as reflected in this table.

SOURCE: *Federal Reserve Bulletin,* October, 1974, Boards of Governors of the Federal Reserve System, Washington, D. C., p. A9.

7 to 14 percent; and for time deposits of all member banks, 3 to 10 percent. Note from Table 4-1 that the legal reserves have been changed frequently. These changes have been effected for the purpose of countering either inflationary or deflationary influences.

Loans and Discounts

It was believed that if the federal reserve banks were to serve effectively as bankers' banks, they would have to provide facilities for lending to their member banks at times when additional funds were required by the banks. Such a lending arrangement was to meet one of the principal objections to the National Banking Act, that of an inflexible currency system. Loans to member banks by the federal reserve banks may take two forms: first, the member bank may receive an "advance" secured by its own promissory note together with eligible paper it owns; or second, the member bank may "discount" its eligible paper with the federal reserve bank. *Eligible paper,* which is defined in considerable detail by the Board of Governors, includes such items as the promissory notes, bills of exchange, and banker's acceptances of customers.

Bonds and notes of the United States government and obligations of instrumentalities of the United States government that carry the guarantee of the government are also acceptable as collateral for advances. The federal reserve banks may make advances to banks that are not members of the Federal Reserve System and to certain nonbanking institutions when direct obligations of the United States government are offered as security.

The use of eligible paper as collateral for a loan from a federal reserve bank involves a contingent liability on the part of the member bank in the case of either a discount or an advance. In discounting eligible paper, the member bank is required to endorse each item. For an advance, the bank must sign a promissory note in addition to submitting eligible paper as collateral. The promissory note, of course, represents a general claim against the bank over and above the value of the eligible paper.

Member banks have generally found that in borrowing from a federal reserve bank the use of the advance arrangement, as opposed to the discount arrangement, is more convenient since the maturity of the various items of eligible paper may not coincide with the needs of the member bank. Under the advance arrangement, paper held by the federal reserve bank as collateral that matures before the due date of the advance is simply replaced by other eligible paper. Also, under the advance arrangement, a single interest rate is calculated on the loan while discounted eligible paper may require varying discount rates, depending upon the quality, length of maturity, and general character of each item. Because of the large bank holdings of United States government securities in recent years, however, and because of their convenience, member banks have generally used these securities instead of eligible paper as collateral for federal reserve bank advances.

The rate charged by all federal reserve banks on advances and discounts as of October 31, 1974, was 8 percent. The rate may be lowered or raised from time to time to encourage or discourage, as may be desired, member banks' participation in the loan program. Also, at times the rate will vary from one federal reserve bank to another. Such variations in rates between banks generally result from a desire to equalize the general flow of credit.

Until late in 1952, the volume of lending operations of the federal reserve banks had reached significant proportions only during World War I and the period thereafter and during the stock market boom of 1928 and 1929. Late in 1952, and again in 1969 and 1970, member banks obtained over $1.5 billion in loans from the federal reserve banks. In 1973 loans to member banks reached an all-time high of more than $2 billion.

Clearance and Collection of Checks

One of the important contributions of the Federal Reserve System to the smooth flow of financial interchange has been that of facilitating the clearance and collection of checks of the banks of the nation. Each federal reserve bank serves as a clearinghouse for all banks in its district, provided that they agree to remit at par on checks forwarded to them for payment. The importance of this service to the banking system of the United States can be readily understood by a brief review of clearance practices prior to the Federal Reserve System.

Although local clearinghouses made it possible for banks within the same city to effect an efficient exchange of customers' checks, it was often difficult and time-consuming to provide for the settlement of claims when checks were drawn on out-of-town banks or when checks drawn on the local banks were presented to out-of-town banks for payment. In addition to the time consumed in routing checks from one bank to another for payment, many banks on which checks were drawn made payment only at a discount; that is, instead of remitting the face value of the check, they would deduct ⅛ to ½ of 1 percent of the face value of the check as a clearance charge. This practice resulted in the establishment of correspondent banking relations between banks in the important commercial centers of the United States.

Correspondent arrangements generally provided that checks exchanged between the two banks would be accepted at par. In this way, a local bank that had received a check drawn on a bank in another community, in order to avoid having the other bank remit at less than par, would send the check instead to a correspondent bank in the same community as the bank on which the check was drawn. That bank, in turn, would either send the check directly to the bank on which it was written, if it were a correspondent of that bank, or pass it on to another bank that might have correspondent relations with it, thus avoiding the penalty. As such checks were forwarded to correspondent banks, the reserves of the forwarding bank were increased because deposits with correspondents were considered to be part of required reserves. The days required to clear checks meant that reserves were greatly padded, increasing their potential for bank lending.

Although it may seem that the bank on which the check was originally presented would be able to pass on such charges to its customers, such practice was avoided if at all possible because of the intense competition for the accounts of businesses and other customers at that time. Hence, banks frequently attempted to absorb these costs, when they could not otherwise be avoided, rather than to pass them on to their customers.

Check Clearance Through the Federal Reserve Banks. Member banks of the Federal Reserve System and nonmembers alike may utilize the check-clearance facilities of the federal reserve banks. Nonmember participating banks, however, like member banks, must remit at par on checks presented to them for payment and must keep a small deposit with the federal reserve bank for check-clearance purposes. As of year-end 1973, the number of banks that continued to charge exchange fees on checks presented for payment was 147. These banks are small and unimportant, and their number is continually decreasing. The Board of Governors of the Federal Reserve System has at times encouraged state legislatures to outlaw this practice. For the vast majority of commercial banks, the federal reserve banks provide an efficient and economical system of check clearance. For member banks the service is particularly appropriate since they must hold legal reserves with the federal reserve banks anyway. As checks are sent through federal reserve banks for collection, the reserve balances of participating banks are decreased or increased, depending upon the day's total of checks drawn against or in favor of a particular bank.

An example of the check-clearance process through the federal reserve banks will demonstrate the facility with which these clearances are made at the present time. Assume that a businessman in Sacramento, California, places an order for merchandise with a distributor in San Francisco. His order is accompanied by a check drawn on his bank in Sacramento. This check is deposited by the distributor with his bank in San Francisco, at which time he receives a corresponding credit to his account with the bank. The distributor's bank will then send the check tó the federal reserve bank of its district, also located in San Francisco, which will in turn forward the check to the bank in Sacramento on which the check was originally drawn. The adjustment of accounts is accomplished at the federal reserve bank through an alternate debit and credit to the accounts of the banks concerned in the transaction. The San Francisco bank, which has honored the check of its customer, will receive an increase in its reserve with the federal reserve bank, while the bank in Sacramento will have its reserve decreased by a corresponding amount. The bank in Sacramento will reduce the account of the businessman who wrote the check. Hence, the exchange is made with no transfer of currency.

In the event that the Sacramento bank found its legal reserve reduced below the point required by its total deposits, it would then be necessary, in one way or another, to supplement its reserves with the federal reserve bank. For the vast amount of check clearance that takes place, however, a negligible amount of cash shipment is required. Although the distributor in this case received an immediate increase in his account for the amount of the check deposited with his bank as is customary, the bank did not receive an immediate increase in its reserves with the federal reserve bank on which it could draw. Had the bank on which the check was drawn been located in San Francisco, there would have been an immediate credit to the account of the depositing bank. The length of time that a bank must wait before checks deposited with a federal reserve bank are added to its active accounts depends on its distance from the federal reserve bank. A schedule of zones exists in which these waiting periods for various geographical areas are specified. In no case, however, is a bank required to wait more than two days before a check deposited with the federal reserve bank will be entered to its credit.

Check Clearance Between Federal Reserve Districts. If at the time the businessman placed his order with the San Francisco distributor, he also placed an order with a distributor of goods in

Chicago, Illinois, his check would be subject to an additional step in being cleared through the Federal Reserve System. The Chicago distributor, like the San Francisco distributor, deposits the check with the bank of his choice and in turn receives an increase in his account. The Chicago bank deposits the check for collection with the Federal Reserve Bank of Chicago, which in turn forwards the check to the Federal Reserve Bank of San Francisco. The Federal Reserve Bank of San Francisco, of course, then presents the check for payment to the bank on which it was drawn. There are, therefore, two routes of check clearance: the *intradistrict* settlement where the transaction takes place entirely within a single federal reserve district, and the *interdistrict* settlement in which there are relationships between banks of two federal reserve districts.

The Interdistrict Settlement Fund. Just as the federal reserve banks are able to minimize the actual flow of funds by increasing or decreasing reserves of the participating banks, the federal reserve banks are able to avoid the flow of funds between the federal reserve banks to effect interdistrict settlements. This is accomplished through the Interdistrict Settlement Fund in Washington, D. C.

The Interdistrict Settlement Fund has a substantial deposit from each of the federal reserve banks. These deposit credits are alternately increased or decreased, depending upon the clearance balance of the day's activities on the part of each federal reserve bank. At a certain hour each day, each federal reserve bank informs the Interdistrict Settlement Fund by direct wire the amount of checks it received the previous day that were drawn upon banks in other federal reserve districts. The deposit of each federal reserve bank with the Interdistrict Settlement Fund is increased or decreased according to the balance of the day's check clearance activities. The Interdistrict Settlement Fund also makes it possible for large sums to be transferred from member banks to banks in other federal reserve districts through the deposit balances of the federal reserve banks with the Fund.

Check Clearance Through Federal Reserve Branch Banks. Branch banks of the federal reserve banks enter into the clearance process in a very important way. If the check is deposited with a bank located nearer to a federal reserve branch bank than to a federal reserve bank, the branch bank, in effect, takes the place of the federal reserve bank.

Check Routing Symbols. The magnitude of the task of assisting in the check-clearance process by the Federal Reserve System is attested to by the fact that over one quarter of the total personnel of the twelve federal reserve banks are engaged in this function. Great effort has been exercised to make this task easier, and much time-saving machinery has been introduced into the operation.

A check routing symbol plan, jointly sponsored in 1945 by the American Bankers Association and the Federal Reserve System, is of great assistance in the more rapid and accurate sorting of out-of-town checks. These symbols are usually found in the upper right-hand corner of the check.

The purpose of the symbol is to reveal to check sorters at a glance the identity, the location, and the proper check collection route to the bank on which the check is drawn. Preceding the hyphen, in the numerator of the symbol, are to be found numbers ranging from 1 through 99. Numbers 1 through 49 are assigned to major cities, while numbers 50 through 99 apply to states and United States territories. The number following the hyphen identifies a specific bank in the locality. The first digit of the denominator (or the first two digits in the case of the tenth, eleventh, and twelfth districts) identifies the federal reserve district. The next digit designates the federal reserve office serving the territory, that is, whether it is a federal reserve bank or one of its branches. The final figure in the denominator is a dual-purpose one. A zero means that credit will be given to the collecting bank's reserve account as soon as the check is received by the appropriate federal reserve office. Any other final number signifies that reserve credit will be deferred because the paying bank is far enough away from the federal reserve office so that one or more days will elapse before the check can be physically presented to that bank for payment. In addition, if a "deferred availability" number (a final number other than zero) appears, it also indicates the district state within which the paying bank is located.

The latest innovation in the clearance process is a machine that has the ability to "read" a system of symbols and numerals. Al-

Figure 4-1

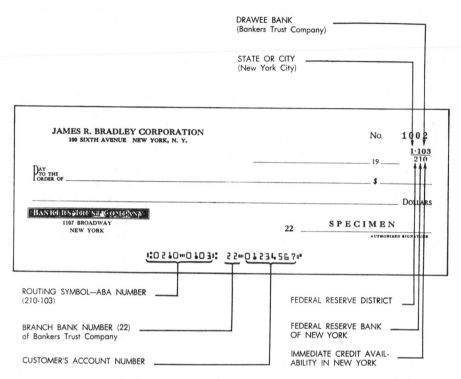

though these symbols are slightly different from conventional numbers, they are easily read by human eyes as well. Information relative to the clearance process is printed on the lower part of the check form in magnetic ink (ink containing iron oxide). This information can be read directly from checks by the processing machines. The system has been named Magnetic Ink Character Recognition (MICR). In addition to the clearance symbol, banks with compatible electronic accounting equipment include a symbol for each customer's account. This makes possible electronic processing of checks for internal bookkeeping purposes.

During the period that banks are converting to magnetic ink symbols, banks will retain the conventional symbol in the upper right-hand corner of the check form to permit visual sorting as well as electronic sorting. An explanation of check routing symbols is given in Figure 4-1.

Federal Reserve Transfer of Credit. The Federal Reserve System provides for the transfer of hundreds of millions of dollars in bank credit about the country daily. In 1953 the Federal Reserve System put into operation a near-automatic system of teletype through which bank credit can be transferred. The communication system, referred to as the *federal reserve leased system,* spans approximately 11,000 miles and makes it possible for the 12 federal reserve banks and their 24 branches to maintain facilities for almost instantaneous transfer of bank credit. Headquarters for the communication system is in Culpeper, Virginia.

The tremendous growth of the check clearance function dictates an entirely new approach to the payment process. While the use of credit cards has taken some pressure off of check clearance facilities, the problem remains. Credit cards, of course, permit the payment for many transactions to be completed with a single check at the end of each billing cycle. The payments system of the future is usually seen as one that combines modern electronic technology with what is known as the *giro transfer system.* This system is one that has been widely used in continental European countries for years but which has been largely untried in the United States. Its characteristics make it especially suitable for the use of computers.

Like the check payments system, the giro system involves deposit balances held by individuals and businesses at a financial or governmental institution, and some systematic arrangement for the transfer of ownership of these balances from payer to payee. Unlike the check system, in the typical giro transaction the payer delivers to the drawee institution an electronic order directing it to transfer a specified sum from the payer's account to that of the payee. This system is more direct and involves less time and paper handling than ordinary check transfers. There are a number of experimental projects in cities around the country aimed toward development of a system of paperless transfers.

Supervision and Regulation

Few fields of activity are so strongly regulated and supervised as that of the banking system. This regulation, of course, results in part from the strategic role played by the commercial banking system in the nation's economy and the sensitivity of business conditions in general to undue disturbances in the banking system. Regulation and supervision are exercised by several different agencies. For example, national banks are subject to examination by the Comptroller of the Currency, and because all national banks must be members of the Federal Reserve System, they are also subject to examination and regulation by the Federal Reserve System. Also, since members of the Federal Reserve System must be insured by the Federal Deposit Insurance Corporation, they are subject to possible examination by that organization.

Regulation of State Chartered Banks. If a member bank is a state-chartered institution, although not subject to the supervision of the Comptroller of the Currency, it is subject to the laws of the state in which it is chartered as well as the regulation of the Federal Reserve System and the Federal Deposit Insurance Corporation. Insured state banks that are not members of the Federal Reserve System are subject to examination by the Federal Deposit Insurance Corporation, while nonmember uninsured state banks are subject only to state examination.

Delegation of Federal Reserve Examination Responsibilities. Examination of member banks by the Federal Reserve System is generally delegated to the regional federal reserve banks; however, the Board of Governors of the Federal Reserve System is authorized by law to examine member banks if it so chooses. In practice, national banks are seldom examined by the staff of the Federal Reserve System since they are normally subject to examination also by the Comptroller of the Currency. National bank examiners, responsible to the Comptroller of the Currency, generally submit a copy of the examination report of each national bank to the examination department of the district reserve bank, and normally no further examination is made by the federal reserve bank. The federal reserve bank may, however, dispatch its own examiners to one of the national banks to secure information not covered by the examination of the national bank examiners. The principal activities of the examination department of the federal reserve banks is that of examining state-chartered member banks of the district.

As in the case of national banks and the national bank examiners, federal reserve authorities cooperate closely with the state banking authorities in an effort to minimize the burden of bank examination on banking operations and in order to simplify the procedure. In many states, state bank officials accept the report of the federal reserve examiners and concentrate their own examination activities on nonmember state banks. State and federal reserve bank examiners may appear jointly for purposes of examination to minimize the inconvenience to bank operations. The Federal Deposit Insurance Corporation confines its examination activities largely to insured state banks that are not members of the System.

GENERAL FUNCTIONS OF THE FEDERAL RESERVE SYSTEM

Open Market Operations

Open market operations are regarded as the most important single instrument available to the Federal Reserve System for purposes of credit control. By purchasing large quantities of securities in the open market, the federal reserve banks increase the flow of funds in circulation. By selling securities, funds are withdrawn from circulation. Obligations of the United States government are the principal kind of securities that the federal reserve banks buy and sell. The Open Market Committee is responsible for such activities.

As an example of an Open Market Committee action, assume that the Committee decides to buy $50 million of United States government securities. These securities are purchased in the open market from whatever source that may be available. A check drawn on the federal reserve bank making the purchase is delivered to the seller of the securities. The seller deposits the check with a member bank, which in turn delivers the check to the federal reserve bank. The seller of the securities has had an increase in his deposit balance with the member bank, and the member bank in turn has increased its reserves with the federal reserve bank. On the basis of the expanded reserves of the member bank with the federal reserve bank, loans and investments may also be expanded. The net effect, therefore, of the purchase of securities is to expand the reserves of member banks and in turn their credit-creating potential.

If it is the desire of the Federal Reserve System to restrain credit expansion and growth in money supply, the federal reserve banks may sell securities in the open market. The purchasers of the securities pay for them by drawing checks on their balances with member banks. This, in turn, reduces the reserves of the member banks with the federal reserve banks, and they must adjust their loan and investment operations to the lower level of reserves on deposit with the federal reserve bank. In this way pressure is brought to bear on the loan and investment activities of commercial banks.

Selective Credit Controls

To supplement the general methods of regulating the flow of funds, the Federal Reserve System has special powers to regulate the credit terms on which transactions in stock market securities are financed. The terms of consumer credit and certain real estate credit have also been regulated by the Federal Reserve System from time to time. In contrast with the other methods of monetary control, selective credit controls act directly on credit rather than on the reserves of member banks. They are also directed to specific lines of business activity to the exclusion of all others. Much controversy has existed as to the merits of a system of monetary control that imposes special restriction on individual segments of the economy.

Margin Requirements on Stock Market Credit. Since 1934 the Board of Governors of the Federal Reserve System has had the responsibility of curbing the excessive use of credit for the purpose of purchasing or carrying securities. It discharges this responsibility by limiting the amount that brokers and dealers in securities, banks, and others may lend on securities for that purpose. Brokers are limited in their lending for the purpose of purchasing or carrying any type of security. The restriction on banks applies only to loans for purchasing or carrying securities registered on national security exchanges. Such limitations do not apply to loans secured by stocks if the purpose of the loans is for regular business activities. Margin requirements are discussed in Chapter 14.

Consumer Credit. The Federal Reserve System has resorted to regulation of consumer credit only in times of emergency to supplement general credit measures. Its first use in 1941 was for the purpose of curbing the use of credit for the purchase of automobiles, household goods, and other such consumer durables. The problem faced by the nation at that time was one of an acute shortage of consumer goods and services accompanied by an increase in consumer purchasing power. Without restrictive measures, such a situation could only bring increased prices. By 1952 all restrictions on the use of consumer credit were eliminated.

The Truth in Lending Act which became effective May 29, 1968, requires the Board of Governors to prescribe regulations to assure a meaningful disclosure of credit terms so that consumers will be able to compare more readily the various terms available and avoid the uninformed use of credit.

Real Estate Credit. Because of the tremendous inflationary pressure on prices in the post-World War II period, it was necessary to restrict the flow of credit for home purchase. Failure to do so would have meant a substantial diversion of manpower and materials from essential defense requirements. In 1950 the Board of Governors of the Federal Reserve System issued Regulation X for real estate credit. It specified the maximum amount that could be borrowed, the maximum length of time the loan could run, and the minimum periodic payments that had to be made to pay off the principal amount of the loan. Restrictions on real estate credit were removed in 1952, and they have not been utilized since.

Government Fiscal Agent

A substantial proportion of the employees of the Federal Reserve System hold duties that are directly related to the provision of fiscal services for the United States government. These services, provided without charge to the government, include the holding of the principal checking accounts of the Treasury of the United States, assisting in the collection of taxes, the transfer of money from one region to another, the sale and redemption of federal securities, and the paying of interest coupons. These duties, under-taken in addition to the general functions of the Federal Reserve System, make it possible for the United States government, in spite of its increased complexity, to handle the mechanics of its fiscal affairs more efficiently and safely than before the establish-ment of the Federal Reserve System.

Reports, Publications, and Research

The federal reserve banks publish a weekly statement of condi-tion for each reserve bank as well as a consolidated statement for all of the reserve banks. This information has become valuable for purposes of studying business conditions in general and for the formulation of forecasts of business activity. In addition to the weekly statement, all twelve of the federal reserve banks, as well as the Board of Governors, engage in intensive research in mone-tary matters. The Board of Governors makes available the *Federal Reserve Bulletin*, which not only carries articles of current interest to economists and businessmen in general but also offers a con-venient source of the statistics compiled by the Federal Reserve System. The *Bulletin* is also a convenient secondary source for certain statistical series and data prepared by other organizations.

QUESTIONS

1. Describe the background of commercial banking activities that resulted in the passage of the Federal Reserve Act of 1913.
2. The Federal Reserve Act of 1913 provided for the establishment of a group of "central banks." How do the operations of a central bank differ from those of a commercial bank?
3. Describe the organizational structure of the Federal Reserve System.
4. Describe the circumstances and conditions under which a commercial bank may become a member of the Federal Reserve System.
5. The board of directors of each federal reserve bank is constituted in such a way that representation is given to banking and to business of large, intermediate, and small size. Explain how this is accomplished.
6. What is meant by a "federal reserve branch bank"? How many such branches exist, and where are most of them located geographically?

7. The Federal Reserve System is under the general direction and control of the Board of Governors of the Federal Reserve System in Washington, D. C. How are members of the Board of Governors appointed? To what extent are they subject to political pressures?
8. What is the number of the federal reserve district in which you reside? In what city is the federal reserve bank of your district located?
9. Discuss the structure, the functions, and the importance of the Federal Open Market Committee.
10. Why did Congress give to the Board of Governors the power to change, within a limited range, the legal reserves of member banks?
11. With respect to their lending power, federal reserve banks have at times been described as banker's banks. What is meant by this statement?
12. Describe the process by which a check drawn on a commercial bank but deposited for collection in another bank in a distant city might be cleared through the facilities of the Federal Reserve System.
13. What is meant by "check routing symbols"?
14. Explain the usual procedures for examining national banks. How does this process differ from the examination of member banks of the Federal Reserve System holding state charters?
15. In what way do the federal reserve banks serve as fiscal agents for the United States government?

SUGGESTED READINGS

BARGER, HAROLD. *Money, Banking, and Public Policy,* 2d ed. Chicago: Rand McNally & Company, 1968. Chapter 8.

FEDERAL RESERVE SYSTEM. *The Federal Reserve System—Purposes and Functions.* Washington: Board of Governors of the Federal Reserve System, 1963.

HUTCHINSON, HARRY D. *Money, Banking, and the United States Economy,* 2d ed. New York: Meredith Corporation, 1971. Chapter 3.

KLEIN, JOHN J. *Money and the Economy,* 2d ed. New York: Harcourt Brace Jovanovich, Inc., 1970. Chapters 10, 11, and 12.

SMITH, HARLAN M. *The Essentials of Money and Banking.* New York: Random House, 1968. Chapter 4.

5 | Savings

In this chapter we are concerned with savings, the ultimate source of capital funds. We discuss the importance of savings to current economic activity and capital formation, the historical significance of savings, types of savers, savings media, and the factors that influence the levels of savings. In speaking of *capital formation*, we refer to the creation of physical productive facilities, such as buildings, tools, equipment, roads, and other facilities for the economic processes of society.

The concept of savings that we deal with is *financial savings* or the accumulation of cash and other financial assets, such as savings accounts, corporate securities, and savings and loan shares. Changes in the level of savings for individuals and corporations are measured by current income less tax payments and total expenditures. Governments, too, may save insofar as their revenues exceed their expenditures. This definition embraces two types of savings: voluntary savings and contractual savings. *Voluntary savings* are simply financial assets set aside for use in the future. *Contractual savings* include such things as the accumulation of reserves in insurance and pension funds. Contractual savings are not determined by current decision; they are disciplined by previous commitments which the saver has some incentive to honor.

Savings may be defined in different ways, each definition having its own significance and application for analytical purposes. Our definition serves our purposes well in the study of finance and capital markets.

HISTORICAL ROLE OF SAVINGS

As the size of American business establishments expanded, it became increasingly important that large amounts of capital be accumulated and converted to business use. The corporate form of organization provided a convenient and flexible legal arrangement for the mobilization of available investment capital. These advantages of the corporation over the proprietorship and partnership are described in Chapter 7.

Developments in transportation were often too costly and speculative for private promoters to undertake. The magnitude of early canal, turnpike, and railroad construction was such that government undertook much of the task of financing such projects. Until the end of the nineteenth century, governmental units contributed more capital to these efforts than did private interests.[1] Since this government financing was largely through bond issues rather than current revenues, the ultimate source of the funds was the savings of the individuals.

Foreign Sources of Savings

Large proportions of the securities sold by both government units and private promoters were purchased by foreigners. Foreign capital played a decisive role in the development of the nation's early transportation system.[2]

The importance of the role that foreign capital played in the economic development of the United States can be illustrated through a comparison of this development with that of the developing nations of today. These nations now face many of the financial problems that the United States experienced during her early development. Private savings in many of these countries

---

[1] Ross M. Robertson, *History of the American Economy* (New York: Harcourt, Brace and Company, 1955), p. 213.

[2] Donald L. Kemmerer and Clyde C. Jones, *American Economic History* (New York: McGraw-Hill Book Company, Inc., 1959), pp. 176-182.

are negligible since almost all current income goes for immediate consumption. Individual nations and such international organizations as the World Bank supply large amounts of capital to the developing nations of the world for purposes of increasing their productive capacity.[3] The flow of development capital not only stimulates economic expansion in these countries but it also makes their capital much more efficient. For example, speedier transportation reduces the amount of goods in transit, thus releasing working capital for other purposes. In due time, as internal capital formation increases, it is hoped that the need for foreign capital will be eliminated and that these countries can then enjoy an autonomous capital formation process.

Domestic Supply of Savings

As capital formation began increasing at a faster and faster rate after the Civil War, the demand for funds also increased. Wealthy individuals and foreigners could no longer provide funds at a fast enough rate. Britain was investing heavily in India because of political commitments, and the other European countries were not of sufficient size and wealth to continue supplying funds in quantities adequate to sustain our growth.[4] The American family soon took over the function of providing savings for the capital formation process. Per capita income had risen to a level where American families could afford luxuries well beyond the subsistence level and also save part of what they had earned. Thus, the United States gradually developed to the stage where she could generate sufficient capital to finance her own expansion. The result was ultimately a change in our status from that of a debtor nation to that of a creditor nation.

Importance of Savings to Economic Growth

The increasing capital requirements of the nation's business enterprises, the ever-increasing levels of consumer credit, and the

---

[3] The World Bank, the popular name for the International Bank for Reconstruction and Development, is a cooperative international organization established for the purpose of promoting long-term capital loans between nations for productive purposes.

[4] Simon Kuznets, *Capital in the American Economy, Its Formation and Financing* (New York: National Bureau of Economic Research, 1961), pp. 131-134.

expanding deficits of governmental fiscal operations make it imperative that an expanding flow of savings be available for these purposes. Capital formation, too, continues as a critical necessity for the modernization of American industry capacity. Technological advances in areas such as automation have meant that more capital per worker is necessary. Today, American manufacturers require a capital investment of over $30,000 per worker in the form of plant and equipment compared with about $4,000 of capital per worker in 1920. There is every indication that this trend will continue in the future.

Sources of Savings, Savings Media, and Trends

All additions to total savings in the United States originate from current income and profits of individuals, corporations, governmental units, and foreign investors. It includes all capital gains, windfalls, and new discoveries of wealth. Not included, however, are such items as gifts and inheritances, since they do not add to total savings. They merely represent transfers between individuals or between savings sectors.

These savings are maintained by savers through a variety of media. The specific form in which savers keep their savings is largely dependent upon the type of saver and the motives for saving. The amount of savings that a saver accumulates is another variable that influences choice of media, since some media are not adaptable to all sizes of savings. A more thorough description of savers and savings media follows, with a discussion of the factors influencing trends in savings and savings media.

PERSONAL SAVINGS

The most important savings sector in the economy is personal savings. Private individuals provide more than 75 percent of all savings in the United States. It is toward the individual that most financial institutions direct their attention in the capital accumulation processes.

Reasons for Saving

Private individuals maintain savings for a number of reasons. They set aside a part of their current income for the acquisition of costly durable consumer goods. Savings are set aside by individuals to meet unforeseeable contingencies. These savings are not set aside for specific future consumption; instead, they represent emergency or "rainy-day" funds. Individuals may also save for such long-term foreseeable expenditures as children's college education or for retirement. For short periods of time people may save a portion of current income simply because desirable goods and services are not available for purchase.

Savings Media for Individuals

Persons have open to them a number of media in which to maintain their savings. These media range in liquidity from cash balances to pension funds. The medium that a person chooses is usually a function of the liquidity he desires and the degree of safety and return that the particular medium provides.

Cash Balances. The most liquid form of savings that an individual can maintain is cash. Cash savings are generally in the form of checking accounts and pocket cash. People maintain this liquidity in order to meet current commitments or to make expenditures in the very near future. Cash savings may also be hoarded. Such hoards are not held for specific consumption purposes but rather out of distrust of banks or because the individual wants his monetary wealth to be close at hand. Funds so hoarded are withdrawn from circulation and add nothing to the capital formation process. The more important form of cash savings, those maintained in bank checking accounts, constitutes a significant part of total bank demand deposits.

Thrift Accounts, Insurance Reserves, and Pension Funds. A wide choice of facilities that provide both safety of principal and a reasonable yield is available to the individual saver. The combination of ready availability of funds and a regular earning power on thrift account investments has resulted in a substantial rate of growth for such accounts. Chart 5-1 reflects the relative growth of the stocks of financial assets held by individuals. Three principal forms of thrift accounts are those maintained as savings or time deposits in commercial banks, the shares and deposits in savings and loan associations, and the shares of mutual savings banks. The item in Chart 5-1 described as "Time and Savings

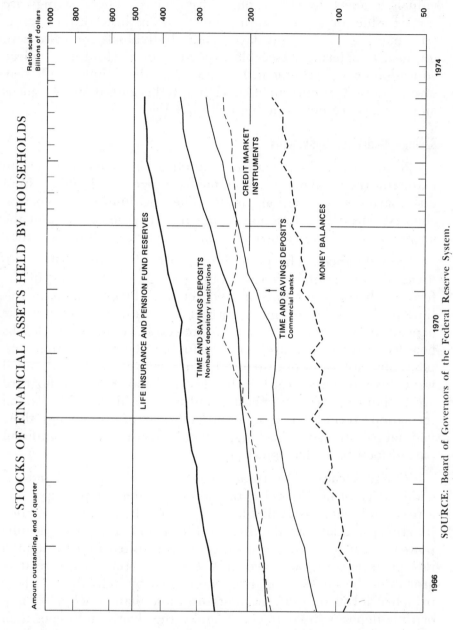

Chart 5-1

STOCKS OF FINANCIAL ASSETS HELD BY HOUSEHOLDS

Ratio scale
Billions of dollars

Amount outstanding, end of quarter

1000 800 600 500 400 300 200 100 50

LIFE INSURANCE AND PENSION FUND RESERVES

TIME AND SAVINGS DEPOSITS
Nonbank depository institutions

CREDIT MARKET
INSTRUMENTS

TIME AND SAVINGS DEPOSITS
Commercial banks

MONEY BALANCES

1966   1970   1974

SOURCE: Board of Governors of the Federal Reserve System.

Deposits—Nonbank Depository Institutions" is made up almost entirely of the assets of savings and loan associations and mutual savings banks.

In the decade of the fifties savings and loan associations enjoyed by far the most rapid rate of growth of these three forms of thrift institutions. During the sixties, however, the growth of time and savings accounts in commercial banks took over the lead. The relative rates of growth of commercial banks and savings and loan associations has apparently been determined by the maximum rates these organizations are legally permitted to pay savers. Since these permissible rates change from time to time, the competitive positions of the institutions in attracting savings also change.

Another, though less important, savings medium for individuals is the credit union. Credit unions have enjoyed one of the most rapid rates of growth of all forms of financial institutions.[5]

The contractual savings embodied in insurance reserves and in pension funds represent another fast-growing commitment of personal savings. It should be mentioned that the contractual savings plans provided by local and state governments and the federal government have also grown at a rapid rate. The principal form of individual savings provided by state and local governments are retirement funds. The federal government accumulates reserves for the accounts of individuals through the Old-Age and Survivors Insurance Trust Fund, the Disability Insurance Trust Fund, the National Service Life Insurance Fund, and others. The total of individual savings committed to government insurance and pension fund reserves at all levels at the end of 1973 was approximately $160 billion.[6] These savings of individuals as represented by government-held reserves are invested primarily in the obligations of federal, local, and state governments. As such, they satisfy a part of the demand for funds of government in general.

Securities. Because of the wide diversity of security forms—corporate stock, corporate bonds, and government securities—private individuals can usually find a security that is well suited

---

[5] Thrift account facilities are described in detail in the chapters as follows: savings and time deposits of commercial banks, Chapter 8; mutual savings banks, Chapter 13; credit unions, Chapter 19; and savings and loan associations, Chapter 20.

[6] *Statistical Bulletin*, United States Securities and Exchange Commission, April, 1974, p. 459.

to their special savings objectives. For those persons desiring growth of principal, corporate stocks with the promise of growth are available. Such stocks usually provide a lower current income to the saver ·than is available from most other securities. Other savers may place primary emphasis on stability of principal for liquidity purposes. The stocks of public utilities and other recession-resistant companies are available for this purpose as are high-grade corporate and government bonds. There is a wide spectrum of risk, growth potential, and yield in which virtually every saver who chooses securities as a savings medium can find a place for his funds consistent with his objectives and preferences.

By far the most important security as a savings medium for individuals is the common stock of corporations. This has been due in part to an increasing number of people entering the market as common stock investors. More important, however, has been the increase in market value of common stocks over the past decade. Such increased values have expanded the share of common stocks as a percent of total savings.

It should be recognized that insofar as the market value of common stock held by an individual reflects a gain due to increased market value, financial saving under our definition has not taken place. A "windfall" or "paper" gain has been experienced without a corresponding restraint on consumption. To this extent, the market value of common shares is inflated beyond the limits of annual increments to individuals' financial savings. In like manner, a substantial decline in market values resulting in large decreases in the market value of common shares would not reduce our measure of annual increment to financial savings.

The shares of investment companies add to the importance of common stock as a form of individual savings. These shares have played an especially important role for the saver with limited funds because of their ready availability in small quantities. The investment companies have also instituted convenient procedures for accumulation of shares on a regular basis out of current income.

CORPORATE SAVINGS

Corporations, broadly described, include not only business enterprises but nonprofit institutions such as colleges, churches, hospitals, and philanthropic foundations. These nonprofit organizations ordinarily acquire their financial assets not through their own saving but through the gifts of individuals and business corporations. The earning power of their endowed funds is usually devoted to their operating expenses, and their savings are small. In the following pages we are concerned with the savings of the nonfinancial business corporation. These financial savings are defined as the financial assets retained by the corporation out of funds generated through business operations that are neither paid out in dividends nor invested in operating assets of the business. Funds generated through business operations include not only corporate earnings but the conversion of operating assets to financial assets through depreciation allowances.

Corporate saving for short-term working capital purposes is by far the most important reason for the accumulation of financial assets. Seasonal fluctuations create an uneven demand for corporate operating assets, such as inventories and accounts receivable. And because of these seasonal fluctuations, cash inflow is seldom in just the right amount and at the right time to accommodate the increased levels of operating assets. Quarterly corporate income tax liabilities also impose upon corporations the necessity of accumulating financial assets for their payment. Although the short-term accumulation of financial assets on the part of business corporations does not add to the level of long-term savings of the economy as a whole, such funds do enter the monetary stream and become available to users of short-term borrowed funds. As such, these short-term savings serve to meet a part of the demand for funds of consumers, government, and other businesses. These savings are typically held by the corporation in the form of checking accounts with commercial banks, short-term obligations of the federal government, commercial paper, and certificates of deposit as issued by commercial banks. These financial assets meet the requirements of safety and liquidity.

Corporations also engage in the savings process for purposes of meeting planned expenditures in the future. Reserves are often set up to provide all or part of the cost of construction, the acquisition of equipment, or major maintenance and repairs to existing facilities. Savings committed to these purposes are often invested in securities having longer maturities and higher yields than those acquired for short-term business purposes. Such securities include the obligations of both corporations and government and, to a limited extent, corporate stock.

FACTORS AFFECTING SAVINGS

In the preceding pages, brief mention was made of the reasons for personal and corporate savings. In the following discussion, we are concerned with the factors at work that influence the total amount of savings that are forthcoming. These factors are as follows: levels of income, economic expectations, cyclical influences, and the life stage of the individual saver. The precise relationship between savings and consumption is the subject of much debate and continuing study, however, and we limit our observations here to broad generalizations.

Levels of Income

For our purposes, savings have been defined as current income less tax payments and consumption expenditures. Keeping this definition in mind, let us explore the effect of changes in income on the levels of savings of individuals. As his income falls, the individual attempts to maintain his plane of living as long as possible. In so doing, the proportion of his consumption expenditures increases and total savings diminish. As income is further reduced, the individual may be forced to curtail his consumption expenditures, and this results in a lower plane of living. Such reduction is reasonably limited, however, since the basic needs of the family must be met. Not only will personal savings be eliminated under circumstances of drastic reductions in income, but the individual may also *dissave*, that is, he will liquidate accumulated savings rather than reduce further his consumption expenditures.

As income increases, the individual will again be in a position to save. He will not necessarily begin saving immediately since it may be desirable to buy many things that had to be foregone during the low-income period. The amount of pent-up demand, notably for durable consumer goods, largely determines the rate of increase in savings during periods of income recovery.

Economic Expectations

The anticipation of future events has a significant effect on savings. If individuals believe that their incomes will decrease in the near future, they may tend to curtail their current expenditures in order to establish a reserve for the period of low income. A worker anticipating a long and protracted labor dispute may increase his current savings as partial protection against the financial impact of a strike.

Expectations of a general increase in price levels may also have a strong influence upon the liquidity that savers will want to maintain. The prospect of price increases on consumer durable goods may cause an increase in their sales as individuals attempt to make their purchases before such price increases take place. Savings are thus quickly converted to consumer expenditures. Corporate savings too may be reduced as a result of price increase expectations. In addition to the commitment of funds to plant and office equipment before price increases take place, corporations typically increase their inventory positions. And as for the individual, the prospect of an interruption in the supply of inventory by reason of a labor strike or other such cause results in a rapid stockpiling of raw materials and merchandise. The prospect of price decreases and of ample production capacity has the opposite influence of increasing the liquidity and financial assets of a business relative to its operating assets.

The influence of both rising levels of income and price increase expectations is reflected in Chart 5-2. The gradual rise in savings until 1968 reflects the steadily growing incomes of individuals. Starting in 1968, however, the rate of savings began to turn down in spite of continuing increases in personal income. This apparent contradiction is explained by the realization on the part of individuals of the impact of prevailing inflationary pressures. Inflationary pressures reached levels that had not been experienced since the Korean War and a philosophy of "Buy it now because it will cost more later" prevailed, providing a classic example of the impact of price increase expectations on the spend-save decisions of individuals. Savings surged upward again in 1970 and then slackened under the pressure of renewed price inflation.

Chart 5-2

PERSONAL SAVINGS UNITED STATES 1960-1973

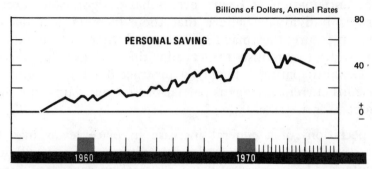

SOURCE: *Historical Chart Book,* Board of Governors of the Federal Reserve System, 1973, p. 76.

Cyclical Influences

While changes in levels of income may be brought about largely by cyclical movements in the economy, they do not represent the complete effect that the cycle has on savings. Cyclical movements affect not only the level but also the media of savings.

To illustrate this point, let us observe the effect that economic recession has on the shifting of savings from medium to medium, notably into time and savings deposits of commercial banks from other media. As short-term interest rates decrease during a period of economic recession for such money market instruments as United States Treasury bills, commercial paper, and obligations of United States government agencies, savings tend to shift into such institutions as commercial banks. The yield available on time and savings accounts in commercial banks has remained fairly constant in relation to the yields of money market instruments in general. Chart 5-3 reveals the strategic relationship between declining yields on United States Treasury bills and the rate of change of time and savings deposits in commercial banks. The years 1969 and 1970 provide an excellent illustration of this relationship. Industrial production and employment showed much strength in 1969. The Consumer Price Index increased strikingly also. The yields on short-term United States obligations increased rapidly while the rates paid on time and savings accounts at commercial banks remained relatively fixed. The result was a sub-

Chart 5-3

INTEREST RATES ON SHORT-TERM
U.S. GOVERNMENT OBLIGATIONS

per cent per annum

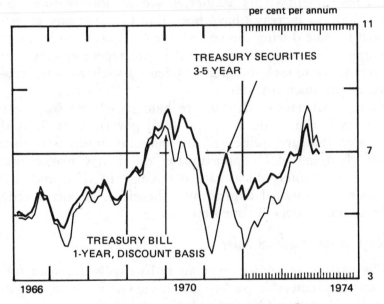

1966   1970   1974

GROWTH OF COMMERCIAL BANK
TIME AND SAVINGS DEPOSITS

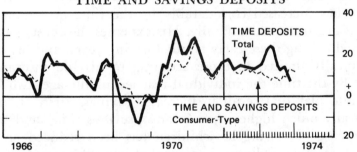

1966   1970   1974

SOURCE: Board of Governors of the Federal Reserve System.

stantial reduction in the absolute level of time and savings deposits. In 1970 conditions were reversed. Industrial production was down somewhat and unemployment rates increased. The rates available on short-term United States Obligations fell rapidly and time and savings deposits at commercial banks increased substantially.

The countercyclical swings in the rate of time and savings deposits in commercial banks must be explained in part by factors other than differential yields. Savings deposits are held almost entirely by individuals. It is doubtful that the average individual shifts heavily into savings accounts because of decreasing money market instrument yields. Rather, it seems more reasonable that savings deposits increases have been due to the steady growth in personal income during the last decade. Savings deposits increases preceding or during periods of economic recession may also be due to a desire to seek the greater safety of such accounts relative to that of the stock market.

Time certificates of deposit are held largely by corporations, foreign institutions, and state and local governments. It is these institutions that are influenced by changing business conditions and by changing yield opportunities on money market instruments. The countercyclical rate of change in time and savings deposits at commercial banks must, therefore, be attributed primarily to the holders of time deposits.

Life Stage of the Individual Saver

The pattern of savings over an individual's life span follows a somewhat predictable pattern when viewed in the aggregate of the total population. An individual saves very little during his youthful years simply because he produces little income. His income has increased considerably by the time he has matured and has begun to rear a family. His expenses, however, have also increased during these early family-forming years; and his savings are typically limited to those accruing to his life insurance reserves. By the time the individual reaches middle age, two factors come into play that result in increased savings. First, his income is typically much higher than at any previous time; and second, the expense of rearing his children has been reduced or eliminated. It is this middle-aged group that saves the most.

At retirement the individual's income is sharply reduced. He may now begin the process of dissaving. His pension fund payments along with accumulated savings now are drawn upon for current living expenses.

The level of savings of individuals is therefore a function of age composition of the population as a whole. Other things remaining the same, a shift in age composition in which the proportion of the young to the elderly increases would cause fewer current savings to be forthcoming. A population shift to a large proportion of individuals in the productive middle-age years would result in a greater savings potential.

Life Stage of the Corporation

Just as the financial savings of an individual are governed in part by his age, so the financial savings generated by the business firm are a function of its life stage. It is true, of course, that all business firms do not proceed through a fixed life-stage cycle. To the extent, however, that the firm experiences the typical pattern of vigorous early growth and ultimate maturity and decline, its flow of financial savings is influenced.

During the pioneering and early expansion years of a successful business, the volume of physical assets typically increases rapidly. So rapid is this growth that the firm is unable to establish a strong position with respect to its financial assets. Indeed, it is during these years of the corporate life cycle that heavy reliance is placed on borrowed capital. At this time the corporation is typically a heavy user of financial assets rather than a provider.

More intensive market penetration and expanding geographic areas of distribution make it possible for the firm to continue its growth. Continuing profitable expansion becomes more difficult, however, as the managerial talent of the firm reaches the limit of its ability to direct and control operations and as competing firms in the industry also grow. The combination of a slowdown in expansion and a continuing large flow of cash generation results in financial savings. As the enterprise matures and ceases to expand, it reaches its peak of savings. Earnings are high, and commitment of funds to increased operating assets is reduced or eliminated.

As the firm begins to decline in the final phase of the life cycle, its ability to create financial savings is reduced. During the early years of the decline of a business, however, it may continue to provide a reasonably high level of financial savings. This is true, notwithstanding lower profits, because of the conversion of physical assets to financial assets through depreciation allowances.

As the final stages of decline are reached, the firm is unable to generate further financial savings and is, in all probability, perpetuating itself largely on the basis of the sustaining power of its previously accumulated financial assets.

QUESTIONS

1. Savings may mean different things to different people. Describe some of the possible differences in the savings concept.
2. Describe the role of personal savings of United States citizens in the early economic growth of the nation. In what way has that role changed in recent generations?
3. Do you consider a high level of continued savings to be of importance to the future economic growth of the nation?
4. Describe your personal saving plans for the next ten years. Do you expect to alter your savings pattern as you become older? Why?
5. Describe the conditions that would appeal to you in investing your savings. Indicate the types of savings media that would meet your requirements.
6. Describe the relative growth rates of the principal thrift institutions, and indicate the reasons for the differences in growth.
7. Describe the special appeal of corporate stocks for the individual saver. Do you consider this appeal to be well founded, or is it possible that corporate stocks may be enjoying a temporary glamour and popularity?
8. In what ways can nonfinancial business corporations save?
9. The purposes for which corporations save have a direct bearing on ways in which savings are held or invested. Give some examples.
10. Describe some of the principal factors influencing the levels of savings forthcoming from individuals and corporations.
11. Explain the countercyclical swings in the rate of time and savings deposits in commercial banks.
12. In what respect does the age composition of a nation's population affect its ability to save?

SUGGESTED READINGS

FRIEND, IRWIN. *Individuals' Savings.* New York: John Wiley & Sons, Inc., 1954.

GOLDSMITH, RAYMOND. *A Study of Savings in the United States.* Princeton, New Jersey: Princeton University Press. Three Volumes. 1955.

————. *The Flow of Capital Funds in the Postwar Economy.* New York: National Bureau of Economic Research, 1965. Chapter 1.

KEMMERER, DONALD J., and C. CLYDE JONES. *American Economic History.* New York: McGraw-Hill Book Company, Inc., 1959.

KUZNETS, SIMON. *Capital in the American Economy, Its Formation and Financing.* New York: National Bureau of Economic Research, 1961. Chapters 1 through 4.

Savings and Loan Fact Book. Chicago: United States Savings and Loan League (1973), pp. 7-17.

"What We Do With Our Savings," *Business in Brief.* New York: The Chase Manhattan Bank (April, 1974), pp. 6 and 7.

6

Expansion and Contraction of the Money Supply

In Chapter 1, the nature of monetary transactions was described in some detail, stressing the use of money for current transactions of all types and also for investments of all kinds. The supply of funds available for investment is determined primarily by the level of savings, and the factors affecting savings were analyzed in the preceding chapter. The supply of funds for investment is also affected by the size of the total money supply in relation to the demands put upon it. This relationship in turn affects the price level and economic activity generally. Therefore, the process by which the money supply is increased and decreased is a very important factor in the economy.

This chapter begins with a discussion of the changes in the volume of federal reserve notes and of coins. Next, the process by which deposit credit is expanded and contracted by the banking system is explored in some detail; and the various factors which affect it are analyzed and summarized. A final section of the chapter shows how these factors have worked out in several periods in our history.

CHANGES IN THE VOLUME OF FEDERAL RESERVE NOTES AND FRACTIONAL COINS

Federal reserve notes may be issued by the Federal Reserve System with a backing of gold certificates, commercial paper, or United States government bonds. The use of notes and drafts is not common in American business transactions, and as a result, the commercial paper held by the banking system has fallen far short of monetary needs. Federal reserve notes, therefore, have been backed by government bonds and gold certificates. On March 27, 1974, for example, the backing for $67.1 billion in federal reserve notes was $2.3 billion of gold certificates, and $66.8 billion of United States government securities.[1]

The volume of federal reserve notes has increased to meet the needs of the country for currency. Large increases took place during World War II, although there was a fairly rapid rate of increase beginning in 1933. The increases before 1933, except for a brief period during World War I, were largely to meet the needs of an increasing population and a rising standard of living. Part of the increase after 1933 was due to government efforts to raise the level of economic activity. During World War II, a major part of the increase was due to the rapid increases in the volume of payments resulting from war activities and in the postwar period it was due to inflation.

Before the onset of the 1929 depression, the backing for federal reserve notes was gold and commercial paper. The volume of commercial paper was large enough and grew rapidly enough to permit increases in this part of the money supply to keep pace with the increasing level of business activity. During the depression, the supply of commercial paper in the portfolios of the federal reserve banks dropped to a level so low that extra gold had to be used as backing for federal reserve notes. When gold flowed out of the country due to the uncertainties of the world economic situation, it became almost impossible to provide sufficient monetary backing. As a result, Congress passed the Glass-Steagall Act in 1932 that permitted government bonds to be used along with gold and commercial paper as backing for federal reserve notes.

---

[1] *Federal Reserve Bulletin,* April, 1974, p. A12.

Since that time government bonds have been used to an increasing extent as backing for the federal reserve bank currency.

The original requirement for gold backing of federal reserve notes was 35 percent and 40 percent against member bank deposits with the Federal Reserve. This was changed in 1945 to 25 percent against notes and deposits combined. In 1965 Congress eliminated the gold-certificate requirement against deposits and in 1968 against federal reserve notes. This action was made necessary by the increase in currency needed to carry on the expanding volume of economic activity and by the sustained loss of gold which occurred after 1958.

Federal reserve notes still maintain their elastic character even though they are not tied to changes in business volume as directly as when they were backed to a large extent by commercial paper. The supply does expand and contract, however, to meet changes in the demand for funds. For example, when the Christmas shopping season ends, the public has less need for funds; and money accumulated in the hands of businessmen is deposited in their banks. The commercial banks turn these excess funds over to their federal reserve bank, which exchanges the excess federal reserve notes for its collateral with the federal reserve agent, thus reducing the supply of federal reserve notes.

Federal reserve notes have also become elastic with respect to government deficit expenditures. As the government debt grows, more bonds are available to be used as collateral for federal reserve notes. Therefore, when large-scale government operations, such as those of World War II, result in a greatly increased demand for currency, the basis exists for meeting this demand by the issuance of additional federal reserve notes.

The money supply is also increased when fractional coins are issued by the Treasury. When the Treasury issues additional coins in response to the demands of one of the federal reserve banks, it receives a credit to its account at that bank. When the Treasury draws checks on such an account, the funds are transferred to the general public. As these funds are deposited in a commercial bank, they become available to the banking system as additional funds. As banks in turn deposit them in a federal reserve bank, they increase their reserve balances.

EXPANSION AND CONTRACTION OF DEPOSIT CREDIT

The banking system of the United States can expand and contract the volume of deposit credit as the needs for funds by individuals, businesses, and governments change. The process by which this is done is not easily understood from a study of the operations of an individual bank but requires a study of the operations of the banks as units in a banking system. Furthermore, an understanding of this process requires a study of the relationship of bank loans to deposits and to bank reserves.

In analyzing the process of bank credit expansion, it is helpful to make a distinction between primary deposits and derivative deposits. The former arise whenever cash and all forms of checks drawn against other banks are placed on deposit in a bank or whenever a bank receives money from a bond coupon or other item left for collection. The derivative deposit arises out of a credit to a depositor's account when he receives a bank loan. Since most businessmen pay all their bills by check except for petty cash items, they do not withdraw the loan funds but leave them on deposit and write checks against them. The commercial banks must keep reserves against deposits, primary or derivative.

Credit Expansion

When reserves were first required by law, the purpose was to assure depositors that the bank had the ability to meet their needs for the withdrawal of cash. This was before the establishment of the Federal Reserve System which made it possible for a sound bank to obtain additional funds in time of need. Confidence of depositors in the ability of a bank to meet their needs has also developed because of deposit insurance and more thorough and competent bank examinations by governmental agencies. The basic function of required reserves today is to provide a means for regulating the process of credit expansion and contraction.

The process of credit creation takes place as a result of the operations of the whole system of banks, but it arises out of the independent transactions of individual banks. To explain the process, therefore, the loan activities of a single bank will first be considered without regard to their effects on other banks, and then in relationship to a system of banks. This approach is somewhat artificial since a bank practically never acts independently of the actions of other banks, but it has been adopted to clarify the process. Furthermore, it helps to explain the belief of some bankers that they cannot create credit since they only loan funds placed on deposit in their bank by their depositors. This analysis shows how a system of banks in which each bank is carrying on its local activities can do what an individual banker cannot do.

For illustration, let us assume that a bank which must keep reserves of 20 percent against deposits receives a primary deposit of $10,000. The bank statement, ignoring all other items, would then show the following:

ASSETS		LIABILITIES	
Reserves	$10,000	Deposits	$10,000

Against this new deposit of $10,000, the bank must keep required reserves of 20 percent, or $2,000, so that it has $8,000 of excess reserves available.

It may appear at first glance as if the banker could proceed to make loans for $40,000 since all he needs is a 20 percent reserve against the resulting demand deposits. If he attempted to do this, however, he would soon find himself in difficulty. Since bank loans are usually obtained just prior to the demand for funds, checks would undoubtedly be written against the deposit accounts almost at once. Many of these checks would be deposited in other banks, and the bank would be faced with a demand for cash as checks were presented for collection. This demand could reach the full $40,000. Since the bank has only $8,000 to meet it, it could not follow such a course and remain in business.

The amount that the banker can safely lend is the $8,000 of excess reserves. If he lends more, he runs the risk of not being able to make payments on checks. After such a loan, his books show:

ASSETS		LIABILITIES	
Reserves	$10,000	Deposits	$18,000
Loans and discounts.	8,000		

If a check were written for the full amount of the derivative deposit ($8,000) and sent to a bank in another city for deposit, the lending bank would lose all of its excess reserves. This may be seen from its books, which would appear as follows:

ASSETS		LIABILITIES	
Reserves	$ 2,000	Deposits	$10,000
Loans and discounts.	8,000		

In practice a bank may be able to loan somewhat more than the $8,000 since banks frequently require their customers to keep an average deposit balance of something in the neighborhood of 15 to 20 percent of the loan. The whole of the additional $1,500 to $2,000 cannot safely be loaned since an average balance of $1,500 to $2,000 does not prevent the full amount of the loan being used for a period of time. With an average balance in each derivative deposit account, however, all accounts will not be drawn to zero at the same time; and some additional funds are available for loans.

It may be argued that a banker will feel sure that some checks written against his bank will be redeposited in his bank and that he can therefore lend larger sums. The banker, however, since his is one of approximately 14,000 banks, can usually not anticipate such redeposits of funds; and he cannot run the risk of being caught short of reserves. Thus, when an individual bank receives a new primary deposit, it cannot lend the full amount of that deposit but only the amount available as excess reserves. From the point of view of an individual bank, therefore, credit creation appears impossible. Since a part of every new deposit cannot be loaned out due to reserve requirements, the volume of additional loans is less than new primary deposits.

What cannot be done by an individual bank is being done by the banking system when many banks are expanding loans and derivative deposits at the same time. To illustrate this point, assume that we have an economy with just two banks, *A* and *B*. This example can be realistic if we assume further that Bank *A* represents one bank in the system and Bank *B*, all other banks combined. Bank *A*, as in our previous example, receives a new primary deposit of $10,000 and is required to keep reserves of 20 percent against deposits. Therefore, its books would appear as follows:

BANK *A*

ASSETS	LIABILITIES
Reserves $10,000	Deposits $10,000

A loan for $8,000 is made and credited as follows:

BANK *A*

ASSETS	LIABILITIES
Reserves $10,000	Deposits $18,000
Loans and discounts. 8,000	

Assume that a check is drawn against it almost immediately and deposited in Bank *B*. The books of the two banks would then show the following:

BANK *A*

ASSETS	LIABILITIES
Reserves .... $ 2,000	Deposits $10,000
Loans and discounts. 8,000	

BANK *B*

ASSETS	LIABILITIES
Reserves .... $ 8,000	Deposits .... $ 8,000

The derivative deposit arising out of a loan from Bank *A* has now been transferred by check to Bank *B* where it is received as a primary deposit. Bank *B* must now set aside 20 percent as required reserves and may lend or reinvest the remainder. Its books after such a loan would appear as follows:

BANK *B*
(After a loan equal to its excess reserves)

ASSETS	LIABILITIES
Reserves .... $ 8,000	Deposits $14,400
Loans and discounts. 6,400	

Assume that a check is drawn against the derivative deposit of $6,400 arising out of the loan by Bank *B*. This reduces its reserves and deposits as follows:

BANK *B*

ASSETS	LIABILITIES
Reserves .... $ 1,600	Deposits .... $ 8,000
Loans and discounts. 6,400	

The check for $6,400 will most likely be deposited in a bank, in our example in Bank *A* or Bank *B* itself, since we have assumed that only two banks exist. In the American banking system, it may be deposited in one of the approximately 14,000 banks.

This process of credit expansion can take place in the same way when a bank buys securities as when it makes a loan. Assume, as we did in the case of a bank loan, the following situation:

BANK *A*

ASSETS		LIABILITIES	
Reserves	$10,000	Deposits	$10,000

Securities costing $8,000 are purchased and the proceeds credited to the account of the seller, giving the following situation:

BANK *A*

ASSETS		LIABILITIES	
Reserves	$10,000	Deposits	$18,000
Investments	$ 8,000		

Assume that a check is drawn against the deposit and is deposited in Bank *B*. The books of the two banks would then show:

BANK *A*

ASSETS		LIABILITIES	
Reserves	$ 2,000	Deposits	$10,000
Investments	8,000		

BANK *B*

ASSETS		LIABILITIES	
Reserves	$ 8,000	Deposits	$ 8,000

Just as in the case of a loan, the derivative deposit has been transferred to Bank *B* where it is received as a primary deposit.

At each stage in the process, 20 percent of the new primary deposit becomes required reserves and 80 percent excess reserves that can be loaned out. In time, the whole of the original $10,000 primary deposit will have become required reserves, and $50,000 of deposits will have been credited to deposit accounts of which $40,000 will have been loaned out.

Required reserves on demand deposits may be as high as 22 percent for reserve city banks and not above 14 percent for other banks. Required reserves in the United States probably average somewhat less than 15 percent. The possibilities of credit creation with a 15 percent required reserve are shown in Table 6-1.

Offsetting Factors

The process of credit creation can go on only to the extent that the activities described actually take place. If for any reason the proceeds of a loan are withdrawn from the banking system, no new deposit arises to continue the process. A new deposit of

Table 6-1

THE MULTIPLYING CAPACITY OF MONEY IN BANK OR COMMODITY TRANSACTIONS

		Amount Received or Deposited	Amount Lent	Amount for Legal Reserves
Transaction	1	$100.00	$ 85.00	$ 15.00
	2	85.00	72.25	12.75
	3	72.25	61.41	10.84
	4	61.41	52.20	9.21
	5	52.20	44.37	7.83
	6	44.37	37.71	6.66
	7	37.71	32.05	5.66
	8	32.05	27.24	4.81
	9	27.24	23.15	4.09
	10	23.15	19.68	3.47
	11	19.68	16.73	2.95
	12	16.73	14.22	2.51
	13	14.22	12.09	2.13
	14	12.09	10.28	1.81
	15	10.28	8.74	1.54
	16	8.74	7.43	1.31
	17	7.43	6.32	1.11
	18	6.32	5.37	.95
	19	5.37	4.56	.81
	20	4.56	3.88	.68
Total for	20	$640.80	$544.68	$ 96.12
Additional transactions		25.86	21.98	3.88
Grand total		$666.66	$566.66	$100.00

SOURCE: Board of Governors of the Federal Reserve System, *The Federal Reserve System—Its Purposes and Functions*, Washington, D. C., 1947, p. 18.

$10,000 permits loans of $8,000 under a 20 percent required reserve; but if this $8,000 were used in currency transactions without being deposited in a bank, no credit could be created. It is the custom of carrying on business by means of checks which are deposited on the same day or next business day after they are received that makes credit creation possible.

In the examples above, no allowance was made for currency withdrawal. In actual practice, as the volume of business in the economy increases, some additional cash is withdrawn for hand-to-hand circulation and to meet the needs of business for petty cash. Larger balances are also kept in the deposit accounts of businesses and individuals. Banks likewise must keep larger sums to meet day-to-day needs for funds and thus must keep larger till reserves over and above the required reserves.

Money may also be withdrawn from the banking system to meet the demand for payments to foreign countries, or foreign banks may withdraw some of the money they are holding on deposit in American banks. The United States Treasury may withdraw funds it has on deposit in commercial banks. The volume of demand deposits may be reduced because individuals shift some of their funds into time deposits or savings accounts. All of these factors reduce the multiplying capacity of primary deposits.

Furthermore, this process can go on only if excess reserves are actually being loaned by the banks. This means that banks must be willing to lend the full amount of their excess reserves and that acceptable borrowers must be available who have a demand for credit.

Contraction of Credit

When the need for funds by business decreases, this process can work in reverse. Expansion takes place as long as the demand for new bank loans exceeds the repayment of old loans. When old loans are being repaid faster than new loans are being granted and banks are not immediately investing the funds so freed, contraction of the supply of deposit credit will take place.

Let us assume that Bank *A* has no excess reserves and see the effect of the repayment of a loan. Before the borrower began to build up deposits to repay the loan, its books were as follows:

BANK *A*

ASSETS		LIABILITIES	
Reserves	$ 2,000	Deposits	$10,000
Loans and discounts.	8,000		

The borrower of the $8,000 must build up his deposit account by $8,000 in order to be able to repay the loan. This is reflected on the books as follows:

BANK *A*

ASSETS		LIABILITIES	
Reserves	$10,000	Deposits	$18,000
Loans and discounts.	8,000		

After the $8,000 is repaid, the books show the following:

ASSETS		LIABILITIES	
Reserves	$10,000	Deposits	$10,000

If no new loan is made from the $10,000 of reserves, credit contraction will result. This is true because $8,000 of funds have been taken out of the banking system to build up deposits to repay the loan and are now being held idle by Bank *A* as excess reserves. The result of taking out $8,000 of reserves may be cumulative on the contraction side just as it was during expansion.

Assume that the $8,000 of deposits built up to repay the loan came from Bank *B*, which before these funds were withdrawn had no excess reserves and showed the following situation on its books:

BANK *B*

ASSETS		LIABILITIES	
Reserves	$ 2,000	Deposits	$10,000
Loans and discounts.	8,000		

The withdrawal of $8,000 of deposits would require a sale of securities that might be held by the bank or a loan from its federal reserve bank or from another bank that might have excess funds to lend. If we assume a loan was made, its books would show:

BANK *B*

ASSETS		LIABILITIES	
Reserves	$ 400	Deposits	$ 2,000
Loans and discounts.	8,000	Loan from federal reserve bank	6,400

Reserves must remain at $400 since this amount is the required reserve on the $2,000 of deposits. In order to pay off its debt to the federal reserve bank, this bank will probably refuse to renew the $8,000 loan when it comes due. In order to pay the loan, the borrower builds up his deposit by $8,000. The books now show:

BANK B

ASSETS		LIABILITIES	
Reserves	$ 8,400	Deposits	$10,000
Loans and discounts.	8,000	Loan from federal reserve bank	6,400

This enables the bank to pay its loan to the federal reserve bank as follows:

BANK B

ASSETS		LIABILITIES	
Reserves	$ 2,000	Deposits	$10,000
Loans and discounts.	8,000		

After the $8,000 loan from the bank is repaid, the situation is as follows:

BANK B

ASSETS		LIABILITIES	
Reserves	$ 2,000	Deposits	$ 2,000

In building up the $8,000 deposit to repay the loan, the lender took $8,000 out of another bank in the system. This in turn led this bank to refuse to renew loans for this amount; and in building up deposit balances to repay the loans, funds were withdrawn from other banks. This process of contraction is thus cumulative just as the process of expansion is and it cannot be stopped if a bank sells securities to meet a demand for funds when it does not have excess reserves. When he buys the securities, the purchaser will withdraw funds from some bank in the system to pay for them, thus leading to contraction just as when the adjustment to a deficiency in reserves is a loan from the federal reserve bank that is repaid by reducing the amount of loans outstanding.

FACTORS AFFECTING BANK RESERVES

The extent to which the process of credit expansion or contraction can and does take place is governed by the level of free reserves which a bank has, that is, reserves above the level of required reserves. This is true for an individual bank and also for the banking system as a whole. Therefore, the factors which affect the level of bank reserves are of basic significance in determining the size of the money supply. There are four kinds of factors which affect reserves: currency flows, gold flows, Federal Reserve transactions, and Treasury transactions.

Changes in the Demand for Currency

Currency flows into and out of the banking system affect the level of bank reserves of the banks receiving the currency for deposit. Let us assume that individuals or a business find that they have excess currency of $100 and deposit it in Commercial Bank *A*. Deposit liabilities are increased by $100 and so are the reserves of Bank *A*. The bank now has excess reserves of $80, assuming a 20 percent level of required reserves; and these reserves can be used by the banking system to create $400 in additional deposits. If the bank does not have a need for the currency but sends it to its federal reserve bank, it will receive a $100 credit to its account. The volume of federal reserve notes is decreased by $100, and this frees the collateral backing them. These transactions may be summarized as follows:

1. Deposits in Bank *A* are increased by $100—$20 in required reserves and $80 in excess reserves.
2. Bank *A*'s deposit at its federal reserve bank is increased $100.
3. The amount of federal reserve notes is decreased by $100.

Just the opposite takes place when the public demands additional currency. Let us assume that a customer of Bank *A* needs additional currency and cashes a check for $100. The deposits of the bank are reduced by $100, and this reduces required reserves by $20. If the bank has no excess reserves, it must take steps to get an additional $80 of reserves either by borrowing from its federal reserve bank, calling a loan or not renewing one which comes due, or by selling securities. The reserves of the bank are also reduced by $100; and if it replenishes its supply of currency from its federal reserve bank, its deposits with this bank are reduced by $100. These transactions may be summarized thus:

1. Deposits in Bank *A* are reduced by $100—$20 in required reserves and $80 in excess reserves.
2. Bank *A*'s deposit at its federal reserve bank is reduced $100.
3. The amount of federal reserve notes is increased by $100.

Changes in Gold Flows

Bank reserves are also affected by gold flows into and out of the Treasury. Since it is illegal to hold gold except for industrial use, in coin collections, or in token amounts, newly mined gold or gold coming into the country from abroad must be sold to the Treasury. The Treasury pays for the gold with a check which is drawn against its account at the federal reserve bank. The person receiving the check deposits it with his bank and receives a credit in his deposit account. His bank sends the check to the federal reserve bank for collection, and funds are transferred from the Treasury account to the account of the bank. The Treasury sends the federal reserve bank gold certificates for the amount of the check, and the federal reserve bank credits the Treasury account for this amount.

The process for a $100 gold inflow, the check for which is deposited in Bank *A*, may be summarized as follows:

1. Deposits in Bank *A* are increased by $100—$20 in required reserves and $80 in excess reserves.
2. Bank *A*'s deposit at its federal reserve bank is increased by $100.
3. The federal reserve bank's holdings of gold certificates are increased by $100.

The Treasury account at the federal reserve bank is unchanged. It was reduced by $100 when the check to pay for the gold was collected but increased by $100 again when the federal reserve bank received the gold certificates.

Just the opposite type of transaction takes place when the Treasury sells gold, for example, to enable an importer to pay for goods. The process for a $100 gold outflow, the check for which is drawn on Bank *A*, may be summarized as follows:

1. Deposits in Bank *A* are reduced by $100—$20 in required reserves and $80 in excess reserves.
2. Bank *A*'s deposit at its federal reserve bank is reduced by $100.
3. The federal reserve bank has $100 less in gold certificates, since it sends a $100 gold certificate to the Treasury.

Federal Reserve System Transactions

Transactions of banks with the Federal Reserve System and changes in reserve requirements by the Federal Reserve also affect either the level of bank reserves or the degree to which credit can be expanded with a given volume of reserves. Such transactions may occur at the initiative of a commercial bank when it borrows from its federal reserve bank, at the initiative of the Federal Reserve when it buys or sells securities, or from a change in Federal Reserve float arising out of the process of collecting checks. These are considered in turn, and then the effect of a change in reserve requirements is described.

When a bank borrows from its federal reserve bank, it is borrowing reserves; and so reserves are increased by the amount of the loan. Similarly, when a loan to the federal reserve bank is repaid, reserves are reduced by the amount so repaid. The transactions when Bank *A* borrows $100 from its federal reserve bank may be summarized as follows:

1. Bank *A*'s deposit at its federal reserve bank is increased by $100. The assets of the federal reserve bank are increased by $100 by the note from Bank *A*.
2. Bank *A*'s excess reserves have been increased by $100. It also has a new $100 liability—its note to the federal reserve bank.

This process is just reversed when a debt to the federal reserve bank is repaid.

When the Federal Reserve purchases securities, such as government bonds, it adds to bank reserves. The **Federal Reserve** pays for the bonds with a check. The seller deposits the check in his account and receives a credit in his deposit account. The bank presents the check to the federal reserve bank for payment and receives a credit to its account. When the Federal Reserve buys a $100 government bond, the check for which is deposited in Bank *A*, the transactions may be summarized as follows:

1. Bank *A*'s deposit at its federal reserve bank is increased by $100. The bank has a new asset—a bond worth $100.
2. Deposits in Bank *A* are increased by $100—$20 in required reserves and $80 in excess reserves.

Just the opposite takes place when the Federal Reserve sells securities in the market.

Changes in Federal Reserve float also affect bank reserves. Float arises out of the process of collecting checks most of which are cleared in one way or another at federal reserve banks. Checks drawn on nearby banks are credited almost immediately to the account of the bank in which they were deposited and debited to the account of the bank on which the check was drawn. Under Federal Reserve regulations, all checks are credited one or two days later to the account of the bank in which the check was deposited. It may take longer for the check to go through the collection process and be debited to the account of the bank upon which it is drawn. When this happens, bank reserves are increased, and this increase is called *float*. The process in which a $100 check drawn on Bank *B* is deposited in Bank *A* and credited to its account before it is debited to the account of Bank *B* may be summarized:

1. Bank *A* transfers $100 from its Cash Items in the Process of Collection to its account at the federal reserve bank. Its reserves are increased by $100.
2. The federal reserve bank takes $100 from its Deferred Availability Account and transfers it to Bank *A*'s account.

Thus, total reserves of member banks are increased temporarily by $100. They are reduced when Bank *B*'s account at its federal reserve bank is reduced by $100 a day or two later.

Changes in reserve requirements change the amount of credit expansion which is possible with a given level of reserves. With required reserves of 20 percent, excess reserves of $80 can be expanded to $400 of additional loans and deposits. If required reserves are reduced to 10 percent, it is possible to expand $80 of excess reserves to $800 of additional loans and deposits. Additional expansion also takes place because when reserve requirements are lowered, part of the required reserves becomes excess reserves. This process is reversed when reserve requirements are raised.

Bank reserves are also affected by changes in the level of deposits of foreign central banks and governments at the federal reserve banks. Such deposits are maintained with the federal reserve banks to settle international balances and also at times as part of the monetary reserves of a foreign country. A decrease in such foreign deposits with the federal reserve banks increases bank reserves; an increase in them decreases bank reserves.

Minor changes in reserve positions also occur because of changes in the federal reserve accounts, such as the Capital and Surplus accounts. A decrease in such accounts makes more reserves available to the banking system; an increase in them reduces reserves.

Treasury Transactions

Bank reserves are also affected by the transactions of the Treasury, being increased by expenditures and other payments and decreased when the Treasury increases the size of its accounts at the federal reserve banks. The Treasury makes almost all of its payments out of its accounts at the federal reserve banks, and such spending adds to bank reserves. The recipient of a check from the Treasury deposits it in his commercial bank. The bank sends it to the federal reserve bank for collection and receives a credit to its account. The federal reserve bank debits the account of the Treasury. When a Treasury check for $100 is deposited in Bank *A* and required reserves are 20 percent, the transactions may be summarized as follows:

1. The deposits of Bank *A* are increased by $100, its required reserves by $20, and excess reserves by $80.

2. Bank A's reserves at the federal reserve bank are increased by $100.
3. The deposit account of the Treasury at the federal reserve bank is reduced by $100.

Treasury funds from tax collections or the sale of bonds are generally deposited in its accounts in commercial banks. When the Treasury has a need for funds for payment from its accounts at the federal reserve banks, it transfers funds from commercial banks to its accounts at the federal reserve banks. This process reduces bank reserves. When $100 is transferred from the account in Bank A and required reserves are 20 percent, transactions may be summarized as follows:

1. The Treasury deposit account in Bank A is reduced by $100, required reserves by $20, and excess reserves by $80.
2. The Treasury account at the federal reserve bank is increased by $100, and the account of Bank A is reduced by $100.

The effect on bank reserves is the same for changes in Treasury cash holdings as it is for changes in Treasury accounts at the federal reserve banks. Reserves are increased when the Treasury decreases its holding of cash, and reserves are decreased when it increases such holdings.

SUMMARY OF TRANSACTIONS AFFECTING RESERVES

The transactions which increase the volume of bank reserves or the ability of banks to expand credit may be summarized:

1. Decrease in the public's demand for currency.
2. Treasury purchase of gold.
3. Federal Reserve purchase of securities.
4. Increase in member bank borrowing.
5. Increase in Federal Reserve float.
6. Lowering of reserve requirements.
7. Decrease in foreign deposits with the federal reserve banks.

8. Decrease in other Federal Reserve accounts.
9. Treasury expenditures out of accounts at the federal reserve banks.
10. Decrease in Treasury cash holdings.

The transactions which decrease the volume of bank reserves or the ability of the banks to expand credit may be summarized as follows:

1. Increase in the public's demand for currency.
2. Treasury sales of gold.
3. Federal Reserve sales of securities.
4. Decrease in member bank borrowing.
5. Decrease in Federal Reserve float.
6. Raising of reserve requirements.
7. Increase in foreign deposits with the federal reserve banks.
8. Increase in other Federal Reserve accounts.
9. Treasury transfer of funds from its accounts at commercial banks to its accounts at the federal reserve banks.
10. Increase in Treasury cash holdings.

THE ROLE OF NONBANK FINANCIAL INSTITUTIONS IN THE CREDIT EXPANSION PROCESS

One of the most debated issues in monetary theory in recent years relates to the role of financial institutions other than banks in the credit expansion process. The Gurley-Shaw thesis [2] holds that there is little real difference in the role of banks and other financial institutions so far as credit expansion is concerned. This thesis minimizes the difference between money and other financial assets. Money is different from other financial assets because it is a means of payment; but so, for example, are shares of common stock different because they carry ownership rights. The multiple expansion of deposits is also not considered as a special case involving the banking system alone. In the general sense, multiple expansion is found everywhere in the economy. For example, farmers create crops in a multiple of land inputs, and cooks create

---

[2] Named after its originators and chief exponents, John B. Gurley, Brookings Institution, and Edward S. Shaw, Stanford University.

omelettes in a multiple of cream inputs. A bank may create $1,000 of demand deposits from a deposit of $1,000 of paper money and use the money in turn to buy bonds, resulting in multiple creation in the general sense. The same is true when $1,000 is placed in a share account in a savings and loan association and then used to buy mortgages.

A significant difference occurs in the case of multiple creation by banks in the legal sense. They must put aside part of all money put on deposit with them as legal reserves, and so their potential of multiple creation is restricted. This thesis thus holds that banks can create credit in a set multiple of funds put into them because of required reserves. If other institutions had the same reserve requirements, the results would be the same as far as multiple expansion is concerned.

There is some significance to such an analogy. All of these institutions channel funds from savers to investors. They do so by issuing their own debt instruments in the form of deposits, shares, and the like for savers and use the funds received for them to buy debt or equity investments, such as bonds, mortgages, and the like. If these institutions did not exist, funds would not flow so freely as they do; economic growth would be slower.

However, a major distinction between banks and other financial institutions must be kept clear. Banks are the only institutions which can create spendable funds. When any institution acquires cash for a debt instrument, there is no net increase in the total purchasing power of the economy. But a bank can acquire an earning asset with a debt instrument, that is, it can make a loan or buy a bond by creating a demand deposit. When this happens, there is a net increase in purchasing power. Under present business practice, this is not a temporary increase until the cash is withdrawn but is a permanent increase for the economy as long as the total demand for credit does not decrease.

This distinction is a real one which cannot be ignored. But financial institutions other than banks exchange for cash debt instruments which serve some of the same functions as money and so reduce the need for it. Funds for emergencies may be held in savings accounts in a savings and loan association and so reduce the need to hold money. Thus, a given amount of money will support a larger volume of economic activity. The financial activities of financial institutions other than banks speed up the velocity of money, even though they do not create spendable funds.

CONSOLIDATED CONDITION STATEMENT FOR BANKS AND THE MONETARY SYSTEM

Since so many factors affect the supply of money, it is helpful to have data on all of them in summary form so as to be able to analyze the changes that have taken place. Such information is sometimes published in the *Federal Reserve Bulletin* in the form of a Consolidated Condition Statement for banks and the monetary system. This statement shows a balance between the assets of the banking and monetary system and the liabilities in the form of deposits and currency and the capital accounts of the banks. The items on each side of this equation are as follows:

ASSETS	LIABILITIES AND CAPITAL
Gold stock and SDR's	Capital and miscellaneous accounts
Treasury currency outstanding	Currency outside banks
Bank credit	Demand deposits
Loans, net	Time deposits
Investment in U. S. government securities	Foreign deposits
securities	U. S. government balances
Investments in other securities	

Table 6-2 on pages 128 and 129 shows this Consolidated Condition Statement for various midyear and year-end dates between 1929 and 1972.

By studying the increases and the decreases in each of these items, it is possible to see the method by which the money supply has been expanded or contracted, and, by studying figures for a period of time, to see trends being developed. For example, the period from December 31, 1941, to December 31, 1945, the period of World War II, shows the following increases and decreases in the various accounts in the statement:

Table 6-2

CONSOLIDATED CONDITION STATEMENT

(In millions of dollars)

| DATE | GOLD STOCK and SDRs | TREASURY CURRENCY OUTSTANDING | ASSETS — BANK CREDIT | | U.S. GOVERNMENT SECURITIES | | | | OTHER SECURITIES | TOTAL ASSETS, NET— TOTAL LIABILITIES AND CAPITAL, NET | LIABILITIES AND CAPITAL | |
			TOTAL	LOANS, NET	TOTAL	COMMERCIAL AND SAVINGS BANKS	FEDERAL RESERVE BANKS	OTHER			TOTAL DEPOSITS AND CURRENCY	CAPITAL AND MISC. ACCOUNTS, NET
1929—June 29	4,037	2,019	58,642	41,082	5,741	5,499	216	26	11,819	64,698	55,776	8,922
1933—June 30	4,031	2,286	42,148	21,957	10,328	8,199	1,998	131	9,863	48,465	42,029	6,436
1939—Dec. 30	17,644	2,963	54,564	22,157	23,105	19,417	2,484	1,204	9,302	75,171	68,359	6,812
1941—Dec. 31	22,737	3,247	64,653	26,605	29,049	25,511	2,254	1,284	8,999	90,637	82,811	7,826
1945—Dec. 31	20,065	4,339	167,381	30,387	128,417	101,288	24,262	2,867	8,577	191,785	180,806	10,979
1947—Dec. 31	22,754	4,562	160,832	43,023	107,086	81,199	22,559	3,328	10,723	188,148	175,348	12,800
1950—Dec. 30	22,706	4,636	171,667	60,366	96,560	72,894	20,778	2,888	14,741	199,009	184,384	14,624
1960—Dec. 31	17,767	5,398	266,782	144,704	95,461	67,242	27,384	835	26,617	289,947	263,165	26,783
1965—Dec. 31	13,733	5,575	399,779	242,706	106,716	65,016	40,768	932	50,357	419,087	383,727	35,359
1968—Dec. 31	10,367	6,795	514,427	311,334	121,273	68,285	52,937	51	81,820	531,589	484,212	47,379
1970—Dec. 31	11,132	7,149	580,899	354,447	127,207	64,814	62,142	251	99,245	599,180	535,157	64,020
1972—Dec. 27	10,800	8,300	722,600	444,400	139,500	68,400	68,200	2,800	138,700	741,700	677,600	64,100

Continued on page 129.

DETAILS OF DEPOSITS AND CURRENCY

| DATE | MONEY SUPPLY | | | | | | RELATED DEPOSITS (NOT SEASONALLY ADJUSTED) | | | | | | | |
| | SEASONALLY ADJUSTED [1] | | | NOT SEASONALLY ADJUSTED | | | TIME [3] | | | | FOREIGN NET [5] | U. S. GOVERNMENT | | |
	TOTAL	CURRENCY OUTSIDE BANKS	DEMAND DEPOSITS ADJUSTED [2]	TOTAL	CURRENCY OUTSIDE BANKS	DEMAND DEPOSITS ADJUSTED [2]	TOTAL	COMMERCIAL BANKS	MUTUAL SAVINGS BANKS [4]	POSTAL SAVINGS SYSTEM		TREASURY CASH HOLDINGS	AT COMMERCIAL AND SAVINGS BANKS	AT F. R. BANKS
1929—June 29	.....	.....	.....	26,179	3,639	22,540	28,611	19,557	8,905	149	365	204	381	36
1933—June 30	.....	.....	.....	19,172	4,761	14,411	21,656	10,849	9,621	1,186	50	264	852	35
1939—Dec. 30	.....	.....	.....	36,194	6,401	29,793	27,059	15,258	10,523	1,278	1,217	2,409	846	634
1941—Dec. 31	.....	.....	.....	48,607	9,615	38,992	27,729	15,884	10,532	1,313	1,498	2,215	1,895	867
1945—Dec. 31	.....	.....	.....	102,341	26,490	75,851	48,452	30,135	15,385	2,932	2,141	2,287	24,608	977
1947—Dec. 31	110,500	26,100	84,400	113,597	26,476	87,121	56,411	35,249	17,746	3,416	1,682	1,336	1,452	870
1950—Dec. 30	114,600	24,600	90,000	117,670	25,398	92,272	59,247	36,314	20,009	2,923	2,518	1,293	2,989	668
1960—Dec. 31	139,200	28,200	111,000	144,458	29,356	115,102	108,468	71,380	36,318	770	3,184	377	6,193	485
1965—Dec. 31	167,100	35,400	131,700	175,314	36,999	138,315	199,427	146,433	52,686	309	1,780	760	5,778	668
1968—Dec. 31	199,600	42,600	157,000	207,347	43,527	163,820	267,627	202,786	64,841	.....	2,455	695	5,385	703
1970—Dec. 31	209,400	47,800	161,600	219,422	49,779	169,643	302,591	230,622	71,969	.....	3,148	431	8,409	1,156
1972—Dec. 27	252,400	55,400	197,000	200,100	56,600	203,500	402,800	311,400	91,400	.....	3,700	400	8,300	2,300

[1] Series begin in 1946; data are available only for last Wed. of the month.
[2] Other than interbank and U. S. Govt., less cash items in process of collection.
[3] After June 30, 1967, Postal Savings System Accounts were eliminated from this statement.
[4] Includes a small amount of demand deposits. Beginning with June, 1961, also includes amounts previously reported as other liabilities.
[5] Reclassification of deposits of foreign central banks in May, 1961, reduced this item by $1,900 million ($1,500 million to time and $400 million to demand deposits).

NOTE.—Includes all commercial and mutual savings banks, F. R. Banks, and Treasury currency funds (the gold account, SDR's, Treasury currency account, and Exchange Stabilization Fund).

SOURCE: *Federal Reserve Bulletin,* September, 1963, p. 1271, February, 1967, p. 259, June, 1969, p. A18, and January, 1973, p. A19.

ASSETS

		MILLIONS OF DOLLARS
Gold		— 2,672
Treasury currency		+ 1,092
Loans		+ 3,782
U. S. government obligations		
Commercial and savings banks	+75,777	
Federal reserve banks	+22,008	
Other banks	+ 1,583	+ 99,368
Other securities		— 422
		+101,148

LIABILITIES AND CAPITAL

	MILLIONS OF DOLLARS
Capital accounts	+ 3,153
Foreign bank deposits	+ 643
U. S. government balances	+ 22,895
Demand deposits	+ 36,859
Time deposits	+ 20,723
Currency outside banks	+ 16,875
	+101,148

From these figures it is apparent that the major factor leading to an increase in the money supply was bank investment in United States government obligations, although some increase also took place in bank loans to business and in the supply of Treasury currency. This increase in bank holding of Treasury obligations made possible the large increases in United States government balances, demand deposits, time deposits, and currency outside banks.

It is interesting and informative to see the contrast in the picture during the inflationary period of the most active phase of the Vietnam War. The increases and decreases that occurred between December 31, 1965, and December 31, 1970, were:

ASSETS

		MILLIONS OF DOLLARS
Gold stock and SDR's		— 2,601
Treasury currency		+ 1,574
Loans		+111,741
U. S. government obligations		
Commercial and savings banks	— 202	
Federal reserve banks	+21,374	
Other banks	— 681	+ 20,491
Other securities		+ 48,888
		+180,093

LIABILITIES AND CAPITAL

Capital accounts	+ 28,661
Foreign bank deposits	+ 1,368
U. S. government balances	+ 2,790
Demand deposits	+ 31,328
Time deposits	+103,164
Currency outside banks	+ 12,780
	+180,091

During this period the major source of the expansion of purchasing power was loans, although the purchase of securities other than those of the government also provided a sizeable sum. Bank reserves were cut down by the loss of gold. There was also a significant increase in bank holdings of government obligations. The major source of funds for the credit expansion during this period was time deposits and demand deposits, although currency outside banks and bank capital accounts also increased significantly.

There is a decided difference between the credit creation of the two periods. During World War II, it took place primarily through the sale of government obligations to the banking system, whereas during the Vietnam War it occurred largely because of the extension of bank loans to business and bank purchases of securities other than government obligations. Studies of figures in the Consolidated Condition Statement for any period show what is happening in the monetary and credit system, and especially the extent and type of inflationary pressures being developed.

QUESTIONS

1. How is the supply of federal reserve notes expanded and contracted to meet the needs of the economy?
2. Explain how changes in the supply of fractional coins change the money supply.
3. Trace the effect on its accounts of a loan made by a bank that has excess reserves available from new deposits.
4. Describe the process of credit expansion in an economy with two banks.
5. How can credit expansion take place when a bank buys securities?
6. Explain the potential for credit expansion when required reserves average 15 percent.
7. Explain the process of credit contraction.
8. Describe the relationship of bank reserves to the money supply.

9. Trace the effect on bank reserves of a change in the amount of cash held by the public.
10. Describe the effect on bank reserves of gold flows into and out of the Treasury.
11. Summarize the effect on bank reserves of various Federal Reserve transactions.
12. How do Treasury transactions affect bank reserves?
13. Summarize the factors that can lead to an increase and a decrease in bank reserves.
14. Discuss the role of financial intermediaries in the process of credit expansion and contraction.
15. Describe the Consolidated Condition Statement for banks and the monetary system.
16. Explain the use of the Consolidated Condition Statement in analyzing the factors which have led to a change in the money supply.
17. Compare and contrast the factors that led to an increase in the money supply during World War II and during the Vietnam War.
18. Using data in Table 6-3, summarize the changes in the factors affecting the money supply between December 31, 1970, and December 27, 1972. Analyze these changes.

SUGGESTED READINGS

BURGER, ALBERT E. "Money Stock Control." *Review,* Federal Reserve Bank of St. Louis (October, 1972), pp. 10-18.

FEDERAL RESERVE SYSTEM. *The Federal Reserve System—Its Purposes and Functions.* Washington: Board of Governors of the Federal Reserve System, 1961. Chapters 2, 7, 9-13.

How to Interpret Federal Reserve Reports. Federal Reserve Bank of Philadelphia, 1962.

JORDAN, JERRY L. "Elements of Money Stock Determination." *Review,* Federal Reserve Bank of St. Louis (October, 1969), pp. 10-19.

Modern Money Mechanics: A Workbook on Deposits, Currency, and Bank Reserves. Federal Reserve Bank of Chicago, 1961.

PART

2

MEETING THE BUSINESS DEMAND FOR FUNDS

7

The Nature of Business Financing

All business firms require money to accommodate their operations. Money is needed to provide plant and equipment and to provide the necessary financial support for current operations. Some firms require very little capital, and it is in these industries that there is a vast number of competitors. Any field of activity that requires little investment capital is an open invitation to a host of people who would try to establish their own business. At the other extreme, there are businesses that require huge amounts of money to operate on even a minimum scale. The cement and steel industries, for example, by the very nature of their capital requirements are representative of situations where a few large firms dominate the market.

FREEDOM OF ENTRY INTO BUSINESS

We have freedom to establish the enterprise of our choice if we have, or can arrange, the necessary financing. Since business activities are pursued for profit purposes, the success of the businessman in raising funds for operations is governed by the extent to which he can produce profits from operations. This means, of course, that the individual starting a new business must possess either the necessary capital to support initial operations until such time as he is able to show a profit from operations, or he must show unusual promise of the prospect for profits. Typically, the would-be businessman must possess some initial capital for the creation of the enterprise that he would establish; the prospect of profit is seldom enough to attract financial supporters.

The nation's resources are limited. There is only a certain amount of manpower, of suitable land, of buildings appropriate for specific purposes, and other factors of production that the businessman would like to have under his command. Our command over these scarce resources is a measure of the extent to which we engage in successful business operation and financing. The financing of business, therefore, is the process of acquiring the factors of production necessary to conduct the business operations of the firm.

Capital Markets and the Established Firm

Just as it is true that the new business labors under the burden of arranging the initial resources to begin operations, the established firm is also subject to the discipline of the marketplace. The firm that has prospered for many years but begins to fail in its profit generation finds itself very quickly in a weak position to command productive resources. The firm's banker is readily aware of the declining profit experience of the firm, and he watches with increasing concern the loans that have been arranged on behalf of the businessman. In due time, of course, such loan commitments may be entirely cancelled. Finance companies may refuse to accommodate the financing of equipment purchases for firms if their profit prospects are slight. Long-term capital needed for land and buildings is especially difficult to acquire when the firm has a poor profit prospect. As the firm finds it difficult to modernize and take advantage of new markets, it also finds it difficult to reward the human resources employed by the firm with the result that key people are lost as they move to other businesses where opportunities are greater.

Risk and Reward

In contrast with controlled economies where factors of production are allocated by central planning authorities, under the free-price system that process is largely automatic. Resources flow smoothly to those businessmen who through their past operations and who through the promise of profitable future operations are able to lay claim to these resources. It is true of course that mistakes are made. Investors often place their funds with businessmen only to find that the performance of the firm in which they have invested does not measure up to expectations. The result, of course, is the loss of or decrease in the value of the investment. This is the risk inherent in the free-enterprise system. By the same token, the investor or the financial institution that assumes an unusually large risk in accommodating a business customer does so with the full expectation that if things go well with the firm the rewards for the investment will be very great. Where the prospective risk is very small, the prospective reward is small. It is on this basis that the investment funds flow to risky enterprises as well as to the very safe enterprises. There is simply a difference in the risk and reward expectation on the part of the investor. Some investors prefer to maintain a minimum risk; and they must, of course, be satisfied with a modest return on their investment. Other individuals and institutions assume large risks in the hopes of achieving substantial rewards.

The Flow of Resources

The free-price system, therefore, serves as an automatic mechanism whereby the resources of the nation move effectively into those uses where their contribution is presumed to be the greatest. The productivity of the nation itself is a function of the mobility of productive resources moving into those uses for which they are best suited, and it is the free-price system that serves as a continuing market for these resources. Like all markets, of course, this one is not perfect; and yet as measured by the success of our economy relative to other economic systems, it works well indeed. It is of considerable interest that when there is a breakdown in the production and distribution functions in economies dependent upon central planning for the allocation of resources, there seems inevitably to be a reduction in central planning and a reversion to some form of free-pricing mechanism to solve the problem.

It is also true that after a prosperous firm has acquired through financing efforts some of the savings of the nation, funds may be allocated within the firm on a central planning basis. As a result, in the large enterprise funds may be allocated to certain divisions of the business where the return is very great. Other funds may be allocated to divisions of the company where the return is very small, and such allocations may continue for many years. The productivity of the more efficient divisions carry, in effect, the poorer producing divisions. If these various divisions existed as separate companies, there could probably be no such support of the operations of weak producing divisions. It becomes critically important, therefore, that financial management, as well as management in general, determine methods of allocating funds within the business in much the same way that funds are allocated among businesses. The roll of financial management, therefore, is far more significant than that of the welfare of the firm. The nation as a whole depends upon the skillful application of productive resources within the firm.

THE FINANCE FUNCTION

The finance function of the business may be lodged with an individual whose sole function is described as that of finance activity. In smaller firms the operator of the business may take the total responsibility of the finance function. In fact, in small firms, the owner usually finds himself engaged in the administration of all facets of the business' operations, and it is on this basis that the small business finds itself at a special disadvantage. Few people have the overall ability to effectively perform the many challenging functions of even the small business. The medium- and large-size business, on the other hand, by virtue of size may assign an individual or group of individuals to these special functions and in so doing achieve the efficiency that comes from specialization of talent. But irrespective of who carries out the finance function it is still true that the function involves far more than the simple raising of funds for business operations.

Beyond the matter of raising capital is that of effective planning and control as well as the wise application of these funds to the business processes. Needless to say, each of these areas of financial management is interesting and challenging. The planning and control functions are commonly overlooked in the small business and all too frequently are found to be poorly carried out even by large businesses. The application of funds to specific investments within the firm also is a matter that requires a great deal of special effort, and there remains even at this time a great deal of debate as to the most appropriate procedures by which alternative applications of funds can be tested for purposes of achieving their most efficient use. The chore of raising funds requires a very careful cultivation of the interest of the financial community, making the community aware of the performance and prospects of the company and keeping it fully informed of the activities of the firm. While it is true that firms have difficulty raising funds in the market if they are not performing effectively or have little promise of such effective performance, it is also true that knowledge of successful operations must be communicated to the community if the full benefits of good performance are to be realized. It is for this reason that corporate officials are pleased to appear before financial analyst groups and other interested investor groups.

FORMS OF BUSINESS ORGANIZATION

The choice of a legal form of organization for a business is a strategic matter from many points of view. Managerial lines of authority and control, legal responsibility, and the allocation of income and risk are all directly related to the form that the organization takes. Our interest at this time is with the relationship of the legal form of organization to sources and methods of financing and with the allocation of risk.

Sole Proprietorship

The *sole proprietorship* is a business venture that is owned by a single individual who personally receives all of the profits and assumes all the responsibility for the debts and the losses of the business. Although the sole proprietorship form of organization far outnumbers all other forms of business organization, the economic power of these enterprises, as measured by number of employees and amount of payrolls, is far less than that of the corporations of the nation.

The savings of the businessman together with the funds that he may be able to borrow from friends, relatives, and his bank may be sufficient for the operation of the typical small business. As the volume of business increases, however, and as larger investments in capital equipment are required, the owner may reach the point where he cannot borrow additional funds without increasing his equity investment. As increased demands are made for borrowed capital, lenders will generally insist on an increase in the equity capital as well, since the equity of a firm provides a margin of safety for the lender. At this point the sole proprietorship form of organization displays its basic weakness. In many cases, the owner's original investment exhausts his personal resources and often those of his friends and relatives; and unless profits from the operation of the venture have proved sufficient to meet increased equity needs, the business either is prevented from achieving its maximum growth or is required to adopt a more appropriate form of organization for capital-raising purposes.

The sole proprietor's position as it relates to liability for debts of the business is an unfavorable one. Creditors have recourse not only to the assets of the business for the settlement of their claims but also to the personal assets of the proprietor. Thus, the sole proprietor may find his home and personal property under claim by his creditors in the event that the assets of the business are not sufficient to meet the demands of creditors. This unlimited liability of the proprietor is, therefore, one of the serious disadvantages of the sole proprietorship.

The Partnership

The *partnership* form of business organization exists when two or more persons own a business operated for profit. Although the partnership resembles the sole proprietorship in a technical sense to some degree, there are many important differences.

Undoubtedly, one of the important reasons for the popularity of the partnership arrangement is the fact that it enables businessmen to pool their resources without the complications that often accompany incorporation. In some instances, the partnership form of organization exists from the beginning of business operation, the property, equipment, knowledge, and skills for business purposes being acquired through the joint contributions of two or more persons. In other cases, an enterprise that began as a sole proprietorship may reach the point where additional growth is impossible without an increase in equity capital, and conversion to the partnership arrangement is one method of increasing the equity capital of the enterprise.

Although the number of partners that may be taken into a business venture is theoretically unlimited, the managerial difficulties and conflicts arising as a result of a large number of partners limits effectively the number of such co-owners. The partnership, therefore, like the proprietorship, eventually suffers from a lack of command over large sums of capital because of the practical limit to the number of partners that a business venture may have. Although it is true that some types of businesses have dozens and even hundreds of partners, a modification of the general partnership arrangement is usually utilized. It is extremely rare to find more than a few partners involved in an industrial or commercial enterprise.

Like the sole proprietor, the members of a partnership team risk their personal assets as well as their investments in the business venture. In addition, if one of the partners negotiates a contract that results in substantial loss, each partner suffers loss in proportion to the previously agreed upon terms of distribution of profits and losses. This is true whether the partner responsible for the loss was pursuing his specified responsibilities or whether he was violating his authorized functions as set out in the articles of copartnership. The other partners may, however, take action against the offending partner because of his violation of the articles of copartnership.

More serious, perhaps, is a partner's liability for the actions of the business. Under partnership law, each partner has *joint and several liability* for the debts of the business, a situation that permits creditors to seek satisfaction from one or more of the partners if the remaining partners are unable to bear their share of the loss.

The Corporation

In the Dartmouth College Case in 1819, Chief Justice John Marshall described the status of the corporation so explicitly and clearly that this description has since become the generally accepted definition of the corporation. It reads in part as follows:

> A corporation is an artificial being, invisible, intangible, and existing only in contemplation of law. Being the mere creature of law, it possesses only those properties which the charter of its creation confers upon it, either expressly, or as incidental to its very existence . . . [Dartmouth College vs. Woodward, 4 Wheaton (U. S.) 518 (1819)]

The small corporation that has been in existence only a short time, like most new ventures, usually finds it difficult to attract investment funds from outsiders. It is only after the corporation has become well established and offers attractive prospects for investors that the special features of the corporate form of organization become significant. One of the important reasons for the suitability of the corporate form of organization as a medium through which large sums of capital may be accumulated is that capital stock may be offered to its existing stockholders or to investors in amounts suited to their purposes. The corporate form of organization, however, does not by itself assure the flow of investment funds into the business. Rather, it removes several of the impediments to the flow of capital that exist for other forms of business organization.

One of the advantages to the stockholders is the limitation on liability. Ordinarily creditors and other claimants may look only to the assets of the corporation for satisfaction of their claims; they do not have recourse to the personal assets of the owners. This advantage is particularly appealing to the owner of the business who has built up considerable wealth and has diverse business interests over which he cannot exercise complete personal control. The limitation on liability may also make it possible for the promoters of new ventures to attract the interest of wealthy investors who would otherwise be unwilling to risk possible claims against their personal property. Unlimited liability may be avoided under certain circumstances in some of the noncorporate forms, but the certainty provided by the corporate form is not present.

The limitation on stockholder liability for debts of the corporation is seldom sufficient reason for incorporation of the small business of which there is an individual owner whose personal assets are largely invested in the business. In this situation there is little risk on the part of the owner beyond his investment in the corporation. Nor is the corporate form of organization necessarily effective in protecting stockholders from personal risk beyond their investment when the business is relatively new or in a weak financial condition. Creditors may simply require that one or more of the stockholders add their personal signatures to the obligation of the corporation, rendering them personally liable for the obligation. After a corporation has established a good credit reputation, creditors and suppliers seldom insist on personal guarantees on the part of the stockholders.

A further important advantage of the corporation is the ease with which ownership may be transferred. Corporate stock may be transferred freely from one person to another, and the purchaser of such stock thereafter has all the rights and privileges formerly held by the seller. The corporation is not a party to the transfer of ownership and has no power to interfere with the sale or purchase of its stock. By contrast, there must be unanimous approval of all members of a partnership before a new partner can be brought into the business.

Other Forms of Business Organization

In addition to the sole proprietorship, the partnership, and the corporation, there are a variety of somewhat less well-known forms of business organization that combine to varying degrees some of the advantages and the disadvantages of the forms of organization which have been discussed. The *business trust*, for example, also known as the Massachusetts trust, the voluntary association, or common-law trust, combines the advantage of limited liability with convenience in raising capital. Yet, the utilization of the business-trust arrangement is limited, for the most part, to the New England states. Under the business-trust arrangement, assets of the company are held by a trustee, the beneficiaries of the company holding trust certificates as evidence of their beneficial interest. Profits of the company are distributed to holders of trust certificates much as dividends are distributed to stockholders. In spite of the convenience of the business-trust arrangement, its general lack of familiarity to persons outside of New England renders it a less desirable form of business organization than the corporation for purposes of raising capital for business operations. Although the business-trust arrangement is noncorporate in form, it is subject to federal income taxes at the same rate as corporations.

The *limited partnership*, another minor form of business organization, is a statutory modification of the common-law partnership in which one or more general partners combine with one or more limited partners. The limited partners, much like the shareholders in a corporation, have liability for debts of the business only to the extent of their investment. The general partners are governed by the usual laws relating to partnerships while the limited partners are governed by state statutes. The limited partnership comes into existence only after acceptance and approval by the state of a proper application by the partners.

In addition to the limited partnership and the business trust, there are many other forms of business organization that attempt to combine the advantages of the more common forms, each of which has its particular place and advantages. Some of these minor forms of business organization include the joint-stock company, the joint venture, the mining partnership, and the partnership association.

THE BALANCE SHEET

For purposes of exploring the interrelationship of uses and sources of funds and the allocation of risk for business enterprises, it is very helpful to refer to the balance sheet. The *balance sheet* is a summary or report that shows the assets and the sources of financing of a business at a particular time. It reveals two broad categories of information: the properties owned by a business, referred to as *assets*; and the creditors' claims and the owners' equity in the business assets. The creditors' claims, which are the financial obligations of the business, are referred to as *liabilities*.

The balance sheet is in the nature of a snapshot, revealing the condition of a business as of a given date. Like a cutaway section of an automobile motor, however, much of the dynamic quality of the structure is revealed. The various classes of assets indicate at once the result of recent business operations and the capacity for future operations. The creditors' claims and the owners' equity in the assets reveal the sources from which the assets of the business were derived. The term "balance sheet" itself conveys a relationship of equality between the assets of the business and the sources of funds for their acquisition that may be expressed as follows:

$$\text{ASSETS} = \text{LIABILITIES} + \text{OWNERS' EQUITY}$$

The simplified balance sheet of a merchandising firm in Figure 7-1 reveals this equality of assets and the financial interests in the assets. The financial interests in the assets, as noted above, comprise the creditors' claims and owners' interests. We shall, in the following pages, discuss the composition of this balance sheet with the specific objective of relating the assets to the sources of funds for their acquisition.

Current Assets

The balance sheet of the ABC Merchandising Company reveals, among other things, that the business had assets as of December 31 of $375,000. The assets of the company have been classified into two groups: current assets and fixed assets.

The *current assets* of a business enterprise include cash and other assets that may reasonably be expected to be converted into cash, sold, or used in the near future through the normal operations of the business. The principal current assets of a business are typically its cash, notes receivable, accounts receivable, inventories, and prepaid expenses.

Cash. In addition to cash on hand and on deposit with banks, such items as postal money orders, bank checks not yet deposited, and bank drafts are included under this heading.

Notes Receivable. A *note receivable* is a written promise by a debtor of the business to pay a specified sum of money on or before

Figure 7-1

ABC MERCHANDISING COMPANY

BALANCE SHEET

December 31, 1974

ASSETS

Current Assets:

Cash	$ 25,000.00	
Notes Receivable	25,000.00	
Accounts Receivable	75,000.00	
Merchandise Inventory	120,000.00	
Prepaid Expenses	5,000.00	
Total Current Assets		$250,000.00

Fixed Assets:

Equipment	$ 50,000.00	
Land and Buildings	75,000.00	
Total Fixed Assets		125,000.00
Total Assets		$375,000.00

LIABILITIES AND OWNERS' INTERESTS

Current Liabilities:

Notes Payable (to bank)	$ 25,000.00	
Accounts Payable	50,000.00	
Accrued Liabilities	25,000.00	
Total Current Liabilities		$100,000.00
Fixed Liabilities:		
Mortgage Payable (due 1994)		60,000.00
Total Liabilities		$160,000.00
Owners' Equity [1]		215,000.00
Total Liabilities and Owners' Interests		$375,000.00

a stated date. Such notes are ordinarily made payable to the order of a specified firm or person or to "bearer." Notes receivable may come into existence from the settlement of accounts receivable, from the sale of goods and services when required by the seller,

---

[1] The student with a knowledge of accounting will understand that in practice the owners' equity is shown in the balance sheet as the proprietorship, partnership, or capital and surplus accounts, depending upon the legal form of organization.

and from short-term loans made by the business to its employees or to other persons or businesses. These notes may be held until maturity or converted into cash immediately through their sale to a bank or other purchaser.

Because most credit sales of goods and services by businesses in the United States are made on the basis of accounts receivable financing, as described in the following paragraph, notes receivable are typically of minor importance. For the bank, loan company, or other such financial institution, however, notes receivable represent one of the principal assets since their customers are required to sign notes as evidence of the loans.

Accounts Receivable. *Accounts receivable* generally arise from the sale of merchandise or services on credit, that is, the oral promise of the customer to pay. An account receivable is not based on a note and is carried on the books of the seller as a claim against the buyer. The buyer generally pays his debts to the business according to the credit terms of the sale. Overdue accounts receivable may be converted to notes receivable at the insistence of the seller or upon special request by the buyer.

Merchandise Inventory. The goods that a merchandising enterprise has on hand for sale are generally shown as merchandise inventory on the balance sheet. A manufacturing firm has raw materials and goods in the process of manufacture as well as finished goods. The balance sheet of a manufacturing firm usually reveals the amount of inventory in each of these categories.

Prepaid Expenses. Supplies on hand and prepayment of operating expenses, such as rent, insurance, and taxes, are current assets of the business. Without them it would be necessary to make early expenditures in approximately equal amounts to support business operations. Although the trend is toward inclusion of such items in the current assets section of the balance sheet, they frequently are to be found under "deferred charges."

Fixed Assets

Fixed assets are the physical facilities used in the production, storage, display, and distribution of the products of a firm. These assets normally provide many years of service to the firm. The principal fixed assets are equipment, land, and buildings.

Equipment. In a manufacturing enterprise large investment exists in equipment. In merchandising operations, also, much equipment is required, such as display cases, cash registers, bookkeeping machines, and delivery equipment.

Land and Buildings. The special characteristic of land and buildings is that they are relatively fixed or permanent. Although the buildings of a firm slowly outlive their usefulness, either from structural deterioration or lack of adaptability to new business methods, their life is generally far greater than that of the most permanent of the equipment and other assets of the firm.

Current Liabilities

The liabilities of a business come into existence through direct borrowing, the purchase of goods and services on a credit basis, and the accrual of obligations for such purposes as wages of employees and income taxes. Liabilities are classified as current and fixed.

The *current liabilities* of a business may be defined as those obligations that must be satisfied within a period of one year. They are the liabilities that are to be met out of current funds and operations of the business. Although the cash on hand for the ABC Merchandising Company is only $25,000 compared with current liabilities of $100,000, it is expected that normal business operations will convert receivables and inventory into cash in sufficient time to meet current liabilities as they become due. In addition to notes and accounts payable, there is a third group of current liabilities—accrued liabilities—described below.

Notes Payable. A *note payable* is a written promise to pay a specified amount of money to the order of a creditor on or before a certain date. These notes may arise from the purchase of goods or services on a credit basis, from direct short-term borrowing, or in settlement of accounts payable that have not been satisfied according to the terms of the purchase agreement. The most common situation giving rise to a note payable is the borrowing of money from a bank on a short-term basis for the purchase of merchandise for resale or for other current operating requirements. The transaction that gives rise to the note payable on our balance sheet is reflected as a note receivable on the balance sheet of the firm to which the money is owed.

Accounts Payable. *Accounts payable* arise primarily from the purchase of goods by a business on credit terms. The account payable is not evidenced by a note. Although it lacks some of the certainty of the note, its convenience and simplicity have resulted in a considerable popularity in its use. Accounts payable, as well as notes payable, arising from the purchase of inventory on credit terms represent "trade credit" financing as opposed to direct short-term borrowing from banks and other lenders. An account payable shown in our balance sheet is reflected as an account receivable on the balance sheet of the firm from which we have acquired the goods.

Accrued Liabilities. Amounts owed but not yet due for such items as wages and salaries, taxes, and interest on notes are classified as *accrued liabilities* and as such are included in the current liabilities section of the balance sheet. Of special importance is the tax accrual, which often is the largest single current liability of the business.

Fixed Liabilities

The *fixed liabilities* of a business represent long-term debts, repayment of which is not required within a period of one year. The long-term debts of a business may extend from one to one hundred years or more, depending upon the confidence of lenders in the business and the nature of the security that the business may offer for such loans. As a long-term debt approaches the date it is to be paid, ordinarily within a year from its maturity date, the debt is transferred to the current liabilities section of the balance sheet to call attention to the fact that its settlement must be made within the year.

One of the most common methods of obtaining a long-term loan is for a business establishment to offer a mortgage to a lender.

A *mortgage* may be described as a conveyance or transfer of title to property given by a debtor to a creditor as security for the payment of the debt, with a provision that such conveyance or transfer of title is to become void on the payment of the debt according to the terms of the mortgage. In the event that the borrowing business fails to meet the obligations of the loan contract, the mortgage may be foreclosed, that is, the property may be seized through appropriate legal channels and sold in order to satisfy the indebtedness.

Owners' Equity

All businesses have an ownership equity in one form or another. This ownership equity initially results from a cash outlay for the purchase of assets with which to operate the business. In other cases, the owners of a business may simply place physical assets, such as machinery, real estate, or equipment, with the firm for its operation. Owners' equity is also increased by allowing profits of the business to remain with the business rather than by making additional contributions of cash or property. On the balance sheet the amount of owners' equity is always represented by the difference between total assets and total debts of the business. It reflects the owners' claims on the assets of the business as opposed to the creditors' claims.

FORMS OF LONG-TERM CORPORATE FINANCING

The principal instruments of short-term financing were described earlier in the chapter. These instruments, notes and accounts payable, are used by all forms of business. The instruments of long-term finance for the corporation, however, are peculiar to the corporate organization, and because of the importance of the various types of corporate securities, they are discussed here in detail.

The long-term capital funds for the corporation are of two broad forms: equity capital and debt capital. Equity capital is obtained through the sale of shares of stock in the corporation. These shares may be divided into several classes, each having specified benefits and privileges with respect to ownership status in the corporation.[2] As opposed to the equity capital of a corporation, debt capital represents funds obtained from creditors rather than from owners. Such capital may be obtained through direct negotiation with a lender or the sale of notes or bonds to many lenders.

Equity Capital

Equity capital is the capital supplied by the owners of the enterprise. This ownership claim in a corporation is evidenced by the *stock certificate*. The stock certificate shows the type of stock held by the owner, the name of the company, the name of the owner of the stock, and the names of certain of the company officers. The stock certificate also carries space for its assignment in the event that it is transferred to another person. As a protection against forgery, all signatures on stock certificates must generally be certified by a representative of a commercial bank, a stockbroker, or other authorized person. In the event of the loss of a stock certificate, however, an individual may request a duplicate certificate. The corporation, in turn, will generally require that a bond or surety be posted by the stockholder to protect the corporation in the event that the lost certificate should later be presented.

Stock certificates are generally made out in terms of one hundred shares or multiples thereof. Stock certificates representing less than one hundred shares are generally referred to as *fractional certificates*. The holder of an odd number of shares, as for example, 523, will probably hold one stock certificate representing the ownership of 500 shares and a fractional stock certificate representing an ownership of 23 shares. (See Figure 7-2.)

When the holder of stock sells his shares, the assigned stock certificate is forwarded to the company by the purchaser, and it is destroyed by the secretary of the corporation. A new certificate is issued to the new owner whose name will then be carried on the stock record. In the larger corporations, an official transfer agent, generally a trust company or a bank, is appointed to accomplish

---

[2] Profits of a business that are retained rather than paid out as dividends are also a form of equity capital since they represent ownership capital reinvested in the business. The importance of this source of financing is discussed later in Chapter 15.

Figure 7-2

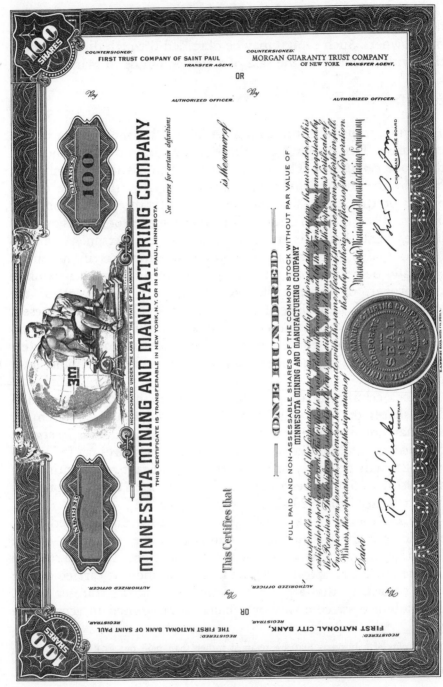

Common Stock Certificate

this task. The larger corporations may also have an independent stock registrar to supervise transfer of its securities.

The capital stock of a corporation may be assigned a *par value* (a fixed value) in the certificate of incorporation. If the corporation sells the stock for less than the par value, the owners of the stock may become liable to creditors for the difference between the selling price and the par value in the event of failure of the company. Thus, the limited liability of the stockholders may be defeated. This technicality seldom creates any difficulty, however, since most stock is sold initially at or above its par value. In addition, certain legal devices may be used to protect against such contingent liability even in those instances when the stock must be sold at less than its par value.

Aside from this significance, par value usually bears little relationship to the current price or book value of the stock. Most states permit corporations to issue no-par stock.

Types of Equity Instruments

Equity instruments of the corporation may be grouped broadly into two classes: common stock and preferred stock.

Common Stock. The outstanding characteristic of *common stock* is its complete claim to the profits of the business that remain after the holders of all other classes of debt and equity instruments have received their stipulated returns. Also, it is generally the voting privilege of the common stockholders that governs the selection of the board of directors of a corporation; the board of directors, in turn, exercises general control of the enterprise. For these reasons, the holders of common stock may be regarded as the basic owners of the corporation.

The favorable position of the common stockholders with respect to dividends and control of the corporation is offset by the fact that during periods when profits from operations are low, the claims of others may completely absorb available funds, leaving little or nothing for the common stockholders. The common stockholders, therefore, may expect less stability with respect to the amount of their dividends, often receiving considerably greater yield than the holders of other instruments during prosperous periods and generally less than other security holders during periods of distress.

Just as the common stockholders receive dividends only after all other classes of security holders have received their specified return, so they have low priority when a business venture is liquidated. All creditors must receive their claims in full; and preferred stockholders must, as a rule, be paid in full before common stockholders may participate in the proceeds of liquidation. As in the case of dividends, all proceeds of liquidation remaining after the settlement of prior obligations accrue to the common stockholders. It is seldom, however, that an enterprise which has been forced to liquidate because of unfortunate business experience will provide enough proceeds to take care of the claims of creditors and preferred stockholders. Common stockholders generally receive little, if anything, from liquidation proceedings. The common stockholders, therefore, suffer the brunt of business failure just as they enjoy the primary benefits of business success.

Common stock may be divided into special groups, generally Class A and Class B, in order to permit the acquisition of additional capital without diluting the control of the business. When a corporation does issue two classes of common stock, it quite often will give voting rights to only one class, generally Class B. Owners of Class A stock, then, have most, if not all, of the other rights and privileges of the common stockholders. The tendency of some corporations to issue nonvoting equity securities is opposed by some government agencies as well as some authorities in the field of corporate finance on the basis that it permits the concentration of ownership control. The New York Stock Exchange refuses to list the common stock of corporations that issue nonvoting classes of common stock.

Preferred Stock. *Preferred stock,* in contrast with common stock, generally carries a limited dividend, specified as either a percentage of par value or as a fixed number of dollars per year. For example, a preferred stock may be referred to as a 5 percent preferred, meaning that its annual dividend participation is limited to 5 percent of its par or stated value. The dividend priority for no-par preferred stock is stated in terms of a dollar amount, for example, "preferred as to dividends in the amount of $5 annually." The holder of the preferred stock accepts the limitation on the amount of dividends as a fair exchange for the priority he has in the earnings of the company.

As has been noted, before the common stockholders receive any dividends, preferred stockholders must be paid the total of their prior claim. The preferred stock, therefore, offers the investor something of a compromise between the basic equity instruments of common stock and credit instruments such as bonds and long-term notes. Because preferred stocks are frequently of a nonvoting nature, the managements of many corporations favor their issuance as a means of obtaining equity capital without diluting the control of the current stockholders.

As in the case of common stock, preferred stock may be classified into Class A, Class B, or First Preferred and Second Preferred. The Class A Preferred or First Preferred usually has priority over other classes of preferred stock of a company in the distribution of dividends and in the proceeds from liquidation.

Preferred stock may have special features. For example, it may be cumulative or noncumulative. *Cumulative preferred stock* requires that before common stock dividends may be paid, preferred dividends must be paid not only for the dividend period in question but also for all previous periods in which no preferred dividends were paid. It is important to remember that since the preferred stockholder technically is an owner of the business, he cannot force the payment of a dividend. The preferred stockholder may be made to wait until such time as earnings are adequate for that purpose, the cumulative preferred stock offering protection for those periods during which dividends were not declared. *Noncumulative preferred stock,* on the other hand, makes no provision for the accumulation of unpaid dividends with the result that management may at times be tempted to declare preferred dividends only when it appears that sufficient earnings are available to make possible common stock dividends also. Practically all modern preferred stock is cumulative.

A preferred stock may be participating or nonparticipating. *Participating preferred stock* is stock that participates, on a share-for-share basis with common stockholders, in any residual profits of a corporation after payment has been made of the basic preferred stock dividend and the common stock dividend. Very few issues of preferred stock carry participation clauses today.

Preferred stock also may be callable, in which case the corporation may retire the preferred stock at its option. Preferred stock may also carry a conversion clause that makes possible its conversion to common stock of the corporation at the stockholder's option.

Many special features that preferred stocks may carry exist primarily as an added attraction to investors to permit the sale of securities at times when distribution would otherwise be difficult.

Debt Capital

In addition to the capital provided by the owners of the corporation, funds may be secured also from creditors on a long-term basis. Debt capital, however, must be preceded by an equity investment in the corporation on the part of the stockholders, inasmuch as creditors generally require a contribution on the part of owners before entrusting their own funds to the use of the corporation. Uses for borrowed funds may be the same as the uses for equity funds, for example, the acquisition of additional land, buildings, and equipment. Debt capital, however, has certain rights and privileges not possessed by the holders of equity capital in a corporation. The holder of a debt instrument issued by a corporation may force the business to abide by the terms of the contract even though it may mean reorganization or dissolution of the enterprise. The periodic interest payments due the holders of such debt instruments must be paid, therefore, if the corporation is to survive. The holders of debt instruments have priority over stockholders up to the limit of their claim against the corporation in the event of liquidation of the concern.

Offsetting the advantage of this preferred position, the yield to which the creditors of a corporation are entitled is usually considerably less over a period of years than that available to the owners of the various classes of equity securities. Also, so long as the corporation meets its contractual obligations, the creditors have little voice in its management and control, except for those covenants and restrictions that are a part of the loan contract.

Types of Debt Instruments

Long-term corporate debt instruments may be classified into two categories—secured obligations and unsecured obligations, generally referred to as *mortgage bonds* and *debenture bonds*. In contrast with the stockholder whose ownership of shares of stock may be evidenced by a single stock certificate, the holder of bonds has a separate instrument for each bond owned. On the face of the bond itself appear the facts relating to the rights and obligations of the corporation and the bondholder, including denomination of the bond (generally $1,000), maturity, interest rate, periods of interest payments, and the specific nature of the claim of the bond.

The bond contract is generally rather complicated, and the ramifications are too extensive to be included on the face of the bond. This supplementary information is set out in a document referred to as the *trust indenture*. This document is generally quite voluminous and includes in the greatest detail the various provisions of the loan arrangement. Although the indenture is seldom seen or utilized by the average bondholder, it is available to the creditor who requires its use. The trust indenture, then, provides the basis for the settlement of disputes relative to the responsibilities and the rights of the parties to the contract and hence it is essential that it be carefully preserved, generally by a trustee designated by the corporation. The trustee has a duty to protect the indenture and to enforce its provisions.

The importance of the function of the trustee is such that in 1939 government legislation came into existence to establish specific duties and obligations of the trustee in this respect. This legislation, known as the Trust Indenture Act of 1939, provides, among other things, that the trustee act impartially in behalf of the creditors of the corporation in such a manner as required by the terms of the Act. Also, the trustee must have a combined capital and surplus of not less than $150,000, must be corporate in form, and must have interests not in conflict with those of the holders of the securities.

When there is a direct loan arrangement established between a borrowing corporation and a single lending institution, corporate notes may be used rather than bonds. Although long-term corporate notes are less formal in nature than bonds, they generally include many restrictive covenants not required in connection with the typical short-term promissory note. Long-term corporate notes may also be used when a group of institutions negotiates jointly with a borrowing corporation.

Mortgage Bonds. The property specifically pledged to secure the mortgage bonds may include all of the assets of a corporation or it may include only a part thereof. As a rule, however, the mortgage applies only to the real estate, buildings, and other assets that are classed as real property. For the corporation that is expanding its plant facilities, the mortgage so offered for expansion purposes usually includes only a lien on the additional property acquired. The opposite has been true of most railway expansions. Originally, railway construction was of a piecemeal nature, providing for extensions of road and facilities over a period of many years. Mortgage bonds issued to finance such extensions of track often included a lien on all of the roadbed previously constructed as well as the additional track.

When a parcel of real estate has more than one mortgage lien against it, the mortgage first filed for recording at the appropriate government office, generally the county recorder's office, has priority; and the bonds outstanding against the mortgage are known as *senior liens*. The bonds outstanding against all mortgages subsequently recorded are known as *junior liens*. Inasmuch as senior liens have priority with respect to distribution of assets in the event of failure of the business, they generally provide a lower yield to investors than do the junior liens. The junior liens of a strong company, however, may be considered by investors to be safer than the senior liens of a less well-established company.

Mortgage bonds may differ to a considerable extent. For example, the mortgage may prevent the issuance of securities over and above those authorized in the initial flotation. The term *closed-end mortgage* applies to this arrangement. Alternatively, the mortgage may provide for continuing sale of bonds against the same mortgage. As a rule when such an *open-end mortgage* exists, there is also a stipulation to the effect that additional real property which the company acquires automatically becomes a part of the property secured under the mortgage.

Debenture Bonds. These bonds are dependent upon the general credit and strength of the corporation for their security. They represent no specific pledge of property, but rather their holders are classed as general creditors of the corporation on a par with the holders of promissory notes and trade creditors that have sold merchandise to the corporation. Debenture bonds are used by governmental bodies and by many industrial and utility corporations as well. Since mortgage bonds would otherwise have a prior claim against the fixed assets of a corporation, even though they are sold subsequent to the debenture bonds, the debenture bonds are sometimes afforded protection against such subsequent sale of senior securities through a covenant of equal coverage. Such a covenant provides that the debenture bonds will be accorded equal rank with any subsequent senior issues of securities.

Like preferred stock, corporate bonds may carry such special provisions as conversion rights and participation rights in order to enhance their original sale. Most modern industrial bond issues are callable at the option of the company.

In the following chapters the various sources of funds for business operations and the instruments used for financing will be described in detail. The sections on short- and long-term financing will each be followed by a chapter setting out techniques and policies of business financing.

QUESTIONS

1. From the viewpoint of society, what is the strategic role of the nation's capital markets in contributing to the maintenance of a high degree of efficiency on the part of the businesses of the nation?
2. From the viewpoint of the financial manager of a firm, how can the capital markets of the nation be influenced to provide a maximum of financial support to the firm?
3. How do the capital markets of the nation accommodate the needs of both the very risky business effort and the well-established firm?
4. The financial executive of the large firm has a special responsibility for contributing to the effectiveness with which funds raised in the capital markets are utilized in his firm. Explain.
5. Describe some of the advantages or disadvantages of firm size as it relates to utilization of the capital markets.
6. Describe the procedures by which owners may invest in the sole proprietorship, the partnership, or the corporation.

7. The ability of a business to obtain capital is in part a function of its legal form of organization. Explain.
8. Compare the practical significance of unlimited liability in the sole proprietorship with that of the partnership.
9. Why do not all business ventures incorporate in order to obtain the advantages of limited liability?
10. Discuss the fundamental difference between equity capital and debt capital as it applies to corporate financing.
11. List the principal features of a stock certificate. How are such certificates transferred from person to person?
12. Distinguish between the types of corporate debt instruments.
13. What type of property is generally under lien in a mortgage bond issue?
14. Debenture bonds, although unsecured in a technical sense, are not necessarily insecure. Explain.

SUGGESTED READINGS

HUNT, PEARSON, CHARLES M. WILLIAMS, and GORDAN DONALDSON. *Basic Business Finance*, 4th ed. Homewood, Illinois: Richard D. Irwin, Inc., 1971. Chapter 1.

JOHNSON, KEITH B., and DONALD E. FISCHER (eds.). *Readings in Contemporary Financial Management*. Glenview, Illinois: Scott, Foresman and Company, 1969. Part I.

MOCK, EDWARD J. (ed.). *Financial Decision-Making*. Scranton, Pennsylvania: International Textbook Company, 1967. Chapter 1.

National Industrial Conference Board, *Organizing and Managing the Corporate Finance Function,* Studies in Business Policy, No. 129. New York, 1969.

VAN HORNE, JAMES C. *Fundamentals of Financial Management*, 2d ed. Englewood Cliffs, New Jersey: Prentice-Hall, Inc., 1974. Chapter 2.

WESTON, J. FRED, and EUGENE F. BRIGHAM. *Managerial Finance*, 4th ed. New York: Holt, Rinehart, and Winston, 1972. Chapter 18.

8 | Lending Operations of Commercial Banks

The tremendous resources of the commercial banking system of the nation make it the largest provider of short-term loan funds for business. In this chapter are detailed the operations of a single bank through its financial statements to determine its manner of operation and its sources of income.

CHANGES IN LOAN POLICIES

According to an early and widely held theory, the only appropriate loans for a commercial bank to make were those for short-term productive purposes to businessmen and farmers exclusively. It was believed that the commercial bank should serve simply as a depositary or a pooling place for the surplus cash funds of the community and that these funds should be available to businessmen and farmers of the community in such form that they could be repaid out of current operations. For example, the use of bank loans by a business to purchase inventory makes possible their repayment from sales. Such loans, it was believed, would provide a high degree of liquidity for the bank in meeting depositor withdrawal demands. Nor was this attitude wholly theoretical, for much of our banking legislation specifically restricted the banks with respect to other forms of loans. The National Banking Act of 1863 prohibited completely the lending of money on the basis of real estate. Later legislation modified this extreme limitation.

Although commercial banks remain the primary source of short-term business funds, there has been a noticeable drift away from this traditional theory of banking practice. This change in attitude became noticeable during World War I when the banks were encouraged to lend to individuals for the purpose of purchasing United States government bonds. This type of lending, of course, represents a far cry from the traditional type of loan for production use. Following World War I, there was much speculation in inventory accumulation by the business enterprises of the country; and many of the loans extended to businesses ostensibly for production purposes were, in fact, loans for speculative purposes. Later, during the stock market boom of the late twenties, the commercial banks played an important part in providing funds for the purchase of stocks and bonds, again representing a considerable shift from the traditional practices of banking. During the period from January, 1922, to September, 1929, when Standard and Poor's index of common stock prices increased by 284 percent, loans to brokers and others for purchasing securities became the largest class of bank loans.

During this period, many of the nation's large companies were becoming more and more self-sufficient financially and required less assistance from the banking system for their short-term financial requirements. This, of course, meant that many commercial banks suffered from a lack of adequate demand for short-term business loans. During World War II, the banks were encouraged to purchase large quantities of United States government securities. Chart 8-1 shows that commercial banks continue to hold a significant amount of government securities. Although commercial banks at the end of 1973 had only approximately 9 percent of their total loans and investments in the form of United States government bonds, in the immediate postwar period the percentage was as high as 72 percent.

Chart 8-1

PRINCIPAL ASSETS OF COMMERCIAL BANKS

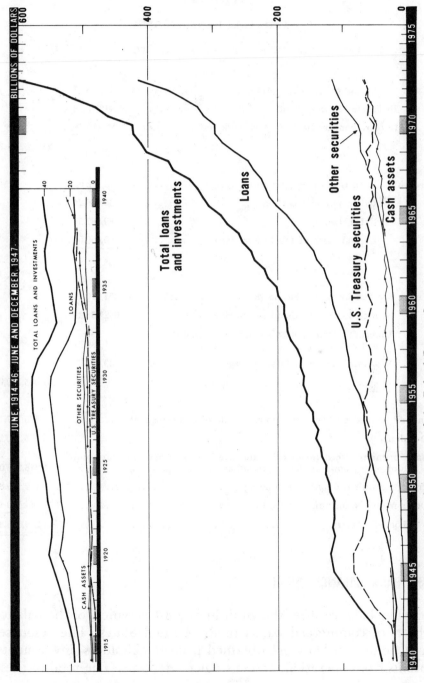

SOURCE: Board of Governors of the Federal Reserve System.

Figure 8-1

THE NATIONAL BANK

CONDENSED STATEMENT OF CONDITION—DECEMBER 31, 197—

RESOURCES

Cash: In our vaults .... $ 5,240,538.21

    In Federal Reserve Bank 13,641,943.38

    In correspondent banks in New York and other cities   5,227,419.78

    $ 24,109,901.37

Securities: U. S. Government Securities $22,838,112.83

        Other public securities 3,436,606.24

        Other bonds 789,687.50

        Capital stock of the Federal Reserve Bank 150,000.00

    27,214,406.57

Loans: Secured loans payable on demand $11,851,310.96

    Secured loans with definite maturities 3,082,958.33

    Unsecured loans and discounts with definite maturities 35,341,182.51

    Real estate loans on first mortgages 10,769,897.27

    61,045,349.07

Interest accrued on bonds and notes to date of this statement 396,787.13

Overdrafts 5,186.36

Bank premises owned (main office and five branches) and furniture and fixtures—less allowance for depreciation 1,248,358.06

Property acquired for branch building 179,110.82

Other resources, including prepaid expenses 44,579.46

    Total Resources $114,243,678.84

THE BANK BALANCE SHEET

The balance sheet shown in Figure 8-1 is typical of the balance sheets of commercial banks in the United States. The resources and funds of a bank are obtained from stockholders' investments, profits from operation, and customers' deposits. The total of these

Figure 8-1

THE NATIONAL BANK

CONDENSED STATEMENT OF CONDITION—DECEMBER 31, 197—

LIABILITIES

Deposits:

U. S. government deposits	$ 2,249,319.22	
Other demand deposits	52,269,505.04	
Savings and other time deposits	49,446,308.18	
		$103,965,132.44

Other Liabilities and Deferred Credits:

Dividends declared, but not yet payable	125,000.00
Interest on deposits, taxes and other expenses accrued to date of this statement	99,758.87
Discounts collected but not earned	237,997.20
Reserve for federal income taxes	391,789.85
Other liabilities	None
Total Liabilities	$104,819,678.36
Reserve for Contingencies	71,012.23

CAPITAL FUNDS

Capital—100,000 shares at $20.00 par value	2,000,000.00
Surplus	4,000,000.00
Undivided profits	3,352,988.25
Total Capital Funds	$ 9,352,988.25
Total Liabilities and Capital Funds	$114,243,678.84

three items plus "Other Liabilities and Deferred Credits" and "Reserve for Contingencies" equals the total assets of the bank. The assets (resources) for this particular bank are shown on the left-hand side of Figure 8-1, and for all commercial banks in the United States they are shown in Chart 8-1.

Bank Assets

The principal assets of a commercial bank are cash, securities, and loans.

Cash. The first category of assets on the "Resources" side of the balance sheet for a bank is Cash. *Cash* includes funds in the bank's vaults, in a federal reserve bank, and in correspondent banks.

A bank must keep a certain minimum of vault cash to meet the day-to-day currency requirements of the bank's customers. The amount of such cash requirements may be small relative to the total of a bank's resources for the simple reason that the typical day's operation will result in approximately the same amount of cash deposits as cash withdrawals. A margin of safety, however, is required to take care of those periods when for one reason or another withdrawals exceed deposits by more than an average amount.

The appropriate amount of cash that a bank should carry depends largely upon the character of its banking operations and on the distance of the bank from its depositary for legal reserves. For example, a bank that has a few very large accounts might be expected to have a larger volume of unanticipated withdrawals (and deposits) than a bank that has only small individual accounts. An erratic volume of day-to-day withdrawals requires, of course, a larger cash reserve. A bank that is located a great distance from its depositary for legal reserves also must maintain larger cash reserves than a bank that can in a matter of minutes or hours draw on such reserves.

The second cash item, designated "In Federal Reserve Bank," is considerably greater than vault cash. Members of the Federal Reserve System are required to keep a percentage of their deposits as minimum reserves either with the federal reserve banks of their districts or in the form of vault cash.[1] As withdrawals are made and total deposit balances decrease, the amount of the required reserves also decreases. These reserves that have been freed may be used by the bank to help meet withdrawal demands. The reserves of state banks that are not members of the Federal Reserve System are subject to regulation by the state in which the banks are chartered. The laws of the states differ as to the form that such reserves may take. In general, however, state required reserves include vault cash, deposits with other banks, and in some cases bonds of the federal government.

---

[1] The system of fractional reserves was discussed in Chapter 4.

Cash "In correspondent banks in New York and other cities" refers to the common practice of keeping substantial deposits with other banks, particularly those banks in large cities. Such correspondent relations with other banks facilitate the clearing of drafts and other credit instruments, and provide an immediate access to information regarding the money markets of the large cities.

The cash items of this bank total approximately $24 million compared with total resources of more than $114 million; hence, a little more than 21 percent of the total resources of this bank are held in such form as to produce no yield whatsoever.

Securities. Securities comprise the second major group of resources on the balance sheet. These securities held by the bank include those of the United States government, those of state governments, and of municipalities. Also included are other bonds and capital stock of the federal reserve bank. The bonds owned by this bank are held as investments. The capital stock of the federal reserve bank owned by the bank is a requirement for all member banks of the Federal Reserve System.

Loans. The third group of resource or asset items includes several classifications of loans: first, those loans that are payable on demand and which are secured; second, those secured loans that have definite maturities; third, and by far the most important, unsecured loans and discounts with definite maturities; and finally, real estate loans on first mortgages.

In a *secured loan*, specific property is pledged as collateral for the loan. In the event of the failure of the borrower to repay his loan, the bank has recourse to the assets pledged as collateral for the loan. In all cases, the borrower is required to sign a note specifying the details of the indebtedness; but unless specific assets are pledged for the loan, it is classified as unsecured. An *unsecured loan* represents a general claim against the assets of the borrower. It is the typical arrangement between the businessmen of the community and the bank whereby periodic amounts are borrowed for the purposes of meeting a payroll, accumulating an inventory, or for other short-term working capital purposes. This section reflects the most important single activity of the commercial bank and, except for the real estate component, it was often thought to be the sole type of activity in which the commercial banks should be permitted to engage. Through these loans, the bank has gained its reputation as being the most important single source of short-term funds for businesses.

The Federal Deposit Insurance Corporation reports that for all insured commercial banks at December 31, 1973, earnings from interest on loans accounted for approximately 67 percent of total earnings.[2] Such loans comprised 59 percent of total assets. Total earnings include not only interest from loans and from other securities but also service charges and fees on loans, service charges on deposit accounts, commissions, trust department earnings, and other current earnings.

The distinction between a loan and a discount is an important one. A loan customarily includes a specified rate of interest that must be paid with the principal amount of the loan at the maturity of the loan contract. A discount, on the other hand, is customarily made with no interest rate specified on the note, a deduction being made from the face amount of the note at the time the money is loaned. The borrower receives less than the face of the note, but he repays the full amount of the note when it matures.

A given discount rate means a higher real cost of borrowing than an interest loan made for the same rate. This is true because under the discount arrangement less actual money is received by the borrower, although the amount paid for its use is the same. For example, if $500 is borrowed on a loan basis at an interest rate of 7 percent for one year, at the maturity of the loan $500 plus $35 interest is repaid. On the other hand, if the $500 is borrowed on a discount basis and the rate is 7 percent, a deduction of $35 from the face of the note is made and the borrower receives only $465. At the end of the year, he returns to the lender the face amount of the note, $500. In the first case, the borrower has paid $35 for the use of $500; in the second case, he has paid $35 for the use of only $465. The effective rate of interest, therefore, on the discount basis is approximately 7.5 percent in contrast with the even 7 percent paid when the $500 was borrowed on a loan basis.

---

[2] *Annual Report of the Federal Deposit Insurance Corporation,* December 31, 1973, p. 212.

Other Bank Assets. The remaining items on the Resources side of the balance sheet are of less importance than the foregoing groups. A brief look, however, should be taken at these individual items. *Interest accrued on bonds and notes* refers to earnings that have not been received although they were earned during the period covered by the statement. *Overdrafts* are, in effect, short-term loans to customers who have overdrawn their bank balances. Banks disapprove of this practice and often will refuse to honor overdrafts. A bank may, however, accept the check and carry the overdraft temporarily until the customer is able to make the necessary adjustments. During the period that overdrafts are accepted by the bank, they are carried as assets.

The next item, *Bank premises owned and furniture and fixtures,* is self-explanatory. These are the bank's physical properties. This particular bank has acquired other real estate that is to be used in the future for additional bank buildings. The final item, *Other resources, including prepaid expenses,* is a catchall account that includes such items as prepaid insurance and expenditures made for supplies which have not been completely used.

Bank Liabilities

The most important liability of a commercial bank consists of its deposits of various kinds, but a bank's other liabilities should be understood also.

Deposits. Three groups of deposits—U. S. government, demand, and savings and time—make up the principal liabilities of all commercial banks. U. S. government deposits are shown separately because by law banks must provide for a segregation of assets to protect such deposits. Demand deposits represent the checking accounts of individuals, businesses, and other institutions. Such deposits are withdrawable by check without the depositor having to go to the bank.

Savings and time deposits are segregated because they are payable on notice of thirty days or more, although most banks now permit customers to draw on their savings accounts as readily as on their checking accounts. *Savings deposits* differ from time deposits in that they are generally represented by a passbook, while *time deposits* are usually represented by printed receipts called *certificates of deposit*. Further, savings deposits are limited to individuals and nonprofit organizations while time deposits may be held by business firms as well as by individuals. In addition to the certificates of deposit that specify withdrawal limitations, usually 30 days after deposit or after 30 days' notice has been given, time accounts may be represented by written agreements. Such agreements provide that no part of the time deposit may be withdrawn before the maturity of the account or without giving 30 days' notice of intent to withdraw the funds. These time accounts are usually associated with "Christmas Clubs," which permit deposits to be withdrawn shortly before Christmas, funds for tax accumulation purposes, and funds for the advance budgeting of vacation expenses. As for savings accounts, the 30-day notice requirement before withdrawal is generally not enforced.

Although records reveal that commercial banks issued certificates of deposit as early as 1900, a major innovation in the early 1960's has resulted in a vastly increased importance for them. This innovation was the issuance of "CD's" (certificates of deposit) in negotiable form. The negotiability feature was not totally unknown before that time; but they were so seldom issued that even though negotiable, it was difficult to sell them in the general money markets. Along with the vastly increased use of negotiable CD's in the 1960's there came into existence a secondary market for them. Today, CD's as issued by banks are purchased and sold in the money markets as readily as most forms of debt obligations. The commercial banks of the nation have used negotiable CD's as a means of attracting vastly increased sums of deposits of business corporations and other institutions. Demand deposits on the part of corporations had been hard hit as treasurers began to take advantage of the higher alternative interest rates in the money markets in the late 1950's. The CD's have served their purpose well in allowing banks to recapture temporary funds of businesses.

Other Liabilities and Deferred Credits. The second category of liabilities is represented by items having a far smaller dollar significance than that of deposits. For this bank, these items total nearly $1 million. In brief, this section represents liabilities not yet payable and the receipt of fees and other charges for which service has not yet been rendered. Funds borrowed from the federal reserve bank or other banks are also reflected here.

Reserve for Contingencies. Reserves set aside out of profits may be established by bank management to provide for unusually large risks. When a bank engages in lending practices that are not common to the bank, such reserves may be established to protect capital and surplus. Such reserves also are established to absorb possible losses from declining prices of bonds and other investments that the bank holds.

Bank Capital Funds

The capital funds section of the bank balance sheet includes capital, surplus, and undivided profits. This bank has 100,000 shares of common stock at $20 par value per share for a total of $2,000,000. Surplus of $4,000,000 was accumulated from the sale of capital stock at a price above its par value and for some banks may include a part of retained earnings. When dividends are paid, the undivided profits section is reduced. These three capital accounts constitute the total capital funds of the bank.

On the balance sheets of many banks today, there is to be found in the capital funds section an item designated as "capital notes." These notes, always subordinated to the claims of bank depositors, reflect long-term borrowing on the part of the bank for purposes of bolstering the capital section. Although, like deposits, they are liabilities of the banks that issue them, reserve requirements do not apply to them. The Comptroller of the Currency of the United States in its regulation of national banks and the bank regulatory authorities of many states consider capital notes to be a part of the capital accounts in determining the adequacy of bank capital. The Board of Governors of the Federal Reserve System, on the other hand, has taken a far less liberal view of such long-term debt and generally ignores capital notes in the measurement of capital adequacy.

Lending Operations of the Commercial Bank

The typical loan made by a bank to a businessman is on an unsecured basis; that is, the prospect for the future of the business is such that the bank believes it to be unnecessary to require the pledge of specific assets of the business as security for the loan. Bankers for many years have held the opinion that if a loan does not qualify on an unsecured basis, it should not qualify on a secured basis. In recent years this attitude has been changing, and we find many banks lending on the basis of a pledge of specific assets. The unsecured loan, however, remains the primary type of bank loan arrangement.

The Bank Line of Credit

There is often an agreement between the business and the bank regarding the amount of credit that the business will have at its disposal. The loan limit that the bank establishes for each of its business customers is called a *line of credit*. These lines of credit cost the businessman only the normal interest for the period for which money is actually borrowed. Under this arrangement, the businessman does not wait until he needs money to negotiate for the loan, but rather he files the necessary financial statements of his business and other evidences of financial condition with the bank in order that the credit may be available when needed. The banker, of course, is interested not only in how well the business has fared in the past but also in the probable future of the business, since the line of credit itself is generally extended in advance for a year at a time. The banker may require that other debts of the business be subordinated to the claim of the bank.

Under a line of credit program, major changes in the operation of a business may be subject to the approval of the bank. A major shift or change in management personnel or a major change in the manufacture or sale of particular products can have a material influence on the future success of a company; hence, the bank, having contributed substantially to the resources of the business, is necessarily interested in such business activities. The bank may also seek information on the business through organized credit bureaus, contact with other businesses having relations with the enterprise in question, and other banks.

In the event that the businessman requires more money than was anticipated at the time the line of credit was established, he may request the bank to increase the limit on his line of credit. He must be prepared, however, to offer very sound evidence not only of the need for additional funds but also of the ability of the business to repay the increased loan from business operations. A request for an increased line of credit frequently occurs when a business is growing and must have ever-increasingly large amounts of capital to make such growth possible. Although banks generally insist that expansion be financed with long-term capital, they do frequently assist such growth by providing a part of increased capital needs. The businessman who is unable to secure additional credit from his bank on an unsecured loan basis may seek funds from other lenders or from his bank on a secured basis. These other forms of borrowing are discussed later in this chapter.

A *compensating balance* (on deposit by the business) of from 10 to 20 percent of unsecured loans outstanding under bank lines of credit is required by nearly all banks. The most frequently cited justification for this requirement is that since banks cannot lend without deposits, bank borrowers should be required to be depositors also.

Banks usually require their business customers to "clean up" their lines of credit for specified periods of time during the year, that is, to eliminate their indebtedness to the bank for this period of time, generally a minimum time span of two weeks.

The Revolving Credit Agreement

Although a businessman may feel rather certain that the line of credit which has been agreed to will provide the necessary capital requirements for the coming year, there is always the possibility that conditions will change to the extent that the bank may have to reduce or withdraw its extension of credit. This possibility is normally part of the original agreement. The bank is obligated to make good on its line of credit only so long as conditions do not change materially.

The well-established business that has an excellent credit rating may find it possible, however, to obtain a commitment in the form of a standby agreement for a guaranteed line of credit. This arrangement is referred to as a *revolving credit agreement*. In addition to paying interest for the use of money for the period of the loan, the business must pay a commission or fee to the bank based on the amount of money it has on call during the agreement period. This additional commission or fee is charged because the bank must provide for such loan demands regardless of changes in business conditions and is, therefore, from time to time denied flexibility in the use of its own funds for other lending purposes.

Bank Credit Groups

The Postwar Small Business Credit Commission of the American Bankers Association (ABA) was largely responsible for the development of bank credit groups. Under this arrangement, if a businessman applies to any bank that is a member of a bank credit group when the bank is not in a position to make the loan, either because of other loan commitments or because the required loan is too large, other members of the bank credit group stand ready to participate in the loan.

Accounts Receivable Financing

For the businessman whose credit does not warrant an unsecured bank loan or for the businessman who has emergency needs for funds in excess of his line of credit, a pledge of his accounts receivable may be offered as security. Accounts receivable, as distinct from notes receivable, represent claims against customers to whom credit sales have been made without requiring them to sign a note or other credit instrument. This development in banking is rather recent and stems in part from the competition offered the banks by the specialized finance companies that have come into existence in recent decades.[3]

In extending loans on this basis, banks of course make the same sort of credit investigation that they do for businesses which are applying for unsecured loans. Particular attention is given

---

[3] These specialized finance companies, commonly referred to as commercial credit companies, are discussed in detail in Chapter 9. In addition to competing against nonbanking institutions by lending against the security of receivables, a very few banks undertake the practice of purchasing such receivables outright—a process referred to as "factoring." Factoring activities, also discussed in Chapter 9, are usually engaged in solely by highly specialized nonbanking finance organizations.

to the collection practices of the company and to certain characteristics of the company's accounts receivable. The bank also spot-checks the receivables of the firm and may in some cases analyze each account to determine the promptness of the customers of the firm in making payments. In addition, the bank will study the type and the quality of goods that are sold, for if the merchandise is of inferior quality, there may be objections from the customers and hence slower payment on the bills. Accounts receivable are of little value as the basis of a loan if large quantities of merchandise are returned and the amount of accounts receivable reduced accordingly. It is also important for the bank to know something of the customers of the business since their ability to pay their debts will have an important influence or bearing on the actual collection success of the business applying for the loan.

Accounts Receivable Loan Limits. The Bank Management Commission of the ABA recommends that a loan based on the security of accounts receivable should generally be no more than 80 percent of the gross receivables and that this amount should be reduced by any trade discounts allowed to customers and by the normal percentage of the merchandise returns. If there is reason to believe that many of the customers of the business which is applying for the loan are not suitable risks, or if adequate credit ratings are not available, the bank will be inclined to lend a correspondingly lower percentage of the face value of such receivables.

Technical Features of Accounts Receivable Financing. Under the accounts receivable loan arrangement, there is, in addition to the basic interest charge, a fee to cover the extra work that such a loan entails. The banks must periodically check the books of a business that has borrowed on the basis of its receivables in order to see that the business is, in fact, living up to the terms of the agreement. At the time the loan is made, it is generally provided that individual accounts on the ledger of the business will be clearly designated as having been pledged for the bank loan. Only those accounts that are suitable for collateral purposes for the bank are earmarked, and these accounts are replaced by other accounts as they are paid in full or in the event any become unsatisfactory.

Figure 8-2

Promissory Note

In addition to "earmarking" pledged accounts in the ledger of the borrowing firm, the bank also requires a schedule of the accounts so pledged along with a copy of each of the invoices involved in the shipment of goods. The businessman must also execute an assignment of the accounts involved. A specimen copy of a note for such a loan is shown in Figure 8-2.

As remittances are received by the business on the individual accounts that have been assigned, they must be turned over to the bank separately from other business funds. The bank also reserves the right to make a direct audit of the books of the business from time to time and to have an outside accounting firm examine the books periodically. The accounting firm frequently verifies a certain percentage of the accounts by mail, much as it does in a regular audit. Verification of the accounts in a routine manner leaves customers of the business unaware of the fact that their accounts have been pledged as collateral for a loan.

In this connection, it is interesting to note that businesses utilizing their receivables as collateral for bank loans often prefer to keep such knowledge from their own customers because this may be interpreted as an indication of weakness on the part of the business. Although businesses participating in this form of loan arrangement are frequently in a financially weak condition, this is not always the case. Some firms that are on a sound basis use accounts receivable financing as a permanent arrangement because they feel it has advantages for them which would not be available through other loan arrangements.

Manufacturing concerns appear to be the largest users of accounts receivable financing. In particular, this is true of manufacturers of food, textiles, leather products, furniture, paper, iron, steel, and machinery.

Inventory Loans

A business enterprise may borrow on the basis of its inventory as collateral in much the same manner that it may borrow on its receivables. A study is made by the bank not only of the physical condition of the inventory but also of the general composition of the inventory that the firm owns. Staple items that have a ready marketability serve well as collateral for a loan; style and fashion items do not serve well as collateral except for brief periods of time. Firms that use inventory as collateral are generally not in a position to procure further funds on an unsecured basis.

The bank may protect itself when lending to a business on the basis of inventory as collateral either by having title to the goods assigned to the bank or by taking a chattel mortgage on the inventory. In other cases, a trust receipt instrument may be used. When an assignment of title to the inventory is made to the bank, clear title cannot pass from the businessman to his customer until the loan is paid off or other collateral is substituted for the merchandise. Under a trust receipt arrangement, the bank retains ownership of the goods until they are actually sold in the regular course of business.

Warehousing of Inventory. In some cases when lending on the basis of inventory as collateral, the bank may insist that the business deposit the inventory in a bonded and licensed warehouse. The receipt issued by the warehouse is then turned over to the bank, which in turn holds it until such time as the loan is repaid. A specimen copy of a warehouse receipt for stored merchandise is shown in Figure 8-3.

It is frequently inconvenient for a business to deliver large bulky items of inventory to a warehouse for storage. This problem is solved through the use of *field warehouses*. A field warehousing

Figure 8-3

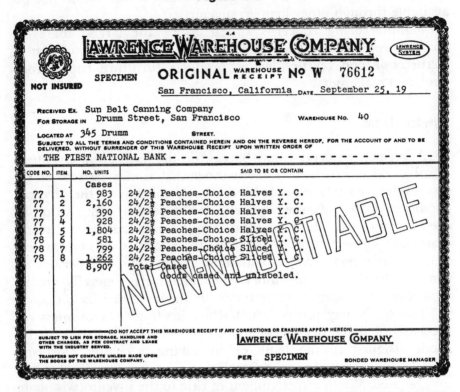

Warehouse Receipt

enterprise has the power to establish a bona fide warehouse on the premises of the borrowing business establishment. Field warehouses differ from the typical public warehouse in that they serve a single customer—that customer on whose property the field warehouse is established. The field warehouse could be a cattle ranch, a grain elevator, or a lake on which logs are temporarily stored.

In setting up the field warehouse, it is generally necessary first for the warehousing establishment to obtain a lease on that portion of the property of the business which is to be used for warehousing purposes. It is then necessary to establish fences, barriers, walks, and other postings to indicate clear possession of the property by the warehouseman in order to avoid accidental or deliberate removal of items by employees of the business during the general course of the business operations. A guard may be posted in order to check on the safety of the goods warehoused, or a room may be sealed and the seal inspected periodically to determine whether or not the company is honoring its agreement.

There must also be a complete statement of the commodities or items that are to be warehoused, and agreements must be made as to the maintenance of the property, proper fire precautions, insurance, and other necessary physical requirements. Under certain circumstances, the warehouseman is authorized to release a certain quantity of goods by the day, week, or month to make possible a rotation of merchandise. Under this arrangement, periodic physical inventories must be taken.

Extent of Field Warehousing. Field warehouses are in operation throughout the United States with a concentration of such activities in the central and Pacific Coast regions. It is estimated that from 10,000 to 12,000 field warehouses are in existence. Nearly all forms of merchandise that may be safely warehoused have at one time or another been used for this purpose. Canned goods, miscellaneous groceries, lumber, timber, and building supplies fill about two fifths of all field warehouses in this country. Those banks that make commodity loans will generally accept field warehouse receipts as collateral.

Cost of Inventory Loans. Inventory loans are somewhat more expensive than are the unsecured loans. The greater cost is due in part to the cost of the warehousing operation itself and in part to the fact that the borrower's credit rating may be low. Bank interest rates for warehouse loans are ordinarily somewhat higher than unsecured loans; and, in addition, a warehouse fee of from ¾ to 2½ percent of the loan, depending upon size and other factors, must be paid.[4] When warehousing facilities must be utilized anyway, there is little additional cost involved.

Inventory loans, like accounts receivable loans, have become popular due to the increasing demand for working capital additions. Also, business firms are understandably anxious to take advantage of cash discounts on their purchases when the money for cash payments can be secured at nominal rates. Unemployment insurance taxes under the federal social security laws have made it advantageous for many firms to stabilize both production and employment of labor throughout the year rather than to bear part of the burden of seasonal employment layoffs. Stabilized production throughout the year rather than production just prior to anticipated sales of the products results in the firm's carrying a larger average inventory. In turn, a larger commitment of funds by the company for carrying inventories is required. Such funds for inventory accumulation may be obtained by placing the inventories in a field warehouse, thus using the inventory itself as the basis for a bank loan.

Loans Secured by Stocks and Bonds

Stocks and bonds constitute a very popular type of collateral for short-term loans. Such securities, when pledged as collateral for a loan, are of interest to the banker primarily because of their marketability and their value. If the securities are highly marketable, and if the value is satisfactory to cover the amount of the loan requested and to provide a substantial margin for shrinkage in value, the banker may have little hesitancy in extending such a loan. The banker, of course, gives preference to those securities that are listed on one of the national security exchanges since frequent quotations of the value of such securities are available.

---

[4] Inventory loans, like receivable loans, are made also by commercial credit or sales finance companies. Interest rates charged by these companies are generally higher than are those charged by the banks.

Banks will usually lend from 60 to 70 percent of the market value of listed stocks, and from 70 to 80 percent of the market value of high-grade bonds. Since 1934, however, the Board of Governors of the Federal Reserve System has established maximum loan limits when the purpose of the loan is to purchase or deal in listed stocks.[5]

Only assignable stocks and bonds are eligible for this type of collateral financing. This restriction excludes United States Savings Bonds that are not assignable. When assignable securities are placed with the bank, a *stock power* or *bond power* is executed that authorizes the bank to sell or otherwise dispose of the securities should it become necessary to do so to protect the loan. (See Figure 8-4.)

Other Forms of Security for Short-Term Bank Loans

Security for bank loans may also include such things as the cash surrender value of life insurance policies, guarantee of a loan by a party other than the borrower, notes, and acceptances.

Life Insurance Loans. Small business establishments frequently find it possible to obtain needed short-term bank loans by a pledge of the cash surrender value of life insurance policies. Such policies must be of the assignable type, and many insurance companies insist that assignment forms prepared by the company be used for such purposes. Because of the safety afforded the bank through the use of these cash surrender values, such loans usually carry a moderate interest rate compared with loans on other types of business collateral. Another reason for the favorable rates is the fact that the borrower has the alternative of borrowing directly from the insurance company. Bank interest rates in general have been much higher in recent years than the contractual rate at which policyholders may borrow directly from their insurance companies. As a result, there has been a spectacular increase in the number of loans made by insurance companies to their policyholders.[6]

---

[5] The operations of the securities exchanges and the limitations on borrowing for purposes of dealing in securities are discussed in Chapter 14.

[6] Chapter 12 is devoted to functions and financial operations of insurance companies.

Figure 8-4

IRREVOCABLE STOCK POWER
Adopted by Washington Stock Exchange

Law Reporter Blank No. 43-A
All Rights Reserved

Know All Men by These Presents

That

For Value Received *have granted, bargained, sold, assigned, and fully and irrevocably transferred and do by these presents grant, bargain, sell, assign and fully and irrevocably transfer for all purposes unto* The Citizens National Bank of Washington, D. C.

- - - - - - - - - - - one hundred - - - - - - - - - - - - - *shares*

of the common *Stock of the* United States

Copper and Brass Company of Baltimore *standing in* my *name on* *the books of* United States Copper and Brass Company of Baltimore

And I *do hereby constitute and appoint* The Citizens National Bank of Washington, D. C. *to be* my *true and lawful attorney, irrevocable, for* me *and in* my *name and stead to sell, hypothecate or dispose of in any manner and for any purpose, assign, transfer and set over to any person or persons the whole or any parts of said stock, at once or from time to time, and for that purpose to make all necessary acts of assignment or transfer, and with power to substitute one or more persons in* their *stead, as to the whole or parts of said stock, with all the powers herein mentioned,* and I do *hereby ratify and confirm all acts that* my *said attorney or any substitute or substitutes under* this power *shall lawfully do by virtue hereof.*

In Witness Whereof John Smith has *have hereunto set* his *hand and seal this* 17th *day of* June *A. D. 19*

Signed, sealed and delivered in the presence of—

Roy Jones

John Smith [SEAL]
(Seal affixed)

Made and Sold by Law Reporter Ptg. Co., 518 9th St., Wash., D. C.

Stock Power

Comaker Loans. Many small businesses find it necessary to provide the bank with a guarantor in the form of a cosigner to their notes. It is to be expected that the cosigner would have to have at least as satisfactory a credit rating as, and usually a far better rating than, the firm requesting the loan.

Discounting Notes and Acceptances. Although the act of discounting a credit instrument with a bank technically may be considered as a sale rather than a pledge of collateral, the fact that such discounted instruments are endorsed by the seller renders the seller contingently liable. The discount of credit instruments by a firm with its bank is a form of bank credit.

The promissory note signed by the customer may be used by a firm when it is not certain of the credit standing of its customer. The use of the promissory note to bind a credit sale, however, as noted earlier, is not common in most fields of business activity. Notes have the advantage to a business of not requiring further proof of the claim against a customer as may be the case for the open-book account. The further advantage of negotiability makes it possible for the business to sell these notes to its bank or other financing agency. Except for the few lines of business activity where the use of the note is customary, however, banks are cautious in their purchase of such instruments because they often arise out of weak credit situations.

Another type of receivable instrument that arises out of the sale of merchandise to a business customer and which may be sold to a bank is the acceptance. An *acceptance* comes into the possession of a business through the sale of merchandise on the basis of a draft or bill of exchange drawn against the buyer or the buyer's bank. The accepted draft or bill of exchange is returned to the seller of the merchandise where it may be held until the date of its maturity. During this period, the business may see fit to discount such acceptances with its bank. Again the seller is contingently liable for these discounted acceptances.[7]

QUESTIONS

1. To what extent have commercial banks changed their lending policies? Do you believe that commercial banks have been wise in altering their original lending practices?
2. Describe the principal types of assets owned by commercial banks at the present time.
3. What bearing does the asset structure of a commercial bank have on the proportion of capital to deposits?
4. What is meant by an "unsecured loan"? Are such loans important as a form of bank lending?
5. Describe what is meant by a "bank line of credit." Describe the "revolving credit agreement" and compare it with the bank line of credit.
6. Describe the nature of accounts receivable lending on the part of commercial banks.

---

[7] The use of the banker's acceptance is shown in detail in connection with an international shipment of goods in Chapter 17.

7. What safeguards may a bank establish to protect itself when it lends on the basis of customer's receivables pledged as collateral for the loans?
8. When a business establishment uses its inventory as collateral for a bank loan, how is the problem of storing and guarding the inventory accomplished for the bank?
9. Discuss other forms of collateral that a business may use in securing loans from a commercial bank.

SUGGESTED READINGS

BARGER, HAROLD. *Money, Banking, and Public Policy,* 2d ed. Chicago: Rand McNally & Company, 1968. Chapters 12 and 13.

COCHRAN, JOHN A. *Money, Banking, and the Economy,* 2d ed. New York: The Macmillan Company, 1971. Chapters 9 and 10.

FRAZER, WILLIAM J., JR. *Introduction to Analytics and Institutions of Money and Banking.* Princeton, New Jersey: D. Van Nostrand Company, Inc., 1966. Chapter 12.

HAYES, DOUGLAS A. *Bank Lending Policies—Issues and Practices.* Ann Arbor, Michigan: The University of Michigan, 1964. Chapter 3.

KLEIN, JOHN J. *Money and the Economy,* 2d ed. New York: Harcourt Brace Jovanovich, Inc., 1970. Chapters 5 and 6.

ROBINSON, ROLAND I. *The Management of Bank Funds,* 2d ed. New York: McGraw-Hill Book Company, Inc., 1962. Part III.

VAN HORNE, JAMES C. *Fundamentals of Financial Management,* 2d ed. Englewood Cliffs, New Jersey: Prentice-Hall, Inc., 1974. Chapter 16.

9 | Other Sources of Short-Term Business Financing

Although the commercial banking system is of great importance to the business community as a source of short-term funds, it is by no means the only source. Trade credit, commercial finance companies, factors, and the Small Business Administration also provide significant amounts of short-term financing for business. In this chapter each of these sources is discussed.

TRADE CREDIT

The most important single form of short-term business financing is that of credit extended by one business organization to another. The open accounts receivable, together with notes receivable, taken by manufacturers, wholesalers, jobbers, and other business units as sellers of goods and services to other businesses are known as *trade credit*. This discussion excludes credit established as a result of sale of goods to the ultimate consumer, for this is considered in Chapters 18 through 20.

Characteristics of Trade Credit

The establishment of trade credit is the least formal of all forms of financing. It involves only an order for goods or services by one business and the delivery of goods or performance of service by the selling business. The purchasing business receives an invoice stating the terms of the transaction and the time period within which payment is to be made. The purchaser enters the liability as an addition to accounts payable; the seller enters the claim as an addition to accounts receivable. In some situations, the seller of goods or services may insist upon written evidence of the liability on the part of the purchaser. Such written evidence generally takes the form of a note and is carried as a note payable by the purchaser and as a note receivable by the seller. In both situations, through the open account and the use of the note, trade credit as a form of short-term financing has been utilized.

Before a business organization delivers goods or performs a service for another business, it must determine, of course, the ability and willingness of the purchaser to pay for the order. The responsibility of such credit analysis in most businesses belongs to the credit manager.

Terms for Trade Credit

Sales may be made on such terms as *cash, E.O.M.* (end of month), *M.O.M.* (middle of month), or *R.O.G.* (receipt of goods). In other situations, such terms as *2/10, net 30* may be provided, in which case the purchaser may deduct 2 percent from the purchase price if payment is made within 10 days; but if not paid within 10 days, the net amount of the purchase is due within 30 days of shipment. Such discounts for early payment are common and are designed to provide incentive for prompt payment of bills by the purchaser. Occasionally net terms, such as net/30 or net/60, may be provided.

A cash sale, contrary to its implication, does involve the element of credit since the purchaser is generally permitted a certain number of days within which to make payment. For example, a sale of merchandise in which the purchaser is permitted up to ten days to remit may be considered a cash transaction, although credit is outstanding to the purchaser for that period of time. Even for the firm that purchases goods and services entirely on a cash basis of this nature, the volume of accounts payable outstanding on its books at any one time may be large.

E.O.M. terms and M.O.M. terms are designed primarily for the convenience of frequent purchasers of goods from a given company. Rather than being paid for within a specified number of days, all sales made to a customer during the month are payable during the following month. For example, under terms of 2/10, net/60 E.O.M., all sales made to a customer during the month of April become payable during the month of May, the discount period running from May 1 through May 10. This arrangement makes it possible for the customer to pay for his many purchases from a particular company with a single remittance. In order to shorten the time lag for payment of credit purchases, M.O.M. terms may be used instead of E.O.M. Under this arrangement, the discount period begins the fifteenth day of the month for sales made from the first to the fifteenth and the first of the following month for sales made from the fifteenth to the end of month.

R.O.G. terms signify that payment is to be made upon "receipt of goods." These terms are used when shipment of goods is made over a long distance, during which period of shipment the seller of the merchandise finances the credit transaction.

Cost of Trade Credit

When trade credit terms provide for no discount for early payment of obligations, there is, of course, no cost for such financing. Even when discounts are available to the purchaser, it may appear that there is no charge for trade credit since failure to take the discount by early payment simply requires the purchaser to pay the net purchase price. An implicit cost is involved, however, when a discount is not taken. For example, with terms of 2/10, net/30 the cost is measured directly by the loss of the discount that might otherwise be taken if payment were made within the first 10-day period. During the first 10-day period, however, the buyer does have trade credit without direct cost.

In order to calculate the comparative cost of trade credit to a business firm as opposed to bank credit, the cost of the trade credit must be reduced to an annual interest rate basis. For example, if the terms of sale are 2/10, net/30, the cost of the trade credit is the sacrifice of the 2 percent discount that the purchaser fails to take if he allows his credit to run for the full 30-day period. Since the buyer may take the discount if he pays within the first 10 days after purchase, payment on the thirtieth day would result in a sacrifice of the discount for the privilege of extending the payment period by 20 days. The loss of the discount of 2 percent may then be represented as the cost of trade credit for 20 days under terms of 2/10, net/30. Two percent for 20 days is at the rate of 36 percent for 360 days, the relevant figure for comparison with bank loan rates. Had the terms of the sale been 2/10, net/60, the cost of the trade credit would have been 2 percent for the use of credit for 50 days. Two percent for 50 days is the same rate as 14.4 percent for 360 days. In like manner, terms of 2/10, net/20 represent a cost of trade credit on an annual basis of 72 percent. The cost of such trade credit is clearly far in excess of bank rates.

It should be noted that these figures reflect discount rather than loan relationships. If the discount is not taken on a transaction with an invoice amount of $100, terms of 2/10, n/30, the cost of the trade credit is $2. The $2 discount loss, however, relates to the discount price of the purchase, $98, rather than to the gross invoice amount of $100. The base amount of the transaction is, in effect, $98 with a $2 penalty added for failure to make payment within ten days from the invoice date. The effective interest rate is, therefore, slightly above these stated percentages.

Volume of Trade Credit

As an indication of the importance and dominance of trade credit as a form of short-term financing, as of September 30, 1973, trade credit shown as a liability for a group of 11,429 manufacturing corporations was $53 billion compared with short-term bank loans of $25 billion.[1] Earlier studies have revealed similar comparisons. The Securities and Exchange Commission reports that as of late 1973 the volume of notes and accounts receivable of all United States Corporations was $252.2 billion. This compares with $241.5 billion for inventories and $62.1 billion for cash. Receivables are, therefore, the most important single category of current assets.[2] Trade credit is particularly heavy in the construction industry and in wholesaling operations.

---

[1] FTC *Quarterly Financial Report* for manufacturing corporations, 3d Quarter, 1973 (Washington, 1973), p. 34.

[2] *Economic Report of the President* (Washington: United States Government Printing Office, 1974), p. 340.

Sources of Funds for Trade Credit

Trade credit, unlike other forms of short-term finance, does not involve the conveyance of money to the user. The net effect as far as the user of trade credit is concerned, however, is very much the same since it enables him to acquire goods or services without an immediate payment therefor. The firm that provides trade credit must be able to do so from its general resources. If the firm has such a strained financial position that it is unable to extend credit terms in line with other firms of its industry, it operates at a severe if not impossible competitive handicap. Since the trade credit provided by a firm is reflected in its balance sheet as a current asset, in particular as notes receivable and accounts receivable, sources of funds for carrying such trade credit are very much the same as for other current assets, namely, purchasing goods and services on the basis of trade credit, short-term borrowing, long-term financing, and retaining profits from operations.

Reasons for Use of Trade Credit

Because the cost of trade credit in most lines of business activity is high, it may be difficult to understand why such a tremendous volume of trade credit would be taken by business. Trade credit is used by financially weak concerns because they have no adequate alternative sources of credit. In any event, it may not be assumed that because of its high cost, trade credit is an undesirable source of short-term financing for the business. It may be, in fact, the most essential form of financing for small and growing business enterprises that are unable to qualify for short-term credit through customary financial channels.

Few of the business enterprises in operation today would have been able to reach their present size and scope of operations without the help of trade credit during the growth stages of their development. For the firm that does not have recourse to a line of credit with a bank or other financial institution, the question is not the cost of trade credit as compared with unavailable bank credit but rather the profit that can be made from the sale of the goods so acquired as compared with the cost of the trade credit itself. For the firm that does have access to low-cost bank credit and credit from other financial institutions, it appears reasonable to expect a wise management to take advantage of discounts.

The firm in a weak financial condition will find trade credit more readily available than bank credit because the bank as a lender of money stands to gain only the stipulated interest on the loan if repayment is made in accordance with the terms of the agreement. It stands to lose up to the total of the sum loaned in the event of the failure of the borrower to meet his obligation. The manufacturer or the merchant, on the other hand, who sells on the basis of trade credit has a profit margin on the goods sold. Failure of the purchaser to meet his obligation results, at most, in the loss of the cost of the goods so delivered to the purchaser. The seller of the merchandise also is encouraged to open a new account, although it may be weaker than his average account because he anticipates repeated orders from the customer. Hence, his profit from the first transaction is measured not simply by the markup but also by the future business that may be brought in by opening the account.

COMMERCIAL FINANCE COMPANIES

Shortly after the turn of the century, the first commercial finance company was chartered. Since that time, the number of such institutions has increased to more than five hundred. Some of these organizations are small, offering limited financial services to their customers, while others have vast resources and engage in broadly diversified programs of business lending. The *commercial finance company* has been defined as an agency without a bank charter that performs one or more of the following functions: advances funds to business concerns by discounting accounts receivable, usually without notice to the trade debtor; makes loans secured by chattel mortgages on machinery or liens on inventory; and finances deferred-payment sales of commercial and industrial equipment.[3] These companies are also frequently referred to as commercial credit companies, commercial receivables companies, and discount companies.

Commercial finance companies, represented by such organizations familiar to the business world as C.I.T. Financial Corporation of New York City, the Commercial Credit Company of

---

[3] Neil H. Jacoby and Raymond J. Saulnier, *Business Finance and Banking* (New York: National Bureau of Economic Research, 1947), p. 113.

Baltimore, Maryland, and Walter E. Heller, International, offer much the same sort of service to business concerns as do the commercial banks in connection with accounts receivable financing and inventory financing. Accounts receivable financing was, in fact, originated by the commercial finance companies and only later was it adopted by commercial banks.

The commercial finance companies gained a foothold in the financial markets and grew to their present size as a result of many factors. Among these factors may be included the fact that they were completely free to experiment with new and highly specialized types of credit arrangements, that state laws were generally more favorable to these nonbanking organizations in lending on the basis of accounts receivable, and finally that these organizations were able to charge rates of such a level as to make possible a profitable return for high-risk loans. Frequently these rates were far above those bankers would want or were permitted to charge their own customers.

As noted in the definition of the commercial finance companies, these organizations also lend money on the basis of inventory as collateral and finance the sale of commercial and industrial equipment on a deferred-payment basis. These companies concentrate their attention, however, on receivables as a form of collateral for their loans. This type of financing is used primarily in fields where there are large numbers of small businesses, such as home appliances, hardware, plastics, drugs, paper, food products, paint, wallpaper, and leather.

Operating Characteristics of Commercial Finance Companies

When a commercial finance company sets up a loan secured by receivables, it enters into a contract with the borrower that provides for the acceptance of the borrower's open accounts receivable as collateral for a loan. The company specifies those accounts that are acceptable to it as collateral and, as a rule, will lend to the borrower an amount less than the total of such receivables pledged for the loan. The excess of the total volume of receivables pledged over the actual amount of the loan provides a margin of safety in the event that the borrower fails to repay the loan, and it also facilitates adjustments in outstanding accounts resulting from the return of goods by customers of the borrowing company.

As in the case of receivables financing with the commercial banks, the commercial finance companies require their borrowers to mark clearly their ledgers to indicate those accounts that have been assigned as collateral for the loan, and all payments received on such accounts must be immediately turned over to the company. As a further protection to the finance company, it is generally provided that the borrower may not assign any of his other accounts to other lenders without appropriate notice to the finance company. Also, representatives of the finance company may make periodic audits of the borrower's books.

Terms and Charges of Commercial Finance Companies

The cost of loans offered by the commercial finance companies on the basis of receivables as collateral varies widely with the size of the lending company. In recent years the effective rates per annum on loans by the largest companies have fallen within the range of 12 to 15 percent. The volume of business of these large companies represents a major portion of all accounts receivable financing by finance companies. Higher rates of interest—up to 18 percent—are not uncommon on business which is handled by small finance companies because these companies generally deal with local firms whose receivables are smaller in amount and more expensive to handle than the receivables of the firms financed by the larger companies. Also, the small finance company cannot achieve the economies of large-scale operation.[4]

In comparing the costs of loans secured by receivables that are extended by commercial finance companies with the typical unsecured line of credit, one factor is commonly ignored. In the case of a bank loan, the term may be for a fixed period, such as 30, 60, or 90 days. During the period of the loan, the borrower must accumulate a sufficient sum to repay the loan at its maturity, during which time the accumulating funds lie idle. The borrower pays interest on the total loan and may be required to maintain with the bank a compensating deposit balance of as much as 20 percent of the amount borrowed. This is a well-established banking prac-

---

[4] Clyde William Phelps, *Accounts Receivable Financing as a Method of Business Finance* (Baltimore: Educational Division, Commercial Credit Company, Studies in Commercial Financing, No. 2, 1957), p. 41.

tice. The net effect of such a required compensating balance is to increase the cost of borrowing from the bank. In accounts receivable financing, however, each amount collected from the customer is immediately turned over to the finance company; the principal of the loan is reduced accordingly; and financing charges, based entirely on the actual number of days the borrowed funds are outstanding, are reduced.

Volume of Commercial Finance Company Lending

At the close of 1973 loans outstanding on accounts receivable by commercial finance companies totaled slightly over $2 billion. These companies also provided a vast amount of credit for businesses through the financing of commercial vehicles, industrial and farm equipment, and other types of business credit. The Board of Governors of the Federal Reserve System estimates the total volume of such business credit outstanding by the commercial finance companies at the end of 1973 to be more than $29 billion.

Sources of Funds for Commercial Finance Companies

The equity position of the commercial finance companies is considerably greater than that of the commercial banks of the nation; however, these organizations do not operate on equity capital alone. Additional long-term capital is acquired through the sale of debenture bonds. In addition, commercial banks lend a large volume of money at wholesale rates to the commercial finance companies, which in turn lend it to business borrowers at retail rates. Banks have been known to refer customers to finance companies for their loans when they do not choose to engage in receivables or inventory financing. Nonbanking financial institutions, as well as commercial and industrial firms, often find it advantageous to invest their temporary surplus funds in the notes of commercial finance companies.

These sources of short-term funds permit the commercial finance companies to meet their peak loan demands without becoming encumbered with long-term debt, only part of which would be used during slack lending periods.

Reasons for Use of Commercial Finance Companies

In view of the average cost of commercial finance company loans as noted above, the question may arise as to why a businessman would under any circumstances utilize the facilities of these companies. As a matter of fact, the businessman who has ample current assets and is in a highly liquid position may be well advised to restrict his borrowing activities to his local bank. The business that is without a short-term financial problem at one time or another, however, is the exception rather than the rule. During periods when business is most brisk and growth possibilities most favorable, the need for additional funds on a short-term basis becomes unusually pressing. The businessman's first action is to request an increase in his customary line of credit at his bank. Failing this, he may secure an additional loan from his bank by pledging either inventory or receivables as collateral.

As noted in Chapter 8, however, not all banks engage in this type of financial arrangement, and it may be necessary to deal with a commercial finance company. Also, under federal banking laws, no bank may lend more than 10 percent of its capital and surplus to any one borrower. Since a majority of the nation's approximately 14,000 banks are capitalized for less than $350,000, it is entirely possible that the businessman's bank may be unable to provide additional short-term funds even though it considers the customer deserving of such increased credit. For the banks with capital and surplus of $350,000, the maximum loan would be no greater than $35,000 to each borrower. Because the commercial finance companies are able to operate through a system of branches on a regional or on a national basis, unhampered by restrictions on branch operations, they can acquire the volume of business necessary to cover overhead and to provide the needed diversification of risks to undertake high-risk financing.

FACTORS

The *factor*, like the commercial finance company, engages in accounts receivable financing for business enterprises. In contrast with the commercial finance companies, however, the factor purchases the accounts outright and assumes all credit risks. Under this arrangement, customers whose accounts are sold are notified that their bills are payable to the factor. The task of collection of accounts is thus shifted from the seller of the accounts to the factor.

Despite the long history of operations of these companies, their growth has taken place largely within the last twenty-five years. The origin of factoring was in the textile industry, and since most of the selling agencies and credit-reporting agencies in the textile field are located in New York City, most of the nation's factors are also located there. In addition to serving the textile industry, factors have also proved useful in such fields as furniture, shoes, bottle making, paper, men's clothing, toys, and furs.

Operating Characteristics of Factors

Assume that a business organization in a field which is amenable to the factoring operation finds that for the first time in several years, because of increasing levels of inventory and receivables, the firm is experiencing financial difficulties. Although the firm is well managed and has for several years been able to secure adequate financing through an unsecured line of credit with its bank, in order to take advantage of expanded business opportunities it finds it necessary to supplement its usual sources of current funds. The factor draws a contract establishing the duties and the obligations of each party. This contract includes the conditions under which accounts may be sold to the factor, the responsibility for the payment of all such accounts, the collection procedures to be followed, and the method of reporting balances due. The contract also provides that the daily invoices for sales of goods to customers, together with the original shipping documents, be delivered to the factor and that the accounts so established be assigned to the factor. All proposed sales must be approved by the factor before the delivery of goods, and they are subject to rejection in the event that the credit rating of the customer does not meet the standards of the factor. Daily reports must be rendered to the factor of all credits, allowances, and returns of merchandise. The contract also indicates the charges to be made for the factoring service.

The credit analysis department of the factor is the heart of that organization since it must serve in such a way as to conserve the factor's assets and also to be in constant contact with the factor's clients. Members of the credit department of the factor not only must be extremely prompt and accurate in their credit analyses but also, because they work closely with the firm's clients, must retain the goodwill of the companies that use the services of the factor.[5]

Terms and Charges for Factoring

The charge for factoring is in two parts. First, interest is charged on the money advanced, based on the actual daily net debit balance. Second, a factoring commission or service charge is figured as a percentage of the face amount of the receivables. Such service charges typically range from 3/4 of 1 percent to 1 1/2 percent of the face amount of the accounts financed. The commission charge is determined after taking into consideration such things as the volume of sales of the client, the general credit status of the accounts being factored, and the average size of individual accounts.

In addition to the interest and commission charges, the factor will also reserve from 5 to 15 percent of the total amount of receivables factored for purposes of making adjustments, such as for merchandise that is returned to the seller. This is not a charge, however, and is returned to the seller after it has served its intended purpose.

Volume of Factoring

In 1973 about $19 billion of financing was supplied to American business firms through the factoring of open accounts receivable. The dollar volume of such factoring operations is increasing and spreading into many lines of business where it was formerly unknown. About 18 firms in the United States engage exclusively in factoring, and each has capital funds of $1 million or more. Several additional firms with capital funds in excess of $1 million engage in both open accounts receivable financing and factoring operations.

---

[5] For three excellent articles on factoring, see *Credit and Financial Management,* the official publication of the National Association of Credit Management, Volume 74, Number 12 (December, 1972).

Sources of Funds for Factors

Like the commercial finance companies, factors obtain their funds for operations through a combination of equity capital, long-term borrowing, short-term borrowing, and profits from operations. Although most factors obtain equity capital directly from the small group of persons actively engaged in the factoring operations, at least one factor has sold common stock to the general public.

Reasons for Use of Factoring Services

Although the services of the factor may be used by a firm that is unable to secure financing through customary channels, financially strong companies may also at times use his services to good advantage. In fact, these facilities are of greatest benefit to those companies that are enjoying unprecedented success with respect to sales and growth. It has been noted before that during such periods companies experience extreme shortages of working capital. The sale of receivables without recourse (no contingent liability for their collection) has the effect of substituting cash for accounts receivable, which may make possible even greater growth and profitability in the long run.

Some firms factor their receivables not because it is the only form of financing available to them but because of other considerations. First, the cost of doing business through credit sales is definite and determinable in advance, since the factor assumes all risks of collection. This is in effect a form of credit insurance. Second, it eliminates overhead including bookkeeping costs, the maintenance of a credit department, and the expenses of collecting delinquent accounts. Unless a firm factors all of its receivables, however, the complete elimination of the expenses of credit department operation could not be accomplished. A corollary of these two advantages, but of a somewhat less tangible nature, is the fact that the management of a business is freed from concern with financial matters and is permitted to concentrate on production and distribution.

Although factoring services are regarded highly by some business firms, others offer several objections to their use. The two reasons cited most frequently are the cost and the implication of financial weakness. The cost of factoring is admittedly higher than the cost of borrowing from a bank on the basis of an unsecured loan; however, it is difficult to conclude without reservation that the net cost is higher. The elimination of overhead costs that would otherwise be required of a business plus the fact that management need not concern itself with financial matters may completely offset the additional cost involved in the factoring process. With respect to the implication of financial weakness, many businessmen prefer to avoid the factoring plan in favor of the non-notification plan available through the commercial finance companies. In this way they avoid having their customers make their payments to the factor.

Outside the textile field, where factoring has long played an important part, the businessman often makes every effort to avoid letting his customers know that he is using their accounts in order to secure financing because of the implication of financial weakness.

TRENDS IN ACCOUNTS RECEIVABLE FINANCING AND FACTORING

Following the great depression of the 1930's, many financial institutions began to broaden their activities and functions. The factors began to engage in activity outside the textile industry, which had been their special field for nearly a hundred years. During this period, several commercial finance companies that were originally established to finance open accounts receivable on a non-notification basis and without assumption of risk began to undertake factoring operations of much the same nature as those of the factors. In addition, some commercial banks began to undertake regular factoring functions for the textile industry and for a few other fields on much the same basis as that provided by the factors.[6] One of the most important commercial banks engaged in direct factoring operations is the First National Bank of Boston, which, because of its interest in the textile industry of New England, very early engaged in this type of operation to accommodate its customers. The volume of commercial receivables

---

[6] Jacoby and Saulnier, *op. cit.*, pp. 120-21.

factored through the facilities of commercial banks now constitutes almost half of the total volume of such financing.

Many of the companies which are engaged solely in factoring operations are wholly owned subsidiaries of larger commercial finance companies or commercial banks. At the present time, therefore, the commercial banks, the commercial finance companies, and the factors have much in common. In many situations they offer identical services, but each retains a special emphasis and a primary interest that allows it to be identified with a basic type of financial operation.

SMALL BUSINESS ADMINISTRATION

The Small Business Administration was established by the federal government to provide financial assistance to small firms that are unable to obtain loans through private channels on reasonable terms. It limits its activities entirely to small firms in contrast with its predecessor, the Reconstruction Finance Corporation, which ceased its lending activities on September 30, 1953. The Small Business Administration, created June 30, 1953, has 65 field offices through which applications for loans are accepted. Preference is given to applicants engaged in producing for military or essential civilian requirements.

If a firm is able to obtain financing elsewhere, its application to the Small Business Administration for a loan is rejected. An applicant for a loan must prove that funds are not available from his own or a competing bank in an appropriate amount, that no other private lending sources are available, that the issuance of securities is not practicable, that financing cannot be arranged through the disposal of assets of the business, and that personal credit of the owners cannot be used. Such loans may not be used for paying existing creditors nor for speculative purposes.

Operating Characteristics of the Small Business Administration

The Small Business Administration assists in the financing of small enterprises in three ways: it may make direct loans to businesses; it may participate jointly with private banks in extending loans to businesses; or it may agree to guarantee a bank loan. On a direct basis, the SBA can make loans of up to $100,000. When participating with banks in making loans, the SBA's share may not be in excess of $150,000. In guaranteeing loans, the SBA may extend its guarantee to 90 percent of a bank loan or $350,000, whichever is less.

Terms and Charges for Small Business Administration Financing

In addition to lending short-term working capital to business, the Small Business Administration may make loans for up to ten years and if a substantial part of the loan is for construction, it may be for as long as twenty years. As of 1974, the maximum interest rate was 5½ percent. A commercial bank participating in a loan with the Small Business Administration may set a higher rate on its share of a loan, provided the rate is legal and reasonable. Or, if it wishes to do so, a bank may charge a lower rate; in this case, the Small Business Administration will lower its rate, though not below 5 percent. In allowing commercial banks participating in a Small Business Administration loan to set their own rates on their shares of the loans, it was assumed that prevailing rates in the area would be reflected.

In addition to the business lending activities of the SBA described above, it has been vested with the responsibility for several corollary financial activities. These include loans to development companies, disaster loans, lease guarantees, surety bond support, minority enterprise programs, procurement assistance, and support for small business investment companies.

Volume of Lending by the Small Business Administration

During the very early days of its operation, the Small Business Administration encouraged lending to small businesses by local credit pools throughout the country. A change in policy, however, resulted in more active direct lending by the Administration. In 1973, 31,506 business loans were approved totaling $2.2 billion. Approximately two thirds of the loans were made on a participation basis with commercial banks rather than independently.

Sources of Funds for the Small Business Administration

The Small Business Administration operates on a revolving fund provided by Congress. The total of business loans which have been approved far exceeds the revolving fund because of repayments and the fact that a portion of the amount approved is the participation share of commercial banks.

Reasons for Use of Small Business Administration Loans

The reason for the use of Small Business Administration loans by businesses is explained by the stated objectives of the Administration, that is, to enable small businesses to obtain financial assistance otherwise not available through private channels on reasonable terms. When the Small Business Administration was established, it was recognized that the economic development of the nation has depended in large part upon the freedom of new business ventures to enter into active operation. Yet the increased concentration of investable funds in the possession of the large institutional investors, such as life insurance companies, investment companies, and others, has made it increasingly difficult for new and small business ventures to attract investment capital. Through the Small Business Administration it is presumed that deserving small businesses may have access to capital on reasonable terms.

QUESTIONS

1. Describe the nature of trade credit as a form of short-term financing.
2. Why do trade credit terms tend to be similar for firms within an industry?
3. Businesses that purchase all of their supplies on a cash basis frequently show sizable amounts as "accounts payable" in their balance sheets. Explain.
4. What is meant by the abbreviation E.O.M. as it applies to trade credit terms? Why would such terms be used?
5. Explain how the cost of financing through trade credit may be compared with financing through bank loans.
6. Compare the importance of trade credit as a form of short-term financing with other forms of short-term financing.

7. What are the principal reasons for using trade credit for short-term financing?
8. Compare the operations of commercial finance companies with those of commercial banks.
9. Why is it difficult to compare the costs of short-term borrowing through a commercial finance company with short-term financing from commercial banks?
10. What are the sources of funds for commercial finance companies?
11. Under what circumstances would a business secure its financing through a commercial finance company?
12. Why are commercial finance companies able to provide their business customers with more liberal financing than are commercial banks?
13. Explain the operations of the factor.
14. Why is it difficult to make a direct comparison of short-term financing through a factor with bank or commercial finance company financing?
15. Why would a business utilize the services of a factor?
16. Discuss the place of the Small Business Administration in the field of finance.

SUGGESTED READINGS

Credit Management Handbook, 2d ed. Edited by the Credit Research Foundation. Homewood, Illinois: Richard D. Irwin, Inc., 1965. Chapters 13 and 26.

GRUNEWALD, ADOLPH E., and ERWIN ESSER NEMMERS. *Basic Managerial Finance.* New York: Holt, Rinehart and Winston, Inc., 1970. Chapter 12.

HUNT, PEARSON, CHARLES M. WILLIAMS, and GORDON DONALDSON. *Basic Business Finance,* 4th ed. Homewood, Illinois: Richard D. Irwin, Inc., 1971. Chapters 11 and 14.

JOHNSON, ROBERT W. *Financial Management,* 4th ed. Boston: Allyn and Bacon, Inc., 1971. Chapters 12 and 13.

"New Trends in Commercial Finance," *Credit and Financial Management,* March, 1962.

PHELPS, CLYDE WILLIAM. *The Role of Factoring in Modern Business Finance.* Baltimore: Educational Division, Commercial Credit Company, Studies in Commercial Financing, No. 1, 1956.

————. *Accounts Receivable Financing as a Method of Business Finance.* Baltimore: Educational Division, Commercial Credit Company, Studies in Commercial Financing, No. 2, 1957.

WESTON, J. FRED, and EUGENE F. BRIGHAM. *Managerial Finance,* 4th ed. New York: Holt, Rinehart and Winston, Inc., 1972. Chapter 21.

10 | Merchandising and Facilitating Agencies for Short-Term Financing

Short-term financing is provided directly by the nation's banks, commercial finance companies, factors, and other agencies and institutions discussed in the previous chapters. Other organizations contribute to the flow of short-term funds from lender to borrower by serving as media through which the flow is channeled. For example, commercial paper houses serve merely to distribute or merchandise to lenders the obligations taken from borrowers, lending no money for their own account. Other organizations serve the business world through a system of insurance on the receivables held by business firms as a result of credit sales. These credit insurance companies serve as facilitating agencies, as do the many forms of special organizations established for the purpose of reporting on the credit standing of prospective customers. The Federal Reserve System, discussed in Chapter 4, is basically a facilitating agency in that it serves to make the commercial banking system more effective in its operation and service to the business community. Commercial paper houses, credit insurance companies, and credit reporting agencies are those agencies specifically discussed in this chapter.

COMMERCIAL PAPER HOUSES

The *commercial paper house* purchases the promissory notes of reputable business organizations for the purpose of resale to banks and other lenders. A fee based on the amount of notes purchased, charged to the issuer of the notes, provides the basic income of the commercial paper house.

Operating Characteristics of Commercial Paper Houses

The businessman who wishes to use the services of the commercial paper house must have an unquestioned reputation for the sound operation of his firm. If after thorough investigation of the firm's financial position by the commercial paper house it appears that the notes of the firm can be sold with little difficulty, an agreement is made for the outright sale of a block of the firm's promissory notes to the commercial paper house. The commercial paper house will resell these notes as quickly as possible to banks, to managers of pension funds, business corporations that have surplus funds, and to other investors. The notes are usually prepared in denominations of $100,000 or more with maturities ranging from a few days to 270 days. The size of the notes and the maturities, however, can be adjusted to suit individual investor requirements.

Terms and Charges for Commercial Paper House Financing

The commercial paper house will pay to the borrower the face amount of the notes less the interest charge and a fee usually of $\frac{1}{8}$ of 1 percent calculated on an annual basis. The interest charge is determined by the general level of prevailing rates in the money market and the strength of the borrowing company. When these notes are resold to banks and other lenders, only the prevailing interest rate is deducted from the face value of the notes; hence, the commercial paper house receives the fee as compensation for the negotiation.

Although the paper is sold without recourse, that is, the commercial paper house has no liability in the event that the terms of the notes are not met by the borrowers, it is generally provided that a bank has ten days after purchase of the notes to investigate the credit standing of the company whose notes are purchased. If the bank determines the credit of the company to be unsatisfactory, it is permitted to return the notes to the commercial paper house. During this ten-day period, the purchaser of the notes may contact other banks for information regarding the borrowing company and make direct inquiries of the company itself for additional information that may be desired. In addition, the purchaser of the notes may request information from Moody's Investors Service, Inc. or Standard and Poor's Corporation. Both firms now report regularly on the quality of commercial paper.

Since a fee of $\frac{1}{8}$ of 1 percent (on an annual basis) on a 30-day note of $100,000 is only $10.42, dealers have little interest in such small transactions. They may do so, of course, in order to develop accounts having greater volume potential.

Volume of Commercial Paper House Financing

Although the activities of the commercial paper houses date back nearly 150 years, the volume of commercial paper sold has varied widely. From a volume of well over $1 billion shortly after World War I, the amount of commercial paper decreased to less than $160 million in 1945. From the low point in 1945, the volume has increased markedly, especially since 1958. As of the end of 1973, the commercial paper houses of the nation had placed approximately $14 billion. In addition to the commercial paper sold through dealer houses, the large sales finance companies of the nation had outstanding approximately $25 billion which they sold directly to borrowers. In 1973, 8 commercial paper houses, located for the most part in New York City, dominated the market. These dealers in commercial paper served such borrowing companies as sales finance companies, manufacturers, wholesalers, retailers, and various other categories, including a significant number of public utilities.

Most of the companies using commercial paper as a means of short-term financing have net worth of $25 million or more. Among the larger firms that have issued commercial paper are General Motors Acceptance Corporation, Atlantic Refining Company, General Mills, Inc., and the May Department Stores Company.

Reasons for Use of Commercial Paper House Financing

Businesses use funds secured through the commercial paper houses in much the same manner as those funds secured through regular banking channels: accumulation of inventory during peak seasons, carrying large volumes of receivables, and general working capital purposes. Funds secured through the commercial paper houses, however, are seldom regarded as an alternative to bank credit, but rather as a supplementary source of short-term financing. Any business that is in a strong enough position to make use of commercial paper facilities would be expected to have a firm line of bank credit. Funds secured through the commercial paper houses may be used to take advantage of special situations that require capital in excess of the regular line of bank credit. They may also be used periodically to retire all bank indebtedness.

The most important reason for the use of facilities of the commercial paper houses, however, is the fact that the cost of such borrowing is generally less than regular bank rates, despite the fact that a commission on the face amount of the notes is charged. The companies borrowing through the commercial paper houses are generally able to obtain interest rates of from $\frac{1}{8}$ of 1 percent to 1 percent lower than regular bank rates. Also, the need for compensating bank balances is avoided, a factor that may add up to 2 percent to stated interest costs on short-term bank loans.

Because the commercial paper houses distribute notes over wide geographical areas, they are able to place them with banks that have fewer profitable alternative uses for their funds. Also, industrial firms and other nonbank lenders often purchase commercial paper as a profitable alternative to the purchase of Treasury bills and other high-grade short-term obligations. In recent years, commercial paper has provided a yield slightly above that of short-term government securities but somewhat under that received by banks from high-grade short-term business loans. Although commercial banks have historically been the principal purchasers of commercial paper, at the present time almost 60 percent of all paper is purchased by industrial corporations. Corporations have increased their purchases of commercial paper as a convenient and profitable means of investing their increasing accumulations of cash. Country banks that rarely have an opportunity to lend directly to the nation's large corporations now account for most of the commercial paper purchased by banks.

CREDIT INSURANCE COMPANIES

Like all forms of insurance, credit insurance serves to spread the risk of loss on the part of a few persons among many persons. A definite and ascertainable cost, the insurance premium, is sub-stituted for an uncertain and perhaps unlimited loss. Just as fire and other forms of property insurance protect the businessman against loss due to damage to his physical properties, *credit insurance* offers similar protection against unusual losses resulting from the sale of merchandise on a credit basis. Credit insurance is written only on trade credit accounts, that is, the accounts receivable that are established from the sale of goods to another business. The history of credit insurance in one form or another has been traced back to 1837. It makes its contribution to the field of finance as a facilitating factor in the flow of credit between borrower and lender and is considered as such in this chapter.

Types of Credit Insurance

Although many types of credit insurance policies have been used in the past, at present credit insurance companies offer two broad types of policies. These are the *general coverage policy*, which insures the company against unusual losses on all of its insurable accounts, and the *extraordinary coverage policy*, which offers protection only against loss from a small proportion of the firm's accounts and often from a single account. The general coverage policy is used when the accounts of the firm are numerous with no single account being of such a size as to have a substantial effect in the event of the customer's failure to meet his obligation. The extraordinary policy, on the other hand, is used by firms having only a few very large accounts, any one of which could cause substantial difficulties to the firm extending the credit should a default in payments occur. In some instances, when a firm has many small accounts and only one or two large accounts, it may use the extraordinary coverage policy to good advantage to protect it against default of these large accounts.

The Risk

The purpose of insurance companies offering credit policies is not to substitute the benefit of risk diversification for thorough and systematic credit investigation. In determining the insurability of accounts, the insurance companies depend heavily upon the regular mercantile credit reporting agencies and on Dun and Bradstreet, Inc., in particular. In general, accounts are classified as either preferred or inferior, the preferred accounts alone qualifying for regular credit insurance. In some instances, both preferred and inferior accounts may be insured on a special combination-policy basis. Under a combination policy, the amount of insurance extended on inferior accounts is severely limited and the cost considerably higher than on preferred risks.

In addition to dividing individual accounts into preferred and inferior categories, the credit insurance companies classify types of businesses as to their desirability for credit insurance purposes based on past experience. These lines or types of businesses range from those dealing in agricultural implements, dairy products, and railroad supplies, which have the most desirable risk characteristics, to businesses dealing in diamonds and patent medicines, which are considered to have generally unsatisfactory risk characteristics and hence are not insurable.

Normal Loss and Coinsurance

Credit insurance attempts to insure only against losses that are in excess of the normal anticipated volume of losses. Since losses on bad debts are a part of all credit sale operations, it would be expecting too much to depend upon credit insurance to eliminate all losses. To do so, it would be necessary for the insurance company to charge a premium equivalent to the normal loss to offset the expected costs of the insurance, plus an additional premium to cover excess losses. Such an arrangement would be unacceptable, for the most part, to both the insured and the insurance company. In determining the normal loss of a firm above which losses are insurable, the insurance companies consider two factors: the line of trade of the applicant, and the past credit experience of the particular firm. An applicant with an excellent record of account collections is afforded a relatively low normal loss volume above which all accounts are insurable. The firm with a poor record, of course, can expect the establishment of a higher normal volume of losses and thus a smaller percentage of insurable losses.

In addition to the protection afforded the insurance company through the establishment of a normal loss ratio, protection is provided through the coinsurance clause. The *coinsurance clause* provides that, although all accounts above the normal loss volume are insurable, the insured must bear a portion of the losses that do occur. Such participation in losses on the part of the insured is generally limited to 10 percent. On the insurable accounts, therefore, the insurance company ordinarily will bear 90 percent of the loss. The coinsurance clause makes possible a lower premium for the insurance and also avoids the complete shift of risk to the insurance company. It is assumed that a complete shift of risk to the insurance company would in some instances encourage laxity in extending credit.

Terms and Charges for Credit Insurance

Policies are generally written for periods of one year and are renewable annually. The policyholder may choose a "back coverage" type that provides protection for a specified 12-month period against losses resulting from sales, shipments, and deliveries made during that period or during a preceding period covered by the "back sales endorsement." Alternatively, he may choose a "forward coverage" type of policy that provides protection on shipments made during a specified 12-month period on which losses may not be realized until later.[1]

The cost of credit insurance over a period of many years has consistently averaged about 1/10 of 1 percent of insured sales. The specific cost to a company is, of course, a function of the total sales volume insured, the policy amount, the terms of sale, and the special endorsements, if any. Certain well-managed firms with very large sales volumes may be charged as little as 1/100 of 1 percent; other firms may be charged 1/5 of 1 percent or more.[2]

---

[1] Clyde William Phelps, *Commercial Credit Insurance as a Management Tool* (Baltimore: Educational Division, Commercial Credit Company, Studies in Commercial Financing, No. 3, 1961), p. 38.

[2] *Ibid.*, pp. 99 and 100.

Volume of Credit Insurance

Although it is difficult to obtain estimates of the total amount of credit insurance in effect at a particular time, The American Credit Indemnity Company of New York, with headquarters in Baltimore, Maryland, reported a premium volume of $13 million in 1973. This company accounts for most of such credit insurance written in the United States and is the only company issuing credit insurance in Canada. The London Guarantee and Accident Company reported premium volume of $4.7 million.

Credit insurance is used by several thousand manufacturers, wholesalers, advertising agencies, and other service organizations that deal with business firms. More than 150 lines of industry are represented by users of credit insurance, including small firms with as little capital as $20,000 and firms with capital of many millions of dollars. Most of the insured companies have annual sales of less than $10 million.[3]

Reasons for Use of Credit Insurance

Among the reasons for the use of credit insurance by business firms may be included the desire to establish a definite loss expense with the accompanying advantage of not needing large reserves to care for unusual losses, the ability to undertake a larger volume of credit business, and the success of the insurance companies in collecting overdue accounts.

Attitudes toward the use of credit insurance vary in great measure, however; the apparent advantages of its use by one firm may be regarded as disadvantages by other firms. In general, the credit managers of business firms display little liking for such insurance, possibly because it shifts much of their own function, that of credit analysis, to the insurance company. The major objection to the use of credit insurance lies in its cost. Over a period of years, credit insurance adds to the cost of doing business by the amount by which the premiums paid exceed the amounts received for losses under the policies.

---

[3] *Ibid.*, pp. 12 and 13.

CREDIT REPORTING AGENCIES

A highly refined system of banking and finance is essential to the processes of a modern industrial economy; it is no less true that the field of finance could not possibly function effectively without readily available sources of credit information. The history of the development of our credit reporting institutions is, in fact, part and parcel of the development of our financial institutions themselves; and it is not surprising that there now exist many large and efficient organizations devoted to the objective of determining the credit position of virtually every person and business organization in the United States and to some extent throughout the world. Nor are the services of these organizations used only by lenders of money and firms selling goods and services on credit. Insurance companies often require credit reports on individuals when considering issuance of life or property insurance contracts and when issuing fidelity bonds protecting against dishonest acts of individuals in the performance of their jobs. Physicians, lawyers, and other professional groups seek such information to determine the ability of prospective clients to pay their bills. The Federal Housing Administration and other government agencies which lend or insure loans to individuals and businesses require that all applications be accompanied by appropriate credit reports. During World War II, the United States government used the services of many credit reporting firms to supplement the efforts of the Federal Bureau of Investigation in determining the suitability and loyalty of individuals for positions of trust.

The sources of credit information are numerous and varied in nature, ranging from informal personal contact with the person or firm requesting credit to the detailed and thorough investigations that are conducted by highly specialized credit reporting agencies. In the remainder of this chapter we shall discuss the operations of credit interchange bureaus, Dun & Bradstreet, Inc., the National Credit Office, and the Retail Credit Company, as representative of the various types of credit reporting agencies.

Credit interchange bureaus are generally established as nonprofit institutions by the businesses they are intended to serve. Such credit interchange bureaus exist to obtain information regarding both business firms and individuals. We shall in this chapter refer to credit information on business firms as *mercantile credit* and credit information on individuals as *retail credit*. Dun & Bradstreet, Inc., is discussed because it is the only mercantile credit reporting agency that provides information on businesses in all lines of activity; the National Credit Office is representative of the type of mercantile agency that provides information on businesses in selected lines of activity; the Retail Credit Company has been chosen as representative of the type of agency that provides information on individuals.

Credit Interchange Bureaus

Information obtained from other creditors of a prospective customer is often of substantial importance for both mercantile and consumer credit purposes. For local business operations it is common for the credit manager of one firm to phone his counterpart with another firm for advice and recommendations regarding applicants for credit. Various attempts have been made to provide a systematic and effective means of transmitting credit information between firms.

Local Mercantile Credit Interchange Bureaus. The *local mercantile credit interchange bureau* provides a central record in the community for credit information on business firms. The typical local credit interchange bureau is a nonprofit organization whose expenses are paid by member businesses. Bureau members submit lists of their customers to the bureau. The bureau determines the credit standing of these customers by contacting other bureau members who have extended credit to them. Thus, a member firm need only contact its credit bureau for information on prospective customers rather than write or telephone many individual firms.

National Mercantile Credit Interchange System. As the scope of business operations expanded with better communication and transportation systems, it became increasingly necessary to have access to the credit experience of firms in other geographical areas, as well as within the area served by the local credit interchange bureau. This problem was solved through the establishment of centralized bureaus to which the records of local bureaus could be forwarded for broader distribution throughout the country. The exchange of mercantile credit information from bureau to bureau is accomplished through the National Credit Interchange System. This system with a central bureau has 55 member credit interchange bureaus. These bureaus have a relationship with the central bureau much like that of the member firms with the local credit interchange bureaus.

Reports of credit exchange bureaus are factual rather than analytical, and it is up to each credit analyst to interpret the facts.

Foreign Credit Interchange Bureaus. United States businessmen selling to foreign customers encounter all of the problems involved in a domestic sale, plus several additional ones. Among these are increased geographical distance, language barriers, complicated shipping and government regulations, differences in legal systems, and political instability. To help exporters with these problems, the National Association of Credit Management established the Foreign Credit Interchange Bureau in 1919.

At the time the Foreign Credit Interchange Bureau was established, credit information on overseas customers was slow and scarce. Just as the local credit interchange bureaus increased their knowledge of business credit risks by pooling their credit and collection experience, so the members of the Foreign Credit Interchange Bureau have established a central file of information extending over forty years of experience. Access to this information on a reciprocal basis is available under special contract to more than 35,000 members who are interested or engaged in international trade activities. The Bureau is located in New York to serve the concentration of export and financial organizations that do business overseas.

The Foreign Credit Interchange Bureau provides eight basic services for its members: (1) worldwide collection service, (2) foreign credit reports, (3) free copies of all reports to which the member contributes experience, (4) weekly bulletins, (5) minutes of monthly Round Table Conferences on foreign credit, collection, and exchange problems, (6) exchange of general information, (7) industry group meetings, and (8) consultation on foreign trade problems.[4]

---

[4] "The Foreign Credit Interchange Bureau," *Credit and Financial Management* (November, 1961), p. 18.

Local Retail Credit Interchange Bureaus. Early retail merchants found that the rapid growth of cities and the increased mobility of consumers from community to community throughout the nation rendered it impracticable to rely on a direct exchange of credit information with other merchants. As for mercantile credit, the local merchants established retail credit bureaus for the purpose of consolidation and distribution of credit information regarding consumers in the community. These organizations are generally owned and operated by participating members on a nonprofit basis. The types of service rendered by the retail credit bureaus differ to a considerable extent, although basically they all provide credit information in one form or another. Some bureaus collect only derogatory information from their members, and this information in turn is distributed to other members. Other bureaus provide a complete reporting service on all customers. In addition, some bureaus publish rating books, cooperate with detective agencies, and operate collection services. A central organization known as the Associated Credit Bureaus of America serves as a medium through which approximately 1,500 retail credit bureaus in the United States are able to transmit credit information from bureau to bureau.

Dun & Bradstreet, Inc.

This organization, with more than a 134-year history of operations, serves commerce and industry as a general credit agency covering all fields of business activity. The information that is assembled and evaluated by Dun & Bradstreet, Inc., is brought into the company through many channels. The company employs full-time and part-time employees for the purposes of direct investigation, communicates directly with business establishments by mail to supplement their informational files, and obtains the financial statements of companies upon which reports are to be made. In addition, careful analysis is made of all information filed with public authorities and financial and trade papers in order to gather bits of information that would be pertinent to a credit analysis. The basic service supplied to the manufacturers, wholesalers, banks, and insurance companies who are subscribers to Dun & Bradstreet, Inc., is rendered in two ways—through written reports on individual businesses and through the Reference Book.

Figure 10–1

Dun & Bradstreet, Inc.

Please note whether name, business and street address correspond with your inquiry.

BUSINESS INFORMATION REPORT

BASE REPORT

SIC	D-U-N-S	© DUN & BRADSTREET, INC.	STARTED	RATING
34 69	04-426-3226 ARNOLD METAL PRODUCTS CO	CD 13 APR 21 19-- METAL STAMPINGS	1957	DD I

53 S MAIN ST
DAWSON MICH   49666
TEL 215 999-0000

SAMUEL B. ARNOLD)
GEORGE T. ARNOLD) PARTNERS

SUMMARY

PAYMENTS	DISC
SALES	$177,250
WORTH	$42,961
EMPLOYS	10
RECORD	CLEAR
CONDITION	STRONG
TREND	UP

PAYMENTS

HC	OWE	P DUE	TERMS	APR 19--	SOLD
3000	1500		1 10 30	Disc	Over 3 yrs
2500	1000		1 10 30	Disc	Over 3 yrs
2000	500		2 20 30	Disc	Old Account

FINANCE

On Apr 21 19-- S. B. Arnold, Partner, submitted the following statement dated Dec 31 19--

Cash	$ 4,870	Accts Pay	$ 6,121
Accts Rec	15,472	Notes Pay (Curr)	2,400
Mdse	14,619	Accruals	3,583
	-----------		-----------
Current	34,961	Current	12,104
Fixt & Equip ($4,183)	22,840	Notes Pay (Def)	5,000
CSV of Life Ins	2,264	NET WORTH	42,961
	-----------		-----------
Total Assets	60,065	Total	60,065

Annual sales $177,250; gross profit $47,821; net income $8,204. Fire insurance mdse $15,000; fixt $20,000. Annual rent $3,000.
Signed Apr 21 19-- ARNOLD METAL PRODUCTS CO by Samuel B. Arnold, Partner.

-----0-----

New equipment purchased last Sep was financed by bank loan. Monthly payments on loan are $200.

Arnold reported sales for the three months ended Mar 31 were up 10% compared to the same period last year. Increase was attributed by management to additional capacity provided by new equipment.

Profit is being made and retained resulting in an increase in net worth. Current debt is light in relation to worth. Inventory turnover is rapid.

BANKING

Balances average high four figures. Loans granted to low five figures, secured by equipment, now owing high four figures. Relations satisfactory.

HISTORY

Style registered Feb 1 1965 by partners. S. ARNOLD, born 1918, married. 1939 graduate of Lehigh University. 1939-50 employed by Industrial Machine Corporation, Detroit, and 1950-56 production manager with Aerial Motors Inc., Detroit. Started this business in 1957. G. ARNOLD, born 1940, single, son of Samuel. Graduated in 1963, Dawson Institute of Technology. Served U.S. Air Force 1963-1964. Admitted to partnership Feb 1965.

OPERATION

Manufactures perforated metal stampings for industrial concerns. Sells on Net 30 day terms. Has twelve accounts. Territory greater Detroit area. Employs ten including partners. LOCATION: Rents 5,000 square feet in one story cinder block building in normal condition. Located in central business section of main street. Premises neat.
4-21 (803 77) PRA

Sample of a Typical Dun & Bradstreet Report

Written Business Information Reports. Dun & Bradstreet, Inc., prepares three major types of reports of interest to the businessman. The first type is the *Business Information Report* which is the firm's regular or general report. The second type of report is the *Analytical Report,* which is written on the larger businesses or/those of an unusually complex nature. The *Key Account Report* is written in response to requests for information bearing on specific problems.

A Dun & Bradstreet, Inc., report is typically divided into five sections as follows: (1) Rating and Summary, (2) Trade Payments, (3) Financial Information, (4) Operation and Location, (5) History. A typical report is shown in Figure 10-1 on page 215. The reports are presented in a color-band system so that the subscriber may know at a glance the nature of the report he is receiving.

Reference Book. Dun & Bradstreet, Inc., publishes six times yearly a composite reference book of ratings on nearly 3,000,000 manufacturers, wholesalers, retailers, and other businesses on which credit reports have been written. Figure 10-2 illustrates a section of the Dun and Bradstreet, Inc., Reference Book. The Standard Industrial Classification Code placed at the left of each concern's name indicates the type of business in which the firm is engaged. The symbols at the right of the firm name indicate the capital and the credit rating. The key to the Dun & Bradstreet, Inc., ratings is shown in Figure 10-3.

In addition to the activities of the Credit Reporting Division, Dun & Bradstreet, Inc., provides additional services to the business world through the operation of collection facilities for overdue accounts, the publication of a business magazine, and intensive research and statistical study on business trends.

The National Credit Office

The National Credit Office (NCO) was established in 1900 to provide credit information on jobbers of textile fabrics. The concept which led to its formation and subsequent growth provides an interesting footnote to economic history. At the beginning of the century home sewing was very much a way of life in both urban and rural communities. Apparel made of woven fabrics

Figure 10–2

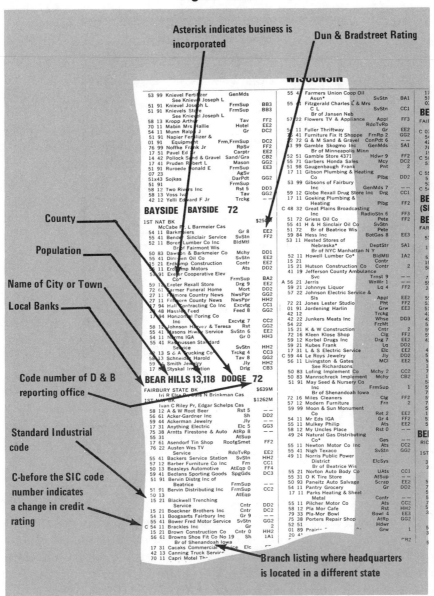

Page Section of Dun & Bradstreet Reference Book with Explanations

was fashioned from piece goods that reached the retail market through jobbers. Because the economy was predominately agricultural, it was customary for the textile mills to grant seasonal

Figure 10–3

Key to Ratings

ESTIMATED FINANCIAL STRENGTH			COMPOSITE CREDIT APPRAISAL			
			HIGH	GOOD	FAIR	LIMITED
5A	Over	$50,000,000	1	2	3	4
4A	$10,000,000 to	50,000,000	1	2	3	4
3A	1,000,000 to	10,000,000	1	2	3	4
2A	750,000 to	1,000,000	1	2	3	4
1A	500,000 to	750,000	1	2	3	4
BA	300,000 to	500,000	1	2	3	4
BB	200,000 to	300,000	1	2	3	4
CB	125,000 to	200,000	1	2	3	4
CC	75,000 to	125,000	1	2	3	4
DC	50,000 to	75,000	1	2	3	4
DD	35,000 to	50,000	1	2	3	4
EE	20,000 to	35,000	1	2	3	4
FF	10,000 to	20,000	1	2	3	4
GG	5,000 to	10,000	1	2	3	4
HH	Up to	5,000	1	2	3	4

**CLASSIFICATION FOR BOTH
ESTIMATED FINANCIAL STRENGTH AND CREDIT APPRAISAL**

FINANCIAL STRENGTH BRACKET	EXPLANATION
1 $125,000 and Over 2 20,000 to 125,000	When only the numeral (1 or 2) appears, it is an indication that the estimated financial strength, while not definitely classified, is presumed to be within the range of the ($) figures in the corresponding bracket and that a condition is believed to exist which warrants credit in keeping with that assumption.

ABSENCE OF RATING DESIGNATION FOLLOWING NAMES LISTED IN THE REFERENCE BOOK
The absence of a rating, expressed by two hyphens (--), is not to be construed as unfavorable but signifies circumstances difficult to classify within condensed rating symbols. It suggests the advisability of obtaining a report for additional information.

EMPLOYEE RANGE DESIGNATIONS IN REPORTS OR NAMES NOT LISTED IN THE REFERENCE BOOK

Certain businesses do not lend themselves to a Dun & Bradstreet rating and are not listed in the Reference Book. Information on these names, however, continues to be stored and updated in the D&B Business Data Bank. Reports are available on such businesses and instead of a rating they carry an Employee Range Designation (ER) which is indicative of size in terms of number of employees. No other significance should be attached.

	KEY TO EMPLOYEE RANGE DESIGNATIONS
ER 1	Over 1000 Employees
ER 2	500 - 999 Employees
ER 3	100 - 499 Employees
ER 4	50 - 99 Employees
ER 5	20 - 49 Employees
ER 6	10 - 19 Employees
ER 7	5 - 9 Employees
ER 8	1 - 4 Employees
ER N	Not Available

Key to Dun & Bradstreet Ratings

dating terms to the jobbers. Not until crops were harvested and cattle sent to market were funds available for the payment of bills.

For the mills, seasonal terms meant long exposure and relatively high credit lines. Jobbers were vulnerable to the effects of erratic crops and agricultural prices. Failures were frequent. This volatile credit relationship created the need for a service that would evaluate each customer in the light of overall industry conditions and facilitate the more frequent exchange of ledger experiences. NCO was formed to fill that need.

As other major industries for which this type of credit service is appropriate emerged, NCO expanded its coverage to include them. Today it provides credit reports on textile weaving, spinning and knitting mills; converters; manufacturers of apparel, industrial and household fabric goods; manufacturers of leather, electronic, wheel goods and aerospace products; manufacturers of mobile homes and recreational vehicles, household appliances, machinery, and transportation equipment. Its service also covers wholesalers of electronic components, soft goods, toys; department stores; mass merchandisers; mobile home and hi-fi dealers.

NCO reports include the suggestion of a dollar line of credit, bank and trade references by name as well as background and financial information. Financial statements as they are received are reproduced by a photographic-offset process so that they can be sent promptly to subscribers who have registered their interest. National Credit Office, a member of the Dun & Bradstreet Group, has branch offices in Boston; Philadelphia; Atlanta; Charlotte; Cleveland; Chicago; Detroit; and Los Angeles.

The Retail Credit Company

This organization, which is more than 50 years old, gathers information not only within this country but throughout the world. Information provided by this organization is almost exclusively restricted to individuals rather than business firms. Although the services of the Retail Credit Company are used primarily by insurance companies, during World War II many companies and government agencies depended upon them to screen applicants for employment. The services of this company are also used by mortgage lenders and trade creditors in general. This organization has more than 1700 offices and direct reporting stations. It has been reported that this company has on file the credit records of more than 48 million individuals. These files are maintained through personal investigation, clippings from newspapers, and information from numerous governmental offices. As reports are requested on individuals who are not currently in their files, the Retail Credit Company makes special investigations.

QUESTIONS.

1. Describe the operations of a commercial paper house.
2. In what manner may the commercial paper houses be considered as facilitating institutions in the field of business finance?

3. What is the commercial paper house's source of profits?
4. Describe a typical commercial paper house transaction.
5. Compare the cost of borrowing through the facilities of a commercial paper house with direct bank borrowing.
6. How important are the operations of commercial paper houses as a part of the entire field of short-term business financing?
7. What are the advantages to a business of financing through a commercial paper house?
8. What is the special role of the credit insurance company in the field of short-term business finance?
9. Describe the principal types of credit insurance policies offered by the credit insurance companies.
10. To what extent does a credit insurance policy reduce the risk of loss on accounts receivable?
11. Of what significance are the terms "normal loss" and "coinsurance" in the credit insurance policy?
12. Explain the special circumstances that would induce a business to utilize the services of a credit insurance company.
13. In what way do credit reporting agencies serve the field of finance as facilitating media?
14. Describe the various types of credit reporting institutions that are available to a business in seeking credit information on its customers.
15. How does Dun & Bradstreet, Inc., accumulate information on which to base its credit reports?
16. Distinguish between mercantile and retail credit information.

SUGGESTED READINGS

CHURELLA, J. A. *An Evaluation of Credit Insurance and Its Effect on Business Management.* Baltimore: American Credit Indemnity Co., 1958.

Credit Management Handbook, 2d ed. Edited by the Credit Research Foundation. Homewood, Illinois: Richard D. Irwin, Inc., 1965. Chapters 27 and 28.

HUNT, PEARSON, CHARLES M. WILLIAMS, and GORDON DONALDSON. *Basic Business Finance,* 4th ed. Homewood, Illinois: Richard D. Irwin, Inc., 1971. Chapters 3 and 14.

PHELPS, CLYDE WILLIAM. *Commercial Credit Insurance as a Management Tool.* Studies in Commercial Financing, No. 3. Baltimore: Educational Division, Commercial Credit Company, 1961.

"The Foreign Credit Interchange Bureau." *Credit and Financial Management* (November, 1961).

VAN HORNE, JAMES C. *Fundamentals of Financial Management,* 2d ed. Englewood Cliffs, New Jersey: Prentice-Hall, Inc., 1974. Chapter 7.

WESTON, J. FRED, and EUGENE F. BRIGHAM. *Managerial Finance,* 4th ed. New York: Holt, Rinehart and Winston, Inc., 1972. Chapter 21.

11 | Short-Term Business Financing Policies

The financial management of a business generally has a significant amount of discretion about the relative amounts of long-term and short-term financing to use to meet its needs. Choices must also be made on the sources of financing and on the type of financing to be used. Such decisions on the time period of financing and on the type of financing are influenced to some degree by conditions in the money and capital markets; and the financing decisions which are made, in turn, have an effect on these markets. As a background for an analysis of the factors which affect financing decisions, consideration will be given to the nature of short-term financing. Then the major external and internal factors which affect short-term financing will be discussed and policy decisions on the amount of short-term financing will be considered. This will be followed by a discussion of policy questions on the type of short-term financing and on the source of such financing.

THE NATURE OF SHORT-TERM FINANCING

Current financing is used primarily to finance part of the current assets of a business. Current funds may be used to finance a building during the construction period or for other temporary financing of permanent capital. But for all practical purposes, fixed capital must be financed on a long-run basis, and current financing is used for only a part of the current assets. That part of total current assets provided through long-term financing is referred to as the *net working capital*. This amount is determined by subtracting the total of current liabilities shown on the balance sheet from the total of current assets. If short-term financing were relied upon entirely by a business for its current asset requirements, the total current assets of the firm would be equal to the total current liabilities. The balance sheet of a successful non-financial business enterprise, however, will reveal an excess of current assets over current liabilities. This excess reflects the extent to which long-term financing has contributed to the support of the current asset requirements of the business firm.

The basic source of net working capital is, in the final analysis, the equity of the owners since intermediate and long-term creditors will not lend a firm all of the money it has invested in fixed assets. The immediate source of working capital may be long-term borrowing, but this can be true only if a concern has maintained additional borrowing capacity. These relationships, ignoring for the time being any intermediate-term borrowing, may be shown in a somewhat oversimplified form as follows:

Current Assets = Current Borrowing
Net Working Capital
(portion of owners' equity)

Fixed Assets = Long-Term Borrowing
Owners' Equity
(amount above net working capital)

The net working capital is a measure of the financial soundness of a firm, since it provides additional resources from which the short-term liabilities may be paid. In general, the greater the net working capital of a firm, the less burdensome are the problems of meeting short-term obligations. So important is the existence of an adequate net working capital to a firm that it has become one of the prime tests of strength, and creditors place great emphasis on it in determining whether or not to extend credit.

The Current Ratio

The net working capital or short-term financial position of a firm is expressed not only in terms of a dollar quantity, that is, the difference between total current assets and total current liabilities, but also in relative terms. This relationship is determined by dividing total current assets by total current liabilities, the quotient being the *current ratio* of the firm. Although the net working capital position and the current ratio are simply alternative ways of expressing the short-term financial position of the firm, each has its particular usefulness. The relationship is explained and illustrated below.

The current ratio concept is particularly useful in comparing the financial positions of firms of varying sizes. For example, a firm may have total current assets of $200,000 and total current liabilities of $100,000, in which case the current ratio is 2 to 1 and the net working capital is $100,000. Another firm, engaged in similar business activities, may have total current assets of $400,000 and total current liabilities of $200,000, the current ratio being 2 to 1 and the net working capital $200,000. In this example, the net working capital of the latter firm is twice that of the former, yet it is clear that it is a matter of proportion, that the latter firm may simply be a larger enterprise doing a larger volume of business. The current ratio of each firm, however, is 2 to 1, revealing the similarity of short-term financial positions. It is the current ratio, therefore, that facilitates comparisons with other firms, while it is the net working capital position that is of primary interest to the management of the firm and in particular to those persons in the firm who are charged with the responsibility for budgeting and controlling the flow of funds into the business and the payment of short-term obligations.

Necessity of Adequate Net Working Capital

The importance of providing for part of the current asset requirements of a business through long-term financing may be illustrated by a theoretical and highly improbable situation in which long-term financing has not been provided for this purpose.

Figure 11–1

ABC MERCHANDISING COMPANY

BALANCE SHEET

December 31, 1974

ASSETS

Current Assets:

Cash	$ 25,000.00	
Notes Receivable	25,000.00	
Accounts Receivable	75,000.00	
Merchandise Inventory	120,000.00	
Prepaid Expenses	5,000.00	
Total Current Assets		$250,000.00

Fixed Assets:

Equipment	$ 50,000.00	
Land and Buildings	75,000.00	
Total Fixed Assets		125,000.00
Total Assets		$375,000.00

LIABILITIES AND OWNERS' INTERESTS

Current Liabilities:

Notes Payable (to bank)	$ 75,000.00	
Accounts Payable	150,000.00	
Accrued Liabilities	25,000.00	
Total Current Liabilities		$250,000.00

Fixed Liabilities:

Mortgage Payable (due 1994)		60,000.00
Total Liabilities		$310,000.00
Owners' Interests		65,000.00
Total Liabilities and Owners' Interests		$375,000.00

The balance sheet of the firm might appear as in Figure 11-1. In this balance sheet, the total of current liabilities equals the total of current assets; there is no net working capital.

The current liabilities of such a firm would fall due periodically and would have to be paid out of cash. Since the cash is $25,000, only that much indebtedness could be retired on the date of the balance sheet. It is true, of course, that the accounts receivable and the inventory would in time be converted into cash. It is even possible to work out a schedule of conversion into cash of receivables and inventory at such a rate that obligations falling due could theoretically be met. The business would be in an extremely precarious position, however; for, in the event of failure of the conversion of receivables and inventory into cash on schedule, the firm would be unable to meet promptly its current obligations. It is improbable that any firm with such a relatively large volume of short-term obligations could always schedule its inflow of funds in such a way as to match its outflow.

The answer to this problem is to provide part of the current asset requirements through long-term financing. Under these circumstances, the total of the current liabilities will be less than the total of the current assets. With current assets amounting to substantially more than current liabilities, the chance of the business having too little cash to meet its obligations is reduced materially.

Advantages of Adequate Net Working Capital

An adequate net working capital makes it possible for the firm to meet its debts promptly and to take discounts that may be available if early payment is made for purchases of raw materials and other goods. Also, the firm that is in a position to make cash payments may pay a lower price for its purchases, or it may have access to a better quality of merchandise at the same price because of the better bargaining position it enjoys. Suppliers of materials as well as banks regard more highly the firm with a strong net working capital position, insuring a continuing flow of funds and supplies during peak periods of seasonal activity and making it possible for the firm to take advantage of overall expansion as long-term growth opportunities become available. Finally, insofar as an adequate net working capital position insures a continuous supply of raw materials and production, steady work is available for employees. The firm that offers steady employment will usually benefit from greater efficiency on the part of its employees.

FACTORS AFFECTING THE AMOUNT OF SHORT-TERM FINANCING

The determination of the proper proportion between current financing and net working capital depends upon an evaluation of many factors which affect the business. The nature of the demand for funds is basic and it will be considered first in this section. Then consideration will be given to a series of other factors such as risks, cost, flexibility, the ease of future financing, and other qualitative factors.

Nature of the Demand for Funds

The nature of the demand for funds depends in part on the industry in which business operates and on the characteristics of the business itself. It also depends on such factors as the seasonal variation in sales and output and on the trend of growth of the company. The need for funds also depends upon fluctuations in sales over the business cycle.

Industry and Company Factors. The nature of a company and the industry of which it is a part have a significant effect on financing decisions. An industry which has a need for large amounts of fixed capital can do more long-term financing than one which has a relatively small investment in fixed assets. Electric light and power companies, for example, have heavy investments in fixed assets to provide light, heat, and power and relatively little investment in current assets. The same is true of telephone companies, railroads, and gas companies. Manufacturing companies are likely to have heavy investments in fixed assets for manufacturing purposes, but will also have significant investments in inventories and receivables. Large retail stores generally lease their quarters and so have a relatively small investment in plant and equipment but a large investment in inventories and receivables. The composition of the asset structure of an industry and of a firm in the industry is a significant factor in determining the relative proportions of long-term and short-term financing done by a firm.

The competitive structure of an industry is also of significance. In an industry in which prices and profits fluctuate widely, as is the case in some of the basic metals industries, it is poor policy to incur a large proportion of debt. The same is true of oligopolistic industries in which price wars can disrupt normal cost and price relationships. In industries in which demand is relatively stable and prices are regulated, such as utilities, a larger proportion of debt financing is generally safe.

The size and age of a company and its stage in its financial life cycle may also be significant in financing decisions. A small, new company may find that its only source of funds is investment by the owners and some of his friends. Some long-term funds may be raised by mortgaging real estate and buying equipment on installment, and some current borrowing may be possible to meet seasonal needs. As a business grows it has more access to short-term capital from finance companies and banks. Further along in its growth in size and record of profitability a business may be able to arrange longer-term financing with banks or with other financial agencies such as insurance companies. At this stage in its financial development it may also expand its group of owners by having stock held by a wider group of people than the owner and his friends.

The next stage in financial development is one in which stock is widely enough held and the financial record of a company is such that brokerage houses will sell the stock over the counter. At this stage they may also be willing to sell stock of the company or bonds or notes in a small-scale public offering. The last stage in the financial life cycle is one in which stock is widely enough held that it is listed on a regional and finally also on a national stock exchange. New issues of stock and bonds can then be sold to the general public through a large group of investment banking houses. At these stages in its financial life cycle a company will be able to obtain short-term credit on reasonable terms.

The growth prospects of a company also have an effect on financing decisions. If a company is growing faster than the rate at which it can finance its funds from internal sources, it must give careful consideration to a plan for long-term financing. Even if it can finance its needs in the current situation from short-term sources, it may not be wise to do so. Sound financial planning calls for raising long-term funds under the most favorable conditions, and this may call for such financing at intervals of several years.

Seasonal Variation. Seasonal variations in sales in a business affect the demand for current assets. Inventories must be built up to meet seasonal needs, and receivables will go up as sales increase.

The peak of receivables will come after the peak in sales, depending on the credit terms and payment practices of customers. Accounts payable will, of course, go up as inventories are purchased, again with a lag depending on terms and payment policies. The difference between the increase in current assets and accounts payable must be financed by current borrowing or additional working capital.

The added need for funds will again disappear as inventories are reduced by sales as the season progresses and accounts receivable are collected. If the added need for funds is financed by a short-term loan, such a loan is said to be self-liquidating since funds are made available to repay it as inventories and receivables are reduced.

Some advocate current borrowing be used only to meet such seasonal needs. In fact, this has been referred to as the "ideal" working capital policy. The requirement of some bankers, which was much more common before 1930, that bank loans should be cleared up at least once a year is based on this type of loan.

It does not follow that because a loan would be self-liquidating in the normal course of business, it will always be made. A concern in a highly seasonal business, such as the manufacture of swimming suits, for example, may have a peak need for current assets which is ten times as high as the minimum need. A loan for this additional sum could be repaid if all went according to plan. But if the season was unusually cool in the sales territory of the concern or its sales were low because of poor styling, the inventory might not all be moved, or only at a loss. A loan which would under normal conditions be self-liquidating could thus result in a loss.

Trend. The trend of sales of a business also affects the current position. Current assets and accounts payable will go up and so will the gap between them. This need for funds, however, is a permanent one unless the trend of sales is reversed. If it is met by current borrowing, the loan could not be repaid, except by added investment by the owners, but would have to be renewed indefinitely. The sum of money involved would go up year by year as the trend continued upward. Even if no season existed and, therefore, there was no seasonal need for funds, short-term borrowing could not be used indefinitely to supply the added funds. In time, the current ratio would drop to such a level that no financing institution would provide additional funds. The only alternative then is working capital.

Cyclical Variation. The need for current funds is also increased when there is an upswing in the business cycle or the cycle in an industry. Since the cycle is not regular in timing or amplitude, it is hard to predict exactly how long the added funds will be needed or what the extent of the need will be. It will, of course, be estimated for a year ahead in the budget and checked quarterly. When the volume of business decreases, the need for funds will again decrease. If a concern is growing, the need will not return to its former level because of the trend. It is also possible that for a time during the downturn the need will not decrease, but may even increase temporarily because the circular flow of cash is slowed down as receivables are collected more slowly and inventories move more slowly and drop in value.

If cyclical needs for funds are met by current borrowing, the loan will, of course, not be self-liquidating in a year. It may be over a complete cycle except for the increased needs due to the trend. There are hazards in financing such needs on a short-term basis. The lending institution may demand payment of all or part of the loan as business turns down. Funds may be needed more severely than ever at this stage of the cycle, and the need may last until receivables can be collected and inventory can be reduced.

This situation was responsible in part for the development of the term loan.[1] During the decline in business from 1929 to 1933, many businesses were asked to repay bank loans at the time they needed them badly. It was recognized when the loan was made that it could not be repaid at maturity, but would have to be renewed. However, as depositors wanted their money and depression psychology affected the banks, they called loans more rapidly than the decline in their business customers' need for funds. If term loans are used to meet cyclical needs, the funds are available for a definite period of time. The loan must be repaid regularly

---

[1] Term loans of commercial banks are described in Chapter 13.

out of earnings and other available cash. When the need for funds declines cyclically, the loan can be repaid ahead of time.

Usually a concern does not negotiate a term loan until business has been increasing for some time and a greater demand for funds exists than can be met by current borrowing. If a term loan is to meet cyclical needs, it must be negotiated before business decreases and the loan becomes difficult or impossible to get. To the extent that a term loan is repaid quarterly or annually from earnings, working capital is increased. If the term loan is to be used primarily for cyclical needs, the repayments from earnings should be large enough to meet the needs due to the trend, and the remainder of the loan should be repaid out of the liquidation of current assets as the cycle turns down.

The Effect of Risks on Financing Decisions

The risks which affect all business operations also affect the financing of the business. Some risks arise out of the operation of the business itself; others, from outside economic forces. The internal risks or business risks arise from several factors. There is a risk of loss of property due to fire, flood, insurrection, and the like. Such risks can and must be covered by insurance before any financing can be done. There is a risk in small and medium-size firms of the loss due to the death of a key figure in the business. Such a risk can be covered by insurance on the lives of key officials. In some cases, however, no amount of money will offset the loss sustained if a business does not progress as it did before a key official died. Profits may be too low to attract new capital, or losses may result because of inept management in any area of a business. This is one of the reasons why a small or medium-size business generally cannot do any significant amount of long-term borrowing except through mortgages on general-use real estate and must rely on short-term borrowing and owners' equity to meet its needs. Suppliers of short-term loans will generally be protected if a reasonable amount of insurance exists since this will allow the business to continue operations and will give the lending institution time to assess the situation. If they feel the risk is too great, they can reduce the loan or call for payment before the business gets into financial difficulties.

Some risks which are primarily of a financial nature also have some effect on short-term financing policies, but primarily affect long-term financing. One of these financial risks is the purchasing-power risk which results from changes in the price level. As the price level increases a business has problems since it takes a larger number of dollars to do the same volume of business. This affects short-term financing almost immediately since part of the purchasing power in cash balances and receivables is lost when the price level increases. This loss is offset to the extent that current assets were financed by current or long-term borrowing since the loan agreement calls for repayment in dollars which now have less purchasing power. But the total dollar amount of current assets to be financed will be greater than before the price rise, and this also means a larger dollar amount of net working capital.

In a period of rising prices a firm benefits from a relatively large amount of debt. But there are also factors which will make it more difficult to borrow. There is always the risk that prices will drop and that such a drop will lead to a reduction in profits or even to losses since the value of goods in inventory is reduced and it may not be possible to cut costs as much as selling prices have declined. The increased price level also requires a larger net working capital and total dollar investment in the business in the form of owners' equity. If this cannot be supplied out of profits or on a reasonable basis from the present owners or others, the financial position of a firm becomes worse and the cost of borrowing increases.

Another financial risk which has some effect on short-term financing is the interest-rate risk. If interest rates rise significantly in a short period of time, the added cost may affect profit margins unless prices can be raised to offset the added cost. Such increases were especially significant in the periods of tight money in 1966, 1969, and 1973-74. Such increases in costs could have been and were avoided by firms that did intermediate- and long-term financing in periods of more moderate interest rates. This risk is offset in part by the possibility of a drop in interest rates. It cannot be ignored, however, on the basis that it will cancel out since interest rates have at various times moved in one direction for years at a time.

Cost of Financing

Another factor to consider is the cost of short-term financing when compared with alternative sources of financing. Short-term interest rates on business loans have generally been lower than long-térm interest rates since the depression of the 1930's. This has not always been true, especially in periods of tight money such as 1966, 1969, and 1973-74. However, when interest rates on short-term borrowing are lower than on long-term borrowing, there is an incentive to use short-term financing as fully as possible.

It is usually less costly to engage in short-term financing than to sell additional equity (ownership) interests in the business. Persons who purchase additional ownership interests in the business, like the existing owners, will share in the profits of the business. During periods of normal business activity, these profits will generally represent a return on investment far greater than the costs of short-term financing. Hence, the existing owners of the business can increase their own earnings through short-term financing to the extent that the earnings on assets acquired through short-term financing exceed the costs of such financing. Even if the owners of a business are in a position to provide the business with needed funds from their personal accounts, that plan may represent a costly investment, since these funds might be employed far more profitably in other uses where equity capital is in great demand. Both forms of long-term financing, debt and equity, may therefore be more costly than are the usual forms of short-term financing.

Many business enterprises are subject to seasonal influences that result in a concentration of sales activity during certain months of the year. The advantages of short-term financing under these circumstances are readily apparent when it is recognized that such financing may extend over only a few months, at the end of which time the obligations may be repaid by a business out of the proceeds of sales. The very nature of most business operations is such that the disbursements of the firm do not coincide with the receipts so far as timing is concerned. The cost of short-term financing is largely confined to the periods during the year when expenses are being incurred or inventories accumulated without a corresponding flow of receipts from sales. If long-term financing were undertaken for such purposes, these funds would be idle during several months of the year and of little use until the next period of increasing seasonal activity. The cost of long-term financing would continue throughout the year, while in short-term financing the costs exist only during the periods when such financing is actually needed and used. Unused funds can be invested on a short-term basis, but the return is usually less than the cost of long-term funds.

Cost can also be a limiting factor in current borrowing. As the percentage of current assets financed by current borrowing goes up, interest charges become higher. If the lending institution feels an increased unsecured loan is not safe, they may lend larger sums on a secured basis, such as an accounts receivable loan or an inventory loan. Not only is the interest charge on such loans higher than on unsecured loans, but the mechanics of the financing arrangement involves added clerical costs, warehouse fees, and the like, and these increase the cost of the financing.

Other Factors

Short-term borrowing has several other advantages over other forms of financing. Short-term borrowing has more flexibility than long-term financing. Only those sums needed currently can be borrowed, whereas long-term financing is usually done to take care of needs for some time in the future due to the cost and time involved in getting the funds. If during periods of general business expansion an enterprise obtains its additional current asset requirements entirely through long-term financing, it might be burdened with excess funds during a subsequent period of general business contraction. In using short-term financing along with long-term financing, therefore, a flexibility of operations is possible that does not exist with long-term financing alone. As the need for assets decreases, the firm may simply retire its short-term obligations. Although the long-term obligations of the business may in some cases be retired when the funds provided through such financing are no longer required, such an action may be awkward; and often a penalty must be paid for prepayment of the obligation.

Short-term financing also has advantages that result from establishing continuing relationships with a bank or other financial institution. The firm that depends almost entirely upon long-term financing for its needs will not enjoy the close relationship with its bank that it otherwise would. A record of frequent borrowing from and prompt repayment to its bank by an enterprise is an extremely important factor in sound financial management. Under these circumstances, a bank will make every effort to accommodate its business customers with loans at all times. The enterprise that has not established such a working relationship with its bank will scarcely be in a position to seek special loans during its periods of emergency needs. Also, the credit experience of a business in connection with its short-term financing may be the only basis on which potential long-term lenders to a business can judge the enterprise. Hence, the business that intends to seek long-term loans may wish to establish a good credit reputation based on its short-term financing. Qualitative considerations relating to the financing arrangements must also be considered. One is the ease of obtaining the funds and also the time required to do so. It may, for example, be convenient and fast to use short-term bank credit regularly. Even though funds from other sources may be cheaper, in the long run there may be a tendency to use what is immediately available without time-consuming negotiation.

Another qualitative consideration is the degree of publicity about financial affairs required to get public financing. A medium-size firm, especially if it is largely owned by a family group, may not care to divulge the financial information which would be required to sell bonds or stocks publicly and may therefore prefer to do short-term financing.

Offsetting these advantages are such factors as frequent renewals and perhaps a greater risk than with more permanent financing. Even though short-term credit is usually easy to obtain, some time and effort must be spent on it at frequent intervals since loans are of short duration. And when business decreases there may be quite a bit of negotiation to get the needed credit.

Frequent maturities also introduce an added element of risk. The bank or finance company can call the loan whenever it is due. Even if a revolving credit agreement is used, it runs for a limited period of time only. A concern may be in a temporary slump due to the business cycle or some internal problem and may be able to work out the problem in time. However, if it is relying heavily on short-term financing, its loans may be reduced or not renewed, which may make it all but impossible to get back on its feet, or may even lead to liquidation. If the loan is from a bank, the banker may be under pressure from bank examiners to cut down on doubtful loans or may be under pressure to reduce loans because deposits have decreased. Therefore, even if the banker would like to go along with a firm and renew the loan, he may not be able to do so. On the other hand, if the concern had raised the money on a long-term basis, it may have worked out of its difficulties, or at least it may have had a chance to do so under more favorable circumstances.

POLICIES ON THE EXTENT OF SHORT-TERM FINANCING

After weighing all of the factors involved, a concern is in a position to develop a policy on the extent of short-term financing. This may be done formally, or an informal policy arrangement may develop out of past experience and practice. One possibility is to have a policy of borrowing on a short-term basis to meet seasonal needs, especially when bank credit on an unsecured basis is available in sufficient quantities to meet peak needs. Or in cases in which seasonal needs do not exhaust the loan potential, a firm may still plan to borrow to the limit so as to finance the maximum of permanent needs on a short-term unsecured basis. A concern with no significant seasonal needs may also have a policy of doing as much current financing as possible on an unsecured basis. Growing concerns may follow the same type of policy, but take the maximum amounts of secured short-term credit. This may be costly credit, but it may be the only way in which enough funds can be raised to keep up with profitable expansion opportunities.

At the other extreme a concern may adopt the policy of doing long-term financing to take care of all regular needs, including seasonal variations. Idle funds are then invested in marketable securities. Short-term credit, under these circumstances, is only used for convenience in the form of accounts payable and to meet unusual situations due to irregular factors. Such a policy usually means that excess cash exists during a good part of the year. The cost of such excess funds may be materially higher than the return which can be earned by investing them in short-term marketable securities. There is less risk of insolvency than when short-term borrowing is used, but this added safety may have been achieved by a reduction in profitability.

A policy between these extremes is frequently followed. A concern may do short-term borrowing so long as it is easy to obtain and there is little risk if the loans are reduced or are not renewed since other sources of funds are available. The policy on short-term financing may also be tied in with the policy on long-term financing. A business may borrow money on a short-term basis to finance an expansion program and then retire the short-term loans with long-term financing at the end of the program or several times during the program. This has been used as a method of financing by many electric light and power companies. Or a concern may do long-term financing ahead of current needs and use the excess funds to finance short-term needs. When all of the funds are expended, short-term borrowing is again resorted to.

THE SOURCE OF FUNDS AND TYPE OF BORROWING

Financial management must also decide on the source of funds, that is, trade creditors, banks, finance companies, factors, or the commercial paper market. If financing is not available from any of these sources, it may be possible for a small business to get a loan from the Small Business Administration. A decision must also be made as to the type of loan to seek. Some types of loans can be obtained readily from several sources, others from only one or two, in which case both decisions are made at the same time.

Trade Credit

There is little question about using trade credit when no discount is involved for payment at a specified date. When discounts are involved, trade credit is generally high-cost credit. If it is possible to borrow funds at a lower cost, it is desirable to do so and take the discounts offered. Unless a concern is in very weak financial condition, it is usually possible to get a finance company loan on a secured basis which will be lower in cost than the discounts which are not taken.

Bank and Finance Company Credit

The basic source of short-term financing is still the commercial bank for most fields of business. If the credit rating of a concern is high enough to get the credit it needs from a commercial bank on an unsecured basis for a reasonable rate of interest, it is generally the most desirable arrangement. If a line of credit can be established at a bank to take care of foreseeable needs, the financing can be carried out with a minimum of "red tape" and usually at the lowest possible cost. If a business is subject to rapid changes in outlook, as is the case, for example, in the nonferrous metals fields in which prices change rapidly, it is often worthwhile to pay the extra costs involved in a revolving credit agreement to be sure of funds for the year.

A loan from a finance company may at times be cheaper than bank borrowing if the need for funds is large for only a few days during the month. Finance companies usually charge higher rates of interest than banks but will in many cases charge only for the days the funds are in use, while banks usually lend on a monthly basis. A business may have a peak need for cash which lasts only a few days. It may send out checks to pay accounts payable on a discount basis on the 9th of the month. Its checks may come in between the 11th and 15th. The biggest cash need may be for only three or four days and a sizeable need for only a week. Interest on a day-to-day loan, even at significantly higher rates may be lower than on a monthly loan.

There may also be a saving in the case of a loan to carry seasonal inventory or receivables; for example, a 90-day loan. Peak needs may build up gradually during the month and so call for less borrowing on a day-by-day basis than on a monthly basis. Also, when the peak is past, needs may drop rapidly after the 10th of the month as receipts come in. Therefore, whenever the need for funds varies widely during the month, bank and finance company charges should be checked for lowest costs.

Factors other than cost must also be considered. Both banks and finance companies offer financial counsel. The value of this depends upon the individuals involved. In a small town, for example, the local banker may not have as wide a range of experience as a representative from a national or regional finance company, but the banker may be more familiar with the local situation. On the other hand, in any emergency a national or regional concern may set general policies not exactly applicable to the local situation, whereas the banker can adapt to it. However, the banker is working with depositors' money and subject to bank examiners' scrutiny and so may not go as far in working out difficult situations as a finance company would. This may be especially true if the bank is reasonably sure of recovering its investment if it decides to call for payment and thus force liquidation.

A finance company operating on a regional or national basis also offers some advantages over banks, which in many states can have no branches and are severely restricted in others. It is easier for a concern operating over a wide territory to finance with one agency than with several. There are also, of course, disadvantages since in a downturn all banks may not reduce credit at one time, thus providing flexibility. These qualitative factors must be weighed in each case before deciding upon bank or finance-company borrowing.

Raising Funds by Selling Unsecured Commercial Paper

A select group of concerns may at times be able to do unsecured borrowing by selling their own notes. There are several factors which would lead to a decision to use such financing. The major one is cost, since the rate on such paper is usually lower than the lowest bank rate on prime loans. A concern may also use this method because its bank cannot legally lend it the funds it needs. Rather than deal with several banks the officers feel they might just as well resort to the open market, deal with one broker, and save money. A concern may also do open-market borrowing to establish its financial reputation. Since only the best concerns can do such financing, it helps the reputation of these firms that can do so. If they want to do public financing later, their names may be better known to financial analysts.

The biggest potential disadvantage which must be weighed in deciding to use this form of financing is the loss of close relationships with a bank or finance company. In a downturn in business, the concern may find that it can no longer sell its own notes and may find it difficult to arrange financing. The strain on financial institutions increases in such periods and they are likely to feel little obligation to a concern which bypassed them in better days.

Secured Loans

A business will usually prefer an unsecured short-term loan when sufficient credit to meet its needs is available on this basis. This is due to the simplicity of the arrangement and the lower cost. Not only is interest usually lower on unsecured loans, but various additional clerical and other costs are involved in secured loans. The major exception is a finance company loan, which may be cheaper than a bank loan because funds are needed for only a part of the month. Even though some finance companies have at times made such loans on an unsecured basis, the typical situation is to have them secured by an assignment of accounts receivable.

Loans Secured by Receivables. When a concern desires to borrow more money on a short-term basis than it can get through unsecured loans, it has two major current assets as collateral—receivables and inventory. A small concern may at times pledge marketable securities, but these are usually personal securities of the owners or securities they do not wish to sell because a capital gains tax would have to be paid. Usually when marketable securities are held by a concern, they are sold to provide current funds before borrowing is resorted to.

In most cases when a secured loan is needed, it is best to look to receivables financing on a non-notification basis first. This involves less interference with the normal activities of a business, in most cases, than a loan on inventories. Receivables financing works best when a concern has quite a number of good accounts of reasonable size. When only a few large accounts exist, the risk of loss is too great if one defaults or does not find the merchandise it receives acceptable. On the other hand, if hundreds of small accounts of $100 or less exist, the paper work involved is costly.

There are several types of situations in which loans on receivables are most frequently used. A concern may be in financial difficulties owing to a decline in business in general or some poor managerial decisions. However, the picture has changed and future prospects look much better. Even though it could formerly get all the credit it needed on an unsecured basis, it can no longer do so owing to the loss of working capital. A bank may lend the business the funds it needs on its receivables, especially if the business will agree to again increase working capital by retained earnings. If the losses of a concern have been large, the banker may not feel he can lend all the funds needed, even on a secured basis. Finance companies often go much further in this type of loan than banks, so they should be investigated before deciding that the desired amount of short-term credit cannot be obtained.

A concern may also use receivables as collateral because it has gotten into serious financial straits during a period in which an unsecured loan was outstanding. Prospects may not look bright at present, but not hopeless either. A banker may suggest a receivables loan to put himself in a preferred position if liquidation is necessary. In such situations of distress some finance companies may be more willing than banks to lend funds, and this should also be explored.

Another situation in which receivables financing is often desirable is in cases of rapid expansion. A business may have opportunities for profitable expansion which arise faster than it can attract outside equity capital or plough back earnings. Loans on receivables can be used to get a larger percentage of current borrowing than would normally be considered safe.

If the expansion prospects are temporary, that is, for a year or two, or more equity capital is in the offing, a banker may go along with such financing; but he is reluctant to be tied to it for an indefinite period. Many finance companies will do such financing regularly for a concern whose need for funds is always greater than its equity capital.

Inventory Loans. Loans secured by inventories may be made in the same types of situations in which receivables are used as collateral. This may be done for various reasons. The lending institution may consider the risk so great that it asks for an assignment of receivables and a pledge of inventories to make the loan. In other cases, receivables may be slow moving, or there may be so many small accounts that inventory is better collateral. Inventory is normally not as good as receivables for collateral since the goods must still be sold or even processed and sold before a claim to cash arises. Inventory is most satisfactory as collateral when it is a staple good having a ready market and a fairly stable price.

In addition to its use as collateral to supplement or replace receivables, inventory is frequently used as security in several special situations. A concern with a very pronounced season often borrows on inventory. For example, a canning factory must put up a year's supply of various fruits and vegetables when they are in season. This gives it an inventory of those items equal to a year's sales. If working capital were large enough to meet all or a large part of such a need, it would be idle a good part of the year. Loans on inventory are used as a regular form of financing in the canning industry and other businesses that have a pronounced season in production.

A similar situation exists when a product has to be cured or aged. Goods are in inventory for a long period of time before they are available for sale. The ratio of inventory to sales increases and a larger investment in inventory is required than when products are ready for sale as soon as they are produced. Inventory loans are thus used as a regular method of financing.

Several alternative procedures may be used to pledge the inventory as collateral for the loan. The goods may be stored in a public warehouse or a field warehouse, and warehouse receipts used as collateral; or a trust receipt or similar instrument may be used which places a claim on the goods until they are sold in the normal course of business. The method which is used depends on bargaining with the lender, on cost considerations, and on the degree to which the arrangement interferes with the normal operation of a business. The use of trust receipts involves the least interference with day-to-day business operations, but the lender will often insist on warehouse receipts as collateral. When such is the case a field warehouse plan is usually preferable, but in some cases public warehouses may exist in distribution centers where goods would have to be kept anyway if customers are to be serviced properly.

Wholesale Financing or Floor Planning. This special form of secured financing is available only to finance the purchase of appliances or automobiles. The rate charged on wholesale financing is low; the percentage of the purchase price of the article which is loaned is high; and the arrangement is worked out with the factory so that it is very convenient. As part of the agreement, retail installment financing on items sold is generally turned over to the finance company. Such financing is probably the best possible for auto and appliance dealers because of the low cost, except in those cases in which a merchant wants to carry all or part of his installment accounts with his own funds. Then he will have to finance his inventory much like other concerns do, either with an unsecured loan or a secured loan since wholesale financing is usually extended at a low rate in order to get the installment financing business.

Factors Involved in Choosing Factoring as a Method for Short-Term Financing

Factoring involves going beyond accounts receivable financing and selling the accounts to a factor. It usually means that the choice of the accounts to which the business can sell and the maximum amount of goods it can sell to an account on credit are set by the factor. In fact, the whole process of credit investigation, handling receivables, and collections are often turned over to the factor. A basic element in the decision of a firm in a sound financial condition to use a factor is cost. A concern may be spending more now for credit checking, record keeping, collection, and bad debt losses than a factor charges for these services.

Also basic is the ability to do the credit job well. A concern may be too small to have an adequate credit department. It may be at a disadvantage in dealing with buyers for large businesses. Or the risk of one large account may be too great to assume safely. Competition may be so keen that answers on shipments of goods must be made before a small business has time to check the account. A factor may help solve all of these problems.

Another basic consideration is the attitude in the field toward factors. They have been accepted for years in the textile field. In recent years, factoring has spread to such fields as the manufacture of shoes, hardware, and furniture. In fields where factoring is little used, the financial standing of a concern using it may suffer; and this must be considered in any decision to engage in factoring.

QUESTIONS

1. Explain the relationship between current assets, current liabilities, and net working capital.
2. What is the basic source of working capital?
3. Define the current ratio and discuss its significance. How does current borrowing affect the current ratio?
4. What effect does the nature of an industry have on financing?
5. Describe the effect of the financial life cycle of a company on its financing.
6. Discuss the relationship of the nature of the demand for funds to the amount of current borrowing a concern plans to do.
7. Describe the various risks which should be analyzed in making a decision on financing.
8. How are the interest-rate risk and the purchasing-power risk related?
9. Discuss cost considerations in financing decisions.
10. Discuss the qualitative factors which make current borrowing attractive.
11. Discuss several disadvantages of short-term borrowing.
12. Summarize the factors which should be considered in deciding upon the amount of current financing.
13. Discuss several policies which might be followed in planning current financing.
14. Discuss the factors involved in deciding on each of the following as a source of funds: merchandise suppliers, banks, finance companies, factors, commercial paper market.
15. Discuss the factors to consider in deciding upon a secured or an unsecured loan.
16. When is it desirable to use accounts receivable financing?
17. When is it desirable to use loans secured by inventory?
18. When is wholesale financing the most desirable form to use?
19. Under what conditions should factoring be used?

SUGGESTED READINGS

ARCHER, STEPHEN H., and CHARLES D'AMBROSIO. *Business Finance.* New York: The Macmillan Company, 1972. Part VII.

BRIGHTLY, DONALD S., and the Prentice-Hall Editorial Staff. *Complete Guide to Financial Management for Small and Medium-Sized Companies.* Englewood Cliffs, New Jersey: Prentice-Hall, Inc., 1971. Chapters 12-14.

FERTIG, PAUL E., DONALD F. ISTVAN, and HOMER J. MOTTICE. *Using Accounting Information.* New York: Harcourt Brace Jovanovich, Inc., 1971. Chapters 9, 11, 15.

MacCORMAC, M. J., and J. J. TEELING. *Financial Management.* Dublin, Ireland: Gill and Macmillan, 1971. Chapter 6.

National Industrial Conference Board. *Organizing and Managing the Corporate Finance Function,* Studies in Business Policy, No. 129, New York, 1969.

PRATHER, CHARLES L., and JAMES E. WEST. *Financing Business Firms.* Homewood, Illinois: Richard D. Irwin, Inc., 1971. Part IV.

SOLDOFSKY, ROBERT M., and GARNET D. OLIVE. *Financial Management.* Cincinnati: South-Western Publishing Co., 1974. Parts 3 and 4.

WELSHANS, MERLE T. "Using Credit for Profit Making." *Harvard Business Review* (January-February, 1967), pp. 141-156.

12 | Lending Operations of Investment Companies, Trust Institutions, and Insurance Companies

Institutional investors, encouraged over the past twenty-five years by social and economic developments, have played an increasingly important role in financing the long-term capital needs of industry. The institutions that have participated substantially in the growth of industrial long-term financing are investment companies, trust companies, and insurance companies.

INVESTMENT COMPANIES

Investment companies engage principally in the purchase of stocks and bonds of other corporations. The investment company permits the pooling of funds of many investors on a share basis for the primary purpose of obtaining expert management and wide diversification in security investments. As of June 30, 1973, investment companies held total assets, consisting primarily of stocks and bonds, of approximately $73 billion. Furthermore, the number and the size of the investment companies have been increasing rapidly in recent years.

Development of Investment Companies

Forerunners of the modern investment company existed in the United States during the early part of the 19th century when insurance companies accepted funds from individuals and professionally administered them. Following World War I, the tremendous growth of the industry of the nation and interest in stock market activity in general gave support for the first time to large-scale development of the investment companies. Such companies in the United States were both victims and cause of the speculative excesses in the securities market during the 1920's, much like the situation at the close of the 19th century in Great Britain. Following the depression of the 1930's, the investment companies, strengthened by the introduction of a new form of operation, again attracted public attention and increased in numbers and strength.

A close resemblance may be observed in the modern-day savings and loan associations, the mutual savings banks, and the investment companies in that they all pool the savings of the public, provide professional investment management for such savings, and diversify investments. In contrast with the savings and loan associations and mutual savings banks, however, funds of investment companies may be invested in equity shares as well as debt instruments in order to provide an increased income for the investor. The depositor or the holder of shares in a mutual savings bank or savings and loan association has a return based entirely upon the yield of real estate mortgages, governmental obligations, and other fixed-income securities.

Many of our present-day investment companies represent an outgrowth of businesses originally established for other purposes. For example, in 1952 both the Electric Bond and Share Company and The United Corporation, having been ordered by the Securities and Exchange Commission to divest themselves of their utility holdings, stated their intention to become investment companies. Until that time these companies had operated as public-utility holding companies. The Adams Express Company, organized in 1854, disposed of its express business to the American Railway Express Company in 1918 and has conducted business as an investment company since that time.

Classification of Investment Companies

The Securities and Exchange Commission classifies investment companies as either *management investment holding companies* or *management investment companies.* The first of these two groups operates for the purpose of influencing or controlling the companies in which it invests. The management investment companies invest for the primary purpose of securing diversification and yield. We are concerned only with the latter classification in this chapter.

Investment companies are classified also into the fixed-trust type, the closed-end fund type, and the open-end fund type. Although all three types have the common objective of securing intelligent diversification for the pooled funds of individuals, the methods by which this objective is accomplished differ to a considerable degree.

The Fixed-Trust Investment Company. The *fixed-trust investment company* operates with a fixed fund which involves an initial selection of a group of securities that are deposited in trust for a fixed number of years. Against this fund are issued shares that remain outstanding for the duration of the trust. Fixed trusts may consist entirely of common stocks of a single type, such as oil stocks, motor stocks, or railroad stocks. Other fixed trusts may have a diversification of investment, including diversification not only with respect to industries but also with respect to type of security, that is, common stocks, preferred stocks, and bonds.

The fixed-trust arrangement was particularly popular during the twenties when there was confidence in the future of common stocks in general. Well-chosen stocks of strong companies were expected to become more and more valuable, and it appeared to be unnecessary to provide for the continuous reevaluation of such securities. Since the twenties, however, experience has revealed the importance of continuing attention to the position of each individual stock.

The Closed-End Fund Investment Company. In contrast with the fixed trust, the *closed-end fund investment company* places great emphasis on portfolio management. Ordinarily, the securities issued by a closed-end fund are sold at one time and additional securities seldom are issued. The total asset value of the closed-end fund increases only through the appreciation in the market value of the securities that it holds or through the retention of a small proportion of the earnings obtained by the company. The holder of the securities of a closed-end fund may liquidate his investment much as the holder of a security in any corporation does, that is, through the sale of the securities to other investors.

Bonds and preferred stocks, as well as common stocks, may be issued by the closed-end fund company. The holders of these senior securities have the same relative priority to earnings as the holder of senior securities in any organization. The bonds issued by the closed-end fund, however, seldom represent a claim against specific securities held by the fund but rather take the debenture form. The holders of the debenture bonds of the closed-end funds, therefore, have only a general claim against the assets of the company. This arrangement makes possible the frequent sale and purchase of securities by the investment company without the necessity of securing a release of pledged collateral, as would be required if secured bonds were issued against the portfolio of securities.

Like the fixed-trust fund, the closed-end fund enjoyed its greatest popularity during the twenties and has since derived its importance from the continuation of the activities begun earlier. As of June 30, 1973, there were 201 closed-end funds registered with the Securities and Exchange Commission [1] with total assets of approximately $10 billion.

The Open-End Fund Investment Company. The *open-end fund investment companies*, commonly referred to as mutual funds, are of American origin. In contrast with closed-end funds, they generally offer only a single class of shares to investors. These shares, held by the public, may be returned to the company for redemption at any time. The bylaws or trust agreement of the investment company provides for the redemption of such shares at the liquidation or net asset value of the investment company. Hence, the price at which shares tendered for redemption to an

---

[1] *Annual Report of the Securities and Exchange Commission,* 1973, p. 149.

investment company will be redeemed depends upon the market value of the securities held by the investment company. New shares are offered to the public continuously. The price of these new shares is determined, as is true for shares that are being redeemed, by the current value of the securities held by the investment company.

The shares of the open-end funds are generally sold at a price that includes a selling charge of from 7 to 9 percent with a prevailing average for all companies of about 8 percent. This means that the purchase of shares having a market value of $1,000 would require an additional fee or premium of approximately $80. As larger volumes of shares are purchased, the selling charge as a percentage of the purchase price is reduced accordingly.

Because the shares of the open-end funds are redeemable with the company, they are not listed on the exchanges. It is unnecessary to find other buyers for the shares when they can be promptly and easily redeemed by the investment company itself. In order to know the price at which shares should be redeemed or sold, the investment company must calculate at frequent intervals the total value of its portfolio of securities. Usually a formula that gives due weight to the amount of securities held in the different companies makes possible a quick and ready calculation of the total value of the portfolio. The legal form of organization taken by the open-end fund is generally that of the corporation or the business trust.

Open-end funds may differ radically with respect to objectives of management. In some cases, an extremely conservative portfolio is maintained, comprised largely of high-grade fixed-income senior securities of well-known companies. In other cases, the objective is to maximize the profits to be obtained through the purchase and sale of securities during changes in the market. Then, the bulk of the fund's investments is placed in common stocks. Between these extremes falls the objective of obtaining a somewhat above-average yield combined with reasonable stability of market value. This type of company objective is generally described as a "balanced-fund operation." Such portfolios generally include both bonds and stocks of leading companies.

As of June 30, 1973, there were 788 open-end funds registered with the Securities and Exchange Commission. These open-end investment companies had total assets of approximately $54.4 billion.[2]

Tax Status of Investment Companies

Under the Revenue Act of 1936, corporations are subject to a tax on the dividends they receive. Strictly applied, this tax would make it almost impossible for investment companies to function in their present form, since it would mean triple taxation: taxation first of the operating corporation, again when the investment company receives its dividends or interest, and finally when these profits are distributed to the holders of the shares of the investment company. A special supplement (Supplement Q) to the Revenue Act of 1936, however, provides that under certain circumstances investment companies are considered as mere conduits through which earnings of a corporation flow to the ultimate shareholders of the investment companies. In order to be so regarded, the investment company must register with the Securities and Exchange Commission and otherwise qualify as a *regulated investment company,* exempt from federal corporate income taxes on earnings distributed to shareholders.

Relative Popularity of Investment Funds

As indicated earlier, the fixed-trust fund and the closed-end fund enjoyed their primary popularity during the twenties. Since that time, the open-end funds have almost completely dominated the investment company field as far as the establishment of new companies is concerned. The growth of the open-end funds has in fact been so rapid as to make them a popular subject of discussion throughout the financial world. *The New York Journal of Commerce* and *Barron's* weekly have added special sections devoted entirely to the affairs of open-end funds. Some states now permit savings banks and fiduciaries to invest in the shares of some of the mutual funds.

---

[2] *Ibid.*

TRUST INSTITUTIONS

Trust institutions administer and control great amounts of wealth and account for a significant portion of all securities purchased. A *trust institution* serves in a fiduciary capacity for the administration or disposition of assets and for the performance of specified acts for the beneficiaries of trust arrangements. A *fiduciary* is one who acts in a capacity of trust and undivided loyalty for another. It implies integrity and fidelity of the person or institution trusted, and it contemplates good faith rather than legal obligation as the dominant basis for transactions.

It was not until approximately one hundred years ago that the institutional form of trustee became important. In earlier times, trust duties were performed primarily by family friends or attorneys. With the growth of the country and the increased complexity of legal and financial matters, however, it became increasingly difficult to find individuals capable of administering properly the matters required of trustees. The amount of trust business administered by individuals in the United States at the present time is of minor importance compared with that undertaken by trust companies and trust departments of banks.

Forms of Trust Institutions

Most of the estimated 3,000 corporations actively engaged in the trust business of the United States are also engaged in the banking business. This is accounted for by the fact that the experiences and skills required for banking and trust work are very much the same. Nearly half of all the corporations engaged in the trust business are national banks that operate trust departments. State chartered banks having trust departments account for most of the remaining institutional trustees. A few independent companies are engaged solely in the trust business; and trust business is carried on by other organizations of a nonbanking nature, such as title companies, property insurance companies, and real estate firms. Finally, a few corporate trust institutions operate as affiliates of banks. The banks may own the trust company or the trust company may own a bank; in other circumstances, the stock of both the trust company and the bank may be owned by a holding company. It is estimated that no more than 100 firms are represented by those corporate trustees not engaged one way or another in banking activities. Most banks that provide trust services include the words "and Trust Company" in the corporate title. In some cases, "and Trust Company" may be found to accompany the title even though the bank has ceased to offer trust services.

Classifications of Trusts

Trusts may be classified according to their functions. These functions may be broadly grouped between those of a personal trust nature and those of a corporate trust nature. Under both classifications, the functions are of tremendous importance to the financial structure of the economy in that they involve the transfer and the management of huge sums of money and the provision of services that make possible the administration of such wealth on the part of others. The personal trust is established for the direct benefit of one or more persons, while the corporate trust exists to handle certain affairs of corporations.

Personal Trust Business

Personal trust business is confined largely to the care of assets included in trust estates and to settling estates of deceased persons. The three principal types of personal trusts are living trusts, trusteeships under will, and insurance trusts.

Living Trusts. In recent years there has been a tremendous increase in the number of living trusts due to many factors. In the first place, a living trust provides a convenient means of providing a reasonably assured income for a person's family without immediately conveying the property to the family. Under these circumstances, the beneficiary of the trust, who may be a widow or a minor child, will receive only the income from the trust principal during the term of the trust. The principal itself is conveyed to the beneficiary only upon the happening of some specified event set forth in the trust agreement. The trust agreement is often used by persons of advanced age who have reason to doubt their continuing ability to manage their financial affairs. In other cases, trusts may be established for the benefit of minor children or for persons who are incapable of managing their affairs for reasons of physical disability or mental incompetence. A businessman may establish a trust that will provide a reasonably comfortable income for a specified period of years to protect against undue hardship that might result from a particularly risky business venture.

Under the laws of most states, living trusts can be revocable, irrevocable, or something in between that may be referred to as short-term trusts. As the term implies, a *revocable trust* is one in which the maker of the trust has the right to revoke the trust arrangement after its creation. Such an agreement makes it possible to plan the transfer of assets and reduces the time required in passing the property to the beneficiaries when the maker dies. Also, probate expenses may be reduced and the publicity of a will avoided by the use of a revocable trust.

An *irrevocable trust*, on the other hand, provides for the complete and final transfer of assets to the trustee. In addition to the advantages cited for the revocable trust, the irrevocable trust may involve substantial tax advantages. As a rule, the maker of the trust can free himself from taxation on the income from the assets transferred to the trust institution. In addition, the property in trust usually escapes estate taxes upon the death of the maker of the trust. The maker of such a trust must pay a gift tax when the trust is established, but the rate on gift taxes is approximately 25 percent lower than that on estate taxes.

The irrevocable trust, because of its fixed and definite nature, presents some disadvantages also. First, the maker of the trust may be so tax-economy minded that he may dispossess himself of an unduly large proportion of his assets, making him dependent upon the beneficiaries of the trust for his care. In other cases, an increase in the general cost of living may leave the beneficiaries of the trust with too little income for their needs since trustees place primary emphasis on safety of principal in the administration of trust funds. Such a policy of trust administration generally provides a steady but rather low yield on trust investments.

A *short-term trust* represents a compromise between the revocable and irrevocable trust. In brief, it is an irrevocable trust established for a specified number of years. The reason for the establishment of the short-term trust is often for tax purposes. If the trust meets all of the requirements of the tax laws, the maker is free of tax on the income derived from the assets while the trust exists, assuming such income is paid to a person or institution other than the maker of the trust; and at the end of the trust term, the maker of the trust gets back his assets that have been placed in trust. Short-term trusts can be used for many purposes, such as the support of parents, contributions to charities, the accumulation of an estate for one's family, or carrying insurance on some other person's life.

Trusteeships Under Will. The trusteeship under will represents a second major classification of personal trust business. For the person who prefers that his estate be maintained and administered for the benefit of the heirs rather than be turned over to the heirs directly, a *testamentary trust* may be established. The person establishing such a trust is reasonably assured that his beneficiaries will be properly cared for and at the same time will be protected against acts of irresponsibility with respect to administration of the estate. A trust institution may be designated as the executor in a will. The duties of the executor are, of course, handling the estate with respect to the accountability for all the assets, liquidating all of those assets of a perishable nature, paying all debts including tax claims that may exist against the estate, and distributing the assets of the estate in accordance with the provisions of the will. The trust institution may also act as administrator, guardian, or conservator under authority of a court appointment.

Insurance Trusts. The *insurance trust* represents a third classification of personal trust business. These trusts come into existence through the voluntary act of placing in trust one or more insurance policies with an agreement that the proceeds of the insurance will be paid to the trust institution upon the death of the maker of the trust. The trust institution is then, as a rule, bound by the terms of the agreement to administer the benefits of the insurance policies for the specified beneficiaries of the trust. Such an arrangement is generally provided when the maker of the trust has reason to doubt the ability of the beneficiary to handle properly the large sum of money that would otherwise accrue to him as the beneficiary under the terms of the life insurance policy.

Investment Policies of Trust Institutions

State laws that apply to the administration of trust funds are many and varied and are generally considered to be very restrictive. In addition to the law, the terms of the trust agreement itself may establish restrictive limitations on the trustee's management of the assets placed in trust. Traditionally, trust institutions have been required to limit the investment of assets placed in their trust to the securities on a legal list prepared by the state. Such a list includes only high-grade bonds and other designated fixed-income investments. Only a few states continue to impose restrictions of this nature on trust institutions. Most states now follow the *prudent-man rule*, which requires that a trust institution be held responsible for the same degree of judgment that a prudent man would exercise in investing his own funds, a substantial liberalization from the legal-list concept.

Several states have taken a position between the legal-list and prudent-man policies by permitting trust institutions to invest only a portion of their trust assets according to the prudent-man rule. The remainder of the assets must be invested in the securities included on the legal list published by the state. Many trust institutions operating in prudent-man rule states have increased yields to beneficiaries by adding high-grade corporate stocks to their portfolios.

The Federal Deposit Insurance Corporation, in conjunction with the Board of Governors of the Federal Reserve System and the Comptroller of the Currency, in its fourth survey of trust assets held by commercial banks in 1972 reported total trust assets of $404 billion. Of this total approximately two thirds was held in the form of stock. Approximately 12 percent was in the form of corporate bonds, 5 percent in the securities of states and municipalities, and 4 percent in the obligations of the United States Government and its agencies. The remainder was invested in real estate, real estate mortgages, and preferred stock.

The Common Trust Fund

Of particular importance to the administration of trust assets was the modification of the law to permit national banks to commingle the trust funds of their customers. Since one of the long-established legal principles required that assets of separate trusts should not be mingled, this represented a major step or modification in trust administration activities. Amendments to the federal tax laws were also necessary in order that income from such invested assets would not be taxed as income to both the trust institution and the individuals named as beneficiaries of the trusts.

Although the assets invested under the common trust fund plan are subject to the same regulatory limitations as the investment of individual trust assets, substantial advantages are offered both to the trust institution and to the beneficiaries. One primary advantage is that the common trust fund makes it possible for trust institutions to solicit smaller trusts. Principal amounts of only a few thousand dollars placed under control of the trust institution under common trust agreement receive the same competent supervision as much larger trusts. Costs are reduced and greater diversification is obtained through the common trust arrangement than is possible for the individual handling of assets for small trusts. Total assets of the commingled trusts are administered under the centralized supervision of the investment section of the trust department. The common trust fund was established, as a matter of fact, primarily for the benefit of the smaller trusts. This is evidenced by the fact that originally under the regulations of the Federal Reserve System the maximum amount of any single trust which could be placed in a common trust fund was $25,000. This was raised in 1945 to $50,000 and later to $100,000.

Several trust companies offer three separate common trust funds. One of the funds will ordinarily have all of its assets invested in bonds, the second fund will have all of its assets in common stocks, and the third fund will have its assets in both bonds and common stocks. The person establishing the trust, therefore, may choose between a fund with emphasis primarily on stability of principal and a fund with emphasis on higher income and appreciation possibilities. Ordinarily a person may invest up to $100,000 in each of these funds without violating the limitations on amount established by federal regulations. Under this arrangement of multiple common trust funds, the similarity to the operations of investment companies becomes quite readily apparent.

In addition to the common trust fund operations of national banks, all states authorize state-chartered corporations engaged in trust business to operate common trust funds. As of the end of 1973 a survey of 759 common trust funds in the United States revealed assets of approximately $10.3 billion. Approximately 46 percent of the assets of common trust funds were in the form of common stock. The remainder was invested in preferred stock, United States obligations, corporate bonds, and other commitments.[3]

Trust Services for Corporations

One of the principal forms of trust service provided for corporations is that of *trusteeship under indenture*. This form of trusteeship was referred to in an earlier chapter under the description of the Trust Indenture Act of 1939. There it was explained that under the provisions of the Act, a trustee of a registered company, among other things, was required to be corporate in form and to have no less than the specified minimum of capital and surplus; also, there could be no conflict of interest between the corporation issuing the securities and the investing public. Trust service for corporations is an important phase of the trust business since under the law all corporations subject to regulation by the Securities and Exchange Commission must seek the services of trust corporations.

The duties of the trust institution when serving in a capacity of trusteeship under indenture generally involve the holding of the mortgage against which bonds are issued by the corporation and the enforcement and accountability of all provisions relating to the mortgage. In addition, trustees under these circumstances may also handle the registration and transfer of ownership of registered securities, may enforce or supervise the insurance requirements that are established in the mortgage, may execute various

---

[3] *Trusts & Estates*, May, 1974, Communications Channels, Inc., New York, p. 310.

releases, and may supervise the administration of sinking funds that may be provided in the mortgage.

As described in connection with the establishment of an investment company, trust institutions serve corporations as transfer agents to handle the details relating to the issuance and recording of stock transfers and as dividend disbursing agents to handle details relating to the distribution of dividends. Trust institutions may also serve corporations as registrars. Many of the stock exchanges require that corporations having stock listed on their exchanges maintain separate registrars and transfer agents. The registrar's responsibility, among other things, involves supervision over issuance of new stock of the corporation in order that the corporation will not issue more stock than is authorized by the charter. The transfer agent and the registrar, therefore, provide an effective check on each other's operations and assure the security holder that his interests are being responsibly administered.

In the event of corporate reorganization, it is customary for creditors, pending the final reorganization, to deposit bonds and other credit instruments with a corporate trustee. In return, they are given transferable certificates of deposit. The property of a corporation in bankruptcy is generally conveyed to a trust institution, which provides, if necessary, for the liquidation and the disbursement of funds to the creditors of the corporation.

Trust institutions maintain safe-deposit facilities, administer security holdings, provide complete records of all security transactions, make monthly reports to customers, and provide investment counsel. The numerous additional services provided by trust institutions for corporations cannot be covered in this text. Further reference, however, is made to trust activities later in this part in connection with corporate financing through the use of equipment trust obligations and in connection with pension funds.

FINANCIAL ASPECTS OF INSURANCE

The basic purpose of insurance is to establish a degree of certainty with respect to the plans and activities of individuals and institutions. This certainty is provided not through the elimination of the hazards that face the insured but by protection against financial loss that may result from such hazards. It is true, however, that insurance companies have done much to reduce the perils of both business and personal life through such activities as accident, health, and fire prevention campaigns and driver education. In addition to the financial aspects of insurance, many other benefits are observable. For example, the peace of mind that is derived from the knowledge that one's property and life are insured adequately may contribute in a significant way to the individual's effectiveness in his work as well as to his health. It is with the financial aspects of insurance that we are primarily concerned here.

In this book, the contribution of insurance companies to the financial affairs of the nation may be said to be twofold: as a source of capital for business and government and as direct benefits to the insured. As a source of capital, the companies serve in three ways: (1) they encourage saving by individuals; (2) they accumulate and invest vast sums of money through the normal course of their business operations; and (3) they provide a basis for the extension of credit on the part of other lenders.

Encouraging Saving

Most types of life insurance policies provide for a combination of insurance and savings programs. Periodic payments to the insurance company include both a fee for insurance protection and a contribution toward the savings element or cash value of the contract. The advantage for many people of an insurance contract that combines a savings program with insurance protection lies in the fact that the insured forms the habit of budgeting out of his income regular payments to the insurance company. Many people regard their insurance premiums as current obligations, much like bills for goods or services purchased on credit, and will not allow policies to lapse and the accompanying savings program thus to be abandoned except under unusual circumstances. For many people, the sole cash savings involves accumulations of cash reserves in life insurance policies.

Accumulating and Investing Funds

The funds accumulated by life insurance companies through their necessary reserves have reached tremendous proportions.

These funds, paid to the companies by millions of individual policyholders, are reinvested in many types of business organizations which, in turn, use the funds for constructing buildings, acquiring equipment, and for other business uses. Such financing results in increased productivity for the businesses in particular and for the overall economy of the country. Insurance companies also invest large sums of money in residential mortgages and government bonds.

Basis for Credit

The lender of money is able to reduce some of the risk involved through the use of various forms of insurance. To the extent that his risks are reduced, the lender is encouraged to increase his volume of lending activities. For example, it is important to the residential mortgage lender that properties on which loans are made be adequately insured against damage due to such things as fire and windstorm that might reduce the value of the property to less than the amount of the outstanding loan against the property. Institutions financing the sale of automobiles always require that the automobiles be insured until the indebtedness is completely retired. When a loan is to be made to an organization whose prosperity and continued operation are dependent upon the talents and efforts of one person, the lender may insist that the business maintain insurance on the life of that person with the lender designated as beneficiary. In these and many other instances, insurance contributes to the flow of credit between lender and borrower.

CLASSIFICATION OF INSURANCE

The field of insurance is a broad one, encompassing nearly every phase of our national economy. Most people think of insurance in terms of the type of policy that is purchased from private companies to protect income and property. However, our vast structures of old-age and survivor's insurance, employment security insurance, and other forms of insurance administered by the federal and state governments are also part of the national pattern of insurance coverage. We may, therefore, divide the field of insurance broadly into public or government insurance and private insurance. In this chapter, only the private insurance plans are considered. These plans may be classified as personal insurance and property insurance.

Personal insurance includes all arrangements whereby the risk of loss of earning power as a result of death, accident, sickness, or retirement is avoided or reduced through insurance contracts. These contracts may be classified as life insurance and accident and sickness insurance.

LIFE INSURANCE

One of the most important functions of life insurance is that of providing an immediate estate for the dependents of the head of a household in the event that he dies before sufficient personal resources have been accumulated to provide for his dependents. Where the amount of life insurance is quite small, the objective may be that of a "clean-up fund" which will defray the costs incident to the death of the insured.

Life insurance may also play an important role in business affairs. For example, where the business organization is a partnership, it is frequently desirable to insure the lives of the partners and to specify the other members of the partnership as the beneficiaries. This arrangement permits the survivors in a partnership to buy the interest of the heirs of a deceased member without serious cash drain on the business. A businessman may carry life insurance for the purpose of settling business debts that may exist at the time of his death; and finally life insurance provides a means of minimizing the drain on an individual's estate as a result of taxes imposed upon his business assets at his death.

Types of Life Insurance

The many applications of life insurance to special requirements and situations require the availability of a wide variety of types of policies. The principal types of contracts sold by life insurance companies are term insurance, whole life insurance, endowment insurance, and annuities.

Term Insurance. The basic feature of *term life insurance* is that the policy is issued for a specified period of time after which time no obligation exists on the part of the insurance company toward the insured. During the period of the insurance contract, however, the insured is entitled to protection to the extent of the face amount of the policy. Term life insurance policies are usually issued for one, five, ten, or twenty years.

Term life insurance is seldom recommended in its basic form as an appropriate contract for general family protection. Modifications of the basic form, including renewal privileges without further physical examination and privileges for conversion to more permanent forms of insurance, have added to the attractiveness of this form of insurance. Because no investment program is combined with term insurance, the annual premiums are less than for other types of insurance. But one of the major disadvantages of term insurance is that the premiums are based on standard mortality tables, and they increase as the age of the insured increases. Term life insurance provides much smaller capital accumulation for the insurance companies than do the other types of insurance discussed in the following pages, since the annual premiums correspond more directly to the basic cost of insurance protection and there is no savings or cash value component.

Whole Life Insurance. The *whole life insurance* policy differs from term insurance in that the benefits under the provisions of the policy are payable to the beneficiaries irrespective of the time of death, while for the term policy such benefits are payable only if the insured dies during the specified term of the insurance. The whole life insurance contract differs from term insurance in another important respect; it combines an investment program with the insurance contract. The premiums are generally for a fixed sum each payment period throughout the life of the insured—straight life—or for a specified number of years—limited payment life. That portion of the premium which applies toward the protection part of the contract represents only a small part of the annual premium during the early years of the contract. Much of the premium is credited toward the savings accumulation of the policyholder. This savings accumulation is referred to as the cash value of the policy. The accumulation of this investment portion of the insurance contract makes it possible for an individual to pay a level or fixed premium throughout his life or a specified number of years despite the higher costs of insurance that accompany advancing age.

Endowment Insurance. Like the term plan of life insurance, *endowment insurance* is written for a specified number of years. In contrast, however, if the insured person survives to the end of the stipulated period, the face amount of the policy is payable to the insured. Such policies may be written as twenty- or thirty-year endowment contracts, or for such other time spans as may be desired. Endowment policies may also be written to mature at a specified age, in which case the term of the endowment is the difference between the age of the insured at the time the policy is contracted for and the age so specified in the policy. Like the limited payment plan of life insurance, the endowment policy may involve a single premium to be paid immediately upon the writing of the contract with the endowment to be made at some specified future period. Some endowment policies provide for payment of benefits over a period of years rather than in a single lump sum. Such policies involve a combination of the endowment and annuity contracts. Endowment policies are especially important as outlets for family savings.

Annuity Contracts. *Annuity insurance* has often been described as "insurance in reverse." The basic purpose of life insurance is to create an estate, while the annuity contract provides for the disposition of an estate through its systematic liquidation. Under an annuity contract, the annuitant agrees to pay a stipulated sum of money to the insurance company, either in the form of a single lump-sum payment or in a series of regular payments, in return for a regular income from the company for a specified time, such as a number of years or for life. Typically, annuities are purchased to meet the possibility that the buyer may outlive his earning period and will need a regular income to sustain him in the years beyond retirement.

Extent of Life Insurance Protection

There are more than 145 million insurance policyholders in the United States. In 1973 this insurance represented more than $1.7 trillion of insurance protection. The average amount of life insurance owned per family in 1973 was $28,800. In addition, there were 2.1 million annuity contracts in force.[4]

Life insurance protection and annuities were provided by 1,810 companies in the United States. Of this total, Arizona had 388 chartered companies; Texas was second with 219 companies; Louisiana was third with 99 companies; and Illinois was fourth with 93 companies. Although the above states claim the largest number of life insurance companies, such companies are, for the most part, relatively small. Since the turn of the century, six states have accounted for between 80 and 90 percent of all of the assets of life insurance companies. The six states are New York, New Jersey, Massachusetts, Connecticut, Wisconsin, and Pennsylvania.

The Investment of Life Insurance Company Funds

Although life insurance companies usually are able to meet the payments for which they are obligated each year out of funds received from insurance premiums and from earnings on their investments, the companies maintain vast reserves. Through the investment of these reserves, the life insurance companies make their principal contribution to the flow of long-term capital in the economy. The investments customarily made by life insurance companies may be described as a *fixed income type* in which the purpose of investment is primarily one of safety of principal and stability of income. Such investments usually take the form of United States government securities, state and municipal bonds, the securities of business and industry, real estate mortgages, direct investment in real estate, and policy loans. In 1972 the policy reserves of United States life insurance companies passed $240 billion.

---

[4] *Life Insurance Fact Book,* Institute of Life Insurance, 1974, pp. 9, 10, and 43.

In recent years, there has been a slow but gradual liberalization of restrictive state laws as they apply to investments of life insurance companies. Among other things, these companies have been permitted to invest directly in such income-producing assets as housing projects, real estate for lease-back purposes, and, to a limited extent, common stocks. Although there has been considerable controversy relative to the merits of life insurance company investment in common stocks, most states now permit such investments.

The tremendous growth of life insurance company assets has posed a major problem for the investment departments of these organizations. Government securities provide only part of the answer to the problem of the insurance company, and the diligent search for new investment outlets will continue. To the extent that the insurance companies are able to expand their areas of investment, the long-term capital needs of the economy are more adequately served.

A vast area of investment has opened up to the life insurance companies through direct investment in income-producing properties. The redevelopment housing programs in the major cities offer an excellent opportunity for financing by the large insurance companies. An example of this is the Garden City Apartments in New York City, which are financed by the Metropolitan Life Insurance Company and others. Some states permit life insurance companies to invest in commercial and industrial real estate properties. In such cases, the properties acquired are leased to commercial or industrial enterprises, generally on the basis of a fixed annual rental.[5]

ACCIDENT AND SICKNESS INSURANCE

When disability strikes a person, he may suffer financial loss in two ways: through his loss of income while disabled, and through the medical costs relating to the disability. *Accident and sickness insurance* provides indemnity to the insured for loss of income because of accident or sickness and provides for the

---

[5] The lease is described in greater detail in Chapter 13.

expenses of hospital and surgical requirements. This form of insurance has enjoyed a far greater rate of growth in recent decades than any other form of insurance.

Types of Accident and Sickness Insurance

Accident or sickness insurance may be written as one or a combination of the following: disability income insurance, hospital, medical, and surgical expense insurance, and major medical expense insurance.

Disability Income Insurance. The increasing recognition that the earning power of the head of a household is usually the most important asset of the family has resulted in a greater consciousness of the need not only for life insurance but also for protection against loss of income because of accident or sickness. Disability income insurance provides this form of financial protection. Under such insurance, a person may receive weekly payments for total or partial disability.

Hospital, Medical, and Surgical Expense Insurance. Hospitalization insurance, together with medical and surgical insurance, as the name implies, agrees to reimburse within stipulated limits either the insured or the hospital for certain hospital, medical, and surgical expenses that result from accident or sickness. Insurance of this type may be issued as a group policy, covering all of the employees of a business firm, for example, or it may be issued to cover an individual or a family. Hospital, medical, and surgical expense insurance, in addition to being written by private companies, is written in large volume by certain organizations formed on a nonprofit basis for this specific purpose. Prominent among the latter group are the "Blue Cross" (designed basically for coverage of hospital care) and "Blue Shield" (for surgical expenses coverage) organizations.

Major Medical Expense Insurance. An increasingly popular form of personal insurance is that which provides for large medical expenses. Although such expenses arise infrequently, when they occur, accumulated family savings may be wiped out. In other instances, needed medical treatment of a costly nature may not be available to a family because of a lack of financial resources. *Major medical insurance,* sometimes called "catastrophe insurance," provides protection against the expenses of the most serious of accidents or sicknesses. Although such insurance is usually written under group policies, a few companies have offered such protection to individuals and to families.

PROPERTY INSURANCE

Basically, the purpose of *property insurance* is either to protect the insured against loss arising out of physical damages to his own property or loss arising from damages to others for which the insured may be held liable.

Types of Property Insurance

For purposes of describing the types of property insurance, it will be convenient to follow the broad classification of fire, marine, and casualty and surety insurance.

Fire Insurance. The basic form of *fire insurance* offers protection to the insured against the destruction of physical property as a result of fire. Such insurance does not provide for protection against loss to the insured of the use of such facilities. For example, the owner of a store would receive payment for the physical damage resulting from fire to the store premises, but he would not receive compensation for the loss of trade caused by the fire loss. Such protection may be provided by the fire insurance companies in the form of a modification of the basic fire policy, but at an increased premium. In addition, fire insurance companies may write policies that protect against such related perils to property as explosion, windstorm, and riot. The fire insurance companies find these risks convenient to undertake, since it is often difficult to determine the extent to which damage results from these perils or from the fires that often follow such disasters.

Marine Insurance. Marine insurance is one of the oldest forms of commercial insurance. These policies were written originally to protect against the perils of the sea. Such protection was offered not only against the natural dangers of sea transportation but also against piracy and other man-created dangers. Marine insurance later was extended to include protection over transportation of merchandise from the seller to the purchaser, including land transportation as well as marine transportation. A distinction is customarily made between insurance written on shipments over land by such carriers as railroads and trucks, which is referred to as *inland marine insurance,* and those that involve sea perils, referred to as *ocean marine insurance.*

Casualty and Surety Insurance. Casualty and surety insurance is of more recent origin than the other forms of insurance discussed. In brief, casualty and surety insurance may be assumed to include all forms of coverage not included as marine, fire, or life insurance. An example of casualty insurance is the well-known automobile liability insurance that owners of vehicles carry as protection against claims resulting from injuries to other persons. Another example of insurance of the casualty type is that offering protection against burglary or robbery. Other forms of casualty insurance include insurance of a business against excessive bad-debt loss as a result of sales to customers on open account and protection against the breakage of plate glass.

Business firms protect themselves against claims resulting from occupational accidents through the purchase of a form of casualty insurance known as *workmen's compensation and employers' liability insurance.* Under workmen's compensation laws of the various states, employers are liable for most of the accidents that take place in connection with their business operations. Even for accidents not covered by workmen's compensation laws the employer may be sued for damages under common law. Workmen's compensation and employers' liability insurance assumes the expenses of compensation and provides for medical, surgical, and hospitalization requirements as determined by the compensation laws of the state.

The *surety contract* generally provides that one party, the surety company, becomes answerable to a third party, the insured, as a result of failure on the part of a second party to perform as required by contract. For example, the businessman who contracts for the construction of a new building may secure a surety bond protecting him against failure of the contractor to complete the structure by a certain time, or protecting him against unsatisfied claims of laborers or suppliers of materials as a result of failure of the contractor to meet his obligations.

The *fidelity bond,* as a special form of surety contract, provides that the surety company reimburse employers for the losses incurred as a result of the dishonest acts of employees. Banks, savings and loan associations, and other businesses in which employees have access to large sums of money invariably carry fidelity bonds for protection.

Property Insurance Companies

Historically, fire and marine insurance on the one hand and casualty and surety insurance on the other have been handled by separate companies. It was believed that the strict separation of these two broad types of insurance operations was to be desired in the light of the risk that a single company could undertake. The tremendous growth of the major property insurance companies, however, has long since provided sufficient diversification of risk to permit *multiple-line insurance underwriting.* Since 1950 there has been a steadily increasing number of multiple-line companies in which fire and marine insurance companies are writing a steadily increasing volume of casualty and surety insurance, and casualty and surety insurance companies are building up fire and marine insurance lines. The practice of affording complete property insurance in one package has encouraged mergers and affiliations of fire and marine insurance companies with casualty and surety insurance companies.

A recent development in the insurance field involves life insurance underwriting along with multiple-line property insurance underwriting.

Multiple-line insurance companies make possible the writing of insurance at lower total costs to the insured than is possible with the use of several companies for different specified risks. This lower cost results from lower administrative and selling expenses. The complete property insurance requirement of an individual or business may be handled in a single contract.

Table 12-1

ASSETS OF 880 STOCK FIRE & CASUALTY INSURANCE COMPANIES

December 31, 1972

BONDS	%		%	
U.S. Government	5.8	3,396,473,792		
Other Government	.3	181,701,870		
State, Municipal, Etc.	12.7	7,430,459,893		
Special Revenue, Etc.	16.2	9,494,776,141		
Railroad	.2	100,627,308		
Utility	2.0	1,197,576,050		
Miscellaneous	5.3	3,092,669,442		
Parents, Subs, Affils.	.5	283,393,972		
TOTAL BONDS			43.1	25,177,678,470
COMMON STOCK				
Railroad	.1	67,107,991		
Utility	3.7	2,146,267,623		
Bank	2.3	1,347,503,934		
Insurance	.4	246,109,380		
Savings & Loan	.0	18,091,471		
Miscellaneous	20.7	12,078,172,897		
Parents, Subs, Affils.	9.6	5,585,495,264		
TOTAL COMMON STOCK			36.8	21,488,748,560
PREFERRED STOCK			3.9	2,257,540,438
OTHER ASSETS			16.2	9,536,721,767
TOTAL ADMITTED ASSETS			100.0	58,460,689,235

SOURCE: *Best's Aggregates & Averages,* 1973.

The Investment of Property Insurance Company Funds

Property insurance, like life insurance, is big business. In order to provide an extra guaranty of ability to pay losses, property insurance companies maintain large capital funds. In addition, they have the reserves accumulated out of premiums that are collected on insurance policies in advance. All of these items provide the funds that must be invested and which in turn produce investment income for the companies.

Life insurance companies are permitted to invest only in high-grade securities and limited amounts of the highest quality common stocks. Fire and casualty insurance companies are not so restricted. Property insurance companies have substantial investments in common stock. The pattern of investments of these companies may be observed from Table 12-1.

QUESTIONS

1. Describe the development of investment companies in the United States.
2. Identify the principal differences between investment companies and other savings institutions such as mutual savings banks and savings and loan associations.
3. Although closed-end investment companies usually sell no additional securities after their initial authorization of securities has been distributed, many such companies have increased substantially in size as measured by the value of their assets. Explain.
4. The closed-end form of investment company enjoyed its principal popularity in the twenties. Open-end funds have become far more important to the investing public since that time. From your understanding of the differences in operations of these two types of institutions, how would you explain this shift in popularity?
5. Explain how the price of open-end investment company shares is determined in contrast with closed-end investment company shares.
6. The price at which a share of an open-end investment company may be purchased differs from the price at which the share may be redeemed. Explain.
7. Describe three situations in which one of the forms of living trust would be appropriate.
8. Explain why the irrevocable trust arrangement is utilized since it removes control over trust assets by the maker of the trust.
9. Discuss the significance of a trust institution's investment of funds under the legal-list limitation as opposed to the prudent-man rule.
10. Explain the development and significance of the common trust fund.
11. Describe the principal trust services provided for corporations.
12. Describe the financial contributions made by insurance companies to the economy of the United States.
13. From the viewpoint of financial contribution to the economy, is there any substantial distinction between term insurance and whole life insurance?
14. Discuss the fundamental difference in objectives of life insurance and annuity insurance.
15. Describe the types of investments made by life insurance companies. Why have life insurance companies invested their funds to only a limited extent in common stocks? Comment on any change in pattern of investments of life insurance companies over the last 15 years.
16. Describe the various major types of property insurance contracts.
17. Compare the pattern of investments of property insurance companies with that of life insurance companies.

SUGGESTED READINGS

BICKELHAUPT, DAVID L., and JOHN H. MAGEE. *General Insurance,* 8th ed. Homewood, Illinois: Richard D. Irwin, Inc., 1970. Parts IV & V.

HAYES, DOUGLAS A. *Investments: Analysis and Management,* 2d ed. New York: The Macmillan Company, 1966.

KENNEDY, JOSEPH C. *Corporate Trust Administration.* New York: New York University Press, 1961.

KULP, C. A., and JOHN W. HALL. *Casualty Insurance,* 4th ed. New York: The Ronald Press Company, 1968. Part I.

LATANE, HENRY A., and DONALD L. TUTTLE. *Security Analysis and Portfolio Management.* New York: The Ronald Press Company, 1970. Chapter 3.

MAGEE, JOHN H., and OSCAR N. SERBEIN. *Property and Liability Insurance,* 4th ed. Homewood, Illinois: Richard D. Irwin, Inc., 1967.

WRIGHT, LEONARD T. *Principles of Investments: Text & Cases.* Columbus, Ohio: Grid, Inc., 1972. Chapter 15.

13

Other Sources of Long-Term Business Financing

In addition to the institutions providing long-term funds for business discussed in the preceding chapters, many other types of institutions play an important part in providing such financing. Some of these institutions are discussed in greater detail elsewhere in this book because they engage in short-term lending as their principal activity. Their long-term lending operations, however, are discussed in this chapter. Other institutions and sources of long-term financing discussed in this chapter are concerned almost entirely with long-term financial arrangements. In still other cases, institutions have been established for the specific purpose of providing long-term financial assistance to businesses that cannot obtain such financing on reasonable terms from other sources. Such institutions are generally sponsored by federal, state, or local governments. The sources to be discussed in this chapter are:

Commercial banks
Mutual savings banks
Business corporations
Eleemosynary institutions
Regional development companies
Small Business Investment Companies
Investment development companies
Lease arrangements and equipment trust financing

COMMERCIAL BANKS

In Part 1 the commercial banking system was described as providing the foundation for business credit throughout the nation. It was observed that commercial banks invest heavily in short-term business loans. These banks, however, must be discussed with respect to two additional forms of lending activity. These are bank investments in long-term corporate securities and term loans to business.

Long-Term Corporate Investments by Banks

During the 1920's commercial banks invested heavily in long-term corporate bonds. Because of heavy losses suffered by the commercial banks of the nation as a result of the forced sale of such securities to meet depositors' demands during the depression of the thirties, there was a widespread shift to municipal, state, and federal securities.

As the law now stands, commercial banks are generally permitted to invest in corporate bonds as long as they are of investment quality and are marketable under ordinary circumstances with reasonable promptness at fair value. Bonds that have a wide public interest and investment holding are preferred in this connection because the breadth of the market enhances the marketability of the securities. The law generally restricts banks to an investment of not more than 10 percent of their capital and surplus in the securities of any one corporation.

Despite these restrictions and the general preference of banks today for government securities, long-term corporate securities continue to be held to a limited extent. As of December, 1973, commercial banks held approximately $11 billion of corporate securities as investments.[1]

Term Loans by Commercial Banks

The *bank term loan* represents an interesting and significant development in the lending practices of commercial banks. This type of loan differs from the usual bank business loan in that it

---

[1] *Federal Reserve Bulletin* (Washington, D.C.: Board of Governors of the Federal Reserve System, January, 1974), p. A26.

has a maturity exceeding one year. Also, the term loan requires repayment in installments throughout the life of the loan. Such installment repayments may be on a monthly, a quarterly, or a yearly basis.

Development of Term Loans by Banks. Term lending on the part of the commercial banks of the nation appears to have begun during the depression years of the thirties. Although the term loan was contrary to the generally accepted concept of bank lending activity, there were several reasons for its rapid growth and acceptance by the banks of the nation. First, banks utilized the term-loan arrangement as a convenient means of investing their surplus funds. These surplus funds accumulated in large part from a decline in the demand on the part of business establishments for short-term credit. Second, a higher return could be realized on the term loans than on the usual business loan. Third, the Securities Act of 1933 made it more difficult for the corporations of the nation to secure money through public distribution of securities, and the incentive was strong on the part of business corporations to negotiate directly with banks to finance their intermediate-term capital needs. Fourth, the commercial banks were encouraged by the federal government to engage in this type of lending activity. This encouragement took the form of direct recommendations, which were reflected in the reports of bank examiners. Finally, the term loan provided banks with an alternative to investment in the securities of the federal government and of the states and municipalities. The yields on government securities had been reduced to unprecedented lows.

In the post-World War II period, the American Bankers Association lent its support to the term-lending arrangement and encouraged its members to explore more fully the potential offered by such loans. By 1940 the tremendous growth and popularity of term loans had established them as one of the most important and significant lending innovations by the banks of the nation. During World War II, term lending declined because of the inability of businesses to establish long-range plans for expansion and because special governmental lending programs were established to care for the financing of war production. In the postwar period, however, the volume of such loans increased at a very rapid rate.

By the end of 1973, the volume of term loans outstanding on the part of 160 large commercial banks was nearly $41 billion. As an indication of the relative importance of this total, it is about 40 percent of the total of all commercial and industrial loans by these banks. The loans of these 160 large banks constitute approximately 70 percent of the loans of all commercial banks.[2]

The Term Loan Agreement. The *term loan agreement* takes the form of a detailed written contract between the bank and the borrower. Term loans may be secured by specific property as collateral or they may be unsecured, depending upon the situation that prevails in each case. Among other things, the bank frequently requires a business to maintain a certain minimum amount of net working capital. In the event the net working capital of the business should fall below the stipulated amount, dividends or the salaries of executives may be reduced or curtailed until such time as the appropriate level of net working capital is reestablished.

It is also frequently stipulated in the agreement that the business is not to dispose of its fixed assets without the permission of the bank or to incur other indebtedness without specific permission. Another common provision is that insurance must be carried on the lives of key men of the business establishment with the bank as beneficiary. Some banks carry blanket insurance policies on the lives of executives of companies receiving term loans. Another requirement may be that changes in management personnel, changes in production methods or items of production, and increases in executive salaries or bonuses be approved by the bank before being undertaken by the business.

Despite the restrictive nature of the many protective covenants that usually accompany the term loan, businessmen have generally found the arrangement to their advantage. In any event, the protective covenants establish only fair and reasonable protection against undesirable business activities of management. Also, the simplicity of the term loan arrangement, as well as its cost, renders it far more desirable under many circumstances than funds that may be secured through the public sale of securities or through other media.

---

[2] *Ibid.*, p. A29.

MUTUAL SAVINGS BANKS

Mutual savings banks are legally regarded as banks and are eligible for insurance under the provisions of the Federal Deposit Insurance Corporation. Similarity to commercial banking operations, however, ends with the deposit of the customer's savings. Mutual savings banks provide no checking account facilities and concentrate entirely upon serving as savings institutions. These institutions are located primarily in New York, New Jersey, and in the New England states.

Mutual savings banks invest in bonds and notes of railroads, utilities, and industrial companies, and in commercial and residential real estate mortgages. In addition, a few of the mutual savings banks own the common stock of business organizations. In 1951 New York State amended its laws to permit savings banks to invest in common stock. As of December 31, 1973, mutual savings banks had total assets of more than $106 billion. Approximately 16 percent of mutual savings banks' total assets are invested in the long-term securities of business enterprises.[3]

BUSINESS CORPORATIONS

The business corporations of the nation not only are large users of funds but also play a significant part in providing long-term capital for other businesses. Such capital is provided in several ways. First of all, a corporation may invest capital in a subsidiary company for purposes of control. In other cases, a corporation may invest in the securities of another company when that company is an important supplier of materials to the investing company. Such investment is often undertaken to insure a smooth flow of materials that are required for manufacture. For example, one of the large automobile manufacturing companies loaned a substantial sum of money to one of the major steel corporations in return for which the automobile company received an appropriate interest return plus a guarantee of a priority over other purchasers of supplies of steel.

In still other cases, corporations in setting up sinking funds for retirement of their own outstanding bonds may direct the sinking

---

[3] *Annual Report of the Federal Deposit Insurance Corporation*, December 31, 1973, p. 7.

fund trustee to invest accumulated contributions to the fund in the securities of other corporations. When the maturity of their own bonds is reached, these investments are liquidated and their own bonds are retired with the funds so received. The practice of investing sinking funds in the securities of other companies is now the exception to the rule. Such funds are generally used to retire regularly the bonds for which the sinking funds are set up. Large sums accumulated by the employee pension funds of corporations are invested primarily in long-term securities.

Employee Pension Funds

The establishment of pension funds for the benefit of workers has been a part of the American economy for many years. A major form of pension planning today is that provided by the Social Security Act. Somewhat earlier than this act, the Railroad Retirement Act provided for a retirement benefit for railroad employees; and still other legislation provided for benefits for retired government employees. In recent years employers have shown a willingness to establish private pension plans for employees, generally as a supplement to the Federal Old-Age, Survivors, and Disability Insurance System.

Although the first private pension was adopted by the American Express Company in 1875, a large proportion of the private pension plans now in existence have been established since 1945. Their rapid development since that time has been due in part to union pressure and to the desire of employers to reduce labor turnover by providing greater economic security for their employees. The governmental wage restrictions of the World War II period also played a direct role in encouraging the establishment of employee pension funds by business corporations. The Steel Industry Board in 1949, while disapproving a direct increase in wages for workers in the steel industry, recommended strongly the establishment of private pension plans for the workers. This made it possible for the unions to satisfy the workers' demands without contributing directly to the inflationary pressures that a direct increase in wages would have produced. Corporations were encouraged further to contribute toward pension funds because of high corporate profits taxes. Corporate pension contributions are

Table 13–1

ASSETS OF ALL PUBLIC AND PRIVATE PENSION FUNDS

(Book Value, in billions of dollars)[1]

	1964	1968	1973
Private	77.7	118.0	179.0
Insured pension reserves	25.2	35.0	54.6
(Separate accounts included above).	.1	2.2	9.8
Noninsured pension funds	52.4	83.1	124.4
Public	69.7	98.8	160.0
State and local government	29.9	46.4	80.2
U.S. Government			
Federal Old-age and Survivors			
Insurance	19.1	25.7	36.5
Federal Disability Insurance	2.0	3.0	7.9
Civil Service Retirement and			
Disability Program	14.7	19.4	31.5
Railroad Retirement	3.8	4.2	3.8
Total Private and Public	147.3	216.8	338.9

[1] Figures may not add to totals due to rounding.

SOURCE: *Securities and Exchange Commission.*

treated as deductible business expenses for corporate income tax purposes.

Extent and Administration. It has been estimated that there are about 405,000 private pension plans in existence with approximately 50,000 new plans being formed each year. At present private pension plans cover about 36 million persons, or slightly less than half of the civilian labor force; government pension plans cover roughly another 16 million persons. The pools of savings channeled through pension plans are an important source of funds in the capital markets. Table 13-1 reflects the accumulated funds for all public and private pension funds for selected years.

The majority of pension funds are administered by trust companies or trust departments of banks. In contrast with the regular trust-management functions of the trust companies, there are no general legal restrictions imposed upon the handling of the private pension plans placed under their management. Rather, each trust

Table 13–2

ASSETS OF PRIVATE NONINSURED PENSION FUNDS

(Book Value, in millions of dollars)

	Annual		
	1964	1968	1973
Cash and Deposits	892	1,590	2,300
U. S. Govt. Securities	3,069	2,760	4,330
Corporate Bonds	21,706	27,000	29,810
Preferred Stock	654	1,330	1,240
Common Stock	20,836	41,740	79,200
Mortgages	2,746	4,070	2,710
Other Assets	2,509	4,580	4,770
Total Assets	52,412	83,070	124,360

SOURCE: *Securities and Exchange Commission.*

agreement is complete in itself and provides all of the details relative to administration of funds. Life insurance companies handle approximately one third of all funds paid into private pension accounts. A few large pension funds, such as those of Sears, Roebuck and Company and United States Steel Corporation, are administered by the companies directly.

The Investment of Pension Funds. The distribution of investments of all pension funds other than those managed by life insurance companies is shown in Table 13-2. Note that common stock has become the most important form of investment.

Trust institutions have generally avoided investing funds in the securities of corporations from which such funds have been derived, partly as a matter of sound financial policy and partly as a result of certain requirements on such investments imposed by the United States Treasury Department. Pension funds managed by life insurance companies are invested largely in corporate debt securities and residential and commercial real estate mortgages.

Recent legislation in most states allows life insurance companies to maintain separate investment accounts, each set up for a given pension plan or group of plans. Considerably more investment latitude is permitted for these separate accounts than in life insurance investments generally.

ELEEMOSYNARY INSTITUTIONS

The assets of such organizations as educational institutions, charitable organizations, philanthropic institutions, hospitals, and religious bodies have been increasing at a rapid rate throughout most of the history of the United States. The assets of these institutions now total many billions of dollars, much of which is currently invested in stocks and bonds of business corporations. The Council for Financial Aid to Education lists 60 colleges and universities with endowments in excess of $35 million. The total amount shown for these endowments is $9.7 billion. In addition there are a host of foundations, public trusts, and registered hospitals with endowments aggregating as much, perhaps, as those of the colleges and universities.

REGIONAL DEVELOPMENT COMPANIES

Another source of long-term capital is that provided by organizations which attempt to encourage the establishment of new businesses in their particular geographical areas. Several of these organizations have been in operation for many years and have a fine record of success. Funds for the operations of regional development companies are usually provided by local business firms or associations. For example, La Crosse, Wisconsin, has an Industrial Association which was organized in 1910 by the Board of Trade of that city. This organization is authorized to assist in the establishment of new businesses in that city by purchasing stock or by making loans to assist individuals or corporations in beginning their operations.

Louisville, Kentucky, has supported such an organization since 1916. This organization, the Louisville Industrial Foundation, will lend up to $100,000 to each concern that it feels inclined to support; and, during the earlier years of the operation of this fund, financial support was occasionally given through the purchase of preferred stock. A long list of very successful corporations in that area owe their establishment and early growth to the support lent them by this organization.

Easton, Pennsylvania, has a Guarantee Fund which is authorized to make loans to prospective business enterprises to be located in that city. Scranton, Pennsylvania, and Baltimore, Maryland, among others, have similar funds for encouraging the establishment of business enterprises in their communities.

An interesting development in the financial support of new enterprises has occurred in New England since World War II. This idea was sponsored by a group of men in private industry in Maine in 1950. This organization, called the Development Credit Corporation, obtained funds from 77 Maine individuals, business concerns, and utilities, which subscribed to $50,000 of capital stock each. In addition, to supplement its capital stock funds, this corporation borrows from commercial banks, savings banks, trust companies, building and loan associations, and insurance companies in that state.

A total of 21 states, including most of the New England states, now have development credit corporations. Laws providing for them are on the books in several other states where they have yet to be organized. These institutions have been of special interest in those states where opposition exists to the use of public funds for credit. The development credit corporations all have certain things in common: they are created by action of a state legislature instead of by a corporate charter, and they are able to sell their stock to businesses and individuals and to obtain pledges of loans from lending institutions based on ratios of their capital and surplus. The pattern is for these corporations to be able to lend out 10 times their paid-in capital stock.

The federal government has recognized the merits of regional development companies by providing financial assistance to them through the facilities of the Small Business Administration.[4] The regional development companies may borrow funds for as long as twenty years from the SBA and may borrow as much as the development company's total outstanding borrowings from all other sources. In addition, the SBA makes loans to both state and local development companies for use in assisting specific small businesses. The SBA may lend up to $350,000 for each small business to be assisted, with a maximum loan maturity of 25 years. These loans may be used for plant construction, expansion, modernization, or conversion, including the purchase of land, buildings,

---

[4] The structure and functions of the Small Business Administration were described in Chapter 9.

equipment, and machinery. The SBA may participate with banks in these loans or may make direct loans.

The development credit corporations are designed to make it possible for businesses with good prospects of success but without adequate financial resources to become established, as well as to permit established companies to expand and employ a greater number of people. Although the total amount of long-term funds provided to business through these regional development companies is not large compared with the total of business credit, it does represent a strategic outlay of funds for the establishment of new businesses and permits the growth of established businesses that are handicapped by a lack of adequate financial resources.

SMALL BUSINESS INVESTMENT COMPANIES

The Small Business Investment Act of 1958 was enacted to help solve the problem of long-term financing for small businesses. Under the Act, the Small Business Administration is authorized to license and regulate certain companies organized to make long-term loans and to supply equity capital to qualifying businesses.[5] These small business investment companies, commonly called SBIC's, may in certain cases borrow from the Small Business Administration to supplement their investment funds. By the end of 1972, the Small Business Administration had licenses outstanding to 274 of these companies. The securities of many of these companies are actively traded in the securities markets.

An important attraction to the promoters and organizers of the SBIC's is the liberal tax treatment to which they are entitled. An SBIC may exempt from corporate income taxes the dividends it receives from investments in small businesses. Both the SBIC and its stockholders may apply against ordinary income any losses sustained from price decline in debentures purchased from small firms, in stock obtained through conversion of such debentures, or in stock obtained through the exercising of stock purchase

---

[5] In Chapter 9 it was noted that the Small Business Administration provides long-term loans as well as short-term loans. Since most of the loans and loan participations of the Small Business Administration have maturities of between five and ten years, it must be regarded as another source of long-term financing. In contrast with the SBIC's, the Small Business Administration limits its financial assistance to loans and does not provide equity capital for small businesses.

warrants. Any profits that have accrued can be taxed as capital gains.

An SBIC may finance a small business through the purchase of debentures that are convertible into stock of the small firm, by the purchase of capital stock or debt securities, or through a long-term loan. Financing provided by an SBIC must be for at least a five-year period, and loans may be for as long as twenty years. During the early years of the Seventies loans and investments by the nation's SBIC's have totaled approximately $160 million each year.

INVESTMENT DEVELOPMENT COMPANIES

Since World War II, a new type of financial organization that has as its primary purpose the provision of venture capital for new and growing business organizations has developed. These companies, in most cases, represent the association of a few wealthy persons interested in taking advantage of growth opportunities of selected speculative enterprises. These venture capital companies, commonly referred to as *investment development companies,* are privately established profit-seeking organizations whose primary function is to provide venture capital not otherwise available to new and growing business ventures. They usually supply equity capital, but some loan capital has been provided when its use seemed appropriate.

In addition to providing the financial backing for new companies, the investment development companies take an active and continuing interest in the companies they finance although they do not necessarily require voting control. They offer expert management counsel and guidance and continuing financial assistance as the companies pass through the various stages of their development. Only one of the investment development companies has offered its securities for public sale.

These organizations generally prefer to invest in enterprises that have new processes or products or make use of new ideas with competitive advantages. They will also provide funds to develop new products or processes that offer prospects for the establishment of profitable business ventures. Investments are usually disposed of by the investment development companies when the success of the venture that has been financed is assured and the securities can be sold at a substantial profit.

Although this type of company is fairly new and the total money invested by all such companies to date is perhaps no more than a few million dollars, it represents an interesting development in the financial field and, if successful, can be expected to become more widespread throughout the United States. It is of particular importance because it represents an attempt on the part of private financial facilities to adapt their operations to the needs of a dynamic economy rather than to depend on government assistance to carry the burden of speculative financial assistance for new ventures.

LEASE ARRANGEMENTS AND EQUIPMENT TRUST FINANCING

The lease arrangement and equipment trust financing do not represent special types of credit flowing from any single form of financial institution; rather, they represent a type of financing arrangement that may be utilized in connection with existing financial institutions.

The Lease Arrangement

It has been estimated that more than 80 percent of all retail establishments rent their places of business under lease arrangements. Many manufacturing corporations also find it to their advantage to rent their plant facilities. One refinement of the typical lease arrangement is that of the construction of certain facilities for the specific use of a particular company. For example, Safeway Stores tries to interest local real estate groups and other persons with the necessary capital to construct buildings to their specifications. After construction, such buildings are leased to Safeway for a period of years in accordance with a predetermined agreement. Through this means the company is benefited by the acquisition of new retail facilities without having to make an outlay of cash or to increase its corporate indebtedness. The extent of plant and general real estate leasing is indicated by the fact that at the end of 1973 life insurance companies alone had outstanding $5.8 billion in rental property.[6]

The lease arrangement is not confined to real estate transactions, and its use has now extended far down the line through the equipment and other facilities of some firms. For example, insurance companies and other types of financial institutions now lease fleets of automobiles and trucks to many of the nation's leading corporations. The increasing use of containers for surface ship transportation has resulted in an extraordinary demand for containers and sources of financing for them. Container leasing has now become significant in volume as their use has been extended from an original emphasis on household furniture to such bulk commodities as fertilizers, cotton, hides, and manufactured products.[7]

The lease arrangement has also found an important use in the electric utility industry. More than 25 companies now lease their nuclear fuel supply or "nuclear cores" for their nuclear power production facilities. The average nuclear power production facility costs more than $1.5 billion at this time and the leasing of the fuel supply represents an attractive form of financing a portion of the required investment.

Municipal Leasing. The lease financing of factories through municipal bonds is especially popular. The process involves the construction of plant facilities by a municipality to the specifications of an industrial firm. Financing is arranged through the sale of municipal bonds to the general public or to individual financial institutions. The plant facilities are leased to the industrial company for a period of years at a rental high enough to cover the interest and retirement of the bonds, plus a small reserve. The advantage to the municipality lies in the attraction of desirable industry. The company is benefited by having at its disposal new and modern physical facilities without an immediate outlay of funds except reasonable rental fees. The fact that interest to the purchasers of municipal bonds is free from federal income tax

---

[6] *Life Insurance Fact Book*, Institute of Life Insurance, 1974, p. 82.

[7] An unusually good article on the subject of equipment leasing has been published in the *New England Economic Review* of the Federal Reserve Bank of Boston (November/December, 1973), pp. 3-30.

liability and often from state income tax liability makes it possible for the municipality to sell its bonds at a much lower cost than could a private corporation. This in turn makes it possible for the municipality to establish a low and attractive rental fee for the tenant corporation.

The popularity and rapid growth of this financial device has led to its severe curtailment by the federal government. The amount of these tax-free municipal bonds for industrial purposes increased from less than $2 million in 1956 to nearly $1.6 billion in 1968. The tax exemptions in this type of industrial aid enabled many large, prosperous firms to obtain low cost financing. At the same time, the federal government was losing tax revenues from many well-to-do individuals and corporations who purchased these bonds.

New federal legislation now eliminates the tax-exempt status of most new issues of industrial aid bonds of over $5 million. Moreover, it prohibits public financing support of large projects by limiting the capital spending of the recipient firm to a total of $5 million in any one location over a period of three years before and three years after the issue. In addition to this new legislation, the Securities and Exchange Commission has issued an administrative ruling requiring issues of industrial revenue bonds of over $300,000 to be fully registered. This regulation adds significantly both to the time and to the cost involved in floating public revenue bond issues. In combination, these changes will severely restrict the use of industrial aid bonds. An exception to the $5 million limitation is the use of industrial revenue bonds to support pollution control projects, solid waste disposal systems, certain transportation facilities, and other specified projects. The use of the lease arrangement for these purposes is growing at a rapid rate.

The Sale and Lease-Back Arrangement. Another lease arrangement involves the sale of property owned by a company and its lease back to the selling company. One important reason for this sale and lease-back arrangement is to acquire additional working capital for business operations. Funds obtained from the sale of fixed assets may be used to take advantage of opportunities at times when a firm finds it either impossible or undesirable to increase the debt or equity of the business. The earnings resulting from the application of these funds may far outweigh the rental cost of the facilities that the company has sold. Also, the rental that is paid thereafter to the new owner of the property is considered to be an expense and, as such, is chargeable against earnings for income tax purposes. It is true, of course, that the business which retains its fixed physical facilities is permitted to charge off against its earnings an amount each year for depreciation purposes; however, the amount that is chargeable for depreciation is limited to a proportion of the improvements on the land. Improvements made on leased property may be amortized for tax purposes over the term of the lease rather than over the number of years specified by the Internal Revenue Service.

As a rule, under the sale and lease-back arrangement, the lessee (the user of the property) is required to carry an appropriate amount of property insurance, to pay property taxes that may be levied upon the property, and otherwise to maintain the property as if he were the owner.

In addition to the benefits that may accrue to a company which engages in the sale and lease-back arrangement with respect to its working capital position, the sale of fixed assets often makes possible the retirement of existing debt that may be carried against such assets on the balance sheet. Under these circumstances, the capital structure of the firm is simplified, which, in turn, may result in a stronger credit position.

Equipment Trust Financing

An important method of financing the purchase of heavy rolling stock, such as locomotives and tank cars, by railroads and expensive equipment in general by other types of businesses is that of the *equipment trust arrangement*. As an alternative to the outright purchase of rolling stock, this device provides for the transfer of title to the equipment by the seller to a trustee. The trustee, generally a trust company or a trust department of a commercial bank, holds title to the equipment but leases it to the business that is to make use of it.

The lessee usually pays from 20 to 25 percent of the cost of the equipment as an initial rental payment. This is comparable to the down payment that is customarily made in connection with a direct purchase. The balance of the cost of the equipment is financed through the sale of *equipment trust obligations* issued by the trustee against the collateral value of the equipment to which the trustee holds title.

It is generally the responsibility of the lessee to maintain the equipment properly, to pay all taxes and insurance charges, and to keep the trustee informed of the location and the condition of the equipment. After the stipulated number of rental payments has been made, title to the equipment is turned over to the lessee. The periodic lease or rental payment is used by the trustee to pay interest on and gradually retire outstanding obligations. When a railroad acquires rolling stock under this arrangement, a metal plate showing the name of the trust institution that holds title to the property is usually attached to each piece of equipment.

Examples of Equipment Trust Financing. As an example of the use of equipment obligations, the Southern Railway Company obtained new equipment at an estimated cost of $18,882,795 on March 19, 1974. The title to the equipment was placed with the Morgan Guaranty Trust Company of New York as trustee. The Railroad paid 20 percent of the cost price in cash, and the trustee sold equipment obligations to finance the remaining 80 percent. These equipment obligations carry rates of from 8 percent for those maturing in 1975 up to 8¼ percent for those maturing in 1989. Among other items of equipment, these obligations financed the purchase of seven diesel electric locomotives, forty 70-ton boxcars, and four hundred 100-ton hopper cars. In addition to the 20 percent payment paid to the trustee for this equipment, the Railroad also unconditionally guarantees the equipment trust obligations. The holders of the equipment obligations, therefore, have a lien on the rolling stock and general claim against the Railroad for the amount of the obligations.

Although in some instances it has been considered desirable for the seller of the equipment to underwrite or guarantee the equipment trust obligations, this is not ordinarily required. In fact, equipment trust obligations have an extremely favorable investment rating, and very few losses on them have been recorded in recent decades. This excellent record of equipment trust obligations has resulted in part from the fact that the rolling stock of

Table 13-3

PARTIAL LIST OF EQUIPMENT OBLIGATIONS OF THE SOUTHERN RAILWAY COMPANY

Name of Issue	Maturity	Original Issue	Cost of Equipment	Paid in Cash	Security
So. Ry. eq. 5⅛s, No. 2 '67	1982	$6,180,000	$ 7,758,000	20%	500 100-ton covered hopper cars
So. Ry. eq. 6s, No. 3, '67 (1st)	1982	$7,200,000	$18,076,031	20%	55 3,600 h.p. diesel electric locomotives
So. Ry. eq. 6½ No. 3 '67 (2nd)	1982	$7,200,000			and 5 3,000 h.p. diesel elec. locomotives
So. Ry. eq. 6s, No. 1 of '68	1983	$8,790,000	$10,988,000	20%	200 100-ton gondola cars and 500 all steel box cars
So. Ry. eq. 6s, No. 2 of 1968	1983	$8,400,000	$10,500,000	20%	500 70-ton boxcars; 84 100-ton boxcars; 50 100-ton bulkhead flatcars

railroads has been in extremely short supply in recent decades, and a trustee can easily reclaim the equipment for the benefit of the holders of the equipment obligations in the event of a default on the part of the railroads. In earlier years, a great proportion of the railroads of the country found it necessary to default on their other fixed financial charges, but they have been loath to miss the regular rental payments on equipment acquired through the equipment trust obligations device, since loss of the equipment would generally impair seriously the efficiency of operations.

Although this financial arrangement came into existence originally as a result of the need on the part of the weaker railroads to obtain new rolling stock, it is now the typical process by which railroads acquire rolling stock. A partial list of the equipment obligations of Southern Railway is shown in Table 13-3.

Advantages of Equipment Trust Financing. For the strong companies, the equipment trust device offers the advantage of a low interest cost because of the security offered the investors. For the weaker companies, it makes possible acquisition of equipment that otherwise could not be obtained. The manufacturer of the equipment is benefited inasmuch as it makes possible the payment to him of cash upon delivery of the equipment. The investor is benefited by being provided with extremely high-grade investment instruments. The trust institution, of course, is benefited to the extent that it earns a fee for serving as trustee in the handling of equipment trust obligations.

Although it may appear that the various parties to the transaction benefit at the expense of the existing creditors of the business, this is not necessarily the case; the acquisition of modern equipment may be required to achieve the efficiency and profits necessary to pay all the debts of a company. The equipment trust device, on the other hand, affords an automatic subordination of claims on the part of existing creditors, inasmuch as the leasing company does not possess title until the equipment has actually been paid for through rental payments.

Equipment trust financing has been used by oil companies for the purchase of tank cars and by air transport companies for the acquisition of airplanes. In these cases and in the railroad industry the arrangement has proved successful and perhaps indispensable, but the profitability of equipment trust financing for other industries is yet undetermined.

Chart 13-1

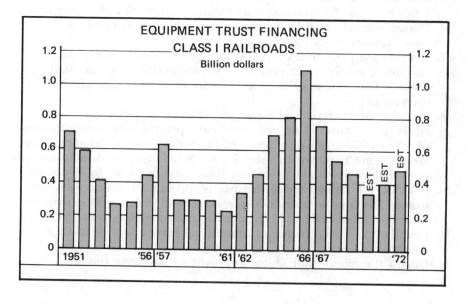

In terms of the dollar volume of equipment trust financing, the figures are not nearly as impressive as those for many other types of financing. Yet, the $500 million volume of such financing estimated by Standard and Poor's Corporation to have been carried out in 1972 was especially vital to an important segment of American industry. The volume of equipment trust financing by Class I railroads from 1951 through 1972 is shown in Chart 13-1 on page 291.

QUESTIONS

1. Describe the role of term loans in commercial banking. As a borrower would you regard a bank term loan to be an acceptable and attractive source of capital?
2. On what logical basis could you as a business borrower object to the protective covenants that are generally incorporated into a term loan agreement?
3. Distinguish between commercial banking and mutual savings banking. Describe the role of mutual savings banks in providing long-term financing for business.
4. Discuss the growth of employee pension funds. How are the pension funds of corporations administered?
5. Discuss the investment of pension funds. In particular, compare the investment of funds administered by life insurance companies with funds managed by administrators other than life insurance companies.
6. Discuss the relationship between eleemosynary institutions and long-term business financing.
7. Describe the pattern of operations of regional development companies. Do you consider such efforts to be worthwhile and generally desirable? Can you describe possible undesirable consequences of such operations?
8. Describe the operations of development credit corporations.
9. Distinguish between the activities and operations of Small Business Investment Companies and those of the Small Business Administration. Would it not have been feasible for the Small Business Administration to extend its operation to include those now provided by the SBIC's?
10. Describe the nature and operations of investment development companies. Discuss the special features of these organizations with emphasis on their basic objectives and methods of long-term financing.
11. Describe the special features of municipal leasing as a financial device to attract industry.
12. Discuss the role of individuals in providing long-term funds.

13. In what way may the lease arrangement be considered a form of long-term financing? As a businessman, would you favor or object to the use of the lease arrangement in general? Describe the reasons for the growing popularity of the sale and lease-back arrangement.
14. Describe the mechanics of financing long-term equipment requirements through the use of the equipment trust arrangement.

SUGGESTED READINGS

HUNT, PEARSON, CHARLES M. WILLIAMS, and GORDON DONALDSON. *Basic Business Finance,* 4th ed. Homewood, Illinois: Richard D. Irwin, Inc., 1971. Chapters 16 and 22.

JOHNSON, ROBERT W. *Financial Management,* 4th ed. Boston: Allyn and Bacon, Inc., 1971. Chapter 14.

JOHNSON, ROBERT W., and WILBUR G. LEWELLEN. "Analysis of the Lease Or Buy Decision." *Journal of Finance* (September, 1972), pp. 815-23.

Leasing in Industry. Studies in Business Policy, No. 127. New York: National Industrial Conference Board, Inc., 1968.

"The Equipment Leasing Industry and The Emerging Role of Banking Organizations." *New England Economic Review.* The Federal Reserve Bank of Boston, November/December, 1973, pp. 3-30.

VAN HORNE, JAMES C. *Fundamentals of Financial Management,* 2d ed. Englewood Cliffs, New Jersey: Prentice-Hall, Inc., 1974. Chapter 17.

14 | Merchandising and Facilitating Agencies for Long-Term Financing

This chapter explores the processes by which the borrowers and the lenders of long-term capital are brought together. Specifically, it describes the activities of the investment bankers as they relate to the origination, distribution, and sale of long-term corporate securities and the activities of the over-the-counter market and securities exchanges in serving as facilitating media for the transfer of outstanding securities.

INVESTMENT BANKING

The process of marketing to the general public securities issued by private corporations is complicated and time-consuming. Corporations usually find it convenient to use independent distributors in selling their products; they find it even more to their advantage to utilize the services of professional groups whose primary activity is that of marketing securities. The average corporation has infrequent occasion to issue long-term securities, and the technicalities of such issues are so great that it is difficult for corporate executives to keep abreast of legal requirements or investor attitudes.

The groups whose function it is to market long-term securities are generally referred to as *investment bankers*. These investment bankers, therefore, are the middlemen between corporations and the general public in the accumulation of investment funds. The legal form of organization used for investment banking purposes includes both the partnership and the corporation.

Functions of Investment Bankers

Although the specific activities of investment bankers may differ, depending upon the size and the financial resources of the company, the primary functions of investment banking in general are:

1. Originating
2. Purchasing and underwriting
3. Wholesaling and retailing

Originating. The investment banker assists the issuing corporation by offering recommendations as to the types and the terms of securities that should be sold and by aiding the corporation in the registration processes required by the Securities and Exchange Commission. Before an investment banking firm undertakes to originate an issue of securities, it makes a detailed study of the corporation in order to determine the feasibility of security distribution. Most of the larger investment banking firms engage in the originating function.

Purchasing and Underwriting. Investment bankers not only offer the facilities through which securities are channeled to the investing public, but they also assume the risk arising from the possibility that such securities may not be purchased by investors. To accomplish this, they enter into a purchase agreement with the issuing corporation. The securities are then purchased in their entirety by the investment bankers after which they are offered for sale to investors at a price sufficiently higher than their cost to assure a profit from operations. Under these circumstances the corporation issuing the securities is free to contract for the construction of additional plant facilities or to make other commitments without having to wait until the securities have been sold.

Under the laws of several states, when a corporation issues additional shares of voting stock or any security that may be converted into voting stock, such securities must be offered for sale first to the existing holders of voting stock in the corporation. The purpose of this regulation is to permit existing stockholders to maintain their proportions of voting power and their claims to assets and earnings of the company. This priority is referred to as the *preemptive right*. Corporate charters may provide for such priority on the part of existing stockholders in states that do not require it. To make the new issues of securities attractive to existing stockholders, the company will generally offer the securities at a discount from the market price.

It may appear, then, that the investment bankers serve their purpose only with respect to the initial issue of securities for public sale by a company and that subsequent issues are simply offered to the holders of the company's earlier issues of voting stock. Despite the discount price at which new issues of securities may be offered to a company's existing stockholders, however, a severe break in the market price of the stock during the period when the additional stock is being issued may eliminate the company-established discount from market price. Under this circumstance, investors will not be inclined to invest further in the company on the basis of the price of the securities set by the company. As a result, the company has an unsuccessful flotation and does not receive the money from the sale of securities on which it may have been depending to carry out its commitments.

In view of the uncertainty of success of an issue of securities, even when offered to existing stockholders at a discount price, the investment bankers may again enter the picture. The investment bankers enter into a *standby underwriting agreement* whereby they agree to purchase from the corporation all securities not taken by the stockholders or the public. This standby function of the investment bankers permits the corporation to proceed with its plans with the assurance of receiving its funds from the sale of securities, notwithstanding the uncertainties of the securities markets. The issuing corporation pays the investment bankers a fee for their assumption of the risk of an unsuccessful flotation of securities. Although there is a clear distinction between the purchasing and the standby underwriting activities of the investment bankers, the term "underwriting" is generally used to include both activities.

Another category of investment banking activity for corporations issuing securities is that of *best-effort selling*. Under this arrangement, the investment bankers make a best-effort to sell the securities of the issuing corporation, but they assume no risk for a possible failure of the flotation. The investment bankers are paid a fee for those securities that they sell. Securities are handled on a best-effort basis for either of two reasons. First, the investment bankers may anticipate so much difficulty in selling the securities that they are unwilling to assume the underwriting risk; and second, the issue of securities may appear to be so certain of successful sale, because of the strength and reputation of the company, that the issuing company itself is willing to assume the risk of an unsuccessful flotation.

Wholesaling and Retailing. A few of the large investment banking houses confine their activities entirely to the originating, underwriting or purchasing, and wholesaling functions, depending upon the sale of securities to retail security brokers for their further disposition. The vast majority of large investment banking houses, however, not only wholesale their securities to independent security brokerage houses, but they also maintain their own retail outlets in the major cities of the country.

In addition to the retail outlets maintained by the large investment banking houses, there are many independently owned and operated retail brokerage outlets. Many of these independent brokerage houses, while of insufficient size and strength to engage in major originating and underwriting functions, purchase small blocks of securities from the underwriters for resale. Like the underwriters, they depend upon the resale of the securities for a price above their cost to cover their expenses and provide profit from operations.

The investment banking firm that is selected by a company to handle the distribution of its securities is called the "originating house." It should be kept in mind, however, that much cooperation exists between investment bankers. For larger issues of securities there may be three or four principal investment banking firms working together in the originating function. These firms are referred to as the "nucleus group." Beyond cooperation in the originating function is a far more substantial degree of cooperation in the underwriting and selling functions. For large issues of securities, thirty or forty investment banking firms may be invited by the originating group to assume part of the risk of the underwriting and to share in the profits resulting from the sale of the securities. For very large issues two or three hundred firms may participate in the underwriting and distribution efforts.

Competitive Bidding

In contrast with industrial companies, where arrangements are typically negotiated between the company and the chosen investment banking group, governmental bodies generally require competitive bidding by investment banking houses before awarding issues for underwriting purposes. This is true also of railroad securities and of some public utilities. Under these circumstances, there may be little initial negotiation between the investment houses and the issuer. Rather, the issuer decides upon the size of issue and the type of security which it wishes to sell and invites the investment banking houses to offer bids for handling the securities. The investment banking group offering the highest price for the securities and providing information to indicate its ability to carry through a successful flotation of the securities will generally be awarded the contract. From that point on, the process of security distribution may be much like that of the handling of securities of an industrial corporation.

A great deal of controversy has existed with respect to the relative advantages and disadvantages of competitive bidding by investment banking houses. Investment bankers contend vigorously that the continuing counsel which they make available to the corporations served is essential to an economical and efficient distribution of the securities of such companies. Others contend that competitive bidding results in a higher price being paid to the issuer for the securities than would otherwise be the case. Much evidence has been presented by both sides, and it is safe to say that securities will continue to be distributed under both arrangements.

Market Stabilization

Investment bankers generally consider the stabilization of market prices for the securities that they are attempting to sell to be an essential feature of their operations. Because the steady flow of the new securities to the market may depress the price temporarily, it is sometimes necessary to "buy in" some of the securities in order to relieve the market of its congestion. Although the action of investment bankers to stabilize the markets for the issues that they are distributing is often regarded as a form of manipulation, its objective is the elimination rather than the creation of wide price fluctuations. It is also argued that market stabilization interferes with the normal operations of supply and demand and that it may lead to the overpricing of securities.

Although the Securities Exchange Act of 1934 prohibits manipulation of this sort on the part of all others, underwriters are permitted to engage in the activity for purposes of reasonably maintaining the price of the securities that they are marketing. When market stabilization is intended, however, it is necessary to state that fact in the information or *prospectus* that is provided for purchasers of registered securities.

Direct Placements

In addition to the securities distributed by investment bankers, corporations sell a substantial volume of securities directly to investors. Because of the unusually large supply of investable funds held by such institutions as life insurance companies and trust companies in the post-World War II period, well-known corporations could sell their securities easily. Such direct placements eliminate the complexities of security registration with the Securities and Exchange Commission. Although the relative proportion of direct placements to those handled through the investment bankers has declined, it remains a substantial amount. The private placement of bonds and other long-term debt obligations has recently constituted approximately 40 percent of all long-term debt financing.

Even in connection with direct placements, the issuing corporation may find it convenient to seek the assistance of the investment banker in negotiating the arrangement. As in best-effort selling, the investment banker serves only as an agent and assumes no risk, receiving a fee based on services rendered.

Regulation of Investment Banking

Federal regulation of investment banking is administered primarily under the provisions of the Securities Act of 1933. The chief purposes of the Act are to provide full, fair, and accurate disclosure of the character of securities offered for sale in interstate commerce or through the mails and to prevent fraud in the sale of such securities. Disclosure is achieved by requiring the filing of a registration statement with the Securities and Exchange Commission and the delivery of a prospectus to prospective investors. The Securities and Exchange Commission does not pass upon the investment merits of securities, and it is illegal for a seller of securities to represent the Commission's approval of a registration statement as constituting a recommendation of investment quality. The philosophy underlying the Act is that the most effective regulatory device is the requirement of furnishing complete and accurate information on which investment decisions may be made. Although the Securities and Exchange Commission does not guarantee the accuracy of any statement made by an issuer of securities in a registration statement or prospectus, legal action may be taken against officers and other representatives of the issuing company for any incorrect statements and misrepresentations.

In addition to federal regulation of investment banking, most of the states have blue-sky laws to protect investors from fraudulent security offerings. *Blue-sky laws* apparently receive their name from the efforts of some unscrupulous operators to sell portions of the blue sky—operators for whom the sky is the limit in their security dealings. Because the laws of the various states differ with respect to the specific nature of regulation of security selling, the efforts of the states are limited in their effectiveness by the difficulties of administering interstate security operations. Thus, the regulatory actions of the federal government provide the principal basis for regulation of investment banking.

OVER-THE-COUNTER MARKET

The security houses that make up the over-the-counter market serve not only to distribute new securities to the investing public but also to provide a secondhand market for securities for the public in general; that is, they stand ready to buy as well as sell securities. It is important at this point to distinguish between over-the-counter operations and security exchange operations.

In the over-the-counter markets, securities are purchased and sold by dealers who act as principals. They buy from and sell to the public, other dealers, and commission brokers for their own account. In a sense, they operate in somewhat the manner of any merchant; they have an inventory, comprised of the securities in which they specialize, which they hope to sell at a figure high enough above the purchase price to provide a profit.

The security exchanges, discussed later in this chapter, provide only facilities where members may buy and sell securities among themselves. The nonmember investor does not have access to the floor of the exchange; hence he must secure the services of a person who does have membership and floor-trading privileges. The brokers that represent the public in floor-trading activities on the exchange serve only as agents and hence must represent their customers to the best of their ability.

Securities Traded in the Over-the-Counter Market

Among the securities handled exclusively through the over-the-counter market may be included real estate bonds, Federal Land Bank and Federal Home Loan Bank bonds, state bonds, municipal bonds, equipment trust obligations, and bank and insurance company stocks. In addition, the over-the-counter market handles the securities of many industrial and utility corporations. Some securities of industrial, utility, and railroad companies are handled both on the exchanges and through the over-the-counter market.

Making a Market

When an over-the-counter dealer stands ready to buy or sell a particular security or group of securities at specified prices, he is said to be *making a market* for the security. Under these circumstances, he will offer for the security a price at which he feels he can profit from a resale of the security to other investors. The quotation which is made by a dealer making a market for a given security is referred to as the *bid-and-asked price*, the bid being that price he is willing to pay for the securities and the asked price being the figure at which the dealer is willing to sell the security. Hence, the margin or spread between bid and asked price for a security is readily apparent from its quotations. Quotations shown in Table 14-1 indicate the spread for a few of the over-the-counter issues as of March 15, 1974.

A security that is traded frequently and has a ready market can be expected to have a narrower spread than a security that is traded infrequently. Since an over-the-counter dealer cannot make a market for the many thousands of securities in existence, he confines his activities to a limited number of securities. However, the over-the-counter dealer will buy securities and will provide a sale for securities in which he does not necessarily specialize. This is accomplished through an arrangement whereby the dealer contacts other investment dealers making a market for the securities in question. The over-the-counter dealer who receives a request for the purchase or sale of securities in which he does not specialize will immediately contact by telephone, wire, or other means dealers who are known to make a market for the security. After a reply is received indicating the quotation, the dealer will contact his customer and negotiate the transaction. A broker serving as an intermediary in negotiating over-the-counter transactions must specify whether he is serving the customer as a principal or as an agent. If the broker is acting in the capacity of a principal, he shares in the proceeds of the sale or purchase. If he acts as an agent, he adds his commission to the best price that he is able to negotiate for his customer.

For the more popular issues, the process of contacting a dealer specializing or making a market in the security may require only a phone call to a nearby dealer in the same community. In some cases, however, a security presented for sale or requested for purchase may be so little known to the dealer that he may have to determine from among the thousands of over-the-counter dealers of the country which dealers make a market for the security in

Table 14–1

SELECTED OVER-THE-COUNTER QUOTATIONS
NEW YORK MARKET

March 15, 1974

	BID	ASKED
Dairy Queen St	9	$9\frac{1}{2}$
Daniel Intl	$29\frac{1}{4}$	30
Danker Wohlk	$2\frac{3}{8}$	$2\frac{7}{8}$
Dant Russ	$13\frac{1}{2}$	$14\frac{1}{2}$
Dart Drug	$4\frac{1}{4}$	$4\frac{5}{8}$
Data 100 Corp	$12\frac{1}{8}$	$12\frac{5}{8}$
Datapoint Crp	15	$15\frac{3}{4}$
Datascope Cp	$13\frac{3}{4}$	$14\frac{3}{4}$
Debron Cp	12	$12\frac{3}{4}$
Decision Data	$11\frac{1}{2}$	12
Dekalb Ag	$45\frac{3}{4}$	$46\frac{3}{4}$
Del Mon Pr	$14\frac{3}{4}$	$15\frac{3}{4}$
Delhi Intl Oil	$4\frac{3}{4}$	$5\frac{1}{4}$
Deluxe CPr	35	$35\frac{3}{4}$
Dento Med Ind	$1\frac{3}{4}$	$2\frac{1}{8}$
Dep Guart	$31\frac{1}{2}$	33
Det Bnk Cp	$41\frac{1}{2}$	$42\frac{1}{4}$
Diagnostic Da	13	14
Diam Crys	$11\frac{3}{8}$	$11\frac{7}{8}$
Diamndhead	$7\frac{3}{8}$	$7\frac{7}{8}$
Dia Shmpf	21	$21\frac{3}{4}$
Digicon Inc	$5\frac{5}{8}$	$6\frac{3}{8}$
Discnt NY	$36\frac{1}{2}$	$38\frac{1}{2}$
Div Earth Sci	$2\frac{7}{8}$	$3\frac{3}{8}$

SOURCE: National Association of Security Dealers, Inc.

question. This process is not so difficult as might seem at first, since the National Quotation Bureau, Inc., provides a service which reveals the dealers throughout the nation that are making markets for or specializing in specific securities.

National Quotation Bureau, Inc.

This organization has three divisions—an eastern division with its main office in New York, a western division with its office in

Chicago, and a Pacific Coast division located in San Francisco. Each day subscribers to this service, that is, participating dealers, who wish to present their quotations on securities on which they are making a market will forward such information by telephone or wire to the office of their district. These quotations, generally sent in the morning, are sorted in the early afternoon and reproduced for distribution. These daily quotations may run more than a hundred pages and contain several thousand bond and stock issues. By early evening the reproduced quotations are ready for delivery to subscribing dealers throughout the country. By the time the dealers open their offices for business the following morning, they have on their desks the quotations offered by specializing dealers that are less than 24 hours old.

Through the use of this service, a dealer in any part of the country is able to quote a recent quotation 'on practically any security for which there is a public market.

For a wide range of quotations, however, it is necessary only for the broker to refer to his desk unit called Quotron, or some similar equipment system. These commercial electronic reporting devices not only provide complete quotation data on all stocks and bonds listed on the major stock exchanges of the nation but a large number of over-the-counter stocks, mutual funds, and major commodities. In February, 1971, the National Association of Security Dealers formally commenced operations of the NASDAQ automated quotations system with approximately 2,300 over-the-counter securities. The system is operated by Bunker-Ramo Corporation for the NASD.

Regulation, of the Over-the-Counter Market

Under the Securities Exchange Act of 1934, all brokers and dealers doing business in interstate commerce must be registered with the Securities and Exchange Commission. Under the Maloney Act of 1938, brokers and dealers were authorized to form national associations to govern and to establish practices of fair trade for their industry. This was one instance where regulation was requested of the government by business itself, and it appears to stem from the fact that reputable dealers in the investment field had little protection against bad publicity resulting from the unscrupulous practices of a few over-the-counter dealers. Under this provision only one such national association, the National Association of Security Dealers, has been formed.

The National Association of Security Dealers has established a lengthy set of rules and regulations intended to insure fair play and responsibility on the part of the member associations. Any broker or dealer engaged in that type of business is eligible to become a member of the NASD as long as he can prove a record of responsible operation and if he is willing to accept the code of ethics provided by the NASD. At present approximately 3,900 registered security firms are members of the Association.

SECURITY EXCHANGES

At present there are 12 security exchanges in the United States. These exchanges are outgrowths of informal arrangements for trading in securities at convenient locations in the nation's cities. The New York Stock Exchange, for example, had its beginning under the shade of a certain buttonwood tree on Wall Street. At a later date, because of the popularity of this meeting place, traders began to transact business as agents of others. Eventually these traders moved indoors, and they now enjoy spacious and well-equipped quarters and facilities.

The stock exchanges of the nation have applied the latest developments in electronic communications. The present methods of transmitting information within cities and between cities is in sharp contrast with the devices used before the introduction of the telegraph in 1844. Quotations were conveyed between New York and Philadelphia through semaphore signals in the daytime and light signals at night from high point to high point across the state of New Jersey. Although cumbersome compared with modern methods, quotations were often transmitted in this manner in as short a time as ten minutes.

The stock exchanges appear to have come into existence primarily to facilitate trading in local issues; and although there are now only 12 such exchanges in operation, records indicate the existence of more than one hundred exchanges during the nation's history. As recently as 1929, 30 exchanges were in operation. Not only has the number of stock exchanges declined, due in part to

Table 14–2

MARKET VALUE AND VOLUME OF SALES EFFECTED ON REGISTERED AND EXEMPTED SECURITIES EXCHANGES

Breakdown of 1973, Data by Exchanges

	TOTAL MARKET VALUE (Dollars)	STOCKS		BONDS	
		MARKET VALUE (Dollars)	NUMBER OF SHARES	MARKET VALUE (Dollars)	PRINCIPAL AMOUNT (Dollars)
All Registered Exchanges	187,323,367	178,037,429	5,730,092	8,301,786	9,429,667
American Stock Exchange	11,413,566	10,429,640	740,358	406,060	641,923
Boston Stock Exchange	1,793,049	1,792,908	42,171	0	0
Chicago Board of Trade	0	0	0	0	0
Cincinnati Stock Exchange	118,869	118,849	2,838	20	29
Detroit Stock Exchange	380,589	380,532	10,676	0	0
Midwest Stock Exchange	8,136,948	8,131,114	241,484	653	1,213
National Stock Exchange	23,987	23,896	7,462	24	145
New York Stock Exchange	154,664,323	146,450,834	4,336,581	7,865,380	8,736,821
Pacific Coast Stock Exchange	6,388,529	6,315,636	206,234	28,934	48,154
Phila.-Balt.-Wash. Stock Exchange	4,395,727	4,386,341	126,991	715	1,382
Salt Lake Stock Exchange	996	996	2,262	0	0
Spokane Stock Exchange	6,685	6,685	13,031	0	0

SOURCE: *Statistical Bulletin,* United States Securities and Exchange Commission, March 20, 1974, p. 334.

the development of better means of communication between investors in the smaller communities and the large city exchanges, but the nature of their operations has also changed. No longer do the stock exchanges of the nation restrict their trading to local issues, but rather they deal in some securities that are traded on other exchanges and in the over-the-counter market.

Of the 12 exchanges, only two may be considered to be truly national in scope: the New York Stock Exchange and the American Stock Exchange, both of which are located in New York City. Together these exchanges account for almost 90 percent of the dollar volume of security trading on all exchanges. The relative importance of the security exchanges may be observed from Table 14-2, which shows the number of shares and market value of stock traded in a month's operations.

Because of the tremendous relative importance of the New York Stock Exchange and because in most respects its operations are typical of those of the other exchanges, the following description of exchange organization and activities will relate primarily to the New York Stock Exchange.

Exchange Organization

The New York Stock Exchange is a voluntary association of 1,366 members. Like all the stock exchanges of the nation, its objective is to provide a convenient meeting place where buyers and sellers of securities or their representatives may transact business. In addition, the New York Stock Exchange provides facilities for the settlement of exchange transactions, establishes rules relative to the trading processes and the activities of its members, provides publicity for the transactions on the Exchange, and establishes standards for the corporations whose securities are traded on the Exchange. The New York Stock Exchange, then, serves primarily to facilitate the transfer of outstanding securities from investor to investor, and in so doing it contributes significantly to the financial processes of the nation. The existence of a highly efficient secondhand market in securities, as in most fields of activity, provides assurance to the purchaser of new securities that his investment can be readily sold should alternative investments appear more attractive or if funds are needed for other purposes.

Although the number of shares, or seats as they are commonly referred to, on the New York Stock Exchange was increased from 1,100 to its present level of 1,366 in 1929, it is improbable that the number will soon be increased because the physical accommodations for trading activity are limited. As might be expected, membership shares carry a considerable value; and in order to purchase a share it is necessary to negotiate with other shareholders who may be willing to dispose of their membership. During the height of stock market activity in 1929, membership shares on the New York Stock Exchange sold for as much as $625,000, while in 1942 shares sold for as low as $17,000. The cost of shares in the post-World War II period has been within the range of $60,000 to $500,000. Memberships on the exchanges may be grouped into four classes: commission brokers, floor traders, specialists, and odd-lot dealers.

Commission Brokers. The largest group of members on the New York Stock Exchange, the *commission brokers,* maintain offices for the purpose of soliciting business from investors. Many members maintain offices throughout the country.

Floor Traders. *Floor traders* hold membership on the Exchange primarily for their own use. Not only do the floor traders avoid commission charges on their transactions by virtue of their access to the floor of the exchange, but also they are able to determine by direct contact with traders the temper and strength of the market for a security at a particular time. The speculative advantage of such a position is apparent. Because the floor traders are constantly in search of opportunities for even modest profits, their activities give breadth to the entire market. They provide bids and offers when they may not be available from other sources.

Specialists. *Specialists* buy and sell securities for their own account and generally limit their interest to a very few stocks. They also serve as floor brokers for other brokers who place transactions with them.

Odd-Lot Dealers. The *odd-lot dealers* facilitate the purchase and sale of securities in less than round lots. Since the customary trading unit on the Exchange is a round lot of 100 shares of stock, the commission broker who receives an order to buy or sell stock in quantities of less than 100 shares must complete the order in a different way than that used for round-lot orders.[1] The odd-lot dealer "makes" a market for these fractional orders by buying full units of a security through the regular trading facilities and selling these securities in odd lots. Similarly, odd lots that are purchased by these dealers are accumulated until they can be resold as full units. For this service the odd-lot dealers charge a commission which is in addition to the commission that the customer would otherwise pay if he were dealing in lots of 100 shares.

---

[1] For a very few stocks listed on the New York Stock Exchange, the round lot is ten shares.

Listing Securities

The New York Stock Exchange requires that all securities be listed before they may be traded on the Exchange. To qualify for listing its security on the Exchange, a corporation must show evidence of its strength and of interest in its security on the part of investors throughout the nation. The corporation agrees to certain requirements stipulated by the Exchange with regard to the publication of periodic reports and the preparation of such other information for public distribution as will make possible an intelligent analysis of the security. If the security is accepted for listing by the Exchange, the corporation then pays a fee for the privilege. The acceptance of the security for listing on the "big board" does not constitute endorsement of the quality of the security by the Exchange. The securities of approximately 1,500 corporations are listed on the New York Stock Exchange. These securities include common stock, preferred stock, warrants, and bonds.

The American Stock Exchange and all of the regional exchanges permit unlisted trading privileges as well as listed trading privileges. The distinction between these two lies primarily in the method by which the security is placed on the exchange for trading. For unlisted securities, the initiative is taken by the exchange itself instead of the issuing corporation in recommending such securities for trading privileges. Unlisted trading privileges must be approved by the Securities and Exchange Commission. The securities of approximately 1,000 corporations carry unlisted trading privileges on the nation's stock exchanges.

Security Exchange Operations

Orders for the purchase or the sale of securities listed on the New York Stock Exchange may be placed with any one of the approximately 3,300 offices maintained for that purpose by members of the Exchange throughout the nation as well as in some foreign countries. In addition, orders may be placed with approximately 2,700 other firms that have correspondent relations with members of the Exchange. The larger firms maintain an electronic board on which security prices are flashed for the customer's observation. Within the city of New York it is possible to dial the telephone for quotations on leading securities.

Market Orders. The firm that receives an order to purchase 100 shares of stock listed on the New York Stock Exchange at the best price immediately available wires the order to the New York office of the firm, where the order is transmitted by telephone to the floor of the Exchange. An order for immediate execution at the best possible price is referred to as a *market order*. The floor of the Exchange is ringed with telephone booths. These facilities are rented by the commission brokers for the purpose of communicating with their central offices. When the message has been relayed to the floor of the exchange, an employee of the commission broker takes the call and signals to the broker. The broker is called to the telephone to pick up the message by two annunciator boards on which a number is flashed. Each broker has a specified number; and upon seeing his number lighted, he immediately goes to his booth to pick up the order.

Having received the order, the broker proceeds to the location on the floor of the Exchange where trading in the security to be purchased is being carried on. Since securities are always traded at the same location or post, the broker knows exactly where to go to make the purchase. These posts carry the names of stocks traded at that location, the last price at which the security was traded, and a plus or a minus sign indicating whether the last transaction was at a price above or below that for the previous transaction.

As the broker in our example approaches the post, he may hear bids and offers being called out by other brokers. Our broker then participates in the bidding until he obtains as low a price as possible for the security that he is commissioned to purchase. Should the activity in that particular security be negligible at that moment, the broker may have to ask for the last quotation. If the quotation is 43¼ bid ($43.25), 43⅞ offered ($43.875), the broker could immediately make the purchase by accepting the existing offer. In attempting to make the purchase at as low a price as possible for the customer, however, he will probably begin by bidding 43⅜, then 43½, and on up by increments of ⅛ of 1 point until the bid is accepted.

When a transaction takes place, a ticker report is sent to the central computer system via direct electronic signals and, in turn, it is conveyed to display devices across the nation. A section of New York Stock Exchange ticker report and an explanation of the symbols are shown in Figure 14-1.

Figure 14–1

SECTION OF TICKER REPORT OF NEW YORK STOCK EXCHANGE

DI	KN	GM	LLT	PE
30	$43\frac{1}{2}$	$72\frac{7}{8}$	$2s23\frac{1}{8}$	$1000s24\frac{1}{4}$

Explanation: Dresser Industries Incorporated, 100 shares sold at 30; Kennecott Copper, 100 shares sold at $43\frac{1}{2}$; General Motors, 100 shares sold at $72\frac{7}{8}$; Long Island Lighting, 200 shares sold at $23\frac{1}{8}$; Philadelphia Electric Company, 1,000 shares sold at $24\frac{1}{4}$.

Ticker abbreviations appear on the upper line of the tape. Immediately below the last letter of the abbreviation are the number of shares and the price. When the sale is for a round lot of 100 shares, only the price is shown. For multiples of 100 shares from 200 through 900, the first digit of the sales figure is followed by an "s." All volume figures are shown for sales of 1,000 shares and over. The letters "ss" are used to separate the volume from the price for stocks traded in units of 10 rather than 100. Errors and corrections are written out.

The purchase transaction is also sent by memorandum to the broker's telephone booth where the information is transmitted to the central office and then by wire to the brokerage office where the order was originally placed. Later the customer will receive a stock certificate indicating his ownership of 100 shares of the stock. If the investor chooses, the stock may be bought in street name, that is, in the name of his brokerage firm. By so doing, the investor may sell his securities by simply phoning his broker without the necessity of signing and delivering the certificates.

In common use today in the brokerage houses of the nation are computerized devices that permit brokers to obtain the latest stock information for their customers. These devices, in effect, accumulate and store reported informatiori and provide an immediate retrieval of the information upon call.

Limit Orders. As an alternative to the market order, the customer may establish a maximum price that he is willing to pay for the security, or, in the case of the sale of securities, a minimum price at which he is willing to sell. When such limitations are placed upon the broker, the transaction is referred to as a *limit order*.

In our example, if a limited purchase order of 43 had been placed by the customer for the security in question, the order could not have been filled at that moment since other brokers were bidding as high as 43¼. The broker then would have waited until such time as a price of 43 or less became available. Usually, such limit orders away from the current market price are turned over to a specialist who enters it in his book and acts upon it for the commission broker when the price comes within the limit. Of course, if the price of the stock progressed upward rather than back down, the order would not be completed. Limit orders may be placed to expire at the end of one day, one week, one month, or on a G.T.C. (good-till-canceled) basis.

Stop-Loss Orders. The holder of stock may limit his possible loss or protect part of a past increase in the price of his stock by placing a *stop-loss order* at a price a few points below the prevailing market price. In this way the stock is automatically offered for sale when the price of the security falls to the stop-loss price. For example, the purchaser of stock in our example may place a stop-loss order on his stock at a price of 40. The commission broker makes no effort to sell the stock until the price falls to that figure, whereupon it is sold for as high a price as possible. This type of order does not guarantee a price of 40 to the seller, since by the time the stock is actually sold, the price may have declined rapidly to well below 40.

Short Sales. The *short sale* may be defined as the sale of securities that the seller does not own but which are borrowed for the purpose in anticipation of a price decline in the security. In the event that a price decline does occur, the short seller covers his short position by buying enough stock to repay the lender.

As an example of the operation of a short sale, assume that a person believes that the price of a certain security is going to fall. If the individual owns that particular stock, he may dispose of it as quickly as possible in order to avoid the loss. In addition, or alternatively, he may turn the situation to his advantage by selling short, that is, by selling stock in excess of that held in his portfolio. Short sales may be made by anyone who has established favorable customer relations with a brokerage firm. It is not necessary that the person have the particular security in his portfolio.

Let us assume that 100 shares of a particular stock are to be sold short. The order is placed through the broker, who in turn arranges to borrow the necessary stock to be sold short. The brokerage house handling the order may secure the stock for the short sale from its other customers, with their permission. When the brokerage house is unable to draw upon its own customers' holdings for this purpose, it generally bargains with another brokerage house.

Having sold the securities which have been borrowed for that purpose, the brokerage house delivers to the lender of the securities the proceeds of the sale of the securities to be held by him as collateral. If the price at which the securities were sold was 50, then the proceeds from the sale of 100 shares, $5,000, would be turned over to the lender of the stocks. Regulation T of the Board of Governors of the Federal Reserve System, as well as regulations of the New York Stock Exchange, require the short seller to maintain a margin or deposit with the broker equivalent to a specified percentage of the value of the stock sold short. Loans of stock are callable on 24 hours' notice. If the short seller covers his short position at the end of thirty days by which time the stock has dropped to a price of 40, he pays $4,000 for 100 shares to be returned to the lender of the stock. The short seller receives the $5,000 that was posted as collateral and has a $1,000 profit from the transaction, minus brokerage fees. Should the price of the security move upward rather than downward, the short seller must, of course, cover his short position by paying more for the stock than the price at which it was sold, with the result that a loss rather than a gain is experienced.

Because short sales have an important effect on the market for securities, the SEC now regulates them.

Margin Purchases. Securities may be purchased by delivering to the broker only part of the purchase price and using the securities so purchased as collateral for a loan to make up the balance of the purchase price. This is known as *buying on the margin.* The purchaser of the securities need not arrange the financing personally since the brokerage houses have constant contact with banks for this purpose. If the price of the securities that have been offered as collateral begins to decline, the customer may be required to reduce the loan by paying additional cash or by placing additional securities as collateral. In the event of a continuing decline in the market for securities pledged as collateral and the failure of the customer to reestablish the required margin, the bank or brokerage house may sell the securities.

Because of the inflationary aspects of a large volume of margin trading, the federal government has limited the extent to which securities may be purchased under this arrangement. In earlier times it was unusual but possible for a person to buy securities by paying in only 10 percent of the purchase price and borrowing the remainder. The leverage that is obtained from such an action is obvious. If the individual should purchase securities having a market price of $10,000 by contributing only $1,000 in cash and by borrowing $9,000, a 10 percent increase in the price of the securities would increase their market value to $11,000, which, if sold, would result in a 100 percent gain to the person making the margin purchase. Of course, if the market price should drop by 10 percent, the purchaser's entire investment is wiped out.

For a period during World War II, the Board of Governors of the Federal Reserve System, through which margin requirements are regulated for the federal government, prohibited margin trading because of its inflationary implications. Since World War II, margin requirements have been changed frequently.

Regulation of Security Trading

At the present time, corporations issuing securities for public distribution are subject to both state and federal regulation. Although state laws and controls, sometimes referred to as *blue-sky laws,* are generally administered well, the very size of many corporations has rendered it necessary to have some form of national control over their activities. The basis of most federal regulation over security trading is the Securities Exchange Act of 1934. It was the purpose of the Act to facilitate the analysis of securities for investment purposes (1) by requiring that information pertinent to that end be made readily available to investors and other interested parties; (2) by maintaining fair and orderly markets and eliminating fraudulent acts, and by establishing rules for the activities of exchange members and others representing investors in the securities markets; (3) by limiting and regulating the use of credit in security trading; (4) by regulating the activities of officers of corporations and other insiders having access to information not available to the general public. These objectives are accomplished in part by requiring the registration of securities, exchanges, and broker dealers.

QUESTIONS

1. Describe the basic economic function of investment banking institutions.
2. Describe in detail each step of the investment banking process.
3. Discuss the assumption of risk by investment bankers in the process of marketing securities of corporations. How do investment bankers minimize their risks?
4. Distinguish between the purchase function and the standby function in investment banking.
5. When additional stock of a company is to be offered to existing stockholders at a discount from the market price, why would the services of investment bankers be utilized?
6. The over-the-counter market has been described as a secondhand market. As a secondhand market, what is the contribution of the over-the-counter market to the economic growth of the nation?
7. Describe some of the types of securities traded in the over-the-counter market.
8. Describe the steps involved in an over-the-counter transaction.
9. Explain how over-the-counter market operations are regulated.
10. Describe the types and nature of operations of the nation's securities exchanges.
11. List the various reasons for ownership of membership shares on one or more of the nation's stock exchanges.

12. Describe the steps involved in the completion of a round-lot market order on the New York Stock Exchange. How does the completion of an odd-lot order differ from that of a round-lot order?
13. Margin purchases of a security are usually made in expectation of a price rise. Short sales are made in expectation of a price drop. Explain.

SUGGESTED READINGS

CAROSSO, VINCENT P. *Investment Banking in America.* Cambridge, Massachusetts: Harvard University Press, 1970.

FRANCIS, JACK CLARK. *Investments: Analysis and Management.* New York: McGraw-Hill Book Company, 1972. Chapter 3.

FRIEND, IRWIN, *et al. Investment Banking and the New Issues Market.* New York: The World Publishing Company, 1967.

HAYES, DOUGLAS A. *Investments: Analysis & Management,* 2d ed. New York: The Macmillan Company, 1966.

JOHNSON, ROBERT W. *Financial Management,* 4th ed. Boston: Allyn and Bacon, Inc., 1971. Chapters 15 and 16.

LOLL, LEO M., and JULIAN G. BUCKLEY. *The Over-The-Counter Securities Market,* 3d ed. Englewood Cliffs, New Jersey: Prentice-Hall, Inc., 1973.

WATERMAN, M. H. *Investment Banking Functions.* Ann Arbor: Bureau of Business Research, University of Michigan, 1958.

WESTON, J. FRED, and EUGENE F. BRIGHAM. *Managerial Finance,* 4th ed. New York: Holt, Rinehart, and Winston, Inc., 1972. Chapter 13.

15

Long-Term Business Financing Policies

In the preceding chapters the various types of securities issued by corporations and the many types of institutions which invest in these securities were described in detail. In this chapter we will explore some of the policies that determine long-term financing decisions. There is a wide difference in the financial practices of companies in various industries and in the financial practices of companies within a given industry, reflecting differing policies with respect to the matter of long-term financing. The intent in this chapter is to explore these aspects of policy that are considered in the process of determining an individual company's long-term financial plan.

As the various aspects of long-term financial planning are explored it will become apparent that the element of personal judgment is quite important. That is, the managements of various companies may place different sets of weights on the factors that enter into the financial decision-making process. It is not the intent, however, to describe the "right" method of long-term financing but only to describe those various considerations that financial management should study with great care before making a decision with respect to long-term business financing. Superior long-term financial planning embodies the systematic analysis of these factors.

INTERNAL VERSUS EXTERNAL FINANCING

Long-term financing for most businesses is usually made up of both internal and external forms. For some types of business, in fact, there may be infrequent occasion to approach the capital markets for any type of financial support. These corporations may rely exclusively upon internally generated funds. Other businesses, by virtue of their rapid rate of growth and of the small amount of funds generated internally, may be forced to go to the capital markets with great regularity to finance their vast financial requirements. But the decision with respect to internal versus external financing is not simply one of resorting to the capital markets only when internal funds are inadequate to serve the needs of the business, but rather to balance these two types of financing in such a way as to provide the best overall financial position for the business.

Dividend Policy

One of the most important policy factors involved in internal financing is that of the firm's dividend policy. A liberal dividend payout may result in a favorable attitude on the part of the stockholders, but it will also result in a reduction of internally generated funds available for investment. It is important for corporate management to adopt a dividend policy that will provide the company with a reasonable amount of retained earnings for internal investment purposes and also hold an appeal to the investor so that public issues of securities will sell at favorable prices.

The company that pursues a policy of paying no dividends and retaining as much of its earnings as possible might find a lack of interest on the part of potential investors in the stock of the company. This is true because many investors depend upon current dividend income to support their personal living expenses. Some investors, in fact, place almost total emphasis on dividend payments in their appraisal of stocks. Other investors may be more interested in the growth of the earnings on their stock.

In general, firms that must approach the capital markets with great frequency find it advantageous to maintain a fairly liberal dividend policy; that is, a policy that provides for a large payout

Table 15–1

CASH DIVIDENDS AS A PERCENTAGE OF EARNINGS FOR SELECTED INDUSTRIES

Average for Years 1968-1972

INDUSTRY	PERCENTAGE PAYOUT
Aerospace	52.5%
Automobiles	73.1
Biscuit Bakers	72.1
Chemical Companies	62.9
Electrical & Electronics	46.7
Industrial Machinery	55.1
Metal & Glass Containers	44.4
Utilities—Electric	69.9

SOURCE: *Standard and Poor's Industry Survey.*

of earnings with a relatively small amount of the earnings being retained in the business. Firms that are able to accommodate a large proportion of their investment requirements through internal financing often find that a conservative dividend policy may be acceptable to the investors. In this case the investor is interested in the growth of earnings and the market price per share.

It should be kept in mind that the capital markets are made up of a host of investors, each with his individual investment goals and objectives. It is the task of the financial manager to so orient the practices of the company that there will be a maximum appeal to a significant group of investors in the capital markets. Table 15-1 reveals the diversity of payout practices among different industries. These averages of the principal companies in these industries, however, tend to cover up the diversity of practices within each industry. For example, the 46.7 percent payout for the electrical and electronics industry is only an average and is hardly representative of more than a few companies. General Electric Company paid out an average of 61.4 percent for the years 1968 through 1972; International Telephone and Telegraph, 33.2; RCA, 55.3; Sperry Rand, 23.1; Texas Instruments, 25.8; and Westinghouse, 47.8 percent. Each company has presumably considered all the factors pertinent to its situation and set its dividend practices accordingly.

Consistency in Dividend Practices

Once a dividend policy is established by a corporation, investors may be disturbed by departures from such established policy. For this reason corporations tend to move slowly in changing their dividend paying practices. Companies in the same industry may have diverse dividend payment practices and yet pursue these practices with great success. For example, one company may have the reputation of being a liberal dividend payer and enjoy strong support in the capital markets. Another firm in the same line of activity may have a very conservative dividend policy and also enjoy strong support in the market. And yet if each company tried to adopt the policy of the other, it is possible that both of them would experience extreme criticism on the part of their stockholders. Consistency, then, plays an important role in the dividend paying practices of the corporation.

The requirement of consistency also results in a lack of coordination between the generation of funds and their need for investment purposes. If firms could arbitrarily use their earnings as needed, paying out the residual as dividends, the convenience of retained earnings would be far greater. For most firms, it is the retained earnings that is the residual, with dividends having first priority in the administration of the income of the firm.

The proportion of internal to external financing varies over the business cycle. During periods of economic expansion it is customary for firms to rely increasingly on external finance as investment opportunities outrun internally generated funds. During periods of economic contraction the reverse is true. As profitable investment opportunities diminish, the rate of investment itself is reduced and the reliance on external capital markets decreases. In the expansion of the 1960's, because of its length and strength, reliance upon external financing was quite marked.

Dividends and Taxes

Corporate income tax matters also influence the decision of internal versus external financing. Although the corporation must pay a corporate income tax on its earnings, no personal income tax liability is incurred on the part of the stockholders if the earnings are not distributed to the stockholders.[1] The case is often made, therefore, that it behooves business to retain a maximum of earnings on behalf of its stockholders since this precludes the creation of a personal tax liability on the part of the stockholders.

While this is undoubtedly true in some measure, not all stockholders may wish to reinvest their funds in the corporations whose stock they hold. For these people, such action on the part of the corporation takes the form of involuntary or forced reinvestment. Presumably a shareholder is aware of the dividend policies of the companies in which he invests and will choose companies whose dividend practices are compatible with his particular tax situation. For the investor who finds his company changing its dividend practice, the alternative is simply to sell the stock. If the company has increased its retained earnings at the expense of the stockholder dividends, the investor who disposes of his stock can only hope that the reinvestment of the earnings of the business has been reflected in the market price of the stock. Table 15-2 on page 322 reflects the internal and external sources of funds for nonfarm nonfinancial corporations in 1972.

The significance of depreciation allowances as a source of internal financing for the business community as a whole is apparent from this table. Depreciation allowances represent an accounting allocation of expense. For an individual firm, depreciation allowances reflect an internal generation of funds only if revenues exceed total cash expense outlays.

LONG-TERM EXTERNAL FINANCING

In reading the balance sheets of many corporations, it may appear that they have pursued erratic practices in their financial activities. It is important to recognize, however, that several specific considerations should be taken into account in deciding upon the best financial plan for a particular business. Among these factors that should be considered are the need for flexibility, control considerations, cost relationships, safety and risk, appropriate timing,

---

[1] Corporate income tax regulations attempt to prevent corporations from using this device as an unfair tax shield. Unless the firm invests retained earnings in due time in business operations, an "undue accumulation of earnings" tax may be levied against the firm.

Table 15–2

SOURCES AND USES OF CORPORATE FUNDS FOR NONFARM, NONFINANCIAL BUSINESSES, UNITED STATES, 1972

	BILLION DOLLARS	PERCENT OF TOTAL
Sources, Total	146.3	100.0%
Internal sources	77.5	53.0
Undistributed profits	21.6	14.8
Corporate inventory valuation adjustment ...	—6.9	—4.7
Depreciation allowances	62.8	42.9
External sources	68.9	47.0
Stocks	10.4	7.1
Bonds	12.2	8.3
Mortgages	15.6	10.7
Short-term financing	29.9	20.4
Profits tax liability	.6	.4
Other liabilities	.2	.1
Uses, Total	131.4	100.0%
Purchases of physical assets	100.7	76.6
Increase in financial assets	30.7	23.4
Discrepancy (uses less sources)	—15.0	

SOURCE: *Board of Governors of the Federal Reserve System.*

and relative availability of funds. We shall look at each of these factors as they relate to the principal types of financial instruments; that is, bonds, preferred stocks, and common stocks. We shall also refer to some of the basic modifications of these types of investment instruments, such as convertible bonds or preferred stock.

Flexibility

As described in the sections relating to short-term financial policies, we saw that one of the important reasons for the use of short-term borrowing was seasonality. If a business needs funds for only six or seven months of the year, it may be far cheaper to engage in short-term borrowing rather than to encumber the firm with long-term funds on which interest would have to be paid throughout the year. By the same token, the business cycle itself results in a change in the financial requirements of the firm. There are always periods in the life of the business in which there will be fewer investment opportunities and in which the market for the firm's products may contract temporarily. It is advantageous to have a capital structure that lends itself to alteration during such periods of time. A large company with many different long-term debt issues with staggered maturities may find during a period of economic contraction that it is wise to simply retire a maturing bond issue out of the increasing liquidity of the firm as working assets move from inventories and accounts receivable into cash.

In other situations the business may engage in temporary ventures that are to be abandoned either at some determinable future date or at the discretion of management. In this case, too, a type of financing that lends itself to elimination if no longer needed becomes appropriate. In both of these cases debt financing holds an important advantage over preferred stock or common stock financing since by the nature of these equity instruments there is no maturity that makes possible their convenient retirement. Debt financing may be accomplished with maturities suited to the expected period of need for funds. It should be mentioned also at this point that the lease arrangement offers as one of its special advantages the fact that the lease term may be established to coincide with the duration of the need for the assets. The lease arrangement was described in Chapter 13.

The flexibility afforded by long-term debt issues may also make it possible for management to refinance bond issues in a period of falling interest rates, if the bonds were originally sold at a time when interest rates were very high. Bonds like preferred stocks typically provide for a premium to be paid by the company if the bonds are called for retirement before their originally scheduled maturity. Even after paying the call premium, refinancing can often be carried out to the advantage of the firm if interest rates have fallen far enough. Ordinarily, the premium that must be paid to call bonds or preferred stock is on a sliding scale.

In the early years of the life of the security the premium is quite high with the amount of the premium being reduced over the life of the security. In very recent years with interest rates at historical peak levels and with borrowers having difficulty in obtaining investment funds in the amounts desired, it has become customary for securities to provide for no call privilege for the first five or seven years of the life of the security.

In short, long-term debt financing provides a greater degree of flexibility than either preferred or common stock financing. It is true that in recent years corporations have been entering the market and buying back their own stock, both preferred and common, and doing so to the benefit of these stockholders who retain their shares. This is practical, however, only when the stock is available at a reasonable price and the firm has adequate financial liquidity to make possible such repurchases.

Corporate Control

Although the control of a corporation is administered generally by its board of directors, ultimate control rests with those stockholders who hold classes of stock with voting rights. The stockholders are responsible for the election of the members of the board of directors, and the members of the board of directors are in turn responsible to the stockholders. Many stockholders in large corporations have little interest in their voting rights, owning such stocks purely for income. Under such circumstances, it is possible and generally true that stockholders owning only a small proportion of the total stock are able to control the election of the members of the board of directors and hence effect ultimate control over all activities of the corporation.

The device of classifying common stock as voting and nonvoting shares facilitates the control of corporate affairs by the ownership of only a small part of all capital investment, and the same is true in some cases of the issue of nonvoting preferred stock. Some states require that all stock, regardless of its class, be voting stock, a provision apparently designed to permit participation on the part of all stockholders in corporate activity. This apparent protection may easily be defeated by numerous devices, one of which is establishment of a much higher par value of the preferred stock or by issuing one class of common stock at a much higher cost than the basic common stock. Since the stockholder is entitled to one vote for each share he owns, an investment in the basic common stock will provide a considerably greater number of votes than would an equal investment in the preferred stock or other class of common stock. The ill-fated promotion and financing of the Tucker Motor Car Company in the post-World War II period serves as an example of the use of classified common stock. This company issued both Class A and Class B stock. The Class A stock, although carrying voting rights, was offered to the public at $5 a share; the Class B stock, also carrying voting rights, had a nominal value of 10 cents a share. Practically all of the Class B stock was held by the promoter of the enterprise. It is obvious, therefore, that a $5 investment in the Class A stock would bring one vote; the same investment in B stock would bring 50 votes.

Although it is true that most corporations have done little to encourage stockholders to participate actively in the election of members of the boards of directors, in recent years some corporations have made very definite efforts to stimulate such activity. One company, The General Mills Corporation, has not only publicized its stockholders' meetings widely in an effort to encourage attendance, but it has also held regional meetings to permit greater attendance. Interest on the part of the stockholders in the affairs of the corporation provides not only a greater feeling of ownership and a sympathy for its problems but also a broadened market for the sale of new securities when such is desirable or necessary. The publicity value of favorable stockholder relationships is important, since the larger firms have thousands of stockholders, each a potential medium of good public relations.

A growing enterprise that has prospered under its existing management may lack the capital necessary to take advantage of the opportunities available. Yet the prospect of bringing additional stockholders into the enterprise may not be attractive to management because of the voting privileges that such new investors in the business would acquire. The volume of additional funds required might make necessary the sale of so much new stock that the existing stockholders would lose control of the affairs of the company because of the concentration of voting power in the hands of the new stockholders. Many firms have avoided expansion rather than risk the loss of control through the sale of stock.

In other cases, the existence of a minority stockholder group would be objectionable to the existing owners even though the minority group would be ineffective insofar as its influence on the affairs of the company were concerned. Although it may be suggested that a nonvoting form of stock can be issued, circumstances might make it impossible to sell such stock to outsiders.

Corporate bonds and notes, on the other hand, provide no voting privilege for their holders; hence, management frequently prefers this form of financing. Although the holders of bonds and notes have no voting privilege, there are frequently contractual provisions that limit the managerial actions of the existing owners of the business. For example, before the loan is made, the borrower may be required to agree that dividends will not be distributed to stockholders if the net working capital of the firm falls below a stipulated minimum. When the debt is retired, of course, the management is freed from such restrictions.

Cost Relationships

Although management may be able to finance either through equity capital or debt capital, the decision may favor debt financing because of its lower cost. Borrowing funds at a cost lower than the return obtained on the use of the funds in the business permits the existing stockholders to retain the added income and to increase accordingly the return on their investment.

The lower cost to a corporation of financing through bonds and notes results from the lower risk involved in such investments from the viewpoint of the investor. Both the interest on and the redemption of the debt is fixed by contract; and if the corporation is to remain in operation, these obligations must be met. From the viewpoint of the corporation, equity claims are willingly subordinated to the claims of creditors in return for the use of creditors' money at a lower rate than that for which the corporation can in turn use the money. The investor is willing to sacrifice the higher yields that are available on equity investments for greater safety and certainty of income.

Trading on the Equity and Leverage. The process of borrowing long-term capital in order to increase the percentage return on the investment of existing stockholders in a business is termed *trading on the equity*. This term is apparently derived from the fact that equity investment must precede debt financing in a business enterprise; hence, the bonds or notes are being sold on the strength of the underlying equity. Frequently a company that is engaged heavily in trading on the equity is referred to as a *high-leverage company*; a company with little or no trading on the equity, as a *low-leverage company*. An example of the effects of this leverage on income is illustrated in Figure 15-1. In this illustration, two companies have similar asset structures and incomes. The Low Leverage Operating Company is financed entirely with equity capital. The $1,000,000 return on the $10,000,000 investment of the stockholders of this company provides a percentage return of 10 percent. The assets of the High Leverage Operating Company, on the other hand, were acquired by the sale of $5,000,000 of 6 percent bonds and $5,000,000 of common stock. The income of this company before interest and dividends, like that of the Low Leverage Operating Company, is $1,000,000. Of this amount $300,000 must be paid to the bondholders (6 percent of $5,000,000), leaving $700,000 for the common stockholders. The $700,000 return on stockholders' investment of $5,000,000 provides a return of 14 percent. The trading on the equity of the High Leverage Operating Company has increased the percentage return to the common stockholders by 4 percent of their investment.

Trading on the Equity and Corporation Taxation. The cost advantage to a corporation of financing through long-term debt arrangements is even more striking when the influence of the federal corporate income tax is considered. This tax is levied against the net income figure of the corporation after deductions for interest expense but before dividends. Interest costs, therefore, reduce the amount of income on which the corporation must pay taxes. In our illustration, the federal corporate income tax would be levied against the entire $1,000,000 of the Low Leverage Operating Company and against the "after interest" figure of

Figure 15–1

LOW LEVERAGE OPERATING COMPANY

BALANCE SHEET
December 31, 197—

ASSETS		LIABILITIES AND CAPITAL	
Current Assets	$ 4,000,000	Liabilities	(none)
Fixed Assets	6,000,000	Common Stock	$10,000,000
Total Assets	$10,000,000	Total Liab. & Cap.	$10,000,000

* Earnings $1,000,000 (all earnings paid out)

Return to common stockholders expressed as a percentage
($1,000,000 ÷ $10,000,000) = 10%

HIGH LEVERAGE OPERATING COMPANY

BALANCE SHEET
December 31, 197—

ASSETS		LIABILITIES AND CAPITAL	
Current Assets	$ 4,000,000	Bonds @ 6%	$ 5,000,000
Fixed Assets	6,000,000	Common Stock	5,000,000
Total Assets	$10,000,000	Total Liab. & Cap.	$10,000,000

* Earnings $1,000,000 before interest and dividends (all earnings paid out)

Bondholders receive	$300,000 (6% of $5,000,000)
Stockholders receive	700,000 ($1,000,000 earnings less bond interest)

Return to common stockholders expressed as a percentage
($700,000 ÷ $5,000,000) = 14%

---

* For purposes of simplification, tax matters have been ignored.

$700,000 for the High Leverage Operating Company. At the basic 1974 federal corporate income tax rate of 48 percent, this would mean a tax saving of $144,000 for the High Leverage Company.

Initial Financing Costs. Another cost item to consider in any financing program is the cost of raising the funds. This will primarily include fees paid to those outside the company to raise money, especially to investment bankers, lawyers, engineers, and so forth. If one method will take more executive time than another, this should also be considered. A final cost factor is the extent to which funds may be raised which will not be used immediately or continuously. Since a great deal of work and cost are involved in the public sale of securities, it may be desirable to raise more funds than are currently needed so as to take care of needs for several years. This, of course, raises the cost of funds because even if idle funds are put into short-term securities, the rate of return earned on them is likely to be less than the cost of the funds. This type of cost consideration is also important in deciding on short-term financing alternatives. One bank may require a minimum balance in the deposit account at all times while the loan is outstanding, another may not. A finance company may lend money to meet a ten-day gap between receipts and disbursements; a bank may prefer to lend money only on a 30-day note or longer.

Safety and Risk

The leverage effect of long-term corporate debt should be recognized as a two-edged weapon. Just as the percentage return to the stockholders is increased substantially during periods of profitable operations, so the percentage return to the stockholders is depressed during periods of low profits. During periods of low income, the fixed charges must be met irrespective of the effect on stockholders, even if it means ultimate liquidation of the business. The student may test the validity of this statement by determining the percentage return to the stockholders of the two companies in our illustration above if earnings before interest and dividends should fall to $200,000.

A study of the relationship of equity capital to borrowed capital for various types of businesses reveals a wide range of practice. Inasmuch as the obligations relating to borrowed capital are of a fixed nature, it is to be expected that if a corporation is wisely managed, fixed charges which would be difficult or impossible to meet during periods of unfavorable business experience will be avoided. Lenders, too, of course, try to avoid making loans that impose a dangerous financial burden on the borrower because of the possibility of loan default. In those industries that are subject to only minor economic fluctuations and reverses over the business cycle, we generally find a greater use of borrowed capital than in those concerns that are subject to wide swings in cyclical experience. The utility companies that have relatively stable revenues can capitalize to a much larger extent through borrowed capital than do most industrial corporations.

There is also a risk in financial decisions due to a change in the tax laws. When taxes on corporate profits are increased, some businesses can pass them on to the consumer in the form of higher prices and maintain the level of profits after taxes. However, in some fields the nature of demand for the product may be such that higher prices will lead to fewer sales and so reduce profits. Thus, an increase in corporate profits taxes may make it impossible to attract capital since the return after taxes is too low. Similar results may follow from raising other taxes, such as a tax on the number of units a retailing firm operates.

Another general economic risk which affects businesses with foreign branches has to do with the relationship between the dollar and foreign currencies. Exchange rates may become unfavorable so that fewer dollars are received in exchange for a foreign currency. In other cases foreign exchange transactions may be restricted so that it becomes impossible to move funds out of a foreign country.

Timing

The sale of securities by a corporation and the type of securities sold depends in large measure upon existing conditions in the capital markets. A wise policy with respect to long-term financial planning makes it possible to capitalize on these changing conditions in the market. For example, during a period of economic recession when business is at a low ebb, interest rates are typically at low levels also. By the same token common stock prices are at low levels. Under these conditions, if additional funds are needed for expansion or to retire maturing debt, it becomes much more attractive to do so through the sale of debt instruments rather than through the sale of common stock.

During the upswing and expansion of the business cycle, when business opportunities and investment plans are increasing, it is also advantageous to borrow on a long-term basis even though interest rates may be rising somewhat. After a long period of economic expansion, however, pressure on capital resources and on the capital markets is such that interest rates reach very high levels and all but the very strongest credit risks may find it difficult to borrow additional funds. At these times common stock prices are typically at very high levels and the corporation that sells stock receives a high price therefor.

The ability of a corporation to take advantage of these changing conditions in the capital markets is a function of the maintenance of a favorable capital structure; one that allows it to maneuver between debt issues and common stock issues on the basis of management's desires. The business that has exhausted its long-term borrowing power may find itself trapped in a situation where it may be forced to sell common stock at a time when the price of the shares is depressed and the return from the sale of the stock is correspondingly low. Long-term financial policy, therefore, must be geared to prospective future needs as well as to the needs of the moment.

Availability

Just as financial management must take into consideration flexibility and timing in its plans, so too it must recognize that sheer availability may dictate the type of securities to be sold. Small firms and medium-size firms, by virtue of their size, may simply not have access to the capital markets for purposes of selling stock. On the other hand, the ownership of plant and equipment may provide entirely suitable collateral for long-term borrowing. At other times a business may be able to borrow only if it provides the lender with a form of override; that is, a form of additional potential return in the form of stock options or other arrangements by which the lender can participate in the prosperity of the company in future years.

In recent years it has become customary for even large institutional lenders such as insurance companies to insist upon additional opportunities for reward in their lending operations. One reason for this has been the strong price inflation of recent years. Lenders try to protect themselves against erosion of the value of the dollar. They try to accomplish this at times through the insistence upon supplementary benefits made available to them by the borrower. Typically, this takes the form of a percentage of gross or net income and at other times through the use of convertible securities or stock options. By the issuance of convertible bonds or preferred stock, the holder of the security not only has the immediate yield and safety provided by the security, but with the increasing prosperity of the business he is provided an opportunity to convert his securities at a predetermined ratio into the common stock of the company. This in turn makes it possible to enjoy the benefits of the common stockholders as the firm prospers.

Obviously, corporations are not anxious to provide investors with securities that provide the best of all worlds; that is, the protection of a fixed-income security in the case of bonds and preferred stock but also the opportunity to convert these securities into the common stock of the company if the company prospers. Yet there may be times when the corporation may simply be forced to issue such securities in order to raise the capital necessary to accommodate investment plans.

In other instances very strong corporations may resort to the use of convertible securities when common stock prices are depressed below levels considered to be acceptable to the company. Convertible securities are issued with the expectation that when the price of the company's common stock recovers, these securities will be called for redemption, thus forcing the holders to convert to the common stock of the company. The holders of convertible securities, of course, have a specified time period within which they may convert their securities once they have been called for redemption by the company. The net effect of this action is to sell stock at a price considered satisfactory to the company through the device of first issuing convertible bonds or preferred stock and then at a later date forcing conversion.

Mergers and Diversification

In addition to the foregoing matters, all of which enter strongly into the policy aspects of long-term financial planning, management must also remain conscious of the fact that mergers or diversification into other product lines may provide the company with a different risk structure than before such acts are carried out. If, for example, a company diversifies its product lines or acquires subsidiaries through merger having a much greater risk than the existing product lines of the company, what had constituted a perfectly acceptable debt to equity ratio may now become too risky for the long-term welfare of the business. By maintaining a somewhat conservative capital structure, therefore, the business is in a position to move into product lines of somewhat greater risk or to introduce entirely new products in which the risk may be very great without excessive concern for the impact on the quality of the credit of the firm.

It should also be mentioned that the various rating organizations, such as Moody's and Standard and Poor's, that make it their job to rate the quality of the securities of the corporations of the nation carry a great deal of weight in the capital markets. And although it is well known that these rating organizations may at times be less than perfect in their judgment and size-up of strength and quality of issues of securities, the public has constantly relied heavily upon them; and for this reason they cannot be ignored for purposes of financial planning. Hence, internal policy decisions with respect to capital structure and debt equity ratios must be tempered by a recognition of how outsiders view the strength of the financial position of the firm. Financial managers of corporations usually make a specific effort to determine how the rating organizations view their securities; and although they seldom become slaves to the judgments of the rating agencies, neither are they oblivious to the attitudes of these organizations.

QUESTIONS

1. In studying the balance sheets of some of the nation's leading corporations, it is immediately apparent that there is a wide variation in methods of financing long-term needs. How is it possible that businesses, with expert leadership, could pursue such diverse financial practices?

2. Describe the relationship between internal and external financing in meeting the long-term financial needs of the firm.

3. Describe a situation in which a firm would be well advised to follow a policy of paying out only a small portion of earnings in dividends.

4. As an owner or an aspiring owner of common stock of a corporation, what dividend policy best suits your requirement? Why?

5. Corporations must pay income taxes on their earnings whether or not they are paid out in the form of dividends. How, then, does the matter of federal income taxes enter into the dividend policy of corporations?

6. Flexibility in the capital structure of a business, as for most things, is a desirable quality. In what ways can long-term debt financing contribute to this flexibility?

7. In planning the capital structure of your firm, under what circumstances would the matter of "corporate control" enter into your decision? If control were important in your planning, what effect would it have on your capital structure decisions?

8. If trading on the equity works out so well mathematically, why do not all firms make use of the concept in their long-term financing?

9. In studying the financial statements of nationally known firms, it is readily apparent that many of them have used trading on the equity to excellent advantage in increasing the earnings on their common equity. In view of this favorable result, could we with confidence recommend to them that they utilize far more long-term debt in their capital structures in order that the return on their common equity would be increased even more?

10. How might a prospective change in the federal corporate income tax laws influence the long-term financing of a firm?

11. Why should the financial executive concern himself with a study of business cycle developments?

12. In all merger and business expansion activities the financial executives of firms play an important role. This role extends beyond the matter of arranging the financing. Explain.

SUGGESTED READINGS

HELFERT, ERICH A. *Techniques of Financial Analysis,* 3d ed. Homewood, Illinois: Richard D. Irwin, Inc., 1972. Chapter 2.

HUNT, PEARSON, CHARLES M. WILLIAMS, and GORDON DONALDSON. *Basic Business Finance,* 4th ed. Homewood, Illinois: Richard D. Irwin, Inc., 1971. Part VI.

JOHNSON, KEITH B., and DONALD E. FISCHER (Editors). *Readings in Contemporary Financial Management.* Glenview, Illinois: Scott, Foresman and Company, 1969. Parts IV and V.

MUMEY, GLEN A. *Theory of Financial Structure.* New York: Holt, Rinehart, and Winston, Inc., 1969. Chapters 9 and 10.

VAN HORNE, JAMES C. *Fundamentals of Financial Management,* 2d ed. Englewood Cliffs, New Jersey: Prentice-Hall, Inc., 1974. Chapter 12.

WESTON, J. FRED, and EUGENE F. BRIGHAM. *Managerial Finance,* 4th ed. New York: Holt, Rinehart, and Winston, 1972. Chapter 26.

WOLF, HAROLD A., and LEE RICHARDSON (Editors). *Readings in Finance.* New York: Appleton-Century-Crofts, 1966. Chapter V.

16

Financing Agriculture

The rapid shift of the population of the United States to urban living since the turn of the century has been one of the results of an expanding industrial economy. Agriculture, with a decreasing proportion of the population devoted to it, has had to provide ever-increasing quantities of food and fibers to sustain a rapidly increasing total population. Such production has been made possible by the more skillful utilization of land through the use of modern machinery, and by improved methods of storage and preservation and of transporting farm products to the population centers. Just as industrial productivity has increased based on scientific research and technological experimentation, agriculture has responded in similar fashion. Agriculture has, in fact, become increasingly commercialized.

PROBLEMS IN FINANCING AGRICULTURE

The demands for increased productivity in agriculture have made it necessary for farmers to invest ever-increasing sums of capital in land, buildings, machinery, livestock, fertilizers, and general supplies. Because the typical farm in the United States remains a combination of home and business, funds for operation of the farm must include operation of the home as well.

Table 16–1

COMPARATIVE ASSET SHEET OF AGRICULTURE
UNITED STATES, JANUARY 1, SELECTED YEARS, 1940-73
[In billions of dollars]

ITEM	1940	1950	1960	1973
ASSETS				
Physical assets:				
Real estate	33.6	75.3	130.2	258.7
Non-real-estate:				
Livestock	5.1	12.9	15.2	34.2
Machinery and motor vehicles	3.1	11.2	22.2	39.0
Crops stored on and off farms	2.7	7.6	7.7	14.1
Household furnishings and equipment	4.3	7.7	9.6	11.9
Financial assets:				
Deposits and currency	3.2	9.1	9.2	14.1
United States savings bonds	.2	4.8	4.7	3.9
Investments in cooperatives	.8	2.1	4.3	8.6
Total	53.0	130.7	203.1	384.5

SOURCE: *Economic Report of the President.* Washington, D. C.: United States Government Printing Office, 1974, p. 349.

As an indication of the size of the investment in agriculture in the United States, as of January 1, 1972, total farm assets approximated $341 billion.[1] Table 16-1 reveals the pattern of agricultural assets for selected years. Note that the item of machinery and motor vehicles has increased from 6 percent of total assets in 1940 to 11 percent in 1972. Such an increase reflects clearly the increasing capital requirements for mechanization of farms.

Methods of Agricultural Financing

The person who is intent on farming but who has no farm of his own nor sufficient capital to acquire one may work for others until he is able to acquire a tract of land of his own. As a possible alternative, the farmer may establish partnership relationships with one or more other persons in order to finance the purchase

---

[1] *Economic Report of the President* (Washington, D. C.: United States Government Printing Office, 1974), p. 349.

of farmland and equipment. He may also lease land for farming purposes, either on the basis of a fixed rental or a fixed proportion of the crops grown on the land. Finally, the farmer may borrow. We are concerned here principally with the facilities that are available for borrowing for agricultural production and for the acquisition of farm assets.

Although many farmers own their farms and have adequate financial resources for current farming operations without recourse to borrowing, other farmers spend many years of their lives repaying indebtedness—indebtedness arising from the purchase of land and from the credit purchases of machinery, livestock, and requirements for the home. Nor is such indebtedness by the farmer to be avoided if the farm is to be operated with efficiency. The farmer who has the capacity and the equipment to cultivate 120 acres but who has only 80 acres of land of his own will do well to acquire additional land with borrowed capital, if such land and borrowing are available at a reasonable cost. Too, the farmer with much land but little equipment may be well advised to use his credit to acquire equipment in order that his land may be utilized fully.

The farmer who has financial resources sufficient only to carry the family through the year would be foolish to reduce his cultivation because he is unable to meet on a cash basis the costs of harvesting his crops. Such a farmer would be expected to borrow prior to the harvest period in anticipation of his expected income. Without ample credit, farms could no more function efficiently than could the business institutions of the nation. Farming, in fact, is only another form of business activity, operating generally as a single proprietorship. There has, however, been a striking increase in the number of publicly held farm corporations.

Special Considerations in Agricultural Financing

Most farm production is highly seasonal in nature. As such, the bulk of the annual income from farming activities may be received by the farmer within a very few weeks during each year. It may be both necessary and profitable to borrow to meet the operational costs of farming, repaying the loan when the crops have been harvested. The traditional source of such financing for the farmer has been the commercial bank. Banks in the farming regions have at times found it difficult to meet adequately the heavy seasonal demands for operating capital on the part of the farmers. In addition, the term of such loans must be adjusted to the growing period of crops and livestock, a term that is generally longer than that of the typical working capital loan to industry.

The small size of the average farm loan as compared with industrial loans and the difficulty of appraising farm resources have resulted in an interest charge somewhat higher than that to industry. Also the purchase of farmland requires a long amortization period, due to the uncertain year-to-year volume and value of agricultural production. Although the twenty-five and thirty-year urban home mortgage is still relatively new, forty-year mortgages have been common for many years in agriculture.

As a result of the complexities and difficulties of agricultural finance, there have been ever-recurring complaints that agricultural financial facilities were not adequate. This special problem of agricultural financing was recognized as early as World War I . by the government. Since that time the government has sponsored several special agencies for the solving of these problems.

SOURCES OF FARM CREDIT

The sources of farm credit may be grouped broadly as private sources and public sources. Although most discussion of farm financing seems to center about the many public agencies established by the government for that purpose, private sources of agricultural credit continue to provide a preponderance of all financing required by the farmer. The public sources serve as supplementary financial facilities. Among the principal sources of private agricultural credit are the commercial banks, life insurance companies, individuals, merchants, and dealers. The governmental facilities for farm financing are almost all within the jurisdiction of the Farm Credit Administration. Both private and governmental facilities for farm financing are discussed here.

Private sources include the following:
1. Commercial banks
2. Life insurance companies
3. Individuals, merchants, dealers, and others

Commercial Banks

The commercial banks of rural areas have been the primary institutional source of short-term agricultural credit throughout the history of this country. In addition, commercial banks provide a substantial amount of long-term farm mortgage credit. Unlike the larger urban communities with many types of financial institutions, the small town in the agricultural area may have the commercial bank as its only financial institution. It is not surprising then that the commercial banks have played such a dominant role in agricultural financing.

Because of the high degree of liquidity required of commercial bank assets, short-term loans for production and operating purposes have been the principal contribution of commercial banks to farm finance. Short-term loans are generally based on the current earnings prospects of the farm rather than on land or equipment as mortgage collateral. The restrictive provisions of federal regulation in connection with real estate lending on the part of national banks have made long-term loans secured by real estate less suitable than short-term loans. Also, the banking laws of many states limit long-term lending based on real estate collateral by state-chartered commercial banks. As indicated by Table 16-2, commercial banks provided only 13.4 percent of all real estate loans, while they provided more than 37 percent of all non-real estate farm loans.

Life Insurance Companies

Life insurance companies have for many years been a significant source of long-term mortgage loans for the farmer. As revealed in Table 16-2, they are one of the most important institutional sources of farm mortgage loans. Life insurance companies of the nation held approximately 16 percent of the farm mortgage debt as of January 1, 1973. Yet, because of the tremendous resources of life insurance companies, farm mortgages represent but a small percentage of their total assets.[2]

Since the objective of life insurance companies for most of their investments in farm mortgages is safety of the loan and a

---

[2] In 1973, approximately 2.4 percent of total life insurance company assets were in farm mortgages. *Life Insurance Fact Book,* Institute of Life Insurance, 1974, p. 78.

Table 16–2

AMOUNT OF LOANS TO FARMERS AND PERCENT OF TOTAL HELD, BY LENDERS, JANUARY 1, 1973

LENDER	AMOUNT	PERCENT OF TOTAL
	REAL ESTATE LOANS	
	(Millions)	
Federal land banks	$ 9,050	26.2
Insurance companies	5,689	16.4
Commercial banks [1]	4,792	13.9
Farmers Home Administration [2]	272	0.8
Individuals and others	17,742	42.7
Total real estate loans	37,545	100.0
	NON-REAL ESTATE LOANS	
Production credit associations	$ 6,607	17.7
Federal intermediate credit banks [3]	251	0.7
Commercial banks [1,4]	14,303	38.3
Farmers Home Administration [5]	779	2.1
Individuals and others	15,360	41.2
Total non-real estate loans	37,300	100.0

[1] Includes national and state commercial, mutual and stock savings, and private banks.

[2] Includes farm ownership loans, farm housing loans, and soil and water conservation loans. Excludes insured loans.

[3] Loans to and discounts for financing institutions other than production credit associations.

[4] Excludes loans guaranteed by Commodity Credit Corporation.

[5] Includes operating loans, rural rehabilitation loans to individuals, disaster loans, and emergency crop and feed loans in liquidation.

SOURCE: *Fortieth Annual Report*, 1972-1973, The Farm Credit Administration, Washington, D.C., p. 4.

modest yield, it is not surprising that the volume of long-term farm mortgage lending by the life insurance companies has diminished during periods of agricultural difficulties. Some authorities believe, however, that the insurance companies were far more lenient toward distressed mortgagors during the depression of the 1930's than most other private mortgagees. The emphasis of the life insurance companies on the factor of safety has resulted in their restriction of farm mortgage loans to the better farming areas and to the better farms.

At the present time, long-term life insurance company loans to the farmer carry maturities of up to forty years, with repayment arrangements based upon the farmer's financial position. In some cases the amortization schedule is such that the payments decrease in size from year to year, while in cases where it is expected that ability to repay will increase, the principal payments increase. The fact that insurance companies restrict their mortgage loans to the better risks makes it possible for them to charge lower interest rates than is true of most other private farm mortgage lenders. The low interest rates of life insurance companies on mortgage loans, together with the fact that prepayments of principal are generally permitted without penalty, make these loans very attractive to the farmer.

The large insurance companies, often located far from the agricultural loan areas of their choice, make such loans through branch offices, local banks, or local loan agents. Branch offices are generally established in choice agricultural areas for the purpose of selecting high-grade long-term farm loans. These branch offices must be staffed with personnel trained both in the mortgage loan field and in agriculture. Farmers needing loans are contacted through the company's local underwriters, through casualty and property insurance underwriters who generally receive a fee for such information, or through individuals who may suggest loan prospects. Branch managers are generally responsible to the home office of the company they represent.

In recent years the insurance companies have made funds available to qualifying farmers in less popular lending areas through the establishment of purchase agreements with local banks. Such purchase agreements involve a commitment to purchase qualifying loans from the bank within a two-year period after the loans are made. To qualify for purchase by the insurance companies, such loans must meet prescribed requirements with regard to appraisal standards, loan-to-value ratios, loan terms, and other pertinent factors. The purchase-agreement arrangement has the advantage to the bank of permitting temporary ownership of long-term investment instruments and the advantage to the insurance company of long-term investments in isolated areas without the trouble of local title and financial settlement details. To the local bank, details of loan settlement and administration are not difficult because they may handle the matters directly rather than by correspondence. The bank generally sells such long-term mortgages to the insurance company at a price somewhat above par as compensation for originating the loan.

Local loan agents also serve the insurance companies in areas where branch offices are not practicable. The loan agents may be real estate agents, contractors, insurance agents, or farm association representatives who have close contact with farmers. Such agents generally receive a fee based on a percentage of the amount of the loan.

Individuals, Merchants, Dealers, and Other Lenders

This group of lenders accounts for well over one third of all short- and long-term agricultural loans. Loans from individuals generally arise out of a property sale in which the seller takes a mortgage as part payment for the sale price, or from a sale in which the purchaser borrows from close friends or relatives. As might be expected, there is little standardization of individual lending practices, and there is generally no appraisal of the property by a trained appraiser.

Typical of the loans from merchants and dealers are the equipment loans. Such loans are offered to facilitate the purchase of heavy farm equipment, such as tractors and combines. Although these loans are arranged to permit systematic and periodic repayment, lending agencies rely to a large extent on the collateral value of the equipment for the safety of the loan. While interest rates are usually quite high, the inability of many farmers to secure adequate financing through customary channels often leaves no alternative to the use of such credit. Credit by merchants is sometimes extended for such purchases as fertilizers, feed, farm supplies, and family living.

Within the category of "other lenders" are the mortgage loan companies that make long-term farm mortgage loans with the express purpose of reselling them to institutional investors. Such mortgages are generally at a premium, and the mortgage companies sometimes continue to service the loans by collecting the payments for a fee. Endowment funds of educational and other institutions are in some cases invested in farm mortgages.

THE FARM CREDIT ADMINISTRATION

The Federal Farm Loan Act of 1916 gave rise to the first of many governmental credit institutions that were to be established to aid the farmer. In 1933 most of these federal credit institutions were consolidated in the Farm Credit Administration, and others have been added since that time. The Farm Credit Administration functioned as an independent agency of the government until 1939 at which time it was placed under the control of the United States Department of Agriculture. Under the provisions of the Farm Credit Act of 1953 the Farm Credit Administration again became an independent agency in the executive branch of the government.

The new act established a 13-member, part-time, policy-making Federal Farm Credit Board to direct, supervise, and control the Farm Credit Administration. Twelve members of the Board, one from each farm credit district, are appointed by the President of the United States, with the advice and consent of the Senate, after giving consideration to nominations made by national farm loan associations, production credit associations, and cooperatives borrowing from the district banks for cooperatives. Thus, farmers through their cooperatives have a voice in the selection of the national board. The thirteenth member is appointed by the Secretary of Agriculture as his representative.

The Farm Credit Act of 1953 provides that the Federal Farm Credit Board shall function as a unit without delegating authority to individual members and prohibits the Board from operating in an administrative capacity. All administrative powers, functions, and duties of the Farm Credit Administration are exercised and performed by the Governor of the Farm Credit Administration, its chief, who is appointed by the Federal Farm Credit Board.

The Farm Credit Administration has three principal credit divisions: the Land Bank Service, the Short-Term Credit Service, and the Cooperative Bank Service. The organizational structure

Chart 16–1

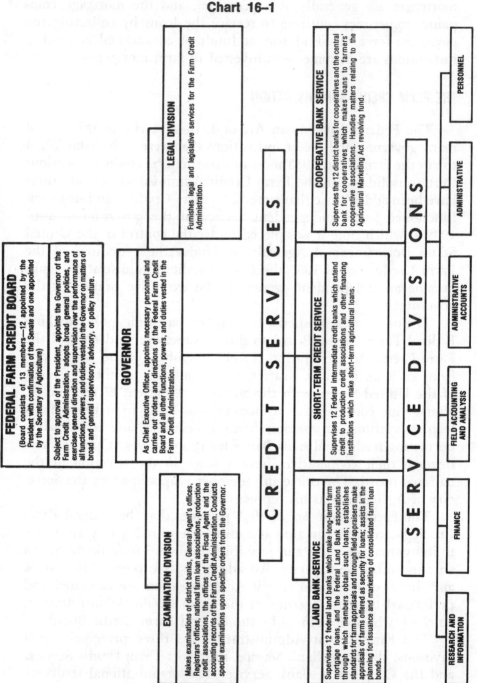

ORGANIZATION OF THE FARM CREDIT ADMINISTRATION

FEDERAL FARM CREDIT BOARD

(Board consists of 13 members—12 appointed by the President with confirmation of the Senate and one appointed by the Secretary of Agriculture)

Subject to approval of the President, appoints the Governor of the Farm Credit Administration, adopts broad general policies, and exercises general direction and supervision over the performance of all functions, powers, and duties vested in the Governor on matters of broad and general supervisory, advisory, or policy nature.

GOVERNOR

As Chief Executive Officer, appoints necessary personnel and carries out orders and directions of the Federal Farm Credit Board and all other functions, powers, and duties vested in the Farm Credit Administration.

EXAMINATION DIVISION

Makes examinations of district banks, General Agent's offices, Registrars' offices, national farm loan associations, production credit associations, the offices of the Fiscal Agent and the accounting records of the Farm Credit Administration. Conducts special examinations upon specific orders from the Governor.

LEGAL DIVISION

Furnishes legal and legislative services for the Farm Credit Administration.

CREDIT SERVICES

LAND BANK SERVICE

Supervises 12 federal land banks which make long-term farm mortgage loans, and the Federal Land Bank associations through which members obtain such loans; establishes standards for farm appraisals and through field appraisers make appraisals of farms offered as security for loans; assists in the planning for issuance and marketing of consolidated farm loan bonds.

SHORT-TERM CREDIT SERVICE

Supervises 12 Federal intermediate credit banks which extend credit to production credit associations and other financing institutions which make short-term agricultural loans.

COOPERATIVE BANK SERVICE

Supervises the 12 district banks for cooperatives and the central bank for cooperatives which makes loans to farmers' cooperative associations. Handles matters relating to the Agricultural Marketing Act revolving fund.

SERVICE DIVISIONS

RESEARCH AND INFORMATION

FINANCE

FIELD ACCOUNTING AND ANALYSIS

ADMINISTRATIVE ACCOUNTS

ADMINISTRATIVE

PERSONNEL

SOURCE: Farm Credit Administration

of the Farm Credit Administration is shown in Chart 16-1. This chart will facilitate an understanding of the administrative relationships of the agricultural lending agencies.

THE FEDERAL LAND BANK SERVICE

Under the authority of the Federal Farm Loan Act of 1916, twelve farm credit districts were created. Each farm credit district is served by a federal land bank located, as a rule, in one of the principal cities of the district. The locations of these banks and the district boundaries are shown in Figure 16-1 on page 348.

Sources of Funds

The original capital of the federal land banks was provided almost entirely by the United States Treasury through the purchase of stock. Each bank was to be capitalized at $750,000 with additional funds to be obtained through the issue of debenture bonds, and these bonds were to be secured by the first mortgages of borrowers or by United States government bonds. With increased subscriptions from other sources, the government-held stock was largely retired by 1932; however, emergency legislation in that year provided for an investment of $125 million in the stock of the banks to increase their supply of loanable funds. No dividends were paid on stock held by the government, and all such stock held by the government has now been retired.

Consolidated federal farm loan bonds, sold to investors, are now the principal source of funds for making land bank loans. These bonds are the joint and several obligations of the twelve federal land banks. They are not guaranteed either as to principal or interest by the United States government. On June 30, 1973, outstanding consolidated federal farm loan bonds amounted to $7.5 billion.[3]

Purposes of Federal Land Bank Loans

Federal land bank loans may be made for these purposes: (1) to buy land for agricultural uses; (2) to provide buildings

---

[3] *Annual Report of the Farm Credit Administration,* 1972-73, p. 62.

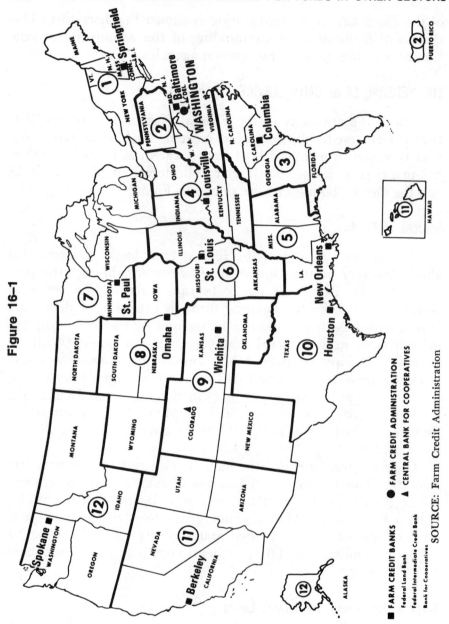

Figure 16-1

SOURCE: Farm Credit Administration

■ **FARM CREDIT BANKS**
  Federal Land Bank
  Federal Intermediate Credit Bank
  Bank for Cooperatives

● **FARM CREDIT ADMINISTRATION**
▲ **CENTRAL BANK FOR COOPERATIVES**

and to improve the farmlands; (3) to buy equipment, fertilizers, and livestock necessary for the proper operation of the farm; (4) to refinance indebtedness of the borrower incurred for agricultural purposes or incurred at least two years prior to the date of the application; and (5) to provide the borrower with funds for general agricultural purposes. A loan may not exceed 85 percent of the appraised normal value of the farm to be mortgaged. The Farm Credit Act of 1971, among other things, expanded the lending authority of the Federal Land Banks to include the financing of certain nonfarm rural homes and of businesses providing on-the-farm services.

Federal Land Bank Associations

Federal land bank loans are negotiated through the federal land bank associations. These associations exist to provide the connection between the farmer and the land bank and to facilitate the orderly and prompt consideration of loan applications through a system of decentralization of functions and responsibilities.

Federal land bank associations may be described as cooperative credit organizations. They are chartered by, and operated under, the supervision of the Farm Credit Administration in accordance with the provisions of the Federal Farm Loan Act. The associations are composed of groups of farmers who assume certain mutual responsibilities to provide a source of long-term farm mortgage credit for their community. They are usually organized on a community or county basis and, to be eligible for a charter, a group of at least ten farmers with a total loan demand of at least $20,000 is required. Where the total demand for funds is less than this amount or the number of persons wanting loans is less than ten, applications may be made directly to the land bank of that district. The stockholders of each association elect a board of directors, which in turn appoints a president, a secretary-treasurer, and a loan committee. The secretary-treasurer, upon whom most of the administrative work falls, is not required to be a stockholder. The primary duties of the federal land bank associations consist of assisting the farmer in the determination of his loan needs, initiating the loan application, and servicing the loan through collecting payments, placing insurance, and in some cases disposing of property upon nonpayment of debt.

Membership. Each borrower is required to purchase stock in his association to the extent of 5 percent of the amount of his loan. As a stockholder-borrower, he is entitled to one vote irrespective of the amount he borrows.

Each loan that is made by a federal land bank through a federal land bank association is guaranteed by the association, resulting in a limited guarantee of each member of the association for all of the loans made through his association. This guarantee is made effective through the requirement that the association hold stock of its federal land bank in an amount equal to 5 percent of total loans made through the association. Should mortgage losses of an association exceed normal dividends due from the federal land bank, recourse may be had to the stock held by the borrower-stockholder.

An example of a loan application and approval may best illustrate the functioning of the federal land bank system. Assume that a farmer has applied for a loan of $6,500 to provide for the purchase of land for agricultural use, or for other reasons acceptable to the land bank. The loan committee of the association examines the application to establish a preliminary appraisal of the property to be mortgaged and the acceptability of the applicant as a mortgagor. If the loan application is acceptable to the loan committee, it is presented to the board of directors of the association where, if acceptable to the board, it is forwarded to the federal land bank of that district. The federal land bank then has the property appraised by one of its own appraisers, a requirement established by the Federal Farm Loan Act. If the appraiser submits a favorable report and the application is satisfactory in other respects, the loan may be granted. The maximum loan-to-value ratio is 85 percent; hence, the property in this example must have an appraised value of at least $7,647.06.

On the assumption that this loan is approved, upon clearance and transfer of title to the property, the $6,500 is delivered to the federal land bank association through which the loan was initiated. The association in turn brings together the parties to the transaction and delivers the money to the seller of the property after the loan settlement arrangements are completed.

The borrower is required to purchase stock in his association in the amount of $325 (5 percent of $6,500). This amount in turn is paid by the association to the land bank for stock. The borrower is liable, therefore, not only for his indebtedness but also to the extent of his stock ownership for the loans of his fellow association members. If losses of the association prove to be negligible, the borrower may surrender his stock upon payment of his loan and receive his $325. Should losses of the association be large because of numerous defaults, the borrower may recover only a part or none of his stock investment, depending on the amount of the stock fund required to offset the loan losses. This system of requiring a joint responsibility for all loans of an association by all borrowers results in a greater selectivity of risks and a local control otherwise difficult to achieve.

Loans, Interest Rates, and Dividends. The federal land banks, through the 566 federal land bank associations, made 58,742 loans for a total of $3 billion during the year ending June 30, 1973. The average size of loan was about $50,000. Under the Federal Farm Loan Act, the contract interest rate on loans made through federal land bank associations cannot be more than 1 percent above the interest rate on the last series of bonds issued by the bank making the loans, except with the approval of the Governor of the Farm Credit Administration. As of June 30, 1972, the interest rate on new loans of federal land banks ranged between 6 and 7½ percent.[4]

Dividends of $148 million were received by member-borrowers through their federal land bank associations from July 1, 1943, to June 30, 1973. During the fiscal year ending June 30, 1973, the federal land banks paid $7.6 million to the associations as dividends on the stock the associations had invested in the banks.[5]

THE FEDERAL SHORT-TERM CREDIT SERVICE

The Federal Short-Term Credit Service supervises and coordinates the operations of the 12 federal intermediate credit banks, which in turn work closely with the 435 production credit associations on all phases of their operations. It provides leadership and guidance in all major phases of the operations of the institutions concerned, including their capitalization, development of credit standards, investment of funds, disposition of earnings, and other factors related to sound lending and management practices. It approves the borrowing of money and the issuance of debentures by the federal intermediate credit banks.

---

[4] *Ibid.*, p. 26.
[5] *Ibid.*, p. 63.

The Federal Intermediate Credit Banks

Federal assistance in the field of long-term credit for the farmer was followed by attempts to provide supplementary sources of intermediate and short-term credit. This was accomplished through the establishment of 12 federal intermediate credit banks under the Agricultural Credits Act of 1923. Congressional inquiry had revealed that agricultural and livestock industries needed a more adequate and stable supply of intermediate and short-term credit than was available to them through existing sources.

The federal intermediate credit banks themselves do not make loans directly to farmers; they discount agricultural and livestock paper and make loans to local financial institutions that do finance the credit needs of the farmer. Representative of the kind of institutions receiving such financing are the production credit associations, agricultural credit corporations, livestock loan companies, and commercial banks. These loans are generally made for production and general farm operation purposes and may carry maturities of up to five years. The usual loan term is one year or less, based on the time for marketing crops or livestock.

Sources of Funds

The federal intermediate credit banks obtain the bulk of their funds from the sale of consolidated collateral trust debentures in the financial markets to the investing public. Although maturities of up to five years are permitted, the average maturity has been from three to forty-two months. For the year ending June 30, 1973, the average maturity was twelve months. Debentures issued carried an average cost to the banks of 6.09 percent. Each bank's participation in the outstanding debentures must not exceed ten times the amount of its capital and paid-in surplus. The twelve banks are jointly and severally liable for these obligations. The debentures are not guaranteed by the federal government either as to principal or interest. Sales and distribution are usually made through security dealers and dealer banks for delivery on the first of each month. Such sales are made on the basis of estimates of cash needs, but unexpected demands make it necessary from time to time to obtain funds for short periods between sales.

The original capital of each federal intermediate credit bank, $5 million, was supplied by the United States Treasury. The total capital and surplus of the twelve banks as of June 30, 1973, was $451 million. This represents $262 million of stock owned by production credit associations and $13 million of participation certificates owned by other financial institutions which use the services of the federal intermediate credit banks.

Management and Supervision

Each intermediate credit bank operates under its own corporate management and under the direction of a board of directors, which serves as the board for the other permanent credit units of each district. The operations of the banks are supervised by the Intermediate Credit Division Commissioner, who is responsible to the Governor of the Farm Credit Administration.

Interest and Discount Rates

The board of directors of a federal intermediate credit bank together with the Commissioner fix the discount and interest rates. Except with the approval of the Governor of the Farm Credit Administration, however, the rate fixed may not exceed by more than 1 percent per annum the rate of the last preceding issue of debentures in which the bank participated. The rate charged by a bank, therefore, is governed primarily by the cost of money which, in turn, is related closely to the prevailing rates on other prime securities in the market. As of June 30, 1973, the interest and discount rate of the federal intermediate credit banks ranged from 6.72 to 7.40 percent.[6]

Institutions that rediscount with an intermediate credit bank are permitted to charge their borrowers on such loans not more than 4 percent per annum in excess of the discount rate of the intermediate credit bank. The twelve federal intermediate credit banks during the fiscal year ending June 30, 1973, had loans and discounts outstanding of nearly $7 billion.[7]

---

[6] *Ibid.*, p. 34.
[7] *Ibid.*, p. 75.

Production Credit Associations

The Governor of the Farm Credit Administration is authorized to charter cooperative lending organizations, known as production credit associations, making short-term loans to farmers for agricultural uses. Typically, such loans are used for purposes of breeding, raising, and fattening of livestock and poultry; dairying; the growing, harvesting, and marketing of crops; the purchase and repair of farm machinery; the purchase and repair of rural homes; and the refinancing of short-term debts. Associations now serve every rural county in the United States and Puerto Rico, each association's territory of operation being prescribed by the Governor of the Farm Credit Administration.

Capital Stock. Each production credit association has two classes of capital stock: Class A, which is nonvoting; and Class B, which is voting. Class B stock may be owned only by borrowing farmers. The Class A stock, owned by the Governor of the Farm Credit Administration, is preferred as to assets in case of liquidation of an association, but all stocks share proportionately in dividends. Borrowers are required to purchase Class B stock of an association to the extent of $5 for each $100 of loan. Such stock may be retained and used regularly for borrowing purposes. Should the borrower prefer to discontinue his membership after his indebtedness to the association has been retired, he may list it for sale to another eligible borrower. As in the case of members of the national farm loan associations, each borrower has one vote. Such voting must be accomplished in person, voting by proxy not being permitted. Holders of Class B stock are required to sell their stock in the event that two years elapse after the loan has been repaid and no new loan has been negotiated. The purpose of this limitation is to restrict control of the production credit association to active borrower members.

Management. Voting stockholders elect their association's board of directors at their annual meetings. The board is generally composed of five members, each selected for three years on a staggered basis. It is the responsibility of these directors to elect the association officers and appoint its employees.

Source of Funds. The production credit associations secure loan funds by borrowing from the federal intermediate credit bank of their district or by turning over to the intermediate credit banks loans that they have made to their customers. Loans are made to farmers and ranchers for general agricultural purposes to finance sound short-term credit needs. These loans are generally secured by a first lien on crops, livestock, and equipment, and interest is charged only on the amount of the loan actually outstanding.

The production loan associations also charge a loan service fee to cover the cost of appraising, reviewing, and administering the loans. Short-term credit secured from the production credit associations is often sufficient to cover a member's entire credit needs for a season or a year. Farmers usually get their installments as they need the money and repay their loans when they sell the products financed. Budgeted loans of this nature reduce the number of days each dollar is outstanding and reduce correspondingly the amount of interest paid by the borrower. Farmers had loans outstanding for a total of $7.5 billion from the 435 production credit associations as of June 30, 1973.[8]

THE COOPERATIVE BANK SERVICE

For many years the federal government has encouraged the establishment of farmers' marketing and purchasing cooperatives. Such encouragement has taken the form of immunity from the antitrust laws, tax advantages, and financial assistance. The provision of financial assistance is accomplished through a system of banks for cooperatives.

Under the provisions of the Farm Credit Act of 1933, the Governor of the Farm Credit Administration chartered twelve district banks and one Central Bank to provide a permanent system of credit for farmers' cooperatives. One of the banks for cooperatives is located in each of the farm credit districts, and the Central Bank is now located in Denver, Colorado.

---

[8] *Ibid.*, p. 84.

Functions of the Banks for Cooperatives

The thirteen banks make loans to cooperatives engaged in marketing agricultural products, purchasing farm supplies, and furnishing farm business services. The Central Bank for Cooperatives makes loans that are too large for district banks to handle and loans to cooperatives operating in more than one farm credit district. The Central Bank also participates in many loans made by the district banks. District banks, in turn, participate in loans made by the Central Bank.

Capital and Other Sources of Loanable Funds

The initial capital for the banks for cooperatives was subscribed by the Governor of the Farm Credit Administration from funds made available by the federal government. Changes in this initial capital have been made from time to time as the demand for credit has varied. All stock originally held by the federal government has now been retired. Borrowing cooperatives must purchase $100 in stock for each $2,000 borrowed.

The banks for cooperatives are authorized to borrow from, or turn their own loans over to, other banks for cooperatives, the federal intermediate credit banks, and commercial banks. The Central Bank for Cooperatives is authorized to issue debentures in an amount not to exceed five times its paid-in capital and surplus.

Management

General supervision of the banks for cooperatives is exercised by the Cooperative Bank Commissioner acting under the direction of the Governor of the Farm Credit Administration. The district banks have as their board of directors the farm credit board of each district. In addition to the officers elected by the board, each of the banks has a staff composed of business analysts, appraisers, accountants, and clerical employees. The Central Bank for Cooperatives has a board of seven directors, six of whom are appointed by the Governor of the Farm Credit Administration. The seventh member is the Cooperative Bank Commissioner, who also acts as chairman of the board.

Eligible Borrowers

To be eligible to borrow from a bank for cooperatives, an association must be a cooperative operated for the mutual benefit of its members in which farmers act together in doing one or more of the following: (1) processing, preparing for market, handling, or marketing farm products; (2) purchasing, testing, grading, processing, distributing, or furnishing farm supplies; or (3) furnishing farm business services.

Types of Loans

Three types of loans are made to cooperatives: (1) short-term loans secured by appropriate commodities in storage; (2) operating capital loans to supplement the borrowing cooperatives' working capital; (3) loans for the purpose of assisting in financing the cost of construction, purchase, or lease of land and the acquisition of buildings, equipment, or other physical facilities. Although maturities of twenty years are permitted, in most cases they are for much shorter periods. As of June 30, 1973, 3,113 cooperatives had loans outstanding from the banks in the amount of approximately $2.7 billion.[9]

OTHER FEDERAL AGRICULTURAL CREDIT FACILITIES

The trend in recent years has been toward administrative centralization of the many sources of government-sponsored agricultural credit under the Farm Credit Administration. There remain, however, several financial operating organizations directly under the control of the Secretary of Agriculture. Two of these are the Commodity Credit Corporation and the Farmers Home Administration.

The Commodity Credit Corporation

The Commodity Credit Corporation was organized in 1933 to provide a more orderly and stable market for farm products. Loans

---

[9] *Ibid.*, p. 94.

and loan guarantees are used by the Corporation in order to support the price of basic commodities, such as wheat, tobacco, corn, and cotton. These basic commodities serve as collateral for Commodity Credit Corporation loans. The maximum loan value on farm products is based on a percentage of "parity" prices established at the beginning of the year. A condition of the availability of such loans, however, is that the borrowing farmer shall have complied with governmental restrictions concerning the number of acres allotted to that farmer for the planting of that crop. He can borrow from the Commodity Credit Corporation a stipulated percentage of the parity value of the crop even though such parity value is above the prevailing market value of that product. Purchase by the government of the farm products used as collateral for the commodity credit loan becomes effective by default if the loan is not repaid. This amounts to a conditional purchase plan by the government to effect a price floor on farm products.

The Commodity Credit Corporation also gives support to farm prices through the outright purchase and storage of crops, and it has participated in general supply programs in cooperation with other federal agencies, foreign governments, and international relief organizations.

The capital of the Commodity Credit Corporation is provided entirely by the United States government. The Corporation has a capital of $100 million. It is authorized to borrow an additional $14.5 billion on the credit of the United States government. From the time of organization of the CCC in 1933 to July 1, 1974, approximately $61 billion in loans and loan guarantees had been issued. Loan guarantees and other private lending agency participation was discontinued after 1969. For the fiscal year ending June 30, 1973, the Commodity Credit Corporation provided more than $1.6 billion in loans.[10]

The Farmers Home Administration

The Farmers Home Administration was created in 1946 by the merger of the Farm Security Administration and the Emer-

---

[10] *Commodity Credit Corporation Report of Financial Condition and Operation.* Quarterly Report, Department of Agriculture, Agricultural Stabilization and Conservation Service, June 30, 1973.

gency Crop and Feed Loan Division of the Farm Credit Administration. It has been authorized to make loans and to insure loans for farmers who are otherwise unable to obtain credit at appropriate rates of interest and suitable maturities. Preference has been given to veterans to enable them to purchase farms. Loans for terms up to forty years are made for purposes of purchase, improvement, or repair of farms and farm buildings.

Responsibility for the following has been given the Farmers Home Administration: (a) administration of rural resettlement projects; (b) financing the purchase of farm property for tenant farmers; (c) financing emergency loans to low-income farmers; and (d) financing loans to facilitate farmers' community and co-operative enterprises that would be classified as rehabilitation or resettlement projects. Loans of up to $50,000 are made for such purposes as the purchase of livestock, seed, fertilizer, farm equipment, supplies, and other farm needs, as well as for financing indebtedness and family subsistence. Such loans have maturities of from 1 to 7 years. Farm ownership loans are repayable over periods up to 40 years. Farmers Home Administration loans plus other debts against the security property may not exceed $100,000. Borrowers may make advance payments in good years so they will be protected against falling behind in their payments in difficult years. Funds for the loans of the Farmers Home Administration are provided by Congress.

QUESTIONS

1. Compare the credit needs for farming with the credit needs of industrial manufacturing.
2. Farm financing is often described as being an especially difficult problem. Explain.
3. Discuss the importance of commercial bank lending for agricultural purposes. Do commercial banks provide credit for all agricultural purposes?
4. To what extent and for what purposes do life insurance companies provide funds for agriculture?
5. How do the life insurance companies of the nation maintain contact with farmers for purposes of extending mortgage loans?
6. Describe some of the private sources of agricultural credit other than commercial banks and life insurance companies.

7. Describe the evolution and present structure of the principal governmental facilities for farm credit.

8. Trace the principal steps involved in the making of a federal land
bank loan from the original application by the farmer to the receipt
of the loan.

9. Discuss the method by which the federal land banks shift part of the
risk of mortgage lending to other groups.

10. Describe the role of the federal intermediate credit banks in agricultural financing.

11. Discuss the sources of loan funds for the federal land banks and for
the federal intermediate credit banks. To what extent are the obligations of these organizations liabilities of the federal government?

12. Describe the role of the production credit associations in agricultural
financing.

13. For what purposes were the banks for cooperatives established?

14. Outline the types of loans available to farmers through the Farmers
Home Administration.

SUGGESTED READINGS

Agricultural Finance Review, published annually by the Agricultural
Research Service, United States Department of Agriculture.

Agricultural Production Financing. New York: Agricultural Commission,
American Bankers Association.

Annual Reports, published by the Farm Credit Administration.

ARNOLD, L. L. *Problems of Capital Accumulation in Getting Started
Farming*. Station Bulletin 638. Lafayette, Indiana: Purdue University,
February, 1957.

Commission on Money and Credit, *Money and Credit*. Englewood Cliffs,
New Jersey: Prentice-Hall, Inc., 1961, pp. 192-96.

DUGGAN, I. W., and RALPH U. BATTLES. *Financing the Farm Business*. New
York: John Wiley and Sons, Inc., 1950.

Farm Equipment Financing by Banks. New York: Agricultural Commission, American Bankers Association.

Farm Real Estate Financing. New York: Agricultural Commission, American Bankers Association.

GOLDSMITH, RAYMOND W. *Financial Intermediaries in the American Economy since 1900*. New York: National Bureau of Economic Research,
1958, pp. 204-14.

Intermediate-Term Bank Credit For Farmers. New York: Agricultural
Commission, American Bankers Association.

TOSTLEBE, ALVIN S. *Capital in Agriculture*. New York: National Bureau of
Economic Research, 1957.

17 | International Finance

The productive capacity of the United States economy is the result of many factors, including vast natural resources, suitable climatic conditions, and a population that has had the courage and the ability to profit by these natural advantages. Of equal importance to the productive growth of the nation has been the existence of a form of government that has encouraged this development through stimulation of individual effort. Not the least of the contributions of the government in this respect has been that of facilitating trade between the areas of the nation, in turn making it possible for each geographical area to specialize in those activities for which its individual natural resources best equip it.

It is difficult to imagine the situation that would exist if each of the fifty states tried to be self-sufficient. Under these circumstances, we could expect the northern industrial states to enjoy little of the citrus fruits that they now import from Florida and the West Coast. Nor could we expect the tobacco-growing states to have the full benefit of farm machinery for their operations, since the market for machinery in a single state is hardly sufficient to warrant production on a scale necessary for economical manufacture.

While these principles of specialization with regard to geographical areas of the United States are obvious enough, it may be somewhat more difficult to appreciate the extension of these principles of specialization beyond the borders of the country; yet the basic principles underlying specialization of effort within a nation hold true with equal force among nations. The very size of the United States is such as to lead a person not otherwise familiar with the vast amount of goods and services transported between the United States and foreign countries to believe that the nation is nearly self-sufficient. It is true that many items which were formerly imported are now produced in the country, making us less dependent upon foreign sources; however, there is an effective limit to the self-sufficiency that any nation can attain. For example, the development of sufficient coffee production within the nation to satisfy the current domestic demand for the product would probably be impossible.

In addition to the many items for which other nations possess a natural productive advantage, other items are not available within our own national borders under any circumstances. Examples of such items include tin, magnesium, and extracts from certain tropical plants used in the preparation of medicines. Although there are some legitimate reasons for curtailing temporarily, and in some cases permanently, certain types of trade flows, it is undoubtedly true that a specialized concentration of effort on the part of the nations of the world is to the general benefit of everybody concerned.

The benefits which arise as a result of specialization of effort are made possible only to the extent that the persons participating in such specialization are assured that there will be a market for the fruits of their effort. A market for goods and services is made effective only if adequate financial facilities exist to make possible the settlement of claims between the parties. Just as there has developed within the United States an intricate and smoothly operating system of finance to provide for the exchange of goods and services among persons and institutions, so too there has developed a system of international finance whereby settlement of international claims may be effected. It is with this process of settlement of international claims that this chapter is concerned.

INTERNATIONAL PAYMENTS

As a citizen of the United States tours our country during his vacation, he desires to pay his lodging bills, his gasoline costs, and other vacation expenses with dollars. Similarly, the motel and hotel operators and the service station attendants wish to be paid for their goods and services in the form of dollars. The large mail-order houses located in Chicago also demand dollars for the goods that they are willing to ship to all parts of the country, and the persons ordering such goods are prepared to pay in terms of dollars. On the other hand, a person who orders leather goods from Mexico, glassware from Italy, or a year's subscription to *The London Times*, may arrange for payment for these items not in dollars but rather in the money of the particular country from which the items have been ordered.

Foreign exporters are usually quite willing to accept United States dollars in payment for their goods and services because of the importance of the dollar in international trade and the ease with which it can be converted into the money of the exporter's country. The importers of many countries, however, must arrange payment to foreign exporters in the money of the exporter's country. The importance of the United States dollar in foreign exchange makes it a popular money for the settlement of transactions among other countries as well as between the United States and other countries.

When it is necessary or desirable to make payments in international trade in the money of another country, actual possession of the foreign money is unnecessary. For example, if a person wishes to pay for a year's subscription to *The London Times* in sterling, the subscriber need only go to the bank and buy a claim against British pounds equivalent to the subscription cost of the paper. This claim, which is purchased in the United States with American dollars, will be in the form of a bill of exchange, a telegraphic order, or similar instrument. An oversimplified example will illustrate how these claims may be purchased and the actual acquisition of the foreign currency avoided.

If the person who is purchasing a subscription to *The London Times* wishes to secure a claim for twenty pounds, he could conceivably seek out a British tourist who at that moment might be touring the United States. If that tourist had brought his check-book with him, he might be induced to write a check against his own local bank in England for twenty pounds, in return for the appropriate number of dollars, which he would expect to spend while a tourist in this country. In addition, of course, the English tourist might expect a slight additional payment to compensate him for the trouble of rendering this service. The individual to whom the check is written could then endorse it and send it together with his order for *The London Times* to England where the check would be deposited for collection with the bank with which that paper does business. The subscriber to the *London Times* purchased, in essence, nothing more than a claim to pounds.

This is rather an awkward process, however, and it is hardly to be expected that an importer would be required to seek out some foreign visitor to this country. Instead, the banking system along with other institutions provides this service for a nominal fee. Although all banks do not have departments that sell foreign exchange to their customers, practically all banks do have correspondent relations with banks located in the major seaport towns or cities which do offer that facility. Hence, it is necessary only to go to a local bank in order to secure a claim against foreign money. If the local bank does not itself have a claim to foreign currency, it can purchase such a claim for its customers from a bank with which it deals for that purpose. The banks that deal directly in foreign exchange may do so by maintaining monetary deposits in banks in foreign countries, against which they may draw drafts for sale to their home customers. In other cases, banks may operate branches in the foreign countries. The Federal Reserve Act authorizes banks to establish branches abroad; as of the end of 1972, there were 627 such branches in 73 foreign countries or dependencies of the United States.

Foreign banking corporations likewise have their own network of foreign contacts. In addition to maintaining correspondent relations with United States banks, foreign banks are permitted to operate agencies and to set up subsidiaries in this country. Most of these organizations are located in New York City and must, of course, comply with the state banking laws. They are limited as to the type of business in which they may engage, primarily that of dealing in foreign exchange. Subsidiary banking corporations established by foreign banks are not subject to any special restrictions because of foreign ownership.

EXCHANGE RATES

The conversion ratio, or *exchange rate* as it is generally referred to, is the rate at which a given unit of foreign currency is quoted in terms of domestic currency. For example, if the British pound is quoted at $2.30 in the foreign exchange rate section of the daily newspaper, it means that purchases of claims on pounds sterling were made on the basis of a ratio of 2.3 dollars for one British pound. For the individual who cares to buy claims on pounds sterling, this exact ratio would not necessarily prevail since it is a record of the exchange ratio of large unit transfers within the foreign exchange market itself. The prices quoted to the individual are always in favor of the seller of the exchange, which, of course, makes possible a margin of profit for the seller. The seller or dealer in our example is a bank.

The balance in the foreign account of a bank is subject to constant drain as a result of the bank's activities in selling claims to individuals in the United States who wish to import goods or services from other countries. These banks may reestablish a given deposit level with their correspondent banks through either the sale of dollar claims in the foreign country concerned or by buying claims from another dealer in the foreign exchange. The question may arise, however, as to what happens if during a period of time the volume of trading is decidedly unbalanced and the demand for claims against British pounds is substantially greater than the corresponding demand by British businesses and individuals for American dollars. Since the exchange ratio reflects the forces of supply and demand for these two currencies, such a situation would be expected to cause the ratio to rise to a point above $2.30 for each pound sterling. At some point, the number of dollars available in exchange for pounds would become high enough to induce owners of pounds to invest in American dollars.

As do the prices of all commodities, exchange rates vary from one period to another, although the degree of variance is as a rule not large over a short period of time. Changes of a few cents may be noticed in weekly comparisons of the exchange ratios of currencies of other countries and of the United States. As a result of varying exchange rates, the importer or exporter may be financially benefited or hurt in much the same manner that he may be affected by changes in the price level of the commodity which he purchases or sells. Foreign exchange rates between the United States and the principal countries of the world as of March 14, 1974, are shown in Table 17-1.

Arbitrage

Arbitrage may be defined as the simultaneous, or nearly simultaneous, purchasing, as of commodities, securities, or bills of exchange, in one market and selling in another where the price is higher. In international exchange, variations in quotations between countries at any time are quickly brought into alignment through the arbitrage activities of international financiers.

For example, if the exchange rate in New York was reported at £1 = $2.31 and in London the rate was quoted at £1 = $2.30, alert international financiers would simultaneously sell claims to British pounds in New York at the rate of $2.31 and have London correspondents sell claims on American dollars in London at the rate of $2.30 for each pound sterling. Such arbitrage would be profitable only when dealing in large sums. If an arbitrager, under these circumstances, sold a claim on £100,000 in New York, he would receive $231,000. The corresponding sale of claims on American dollars in London would be at the rate of £100,000 for $230,000. Hence, a profit of $1,000 would be realized on the transaction.

The effect of such arbitrage activities on exchange rates would be the elimination of the variation between the New York and the London quotations, for example, since the sale of large amounts of claims to American dollars in London would drive the price for pounds sterling up; and in New York the sale of claims to pounds sterling would force the exchange rate down. A quotation differential of as little as one-sixteenth of one cent may be sufficient to encourage arbitrage activities.

Table 17–1

FOREIGN EXCHANGE

Friday, March 14, 1974

Selling prices for bank transfers in the U.S. for payment abroad, as quoted at 4 p.m. Eastern Time (in dollars):

COUNTRY	FRIDAY	THURSDAY
Argentina (Peso)	.1020	.1020
Australia (Dollar)	1.4925	1.4925
Austria (Schilling)	.0513	.0513
Belgium (Franc)	.024940	.024850
Brazil (Cruzeiro)	.1595	.1595
Britain (Pound)	2.3330	2.3420
Canada (Dollar)	1.0281	1.0278
Colombia (Peso)	.0400	.0400
Denmark (Krone)	.1594	.1590
Ecuador (Sucre)	.041	.041
Finland (Markka)	.2607	.2605
France (Franc)	.2065	.2074
Greece (Drachma)	.0338	.0338
Hong Kong (Dollar)	.1977	.1979
India (Rupee)	.1250	.1245
Iraq (Dinar)	3.4025	3.4025
Israel (Pound)	.2385	.2385
Italy (Lira)	.001566	.001562
Japan (Yen)	.003546	.003538
Lebanon (Pound)	.4220	.4220
Mexico (Peso)	.08006	.08006
Netherlands (Guilder)	.3607	.3594
New Zealand (Dollar)	1.4475	1.4475
Norway (Krone)	.1763	.1762
Pakistan (Rupee)	.1020	.1020
Peru (Sol)	.0234	.0234
Philippines (Peso)	.1490	.1490
Portugal (Escudo)	.0395	.0395
Singapore (Dollar)	.4049	.4052
South Africa (Rand)	1.4925	1.4925
Spain (Peseta)	.0169	.017
Sweden (Krona)	.2165	.2160
Switzerland (Franc)	.3226	.3217
Uruguay (Peso)	.00077	.0008
Venezuela (Bolivar)	.2340	.2340
West Germany (Mark)	.3779	.3765

SOURCE: Bankers Trust Co., New York.

Exchange Quotations

In inquiring at the local bank as to the exchange rate for a foreign currency at a specific time, a banker's sight draft rate will generally be given. A *banker's sight draft,* or *banker's check* as it is more commonly termed, differs from the common bank check only in that it is drawn by one bank on another bank. When presented for payment at the foreign bank, the balance of the drawing bank is reduced. Several days or weeks may elapse between the time the check is issued by the bank and the time it is presented for payment at the foreign bank or foreign correspondent bank. During this interval, the foreign balance of the issuing bank is not affected by the transaction.

If specifically requested, the quotation may be based on a cable rate. The bank may cable to its foreign correspondent or foreign branch to credit to the account of a specified individual or business establishment a certain amount of money. The cost of a cable order of this sort is more than a banker's check because it reduces the balance of the bank's foreign deposit almost immediately. A rate which is lower than either the banker's check rate or the cable rate is that of the *banker's time draft,* sometimes called long exchange or a long bill. Such instruments are payable at specified future dates, usually thirty days or some multiple thereof. The quotations on these time drafts are, of course, lower because they involve a reduction in the balance of the foreign branch or correspondent only after a specified period of time.

FINANCING INTERNATIONAL TRADE

One of the substantial financial burdens of any industrial firm is that of carrying the cost of the goods being produced through the process of manufacture itself. In the case of a United States manufacturer who ships his goods to such far distant places as India or Australia, his funds are tied up not only for the period of manufacture but also for a lengthy period of transportation. In order to solve this problem and so reduce the burden of carrying these financial costs, the manufacturers may stipulate that the foreign importer is to provide payment for the goods as soon as the goods are placed in transportation to their destination. In any case, a substantial financial burden exists either on the part of the exporter or on the part of the importer.

Financing by the Exporter

Should the exporter have confidence in his foreign customers and be in a financial position to carry sales to his customers on open-book account, there is no reason why the arrangement should not operate very much as it operates in domestic trade, subject, of course, to the complications involved in any international transaction.

Sight and Time Drafts. As an alternative to the shipment of merchandise on the basis of open-account financing, the exporter may use a collection draft. A *draft* or bill of exchange is an unconditional order in writing, signed by the person drawing it, requiring the person to whom it is addressed to pay on demand or at a fixed or determinable future time a sum certain in money to order or to bearer. A draft may require immediate payment by the importer upon its presentation, or it may require only acceptance on the part of the importer, providing for payment at a specified future time. Those instruments requiring immediate payment are classified as *sight drafts*; those requiring payment later are classified as *time drafts*. These drafts may require remittance in the currency of the country of the exporter or of the importer, depending upon the terms of the transaction. An example of a sight draft form is shown below.

Figure 17–1

$2,500.00	New Orleans, Louisiana,	August 15, 19____

At sight – PAY TO THE

ORDER OF____John Smith_____

Two thousand five hundred no/100 – – – – – – – – – – – – – – – – – DOLLARS

VALUE RECEIVED AND CHARGE TO ACCOUNT OF

TO Brazilian Import Company   }   NEW ORLEANS EXPORT COMPANY

No. 11678   Rio de Janeiro, Brazil   *Thomas Jones*

Sight Draft or Bill of Exchange

Drafts may be either documentary or clean. A *documentary draft* is accompanied by an order bill of lading and such other papers as insurance receipts, certificates of sanitation, and consular invoices. The *order bill of lading* represents the written acceptance of goods for shipment by a transportation company and the terms under which the goods are to be conveyed to their destination. In addition, the order bill of lading carries title to the merchandise being shipped, and only its holder may claim the merchandise from the transportation company. (See Figure 17-2.) The documentary sight draft is generally referred to as a D/P draft (documentary payments draft) while the documentary time draft is referred to as a D/A draft (documentary acceptance draft).

A *clean draft* is one that is not accompanied by any special documents and is generally used when the exporter has confidence in the importer's ability to meet the draft when presented. In such a case, once the merchandise is shipped to the importer, it is delivered to him by the transportation company irrespective of any action he may take with regard to acknowledgment of the draft.

Bank Assistance in the Collection of Drafts. An importer will generally try to avoid making payment for a purchase before the goods are actually shipped because he must wait several days and perhaps weeks before receiving the goods. It is equally true that the exporter is seldom willing to send the draft and documents directly to the importer for payment or acceptance unless he has confidence in the importer. Therefore, the exporter will work through his commercial bank.

A New York exporter who is dealing with a foreign importer with whom he has had little relationship in the past may ship goods on the basis of a documentary draft that he deposits for collection with his local bank. That bank, following the specific instructions set out regarding the manner of collection, then forwards the draft together with the accompanying documents to its correspondent bank in the foreign country involved. The correspondent bank is instructed to hold the documents until payment is made if a sight draft is used, or until acceptance is obtained if a time draft is used. Remittance is made to the exporter when collection is made on the sight draft.

Figure 17–2

UNITED STATES LINES CO.
(SPACES IMMEDIATELY BELOW FOR SHIPPERS MEMORANDA—NOT PART OF BILL OF LADING)

FORWARDING AGENT—REFERENCES	EXPORT DEC. No.
John Doe Shipping Co., #E6776 F.M.B. #9786	X67-90687

DELIVERING CARRIER TO STEAMER:	CAR NUMBER — REFERENCE
Penn Central Company	876528

BILL OF LADING
(SHORT FORM)

(NOT NEGOTIABLE UNLESS CONSIGNED "TO ORDER")

SHIP American Banker	FLAG	PIER 61 N.R.	PORT OF LOADING
PORT OF DISCHARGE FROM SHIP Liverpool	AM.	THROUGH BILL OF LADING	NEW YORK

(Where goods are to be delivered to consignee or On-carrier)
If goods to be transshipped beyond Port of Discharge, show destination Here ☞ To

SHIPPER Midwest Printing Company

CONSIGNED TO: ORDER OF M. T. Wilson & Co.

ADDRESS ARRIVAL NOTICE TO Same at 15 Dock St., Liverpool, E.C. 3

PARTICULARS FURNISHED BY SHIPPER OF GOODS

MARKS AND NUMBERS	NO. OF PKGS.	DESCRIPTION OF PACKAGES AND GOODS	MEASUREMENT	GROSS WEIGHT IN POUNDS
M. T. W. & CO. Liverpool	56	Books		10,145

SPECIMEN

FREIGHT PAYABLE IN NEW YORK

(10,145)	●	PER 2240 LBS. .$		
	●	PER 100 LBS. .$		
	FT. ●	PER 40 CU. FT.$		
545	FT. ● $1.05	PER CU. FT...$	572	25
		$		
		$		
		$		
	TOTAL . . $			

(TERMS OF THIS BILL OF LADING CONTINUED FROM REVERSE SIDE HEREOF)
IN WITNESS WHEREOF,
THE MASTER OR AGENT OF SAID VESSEL HAS SIGNED___3
BILLS OF LADING, ALL OF THE SAME TENOR AND DATE, ONE OF WHICH BEING ACCOMPLISHED, THE OTHERS TO STAND VOID.

UNITED STATES LINES COMPANY

BY_____J. J._____
FOR THE MASTER

B/L No. ISSUED AT NEW YORK, N. Y.
M-105

January	12	19
MO.	DAY	YEAR

Order Bill of Lading

Financing Through the Exporter's Bank. It is important to recognize that throughout this transaction the banking system has only provided a service to the exporter and has in no way financed the transaction itself. The exporter's bank, however, may offer considerable assistance in this respect by allowing the exporter to borrow against the security of a documentary draft. The amount of the bank loan under these circumstances is less than the face amount of the draft. Such loans have not only the financial strength of the exporter to support them but also that of the importer, since the documents permitting acquisition of the merchandise are released only after the importer has accepted the draft. The amount that the exporter can borrow against the draft depends in large measure upon the credit standing of both the exporter and the importer. In some cases, a substantial percentage of the draft may be advanced when the exporter is financially strong, even though the importer may be little known to the exporter's bank, since the credit position of the exporter will offer suitable protection to the bank. In other cases, a substantial advance may be made where the exporter has only modest financial strength but the importer is financially strong.

In addition to the financial strength of the exporter and the importer, the character of the goods shipped will also have an important bearing upon the amount loaned against a draft since the goods shipped offer collateral security for the advance. Goods not subject to breakage or perishability offer a better form of collateral than goods of a highly perishable nature. Also, goods for which there is a ready market are preferred as collateral over those for which the market may be very limited.

Financing by the Importer

As in the case of the exporter, the importer may arrange for the payment of goods that he orders without access to the credit of his bank. Payment may be made in full with the order, or a partial payment may be offered. The partial payment offers some protection to both the exporter and the importer. It protects the exporter against arbitrary rejection of the goods so shipped on the part of the importer. It also assures the importer of having some control over the transactions in the event the merchandise purchased is damaged in shipment or does not meet specifications. Where the importer is required to make payment with his order but wishes some protection against failure of the exporter to make shipment in accordance with the provisions of the order, the order may be sent directly to the exporter; but payment therefor is sent to a representative bank in the country of the exporter. The bank is instructed not to release payment until certain documents are presented to the bank to evidence shipment of the goods according to the terms of the transaction. The bank, of course, charges a fee for providing this service.

Financing Through the Importer's Bank. In the field of foreign trade, because of the language barriers that exist and because of the difficulty in obtaining credit information about companies in the various countries, the use of the banker's acceptance is common. The *banker's acceptance* differs from the trade draft in only one respect. The former instrument is drawn on a bank and is accepted by a bank rather than by the importing firm. An example of a banker's acceptance is shown in Figure 17-3. The importer must, of course, make arrangements with his bank in advance of such an action. The exporter, too, must know before shipment is made whether or not the bank in question has agreed to accept such a draft. This arrangement is facilitated through the use of the commercial letter of credit. The *commercial letter of*

Figure 17–3

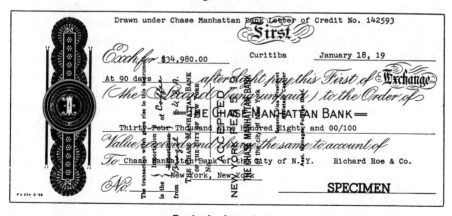

Banker's Acceptance

credit may be described as a written statement on the part of the bank to an individual or firm guaranteeing acceptance and payment of a draft up to a specified sum if presented to the bank in accordance with the terms of the commercial letter of credit. (See Figure 17-4.)

Importer Bank Financing—An Example. The issuance of the letter of credit and its application to international finance may be observed from the following example. The owner of a small but exclusive shop located in Chicago may wish to import expensive perfumes from Paris. Although the firm is well known locally, its financial reputation is not known widely enough to permit it to make direct purchases from foreign exporters on the basis of an open-book account arrangement or on the basis of drafts drawn on the firm. Under these circumstances the firm would substitute for its own credit that of its bank through the use of a commercial letter of credit. This would be accomplished by the firm's applying to its bank for a letter of credit. Before the bank will issue such a commitment, it must be entirely satisfied that its customer is in a satisfactory financial condition.

The letter of credit is addressed to a specific French exporter from whom the perfumes are to be purchased. The exporter, upon receipt of the commercial letter of credit, has little reason to hesitate in making the shipment. Although he has perhaps never heard of the firm that has placed the order, the bank which has issued the commercial letter of credit may be well known to the exporter or to the exporter's bank. The French exporter, then, makes shipment of the perfumes and at the same time draws a draft in the appropriate amount on the bank that has issued the letter of credit. He presents this draft to his bank along with the other papers as required by the commercial letter of credit. The exporter's bank transmits the draft and the accompanying documents to its New York correspondent who forwards them to the importer's bank. The importer's bank, upon receipt of the documents, makes a thorough inspection of the various papers that accompany the draft to determine if all the provisions of the letter of credit have been met. If upon examination of the document the bank is satisfied that the terms of the commercial letter of credit have been met, the draft is accepted and the

Figure 17–4

IRREVOCABLE
COMMERCIAL
LETTER OF CREDIT
The Chase Manhattan Bank
INTERNATIONAL DEPARTMENT
EIGHTEEN PINE STREET
NEW YORK 15, N. Y.

...**$35,000.00 U.S.Cy**...

No. 142593   **New York**   January 29, 19

```
┌                            ┐
  Richard Roe & Co.
  Curitiba
  Brazil
└                            ┘
```

GENTLEMEN:
WE HEREBY AUTHORIZE YOU TO DRAW ON The Chase Manhattan Bank, New York City

BY ORDER OF   John Doe & Co.
     New York, N. Y.
AND FOR ACCOUNT OF John Doe & Co.
UP TO AN AGGREGATE AMOUNT OF THIRTY-FIVE THOUSAND DOLLARS U.S. CURRENCY.....

AVAILABLE BY YOUR DRAFTS AT 90 days sight, for full invoice value, in duplicate..
ACCOMPANIED BY Commercial Invoice in triplicate....
     Consular Invoice in duplicate...
     Full set of onboard Bills of Lading to order of The
Chase Manhattan Bank, New York, marked Notify John Doe & Co., New York,
N. Y., and bearing a separate onboard endorsement signed by the Master
and dated not later than January 31, 19   , also marked freight collect
at port of destination...

evidencing shipment of 500 Bags of Coffee, FOB vessel at Paranagua from
Paranagua, Brazil to any U.S. Atlantic and/or U.S. Gulf Port.

...Any charges for negotiation of the draft(s) are for your account.
...Marine and war risk insurance covered by buyers.

DRAFTS MUST BE DRAWN AND NEGOTIATED NOT LATER THAN   February 5, 19

EACH DRAFT MUST STATE THAT IT IS "DRAWN UNDER LETTER OF CREDIT OF THE CHASE MANHATTAN BANK,
NEW YORK, NO. 142593   DATED January 29, 19   ", AND THE AMOUNT ENDORSED ON THIS
LETTER OF CREDIT.
     WE HEREBY AGREE WITH THE DRAWERS, ENDORSERS, AND BONA FIDE HOLDERS OF ALL DRAFTS DRAWN
UNDER AND IN COMPLIANCE WITH THE TERMS OF THIS CREDIT, THAT SUCH DRAFTS WILL BE DULY HONORED
UPON PRESENTATION TO THE DRAWEE.
     EXCEPT SO FAR AS OTHERWISE EXPRESSLY STATED, THIS CREDIT IS SUBJECT TO THE UNIFORM
CUSTOMS AND PRACTICE FOR COMMERCIAL DOCUMENTARY CREDITS FIXED BY THE THIRTEENTH CONGRESS
OF THE INTERNATIONAL CHAMBER OF COMMERCE.

YOURS VERY TRULY

SPECIMEN

ASSISTANT VICE PRESIDENT   ASSISTANT TREASURER
ASSISTANT TREASURER   PER PROCURATION

Irrevocable Commercial Letter of Credit

appropriate officials of the bank enter their signatures on the draft. The accepted draft, now a banker's acceptance, may be held until maturity by the exporter, then rerouted to the accepting bank for settlement or sold to other investors.

After having accepted the draft, the bank notifies its customer that the shipping documents are in its possession and that he is to come to the bank and make arrangements to take over the documents. As the merchandise is sold, the firm is able to build up its account with the bank by daily deposits until sufficient deposits are available to retire the acceptance. The bank then is in a position to meet its obligation on the acceptance without advancing its own funds at any time.

In releasing shipping documents to a customer, the bank may prefer to establish an agency arrangement between the firm and the bank whereby the bank retains title to the merchandise. The instrument that provides for the retention of title to the merchandise by the bank is called a *trust receipt*. (See Figure 17-5.) Should the business fail, the bank would not take the position of an ordinary creditor in order to establish its claim on the business assets, but rather it would be able to repossess the goods and place them with another agent for sale since title had never been transferred to the customer. As the merchandise is sold under the trust receipt arrangement, it is generally required that the business deliver to the bank the proceeds from the sale until such time as the total amount of the acceptance has been deposited with the bank.

In summary, the banker's acceptance and the commercial letter of credit involve four principal parties: the importer, the importer's bank, the exporter, and the exporter's bank. Each benefits to a substantial degree through this arrangement. The importer benefits in that he is able to secure adequate credit even though his own financial credit is not established on an international basis. The importer's bank benefits because it has charged a fee for the issuance of the commercial letter of credit and for the other services provided in connection therewith. The exporter has been benefited in that he has been given the assurance of definite payment for the shipment of merchandise. A sale is made possible that may otherwise have been rejected because of lack of certainty of payment. Finally, the exporter's bank benefits if it discounts

Figure 17–5

RETURN TO	THE CHASE MANHATTAN BANK	INTERNATIONAL DEPARTMENT
	EIGHTEEN PINE STREET	COMMERCIAL L/C DIVISION

TRUST RECEIPT AND RECEIPT FOR DOCUMENTS

NEW YORK, Feb. 5, 19___

FROM

John Doe & Co.
New York
N.Y.

WE HAVE ACCEPTED DRAFT OF	DRAWN UNDER L/C NO.	
Richard Roe & Co. Curitiba, Brazil	142593	COMMISSION %

FOR ACCOUNT OF

John Doe & Co.

WE DEBIT YOUR ACCOUNT

TENOR	PAYABLE DATE	MATURITY DATE	AMOUNT
90 D/S	May 6, 19	May 6, 19	$34,980.00

COVERING SHIPMENT OF   500 Bags Coffee   PER S/S

FROM Parangua, Brazil TO New York, N.Y.   MORMACSURF

ACCEPTED AGAINST	INVOICE	INSURANCE CTF.	CONSULAR INVOICE	B/L	PAR. POST RECEIPTS	DELIVERY ORDER	FORWARDERS RECEIPT	CERTIF. OF ORIGIN	SPECIF.	INSPECTION CTF.	WEIGHT CTF.
ORIGINAL DOCUMENTS ENCLOSED	-1		1	2/4							
DUPLICATE DOCUMENTS TO FOLLOW											

Please officially sign the trust receipt appearing on the reverse side hereof, and return this form to us.

Trust Receipt No. 1675

MARKS AND NUMBERS	REMARKS
	We are advised remaining documents are coming by second mail and will be delivered as soon as received.

SPECIMEN

HRC/MIO

Trust Receipt and Receipt for Documents

the acceptance for the exporter since it receives a high-grade credit instrument with a definite, short-term maturity. Acceptances held by commercial banks provide a low but certain yield, and a bank can liquidate them quickly if it should need funds for other purposes.

The Volume and Significance of Bankers' Acceptances

The Board of Governors of the Federal Reserve System authorizes member banks to accept drafts that arise in the course of certain types of international transactions. These include the import and export of goods, the shipment of goods between foreign countries, and the storage of readily marketable staples in any foreign country. The maturity of member bank acceptances arising out of such transactions may not exceed six months. This authority to engage in bankers' acceptance financing is designed to encourage banks to participate in the financing of international trade and to strengthen the United States dollar in international exchange.

Bankers' acceptances are used to finance international transactions in a wide variety of items. Such items include coffee, wool, rubber, cocoa, metals and ores, crude oil, jute, and automobiles. Due to the growth of international trade in general and the increasing competition in foreign markets, bankers' acceptances have become increasingly important. Exporters have found it necessary to offer more liberal terms on their sales to compete effectively; the banker's acceptance permits them to do so without exposure to undue risk. Dollar acceptances outstanding as of December, 1973, totaled nearly $9 billion.[1]

The Cost and Market for Bankers' Acceptances

The cost of financing an international transaction with the banker's acceptance involves not only the interest cost involved in the discounting of the acceptance by the exporter but also the commission charge of the importer's accepting bank. From 1961 through 1973 interest costs on bankers' acceptances moved up steadily from slightly less than 3 percent to more than 10 percent.

Foreign central banks and commercial banks have regarded bankers' acceptances as attractive short-term commitments for their funds. More than half of all dollar acceptances have been held by foreign banks in recent years. Domestic commercial banks as of December, 1973, held approximately 32 percent of all dollar acceptances outstanding at that time.[2] Nonfinancial corporations have played a very small role as investors in acceptances.

There are only five firms that deal in bankers' acceptances, all of them located in New York City. The dealer is interested primarily in trading acceptances; that is, in arranging nearly simultaneous exchanges of purchases and sales.

---

[1] *Federal Reserve Bulletin* (Washington, D.C.: Board of Governors of the Federal Reserve System, February, 1974), p. A31.

[2] *Ibid.*

THE EXPORT-IMPORT BANK

The Export-Import Bank was authorized in 1934 and became an independent agency of the government in 1945. The purpose of the Bank is to aid in financing and to facilitate exports and imports between the United States and other countries. It is the only agency engaged solely in the financing of the foreign trade of the United States.

The Export-Import Bank is a government-owned corporation with capital of $1 billion in nonvoting stock paid in by the United States Treasury. It may borrow from the Treasury on a revolving basis and sell short-term discount promissory notes. Interest is paid on these borrowings, and dividends are paid on the capital stock. In performing its function of aiding and facilitating the foreign trade of the United States, the Bank makes long-term loans to finance the purchase of United States equipment, goods, and related services for projects undertaken by private enterprises or governments abroad. The Bank has also aided substantially in the economic development of foreign countries. Emergency credits are provided to assist other countries in maintaining the level of their imports from the United States when they experience temporary balance-of-payments difficulties. In addition, the Bank finances or guarantees the payment of medium-term commercial export credits extended by exporters and in partnership with private insurance companies, offers short- and medium-term credit insurance. It lends and guarantees only where there is reasonable assurance of repayment but avoids competition with sources of private capital.

Since its formation in 1934, the Export-Import Bank has supported $53 billion of export sales. Forty-one percent of this total has been made in the last three years. It has accumulated reserves available for future contingencies of $2.3 billion.[3]

TRAVELER'S LETTER OF CREDIT

A purchaser for a firm traveling abroad may not know in advance from whom purchases are to be made. For example, an

---

[3] Export-Import Bank of the United States, *Report to Congress for the Twelve Months Ended June 30, 1972* (Washington, D.C.), p. 27.

art buyer who tours several countries may not know in advance from which individuals or firms purchases may be made. In this case, the buyer might carry American currency that could be exchanged in the foreign countries for their currency. This involves the possible physical loss of the money, and occasionally conversion into the currency of the foreign country is accomplished only at a substantial discount. A traveler's letter of credit provides the necessary convenience and protection for this purpose.

The *traveler's letter of credit* is issued by a bank in one country and is addressed to a list of banks abroad. These foreign banks to which the letter of credit is addressed are usually correspondents of the issuing bank and have agreed to purchase upon sight drafts presented to them by persons displaying such letters of credit. At the time a letter of credit is issued by a bank, a copy of the signature of the person to whom the letter of credit is issued is sent to each of the foreign correspondent banks. When the individual presents a draft for payment in foreign currency to one of these foreign correspondent banks, he is asked to present his signature, which is then compared with the signature forwarded directly to these banks by the issuing bank. In addition, the individual presenting the draft may be asked for supplementary identification.

As in the case of the regular letter of credit, a maximum amount is stipulated for draft purposes on the part of the holder of the letter of credit. In order that an individual holding such a letter of credit may not exceed his authorized withdrawals, each bank to which the letter of credit is presented will enter on the letter of credit the amount of the draft that it has honored. In this way the individual presenting the letter of credit is unable to draw an amount in excess of that authorized.

TRAVELER'S CHECKS

Traveler's checks, which are offered by banks, express companies, and other agencies, are generally issued in denominations of $10, $20, $50, and $100. These checks, generally purchased by an individual before leaving for a trip, involve a promise to pay on demand even amounts as indicated by the face of the traveler's check. Each check must be signed twice, once at the time it is purchased and again at the time it is presented for payment. In this manner, the firm or institution to which the traveler's checks are presented for payment may be able to determine the authenticity of the signature by requiring the signing in its presence. Such traveler's checks are usually sold for their face amount plus a charge of one percent. The use of the traveler's check is widespread and offers many advantages to the traveler, including protection in the event of loss of the traveler's checks and certainty of acceptance on the part of the firms to which they are presented for payment.

QUESTIONS

1. Describe the process by which an importer in the United States is able to purchase goods from suppliers located in many countries, paying for each purchase with money of the country of the exporter.
2. How do commercial banks provide for the financial settlement of international transactions? Describe the institutional arrangements of commercial banks for maintaining deposits in foreign countries.
3. Explain the role of supply and demand as it relates to the establishment of exchange rates between countries.
4. Describe the activities and economic role of the arbitrager in international finance.
5. Foreign exchange quotations may be given in terms of sight drafts, cable drafts, and time drafts. What is the relative cost of these different types of drafts? Why should such cost differentials exist?
6. Describe the various ways by which an exporter may finance an international shipment of goods. How may commercial banks assist the exporter in the collection of drafts?
7. How may an importer protect himself against improper delivery of goods when he is required to make payment with his order?
8. Describe fully the process by which an importer may substitute the credit of his bank for his own in financing international transactions.
9. How may a bank protect itself after having issued a commercial letter of credit on behalf of a customer?
10. Describe the costs involved in connection with the financing of exports through bankers' acceptances.
11. Describe the ultimate sources of funds for export financing with bankers' acceptances. How are acceptances acquired for investment by these sources?
12. Explain the role played by the Export-Import Bank in international trade. Do you consider this Bank to be in competition with private lending institutions?
13. Distinguish between a commercial letter of credit and a traveler's letter of credit.

SUGGESTED READINGS

KREIDLE, JOHN R., and PAUL O. GROKE. "How to Finance your Exports." *Credit and Financial Management* (March, 1969).

MARCUS, EDWARD, and MILDRED RENDL MARCUS. *International Trade and Finance.* New York: Pitman Publishing Corporation, 1965. Chapters 5, 6, 7, and 16.

SHATERIAN, WILLIAM S. *Export-Import Banking,* 2d ed. New York: The Ronald Press Co., 1956.

VAN HORNE, JAMES C. *Fundamentals of Financial Management,* 2d ed. Englewood Cliffs, New Jersey: Prentice-Hall, Inc., 1974. Chapter 24.

VERNON, RAYMOND. *Manager in the International Economy,* 2d ed. Englewood Cliffs, New Jersey: Prentice-Hall, Inc., 1972.

WESTON, J. FRED, and BART W. SORGE. *International Managerial Finance.* Homewood, Illinois: Richard D. Irwin, Inc., 1972.

18

Consumer Credit in the Financial Structure

This chapter considers the nature of consumer credit and its role in the financial structure of our economy.

Consumer credit is defined so as to distinguish it from other forms of credit. The functions of consumer credit are then considered, showing how development and adaptation took place to meet changing needs. Changes in the volume of consumer credit are analyzed in the light of the factors that affect the demand for such credit. Then attention is directed to the users of various types of installment credit.

NATURE OF CONSUMER CREDIT

Consumer credit may be defined as credit used by consumers to help finance or refinance the purchase of commodities and services for personal consumption. Its use to finance personal consumption distinguishes it from business credit used for production purposes. For example, when an individual uses credit to buy an automobile for personal or family use, the credit extended to him is consumer credit; when a cab driver uses credit to buy a similar automobile for use as a taxi, the credit extended to him is business

383

credit. The distinguishing feature is the use to which the goods or services bought on credit are to be put.

Problems of Classification

Such a definition of consumer credit presents several practical problems. Credit extended to farmers who are operating a family farm may be used for consumption, for production, or for both. It is often difficult for a farmer himself to know just how the money will be divided among different uses. Banks therefore make no attempt to divide farm loans into loans for production and loans for consumption. Agricultural credit is usually treated as a separate category of credit since it is part consumer and part producer credit, and there are many institutions that loan money exclusively to farmers.

A similar problem of classification of credit arises at times in the nonagricultural sector of the economy. A consumer may use credit to buy an automobile that is intended primarily for personal use. It may be used in part, however, for business purposes. Since there is no practicable way of allocating such credit to consumption and production, all of it is assigned classification as consumer credit.

Long-Term Consumer Credit

Our definition of consumer credit includes credit used to purchase residential real estate and to make repairs or to modernize such property, since in each of these cases the purpose is to finance or refinance the purchase of goods or services for personal consumption. The major difference between financing the purchase of an automobile and a home is usually in the time period involved in repayment of the loan. Both are durable goods, but a house obviously lasts much longer than a car and costs considerably more; therefore, payments for a house are made over a longer period of time.

Credit used to purchase homes is treated as long-term consumer credit; that used for other purposes, as intermediate- and short-term credit. Such a distinction is frequently made in practice and in studies of consumer credit. Following such a division, credit for home repairs and modernization is treated as part of short-term and intermediate-term consumer credit. Credit for financing the purchase of a home is, then, the only case of long-term consumer financing.

FUNCTIONS OF CONSUMER CREDIT

The basic function of consumer credit is to enable the consumer to maximize the satisfaction he obtains by using his income for consumer goods. This assistance to the consumer takes several forms: (1) the provision of a convenient form of payment, (2) help in periods of financial stress, and (3) a plan for the payment for durable goods while they are being used.

Convenient Form of Payment

One reason for using consumer credit is the convenience of paying for goods and services. The typical charge account involves purchases from a retail store that are paid for once a month, usually by check. This plan makes small purchases more convenient than paying cash at the time of each purchase. Normally, about the same amount is spent each month whether goods are charged or paid for in cash. Since many people are paid monthly or semimonthly, it is a convenience for them to be able to pay for goods as their wages and salaries are paid to them. At times charge accounts may carry the consumer for a longer period of time. Some customers occasionally are one or two months in arrears in paying their bills. This is especially true after the heavy purchasing for the Christmas season. Many retail establishments, banks, and groups of banks have set up revolving charge accounts on which interest is charged if they are not paid on a monthly basis. The most frequent rate of interests is $1\frac{1}{2}$ percent per month on the unpaid balance. Limits to the total unpaid balances are set based upon an analysis of the financial position of the customer.

Services are also frequently paid for on a charge basis. This is true of electric, gas, and some telephone services that are billed once a month. Utilities companies may require cash deposits by those customers whose credit records and reputations reflect the prospect of difficult collections or possible losses. The usual arrangement, however, is to grant credit for a period of about six weeks since bills are sent out once a month and ten days to two weeks are allowed for payment. As a rule, doctors, dentists, lawyers, and other professional people send out statements once a month, thus providing a convenient method of monthly payment for their patients and clients.

Aid in Financial Emergencies

A second function of consumer credit is to help consumers through periods of financial stress. This function has been referred to as the safety-valve function of consumer credit. Most families with incomes of $10,000 or less, and many with larger incomes, do not have sufficient liquid assets to meet emergencies. They have such assets as homes, life insurance policies, automobiles, and household equipment of considerable value, but they do not have much cash to meet contingencies. When an emergency strikes, such as a serious illness, an accident, loss of a job, or loss of property due to a fire, a tornado, or a theft not covered by insurance, the cash reserves of such families are soon depleted. Consumer credit can perform a valuable function in tiding a family over an emergency. In many cases, the financial difficulty results from poor planning of family expenditures or poor budgeting of family resources. Unpaid bills probably accumulate, and a consumer loan to consolidate these bills may provide a way out of the difficulty.

Buying Durables on Installments

The third function performed by consumer credit is to aid consumers in financing the purchase of durable goods by paying for them in installments. The demands by consumers for housing, refrigeration, transportation, and so on are satisfied in our economy by means of consumer goods that provide such services for a period of time. A house may provide a place to live for 40 to 50 years, an electric refrigerator may provide refrigeration service for 10 or more years, and an automobile may provide transportation for 5 or more years.

The day-by-day satisfactions from durable goods are made available to consumers in several ways. As is the case with houses, and increasingly with cars and some appliances, it is possible to enjoy them by renting them.

Another way of enjoying durable goods is to purchase them, either new or used. These goods may be bought with cash or on the installment plan. To pay cash, the average consumer would have to save for a period of time until he accumulated the purchase price. For most consumers, this is not feasible as a method of acquiring a home since by the time a sufficient amount could be saved, the children would be grown and away from home. Therefore, most houses are paid for while the owners are deriving housing services by living in them.

The situation in regard to durables other than housing is similar. Most consumers would take several years to save enough to buy an automobile, furniture, and other major durable goods even if they followed through with a savings program. In the meantime they would have to do without these goods, and the price of waiting could be very high or even prohibitive. It does little good to save enough money to buy a refrigerator two years after the old one has failed to function, or to buy a car to drive to a new job at a place inaccessible to public transportation a year after the job has begun. Therefore, a system of systematically paying for such durables as they are being used is a real service to consumers.

Under most payment plans, these durable goods are paid for in a period that is materially shorter than their useful life. For example, a house that usually is serviceable for 40 years or more, is paid for in installments in 20 to 25 years; a refrigerator, which lasts 10 years or more, is usually paid for in 2 years. Financing such purchases on installments, therefore, is also an aid to the consumer in building up his stock of durable goods since, when the article is paid for in full, a substantial period of service still remains.

Another effect of selling durable goods on installments is the acceleration of the movement of manufactured goods, since consumers buy such goods sooner than they could if they first had to save the full purchase price. This effect is especially important in the case of a new durable good because manufacturers are able to achieve volume sales more rapidly than they could in a cash-sale economy.

DEVELOPMENT OF CONSUMER CREDIT

Consumer credit is probably as old as the human race itself. Before money was used, primitive peoples developed credit to make barter more flexible. This was consumer credit because almost all goods were consumer goods in those days. Such a form of consumer credit based on a barter system is still used by primitive societies in remote parts of the world today.[1]

In a primitive economy, no charge was made for the loan of goods because it was a problem for a nomadic people to carry around excess goods, such as food and clothing. If such articles were repaid in kind later on, the borrower and the lender both benefited because the borrower had the goods when needed and the lender did not have to move them around with him.

Development of Cash Lending

Records indicate that the lending of money for use in buying consumer goods developed almost simultaneously with the development of money as a medium of exchange. The business of lending cash to wage earners in the United States probably began after the Civil War in the cities of the Middle West. Such loans were made for short periods of time, the smallest payable in a week, two weeks, or a month; the largest, in less than a year.

Some degree of specialization developed in this early business of lending cash to consumers. One group of lenders attached wages as security, that is, they had the borrower sign an agreement to have a part of future wages paid to the lender in the event the loan was not paid on time. Another group loaned on unsecured notes, relying on their ability to get a court order to attach wages to collect on defaulted loans. A third group used chattel mortgages on household furniture as security. These loans gen-

---

[1] *Consumer Credit Today*, Proceedings of the Consumer Credit Conference for 1950 (Urbana: University of Illinois, 1951), p. 6.

erally ranged from $15 to $300, and the charges were between 5 percent and 40 percent a month.

This loan business was illegal under the usury laws that existed in most states then, just as it is now. But it was difficult to prove the usurious nature of the transactions since interest charges were disguised as fees for services, notes often had to be signed before the loans were completed, the cash being loaned was turned over without witnesses, receipts were not given, and so on. Many borrowers were also so glad to be accommodated that they did not press charges of usury.

As these abuses were brought to light, especially by the Russell Sage Foundation, small-loan legislation was passed in state after state; and legal lending of cash to consumers was subsequently developed by consumer finance companies and still later by commercial banks.

Factors Responsible for the Development of Cash Lending

Several factors account for the development of cash lending to consumers on an organized basis. The structure of our society was undergoing some pronounced changes in the period following the Civil War. One of the most important was the shifting of workers from rural to urban areas. A farmer can get along for a period of time during an emergency with practically no cash. As soon as he moves to an urban area, however, he is dependent upon current income, past savings, credit, or charity. Thus, the growing urbanization led to a demand for cash loans to meet emergencies.

This need was further accentuated by the changing character of industry and the position of the laboring class. In 1860 this country was primarily agricultural, but by 1900 it had an established factory system and a permanent body of industrial workers. The average size of the factory increased markedly, and relationships between employer and employee became more and more impersonal. Small independent producers began to disappear, and laborers were organized into plants of a thousand men or more. In many cases, employers continued to maintain a close relationship with employees and financed them during periods of difficulty. In other cases, there was no such relationship, and emergencies found the workers on their own.

Development of the Financing of Durable Goods Purchases

The use of credit for the payment for durable goods while they were being used also developed early in our economy. At first it was extended in the form of sales credit with long periods for repayment. A very large part of the trade in colonial Philadelphia was carried on by means of credit sales. For example, the records of a cabinetmaker for the period from 1775 to 1811 showed that 92 percent of all sales were on credit. A linen merchant of the same period expected few of his customers to pay him in less than a year. Benjamin Franklin took over nine months, on the average, to pay for the books he bought.[2]

Under such conditions, the volume of bad debts was bound to be high. One bookseller who allowed some customers to pay their bills over a period of two years had bad debts averaging 10 percent of sales. As was to be expected, some people misused credit and got into financial difficulties. The debts of some southern planters to mercantile houses in London were passed from father to son for several generations.[3]

Debts that could not be repaid during a lifetime gave rise to a peculiar marriage custom in colonial days. A man who married a widow whose former husband left unpaid debts was required to have the marriage ceremony take place in the middle of the King's highway with the bride dressed only in her petticoat to avoid taking on her former husband's debts.[4]

The first known examples of installment selling occurred in eastern cities. Stores that sold factory-made furniture on installments were established, but no records remain to show the extent of such trade or the terms of such sales. Early in the 19th century, clock manufacturers in New England also began to sell their products on installments. By 1850 a considerable business was done in the sale of pianos and organs on installments. By that year, Singer Sewing Machine Company also had begun to sell its machines through agents on the installment plan, and its competitors soon copied this practice. By the end of the century, the installment system had spread to most of the country east of the Mississippi,

2 *Ibid.*, pp. 6, 7.
3 *Ibid.*, p. 7.
4 *Ibid.*, pp. 7, 8.

and even west in some cases. This plan was used for a wide variety of goods and was made available to consumers with relatively low incomes.[5]

The real giant of installment sales, the automobile, appeared shortly after 1890, but it did not develop into a widely used consumer good until World War I days and later. In 1900 fewer than 4,200 cars were built, and the total production of cars and trucks first passed 100,000 in 1909.[6] Sales of cars paid for on installments probably began in 1910, and advertisements offering cars on time payments appeared in New York City in 1914. Thereafter such financing developed at a phenomenal rate, especially after the end of World War I in 1918. As new consumer goods, such as refrigerators, vacuum cleaners, washing machines, and air conditioners, were developed, they also were sold on installments, which helped increase the volume of such financing.

Factors Responsible for the Growth of Installment Buying

One of the basic reasons for the growth of installment credit was the increase in the investment in durable goods by consumers. It is impossible to estimate the amount of durable goods in the hands of consumers before 1900. It is possible, however, to obtain a fairly accurate picture of the durable goods owned by typical families in 1860.[7] In the homes of the better-housed workers in northern cities, a kitchen range was generally the only stove in the house. Candles frequently were the only source of light. Furniture was often homemade or, if factory-made, it was of very poor quality and there was little of it in the house. Dishes, silverware, and cooking utensils were of the cheapest grades. The poor, of course, got by with even less equipment. Farmers, especially those in the West, lived in log houses. What little furniture they had was homemade, and a fireplace served both for cooking and for heat.

---

[5] Reavis Cox, *The Economics of Installment Buying* (New York: The Ronald Press Company, 1948), pp. 62-63.

[6] Clyde William Phelps, *The Role of Sales Finance Companies in the American Economy* (Baltimore: Commercial Credit Company, 1952), p. 23.

[7] E. W. Martin, *The Standard of Living in 1860* (Chicago: The University of Chicago Press, 1942).

The stock of durable equipment in American homes increased between 1860 and 1900, but at the turn of the century it was still not large by today's standards. The moderately well-to-do home in 1900 probably had an original investment of not over $200 in such devices as a sewing machine, an ice refrigerator, a cooking stove, and a few odds and ends of laundry, cleaning, and transportation equipment. Today such a home will probably have an automobile, a mechanical refrigerator, a vacuum cleaner, an automatic washing machine and dryer, several radios, a television set, many small appliances, such as irons and toasters, and perhaps other items, having a total purchase price of $4,500 to $8,000. This increase in the ownership of durable goods has created a large total investment in such goods. According to one estimate, the total value of the durable goods owned by consumers at the end of 1973, was almost $350 billion.[8]

Basic Causes of Increased Investment in Durables

This increase in consumer expenditures on durables was the major factor leading to an increase in installment credit. Several factors were responsible for these increased expenditures. Methods of producing durable goods in large quantities at a low price were important. It is, of course, also true that a market had to exist for large quantities of goods to make the economies of large-scale, assembly-line production possible, and the development of installment financing helped to provide such a market.

This mass market was made possible because incomes were increasing and money was available for items other than necessary food, clothing, and shelter. Changing modes of living also provided the incentive to purchase such goods. More and more people moved to the cities and wanted conveniences equal to those of their neighbors. Increased activities put a greater premium on leisure time, thus leading to a demand for labor-saving devices.

Development of Urban Residential Real Estate Financing

Lending money to individuals to buy homes appears to have begun almost as soon as people established communities. The

---

[8] *1974 Finance Facts Yearbook* (Washington: National Consumer Finance Association, 1974), p. 45.

earliest form of real estate financing was through loans by one individual to another, and such direct loans are still one source of financing in this field. The first formal organization to set up a plan for home financing was organized in Frankford,[9] Pennsylvania, in 1831.[10] It was a cooperative agency for the purpose of lending funds pooled by the shareholders to the members for building or purchasing houses. It was not an American invention but was patterned after similar European institutions with which some of the immigrants were familiar. As time went on, more of these institutions were established; and they developed into the present-day savings and loan associations. Over the years, other agencies have entered the field of home financing.

Factors Responsible for the Development of Lending on Urban Real Estate

The growth of manufacturing and of urbanization after the Civil War led to an increased demand for housing in the cities. In rural areas it was frequently possible to build a log house with the help of the neighbors, but this was impossible in urban areas. The demand for housing was also increased by the large numbers of immigrants entering this country, most of whom were between 15 and 45 years of age. Some of them went onto farms, but most of them remained in cities, especially in the East.

Few families had the necessary cash to buy or build a house. Many rented their homes, but over the years an increasing number became homeowners. Increase in home ownership was possible not only because of increased incomes but also because financial institutions developed procedures by means of which homes could be paid for while the owners lived in them.

VOLUME OF CONSUMER CREDIT

Consumer credit has become one of the most important segments of financing. Statistics compiled by the Federal Reserve System show that total short- and intermediate-term consumer credit outstanding at the end of 1973 was $180.5 billion. The magnitude of this figure can better be appreciated when it is

---

9 Now a part of the city of Philadelphia.

10 Henry M. Bodfish and A. D. Theobald, *Savings and Loan Principles* (New York: Prentice-Hall, Inc., 1938), p. 27.

compared with short- and intermediate-term lending to business. As of December 31, 1973, all insured commercial banks had commercial loans to business of $157.6 billion outstanding.[11]

The largest segment of consumer credit is represented by *installment credit*, that is, loans which are to be repaid in regular installments, usually on a monthly basis. At the end of 1973, this was $147.4 billion or 82 percent of the total. About 67 percent of all installment credit was sales credit used to finance the sale of durable goods, and the rest was installment cash loans and home repair and modernization loans. Sales credit was higher than these figures show because some personal installment loans are used to finance the purchase of other durables, particularly automobiles. Credit used to buy automobiles on time was the largest part of installment sale credit, accounting for almost 52 percent of such credit outstanding at the end of 1973.[12]

The biggest part of noninstallment credit is convenience credit in the form of charge accounts and monthly payments for services. At the end of 1973, charge account credit was 30 percent and service credit 30 percent of noninstallment credit. The remaining 40 percent consisted of single-payment loans made by commercial banks and other financial institutions.[13] Complete figures on consumer credit outstanding by types for selected years since 1940 are presented in Table 18-1.

Relationship to Disposable Income

Another way to gauge the importance of consumer credit is to compare it with disposable personal income, that is, income available for personal consumption expenditures after paying personal taxes. Since 1929 the quarterly average of consumer credit extended has been between 5 percent and 19 percent of disposable personal income, except during the period 1943-46 when consumer durables were in short supply because of World War II restrictions. In prosperous years, when goods are freely available, consumer credit extended has averaged between 13 and 19 percent of disposable personal income and since 1965 between 15 and 19 percent.[14]

---

[11] *Federal Reserve Bulletin*, May, 1974, pp. A18 and A50.
[12] *Ibid.*, p. A50.
[13] *Ibid.*
[14] Based on Department of Commerce and Federal Reserve Board data.

SHORT- AND INTERMEDIATE-TERM CONSUMER CREDIT OUTSTANDING

[In millions of dollars]

END OF PERIOD	TOTAL	INSTALLMENT					NONINSTALLMENT			
		TOTAL	AUTO-MOBILE PAPER	OTHER CONSUMER GOODS PAPER	HOME IMPROVE-MENT LOANS 1	PERSONAL LOANS	TOTAL	SINGLE-PAYMENT LOANS	CHARGE ACCOUNTS	SERVICE CREDIT
1940	8,338	5,514	2,071	1,827	371	1,245	2,824	800	1,471	553
1950	21,471	14,703	6,074	4,799	1,016	2,814	6,768	1,821	3,367	1,580
1955	38,830	28,906	13,466	7,641	1,693	6,112	9,924	3,002	4,795	2,127
1960	56,141	42,968	17,658	11,545	3,148	10,617	13,173	4,507	5,329	3,337
1965	89,883	70,893	28,437	18,483	3,736	20,237	18,990	7,671	6,430	4,889
1966	96,239	76,245	30,010	20,732	3,841	21,662	19,994	7,972	6,686	5,336
1967	100,783	79,428	29,796	22,389	4,008	23,235	21,355	8,558	7,070	5,727
1968	110,770	87,745	32,948	24,626	4,239	25,932	23,025	9,532	7,193	6,300
1969	121,146	97,105	35,527	28,313	4,613	28,652	24,041	9,747	7,373	6,921
1970	127,163	102,064	35,184	31,465	5,070	30,345	25,099	9,675	7,968	7,456
1971	138,394	111,295	38,664	34,353	5,413	32,865	27,099	10,585	8,350	8,164
1972	157,564	127,332	44,129	40,080	6,201	36,922	30,232	12,256	9,002	8,974
1973	180,486	147,437	51,130	47,530	7,352	41,425	33,049	13,241	9,829	9,979
1973—Mar.	159,320	129,375	45,610	39,951	6,328	37,486	29,945	12,540	7,702	9,703
Apr.	161,491	131,022	46,478	40,441	6,408	37,695	30,469	12,686	8,036	9,747
May	164,277	133,531	47,518	41,096	6,541	38,376	30,746	12,817	8,319	9,610
June	167,083	136,018	48,549	41,853	6,688	38,928	31,065	12,990	8,555	9,520
July	169,148	138,212	49,352	42,575	6,845	39,440	30,936	12,968	8,479	9,489
Aug.	171,978	140,810	50,232	43,505	7,009	40,064	31,168	13,111	8,605	9,452
Sept.	173,035	142,093	50,557	44,019	7,120	40,397	30,942	13,088	8,335	9,519
Oct.	174,840	143,610	51,092	44,632	7,235	40,651	31,230	13,145	8,590	9,495
Nov.	176,969	145,400	51,371	45,592	7,321	41,116	31,569	13,161	8,785	9,623
Dec.	180,486	147,437	51,130	47,530	7,352	41,425	33,049	13,241	9,829	9,979
1974—Jan.	178,686	146,575	50,617	47,303	7,303	41,352	32,111	13,117	8,875	10,119
Feb.	177,522	145,927	50,386	46,781	7,343	41,417	31,595	13,159	8,018	10,418
Mar.	177,572	145,768	50,310	46,536	7,430	41,492	31,804	13,188	7,939	10,677

1 Holdings of financial institutions; holdings of retail outlets are included in other consumer goods paper.

NOTE.—Consumer credit estimates cover loans to individuals for household, family, and other personal expenditures, except real estate mortgage loans. The estimates include data for Alaska beginning with Jan. 1959 (except for installment credit held by sales finance cos.) and for Hawaii beginning with Aug. 1959.

SOURCE: *Federal Reserve Bulletin,* May, 1974, p. A50.

Chart 18-1

SHORT- AND INTERMEDIATE-TERM CONSUMER CREDIT OUTSTANDING

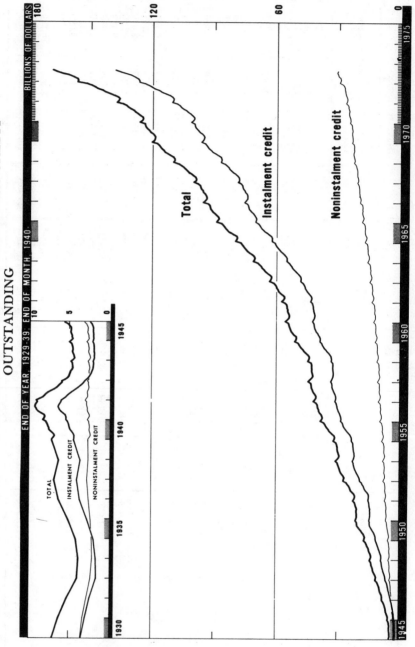

SOURCE: *Federal Reserve Historical Chart Book,* 1973, p. 60.

Since consumer credit fluctuates with disposable personal income, the volume of credit outstanding changes in response to changes in economic activity. Total consumer credit reached a high point at the end of 1929 and again in 1937, and turned down in each case with business activity. The next high point was at the end of 1941 when World War II restrictions cut the supply of durable goods. In 1946 credit started upward again and has continued upward except for minor dips in 1954, 1958, 1961, and 1970-71 when the economy experienced minor recessions and in 1966-67 when there was a minor slowdown in economic activity.

The volatile segment of consumer credit is installment credit, as Chart 18-1 clearly shows. The other forms of credit have remained fairly stable, but they do show adjustments to rising income levels and to changing price levels.

The most pronounced fluctuation in installment credit is in that type used to finance the purchase of durable goods. It fluctuates widely because the sales of such goods have wide fluctuations as economic conditions change.

Relationship to Consumer Expenditures

Another measure of the importance of consumer credit is the amount of new credit granted in relationship to personal consumption expenditures. Total installment credit extended was 5.8 percent of personal consumption expenditures in 1946. It increased year by year until it reached 11.1 percent in 1950. It stayed at about this level in relation to consumption expenditures in 1951 and then increased to over 13 percent in 1952, 1953, and 1954. In 1955 it increased to over 15 percent and remained at about this level in 1956 and 1957. It decreased somewhat in the recession year of 1958 and then reached a new high of 15.5 percent in 1959. It declined again somewhat in 1961, a year of a minor recession, but increased again after that reaching a level of 18.8 percent in 1969. It declined very slightly in the recession of 1970-71 and then increased to 20.5 percent in 1973. Such figures for the period from 1946 through 1973 are shown in Table 18-2 on the next page.

Table 18–2

THE RELATIONSHIP OF INSTALLMENT CREDIT EXTENDED TO PERSONAL CONSUMPTION EXPENDITURES
1946-1973

YEAR	PERSONAL CONSUMPTION EXPENDITURES	INSTALLMENT CREDIT EXTENDED	INSTALLMENT CREDIT AS A PERCENTAGE OF CONSUMPTION EXPENDITURES
	(Billions of Dollars)		
1946	146.6	8.5	5.8
1947	165.0	12.7	7.7
1948	177.6	15.5	8.7
1949	180.6	18.1	10.0
1950	195.0	21.6	11.1
1951	209.8	23.6	11.3
1952	219.8	29.5	13.4
1953	232.6	31.6	13.6
1954	238.0	31.1	13.1
1955	256.9	38.9	15.1
1956	269.9	39.8	14.7
1957	285.2	41.9	14.7
1958	293.2	40.0	13.6
1959	314.0	47.8	15.5
1960	328.9	49.3	15.0
1961	339.0	48.0	14.2
1962	355.1	56.2	15.8
1963	375.0	63.6	17.0
1964	401.2	70.7	17.6
1965	432.8	78.7	18.2
1966	466.3	82.8	17.8
1967	492.1	87.2	17.7
1968	536.2	100.0	18.6
1969	579.5	109.1	18.8
1970	617.6	112.2	18.2
1971	667.2	124.3	18.6
1972	726.5	143.0	19.7
1973	804.0	165.1	20.5

SOURCE: *Economic Indicators* and *Federal Reserve Bulletin.*

Real Estate Credit

At the end of 1973, $386.5 billion of mortgage debt was outstanding on one- to four-family houses in urban areas. Of this total, $322.3 billion was loaned by financial institutions, $28.7 billion by individuals and other lenders, and $35.5 billion by the federal government and related agencies.[15] The volume of nonfarm mortgage debt since 1940 can be seen in Chart 18-2.

Chart 18–2

NONFARM RESIDENTIAL MORTGAGE FINANCING
1-TO-4 FAMILY PROPERTIES

TOTAL AND GOVERNMENT UNDERWRITTEN

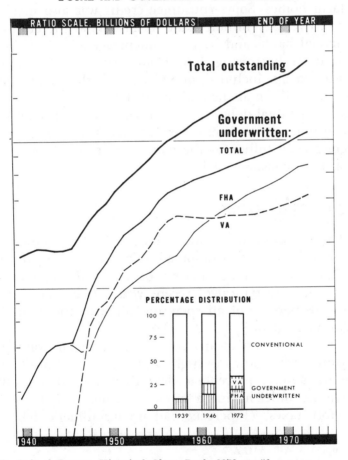

SOURCE: *Federal Reserve Historical Chart Book*, 1973, p. 53.

---

[15] *Federal Reserve Bulletin.* June, 1974, p. A44.

Total Consumer Credit

The full significance of the debts of consumers in urban areas can be gained by combining all types of consumer credit. At the end of 1973, the total of short-term, intermediate-term, and long-term consumer credit outstanding was $567 billion. To get the complete picture, it is necessary to add the consumer credit portion of farm real estate credit and of short-term and intermediate-term farm credit. At the end of 1973, $39.4 billion of farm real estate credit was outstanding. Much of this credit was used to finance farm homes. Some consumer credit was also involved in the loans of over $27 billion made to farmers at the end of 1973 by commercial banks and by government agencies.[16] When additional consumer borrowing done from insurance companies and other institutions is included, one estimate is that total consumer debt was $608 billion at the end of 1973.[17]

Large as this total debt appears to be, it is but a small portion of total consumer assets. It has been estimated that total consumer assets were $3,459 billion at the end of June, 1973, or 5.7 times as great as total consumer debt.[18]

WHO USES CONSUMER CREDIT

The large amounts of consumer credit of all types outstanding indicate that its use is widespread. This is borne out by the Survey Research Center's surveys of consumer finances. The figures for 1971 are typical of recent years. The survey revealed that about 48 percent of all spending units in the country had some installment debt.[19]

This debt is by no means concentrated in any one income classification, either low or high, although the lowest income group shows a lower percentage debt than any other group. Of those spending units having a money income in 1971 of under $3,000 before taxes, 71 percent had no installment debts. This

---

[16] *Ibid.*, pp. A18, A40, A44, A47.

[17] *1974 Finance Facts Yearbook, Op. Cit.*, p. 45.

[18] *Ibid.*

[19] These data and those which follow on the distribution of consumer debt are taken from *1974 Finance Facts Yearbook, Op. Cit.*, pp. 52, 53.

percentage drops to 40 for units with incomes between $10,000 and $15,000. It is 54 percent for those in the $15,000 and over income bracket.

There is also some variation in the frequency of debt by the age of the head of the family or spending unit. The highest percentage of units having some debt is for the group in which the head is under 25 years of age. In this group, over 60 percent had some debt. The percentage decreases as the age of the head of the unit advances.

CALCULATING THE INTEREST RATES ON INSTALLMENT LOANS

In comparing costs of alternative sources of credit, the total dollar cost for the loans should be used. It is also helpful to calculate the annual rate of interest that is being paid. Suppose that a borrower receives a loan of $100 repayable in 12 monthly installments and that the charge for the loan is $10. The $100 loan and $10 charge will most likely be repaid in equal monthly installments of $9.17 ($110 ÷ 12). Since the loan is being repaid monthly, the borrower has the use of $100 for the first month, $91.67 for the second, and so on as follows:

1st month	$100
2nd "	91 2/3
3rd "	83 1/3
4th "	75
5th "	66 2/3
6th "	58 1/3
7th "	50
8th "	41 2/3
9th "	33 1/3
10th "	25
11th "	16 2/3
12th "	8 1/3
Total	$650

The borrower has owed an average amount of $54.17 for the year ($650 ÷ 12). Then, dividing the loan charge of $10 by the average amount owed of $54.17 gives an interest rate of 18.5 percent.

This rate may also be calculated by means of a simple formula:

$$R = \frac{2mI}{P(n+1)}$$

R   equals the annual interest rate expressed in decimal form.
m   equals the number of installment payment periods in a year (12 for monthly payments; 52 for weekly payments).
I   equals the total charge for the loan in dollars and cents.
P   equals the net amount of the credit made available to the borrower (in the case of an installment sale contract, this is the amount of the unpaid balance after the down payment including trade-in allowance; in the case of a cash loan, this is the amount of cash actually received by the borrower).
n   equals the number of installment payments specified in the contract.

In the example above, m is 12 since the loan is repaid monthly, and I is $10. P is $100 since that is the amount he has actually received, and n is 12 since the loan is for 12 months.

$$R = \frac{2 \times 12 \times \$10}{\$100 (12+1)} = \frac{\$240}{\$1300} = .185 \text{ or } 18.5 \text{ percent per year.}$$

INSTITUTIONS GRANTING CONSUMER CREDIT

A large number of institutions are engaged in granting consumer credit. Cash is loaned to consumers by many institutions. The major ones are consumer finance companies, credit unions, sales finance companies or their cash-loan subsidiaries, and commercial banks.

A number of agencies are also engaged in lending money to consumers to aid them in purchasing goods and services. Retail stores, utilities, other service agencies, and professional persons grant credit as a convenience to their customers. Installment sales credit is extended primarily by sales finance companies and commercial banks, but also to some extent by other financial institutions. The lending activities of these institutions are discussed in the chapter that follows.

QUESTIONS

1. Define consumer credit in such a way as to distinguish it from other types of credit.
2. Briefly discuss several problems that arise in applying your definition of consumer credit.
3. What difference, if any, is there between credit used to finance the purchase of a house and to finance the purchase of an automobile?
4. Describe the economic functions performed by consumer credit.
5. Discuss several alternative ways in which consumers may provide themselves with the services of durable goods. Give examples of each.
6. Describe the early development of consumer lending.
7. Describe the development of cash lending to consumers in the United States.
8. Briefly trace the development of the financing of durable goods.
9. Discuss the factors responsible for the growth of installment buying.
10. Briefly describe the factors responsible for the growth of lending on urban real estate.
11. Discuss the relationship of consumer credit to disposable income.
12. Why is installment credit the volatile element in consumer credit?
13. From data in the latest *Federal Reserve Bulletin*, bring Table 18-1 on page 395 up to date. From a knowledge of the factors that cause changes in the volume of various types of consumer credit, account for the changes in the volume of consumer credit from 1960 to the present.
14. Using data from the latest *Federal Reserve Bulletin*, analyze changes in the volume of consumer credit of various types (automobile paper, other consumer-goods paper and personal loans) which has been extended and repaid since 1965. Account for the changes insofar as possible on the basis of the factors which affect each type of credit.
15. Calculate the annual rate of interest on the following loan: $300 loaned for a period of one year to be repaid with a loan charge of $45 in equal monthly installments.

SUGGESTED READINGS

Consumer Credit in the United States. Report of the National Commission on Consumer Finance. Washington: Office of the White House Press Secretary, 1973.

DAUTEN, CARL A. *Financing the American Consumer.* St. Louis: American Investment Company, 1956.

Finance Facts Yearbook—1974. Washington: National Consumer Finance Association, 1974.

"Pattern of Growth in Consumer Credit." *Federal Reserve Bulletin* (March, 1974), pp. 175-188.

"Recent Developments in Consumer Instalment Credit." *Federal Reserve Bulletin* (September, 1971), pp. 703-712.

"Revision of Consumer Credit Statistics." *Federal Reserve Bulletin* (October, 1972), pp. 878-898.

What Truth in Lending Means to You. Washington: Board of Governors of the Federal Reserve System, 1970.

19 | Institutions and Procedures for Financing the Consumer

The development and present status of each of the types of institutions that finance the consumer for short-term and intermediate-term needs are analyzed in this chapter. Consideration is also given to their organization and methods of operation, the results of their operations, and to their current problems.

First to be considered are the institutions in the consumer installment credit industry, which include consumer finance companies, sales finance companies, and industrial banks and loan companies. Next to be discussed are credit unions, followed by commercial banks in their consumer lending role. Also considered are institutions which facilitate consumer financing, including various credit-checking agencies that report on the credit standing of individuals and some specialized insurance companies which insure consumer loans of various types.

THE CONSUMER INSTALLMENT CREDIT INDUSTRY

Many institutions are involved in making personal loans to consumers and financing consumer purchases of goods and services. Some of the institutions such as banks and credit unions have a basic collateral role, that of serving as a depository for savings of individuals and using such savings as the major source of funds for lending to consumers and others. The consumer installment credit industry includes those finance companies whose primary role is to make installment credit available to consumers. The various types of institutions in this industry began as different types of organizations to meet different needs, but by the 1970's many of the early distinctions had disappeared. The development of each type of institution will be considered first, beginning with consumer finance companies.

Development of Consumer Finance Companies

Consumer finance companies were developed to perform the second function of consumer credit, that is, to provide aid in time of financial emergency. They made loans in the early years of their existence primarily to low-income borrowers who found it impossible to obtain credit elsewhere. As time went on they expanded their scope of operations until today most of them make loans to a cross section of middle-income as well as low-income families.

As was pointed out in the last chapter, organized cash lending to consumers in this country probably began in cities of the Middle West after the end of the Civil War. Since the laws of the states not only made no provisions for institutions to lend money to consumers but also made profitable legal operation impossible because of usury laws, such lending was carried on in violation of the law. Illegal lending by loan sharks flourished because there was a need for credit for emergencies that was not being met in any other way. Several steps were taken to combat the loan-shark problem in the period before World War I. Late in the nineteenth century, legislation was passed that was designed to encourage the establishment of semiphilanthropic organizations to make small loans to consumers. As a result, in several cities, especially in the East, remedial loan societies were sponsored by social-minded citizens who devoted their time to these organizations without compensation. Although these societies helped many people, they hardly made a dent in the loan-shark problem. The first comprehensive small-loan legislation was passed in Massachusetts in 1911, and New Jersey followed suit in 1914.

In the next year, such legislation was passed in New York, Ohio, and Pennsylvania. With the experience in these states as a guide, the Russell Sage Foundation published a model Uniform Small Loan Law in 1916.

Several features are basic in a small-loan law if illegal lending is to be eliminated. Maximum charges must be set and these must be high enough to permit profitable operations. The charge is an overall fee for expenses, services, and interest; and it is the only charge permitted. It is computed on the unpaid balance of the loan each month or oftener if payments are made more frequently. Provision must be made for licensing lenders based on character, fitness to conduct the business, and financial responsibility. There must also be state supervision of the business and penalties against nonlicensees and licensees who violate any of the provisions of the law.

Development of Sales Finance Companies

A few years after the development of consumer finance companies, another type of institution, the sales finance company, was developed to finance the sale of durable goods on installments. This is accomplished by purchasing from retail merchants or dealers the promissory notes signed by consumers who have bought goods on time payments. A second function involves the financing of wholesale purchases by the merchant or dealer from the manufacturer. Since cash payment is required by the manufacturer for automobiles and most appliances, the majority of dealers need continuous financing of their stocks. Such financing is business credit, but for convenience it is provided by the same company that finances retail sales.

The sale of durable goods on installments goes back to the early years of the nineteenth century when furniture was sold by some cabinetmakers on that basis. It received its real impetus in the last part of that century when sewing machines, pianos, and sets of books were frequently sold on installments.

The big growth of sales financing came with the rapid development of the automobile industry. The first corporation to finance auto sales, organized in 1915, was immediately swamped with business.[1] Shortly thereafter, the Commercial Credit Company developed a plan to finance automobile sales. This company had been founded earlier to finance accounts receivable for manufacturers and wholesalers. It developed its automobile sales financing activities rapidly and is today one of the major companies in the sales finance field. General Motors Acceptance Corporation was incorporated in 1919 to do sales financing but also to make wholesale loans to General Motors dealers who were having trouble getting enough funds to finance the purchase of new cars from the manufacturer.[2] Many other sales finance companies were established especially during the 1920's.

Before 1938 the major sales finance companies had arrangements with automobile dealers to handle the financing of the sales of their cars. The Department of Justice, questioning these preferred relationships, brought antitrust proceedings against the major companies and their related automobile companies. Late in 1938 Chrysler and Ford entered into consent decrees under which the companies agreed to discontinue preferential arrangements with any of the sales finance companies. General Motors and General Motors Acceptance Corporation, after years of legal bickering, agreed to a consent decree in 1952, freeing their dealers to finance their sales as they see fit.

A new type of institution was developed to meet the need for installment sales financing because commercial banks did not engage in sales financing on a large scale until twenty years or more after the sales finance companies pioneered in its development. The basic philosophy under which commercial banks were operating held that they should restrict themselves to short-term business loans that were self-liquidating. Automobile financing was a new type of business that required new methods and a different outlook from regular banking. Risks were likely to be great until a substantial volume was built up. Bankers also had an obligation to depositors that did not exist in sales finance companies. It was not until the depression of 1929 had run its course that it became clear that sales credit could be extended safely. The ability of sales finance companies to set up branches

---

[1] Clyde William Phelps, *The Role of Sales Finance Companies in the American Economy* (Baltimore: Commercial Credit Company, 1952), p. 55.

[2] *Ibid.*, p. 56.

where they chose also gave them an advantage over banks, which can have no branches in many states and are greatly restricted in others.

A last factor was the usury laws that limited banks to rates lower than those necessary to cover costs of this type of lending. These laws were changed and regulations revised when banks began to enter the field.

Development of Industrial Banks and Loan Companies

A third type of institution in the consumer installment loan industry is the industrial bank or loan company. These institutions are at times called *Morris Plan* companies, a name associated with one of the earliest groups of such institutions.

The first financial institution of this type was established in the United States in 1901 when an immigrant from Latvia, David Stein, founded the Merchants and Mechanics Savings and Loan Association at Newport News, Virginia. It was patterned after the consumer banks and loan associations that had been developed in Europe to make loans to workers. Its name is similar to that of present-day organizations granting real estate credit, but it was established to make general consumer loans for small amounts and to provide a means of saving small amounts.

Other banks of this type were not started until 1910, when Arthur J. Morris set up the Fidelity Savings and Trust Company at Norfolk, Virginia. This institution proposed to lend money to people employed in industry; hence the name industrial bank or loan company. Morris also planned to obtain at least part of his funds by selling investment certificates that would carry a definite rate of interest. Since these certificates could be paid for in installments, they also provided a means of saving in small amounts.

In 1911 Mr. Morris copyrighted the name "Morris Plan" and began to promote such units actively in large cities throughout the country. By 1917 he had established over seventy companies in the major cities of the country and also in some smaller ones. While the Morris Plan banks were being developed, other organizations and individuals were setting up similar units. Several other systems of banks were established, but these have all been dissolved.

The distinguishing characteristic of industrial banks is that they have a thrift function as well as a loan function. When the law permits, they accept deposits; in other cases they sell investment certificates that pay interest. These certificates may be bought on installments, and thus they provide a means of saving in small sums. Since they are cashable on demand, they become essentially the equivalent of a time deposit in a regular bank.

Many states have special statutes governing industrial banks. These provide for consumer loans repayable in installments and for the acceptance of deposits or the issuance of investment certificates. In addition to personal cash loans, loans for home repair and modernization and purchase of retail installment paper from dealers to aid in sales financing are allowed. There is no uniformity in these laws among the various states, such as exists in the consumer finance company field, because the approach to the problem was piecemeal. Some laws give these institutions bank status and allow them to call their savings accounts "deposits."

In about twenty states, industrial-loan laws authorize corporations chartered under them to accept savings under some form of investment certificate, but they cannot call themselves banks or call the money received under savings plans "deposits." The remaining states have no special laws, but in some a few industrial banks have been established under the general corporation law or general banking statutes.

When industrial banks were first set up, they frequently were able technically to operate within an 8 percent usury statute by combining an investment certificate with a loan. During the life of the loan an investment certificate equal to the face of the loan was bought on installments. At the maturity of the loan, this certificate was offset against the loan account. Thus, technically, the whole sum was in use for the life of the loan. Some companies still use this technique even though most laws allow a certain maximum percent of discount on loans paid in installments.

The industrial banks in the states which permitted the acceptance of deposits gradually expanded their scope of activities. The larger banks, especially, increased their percentage of demand deposits. Industrial banks also made loans with real estate as security and some commercial loans.

Many industrial banks have taken out charters as state banks. Several states have abandoned industrial bank laws and have given these banks the status of state banks. This changing pattern has progressed rapidly in those states in which industrial banks can accept deposits and call themselves banks.

In some states there are financial institutions that are a modified form of industrial bank having a loan function but no thrift function. They are designated as industrial loan companies to distinguish them from the deposit-taking industrial banks. Even these institutions, however, are not so clear-cut a type as they once were. Various states have raised the limits on the size of loans of consumer finance companies so that industrial loan companies compete in the same loan class.

Current Status of the Consumer Installment Credit Industry

By the middle 1970's many of the distinctions between consumer finance companies, sales finance companies, and industrial banks and loan companies had disappeared and the trend was clearly toward finance companies with diversified activities. Industrial banks all but disappeared as a separate class of institution and became regular state banks offering a broad group of banking services. As the size of loans which could be made by consumer finance companies was increased, the distinction between them and industrial loan companies disappeared to a large extent. Consumer finance companies and industrial banks and loan companies entered the sales finance field primarily by discounting the sales finance paper of companies selling household durable goods. Sales finance companies also entered the direct cash loan field and the independent companies did so to a significant degree. This happened in part because manufacturers and retail chains established their own sales finance subsidiaries and also because commercial banks entered the automobile financing field in a significant way.

The companies in the consumer installment credit industry vary in size and ownership from one-office concerns to large national chains which operate hundreds of offices. Some companies and chains are independently owned, others are subsidiaries of industrial and commercial concerns, bank holding companies, or insurance companies. At the end of 1970 when the Board of Governors of the Federal Reserve System made its fourth quinquennial survey of finance companies, there were 2961 finance companies in operation. This number had decreased by over 30 percent from 1965 largely as a result of mergers.[3] The number of companies having credit outstanding of $100 million and over increased from 27 in 1960 to 58 in 1970.[4]

Finance companies had $37.2 billion of consumer installment credit outstanding at the end of 1973. This total was distributed as follows: [5]

Personal loans	$16.6	billion
Retail automobile paper	11.9	"
Mobile home loans	3.4	"
Other consumer good loans	4.4	"
Repair and modernization loans	0.9	"

Organizations and Operations

In the early years of licensed lending, most of the lenders were individual proprietorships and partnerships, and most lending was done by individual offices, but since 1920, the corporate form and chain operations have become increasingly important. Chains have grown because they enjoy some advantages over independent offices. They have easier access to capital because they are able to raise funds in the security markets. They also find it easier and cheaper to obtain short-term bank loans. In addition they benefit from the mobility of capital, since they can shift funds from office to office as they are needed. They gain a further advantage from geographic diversification of risks, not only economically but also in reduced legal rates of charge.

In the earliest stages, finance companies were financed almost entirely through the investments of the owners and the retention

---

[3] *Finance Facts Yearbook* (Washington: National Consumer Finance Association, 1974), p. 58.

[4] *Ibid.*, p. 56.

[5] *Ibid.*, p. 58.

of earnings. As time went on, the larger companies gained access to sizable amounts of credit from commercial banks and were also able to sell their own promissory notes to investors through the commercial paper market. They also found it possible to sell securities to the investing public and to sell some issues of notes and bonds directly to institutional investors, such as insurance companies and banks. Finance companies raise about half of their funds through short-term borrowing and another quarter from long-term borrowing. Short-term borrowing is done from commercial banks for about a quarter of the total. The major source of short-term funds is commercial paper, most of which is placed directly. About a quarter of long-term debt is subordinated debentures; the rest is largely senior long-term debt. Capital, surplus, and undivided profits make up about a sixth of the total of funds. The various sources of financing in 1970 are shown in Table 19-1.

Table 19–1

LIABILITIES, CAPITAL AND SURPLUS OF FINANCE COMPANIES—June 30, 1970
(In millions of dollars)

Short-term borrowing	$29,629
Long-term borrowing	16,470
Total borrowing	46,099
Deposit liabilities and thrift certificates	639
Other liabilities	3,892
Total liabilities	50,630
Capital, surplus, and undivided profits	9,947
Total	60,577

SOURCE: *1974 Finance Facts Yearbook* (Washington: National Consumer Finance Association, 1974), p. 57.

Operations. The major purpose of cash loans made by finance companies is to tide consumers over a period of financial emergency. Before a loan is made, the complete financial position of the applicant is usually reviewed. It may be possible to plan his finances in such a way that with a larger loan he can pay off some of his pressing debts and reduce his monthly payments to a level that he can meet.

In the early days of lending, all loans were made with chattel mortgages on automobiles, furniture, or store fixtures as collateral or with a comaker or guarantor of the loan. Today about a fourth of the loans are being made without security or comaker.

The original plan of consumer finance companies was to have the borrower repay an equal amount of principal each month and a smaller sum as interest each month as the balance was reduced. Most lenders have now changed their loan schedules to provide for equal payments each month.

Rates of charge were stated in the early consumer finance laws as the maximum percent per month on the unpaid balance and often with rates that were higher for the first dollars of a loan. The Illinois law, for example, set a maximum rate of 3 percent per month on the first $150 of a loan which was outstanding, 2 percent per month on the amount between $150 and $300, and 1 percent per month on the amount between $300 and $800 which was outstanding. In recent years many states have used a maximum dollar add-on to state rates just as is done by many commercial banks. The Ohio law, for example, provides for a maximum add-on of $16.00 per $100 per year up to $500, $9.00 per $100 per year on the amount between $500 and $1,000, and $7.00 per $100 per year on the amount between $1,000 and $2,000.

Financing the purchase of consumer durable goods is somewhat different from making cash loans. Since most retailers do not have sufficient capital to carry credit obligations to maturity, they refinance them through sales finance companies or other financial institutions. The contracts between the seller and the buyer calling for time payments are sold to a financial institution at a discount. The courts held that this sale of the paper is also a sale of a thing rather than a loan of money. Thus, this whole process has been exempted from the usury statutes. Beginning with Indiana in 1935, however, most of the states have passed special statutes dealing with installment sales and financing. About half of these statutes govern the sale of all goods on installments; the rest apply only to the sale of automobiles on time payments. Some of the laws control charges that can be made, while others require only a detailed disclosure of the items added to the cash price to establish the installment sale price. Practically all of the statutes have provisions regarding the refund of charges if the contract is paid in full before final maturity. Some govern repossession practices, and some, charges for delinquency.

Most of the laws require sales finance companies to be licensed. Generally, the licenses are issued on application and the payment of a license fee, but without specific requirements that must be met or investigation of the applicants. The licenses may generally be revoked if a material misstatement is made in the application, for a willful violation of the law, or for fraud.

The standard down payment in most of the auto industry is 15 percent for new cars and even less for used cars, but some dealers make loans on smaller down payments. The maximum repayment period varies from 36 to 42 months. On late-model used cars (the current model and two previous models) the maximum period is usually 24-36 months and on other used cars usually 12-24 months. Down payments are generally a lower percentage of the purchase price for appliances and furniture than for automobiles. They are frequently 10 percent or less. Most loans do not run longer than a year or a year and a half for most purchases, and two years on larger purchases.

The basic procedures for financing the sale of automobiles and other consumer goods are the same. The original contract is drawn up between the automobile dealer and the purchaser. The usual procedure is to have the purchaser sign a *conditional sales contract*, which provides that the seller retain title to the car until the agreed purchase price has been paid. In some cases, a separate note is signed for the unpaid balance; in other cases, the sales contract is all that is required. Payments are usually made by the purchaser direct to the sales finance company.

Automobile manufacturers insist on cash payment before delivering cars to dealers, and most dealers must finance their inventories. As part of their service, sales finance companies handle this financing.

The rate for wholesale financing is usually just about equal to costs. It consists of a small flat charge, plus interest for the actual time that the money is used. Low charges for wholesale financing are generally used as a promotional device to obtain retail financing business.

The major difference in appliance wholesale financing from automobile financing is that manufacturers or distributors at times agree to repurchase merchandise that the dealer does not sell. Advances are usually for only 90 percent of the wholesale price, whereas they are almost always 100 percent for cars. Charges are higher, especially the flat charge, and the interest rate may also be somewhat higher.

The majority of loans by finance companies are made to middle income families. In 1972 somewhat over two thirds of all loans were made to households having an income of $3,500 to $8,999. However, almost 20 percent of the number of loans were made to households having an annual income of $12,000 or more. The largest percentage of loans are made to young families. Almost half of all loans in 1972 were made to households in which the head of the family was under 35 years of age, and another quarter of all loans were made to households in which the head was between 35 and 44 years of age. About 40 percent of all loans were made to consolidate existing bills, 12 percent were made for automobile purchases or repairs, and the rest for a wide variety of purposes.[6]

Rates of charge vary by types of loans. The average rate in early 1974 on loans made, as reported to the Federal Reserve, was 20.52 percent on personal loans. It was 12.28 percent on loans to finance the purchase of new cars and 16.76 percent on loans to finance used cars. Average rates were 13.15 percent on loans to finance mobile homes and 18.68 percent on loans to finance other consumer goods purchases.[7]

Rates of return on invested capital compare favorably with those in other fields. Consumer finance companies had an average rate of profit on net worth of 12.5 percent in 1972, up from 10.9 percent in 1971.[8] Rising interest rates on borrowed money reduced this return in 1973 and 1974, since finance companies were not able to make comparable increases in rates due to legal restrictions.

Problems

The consumer installment credit business, like any dynamic business, always has problems that it must meet in adapting to

6 *Ibid.*, p. 67.

7 *Federal Reserve Bulletin*, June, 1974, p. A48.

8 *Finance Facts Yearbook, 1974, Op. Cit.*, p. 74.

changing demands by the consumer and changing economic conditions.

One of the biggest problems facing the consumer finance companies is the lack of understanding of the nature of their operations. The idea is still current in some quarters that these companies are charging rates far above the cost of the services they render.

In considering the rates of consumer finance companies, several things should be kept in mind. First of all, the charge is only on the unpaid balance, while competing institutions usually quote rates as a percent of the original amount of the loan. Secondly, consumer finance companies make no other charges of any kind in most states, that is, they have no investigation fee, notary fee, recording fee, and the like. Many states do permit insurance to be sold to cover the borrower in case of death or accident.

In the third place, many costs are almost as great for a small loan as for a large loan. The provision of the small-loan law that payments must be accepted in advance and that the borrower can be charged only for the time he has had the money also increases clerical work and raises costs.

Another major problem is that of maintaining profits in the face of cost increases due to inflation since World War II and especially during and after the period of the Vietnam War. Maximum loan charges in many states have not been increased since before World War II, although the price level has tripled. Consumer finance companies have been able to operate profitably under such conditions because they have automated many operations. The size of companies has also increased through mergers and the larger firms have been able to raise funds at lower rates than smaller firms. Also the size of the average loan on which the interest income is calculated has increased as the price level has risen. Since many costs do not vary with the size of the loan, revenue has increased sufficiently to keep up in large part with increased costs. However, the maximum loan limit must be raised if the companies are to gain the full cost advantage of larger loans, and this has not been done in some states.

The cost problem has become very serious since 1970 due to Federal Reserve action to restrain inflation which raised interest rates. This increased a major variable cost and so offset in part the advantage of larger loans. If interest rates stay up for several years, consumer finance companies will be hard put to keep up profit rates unless they are permitted to charge higher interest rates or can make larger loans. To maintain earnings, several have acquired chains of retail stores and diversified operations in other ways.

When the small-loan laws were first passed, they contained many restrictions on lenders because they were designed to eliminate loan shark operations. One such regulation is the ceiling on the size of loan which may be made. Even though ceilings have been raised in many states, they are still frequently too low to meet the legitimate credit needs of many borrowers. Some state laws also prohibit consumer finance companies from engaging in other types of business such as buying installment sales contracts or making loans under other laws. This restricts companies in such states from meeting many of the credit needs of their customers while competitors are not so restricted. Regulations on loan forms, reporting, advertising, stating charges, and the like are also unduly restrictive in some states and so put consumer finance companies at a disadvantage.

There are also some problems in the sales financing field. Since the late thirties, and especially since World War II, commercial banks have taken over a substantial proportion of the sales finance business, both by engaging in sales financing and by making loans to consumers directly to buy durables. There is every indication that banks will remain in this field. The sales finance field therefore promises to become even more competitive in a period of rising costs, and this makes it difficult to earn an adequate rate of return.

As the automobile business has become intensely competitive, a problem has arisen because some dealers feel that in order to sell cars, they have to lengthen the time period for installment payments and reduce the down payments. It may appear as if terms of 36 or 42 months are sound because automobiles last for eight or ten years. However, under terms of 36 months and a down payment of 15 or 20 percent, the owner does not have an equity in the car for the first year and one half to two years because its value as a used car drops faster than he is retiring his debt. This has resulted in losses of several hundred dollars on cars which have had to be repossessed because payments on them were not being met.

Another problem is one of increasing regulation, which creates new problems for the industry. Every year bills are introduced into state legislatures to regulate one or more phases of consumer financing. Pressure for regulation comes in part because of the undesirable practices of a few companies.

Another area of criticism regards the fees or kickbacks paid to dealers by some finance companies. Under the plan in which there is full recourse to the dealer in the event of default, the finance company frequently returns to the dealer part of the finance charges to cover his losses. Larger sums may be returned to compensate the dealer for obtaining business for the finance company. This practice can lead to abuses and overcharging of the customer. Compensation for losses and for services rendered to the finance company is justifiable, but larger payments to attract business that are passed on to the consumer are not.

CREDIT UNIONS

Another agency that extends credit to consumers is the credit union. The *credit union* is a cooperative society that supplies its members with consumer credit. It is organized in an industrial plant, in a parish, in a social group, or in a small community to provide a means for accumulating savings of its members and lending them at moderate rates of interest to those in the organization who express a need for funds for a provident or productive purpose.

Development and Current Status

The American credit union is an adaptation of the cooperative financial institutions that developed in Germany and other parts of Europe in the latter half of the nineteenth century. The first credit union on the American continent was set up in 1900 near Quebec by a member of the Canadian Dominion legislature, Alphonse Desjardins. Some nine years later, he also helped organize one of the first American credit unions among French

Canadians residing at Manchester, New Hampshire, which was given a special charter in 1909. Prior to that time, several cooperative credit associations had been operating in Massachusetts, and in 1909 that state passed the first credit-union law. Real progress began in 1921 when the late Edward A. Filene, a Boston merchant, became interested in credit-union development and set up the Credit Union National Extension Bureau. Filene put a large sum of money into his organization and, under the guidance and outstanding leadership of an excellent promoter, Roy F. Bergengren, adequate credit-union laws were subsequently passed in state after state.

In 1934 Congress was persuaded to pass a national credit union law. A Credit Union Division was created in the Farm Credit Administration to supervise credit unions with United States charters and to render various services to such organizations. This division has been shifted several times and is now organized as the Bureau of Federal Credit Unions in the Department of Health, Education, and Welfare.

As the number of credit unions in a state grew, a state credit-union league was formed. In 1935 these leagues formed the Credit Union National Association, which took over the promotional work of the Credit Union National Extension Bureau. In 1958 CUNA became a worldwide association, and in 1964 its name was changed to CUNA International.

The number of credit unions grew rapidly until World War II and again after the war. As of the end of 1973, there were almost 23,000 credit unions in the United States with almost 28 million members and assets of over $28 billion. About half of these are still state-chartered credit unions, but the federally chartered credit unions have been growing faster than the state.[9] At the end of 1973, credit unions had $19.6 billions of installment loans outstanding; and the loan volume of credit unions has been increasing over the years. At the end of 1939 their loans outstanding amounted to 4.3 percent of the total of consumer installment loans outstanding at financial institutions. At the end of 1973, this item had increased to 15.2 percent of the total volume of installment loans outstanding at such institutions.[10]

---

[9] *The Credit Union National Association, Inc., Yearbook,* 1974 (Madison, Wisconsin: Credit Union National Association, 1974), p. 17.
[10] *Federal Reserve Bulletin,* June, 1974, pp. A47 and A48.

Organization and Operations

Since the credit union is a cooperative, the power to run it resides in the general meetings of the group. All who have paid the entrance fee, which is usually 25 cents, and have subscribed to at least one share are eligible to vote. The general administration of the organization is placed in the hands of a board of directors elected at the annual meeting.

A credit committee is the heart of the organization since it must pass on all loan applications. Also elected is a supervisory committee. It is an auditing committee that has the duty of going over the books at frequent intervals to be sure that operations are being carried on in line with the bylaws of the association and the law under which it was chartered. Many credit unions also have an education committee that tries to educate the members in thrift and the proper use of credit.

The funds of the credit union and its financial records are handled by the treasurer, who is elected at the annual meeting. He may employ clerical assistance to aid him in his duties and may also be paid for his duties. He is the only elected official who may receive any compensation. Since most of the time spent on credit union affairs is donated by the elected officers and committees and office space is generally donated by the firm or organization sponsoring the credit union, total costs can be kept at a low level.

The typical credit union is a fairly small organization. About 25 percent had assets of $100,000 or less at the end of 1973 and two-thirds had assets of $500,000 or less. At the other end of the scale just over 22 percent of credit unions had assets of $1 million or more.[11]

Almost the only source of funds of credit unions is the money invested in them by the members. Shares are usually sold for $5 each and may be paid for in installments. Some of the state laws, but not the federal law, permit credit unions to accept deposits from members as well as to sell shares. Even where this is possible, the bulk of the funds has come from shares. When deposits are accepted, they are treated as creditor obligations and as such have priority over shares in liquidation. They also usually receive a somewhat lower rate of return than is paid on the shares. Some

---

[11] *The Credit Union National Association, Inc., Yearbook,* 1974, *Op. Cit.,* p. 19.

credit unions have at times obtained additional funds to meet their loan demands by borrowing from other credit unions that have an excess of funds.

Operations. Credit union loans are made for any provident or productive purpose. Some are made for very small amounts, but the average loan is about the same as that of many consumer-finance company offices.

Under most laws, loans can be made on the borrower's signature and for larger sums when secured by a chattel mortgage. The maximum amount loaned to one individual cannot exceed 10 percent of the assets of the credit union. A growing number of credit unions are making mortgage loans when the law permits and funds are available, but this practice is not general and is not encouraged by most credit union officials. Little information is available on the borrowers from credit unions, but they are probably somewhat similar to those of consumer finance companies.

Most laws set 1 percent per month on the unpaid balance of a loan as the maximum charge allowed, and some credit unions charge less. A growing number of credit unions are making an annual refund to borrowers of a part of the interest they paid, the most common proportion being 10 percent.

Life insurance on the unpaid balance of the loan is provided through a mutual insurance company, Cuna Mutual Insurance Society, at no additional cost to the borrower. Under most of the laws, penalties may be charged for being late in payment on loans, but in actual practice this is seldom done. At times some credit unions, especially the larger ones, have funds that are not being used by members of their group. These may be loaned to other credit unions that have a demand for funds greater than the available savings of the group. Most state laws allow credit unions to invest in bonds of various governmental units. Most investments have been made in United States government bonds.

The credit-union laws provide for setting up a reserve as insurance against losses on accounts. All entrance fees and also a percentage of net earnings are put into this reserve fund. The federal law requires that a minimum of 20 percent of net earnings must be put into this fund each year before any dividends can be paid. This fund, however, need be built up only until it equals 20 percent of the total value of shares outstanding. Some credit unions have, by a vote of the members, put a larger amount into the reserve fund.

Credit unions are usually successful enough to pay dividends of at least 3 percent on shares outstanding. Over three fourths of all credit unions are paying 5 to 6 percent, with many paying as much as 6 percent.[12] This is possible on their rates of charge because, as cooperatives, they pay no income taxes. Profits are larger than dividend payments, as a rule, and some funds are retained in the business.

Problems of Credit Unions

Several problems have been encountered in the expansion of the credit-union program. One is to get trained workers to handle the work of the treasurer's office, the loan committee, and the supervisory committee. This is usually not a serious problem in groups of office workers, but it is a real problem in groups of laborers, mechanics, and the like. The Credit Union National Association has sought to overcome this problem by training workers in new credit unions and by developing simplified forms for record keeping.

Another problem is to maintain the interest of the members in the group. Most members use a credit union as an institution for saving and borrowing money, and they have little interest in its affairs beyond that. The spirit of belonging to a cooperative effort has not taken hold as it has in some European cooperatives. If it is just another form of bank, it has no right to expect service to be donated to it.

As cooperatives, credit unions have been exempt from income taxes and from some excise taxes. This tax-exempt status is being questioned by other financial institutions and by some students of public finance. It may be justified in a small credit union in which members help meet each other's financial needs. As credit unions become large institutions, there is a serious question about the equity of tax exemption in a free-enterprise, competitive economy. Most life insurance companies and savings and loan

---

12 *Ibid.*, p. 21.

associations are also mutual organizations owned by their members, but over the years they have been paying taxes to an increasing degree. The issue of tax exemption thus becomes even more serious when credit unions are allowed to make mortgage loans on real estate.

COMMERCIAL BANKS

The largest volume of consumer credit is granted by the commercial banks of the country. Banks have achieved this position even though they entered the field of consumer financing after specialized institutions had been developed in this field. Banks now make all types of consumer loans and most banks are competing vigorously for consumer loans.

Development of Consumer Lending and Current Status

Before consumer financing became widespread some banks made loans to consumers on a 30-, 60-, or 90-day basis in the same way that they made commercial loans to business. In the middle 1920's a few smaller banks set up personal loan departments, but the growth was slow. In 1928 impetus was given to the movement when the National City Bank of New York, one of the largest banks in the country, set up a personal loan department. In 1929 the Bank of America in San Francisco, California, which has branches all over the state, entered the field. Growth was somewhat faster after that, but by the end of 1933 there were still probably fewer than 250 banks engaged actively in the consumer lending field.[13]

In the summer of 1934, the United States government initiated a program that gave real impetus to the expansion of bank lending to consumers. In an effort to stimulate employment and economic activity in general, the Federal Housing Administration was authorized to guarantee loans to authorized lenders who would extend credit for home repair and modernization. These loans, which had to be repaid in equal monthly installments, were

---

[13] Rolf Nugent, "A Census of Personal Loan Departments," *Banking* (November, 1937), p. 29.

known as FHA Title I loans. During the first 20 months under Title I, almost 6,000 banks reported loans made. Losses paid to the banks by the FHA were only 2.4 percent of the loan volume, and a substantial part of such losses were later recovered by the FHA. The record of FHA loans and their experiences with them convinced many bankers that consumer loans could be made without undue losses so as to yield a reasonable profit.

The Bankers Association for Consumer Credit, which was formed in 1938, gave added impetus to the movement. In 1940 it merged its activities with those of the American Bankers Association, which had recognized the importance of consumer financing by banks. Consumer lending by banks became more widespread, especially during the World War II years.

At the present time almost all commercial banks make consumer loans. At the end of 1973 commercial banks had $69.5 million of installment credit outstanding or 47 percent of the total. About 45 percent of this was credit to finance the purchase of automobiles and 29 percent to finance other durable goods including mobile homes. Home repair and modernization loans accounted for 6 percent of the total and personal loans for 20 percent.[14]

Organization and Operations

One problem that had to be met in the development of consumer loan business by banks was the passage of enabling legislation. Until recently most states have set 6 to 8 percent interest as the maximum that banks may charge on regular loans, but consumer financing in small sums cannot be done at this rate. It was necessary for most states to pass enabling legislation to permit Title I FHA loans at a 5 percent discount rate.

Most states have passed legislation permitting interest rates up to a maximum of 8 to 10 percent discount, which amounts to almost double that rate of simple interest per annum. Many of the states also allow fees to be charged for credit investigation, for late payments, and for insurance premiums, or they permit a

---

[14] *Federal Reserve Bulletin*, June, 1974, p. A47.

general service charge. Some of the states have passed special legislation covering other phases of consumer lending, such as licensing and examination.

Banks have generally set up a separate department to handle consumer loans. Consumer loan departments usually are open for more hours than the rest of the bank. This is done to accommodate borrowers and also to remain competitive with other agencies that are open more hours during a week than most banks. Another reason for setting up a consumer loan department is to dispel the feeling many people have that a bank is interested only in business loans.

Commercial banks secure a part of their funds from the investment of the owners in original capital contributions, reserves, and retained earnings, but the bulk of their funds comes from depositors. These deposits are, in the main, demand deposits on which the banks are not allowed to pay interest; however, in recent years increasing funds have come from savings deposits on which interest must be paid. This use of depositors' money on which no interest is paid does not mean that funds are available to the bank without cost. In exchange for the use of such funds, banks furnish services such as checking privileges to their customers. In periods of prosperity when all bank funds are in use, the opportunity cost of using the funds for other types of loans must also be considered.

Operations. The procedure for handling personal loans is much the same as that used by other institutions making such loans. Some personal loans are still made on a comaker basis and other banks achieve the same end by having a note endorsed or guaranteed by one or two individuals. As personal loan departments have had more experience and have tried to increase their volume, they have shifted from comaker loans to loans on an individual signature. Some personal loans are made with collateral, but banks rely much less on household goods than do other institutions. Collateral may consist of savings accounts, marketable securities, the cash value of life insurance policies that have been assigned to the bank, savings and loan shares, and the like.

The most important field for many of the larger banks is automobile financing. Under an arrangement with a dealer, a bank usually finances his stock of cars in order to get the note business. The methods used follow closely those developed by the sales finance companies. The practice of making direct loans to individuals to finance car purchases has been developed by many commercial banks into a major outlet for funds. Frequently it is based upon an arrangement between insurance agents or brokers and the bank. Since sales finance companies often require that insurance be carried in specified companies, insurance agents and brokers have lost regular accounts when a new car was purchased with such financing. To keep this business, they have teamed up with commercial banks that finance purchases directly.

Banks also do a substantial volume of business in financing the purchase of other durable goods. A part of this is direct financing, most of which arises from the purchases of notes from dealers. This financing is done in much the same way as sales financing by sales finance companies. Banks also do wholesale floor planning for the dealers as a method of securing their consumer notes.

An innovation of the middle fifties is the financing of charge accounts. Several stores arrange the plan with a bank and receive application blanks for their customers to fill in. The bank screens these applications and, if a customer is approved, he receives a credit card that is good at any member store. The bank bills the customer monthly for all of his purchases. Such plans generally also provide for revolving credit with payments geared to the size of the outstanding balance and with a credit limit based on the financial position of the customer. The customer pays interest on the outstanding loan balance just as he does on a revolving charge account at a department store.

Banks usually set the service charge to the stores at 5 percent on charge-account loans but may do it for less at times. There has been some criticism that such charges are too high. In some retail fields, credit department costs probably approach 5 percent of credit sales. The bank fee, however, includes a charge for the store's use of money since its account is credited immediately; the bank does not collect the money until after the first of the next month. In addition to objecting to the cost, some merchants do not favor bank charge-account loans because they do not believe that it is good merchandising to turn credit decisions over to an outside agency. They believe that in order to maintain a hold on their customers, they should retain control over who gets credit at their stores and how much he gets.

In the middle sixties bank credit card plans began spreading throughout the country, but the largest concentration remained on the West Coast and in the Chicago and New York areas. The trend is toward plans sponsored by a group of banks, such plans becoming regional and even national in scope. The two largest plans, BankAmericard and Master Charge, have become national plans. By the middle seventies over 60 percent of all banks offered their customers credit card plans.

Some credit is also granted by check-credit plans which provide for credit within preset limits simply by writing a check which is larger than the balance a customer has in his account. By the middle seventies about 10 percent of all banks had such plans and the amount of credit extended through them was in excess of $2 billion in 1974.[15]

Little definite information is available on the average size of consumer loans made by commercial banks. Loans to finance automobiles are usually made for two thirds or more of the purchase price, which often means a loan of $2,500 or more. Loans on appliances and other durables are, of course, much smaller. Personal loans are probably somewhat larger on the average than those of the consumer finance companies.

Borrowers. The individuals who borrow from banks to make repair and modernization loans, auto loans, and personal loans are probably a cross section of the middle-income groups. Bank borrowers, in the main, come from a somewhat higher income group than consumer finance company borrowers.

Rates charged by banks are lower than those of consumer finance companies and some sales finance companies. Charges of 5 to 9 percent on a discount basis are normal, which means effective interest rates between 10 and 18 percent. Average interest rates charged per annum at the end of 1973 were as follows: [16]

---

[15] *Ibid.*

[16] *Ibid.*, p. A48.

New automobiles (36 month maturity) ...... 10.49 percent
Mobile homes (84 month maturity) .... 11.07   "
Other consumer goods (24 month maturity).. 12.86   "
Personal loans (12 month maturity) .... 13.12   "
Credit card plans .... 17.24   "

In addition, there may be a flat service charge for small loans, insurance requirements, and penalties for late payments.

General profit figures on bank consumer lending are not available. Many banks do not calculate such figures. Indications are, however, that the business is profitable, or it would not be pushed so vigorously nor would it have spread to so many banks.

Problems of Commercial Banks

Banks are at a competitive disadvantage in the consumer lending field since they are forbidden to set up branches in many states and are restricted as to their location in others. National sales finance companies have the advantage of being able to work out uniform policies for financing in various parts of the country. As a result, concerns that distribute their products over a wide area find it simpler to deal with branches of a large sales finance company than with individual banks with varying requirements. Sales finance companies can also achieve the advantages of diversification. This has been possible for banks in the western part of the United States where the Bank of America has a large number of branches and the Transamerica Corporation holds stock in subsidiary banks in several states. Banks have also achieved some diversification in recent years through the holding company devices. Offsetting this disadvantage, however, banks are able to meet the needs of their communities by adjusting their policies to changing local conditions.

Banks also have a problem in regard to rates, especially in used-car financing. The typical discount rate of 6 to 9 percent is not high enough to cover the cost of financing older used cars. If costs continue upward and general interest rates remain at the high levels of the middle seventies, this problem will become more serious.

Some banks are still faced with the problem of customers accepting them as a source of consumer loans. Banks were traditionally austere institutions that frightened many would-be borrowers, and some of them have not succeeded in completely dispelling this attitude.

There has also been a hesitancy on the part of some banks to cooperate with other consumer-lending agencies. If consumer lending is to be carried on safely, it is necessary for lenders to exchange information on the amount of credit that has been extended to individuals because some people will get hopelessly into debt if given a chance.

Banks along with other financial institutions have also had a problem of increasing percentages of delinquent accounts as consumers were hit by high rates of inflation in the middle 1970's. The overall rate for delinquent installment loans, that is loans on which payments are past due from 30 to 89 days, rose from 1.5 percent at the end of 1971 to 2.0 percent at the end of 1973, the highest level since 1949.[17]

FACILITATING AGENCIES

The merchandising function plays only a minor role in the intermediate- and short-term consumer credit fields. Some selling of consumer paper to other institutions or individuals is done especially by the larger companies. Some sellers of durables carry their own paper for a period and later look for a purchaser for such paper, but there is little organized activity of this kind carried on by brokers or separate institutions.

Credit Exchanges

Several facilitating agencies, however, play a role in the consumer credit field. In most cities of any size the consumer finance companies operating under the small-loan laws have set up a credit exchange to provide information on loans. Some of the earliest of these exchanges operated on a one-loan plan under which an individual or a married couple could have only one

---

[17] *Federal Reserve Bulletin*, March, 1974, pp. 185-186.

loan from a small-loan company outstanding at any time. This was in keeping with the philosophy that one of the functions of a small-loan company is to help a man plan his finances so as to get out of debt and that this can be done best if he has to deal with only one company.

The one-loan exchanges met with opposition from new companies entering a territory. When some of the small-loan companies entered the field of durable goods financing, a new problem was created for restricted-loan exchanges since these loans were of a somewhat different nature from the regular loans to help an individual in financial difficulty. As a result, some exchanges amended their rules so as to allow several loans to an individual so long as the same collateral was not used as security for more than one loan. More recently, the consumer finance companies in some cities, for example, St. Louis, have developed clearing-house exchanges in which no restrictions are placed on loans; but each company furnishes the exchange with complete information on all loans and on all notes they purchase.

Credit Bureaus

Another important facilitating agency is the credit-checking agency or credit bureau. It is organized by local merchants and finance companies to serve as a central exchange for data on the credit extended to individuals. The latest data in the file is usually furnished by telephone, teletype, TelAutograph,[18] or messenger. When more detailed information is required, a special report may be prepared which gives data on the applicant such as his age, marital status, family, permanence of residence, mode of living, reputation, estimated income, investments, bank accounts, suits or liens against him, and information on his charge-account buying and paying habits.

For information on an individual who lives out of town, data may be obtained from a credit bureau in his town. Several national concerns also prepare reports on the financial status of individuals, primarily for insurance purposes but also for credit evaluation.

---

[18] The TelAutograph is a device that electrically transmits and receives handwritten messages instantaneously.

Credit bureaus work well when all important credit-granting agencies cooperate. It is especially difficult to get some used-car dealers to furnish information, and their data are very important since a used-car loan may represent by far the largest debt of a borrower, especially if he does not own his home. Some progress toward cooperation by all is being made, but the problem is one that probably never will be solved completely or permanently.

Insurance Agencies

Insurance of various types, such as fire, theft, and comprehensive, is usually carried on durables when they are financed. This may be handled by regular insurance companies or by special companies writing insurance only in connection with financing. In automobile financing, collision insurance is also required.

To an increasing extent, group life insurance is being used to insure the unpaid balance of consumer loans. Special companies are active in this field and some of the leading life insurance companies have entered it. There is also increasing emphasis on accident and disability insurance on a group basis to protect borrowers against these contingencies.

Even though all types of insurance coverages are growing, there is disagreement as to the advisability of some types. Some feel that although group life insurance is desirable, accident, disability, and similar forms of insurance are of limited usefulness. Limited surveys made by some companies indicate that consumers, by and large, want group life coverage; but they are not agreed on the desirability of other types.

RECENT TRENDS IN REGULATION

Until recent years regulation of institutions financing the consumer was done by the state governments. In mid-1968 Congress passed the Consumer Protection Act which regulates the disclosure of consumer credit costs and also garnishment procedures and prohibits exhorbitant credit transactions. The regulation to put the Truth in Lending section of the Act into effect was drafted by a Federal Reserve task force and designated as Regulation Z. The purpose of the law and the regulation is to make consumers aware of the cost of credit and to enable them to compare the costs of alternate forms of credit. Regulation Z applies to consumer finance companies, credit unions, sales finance companies, banks, savings and loan associations, residential mortgage brokers, credit-card issuers, department stores, automobile dealers, hospitals, craftsmen such as plumbers, doctors, dentists, and any other individuals or organizations which extend or arrange credit for consumers. Credit transactions of more than $25,000 are exempted from the law except for transactions secured by real estate which are covered regardless of amount. The law also instructs the Board of Governors to exempt from federal disclosure requirements classes of consumer credit transactions within a state if the Board finds that state law imposes substantially the same requirements and that the law is enforced.

The law requires disclosure of the total finance charge and the annual percentage rate of charge. The finance charge includes all costs for getting the loan including not only interest or discount but service charges, loan fees, finder fees, insurance premiums, points, and the like. Charges for such items as taxes not included in the purchase price, licenses, certificates of title, and the like may be excluded from the finance charge if they are itemized and disclosed separately. The annual percentage rate of charge is the relationship of total finance charges to the amount financed and must be computed to the nearest one quarter of 1 percent annually. The creditor must also make a series of disclosures to the customer including such items as the method of determining the balance on which the finance charge is calculated, the conditions under which a creditor may acquire a security interest in any property owned by the customer and the nature of such an interest.

Action was also taken by Congress in the fall of 1970 to prohibit the distribution of credit cards which were not requested by a prospective user and to limit the liability of a credit card owner for purchases made by others on lost or stolen cards. In 1971 Congress also passed the Fair Credit Reporting Act which is designed to protect consumers from the distribution by credit agencies of incorrect or outdated information.

In 1968 a Uniform Consumer Credit Code was published by the National Conference of Commissioners on Uniform State

Laws. In mid-1974 this Code has been adopted by seven states. It provides for one comprehensive regulatory law to replace all consumer credit laws. It regulates credit transactions to individuals up to $25,000 and larger amounts when real estate is involved. It fixes uniform maximum rates for all types of credit grantors. The maximum rates for installment credit loans or for the financing of credit sales are 36 percent per year on the first $300, 21 percent on the next $700, and 15 percent on the remainder. When these maximum rates yield less than 18 percent per year, the maximum is still set at 18 percent.

QUESTIONS

1. Which institutions are included in the consumer installment credit industry?
2. Describe the early development of consumer finance companies.
3. (a) Outline the provisions of an effective consumer finance act.
   (b) Discuss the need for each provision as part of an effective law.
4. (a) What is the status of chains in the consumer finance company field?
   (b) Discuss the advantages and disadvantages of chains compared with individually owned offices.
5. Briefly describe the functions of sales finance companies.
6. Trace the development of sales finance companies before World War II.
7. Account for the development of a specialized type of institution to do sales financing.
8. Discuss the development and current status of industrial banks and loan companies in the consumer financing field.
9. Discuss the sources of funds, the purpose of loans made, and the characteristics of borrowers from finance companies.
10. Discuss the charges and profits of finance companies.
11. Discuss the problems of consumer finance companies and cash lending to consumers.
12. Discuss current problems and trends in sales financing.
13. What are the distinguishing features of a credit union?
14. Briefly trace the development of credit unions.
15. Discuss the operations of credit unions including such items as sources of funds, organizational structure, types of loans made, charges, and the results of operations.
16. Discuss the current problems in the credit union field.
17. Discuss the development of consumer financing by commercial banks.
18. How does the source of funds of commercial banks differ from that of other financial institutions?
19. Describe bank lending in the personal-loan field.

20. How does the development of bank charge-account financing and check credit financing fit into the long-range development of monetary and credit instruments?
21. Discuss current problems in the field of bank lending to consumers.
22. Describe the services of facilitating agencies in the consumer finance field.
23. Describe recent federal legislation in the consumer credit field.
24. Outline the major features of the Uniform Consumer Credit Code.
25. From your knowledge of the nature and operations of consumer finance companies, credit unions, and consumer finance divisions of banks, discuss the effect of the following on each:
    (a) Increases in salaries paid office workers over increases in wages in other fields.
    (b) Inflation of the price level at a rate of 5 percent per year.
    (c) Substantial increase in interest rates.

SUGGESTED READINGS

"Bank Credit-Card and Check-Credit Plans." *Federal Reserve Bulletin* (September, 1973), pp. 646-653.

CHRISTOPHER, CLEVELAND A. *Competition in Financial Services.* New York: First National City Corporation, 1974.

Consumer Credit in the United States. Report of the National Commission on Consumer Finance. Washington: Commerce Clearing House, Inc., 1972.

DAUTEN, CARL A. *Financing the American Consumer.* St. Louis: American Investment Company, 1956.

Finance Facts Yearbook, 1974. Washington: National Consumer Finance Association, 1974.

"Rates on Consumer Installment Loans." *Federal Reserve Bulletin* (September, 1973), pp. 641-645.

"Survey of Finance Companies, 1970." *Federal Reserve Bulletin* (November, 1972), pp. 958-972.

The Credit Union National Association, Inc., Yearbook, 1974. Madison, Wisconsin: Credit Union National Association, 1974.

"The Pattern of Growth in Consumer Credit." *Federal Reserve Bulletin* (March, 1974), pp. 175-188.

20 | Financing Urban Real Estate

Financing the purchase of residential real estate is classified as long-term consumer financing. The volume of such credit extended annually is smaller than the volume of intermediate- and short-term credit; but since the loans run for a much longer period of time, the total volume outstanding is several times larger. At the end of 1973 the total of mortgage loans outstanding on one- to four-family nonfarm homes was $386 billion. Of this amount 48 percent was held by savings and loan associations, 17 percent by commercial banks, 11 percent by mutual savings banks, and 6 percent by life insurance companies. Eight percent was held by individuals and other institutions and 9 percent by agencies of the federal government. The relative proportion of credit supplied by the several lending agencies and individuals has changed over the years. In 1973, for example, life insurance companies decreased somewhat the dollar volume of their portfolios of mortgages on one- to four-family dwellings and federal government agencies provided 14 percent of the net increase in funds. The decrease in the proportion of funds made available by insurance companies and the increased percentage of funds supplied by federal government agencies has been going on since the period of credit stringency in 1966. Commercial banks also supplied a larger proportion

Table 20–1

DISTRIBUTION OF MORTGAGE DEBT ON ONE- TO FOUR- FAMILY NONFARM HOMES BY TYPES OF LENDERS

(For the Year 1973 and on December 31, 1973)

	PERCENTAGE OF INCREASE IN LOANS OUTSTAND- ING IN 1973	PERCENTAGE OF TOTAL OUTSTANDING DEBT HELD AS OF DECEMBER 31, 1973
Savings and loan associations	51.3	48.4
Commercial banks	27.2	17.4
Mutual savings banks	7.0	11.5
Life insurance companies	—1.7	5.7
Individuals and others	2.4	7.9
Federal government agencies	13.8	9.2

SOURCE: Based on data in the *Savings and Loan Fact Book, 1974,* pp. 37, 38, 39.

of funds in 1973 than their share of total mortgage debt outstanding, and mutual savings banks a smaller share.[1] See Table 20-1.

The basic procedures followed by all of the agencies financing urban residential real estate are considered first. Then consideration is given to special features of each of the major financing agencies and to the results of their operations in this field. The role of real estate brokers and mortgage companies in merchandising mortgages is also analyzed. Some consideration is also directed to those agencies that facilitate this process of financing. This is done by such organizations as appraisal companies and title insurance companies but primarily by various governmental agencies. The activities in this area of several federal agencies are so important that consideration is given not only to the governmental financing programs but also to the influences they have had on real estate financing.

PROCEDURES IN RESIDENTIAL REAL ESTATE FINANCING

As in all lending operations, the procedures used in urban residential real estate financing are determined in large part by

---

[1] *Savings and Loan Fact Book, 1974* (Chicago: United States Savings and Loan League, 1974), pp. 37-39.

the characteristics of such financing. The financing is almost entirely long-term except for loans for construction, and even these are usually replaced by long-term loans. Long-term loans are possible because houses last for long periods of time, often 40 or 50 or more years.

Special risks are involved in real estate financing. The value of the collateral is affected by such factors as the changing economic status of the area, the city, and the neighborhood, as well as by business fluctuations, changing price levels, and the like. There are legal technicalities to consider to insure that the prospective borrower can get a clear title. The property must be maintained adequately if it is to maintain its value. The present and prospective income and other obligations of the borrower are also significant in determining the safety of a loan.

The Mortgage

A loan made to finance the purchase of residential real estate is typically secured by means of a mortgage against such property. The real estate mortgage, in one form or another, has probably been used as long as the right of private property has been recognized. The borrower in such a loan transaction is called the *mortgagor*; the lender, the *mortgagee*. The form used in this country is patterned after that of the English common law and equity law. In early England, a borrower of money would actually turn over possession of his land to the lender, and the lender would have use of the land until the debt was paid. The word "mortgage," which stems from the term "mort-gage" or "dead-pledge," was therefore rather appropriate in that the land was, to all intents and purposes, dead so far as the borrower was concerned until such time as the loan was repaid.

Modifications of this form of mortgage arrangement were developed which provided in some cases that the income from the land should apply to the payment of the debt, and in other cases that possession of the land by the lender was not to be obtained unless the borrower failed to abide by the terms of the contractual agreement. Later the English Court of Equity began to take the view that it was unreasonable that a mortgagee should retain the full value of the property if the borrower defaulted since it was merely conveyed to him to secure a debt and, therefore, a mortgagor had a right in equity to redeem his property upon full payment of the obligation, even though the maturity date of the loan had passed. This right is known as the *equity of redemption.*

Along with the development of the equity of redemption came the procedure of foreclosure. The foreclosure was necessary to prevent an undue burden upon the lender because of the uncertainty of the period of equity of redemption. It provided that on the petition of the mortgagee the courts would fix a time within which the mortgagor was required to pay the debt. If the mortgagor failed to pay within this time, the decree provided that his equity of redemption was thereby "barred and foreclosed."

Junior Mortgages. At times a mortgagor may want to borrow more money on a piece of property than the lender on a mortgage is willing to lend him. Then the borrower may find a lender who will lend him the additional sum, usually at a higher rate of interest, provided he gives him a claim on his equity in the property that is not covered by the existing mortgage. When this is done, the existing mortgage is called the first mortgage; the new mortgage, the second or junior mortgage. At times three or more mortgages may be placed on one piece of property.

State laws provide for the recording of mortgages in order to protect the interests of all parties. An unrecorded mortgage is binding between the parties to the agreement, but the law provides that the first mortgage to be recorded is the senior mortgage; so all mortgages should be recorded promptly.

Foreclosure Procedure. In the event of default by the mortgagor, the mortgagee will usually try to work out an arrangement whereby the payments in default may be met. If he feels that his interests are in jeopardy, he will bring a suit asking the court to foreclose on the mortgage and to hold a foreclosure sale. The mortgagee may bid at the foreclosure sale, and he has an advantage because he can use his claim to pay for his bid while other bidders must pay cash. Foreclosure costs are paid first out of the proceeds of the sale of the property. If a surplus exists after foreclosure costs and the mortgage debt are paid, the mortgagor is entitled to it. If part of the debt is unpaid, the court grants the mortgagee a deficiency judgment for the amount. This may be collected from other assets of the mortgagor. If he has insufficient assets, the claim will remain on record for a period of time. Such an unpaid claim makes it almost impossible for the mortgagor to get a mortgage loan in the future.

Land Contracts. In some cases a *land contract* instead of a mortgage is used to finance the sale of real estate. This is a contract for the sale of property in which the deed to the property does not pass to the purchaser until the terms of the contract have been fulfilled. It generally provides for regular payments, usually monthly, of interest and part of the principal. In cases in which the purchaser does not have sufficient money to finance the purchase of property by means of a mortgage, he may be able to do so by means of a land contract; and in this way he can build up enough equity to get mortgage financing or to pay the full cost of the property. The seller may be willing to make such an arrangement since he holds the deed to the property until the terms of the contract have been fulfilled.

Government Guarantees. During the depression of the thirties, the federal government set up the Federal Housing Administration to stimulate home building by guaranteeing mortgages on urban residential real estate. A prospective borrower who wants to obtain an FHA loan applies for such a loan at a savings and loan association, a commercial bank, or other lending institution approved for such loans. The required application papers are sent for approval to the local FHA office which appraises the property and checks the applicant's ability to make payments.

The Servicemen's Readjustment Act, or GI Bill as it is popularly called, authorized the Veterans' Administration to guarantee loans on homes purchased by veterans. Such loans were first made available to World War II veterans and later also to veterans of the Korean and Vietnam Wars. Details of FHA and VA loan guarantee problems are covered in the discussion of government agencies and programs in the real estate field.

Amortized Loans. All loans guaranteed by the Federal Housing Administration and by the Veterans' Administration must be *amortized loans,* that is, loans on which the borrower agrees to make regular payments on principal as well as on interest. Many loans made without such guarantees are also made on this basis.

The payments are calculated so that the loan is retired within an agreed period of time. Often the lender also requires that the borrower add to his payments an amount equal to one twelfth of the annual property insurance and annual property taxes.

Monthly payments required to repay the principal and to pay interest are reduced materially as the time period of the loan is extended. For example, a $1,000 amortized loan at 6 percent interest requires monthly payments of $11.11 if amortized in 10 years and $6.45 if amortized in 25 years.

SAVINGS AND LOAN ASSOCIATIONS

After the first savings and loan association was established in the Philadelphia area in 1831, the movement spread to surrounding towns and cities and gradually to most of the eastern part of the country. Many of these early associations were called building and loan associations, and this name is still used by some associations today. After 1855, the establishment of new associations spread into the Mississippi and Ohio valleys and also into Texas, California, and a few other states. Between 1880 and 1890, associations were chartered at a rapid rate in all sections of the country. Up to this time, all associations were local institutions serving their immediate communities. Late in the decade, many national associations were chartered. Many were organized as promotional ventures for the benefit of the organizers. Most of these organizations failed during the several periods of depressed business activity between 1890 and 1901. As a result, several states passed laws preventing national organizations from doing business in their states. This experience has kept the business largely local in character since that time, although a few holding companies have been formed in recent years, especially in California. The big development came after 1920 and again after World War II. Today savings and loan associations do a greater volume of residential real estate financing than any other type of institution.

There were about 5,200 savings and loan associations with total assets of $272 billion at the end of 1973. About 150 have passed the $300 million mark in assets, but most of them in metropolitan areas have assets of $5 million to $100 million. In suburban areas and in small communities, they are much smaller.

Savings and loan associations may have branches under the laws of almost all of the states and under the federal statutes. The number of branches has grown substantially in recent years from 2 percent of all offices in 1950 to 57 percent in 1973, or 7,100 branch offices out of a total of over 12,000 operating sites.[2]

Organization and Operation

A savings and loan association may be chartered under a state charter or, since 1933, under a federal charter. At the end of 1973, about 60 percent had state charters. The average size of the federal associations was larger than that of the state associations so that the federal group had over 55 percent of the total assets of all the associations.[3]

Usually five or more responsible citizens may apply for a charter. To obtain a state charter, they must demonstrate their fitness to receive a charter and the need for the services of the proposed savings and loan association. To obtain a federal charter, they must demonstrate: (1) the good character and responsibility of the applicants, (2) the necessity for such an institution in the community, (3) the reasonable probability of its usefulness and success, and (4) that it can be established without undue injury to properly conducted existing local thrift and home-financing institutions.[4]

Savings and loan associations are of two types—mutuals and corporations owned by shareholders. All of the associations with a federal charter are mutuals; but almost half of the states allow savings and loan associations to issue shares of stock, and these associations are controlled by the shareholders. Almost 90 percent of all savings and loan associations are mutual companies.

Both savers and borrowers are members of mutual savings and loan associations. Since these associations are cooperatives, the savings put into them are shares of ownership in the association. This distinguishes them from deposits in a commercial bank, which are liabilities of the bank. Payments on savings and loan shares are *dividends*, not interest. In recent years, as part of their competitive strategy to attract savings, savings and loan associations

---

[2] *Ibid.*, pp. 61, 62.

[3] *Ibid.*, p. 60.

[4] Federal Savings and Loan Association (Washington: Federal Home Loan Bank Board, 1951), p. 5.

have, to a large extent, dropped the use of the word "shares" in their literature and referred instead to "savings accounts." The Housing and Urban Development Act of 1968 authorized federal savings and loan associations to call their savings accounts "deposits." This Act also expanded the types of savings instruments available to federal savings and loan associations by liberalizing the power of the Federal Home Loan Bank Board to authorize new forms of savings accounts and savings certificates. Regulations have been changed to provide for a variety of certificate accounts which pay higher rates of return than passbook accounts but have a minimum balance and maturity restrictions. Most savings and loan associations have issued 90-day-notice passbook accounts at a somewhat higher interest rate than regular passbook accounts and have issued certificates for time periods ranging up to four years. Minimum amounts for different types of certificates are usually $1,000, $5,000, and $10,000. Savings and loan associations have also been permitted to issue $100,000 and over negotiable certificates of deposit with maturities ranging from 30 days to 10 years.

The Federal Home Loan Bank Board was given authority under the Interest Rate Adjustment Act passed in 1966 to set maximum interest rates on various types of passbook accounts and savings certificates. The Federal Reserve Board of Governors has had this power over savings accounts at commercial banks since 1933. Rate ceilings have been set and have been altered several times. In the summer of 1974 they varied from 5.25 percent on regular passbook accounts to 7.5 percent on 4-year certificates. No ceilings were in effect for certificates of $100,000 or more. The ceiling on savings and loan regular passbook accounts was ¼ of 1 percent higher than for savings accounts at commercial banks and ¼ to ½ of 1 percent higher on certificates up to $100,000.

Many account holders treat their accounts as a deposit account rather than a share of ownership. In 1973, for example, over $113 billion was put into savings accounts and almost $93 billion was withdrawn, leaving a net increase in savings accounts of over $20 billion. This brought the amount in savings accounts at the end of the year to over $227 billion.[5]

---

[5] *Savings and Loan Fact Book, 1974, Op. Cit.,* pp. 67, 69.

The Housing Act of 1968 authorized federal associations to accept orders from customers to pay money from savings accounts directly to third persons. The instrument used to make the transfer must not be negotiable or transferable. Regulations have restricted such payments to expenditures related to housing including mortgage payments, real estate taxes, and utility bills. Little use has been made of such payment powers. Massachusetts and New Hampshire have allowed state associations to issue negotiable orders of withdrawal called NOWs, and in the summer of 1973 Congress extended this authority to all depository institutions in these states except credit unions.

The usual provision is that a borrower must buy at least one share in the association, so he usually has just one share and one vote. A saver has one vote for each $100 or fraction thereof he has invested in the association with a limit of 50 votes per member. The members consider the affairs of the association and elect the board of directors at an annual meeting.

In addition to savings shares and accounts and certificates, savings and loan associations have several other sources of funds. Stock companies have capital from the sale of stock and all associations have net worth in the form of reserves arising from undistributed earnings. They also obtain some funds in the form of advances and loans from their Federal Home Loan Bank. Since early 1973 they are permitted to issue uninsured capital notes and debentures, which are subordinated to savings deposits and certificates. They must have a minimum denomination of at least $50,000 and a term of at least 7 years. By the end of 1973 more than $70 million of debentures had been issued.[6]

The directors have full responsibility for conducting the business of the association. They usually engage a full-time executive to run the association and restrict their function to the determination of general policies.

Loans and Investments

Savings and loan associations devote themselves primarily to making loans on single-family, owner-occupied houses. Federally chartered associations normally lend up to 90 percent of the

---

[6] *Ibid.,* p. 102.

appraised value of the property on a monthly amortized basis for from 20 to 30 years. The average loan made in 1973 to purchase an existing home was $22,775.[7] Unamortized loans may also be made for not over 5 years. FHA and VA loans may be made in accordance with the terms specified by these agencies.

Many savings and loan associations make loans to finance the construction of new homes. In recent years such loans have represented less than 20 percent of all loans made.

Federal associations may also, under restrictions in the law and by the regulatory authorities, make loans on commercial property and on multifamily structures. The total volume of these loans and other types of exceptional lending may not exceed 20 to 25 percent of assets. Federal associations and those state associations whose accounts are insured by the Federal Savings and Loan Insurance Corporation may also acquire a participating interest in first-mortgage loans held by other insured associations. The selling institution must retain an interest in the loan of at least 25 percent. Federal associations may, under limitations, make conventional loans to finance the acquisition and development of land which is to be used primarily for residential purposes. They may also, within well-defined limits, make loans or investments in business development corporations. Federal savings and loan associations are permitted, within carefully prescribed limits, to make some home loans in excess of 80 percent of the appraised value of property. State laws usually allow broader discretion in the type of property that can be used to secure a loan, but the typical loans are on single-family dwellings.

Loans to consumers for purposes other than mortgages have expanded rapidly in recent years. By the end of 1973 the volume at insured savings and loan associations had exceeded $5 billion. Over a third of all such loans outstanding are to finance the purchase of mobile homes and over a quarter are home improvement loans. Most of them are closely related to some form of residential financing, but almost 10 percent were education loans.[8]

Both federal and state associations may invest in direct and guaranteed obligations of the United States government and federal associations may invest in the general obligations of any state or political subdivision. About three fourths of the states allow

---

[7] *Ibid.*, pp. 82, 83.
[8] *Ibid.*, pp. 81, 84.

investment in bonds of their states and municipalities. Some grant wider investment powers.

Membership in the Federal Home Loan Bank System

Federal savings and loan associations must join the Federal Home Loan Bank System. State associations may join, and over 80 percent have done so. This gives them access to their regional home loan bank for credit. The associations may obtain loans from this bank by using their mortgages as collateral.

Supervision

Federal savings and loan associations are supervised by the Federal Home Loan Bank Board and state associations by agencies in their states. The associations must submit reports at least annually, and they are subject to examinations that are usually made once a year. The purpose of such examinations is to insure that the associations are complying with the law, that they are not insolvent, and that they show no signs of future difficulties. The integrity of the management and personnel in handling the affairs of the association is also checked.

Results of Operations

Most savings and loan associations have operated successfully. The maximum interest rate they can charge is influenced by FHA rates. Usually, charges on other than FHA or VA loans are not above $8\frac{1}{2}$ to 9 percent. Expenses range between 1 and $1\frac{1}{2}$ percent of the volume of loans outstanding. Although some losses occur on mortgages, they have seldom been serious enough to cause difficulty for the association except during the depression of the thirties. Since 1940 the number of failures has been small; and in most years since World War II, none have failed.

In 1973 operating expenses of all savings and loan associations were 16.5 percent of operating income, leaving a net operating income of 83.5 percent. Interest on savings deposits was 64.8 percent of operating income and interest on borrowed money was 4.9 percent, leaving almost 14.0 percent as net income before taxes.

Taxes were 4.0 percent, leaving 9.9 percent of operating income as net income after taxes.[9]

COMMERCIAL BANKS

State banks have made loans on real estate mortgages almost from their beginning, helping to finance the westward movement of the population. National banks were not permitted to loan money on real property as security under the National Banking Act of 1864, but there was some evasion of this provision. The Federal Reserve Act allowed loans on farmland, and an amendment in 1916 provided for one-year loans on urban real estate. In later years, much more liberal provisions for real estate loans were enacted. National banks may make FHA and VA loans according to the provisions of these programs.

State banking laws are much more liberal than the national banking laws. Over half of the states have no restriction on the length of the loan or on the loan-to-value ratio. Those states which do have restrictions, as a rule, have more liberal provisions than those of the national banking acts.

Loans

The length of time of the loan, the ratio of the loan to the appraised value of the property, and the interest rates for FHA and VA loans are generally at or near the upper limits allowed under these programs. Conventional loans on one- to four-family properties are usually amortized loans made for periods of 30 years or less with loan-to-value ratios between 40 and 90 percent and interest rates from 7 to 9 percent or even more in periods of credit stringency such as 1974.

MUTUAL SAVINGS BANKS

Mutual savings banks are an important source of real estate credit in a few geographical areas. Of almost 500 such banks in operation, practically all are in the New England states and in New York and New Jersey.

---

[9] *Ibid.*, p. 105.

Loans

Mutual savings banks invested in real estate mortgages from the beginning of their existence. In fact, until the depression in 1929 such mortgages were their preferred form of investment. Due to losses in the thirties, however, many banks no longer considered mortgages attractive forms of investment. Since World War II, mutual savings banks have again invested heavily in mortgages on residential property, especially owner-occupied buildings. After 1935, FHA loans could be made in line with the regular procedures for such loans; and after World War II, VA-guaranteed loans were also permitted. The average new loan acquired by mutual savings banks in 1972 was $34,874, but it was about $44,000 for conventional loans and somewhat over $23,000 for FHA loans and somewhat over $21,000 for VA loans.[10]

Results of Operations

The record of mutual savings banks in lending on real estate as security has been, good. Foreclosures were negligible before 1928. Beginning with 1929, foreclosures went up rapidly, reaching a high point in 1933. During and after World War II, foreclosures decreased just as rapidly and again became negligible.

Mutual savings banks earned 6.53 percent on mortgages in 1972 and 6.35 percent on securities, yielding an average return of 6.39 percent on assets. They paid an average rate of 5.23 percent on deposits in 1972,[11] a rate somewhat below that earned at savings and loan associations because mutual savings banks issue fewer time certificates.

LIFE INSURANCE COMPANIES

Life insurance companies have been lending substantial sums on real estate for over a century. Mortgages have varied somewhat in importance as a source of investment for their assets. In 1890 over 40 percent of their assets were in mortgages. This figure

---

[10] *National Fact Book-Mutual Savings Banking* (New York: National Association of Mutual Savings Banks, 1973), p. 30.

[11] *Ibid.*, pp. 37, 39.

declined, especially after 1929, until in 1945 it was but 15 percent. Mortgages have been purchased in large amounts since World War II and at the end of 1973 accounted for 32 percent of the assets of life insurance companies, and 25 percent of such holdings were on one- to four-family residential properties.[12]

Loans

The state laws under which insurance companies operate place some restrictions on their investment in mortgages. Loans are generally restricted to first liens on improved real estate. The maximum amount of a loan is often restricted. FHA and VA loans are permitted under regular provisions for such loans.

Geographic restrictions on the location of property are quite liberal. Many states allow loans in all 50 states; some allow loans in several states in the region in which the company is located.

Insurance companies frequently concentrate in particular types of loans. Small companies usually limit themselves to FHA and VA loans and/or to conventional loans on one- to four-family dwellings and large companies often concentrate heavily in nonresidential lending.

Insurance companies make some loans directly through either the home office or branch offices. Most loans, however, are purchased from brokers, mortgage companies, or other institutions. This may be done through branch offices, by appointing a broker or mortgage company as a correspondent to bring loans to the attention of the loan department of the insurance company, or by buying mortgages in blocks from mortgage companies that have made the loans with the intention of selling the mortgages to permanent investors.

Results of Operations

The overall record of life insurance company investments in mortgages has been good. Just as with other institutions, however, foreclosures were numerous during the depression of the thirties. When final losses are spread over the period from 1920 through

---

[12] *Life Insurance Fact Book, 1974* (New York: Institute of Life Insurance, 1974), p. 78.

1946, they are not high. Losses since World War II have been negligible for most companies. Detailed cost records are not available on the net income earned on mortgage loans. Such evidence as is available indicates that insurance companies have earned on the average about the same rate on mortgage loans as have commercial banks.

MERCHANDISING AND FACILITATING AGENCIES

In real estate financing, the merchandising function is performed by some real estate brokers but primarily by mortgage companies. The procedures involved have already been covered in the discussion of mortgage financing. The nature of mortgage companies is considered somewhat more fully in this section. The activities of several facilitating agencies are also considered.

Mortgage Companies

One of the developments that has made possible a national market for real estate mortgages has been the growth of mortgage companies. These companies not only negotiate the loans but continue to service them by collecting interest and principal payments and forwarding them to the owners of the mortgage. This requires facilities for receiving such payments and for sending out notices of accounts due and past due. Servicing also includes making sure that proper insurance is carried and that all taxes are paid.

Mortgage companies as they operate today, for all practical purposes, began with the introduction of FHA mortgage insurance in 1934. These companies first concentrated their activities on FHA loans and later also on VA loans, but they now also handle conventional loans. Their growth was especially rapid in the decade from 1945 to 1955.[13]

Mortgage companies are usually closely held private corporations. They have a relatively small capital investment compared with the volume of business they do. They get most of their money for holding mortgages until they are placed with lenders from short-term bank borrowing.

---

[13] Saul B. Klaman, "Mortgage Companies in the Postwar Mortgage Market," *Journal of Finance* (May, 1957), p. 151.

Real Estate Investment Trusts

Another type of organization which has grown rapidly in recent years, especially since 1968, is real estate investment trusts known as Reits. They came into being in 1960 when Congress extended the same exemption from double taxation which had been granted earlier to mutual funds if they distributed at least 90 percent of their income to shareholders. They engage in a whole series of lending activities in the real estate field and some have taken equity positions in real estate projects. Most activity, however, is in financing construction from land acquisition until completion. At this stage mortgages are often sold to more traditional lenders such as insurance companies. Some Reits have been very successful; others encountered difficulty in the inflationary period of late 1973 and 1974.

Facilitating Agencies

Several agencies also facilitate the process of mortgage financing. One is the professional appraisal concern that makes careful appraisal of all types of property based on such factors as location, the trend of the neighborhood, the type of construction, and the condition of the property. This is done by government appraisers for FHA and VA loans.

Another facilitating agency, the title company, assures the purchaser of real estate or the mortgagee who is loaning money on real estate that the title to the property is clear. The title to most land in the United States was originally held by a state or by the federal government. It has gone through a series of title transfers until it has reached the present owners. Such transfers are recorded in public record books in chronological order. If all titles in the series of sales were defined completely and accurately at the time a transfer was made, if all the proper instruments that might affect the title were properly recorded, and if all complicating factors, such as suits over title arising out of litigation over the bequests in a will, were properly handled, the present title would be clear. There are so many chances for defects in a title that checking the records to be sure a title is clear has become a specialized activity carried on by title companies. They will, for a fee, search the records and issue an opinion on the character of the title being examined.

Important as a clear title to property is, there are very few titles about which there is absolutely no question. Most defects are minor and do not affect the transfer of title. Since it is impossible in most cases to be absolutely sure about a title, some companies have developed title insurance. They, of course, insure only titles that they believe from their examination are sound. The amount of insurance is stated in the policy and is usually the full value of the property at the time the insurance is written. The premium is paid only once, at the time the policy is purchased.

In recent years beginning with the late 1960's private firms have entered the mortgage insurance field on a large scale. Such insurance was developed by the federal government first for FHA loans and then for VA loans. In recent years private insurance of mortgages has grown to such an extent as to rival federal insurance.

In the summer of 1974 a new facilitating agency was set up in the form of a computerized central information system for offers to buy and sell residential mortgage investments. It is called the Automated Mortgage Market Information Network, Inc., or AMMINET. It provides a central data bank on secondary mortgage markets useful to both buyers and sellers of mortgages. It is not an exchange, but provides information to buyers and sellers who conduct their transactions privately, usually by telephone.

GOVERNMENTAL ASSISTANCE IN REAL ESTATE FINANCING

Several agencies of the federal government are instrumental in facilitating the financing of urban residential real estate. One group is the Federal Home Loan Bank Board and the Federal Home Loan Banks and the Federal Savings and Loan Insurance Corporation that are under its jurisdiction. Another group includes the Federal Housing Administration, the Federal National Mortgage Association, the Government National Mortgage Association, and the Federal Home Loan Mortgage Corporation. The Veterans' Administration is also engaged in facilitating real estate financing through its program of loan guarantees under the "GI Bill" and the Farmers Home Administration guarantees loans and makes some loans in rural areas.

Federal Home Loan Bank Board

The Federal Home Loan Bank Board directs operations of the Federal Home Loan Bank System and the Federal Savings and Loan Insurance Corporation. These two agencies were established by Congress during the depression period following 1929 as permanent organizations that were to encourage home ownership and sound home financing and protect the savings of small investors. The Board is responsible also for the supervision of federal savings and loan associations.

Federal Home Loan Bank System. The act establishing the Federal Home Loan Bank System in 1932 provided for twelve regional banks, their number was later reduced to eleven, but raised again in 1964 to twelve. Each bank is administered by a board of twelve directors, four of whom are appointed by the Federal Home Loan Bank Board for terms of four years and eight of whom are elected by the members for terms of two years. Membership is open to all state and federally chartered financial institutions, other than commercial banks, that are engaged in long-term home financing, provided the character of their management and their policies are consistent with standards established under the act. The great majority of the present member institutions are savings and loan companies. A few mutual savings banks have also become members of these federal home loan banks.

The funds of the federal home loan banks are obtained from the proceeds of sales of their capital stock to members, retained earnings, sales of consolidated Federal Home Loan Bank obligations to the public, and deposits of surplus cash by member institutions. Each member institution of the system is required to buy stock in its federal home loan bank equal to at least 1 percent of the total of the unpaid principal of its home mortgage loans and other home purchase contracts. The original capital was provided by the purchase of stock by the United States government as well as by member institutions, but the members took over all of the government-owned stock after World War II.

The system of banks also raises funds by issuing consolidated Federal Home Loan Bank obligations. In the early years they were usually notes that ran for 18 months or less, but one issue in 1972 was a 25-year bond, and 10- and 20-year bonds were issued in 1973. At the end of 1973, $15.4 billion was outstanding in such notes and bonds.[14] These obligations are jointly and severally guaranteed by the twelve banks.

The excess cash of a district federal home loan bank may be deposited with another of the district banks of the system. This is one means by which credit may be transferred from a region of surplus funds to an area of need for funds.

The district banks make long-term or short-term advances to their member institutions on the security of the home mortgages that the members have in turn obtained from their borrowers or on the security of government bonds. Advances outstanding on December 31, 1973, reached a total of $15.2 billion.[15]

These advances of funds have been used in recent years to help make funds available for housing in an economy in which periods of severe credit stringency and rising interest rates are followed by some easing of credit. In early 1970, for example, it became apparent that easing interest rates would lead to increased deposits at savings and loan associations and prompt them to repay advances from their home loan bank. To offset this, they were offered a one-year advance at a rate well below the then current rate for advances. In late 1971 the Federal Home Loan Bank Board announced that it was emphasizing decentralization and diversity. Each home loan bank was urged to develop credit policies that would meet the needs of member institutions and housing finance needs in its district.

In order to provide funds for housing at attractive rates, as interest rates rose the rates on advances were set below the then current rate on consolidated obligations of the home loan banks.

The federal home loan banks are entirely self-supporting and have paid dividends regularly since their establishment. The twelve banks do not pay uniform dividends since their operations are not uniformly profitable. In 1973 dividends ranged from 4 percent

---

[14] *Federal Reserve Bulletin*, June, 1974, p. A40.
[15] *Ibid.*

to 5.5 percent. This was a significant increase from 1972 when the range was from .12 percent to 4 percent.[16]

Federal Savings and Loan Insurance Corporation. The Federal Home Loan Bank Board also has supervision over the Federal Savings and Loan Insurance Corporation. Although this agency is entirely separate from the Federal Deposit Insurance Corporation, it functions in much the same manner and has increased public confidence in and encouraged the flow of savings to savings and loan associations. The law requires federal associations to be insured, while state-chartered associations may become insured upon application and approval. Insured associations are subject to annual examination and to the rules and regulations of the Federal Savings and Loan Insurance Corporation.

As of December 31, 1973, there were 4,163 insured institutions with the total assets of almost $265 billion. Over 97 percent of the assets of the entire savings and loan business are held by the insured group.[17]

The Federal Savings and Loan Insurance Corporation insures the safety of savings against loss up to a maximum of $40,000 for each account holder. If an insured association must be liquidated because it is in financial difficulties, the Corporation may pay the insured accounts in cash or may make accounts in other insured associations available to the account holders of the association in liquidation.

Besides its function of paying off investors in case an insured association is ordered liquidated, the Federal Savings and Loan Insurance Corporation possesses broad preventive powers by coming to the assistance of an association in the early stages of any difficulty. For instance, in order to prevent a default or to restore an insured association in default to normal operations, the Insurance Corporation may make a cash contribution or loan to such an institution.

Insured associations other than the federal associations which are required by law to be insured have the right of terminating their insurance, provided they meet certain legal requirements. Also under the provisions of the insurance law, the Corporation

---

[16] *Savings and Loan Fact Book, 1974, Op. Cit.,* p. 119.
[17] *Ibid.,* p. 122.

has the right to cancel the insurance of any insured association for a violation of the law or the rules and regulations of the Corporation, but it has never found it necessary to do so.

The Federal Housing Administration

The Federal Housing Administration was established under the provisions of the National Housing Act in 1934 for the purpose of stabilizing the mortgage market and to make money available to finance the construction of new homes and also to finance needed repairs to homes and other property. This organization was to accomplish its objectives through the insurance against loss of certain types of loans made by private lending institutions.

Insurance of property improvement loans is authorized under Title I of the National Housing Act. The principal activity of the Federal Housing Administration is the insurance of mortgages on both new and existing one- to four-family homes, authorized under Title II of the Act. All FHA loans are amortized loans. The payments include part of the principal, interest, a mortgage insurance premium of ½ percent,[18] fire and other hazard insurance premiums, real property taxes, and special assessments, if any. Maximum interest rates were set by law until 1968 when the Secretary of the Department of Housing and Urban Development was authorized to set ceilings at a level to meet market conditions. This rate was 9 percent in the summer of 1974. The maximum maturity on FHA loans is 30 to 35 years. The Commissioner of the FHA may reduce this maximum period by administrative action when he feels this is desirable. The maximum loan cannot exceed 97 percent of appraised value up to $15,000, 90 percent for the next $10,000, and 80 percent on the remainder. On a $30,000 home, for example, the loan may be as high as $27,550 or 91.8 percent of the appraisal value.

The FHA is also authorized to insure mortgages on cooperative housing projects. The mortgagor must be a nonprofit housing corporation in which the permanent occupancy of the dwellings is restricted to members or a nonprofit corporation organized for

---

[18] Payments of mortgage insurance premiums to the Mutual Mortgage Insurance Fund are of a mutual nature, and if the loss experience of a given class of mortgages is favorable, a portion of the paid-in insurance may be returned to the mortgagor upon termination of the loan.

the purpose of building homes for its members. Special, more liberal provisions are made if such cooperative housing is for occupancy by elderly persons. FHA insurance is also available to assist in financing the rehabilitation of existing housing, the replacement of slums with new housing, and the construction of housing for essential civilian employees of some defense installations. The Federal Housing Administration also provides insurance on mortgages on certain types of rental property both during and after construction. Beginning in 1965 the FHA was authorized to subsidize some housing in these special categories through interest rate subsidies and rent supplements.

Veterans' Administration

The "GI Bill" provided for the guarantee of insurance of loans made by private lending institutions to veterans of World War II and subsequent laws have extended the benefits to those veterans serving 180 days or more after January 31, 1955. The insurance provided by the Veterans' Administration was patterned after that of the Federal Housing Administration. The terms, however, are somewhat more liberal than those of the conventional insured loan requiring little or no down payment. The Veterans' Administration offers a guarantee for real estate loans to qualified veterans of $7,500 or 60 percent of the total loan, whichever is smaller. Since 1966 the borrower pays a one-half percent fee into a fund to protect the VA from losses.

The large surpluses of loanable funds at the end of World War II resulted in widespread participation in the VA loan insurance program. As these funds were substantially reduced, however, the interest rate limitation on such loans resulted in a lack of interest on the part of many lenders to continue lending on this basis. In 1968 the statutory interest rate ceiling was removed and the VA was given power to set the ceiling. It reached 9 percent in the summer of 1974.

Other Government Agencies

The Farmers Home Administration is an agency of the Department of Agriculture which provides insured loans and some grants and direct financing for rural housing programs. To qualify, the real estate must be in a town of not more than 10,000 people and the family must show that credit is not available elsewhere. Most loans are made on an insured basis and then sold to private lenders. Guarantees are also available for loans on commercial and industrial property in small towns.

The Federal National Mortgage Association was organized in 1938 as a subsidiary of the Reconstruction Finance Corporation and was later transferred to the Housing and Home Finance Agency. It originally was brought into existence to provide an additional market for the FHA insured mortgages of lenders. In the postwar period its authority was broadened to include mortgages insured by the Veterans' Administration and mortgages under special housing programs, such as urban renewal projects, housing for the armed forces, cooperative dwellings, and housing for the elderly. The plan was to help to maintain a more stable construction industry by providing a reservoir of funds that would supplement the flow of mortgage money when it was low and would drain off an excess flow of funds at other times through the sale of mortgages previously purchased.

The Federal National Mortgage Association accumulated a rather substantial portfolio of mortgages prior to World War II, but during the war this process was reversed because construction of new homes was largely curtailed. Following the war, the volume of mortgages purchased by the Association again began to increase as it purchased large sums of mortgages insured by the Veterans Administration and the FHA. As credit became more difficult to obtain from private institutions in the period after 1955, especially at the maximum rates established on FHA and VA loans, the Federal National Mortgage Association increased its activities greatly. The Housing Act of 1968 divided the Federal National Mortgage Association into two organizations, one of which kept the original title and the other named the Government National Mortgage Association. The GNMA took over the functions of assisting in the financing of special areas which cannot be financed adequately through the usual channels and the management and liquidation operations of the FNMA portfolio acquired under contracts entered into before 1954. It is also empowered to guarantee obligations issued by lenders on earmarked pools of mortgages, backed by the full faith and credit of the United States.

The new FNMA is a government-sponsored private corporation which has taken over the secondary market operations in FHA, VA, and Farmers Home Administration backed residential mortgages. The 1970 Housing Act also authorized it to operate as a secondary market for conventional loans. It introduced the Free Market System under which it deals in commitments to buy mortgages three, six, or twelve months in the future. The amount of mortgages it will buy is announced; and mortgage bankers bid on the price at which they are willing to sell, thus allowing market forces to set the price.

FNMA has several sources of funds for its mortgage-buying activity. The principal source is debenture bonds that are sold to private investors and some notes are also sold at a discount. A second source is preferred stock and a third is common stock.

GNMA and FNMA have cooperated in a special program called a Tandem Program to absorb some of the risks in investing in mortgages as interest rates rise. When interest rates rise, mortgages sell at a discount as do all fixed-rate obligations. To cushion some of this risk in a period of rising interest rates, GNMA issues a commitment to purchase a mortgage at a fixed price. It is then sold to FNMA at the prevailing market price at the time of such sale, GNMA absorbing any discount from the price paid to seller.

In 1970 Congress created another agency, the Federal Home Loan Mortgage Corporation. It is funded by a stock subscription of $100 million held by the regional Federal Home Loan Banks. It gets its funds by issuing bonds backed by GNMA guaranteed mortgages and by borrowing from the Federal Home Loan Banks. Its declared goal is to establish mechanisms which will make the secondary mortgage market highly liquid so as to make mortgages attractive to investors. It is to do this by purchases of conventional, FHA, and VA mortgages and participation in conventional loans. Such purchases may be over the counter or in the form of commitments for future purchases. It is also to be a major seller of mortgages so as to provide a true secondary market.

GOVERNMENTAL INFLUENCES ON FINANCING

The difficulties of real estate financing institutions in the early phases of the depression of the thirties were of such a magnitude that even the best-run organizations were strained to remain solvent. It is possible that another experience of this nature would again plunge many institutions into bankruptcy and homeowners into foreclosure. Yet, there is reason to believe that much of this may be averted because the difficulties of real estate finance in the early thirties were due in part to the techniques of mortgage lending, which have been substantially altered since that time. These changes relate to loan maturities, interest rates, loan-to-value ratios, and other terms of the loan.

Loan Maturity and Repayment

One of the most obvious changes in mortgage lending practice is the loan maturity and repayment. Before 1933 in many parts of the United States, loans were commonly written on a one-, three-, or five-year basis, and on occasions were even written "on demand." It was commonly understood that these notes and mortgages would be renewed periodically, if the interest, taxes, and other obligations were paid currently. Not only did the short maturities carried by these loans make it difficult to retire them without several renewals, but also, since amortization of the principal was seldom required, there was no plan for a systematic reduction of the loan. Although mortgage lenders of this period generally cooperated in renewing the notes of borrowers, it was often necessary during depression periods to insist upon payment. Such action frequently resulted in loss of property on the part of the borrower. The FHA and other governmental loan programs were based upon maturities of twenty or more years and the insistence upon amortization of loan principal during the entire period of the loan term. The success of the FHA program and later the VA program led many lenders to make conventional loans on the same basis so that today the typical loan is an amortized loan for a long period of years.

Loan-to-Value Ratio

Another influence of the federal agencies on real estate finance concerns the loan-to-value ratio. The high loan percentage relative to the appraised value of the property replaced the multiple-mortgage system that was prevalent prior to the depression. The effect of the multiple-mortgage system was to place a very high, if not unbearable, debt obligation on the mortgagor at interest rates that added to the difficulty of retiring the indebtedness. The modern mortgage, therefore, not only extends the term of the loan, making possible smaller installment payments, but also reduces the cost of home purchase financing because it eliminates the high cost of second and third mortgages.

Control Over Planning and Construction and the Development of Insurance

A final factor that should be mentioned relative to the influence of federal institutions on real estate finance is that of control over the planning and construction of new houses. Prior to the establishment of the Federal Housing Administration, loans were negotiated between borrower and lender on a take-it-or-leave-it basis. If the lender did not approve of the location or construction of an improvement, he simply refused the loans, in which case the applicant had to seek another lender. The Federal Housing Administration established definite standards of location, construction, and materials on the loans it was willing to insure. The borrower generally found it convenient to conform to these standards in order to qualify for the favorable terms that accompanied the insured loan. A related development was the use of standardized mortgage forms on FHA loans and the insurance of such loans by the federal government. The success of such insurance has led to the development of private insurance in this field in recent years. These factors make it possible to develop a national market for mortgages.

CURRENT PROBLEMS

Even though there are many agencies which supply credit to the housing field, the amount of credit has varied widely in recent years, especially during the periods of tight money. In 1966, for example, the inflow of savings to deposit-type financial institutions was reduced, but the reduction was far greater in savings and loan associations than in commercial banks or mutual savings banks. To try to stem this reduction some savings and loan associations increased rates, and it looked as though a "rate war" with commercial banks was under way. Congress passed legislation which broadened the powers of the Federal Reserve and the FDIC to regulate interest rates on time and savings deposits and gave the Federal Home Loan Bank Board new authority to regulate rate ceilings over savings and loan accounts. But even under regulated rates, savings and loan associations are getting a smaller share of savings. In 1961 about half of all savings gains at financial institutions were made by savings and loan associations; but in 1967, when money was not unusually tight, it was only one third. It dropped materially again in 1969 and in late 1973 and 1974 when the money supply was under pressure just as it had done in 1966. Even though the rates paid on savings are too low in periods of tight money to attract sufficient funds, savings and loan associations cannot afford to pay more because net income after paying dividends and interest to savers is not sufficient. Mutual savings banks have also experienced some of the same problems as savings and loan associations.

Several solutions have been proposed to these problems of savings institutions. One is to make rate regulation permanent and to guarantee a rate differential between commercial banks and savings institutions. But experience would indicate that even though such regulation may prevent the near-crises problems of 1966, it cannot solve the problem of adequate credit for housing. Others have advocated a variable-rate mortgage in which interest rates change as market conditions change. This has been done in some European countries, but it is unlikely to be accepted by borrowers in America, at least not so long as alternative sources of credit are available. A third proposed solution is to allow savings institutions to diversify by making other types of loans, such as consumer loans and a larger proportion of loans on property other than homes. There is also some sentiment for allowing them to offer limited checking account facilities and other services offered by commercial banks.

Even if the problems of savings institutions are solved, it is doubtful whether the total system of real estate financing is organized so as to function effectively under all conditions. Even with the existence of the twelve federal home loan banks, the Federal National Mortgage Association, and the Federal Home Loan Mortgage Corporation, there is still some question that an effective national mortgage market exists. A single secondary mortgage market should exist in which lenders could convert their mortgages into cash when they need funds, either by selling mortgages or by getting a loan on the basis of such mortgages as collateral. A true secondary mortgage market must have an assured source of emergency funds that is available even if debentures cannot be sold or sold at reasonable rates. This means access to the federal reserve banks for loans or to the Treasury, preferably the former. Such a secondary market could also encourage a wider geographic distribution of mortgage funds and could cushion sudden wide fluctuations of funds to the mortgage market. In inflationary periods, such an institution could help achieve stability by operating only on a restricted basis or not at all, and interest rates could be free to equate the supply of and demand for mortgage funds.

It is still too early to tell to what degree the Federal Home Loan Mortgage Corporation can develop into a true national secondary mortgage market. It can do so if it is given access to sufficient funds and pressure is not put on it to become a permanent source of funding for housing at rates below market rates. This is in effect what has happened to FNMA which increased its holding of mortgages in every year from 1965 on. Sales in most years were negligible so that the holdings of mortgages increased from about $2.5 billion at the end of 1965 to over $24 billion at the end of 1973.[19] An effective secondary mortgage market can only exist if private funds are made available for housing in adequate amounts over the years and with some reasonable measure of stability of available funds.

QUESTIONS

1. Indicate the importance of various financial institutions in financing the purchase of urban residential real estate.
2. Discuss the characteristics of residential real estate financing that distinguish it from other forms of financing.
3. Describe a typical mortgage and explain its use in real estate financing.
4. Describe the mortgage loan procedures followed in financing real estate.
5. Discuss the role of government guarantees in real estate financing.
6. Describe the development of savings and loan associations.
7. Describe the organization of a savings and loan association and the procedures followed in making loans.
8. Discuss the results of loan operations of savings and loan associations.
9. Describe the place of commercial banks in real estate financing.

---

[19] *Savings and Loan Fact Book, Op. Cit.,* p. 130.

10. Discuss the operations of commercial banks in the real estate field.
11. Describe the role of mutual savings banks in real estate financing.
12. Describe the activities of life insurance companies in real estate financing.
13. Describe merchandising and facilitating agencies in the real estate financing field.
14. It is often said that the nature of the liabilities of a financial institution determines the use it makes of its funds. What relationship, if any, exists between the nature of the liabilities of savings and loan associations, mutual savings banks, commercial banks, and life insurance companies and their positions in the field of urban real estate finance?
15. Compare and contrast short- and intermediate-term consumer financing with long-term financing of urban real estate. Account for differences.
16. Describe the organization and operation of the Federal Home Loan Bank System.
17. Discuss the operations and record of the Federal Savings and Loan Insurance Corporation.
18. Describe the mortgage loan policies of the Federal Housing Administration.
19. Describe the role of the Veterans' Administration in urban real estate financing.
20. What are the functions of the Federal National Mortgage Association, the Government National Mortgage Association, and the Federal Home Loan Mortgage Corporation?
21. Discuss the major influences that government agencies and regulations have had on real estate financing.
22. Discuss current problems in the field of real estate financing.

SUGGESTED READINGS

"Construction, Real Estate, and Mortgage Markets." *Federal Reserve Bulletin* (June, 1974), pp. 407-419.

Federal Home Loan Bank Board—Annual Report—1973. Washington: Federal Home Loan Bank Board, 1973.

Financing the Nation's Housing Needs, a statement on National Policy by the Research and Policy Committee of the Committee for Economic Development. New York: Committee for Economic Development, 1973.

KENDALL, LEON F. *The Anatomy of the Residential Mortgage.* Chicago: United States Savings and Loan League, 1964.

PEASE, ROBERT H., and LEWIS O. KERWOOD. *Mortgage Banking.* New York: McGraw-Hill Book Company, 1965.

Savings and Loan Fact Book, 1974. Chicago: United States Savings and Loan League, 1974.

The Effect of Government Housing and Mortgage Credit Programs on Savings and Loan Associations, Occasional Paper Number 6. Chicago: United States Savings and Loan Association, 1973.

"Ways to Moderate Fluctuations in the Construction of Housing." *Federal Reserve Bulletin* (March, 1972), pp. 215-225.

21 | Financing State and Local Governments

Our discussion of the various segments of our economy that make demands upon the capital markets would not be complete without giving recognition to the role of government as a part of such overall demand. In this chapter the financing of state governments and all political subdivisions within the state is considered. These political divisions include municipalities, counties, and special tax districts. *Special tax districts* are those governmental units that are set up for the fulfillment of a particular community need. Representative of such districts are county school districts, fire districts, and intragovernmental districts which exist for the financing of sewers or watershed areas.

MAGNITUDE OF STATE AND LOCAL GOVERNMENT FINANCING

Total outlays of state and local governments have grown at a very rapid rate since World War II. In fact, outlays at these governmental levels have increased at a greater rate than have the expenditures of the federal government. The magnitude of such outlays and their rapid rate of growth can be seen by comparing year-to-year total state and local government outlays. As measured in national income accounts, outlays increased from $40.6 billion in 1958 to $179 billion in 1973.

Some of these increased outlays have been due, of course, to the higher cost of providing the same services. For the most part, however, these increasing expenditures represent government's expanded responsibilities and the continuing pressure placed upon existing facilities. Another major factor leading to the post-World War II expansion in state and local government expenditures was the tremendous backlog of projects. The financial pressures of the depression years of the thirties and the shortage of building resources during the war left practically all state and local governments with large accumulations of urgent needs. After this backlog of projects was met, general urban expansion and the movement to suburban areas gave continued support to the upward impetus of governmental expenditure. The suburban movement gave rise to new demands for many kinds of public facilities such as schools, hospitals, and highways. In addition to these reasons for increased state and local government expenditures, there is the fact that the age groups that draw most heavily on governmental services have increased relative to the total population. The growth of school-age population is one example of this increased demand. These factors have led to a rather rapid increase in per capita state and local expenditures as well as total expenditures. Per capita growth in state and local spending is reflected in Table 21-1.

Purchases of goods and services by state and local governments constitute a considerable portion of total expenditures for all levels of government. Approximately 84 percent of all governmental outlays for nondefense goods and services are made through these governmental units. This represents about 13 percent of the gross national product. Approximately 50 percent of the goods and services purchased by state and local governments are used for education and highways. Health and sanitation, public welfare, and police and fire are the remaining major expenditure areas. More than 70 percent of the direct purchases for education are made by local governments, and almost two thirds of the expenditures for highways by the states.

In addition to expenditures for goods and services, transfer payments have become an increasingly important part of the budgets at these levels of government. Transfer payments are

Table 21–1

PER CAPITA EXPENDITURES
BY STATE AND LOCAL GOVERNMENTS

(For twelve months ended June 30 for selected years.)

	TOTAL EXPENDITURES	EDUCATION	HIGHWAYS	PUBLIC WELFARE	OTHER
1965	$385.30	$147.37	$63.05	$ 32.58	$142.30
1967	471.79	191.64	70.41	41.53	168.21
1969	577.96	233.94	76.35	59.97	207.70
1971	730.52	288.05	87.73	88.36	266.38
1973	862.93	331.54	88.71	112.37	330.31

SOURCE: U. S. Department of Commerce, Bureau of the Census.

those for which no current productive service is rendered. Examples of government transfer payments include pensions, direct relief, and veterans' allowances and benefits. With increased emphasis being placed by our society on government's responsibilities to the aged, unemployed, and dependent children, it is anticipated that this type of governmental expenditure will continue to grow. At the present time, transfer payments by state and local governments amount to $20 billion a year and have been increasing at the rate of $1.5 billion each year.[1] A comparison of the major items in the budgets of state and local governments is shown in Table 21-2.

METHODS OF FINANCING

In its simplest form, government financing is the process of securing funds with which to pay for the goods, services, and benefits governments provide for their citizens. Essentially, this task becomes one of securing enough current revenue to meet the demands of operating expenditures. There are occasions, however, when it becomes necessary or desirable for governments to borrow funds to meet their expenditure needs. One of these occasions arises when a highly uneven flow of receipts is combined with a rather stable governmental expenditure pattern.

---

[1] *Economic Report of the President* (Washington: United States Government Printing Office, February, 1974), p. 330.

Table 21–2

PERCENTAGE OF STATE AND LOCAL GOVERNMENT DIRECT EXPENDITURES BY FUNCTION—1971

(For twelve months ended June 30, 1973.)

	STATE	LOCAL GOVERNMENT
Education	38.5%	44.8%
Public Welfare	20.1	8.5
Highways	13.9	5.8
Health and Hospitals	6.8	6.6
Other	20.7	34.3
	100.0%	100.0%

SOURCE: U. S. Department of Commerce, Bureau of the Census.

This often necessitates temporary borrowing on the part of the government in anticipation of the next tax payment period.

The financing of capital expenditures is the second major reason for governmental borrowing. The logic behind such action lies in the fact that capital expenditures are often made to finance improvements which will benefit the community over a long period of time. It is reasoned that because those who will live in the community in the future will benefit from such expenditures, the payment for these improvements should be spread over the useful life of the improvement. This can be accomplished by increasing taxes in the future to finance the repayment of the debt and the interest on the debt.

It may be said that the types of expenditures being made out of current revenues and the capital expenditures being financed through borrowed funds largely dictate the sources of funds for financing governments. In many ways, this can be likened to the financing of a business enterprise. The operating revenues of government are comparable to the internal financing of a business enterprise, while the borrowed funds are much like the external financing of a business. The credit reputations of state and local governments are related to the extent of indebtedness and the ability of the governments to maintain their contractual debt obligations. It is the purpose of this chapter and the next to survey the financing of government expenditures at all levels.

Tax Revenues

The major sources of revenue for state and local governments are sales, income, property, and other incidental taxes. With the increase in expenditures mentioned above, it has been a challenge for these governments to increase revenues at the same rate. Many states have enacted an income tax for the first time, while others have either increased the tax rate or started a withholding procedure to achieve greater effectiveness of the existing tax.

Sales taxes, too, have been increased by states and localities to finance the waves of increasing expenditures. Local governments, however, depend largely upon property taxes for their current revenues; and they have relied upon more realistic property assessments, higher tax rates, and a larger tax base arising from new construction. Table 21-3 reveals the relative importance of various sources of revenue for state and local governments.

Intergovernmental Transfers

An increasingly important source of revenue for state and local governments has been advances from one governmental unit to another. In recent years there has been a significant increase in the amount of grants-in-aid made by the federal government to the states for such purposes as unemployment compensation and highway construction. There has also been an increase in the amount of funds given to local governments by the state governments. In addition, there have been direct grants-in-aid to municipalities by the federal government for such purposes as public housing and urban renewal.

In 1973, federal grants-in-aid amounted to $41.2 billion and covered about 22 percent of the total direct outlays of the state and local governments.[2]

Debt Financing

In recent years, state and local governments have tended to incur annual deficits, and as a result their total debt has increased.

---

[2] *Ibid.*

Table 21-3

DISTRIBUTION OF STATE AND LOCAL GOVERNMENT
TAXES AND NONTAXES

(For twelve months ended June 30, 1965, 1968, and 1973.)

	1965	1968	1973
	PERCENT		
States			
Total	100.0	100.0	100.0
Sales	25.7	28.7	38.2
Income (Personal and Corp.)	21.4	24.1	21.6
Motor vehicle licenses	7.7	6.8	3.5
Property	2.9	2.5	1.4
Death and gift	2.8	2.4	1.5
Other	39.5	35.5	33.8
Local governments			
Total	100.0	100.0	100.0
Property	57.4	56.1	54.1
Sales	5.3	4.0	6.1
Income (Primarily Personal)	1.1	2.2	3.0
All other taxes	2.1	2.8	1.8
Nontaxes	34.1	34.9	35.0

SOURCE: U.S. Department of Commerce, Bureau of the Census.

In addition to debt financing to support annual deficits, in recent years large sums have been borrowed on a short-term basis to bridge the time gap between current expenditures and tax collection. For a particular community, such short-term financing is retired out of tax revenues and total debt is not increased. Because of the general increase in operating budgets of state and local governments, however, the amount of short-term borrowing increases from year to year. In 1973, total state debt was $59.4 billion and total local government debt was $129.1 billion.

Notwithstanding the tremendous increases in capital expenditures by state and local governments, the proportion of these expenditures that has been financed through long-term borrowing has dropped steadily since World War II. This has not been due to budgetary surpluses on the part of such governments but rather to the steadily increasing volume of grants by the federal government. Passage of the Federal Highway Act of 1956 has accounted for a particularly significant increase in grants by the federal government. Although the proportion of capital expenditures financed through long-term borrowing has decreased, state and local governments continue to claim about the same percentage of total funds made available in the capital markets.

State and Local Government Bonds

In investment circles, *municipal bond* is commonly interpreted to mean the obligations of a state itself or of any of its political subdivisions. The description is not technically correct, but it is understood by all parties in the investment world. As with debt financing, municipal bonds are seldom issued with a maturity that exceeds the estimated life of the capital improvement. Exceptions to this rule, such as the issuance of bonds to finance veterans' aid programs, account for a very small part of total long-term debt financing. Specific maturity limits for various types of capital projects have been enacted into law by many states.

Most bonds of state and local governments are issued with *serial maturities*, that is, the bonds mature in installments over the scheduled life of the issue. For example, an issue of bonds for $20,000,000 may have maturities ranging from one to twenty years, with $1,000,000 making up each maturity group. This in effect constitutes twenty separate bond issues, each maturity having its own rate of interest. Typically, the interest rate is lowest on the shortest maturity and increases on the longer maturities. The serial-bond arrangement permits the issuing government to pay off its indebtedness on a predetermined schedule. It also serves the investor well in that it makes possible the selection of maturities to meet his special requirements or preferences. Serial bonds do have the disadvantage to the issuing government of making the repayment schedule more rigid, resulting in possible embarrassment during years when revenues are unusually low or current expenditures unduly high. The occasional use of *sinking fund bonds* by state and local governments requires the issuer to set aside regularly a certain sum for the purpose of retiring the outstanding bonds. Such sinking fund payments are generally paid to a trustee who may invest such funds pending ultimate redemption of the sinking fund issue. As a more frequent alternative, he may retire the issue regularly through purchases on the market or through the call of selected bonds for sinking fund purposes. Few municipal securities are issued on a sinking fund basis, but this arrangement is typical of corporate bond issues.

Tax Status of State and Local Government Bonds

The interest income on state and local government bonds is not subject to federal income taxes. This freedom is based on the sovereignty of the state and the presumed unconstitutionality of a federal levy. In turn, the states are not free to tax the interest income on the bonds of the federal government. The mutual restriction of such taxing power is based on the burden that each governmental level could impose on the other with respect to deficit financing. Although there is no limitation on the power of the states to tax the income received from obligations of state and local governments, most states do exempt from tax liability the income of their residents from their own obligations or those of their political subdivisions. Because the levels of federal taxation are so much higher than those of the states, the tax status of state and local government bonds is of special significance to investors in the higher income tax brackets.

Major Types of State and Local Government Bonds

The extent of the liability of the issuing governmental unit for the payment of principal and interest and the sources of revenue from which such payments are to be made distinguish the major classes of municipal obligations, the term "municipals" being used here in the customary sense to include all state and local government obligations. The two major classes of municipal obligations bonds are general obligation bonds and limited obligation bonds.

General Obligation Bonds. A *general obligation bond* is secured by the full faith and credit of the issuing governmental unit, that is, the bond is unconditionally supported by the full taxing power of the issuing government. General obligation bonds constitute by far the largest class of municipal obligations. Although such issues have at times resulted in losses to investors, municipalities and other political subdivisions of the states are reluctant to permit such defaults to occur. Very seldom have defaults on municipals resulted from bad faith on the part of the issuing unit. Rather, economic pressure on a community and a resulting inability to meet its financial obligations has been the principal cause of default. The reluctance of governmental units as well as business enterprises to default on their obligations is due to the resulting blemishes to their credit ratings, blemishes not easily nor quickly eliminated. The governmental unit has a special incentive for maintaining its good credit rating because, unlike the business corporation, it cannot reorganize under another name. The credit reputation of general credit municipals is very strong, and such securities play a prominent role in the investment portfolios of some of the most conservative institutional investors. Figure 21-1 shows the principal features of a new issue of general obligation municipals.

Limited Obligation Bonds. The limited obligation bonds of principal importance are the *revenue bonds. Limited obligation bonds* are issued by a state or local governmental unit for the purpose of financing a specific project. Examples of such projects are bridges, transportation terminals, sewer facilities, and general public utilities. These bonds are issued with the understanding that principal and interest will be paid only from the revenues produced by such projects, the issuing governmental unit having no contingent or direct liability otherwise. In recent years a much publicized form of revenue bonds has been that sold to make possible the construction of toll roads. The issuance of bonds by states and municipalities to construct industrial plants for lease to private industry may be of the revenue type. This type of financing was described in Chapter 13.

Figure 21-1

New Issue   Moody's Rating Aaa

Interest Exempt from All Present Federal Income Taxes

$22,135,000
City of Milwaukee, Wisconsin
General Obligation Corporate Purpose Bonds
Public Improvements, Series V

Dated April 1, 1974   Due April 1, 1975-1989

Principal and semi-annual interest (April 1 and October 1) payable at the office of the City Treasurer, Milwaukee, Wisconsin, or at Morgan Guaranty Trust Company of New York, New York City. First coupon due October 1, 1974. Coupon bonds in $5,000 denominations registerable as to principal only.

Legal investment, in our opinion, for trust funds and savings banks in New York, and savings banks in Connecticut and Massachusetts.

These bonds will constitute, in the opinion of counsel, general obligations of the City of Milwaukee, Wisconsin, and will be payable as to principal and interest from ad valorem taxes to be levied against all the taxable property located therein, without limitation as to rate or amount.

Amount	Rate	Maturity	Yield	Amount	Rate	Maturity	Yield or Price
$1,480,000	4.90%	1975	4.30%	$1,475,000	4.70%	1982	4.60%
1,480,000	5.00	1976	4.35	1,475,000	4.70	1983	4.65
1,475,000	5.00	1977	4.40	1,475,000	4.70	1984	100
1,475,000	5.00	1978	4.45	1,475,000	4.90	1985	4.75
1,475,000	4.70	1979	4.50	1,475,000	4.90	1986	4.80
1,475,000	4.70	1980	4.50	1,475,000	4.90	1987	100
1,475,000	4.70	1981	4.55	1,475,000	5.00	1988	100
				1,475,000	5.00	1989	100

(Accrued Interest to be Added)

These bonds are offered when, as and if issued and received by us and subject to the approving legal opinion of Messrs. Wood, Dawson, Love & Sabatine, Attorneys, New York, New York, a copy of which will appear on each bond.

First Wisconsin National Bank of Milwaukee

Banc Northwest

Smith, Barney & Co.
Incorporated

E. F. Hutton & Company Inc.

Harris, Upham & Co. Incorporated	The First National Bank and Trust Company Oklahoma City, Oklahoma	Industrial National Bank of Rhode Island
Underwood, Neuhaus & Co. Incorporated	The National City Bank of Cleveland	Manufacturers National Bank of Detroit	Bank of the Commonwealth

Austin Tobin & Co.
Incorporated

Traub and Company, Inc.

March 20, 1974

Although general obligation municipals continue to be far more important in volume, the proportion of revenue bonds to total municipal issues has increased greatly since World War II. Among the reasons for the increasing volume of revenue bonds may be included the expanding scope of state and local governments in the area of public services and the feeling that the cost of new projects should be borne by the users of such facilities. Through the use of revenue bonds the users of new projects pay the fees that support specifically each project.

Special assessment bonds are issued for the purpose of financing improvements that in turn increase adjacent property values. For example, the construction of streets and highways, although for the benefit of all users, is expected to increase the value of nearby properties. These bonds are payable from assessments on the properties that are assumed to have been benefited. Since the safety of special assessment bonds depends upon the ability and willingness of individuals and corporations to pay their special assessments, these securities have found less favor with the investing public. Some special assessment bonds have been issued with contingent general liability of the issuing governmental unit, that is, the obligations of an issue are met from general revenues if assessments are not adequate for the purpose. This type is more appropriately classified as a general obligation.

Underwriting State and Local Bond Issues

New issues of municipal obligations are generally sold to investment banking syndicates on the basis of competitive bids. The issuing municipality first secures competent legal opinion. With legality of the issue confirmed, the issuing unit then consults specialists in the field to determine appropriate timing, suitable interest rates, and other technical aspects of the issue.

Having decided upon the appropriate terms and timing of the issue, the governmental unit will advertise such information in local newspapers and financial trade papers (see Figure 21-1) and send special notices to investment banking houses and large commercial banks with bond departments. These notices clearly set forth the terms of the issue and the date by which competitive bids from underwriting firms must be received. After that date, bids are opened, and the award is made to the highest bidder, who then offers the bonds to the public.

The Market for State and Local Government Bonds

The ownership of municipals is most heavily concentrated in commercial banks, personal trusts, and government trust funds. Investors are attracted to municipals because of their quality and their exemption from federal income taxes. The investor who is in a 50 percent tax bracket, both corporate and individual, must receive a yield of 12 percent on taxable securities to have an after-tax yield equivalent to the 6 percent from tax-free municipal obligations. As indicated by Chart 21-1, the highest grade municipal obligations have averaged a yield of approximately two percent less than the yield on the highest grade corporate bonds. Because of the tax-free status of the income from municipal obligations, their yields are closely related to income tax levels and the number of investors in the higher income tax brackets. Yields are also a function of the volume of tax-exempt bonds available and comparative yields on all types of obligations.

It is estimated that more than three fifths of the net external financing of state and local governments is provided by financial institutions. Most of the remainder is provided by wealthy individuals. The two types of financial institutions that are the principal holders of state and local obligations are the commercial banks and property insurance companies. It is not surprising that these two types of institutions are subject to full corporate income tax liabilities. Commercial banks provide about one half and property insurance companies about one seventh of the total external financing of state and local governments.[3] It is interesting also to note that as corporate taxes have increased since World War II, the share of these two types of financial institutions in the obligations of state and local governments has increased.

CYCLICAL CHANGES IN BORROWING

Although state and local government outlays for construction have been increasing at a steady rate since 1952, the financing

---

[3] Goldsmith, Raymond W. *Financial Institutions* (New York: Random House, 1968), p. 151.

Chart 21–1

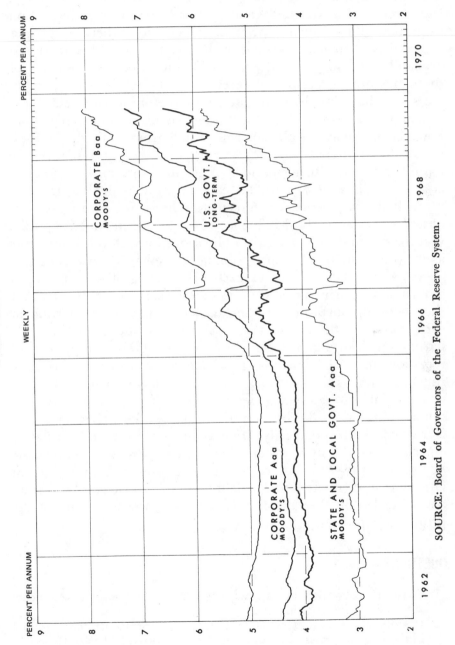

BOND YIELDS

SOURCE: Board of Governors of the Federal Reserve System.

to accommodate such outlays has been very irregular. Further, borrowing by state and local governments has tended to follow a countercyclical pattern. Several factors explain this fluctuation in timing. First, during periods of recession, there is greater availability of bank funds for such investments. This increased availability results from the normally increased free reserves of the banks during periods of recession without corresponding increases in business demands for funds. Running counter to the availability of bank funds during periods of economic recession, however, is the availability of bank funds from individuals. Individuals tend to have greater savings available and higher tax liabilities to face during periods of economic expansion. The increased attractiveness of the tax-exempt municipals does increase individual investment in such securities, but this increase does not offset the countercyclical influence of bank investments. It appears that the demand for municipal obligations by such other investors as fire and casualty insurance companies remains quite constant.

Another reason for the extensive borrowing of state and local governments during periods of economic recession is the fact that the operating surpluses of these governmental units decline at such times. To the extent that operating surpluses provide only partial financial support for construction outlays in periods of recession, increased borrowing is a necessity. Interest rates, too, influence the willingness of state and local governments to borrow. As interest rates in general decline during periods of economic contraction, the burden of prospective long-term financing is reduced correspondingly. The reduction in interest rates is especially significant in connection with the issuance of revenue bonds since the feasibility of the revenue-producing project is, in large measure, related to its debt-servicing capacity. As the interest burden on the financing is decreased, the feasibility of the project is improved.

QUESTIONS

1. Contrast the growth in expenditures of state and local governments with that of the federal government.
2. Describe the pressures on state and local governments that resulted in the large increases in expenditures in the post-World War II period.

3. Describe the various sources of financing for state and local governments, and comment on the role that each plays in the overall expenditures of these governmental units.
4. Account for the fact that long-term borrowing has been declining as a percent of the capital expenditures of state and local governments.
5. Describe the general claim to funds of state and local governments as a percent of funds raised by all users. Has any significant trend in such claims taken place in recent years?
6. The term "municipal bond" as it is generally used is something of a misnomer. Explain.
7. The typical municipal bond issue involves serial maturities. How do such maturities differ from those of the typical industrial bond issue?
8. Describe the special appeal of municipal bonds to investors in high income tax brackets.
9. Distinguish between general obligation and limited obligation municipal bonds. Would it be safe to say that general obligation bonds are always to be preferred by investors over limited obligation bonds?
10. Contrast the yields on high-grade municipal bonds with those of federal government bonds. Does the spread in yields seem reasonable?
11. Describe the factors that influence the yield on municipal bonds at any particular time.
12. Describe the cyclical pattern of state and local government borrowing.

SUGGESTED READINGS

BOWYER, JOHN W., JR. "The Use of Small Area Income Estimates in Municipal Credit Analysis." *The Journal of Finance,* Vol. XII, No. 1 (March, 1957), pp. 16-23.

BUCHANAN, JAMES M. *The Public Finances,* Rev. ed. Homewood, Illinois: Richard D. Irwin, Inc., 1972.

Facts and Figures on Government Finance, 17th ed. New York: Tax Foundation, Inc., 1973, Sections IV, V, and VI.

GOLDSMITH, RAYMOND W. *Financial Intermediaries in the American Economy Since 1900.* Princeton, New Jersey: Princeton University Press, 1958, pp. 258-65.

_____. *Financial Institutions.* New York: Random House, 1968. Chapter 4.

GROVES, HAROLD M., and R. BISH. *Financing Government,* 7th ed. New York: Holt, Rinehart, and Winston, Inc., 1973.

ROBINSON, ROLAND I. *Postwar Market for State and Local Government Securities.* Princeton, New Jersey: Princeton University Press, 1960.

_____. *The Management of Bank Funds,* 2d ed. New York: McGraw-Hill Book Company, Inc., 1962. Chapter 21.

The Financial Outlook for State and Local Government to 1980. New York: Tax Foundation, Inc., 1973.

22

Financing the Federal Government

The magnitude of the expenditures of the federal government is such that those of all other institutions and governments seem small in comparison. The financing of these expenditures is equally impressive. As is true for state and local government financing, the federal government relies primarily on tax revenues to support its various expenditure programs. In addition, revenues for general expenditure purposes are received for the performance of specific services benefiting the person charged. Examples of these revenues include such things as postal receipts, rental receipts from federal housing projects, and charges for subsistence and quarters collected from some government personnel.

The federal government also receives substantial insurance trust revenues from contributions to such programs as Old-Age, Survivors, and Disability Insurance and, in turn, makes large disbursements from these revenues. Although these trust fund receipts and expenditures represent a tremendous flow of funds, it is primarily with the general revenues and expenditures of the federal government that we are here concerned. And finally, as do state and local governments, the federal government relies on borrowing to bridge the gap between revenues and expenditures. In nine of the ten years after 1963, the federal government depended upon borrowed funds to support its program of expenditures. The national debt increased accordingly.

EXPENDITURES AND RECEIPTS OF THE FEDERAL GOVERNMENT

The most striking feature of federal government expenditures is that of the size of outlays for national defense. Although the United States has traditionally supported a relatively small military force, national defense expenditures have constituted the largest single item in the budget throughout most of the history of the country. As a result of the slowdown in defense spending and the growth of general expenditures, the proportion of defense expenditures is expected to fall significantly in the 1970's. Beyond the matters of national defense and the financial burden of past military operations, the next most important expenditure items are those for the welfare of specific individual groups. Such items include agricultural aid, commerce, and public assistance programs. It is interesting to note that one of the smallest items in the budget is that of the general operations of the government itself. This item includes the operations of the judicial system, the executive branch, the Congress, all regulatory agencies, and most of the departments of government, with the exception of the Department of Defense. (See Table 22-1)

As noted in the previous chapter, local governments depend primarily on property taxes, while state governments depend largely on sales taxes and such special taxes as those on motor fuel, liquor, and tobacco products. In contrast, the federal government relies primarily on income taxes for its revenues. Personal income taxes provide approximately 43 percent of general revenue, and corporate income taxes provide approximately 16 percent.

THE BUDGET

Until 1968 the form of budget presented annually to Congress did not include the expenditures and receipts of the various trust funds of the federal government, such as those for Old-Age, Survivors, and Disability Insurance. As such it failed to reflect the full effect of government activity on the economy. Many economists preferred to use the so-called "cash budget" for analytical purposes.

Table 22-1

BUDGET RECEIPTS, OUTLAYS, AND DEFICITS

Fiscal Years 1971, 1972, 1973

(Millions)

SOURCE OR FUNCTION	1971	1972	1973
Budget receipts	$188,392	$208,596	$220,785
Individual income taxes	86,230	94,824	93,900
Corporation income taxes	26,785	32,038	35,700
Employment taxes	41,699	46,119	55,113
Excise taxes	16,614	15,484	16,300
Estate and gift taxes	3,735	5,412	4,300
Customs	2,591	3,285	2,850
All other	10,737	11,434	12,622
Budget expenditures and net lending	211,425	231,619	246,257
National defense	77,661	78,150	78,310
International affairs and finance	3,095	3,659	3,844
Space research and technology	3,381	3,424	3,191
Agriculture and rural development	5,096	7,276	6,891
Natural resources	2,716	3,754	2,450
Commerce and transportation	11,310	11,055	11,550
Community development and housing	3,357	4,230	4,844
Education and manpower	8,654	10,200	11,281
Health	14,463	16,982	18,117
Income security	55,712	64,511	69,658
Veterans benefits and services	9,776	10,748	11,745
Interest	19,609	20,607	21,161
General government	3,970	4,888	5,531
Special allowances	—	—	6,275
Undistributed adjustments to amounts above ..	—7,376	—7,864	—8,590
Net lending	1,117	—1,105	—206
Budget surplus (+) or deficit (—)	—23,033	—23,023	—25,472
Means of financing	23,033	23,023	25,472
Borrowing from the public	19,448	19,442	27,500
Reduction of cash and money assets, etc.	3,585	3,581	—2,028

SOURCE: Treasury Department and Office of Management and Budget.

The cash budget recorded transactions with the public, including such items as trust fund expenditures and receipts. It was concerned primarily with cash transactions between the public and the federal government. But even the cash budget did not include all cash expenditures and receipts. For example, the various enterprises operated by the federal government were reflected on a net earnings or net deficit basis rather than on the basis of total expenditures and receipts.

In October, 1967, the President's Commission on Budget Concepts recommended the use of a new "unified budget" to replace all of the older budget concepts. This change has now been made with the result that the best features of the several previous budget concepts have been incorporated in the new budget. All receipts and expenditures are included on a consolidated cash basis. The "unibudget" covers lending as well as spending, but these two categories are shown separately to facilitate analysis. Lending is included because of the obvious impact it has on the economy. It is separated from spending because it is believed that these two types of outlays differ significantly in their impact on economic activity.

The excess of total expenditures (excluding net lending) over total receipts reflects the deficit in expenditures. The relationship of total outlays relative to total receipts reflects the total budget surplus or deficit. Table 22-1 reveals the 1971 and 1972 budgets and budgetary estimates for 1973.

DEBT FINANCING

As we have observed, the federal government obtains its funds for expenditures primarily through tax revenues. To the extent that such tax and other general revenues fail to meet the expenditures of the federal government, deficits are incurred. Although these deficits in most years have been of modest size relative to the level of government expenditures, their cumulative impact has resulted in a vast increase in the total federal debt. Although statutory debt limits have been set by Congress, it has been necessary to raise such limits at frequent intervals to accommodate the continuing deficits of the federal government. For example, as of December, 1973, the debt ceiling was $476 billion—only $7 billion greater than the national debt at that time. Chart 22-1 vividly reveals the frequency of budgetary deficits over the course of the last 30 years.

While the federal debt continues to rise, it is important to recognize that the present debt stems primarily from the financing of war efforts. The financial burden of war has increased with the cost of waging war, and each conflict has made all previous

Chart 22–1

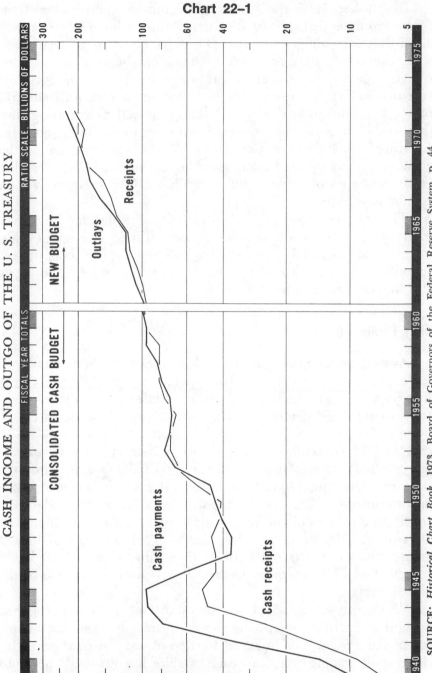

CASH INCOME AND OUTGO OF THE U. S. TREASURY

SOURCE: *Historical Chart Book,* 1973, Board of Governors of the Federal Reserve System, p. 44.

wars inexpensive by comparison. It has been estimated that the per capita figure for debt following the Civil War was $78; following World War I, $240; and following World War II, $1,720.

In contrast with that of some nations, the federal debt of the United States is owned to a large extent by its own citizens and institutions. Indeed, part of our debt is due to our role as a creditor nation, having advanced many billions of dollars to our foreign allies. This has not always been so, however, and until World War I, this nation depended heavily upon foreign investors for support of both government debt and nongovernment debt.

Nowhere in the economy is the significance of a smoothly functioning financial system more apparent than in connection with the federal debt. Not only does the financial system accommodate the federal government in the financing of its frequent budgetary deficits, but it also provides for the smooth transition from old debt issues that mature to the new issues that take the place of the old. The financial markets face a greater challenge in refunding government issues than in absorption of net new debt. Just as the nation's industrial development has depended upon an equally efficient development of financial institutions, so too, many of the financial activities of modern government depend upon the same institutions.

It is interesting to note that public borrowing is a relatively modern development. During the Middle Ages, governments were forced to borrow from wealthy merchants and others on an individual basis. Often crown jewels were offered as collateral for such advances. Large public borrowing by governments, as for businesses, became possible only with the refinement of monetary systems and the development of efficient financial institutions to facilitate the transfer of monetary savings.

In the following pages of this chapter, we are concerned with the manner in which the federal government finances its debt and the financial system that makes it possible. The impact of the federal debt on the economy of the nation is great indeed. These considerations are discussed at length in Chapter 24. It is important here to note only that the growth of the federal debt has taken place in the context of an expanding economy and that the burden of the debt is a function of the interest on the debt to the ability of the nation to pay. Today the federal debt bears a lower ratio to national income than it did immediately after World War II, and it is hoped that fiscal discipline combined with an expanding economy will contribute significantly to reduction of the burden.

OBLIGATIONS ISSUED BY THE UNITED STATES

The obligations that constitute the federal debt have become the largest and most important single class of investment instruments. These obligations dominate both short-term and long-term capital markets and play an important role in investment patterns of most financial institutions. Commercial banks, for example, invest heavily in short-term federal government obligations for liquidity and safety. The short-term obligations provide the investor with a near cash position and an income as well. Life insurance companies and pension funds invest heavily in long-term federal obligations for safety and income.

Because the obligations of the federal government are the highest quality available to any investor and because of the breadth of the market for these obligations, interest rates on all securities are geared to those of federal obligations. Table 22-2 reflects the rate structure for both selected short-term and long-term obligations. In both instances, the rate on the federal obligations becomes the base for the spread of rates. As the interest rates on federal obligations increase or decrease, there is pressure on other obligations for movement in a similar direction. The obligations issued by the federal government may be described as marketable, nonmarketable, and special issues. *Special issues* include those obligations issued specifically for ownership by government agencies and government trust funds. In addition to these direct issues of the federal government, the obligations of certain federal government controlled agencies are either general obligations of or guaranteed by the federal government. The new Federal Financing Bank, created by Congress in December, 1973, coordinates under a single agency the marketing of several federal credit programs. Such programs as the Farmers Home Administration, Rural Electrification Administration, and Amtrak may issue their obligations to the Federal Financing Bank which, in turn, issues obligations to the public which are backed by the full faith

Table 22–2

MONEY MARKET RATES FOR SELECTED OBLIGATIONS
February 2, 1974

Short-term obligations

Three-month federal obligations (Treasury bills)	7.78	Percent
Prime bankers' acceptances—90 days	8.55	"
Prime commercial paper 4 to 6 months	8.38	"
Prime rate on short-term business loans	9.50	"

Long-term obligations

Government bonds—10 years or more	6.55	Percent
Aaa corporate bonds (highest grade)	7.87	"
Baa corporate bonds (medium grade)	8.58	"

SOURCE: *Federal Reserve Bulletin*, Board of Governors of the Federal Reserve System, Washington, D. C., February, 1974, pp. A32, A33, and A34.

and credit of the federal government. We are interested here, however, only in the marketable and nonmarketable direct issues of the federal government.

Marketable Obligations

Marketable securities, as the term implies, are those that may be purchased and sold through customary market channels. Markets for these obligations are maintained by large commercial banks and securities dealers. In addition, nearly all securities firms and commercial banks, large or small, will accommodate their customers' requirements for purchase and sale of federal obligations by routing such orders to institutions that do maintain markets in them. The investments of institutional investors and large personal investors in federal obligations are centered almost exclusively in the marketable issues. These marketable issues are bills, certificates, notes, and bonds, the differentiating factor being their maturity at time of issue. Although the maturity of an obligation is reduced as it remains in effect, the obligation continues to be referred to by its original descriptive title. Thus, a 30-year Treasury bond continues to be described in the quotation sheets as a bond throughout its life.

Treasury Bills. These Treasury obligations bear the shortest of the maturities and are typically issued for 91 days, with some issues carrying maturities of 182 days. A very few issues of Treasury bills have been issued with a maturity of as long as one year. In addition, special issues of bills are provided with maturities to coincide with tax payment dates. Businesses ordinarily invest in these *tax anticipation bills*, referred to as TABS, as a convenient method of arranging to meet tax liabilities while at the same time providing an interest income.

Issues of Treasury bills are offered each week by the Treasury to refund the part of the total volume of bills that matures. In effect, the 91-day treasury bills mature and are "rolled over" in 13 weeks, and each week approximately 1/13 of the total volume of such bills is refunded. Insofar as the flow of cash revenues into the Treasury is too small to meet expenditure requirements, additional bills are issued. During those periods of the year when revenues exceed expenditures, Treasury bills are allowed to mature without being refunded. Treasury bills, therefore, provide the Treasury with a convenient financial mechanism to adjust for the lack of a regular flow of revenues into the Treasury. The volume of bills also may be increased or decreased in response to general surpluses or deficits in the federal budget from year to year and may be increased or decreased also for general monetary control purposes.

Treasury bills are issued on a discount basis and mature at par. Each week the Treasury bills to be sold are awarded to the highest bidders. Sealed bids are submitted by dealers and other investors. Upon being opened, these bids are arrayed from highest to lowest; that is, those bidders asking the least discount (offering the highest price) are placed high in the array. The bids are then accepted in the order of their position in the array until all bills are awarded. Bidders seeking a high discount (and offering a low price) may fail to receive any bills that particular week. Investors interested in purchasing small volumes of Treasury bills ($200,000 or less) may submit their orders on an "average competitive price" basis. In so doing, the Treasury deducts from the total volume of bills to be sold the total of these small orders. The remaining bills are allotted on the competitive basis described above. These small orders are then executed at a discount equal to the average of the competitive bids that are accepted for the large orders.

Although some business corporations and wealthy individuals invest in Treasury bills, by far the most important holders of these obligations are the commercial banks of the nation.

Certificates of Indebtedness. These obligations may be issued by the federal government with maturities not to exceed one year at specified interest rates in contrast with the discount arrangement for Treasury bills. Since 1966, however, their use has been limited to transactions between the United States Treasury and official institutions of foreign countries, and under those circumstances such obligations are nonmarketable.

Treasury Notes. Treasury notes are issued for maturities of more than one year but not more than seven years and are issued at specified interest rates. These intermediate-term federal obligations are also held largely by the commercial banks of the nation.

Treasury Bonds. Treasury bonds may be issued with any maturity but generally have had an original maturity in excess of five years. These bonds bear interest at stipulated rates. Many issues of these bonds are callable by the government several years before their maturity. For example, the 30-year issue of $3\frac{1}{4}$ percent bonds issued in 1953 is described as having a maturity of 1978-83. This issue may be called for redemption at par as early as 1978 but in no event later than 1983. As of 1974 the longest maturity of Treasury bonds was 24 years. As for the other marketable securities of the government, active markets for the purchase and sale of these securities are maintained by dealers.

All marketable obligations of the federal government, with the exception of Treasury bills, are offered to the public through the federal reserve banks at predetermined prices and yields. Investors place their orders for new issues, and such orders are filled from the available supply of the new issue. If the issue is oversubscribed, investors may be allotted only a part of their original orders. A striking exception to this method of selling Treasury bonds was begun early in 1963, and by midyear had been tried a second time. This departure from the customary solicitation of orders at fixed prices involved the sale of bonds through investment banking syndicates on much the same basis that the securities of business enterprises are sold. Competing syndicates bid for the issue, and the highest bidding group received the entire issue for resale to the general public. The first of the two issues was most successful. According to Treasury officials, the price received for the bonds from the syndicate was higher than would have been received by the Treasury through a customary direct issue. In turn, the syndicate was able to distribute the issue with speed and profit to the investing public. The success of this effort was enhanced by the existence of a stable market in bonds. The second issue of bonds through syndicate bids was also a success from the point of view of the Treasury in that a relatively good price for the bonds was received by the Treasury. The syndicate, however, found the issue to be slightly overpriced, and it was distributed to the public only with much effort. The future of bond sales through investment banking syndicates remains uncertain.

Nonmarketable Issues

As the name implies, *nonmarketable issues* of federal obligations are those that cannot be transferred to other persons or institutions and can be redeemed only by being turned in to the United States Treasury. Savings bonds comprise the bulk of the nonmarketable issues and as of the end of 1973 were outstanding in the amount of approximately $60.8 billion. The relative importance of various classes of federal debt and general increase in obligations outstanding since World War I are shown in Chart 22-2.

Savings bonds are redeemable at the option of the holder, and their nonmarketability derives from the fact that they may be redeemed only by the person to whom they were issued. Some of the savings bonds are sold at a discount while others pay interest semiannually. Savings bonds sold at a discount earn interest according to a fixed schedule, such interest being paid only upon redemption of the bond. The most popular of all savings bonds, the Series E, are of this type. They are sold at a discount of 25 percent of their redemption value and if held to maturity, five years, earn an average annual rate of interest of 6 percent. The smallest denomination of Series E bonds is $25, and it is

Chart 22–2

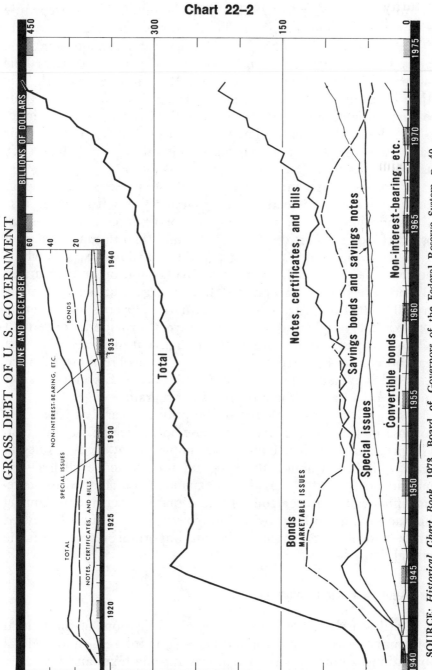

GROSS DEBT OF U. S. GOVERNMENT
JUNE AND DECEMBER

BILLIONS OF DOLLARS

Total

Notes, certificates, and bills

Savings bonds and savings notes

Non-interest-bearing, etc.

Special issues

Convertible bonds

Bonds

MARKETABLE ISSUES

TOTAL

NON-INTEREST-BEARING, ETC.

SPECIAL ISSUES

BONDS

NOTES, CERTIFICATES, AND BILLS

SOURCE: *Historical Chart Book, 1973*, Board of Governors of the Federal Reserve System, p. 40.

sold to the public for $18.75. It should be noted that the schedule of interest accrual on these bonds increases during the life of the bond, thus tending to discourage early redemption. The Series E bonds also have the privilege of extension after their maturity permitting them to continue their interest accrual. The other series of savings bonds, G, H, and K, pay interest to their holders semiannually. Only Series H of these three series continues to be sold to the public. They are sold at 100 percent of their maturity value in denominations no smaller than $500. They mature in ten years.

It has been estimated that 57 million persons own savings bonds. Their appeal to the small investor stems from their ease of redemption, lack of risk, and ease of replacement in case of loss, theft, or destruction. One of the most significant attractions of these savings bonds, however, is the convenience with which they may be purchased. Commercial banks and other institutions sell and redeem Series E bonds without charge. Further, automatic payroll deductions on the part of many employers, now covering approximately eight million payroll savers, provide a convenient method of budgeting savings out of current income. The fact that more than 40 percent of all savings bonds are more than ten years old is evidence that many holders of Series E bonds consider them to be a part of their retirement program.

Savings bonds were offered to the public as early as 1935. The purpose of this early effort was to democratize the public debt. The program of savings bonds as we know it, however, was begun in May, 1941. Although the program was started exclusively to help finance World War II, it was expanded and adapted to peacetime financial requirements of the federal government. During the war, savings bonds provided nearly 20 percent of all borrowed funds, and they continue to be an important segment of the federal debt.

Tax Status of Federal Obligations

Until March 1, 1941, interest on all obligations of the federal government was exempt from all taxes. The interest on all federal obligations is now subject to ordinary income taxes and tax rates. The Public Debt Act of 1941 terminated the issuance of tax-free federal obligations. Since that time, all issues previously sold to the public have matured or have been called for redemption. Income from the obligations of the federal government is exempt from all taxing authority of state and local governments. Federal bonds, however, are subject to both federal and state inheritance, estate, or gift taxes.

OWNERSHIP OF THE FEDERAL DEBT

The federal debt plays a role in the portfolios of most of the financial institutions of the nation, many business corporations, and millions of individuals. Indeed, the very size of the federal debt dictates that it be represented in almost all investment programs. Ownership of the debt by individual groups is shown as a percentage of the total debt in Table 22-3.

Much of the challenge in managing the federal debt has centered around the individual ownership of obligations, particularly the savings bonds. Throughout World War II, the effective savings bond sales drives resulted in more than $10 billion sales each year. Following the war, not only did the purchase of bonds slow down markedly, but also vast numbers of bonds were redeemed

Table 22–3

OWNERSHIP OF THE FEDERAL DEBT
June 30, 1974

	PERCENT OF TOTAL DEBT
U. S. Government agencies and trust funds	29.1
Individuals	17.0
Federal reserve banks	16.9
Foreign and international	12.1
Commercial banks	11.2
State and local governments	6.0
Insurance companies	1.2
Mutual savings banks	.6
Other miscellaneous groups of investors	5.9
	100.0

SOURCE: *Federal Reserve Bulletin,* Board of Governors of the Federal Reserve System, Washington, D. C., August, 1974, p. A36.

by individuals anxious to acquire homes and other durable goods that had been in short supply during the war. In addition, alternative investments became more attractive as interest rates increased and as the stock market began to gain the momentum of a long rising market. Commercial banks, too, were finding profitable alternative investments for their funds, and they reduced their commitments to federal debt obligations. Although the expenditure requirements of the federal government were reduced substantially in the postwar period, they remained relatively high compared with the prewar period. It became necessary for the Treasury to make strong efforts to stabilize the redemption of savings bonds. That they were able to do so is indicated in Chart 22-3. This chart reflects the ownership of the federal debt by ownership groups since World War I.

The series of actions begun in 1951 by the Treasury to halt the drain of cash due to savings bond redemptions included the first of the ten-year extension privileges on Series E bonds and the introduction of additional series of savings bonds at higher interest rates. Rates have since been raised several times. Notwithstanding the difficulties of the Treasury in maintaining the volume of savings bonds since World War II, it is obvious that had their sale been terminated at the end of the war, the task of selling other bonds in the financial markets would have been increased greatly. In short, the Treasury has required the investment interest of all possible groups of investors. The increase in ownership of federal debt obligations by federal agency and federal trust funds as well as corporate pension funds (included under "others") is reflected in Chart 22-3. These groups not only have borne the general increase in the total federal debt but have absorbed the declining share of commercial banks, insurance companies, and mutual savings banks as well.

MATURITY DISTRIBUTION OF THE FEDERAL DEBT

In the earlier pages of this chapter the various types of marketable obligations of the federal government are described. The terms "bills," "certificates," "notes," and "bonds" describe the general maturity ranges, however, only at the time of issue. As time passes, all of these obligations approach maturity. In order to

Chart 22–3

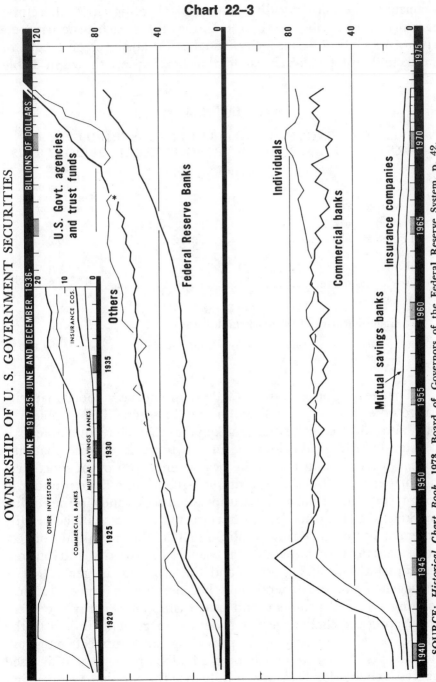

OWNERSHIP OF U. S. GOVERNMENT SECURITIES

JUNE, 1917-35; JUNE AND DECEMBER, 1936-

BILLIONS OF DOLLARS

U.S. Govt. agencies and trust funds

Federal Reserve Banks

Individuals

Commercial banks

Insurance companies

Mutual savings banks

Others

SOURCE: *Historical Chart Book, 1973,* Board of Governors of the Federal Reserve System, p. 42.

determine the maturity distribution of all obligations, therefore, it is necessary to observe the remaining life of each issue irrespective of its class. The maturity distribution and average length of marketable interest-bearing federal obligations are shown in Table 22-4.

Table 22–4

AVERAGE LENGTH AND MATURITY DISTRIBUTION OF MARKETABLE INTEREST-BEARING FEDERAL OBLIGATIONS

December 31, 1973

MATURITY CLASS	PERCENT OF TOTAL MARKET- ABLE DEBT
Within 1 year	52.4
1-5 years	30.2
5-10 years	9.3
10-20 years	5.8
20 years and over	2.3
All issues	100.0

Average maturity of all marketable issues .... 3 years.

SOURCE: *Federal Reserve Bulletin,* February, 1974, Board of Governors of the Federal Reserve System, p. A43.

The heavy concentration of debt in the very short maturity range poses a special problem for the Treasury. This problem is one also for the securities markets in that the government is constantly selling additional securities to replace those that mature. Nor is the solution to the heavy concentration of short-term maturities to be found in the simple issuance of a large number of long-term issues. Like all institutions that seek funds in the capital markets, the Treasury has to offer securities that will be readily accepted by the investing public. Further, the magnitude of federal financing is such that radical changes in maturity distributions can upset the capital markets and the economy in general. The management of the federal debt has become an especially challenging financial problem, and much time and energy are spent in meeting the challenge. Nor is debt management limited to the matter of refunding issues and providing funds to meet budgetary deficits. As described in Chapter 24, debt management is used aggressively by the Treasury to influence the supply of money and credit. We are here concerned only with a general description of the maturity distribution of the debt.

If the Treasury refunds maturing issues with new short-term obligations, the average maturity of the total debt is reduced as the passage of time constantly brings all issues closer to maturity. As time passes, longer-term issues are brought into shorter-dated categories. Net cash borrowing resulting from budgetary deficits must take the form of maturities that are at least as long as the average of the marketable debt if the average maturity is not to be reduced.

One of the new debt management techniques used to extend the average maturity of the marketable debt without disturbing the capital markets is that of *advance refunding* which involves the offer by the Treasury to owners of a given issue of the opportunity to exchange their holdings well in advance of their regular maturity for new securities of longer maturity.

In summary, the Treasury is the largest and most active single borrower in the financial markets. The Treasury is continuously in the process of borrowing and refinancing. Its financial actions are tremendous in contrast with all other forms of financing, including that of the largest business corporations. Yet, the financial system of the nation is suitably adapted to the smooth accommodation of these requirements. Indeed, the very existence of a public debt of this magnitude is predicated upon the existence of a highly refined monetary and credit system.

QUESTIONS

1. Indicate some of the principal budgetary expenditures of the federal government. Do you anticipate any substantial change in this expenditure pattern in the near future?
2. Although the federal government and local governments rely heavily on taxes for their revenues, the type of taxes on which they rely are quite different. Explain.
3. Comment on the evolution of the new "unified federal budget."
4. Why is government lending now included in the federal budget? Why is such lending identified and shown separately in the budget?
5. Trace the growth of the federal debt and the reasons for its growth pattern.
6. Explain the relevance of the federal debt to a study of the monetary and credit system of the United States.

7. By reference to the *Federal Reserve Bulletin, Wall Street Journal*, or other such sources of financial information, construct a schedule of interest rates for both short-term and long-term obligations of the federal government and business enterprises.
8. Compare the yields available on high-grade, long-term municipal obligations with those of the federal government. How do you explain the differential?
9. Explain the mechanics of issuing Treasury bills, indicating how the price of a new issue is determined.
10. What are the factors that determine the volume of Treasury bills in existence at a particular time?
11. Describe the maturity distribution of the federal debt at the present time. What is the nature of the problem involved in the management of the maturity distribution?
12. What have been the special contributions of savings bonds to the financing of the federal government over the years? Has the nature of these contributions changed?
13. Explain the tax status of income from federal obligations.
14. Describe the significant changes in the ownership pattern of the federal debt.
15. Describe the process of advance refunding of the federal debt.

SUGGESTED READINGS

"Advance Refunding: A Technique of Debt Management." *Monthly Review*, Federal Reserve Bank of New York, December, 1962, pp. 169-175.

BUCHANAN, JAMES M. *The Public Finances*, Rev. ed. Homewood, Illinois,: Richard D. Irwin, Inc., 1972.

DAVIE, BRUCE F., and BRUCE DUNCOMBE. *Public Finance*. New York: Holt, Rinehart and Winston, Inc., 1972. Chapter 18.

GAINES, TILFORD C. *Techniques of Treasury Debt Management*. New York: The Free Press of Glencoe, 1962. Part III.

GROVES, HAROLD M., and R. BISH. *Financing Government*, 7th ed. New York: Holt, Rinehart and Winston, Inc., 1973.

"Securities of U. S. Government Agencies." *Economic Review*, Federal Reserve Bank of Cleveland, October, 1969, pp. 19-30.

Tax Foundation, Inc. *Facts and Figures on Government Finance*, 17th ed., 1973. Section III.

"The Role of Savings Bonds in Government Finance." *Monthly Review*, Federal Reserve Bank of New York, June, 1961, pp. 109-111.

WOODSWORTH, G. WALTER. *The Money Market and Monetary Management*. New York: Harper & Row, 1972. Chapter 18.

PART 4

MONETARY AND CREDIT POLICIES AND PROBLEMS

23 | The Role of the Federal Reserve in Monetary and Credit Control

When the Federal Reserve System was set up, it had almost exclusive authority in the field of monetary and credit control. The government did have the right to set the monetary standard and to regulate the value of the dollar, and it had some influence on money and credit through its fiscal policy. Monetary standards, however, were changed infrequently, and the impact of fiscal policy was small except in wartime.

OBJECTIVES OF THE FEDERAL RESERVE SYSTEM

In line with the philosophy of government at the time, the original objectives of the Federal Reserve System were conceived in narrow terms. The founders of the System felt that it should provide an elastic currency for the country, that it should provide facilities for the discounting of commercial paper held by member banks, and that it should improve the supervision of banks. Over the years, however, as the attitude toward the role of government in economic affairs has changed, the objectives of the Federal Reserve System have been broadened. Amendments to the original law contained phrases such as "the maintenance of sound credit conditions and the accommodation of commerce, industry, and agriculture" and "preventing the excessive use of credit" for speculative purposes. The law as amended also refers to the effect of certain actions "upon the general credit situation of the country." The objectives were expanded during World War I to include aid in financing the government. The Board of Governors stated in a publication in 1961 that the objectives of the System are to help counteract inflationary and deflationary movements and to share in creating conditions favorable to sustained high employment, stable values, growth of the country, and a rising level of consumption, as well as to carry out the original objectives for which the Federal Reserve System was established.[1]

MONETARY AND CREDIT CONTROL POLICIES

In attaining these basic objectives, general policies directed toward these ends must be followed. Though there is general agreement on basic objectives, opinions on the policies needed to attain these objectives vary. Furthermore, there is disagreement as to the possibility of carrying out some of the policies. The important policies that have been advocated to achieve the objectives of the System will be considered as a background to the study of the instruments of Federal Reserve policy and their use by the System. These are:

1. Protecting the monetary standard and balance of payments equilibrium.
2. Regulating the use and availability of money.
3. Stabilizing price levels and promoting full employment.
4. Creating conditions favorable for economic growth.
5. Promoting sound banking.

Protecting the Monetary Standard and Balance of Payments Equilibrium

The earliest central bank policy, as developed in Europe and especially by the Bank of England, was to protect the monetary standard; that is, to make certain that a sufficient supply of gold remained in the vaults of the government and of the banks and

---

[1] The Board of Governors of the Federal Reserve System, *The Federal Reserve System, Its Purposes and Functions* (Washington: 1961), p. 1.

in general circulation for the gold standard to operate effectively. For example, during most of the nineteenth century whenever gold was being sent out of England in a volume so large as to threaten the effective operation of the gold standard, the Bank of England acted to raise interest rates so as to make investment of funds at home more profitable, thus reducing the export of gold. This policy was of some importance in this country while we were on an unregulated gold standard; but under the modified gold-bullion standard, it became of less significance since Federal Reserve action was replaced in part by direct Treasury controls over gold. In recent years and especially since 1958 when gold started to flow out of the country in sizeable amounts due to an unfavorable balance of payments, the policy of helping to achieve a balance of payments equilibrium again became of prime significance. Achieving such equilibrium is much more complex than it was in earlier days. It involves not only regulating interest rates, but affecting growth rates to slow imports, swapping currency with foreign monetary authorities to stabilize exchange rates, and the whole range of Federal Reserve instruments for implementing monetary policy.

Regulating the Use and Availability of Money

Another central banking policy is to regulate the use of money so that it is channeled into productive activities rather than speculative activities. Allied to this is the use of monetary policy to prevent inflation. The Federal Reserve System as originally set up provided for an elastic supply of currency, which expanded as business needs for currency expanded, thus providing money for productive activities. Since the Federal Reserve has acted from time to time to curb speculation and to help prevent inflation, it has followed this policy in a general way.

Central banking policy has also traditionally been concerned with the availability of money and with interest rates. Interest rates do have some effect on the flow of funds into and out of the economy and on the rate of use of capital in the domestic economy, but economists are not in agreement as to the extent of this effect or its exact nature. As a result, there has been disagreement as to the general interest-rate policy, if any, to pursue.

There has been little disagreement with the policy to reduce, insofar as possible, seasonal variations in interest rates due to different demands for funds at different times during the year, as for example during the Christmas shopping season. Likewise, there is general agreement on the policy to eliminate regional differences in interest rates due to the uneven distribution of available funds in various sections of the country and the lack of complete mobility of such funds.

Another policy is to regulate the supply of money so as to aid the Treasury in its financing. There is no question about the Federal Reserve helping the Treasury in financing emergency needs, such as those of World War I, the 1929 depression, and World War II. In recent years, however, a controversy has developed concerning Federal Reserve policies of monetary ease to aid Treasury financing in a period of inflationary pressures and a large government debt.

Stabilizing Price Levels and Promoting Full Employment

The third group of policies advocated to attain the objectives of the Federal Reserve System is concerned with the stabilization of price levels and high levels of employment. During periods of excess demand, such as occurred after World War II and during the Korean and Vietnam Wars, there is general agreement that the Federal Reserve should follow a policy of restraining price rises. There is also widespread support for such a policy at other times, but it is by no means shared by all. Some economists have favored a gradually rising price level, since they feel that full employment is easier to maintain when prices are rising.

There is more or less general agreement that monetary policies should be designed so as to help maintain a high level of employment. There is some question about the possibility of having both high employment and stable prices in our economy as it is organized today. Some economists believe that in an economy of powerful national labor unions and industry-wide bargaining, stable prices can be maintained only if unemployment is increased to intolerable levels. The period of the early sixties was one of reasonable price stability, but some unemployment continued to exist. When unemployment dropped to lower levels during the Vietnam War, prices began to rise at an unacceptable rate. Some economists hold that different monetary and fiscal policies would have prevented inflation and that with proper policies both goals can be achieved at the same time.

Creating Conditions Favorable to Economic Growth

During the last several years, increasing stress has been placed on economic growth as a major American goal. Growth makes it possible for America to meet commitments to the free world and also to improve standards of living at home and abroad. The adjustments which technological advances such as automation are forcing on our economy are also easier to make in an expanding economy.

In order to create conditions favorable to economic growth, it is necessary for the money supply to grow. The rate of growth of the money supply need not be the same as the overall growth rate since the rate of use of money in relationship to economic activity changes over time and also on a cyclical basis. It must, however, be fast enough to not only permit growth in total activity but also to develop credit conditions which are favorable to growth.

There is little debate about the desirability of creating conditions favorable to economic growth. But there is a considerable amount of disagreement about the relationship of this policy to that of policies for promoting price stability. These policies taken alone can be at cross purposes and must therefore be coordinated and balanced. For example, the money supply may be allowed to grow little or not at all to promote price stability, but such a policy may restrict economic growth and lead to unacceptable levels of unemployment. The growth in the money supply must be so adjusted as to lead to an acceptable balance between the price level and the rate of growth of total economic activity.

Promotion of Sound Banking

Another general policy of the Federal Reserve is the promotion of sound banking. This includes the promotion of not only sound individual banks but also an effective and efficient system of banks that can meet the needs of the economy as a whole. This objective is accomplished in part by bank examinations, which were discussed in the section on commercial banks. It is also accomplished by regulations governing bank activities, such as those designed to prevent speculative loans. The services of the Federal Reserve in expeditiously clearing checks, holding reserves of member banks, transferring funds, and providing banks with currency to meet regular as well as unusual demands for funds all help to achieve this objective.

Operating Guides for Monetary Policy

After a decision has been reached on the general monetary policies to follow, it is necessary to set some general guides to follow in achieving the goals which have been set. In actual practice the Federal Reserve seems to try to strike a balance between keeping the money supply and bank credit growing at a particular rate and attempting to establish a desired set of money market conditions. Prior to 1970 the Federal Reserve put primary emphasis on money market conditions and on interest rates in setting policies. Beginning in 1970 the Federal Open Market Committee included the rate of growth of the money stock as one of its important objectives. In 1972 the Committee began to use ranges for the growth of reserves available to support private nonbank deposits (RPD's) as its immediate target. They reasoned that maintaining a desired rate of growth in RPD's would after a lag lead to the desired growth in the money supply.

The operating instructions and a consensus on policy growing out of the March 18 and 19, 1974, meeting of the Open Market Committee are typical and are given at the top of the next page.[2] The instructions call for a slower growth in monetary aggregates over the months ahead which will, of course, result in higher interest rates. But this policy directive is to be implemented while taking account of domestic and international financial market developments.

There is some question about the desirability of setting goals so as to achieve a balance between the money supply and credit market conditions. For example, in 1968 the Congressional Joint

---

[2] *Federal Reserve Bulletin*, June, 1974, p. 437.

POLICY CONSENSUS	OPERATING INSTRUCTION
. . . to foster financial conditions conducive to resisting inflationary pressures, supporting a resumption of real economic growth, and maintaining equilibrium in the country's balance of payments.	. . . To implement this policy, while taking account of international and domestic financial market developments, including the prospective Treasury financing, the Committee seeks to achieve bank reserve and money market conditions that would moderate growth in monetary aggregates over the months ahead.

Economic Committee endorsed a proposal to keep the growth of the money supply within a range of 2 percent to 6 percent a year during each quarter except in abnormal conditions. The Federal Reserve would under this proposal have to justify actions in periods it considered abnormal. In recent years changes in the money supply have generally been in excess of the 2 to 6 percent range proposed as guidelines. The major argument for moderating interest rate fluctuations in the credit markets arises out of institutional arrangements in those markets. Financial institutions have a low ratio of equity capital and perform underwriting functions for private and public borrowers at very low margins which could not be done if they had to assume the risks of widely fluctuating interest rates from irregular short-term movements. The counter argument is that short-run changes in the money markets are of two basic types, those which are temporary and will reverse themselves and those which are sustained and do not reverse themselves. Since the money managers cannot always or easily distinguish between the two types of changes at a particular moment of time, their policy often puts short-run stability of interest rates above the more fundamental objective of economic stability.

Consideration is given now to the instruments in the hands of the Federal Reserve System to carry out its policies. Later chapters discuss the relationship of Federal Reserve and Treasury policies to price levels, interest rates, and economic stability.

THE DISCOUNT RATE

One of the most important instruments of Federal Reserve policy, in the minds of the framers of the Act, was the use of the discount rate for making the amount of currency and credit correspond to the needs of business. The discount power was given to the reserve authorities as a basic part of the monetary and credit system because it was felt that it would be effective in regulating the volume of money and credit in use in the economy. This expectation was based upon the experience of the Bank of England, which for decades had been successful in controlling the general credit situation in Great Britain by the manipulation of discount rates.

Experience with the Discount Rate

Discount-rate policy helped finance World War I largely because the discount rate was kept below the interest rate on government bonds used as collateral for loans that were encouraged by the Reserve authorities. It contributed to easy money conditions in the twenties and may have helped to start the stock market boom. Increases in discount rates in 1928 and 1929 were too late to stop the boom, and there is a question as to whether that boom could have been stopped even if discount rates had been raised sooner. Profits in a rising stock market, in which stocks could be bought with 10 percent cash and a 90 percent loan, were too large to be influenced by a difference between 4 and 5, or 6, or even 8 percent a year in interest charges. Low rates during the depression were powerless by themselves to increase business materially. During World War II, low rates helped war financing. Banks were encouraged to expand credit since they knew that additional funds were available at very low rates if needed, and they were urged to make use of such borrowing to help meet the credit needs of the war effort. After World War II and especially during the Vietnam War and early postwar period, discount rates were raised to help restrain inflation. In the summer of 1974 the discount rate was raised to 8½ percent as part of a program to restrain unusual inflationary pressures.

Discount policy alone has not been effective as a method of monetary and credit control. It has been augmented over the years by open-market operations, authority to change reserve requirements, and direct controls over various types of lending. It has had some effectiveness, however, as part of a coordinated monetary and credit policy.

The early experience with discount rates, and especially the experience in the thirties, led to some modifications in discount policy. The Federal Reserve Act was revised to broaden the access to reserve bank credit. A bank may now get credit from its federal reserve bank by (a) discounting eligible commercial paper which matures in 90 days (nine months for agricultural paper), (b) borrowing on its own notes secured by eligible paper or government securities, or (c) borrowing on its own notes secured by other assets satisfactory to the reserve bank. Borrowing was also clearly established as a privilege, not as a right. The Federal Reserve is to extend credit to member banks with due regard to the maintenance of sound credit conditions as well as the needs of commerce, industry, and agriculture.

Rationale of Discount Policy

The early rationale of discount policy was developed by the Bank of England before the Federal Reserve System was established. Stated in somewhat oversimplified terms, discount policy was intended to work in the following fashion. An increase in the discount rate would lead to a general increase in interest rates and a restriction of the extension of credit. This would tend to decrease the demand for short-term credit for additions to inventory and to accounts receivable. This in turn would lead to a postponement of the establishment of new production facilities and therefore to a decreased demand for capital goods. As a consequence, the rate of increase in income would slow down, and in time income would decrease and with it the demand for consumer goods. Holders of inventories carried by means of borrowed funds would liquidate their stocks in an already weak market. The result would be a drop in prices that would tend to stimulate the demand for and reduce the supply of goods, thus restoring economic balance. A reduction in the discount rate was expected to have the opposite effect.

Few economists would ascribe such influence to interest rates today. Business fluctuations depend upon a whole series of real and psychological factors that affect the demand for and the supply of capital, not upon interest rates alone. Increases in the discount rate, however, along with other actions of the reserve authorities, cause banks to curtail their lending activities. Banks not only raise interest rates on their loans to meet the higher cost for money, but also they reduce the amount of credit extended to their customers since the available supply is being restricted.

In the early years of the Federal Reserve System, the discount process was the primary means by which bank reserves were increased, and the discount rate was the primary instrument of monetary policy. Over the years, open-market operations have become the principal means of regulating bank reserves, but the discount process and discount rate still play an important role in Federal Reserve policy. Banks borrow from their federal reserve banks to meet temporary, unplanned for needs for bank reserves, not to obtain capital to supplement their own resources. Such needs may arise in several different ways. A bank may find that loan demand is unusually large or the withdrawal of deposits to meet seasonal needs is greater than expected. A bank may find that its secondary reserves of bonds are not large enough to meet such needs, or it may feel that the needs are of a very short duration and it therefore prefers not to liquidate bond holdings. Borrowing from the federal reserve bank may be the most appropriate action to meet reserve requirements.

A bank may also need additional reserves because of an emergency in its area. The results of a flood or tornado, or a protracted strike at a major plant, for example, may increase the demand for funds in an area and so lead to a temporary, unplanned shortage in reserves. A bank may meet this need by borrowing for a time from its federal reserve bank.

All banks from time to time find that there are withdrawals of deposits for which they have not planned; and, as a result, their daily average reserve balances are below the legal minimums. They can meet such needs by borrowing for a short period of time from their federal reserve banks. If the shortage in reserves turns out to be more extended than a few days or at the most a week or two, the bank will need to get funds by selling bonds or restricting loans. Borrowing from its reserve bank gives it time to make the necessary adjustments. Such unexpected shortages of reserves are most likely to arise in a period of active loan demand, especially when available free reserves are in use to a large extent.

Changing the discount rate affects the cost and availability of credit and, in turn, total spending, in several different ways. The first influence is the direct one: an increase in the discount rate makes member-bank borrowing more expensive and tends to discourage it; and a reduction tends to encourage such borrowing. A more important factor is the effect of the discount rate on the whole structure of interest rates. This is true primarily because a bank can obtain needed reserves either by liquidating short-term securities or by borrowing from the federal reserve bank. If the discount rate is higher than the market rate on short-term securities, banks will generally get funds by selling such securities. Such sales tend to increase rates up to the discount rate. On the other hand, if the discount rate is below short-term rates, banks tend to borrow from their reserve banks. Since fewer securities are sold, the tendency is for rates of return to decrease. Since some investors, especially large institutional investors, are constantly adjusting their proportion of short-term and intermediate- and long-term securities based on the relative yields of each, a change in short-term interest rates also has some effect on other interest rates.

The discount rate also affects interest rates and spending decisions because of its effect on expectations. A lowering of discount rates is generally interpreted as a step to make credit more easily available, and a rise in the discount rate is interpreted as a step to restrict it.

Evaluation of Discount Policy

Discount policy is no longer expected to be the major instrument of credit policy but only one in a series of instruments. Nevertheless, it has come under some criticism, and proposals have been made to modify it or even eliminate it altogether. One criticism of discount policy is that the discount rate is generally changed only at intervals of time which vary from a month or more to several years and then by substantial amounts. Critics feel that this feature introduces unnecessary uncertainty and instability into the economy. Other criticisms are that it is hard to make discount policy effective because of the great difficulty in

predicting how a change in the discount rate will affect the amount
of discounting and in turn the money supply and that the change
in the discount rate is misunderstood. It needs to be changed from
time to time to keep the general monetary situation more or less
unchanged. But since changes are made infrequently, each change
is interpreted as a major change in policy and may have un-
intended effects.

Several proposals have been advanced to modify the use of the
discount rate. One proposal is for the Federal Reserve to change
the discount rate much more frequently than it does now. Another
proposal is to eliminate Federal Reserve discretion in setting the
discount rate and to tie it to the rate on short-term Treasury bills.
A third proposal would tie the rate to the Treasury bill rate, but
the spread between the rates would be changed from time to time,
depending on the nature of monetary policy at the time of the
change. The most drastic proposal calls for eliminating the discount process completely. The Commission on Money and Credit
established in the early sixties by the Board of Trustees of the
Committee for Economic Development concluded that the discount facility should be maintained in its present form. However,
they recommended a uniform discount rate and policy for all
twelve federal banks in place of the current discretion of each
bank.

In the summer of 1968 the Federal Reserve published a report
of a System committee which had made a three-year study of
Federal Reserve lending operations and policies. This report
reaffirmed the basic principles governing Federal Reserve lending
but recommended several changes. The first was that a soundly
operated bank should be given a "basic borrowing privilege" which
would allow it to borrow a limited amount of money on request
in as many as half of its weekly reserve periods. The amount of
the basic borrowing privilege would be set as a proportion of a
bank's capital stock and surplus, and the loan would be made
virtually upon request unless the bank has been notified that its
condition is unsatisfactory and is not being corrected to the satisfaction of the Federal Reserve Bank. The only other restriction is
a rule which is already in force that net sales of federal funds are
not to be made in periods in which the bank is borrowing from
the Federal Reserve.

The second recommendation was that banks which had large seasonal fluctuations in their need for funds could arrange for a "seasonal borrowing privilege." The amount of seasonal borrowing privilege would be set at a specified percentage of the average deposits in the preceding year, and the Reserve Bank would agree to extend credit up to the qualifying amount for the time it was expected to be needed up to 90 days. These seasonal borrowings would not be counted in determining a bank's eligibility to use its basic borrowing privilege. In the spring of 1973 the Federal Reserve Board put seasonal borrowing privileges into effect for banks needing seasonal funds for at least eight weeks which did not have reasonably reliable access to national money markets.

The role of the Federal Reserve in supplying emergency credit when all other sources of credit had been exhausted would also be extended to financial institutions other than member banks. In such lending the Federal Reserve would act in cooperation with the relevant supervisory authority. The final major proposal is to make the discount rate more flexible. It would be changed much more frequently in order to keep it in line with movements in other money market rates.

This report has been made available for study and suggestions by banks and the public at large. The Board announced that it will allow time for careful study of the proposals before any changes are made.

RESERVE REQUIREMENTS

The Board of Governors of the Federal Reserve System has the power to raise or lower the requirements for reserves against deposits to be held by member banks at the federal reserve banks within limits prescribed by law. For time deposits these limits are 3 and 10 percent; for demand deposits the limits are set by the amount of net deposits of the bank. For reserve city banks, that is, those with net demand deposits of more than $400 million, the limits are 10 and 22 percent; for other banks, they are 7 and 14 percent.

When the Federal Reserve Act was passed, reserves were set by law at a fixed amount without provision for change except by an act of Congress. Banks were divided into three groups, that is, central reserve city (New York, Chicago, and at first also St. Louis) banks, reserve city banks, and country banks. In 1933 an amendment to the Agricultural Adjustment Act provided for the present authority of the Board of Governors to set reserves within prescribed limits. In 1948 the Board was given temporary powers to increase maximum reserve requirements as part of the program to combat inflation,[3] but this provision was allowed to lapse the following year. In 1962 the present classification into reserve city and country banks was put into effect and in 1972 the designation as a reserve city bank was related to volume of net demand deposits and reserves of other banks were set on the basis of net deposits.

Early Developments in Bank Reserves

The original provision for fixed legal reserve requirements was based on banking experience in pre-Federal Reserve days. The practice of keeping reserves against deposits dates back to the beginning of banking when money was placed on deposit with goldsmiths for safekeeping in their vaults. They not only kept gold, silver, and precious stones on deposit, but they also bought and sold them and made loans on them.

The goldsmiths soon discovered that most of the deposits were not called for at one time, and that, in fact, the bulk of them continually remained on deposit. They found, therefore, that they could lend some of the money placed on deposit and thus carry on lending operations with reserves equal to only a portion of deposits. Conservative bankers kept a large percentage of the deposits on hand to meet any and all demands of depositors. Reserves thus served to provide liquidity for these early bankers. As the banking system developed in Europe, bankers themselves determined the amount of reserves needed for liquidity and safety of note issue, and a tradition of conservative banking developed.

Early American Experience with Bank Reserves

In colonial days American banks were not required to keep reserves against notes or deposits. Many American banks printed

---

[3] Maximum reserve requirements were set as follows: time deposits, 7½%; demand deposits: central reserve cities, 30%; reserve cities, 24%; country, 18%.

and issued their own money in the form of bank notes with very little backing and failed to keep adequate reserves against deposits. In the early part of the nineteenth century voluntary plans for keeping reserves in key centers developed, and gradually state laws setting minimum reserves were enacted. However, these laws, except in Massachusetts and Louisiana, required reserves against notes only, not against deposits. When the National Banking Act was passed, reserves were required against deposits as well as notes. A geographic division of banks for reserve purposes into country, reserve city, and central reserve city banks was adopted, and different reserve requirements were set for each division of banks. The original fixed reserve requirements of the Federal Reserve Act were based on the procedures developed in the National Banking System.

Functions of Required Reserves

The difference between the total reserves of the banking system and those required to be held at the federal reserve banks constitute the excess reserves available for credit expansion. Thus, the major function of required reserves is to control the process of bank credit creation. If required reserves are increased, a smaller amount is available for credit expansion. For example, assume that required reserves are at a level of 20 percent of deposits and excess reserves of $1 billion exist in the banking system. These reserves could lead to a total extension of credit of $5 billion if no offsetting factors, such as an increase in currency in circulation, were at work. Suppose the Federal Reserve increases required reserves to 21 percent and as a result of this increase $800 million more is needed to meet reserve requirements. Excess reserves are now reduced to $200 million and the potential for credit extension to somewhat less than $1 billion. The potential for credit expansion has been reduced primarily because a large part of the excess reserves are now required reserves and are no longer available for expansion and also because the potential for expansion is somewhat smaller when required reserves are 21 percent than when they are 20 percent.

Another function often associated with required reserves is liquidity. This is provided directly to only a very limited degree since required reserves are not available for use. As depositors call for their funds, reserves on such funds are freed, and this does provide a limited degree of liquidity. Of more importance for liquidity are the indirect effects. Since bankers are under pressure not to be in debt to their federal reserve banks for any length of time, they have to provide for reserves over and above the required reserves. They do this by keeping vault cash to meet any demand for funds that might normally be expected, and they do this also by keeping secondary reserves in short-term government securities.

Many banks, especially the smaller ones, also keep more than the required amount of reserves with their federal reserve bank. They do this to make certain that an error in their books, or in calculating reserves, or an unexpected reduction of their reserve account because of an unusual volume of checks charged against it in the process of clearing checks will not find them short of required reserves. Not only are banks reluctant to be short of required reserves because it is considered a sign of poor bank management, but there is also a monetary penalty assessed them.

Recent American Experience with Changing the Level of Required Reserves

During World War II required reserves were cut in central reserve city banks, but they were raised again in the postwar period. They have been changed several times since then as the Federal Reserve has used them to make credit more easily available when the pace of business slackened and to restrict credit expansion when the economy was operating at or near full employment. From early in 1951 to the summer of 1966, changes in reserve requirements were not used to help restrict credit expansion but only to make credit more easily available. Reserve requirements on demand deposits were lowered in the 1954, 1958, and 1960 recession periods. Reserves on time deposits were lowered in the 1954 recession period and again in 1962. They were lowered in the latter year to help banks compete more effectively with other savings institutions for the available supply of savings deposits. Lower reserve requirements made it possible for banks to pay higher interest rates on time deposits since a larger percentage of their assets was available for loans and investments.

In July, 1966, the reserve requirement on time deposits of over $5 million was raised from 4 to 5 percent and in September to 6 percent as a means of restricting the growth of certificates of deposit. In March, 1967, the reserve requirement on savings deposits and on time deposits under $5 million was first reduced to 3½ percent and then to 3 percent. In January, 1968, reserve requirements on demand deposits of over $5 million were raised ½ point to 17 percent for reserve city banks and 12½ percent at country banks. Reserve requirements on all demand deposits were raised ½ percent in April, 1969, as part of a general program of monetary restraint.

During the recession of 1970 reserves on time deposits of over $5 million were reduced from 6 percent to 5 percent. In November, 1972, the change was made which designated reserve city banks as those with net demand deposits of over $400 million. Reserve percentages for smaller banks were also based upon the level of net demand deposits. The following reserve requirements were put into effect in the summer of 1973:

NET DEMAND DEPOSITS
(Millions of dollars)

0–2	2–10	10–100	100–400	Over 400
8	10	12	13	17½

In the summer of 1973 reserve requirements were raised to 8 percent on increases in the total of time deposits of $100,000 and over in an effort to discourage banks from obtaining funds through large certificates of deposit.[4] In the late fall of 1974 as the economy moved into a recession reserve requirements on demand deposits of the largest banks were reduced to 17.5 percent. Reserves on time deposits maturing in four months or more were reduced to 3 percent and increased to 6 percent on time deposits maturing in less than four months. The first $5 million of such deposits at each bank are subject to a 3 percent requirement.

Evaluation of Changing Reserve Requirements

There has been some question about the effectiveness of changing reserve requirements as an instrument of monetary policy and about the desirability of this form of control even if

---

[4] *Federal Reserve Bulletin,* September, 1969, p. A10, and October, 1974, p. A9.

effective. Excess reserves are not spread evenly throughout the banking system. When requirements are raised, some banks are forced to restrict credit to meet the requirements, whereas others can do so without a change in lending policy because they have excess reserves. Reserves are not necessarily short in those areas in which credit should be restricted most, and so the change may not work equitably or effectively. Thus, most monetary authorities feel that reserve requirements should be changed only when it is demonstrated that some basic monetary or economic change has taken place.

Some monetary authorities have advocated using frequent small changes in reserve requirements as an alternative to major reliance on open-market operations as an instrument of credit control. Their position is based on two major arguments. The first is that such changes affect all banks directly and immediately, whereas changes due to bond purchases and sales spread through the system with a lag and may not affect some banks at all. A second argument for using frequent, minor changes in reserve requirements is to eliminate the influence which open-market operations have on the market for government securities. Federal Reserve purchases and sales are so large from time to time that they dominate this market.

Those opposed to this policy change have some convincing counter arguments. The first is that there are few if any excess reserves in many medium-size and smaller banks even in periods of credit ease. Raising reserve requirements would create an undue and unnecessary hardship on economic activity in the areas served by these banks. The argument that using frequent, small changes in reserve requirements as a partial substitute for open-market operations would have less effect on government security markets is also open to question. If banks have their funds fully committed, a rise in reserve requirements would cut the volume of their earning assets. To make up for the loss of income, they would try to shift to assets with higher earnings. Since demand for loans is high at such a time, they would tend to sell bonds to make funds available for loans on which earnings are higher. Thus, the government bond market would still be affected. After studying the alternative, the Commission on Money and Credit recommended that the power to change reserve requirements be used only sparingly and that major reliance continue to be placed on open-market operations as a countercyclical measure.

Determining the level of required reserves to maintain on a long-run basis poses different problems. If required reserves are too high, bank earnings on free assets may be too low to attract the necessary capital; and if reserves are too low, bank earnings may be excessive. The level of required reserves also has an effect on the government security markets since banks keep most of their funds not needed for required reserves, vault cash, and loans in government securities. A lower level of reserves frees more funds for bond investment; a higher level makes a smaller volume of funds available for this use. The Federal Reserve needs to balance these factors in determining the long-run level of required reserves.

The 100 Percent Reserve Proposal

From time to time proposals have been made for changing the law on required reserves. The most drastic proposal is the 100 percent reserve plan. Under this plan banks would have to keep 100 percent reserves against all checking accounts and could make loans only out of time deposits. This would stop credit expansion by the banks. It is proposed that such powers be put in the hands of the Treasury. To start the plan, banks would have to be given reserves by the Federal Reserve or the government.

The 100 percent reserve plan would affect the American economy materially. Its sponsors hope that it would stabilize business by preventing credit expansion and thus also speculative booms, but this is not generally agreed upon. The adoption of such a plan would present some new problems. Political pressure would no doubt be brought to bear on the officials in the Treasury from time to time for credit expansion. Banks would also have to raise service charges to operate profitably, since bank funds available for lending would be greatly reduced.

Other Proposals

A more moderate proposal is to require reserves in government bonds above the present maximum reserves. This action would force banks to hold these bonds and so not make them available for sale or as collateral for a federal reserve loan. This would prevent further expansion of credit for business purposes. Such a bond reserve could be used, however, to help insure credit expansion by means of government deficits since, if bond reserves were raised, banks would have to buy bonds to comply with the rules.

Another proposal is to keep present requirements but to grant authority to the Board to impose higher requirements on all new deposits received after a certain date. This would not force contraction of loans by any bank but would provide the means to stop further credit inflation. Such a plan would allow up to 100 percent reserves against new deposits and could at any time prevent further credit expansion. In a war period the plan would make it possible for reserve banks to buy government bonds but would subject the funds paid out by the government to 100 percent reserves and so prevent their use for further credit expansion, as was done in World War II.

A proposal of a technical nature is to abolish the present distinction between required reserves for reserve city banks and other banks based on the amounts of their deposits and to have uniform reserves for the nation based only on types of deposits. Usually suggested as classifications for different regulations are time deposits, deposits of other banks, and all other demand deposits. Some proposals would classify demand deposits further, separating those of individuals, financial institutions, and businesses generally. Advocates of this scheme feel that geographic and size differences are much less significant than they were when reserves were first required, some 100 years ago, and therefore the present differentials are inequitable. The types of deposits held at different banks vary and so do the uses of such deposits during various stages of the business cycle. Varying reserve requirements on different types of deposits would give the Federal Reserve more direct control over various areas of the economy. The issues involved in doing so are similar to the issues involved in selective credit controls which are discussed in some detail in a later section of this chapter. A related proposal would have reserve requirements apply to all banks whether or not they were members of the Federal Reserve System or, as an alternative, require all banks to become members.

Another modification in reserve requirements calls for an end to required reserves on time deposits. The arguments for doing so are based on two factors. The first is that deposits arising out of current saving do not have the inflationary potential of demand deposits resulting from credit expansion and therefore do not need to be controlled. The second is that there are no reserve requirements on savings in some competing institutions and as a result the present system is inequitable. This proposal has less support today than it had a few years ago because of the large volume of funds put on deposit in large commercial banks in the form of certificates of deposit when market interest rates make such certificates attractive.

A proposal of a somewhat different nature is to base reserve requirements on the rate of turnover of deposits. The rationale for such a policy is that it would make it possible to restrict the deposits having the highest rate of use and so exert the most effect on the economy in an expansionary period. Such a policy would create technical problems in measuring and reporting velocity, but the main argument against it is that it would have undesirable effects. Some deposits turn over rapidly at all times, for example, the funds deposited in a local bank and shifted to a bank in the city of the main office of a firm, but such turnover has no stimulating effect on economic activity in an expansionary period.

OPEN-MARKET OPERATIONS

One of the most important instruments of monetary and credit policy is open-market operations, that is, the purchase of securities by the federal reserve banks to put additional reserves at the disposal of member banks or the sale of securities to reduce member bank reserves. The original Federal Reserve Act did not provide for open-market operations. This policy instrument developed out of the experience of the early post-World War I period.

From the beginning of their operations, the reserve banks bought government securities with funds at their disposal to earn money for meeting expenses and to show a profit in order that dividends on the stock held by member banks could be paid. All twelve banks usually bought and sold such securities in the New York market, and at times their combined sales were so large that they disorganized that market. Furthermore, the funds used to buy the bonds got into the hands of New York member banks and enabled them to reduce their borrowing at the Federal Reserve Bank of New York. This made it difficult for the Federal Reserve Bank of New York to maintain effective credit control in its area. As a result, an open-market committee was set up to coordinate buying and selling of government bonds. In 1933 the Open Market Committee was established by law, and in 1935 it was given its present composition of the Federal Reserve Board of Governors, plus five members elected by the twelve federal reserve banks.

The Open-Market Process

Open-market operations differ from discount operations in that they increase or decrease reserves at the initiative of the Federal Reserve, not of individual bankers. The process in simplified form works as follows. If the Open Market Committee wants to buy government securities, it contacts dealers in such securities to ask for offers and then accepts the best offers which meet its needs. The dealers receive checks for the securities from the federal reserve banks, and these checks are deposited with member banks. They in turn deposit the checks at their federal reserve banks, thus adding new reserves that form the basis for additional credit expansion. Since 1966 the Federal Reserve also has the authority to buy or sell issues of government agencies such as the Federal Home Loan Banks.

If the Federal Reserve wants to reduce reserves, it sells government securities to the dealers. The dealers pay for them by a check in favor of a federal reserve bank drawn on a member bank, and the reserve bank then deducts the amount from the reserves of the member bank.

Open-market operations may not lead to an immediate change in the volume of bank credit. This is especially true when bonds are sold to restrict credit. As bonds are sold by the reserve banks, some banks lose reserves and are forced to borrow from their reserve bank. Since they are under pressure from the Federal Reserve to repay the loan, they use funds from loans that mature to repay the reserve bank. Thus, credit is gradually restricted as a result of the adjustments banks make to the effects of open-market operations.

Reserve banks also buy banker's acceptances in the open market, but the amount has not been large in recent years. Such purchases are similar to discounts in that the initiative to sell them comes from the individual bank. They are, however, similar to open-market bond operations in that the reserve banks will buy the banker's acceptances from other than member banks, and they do not place member banks in debt to the reserve banks. The effect of these operations in increasing or decreasing bank reserves is the same as purchases and sales of government bonds.

Experience with Open-Market Operations

From the beginning of the use of open-market operations in 1922 until 1941, such operations were gradually coordinated with changes in the discount rate. For example, between 1929 and 1933 large-scale purchases of government securities were made, and discount rates were reduced. These were important factors in the decline of interest rates during this period. During World War II, open-market operations were directed toward war financing. Bank reserves were kept adequate to insure a low interest-rate pattern. Between the bond drives, large sums of government bonds were purchased to support the market and to place banks in a liquid position for additional war financing.

In the early postwar period, Federal Reserve open-market operations in the money market were hampered by the large holdings of government bonds by member banks and the policy of supporting such bonds at par or above. The sale of bonds by the reserve banks to reduce reserves was met by the sale of bonds by member banks which had their reserves reduced. Since the Federal Reserve stood ready to buy such bonds at par or above to maintain their price, the net result was a purchase of bonds that offset the prior sale. Thus, open-market operations were rendered ineffective as long as bonds were purchased at par or above. This policy was abandoned early in the Korean War for a more flexible bond-buying policy, and open-market operations again became an effective instrument of credit policy.

Between 1951 and 1953, open market policy was directed toward maintaining orderly conditions in the government securities market as well as influencing the volume of bank reserves. In 1953 the Federal Reserve announced a policy of using open-market operations to affect bank reserves only as economic conditions warranted. This was to be done by buying and selling short-term securities only, except when necessary to correct already disorderly markets in longer-term securities. This policy has been known as the "bills-only" policy. It was modified in 1961 to permit some dealing in longer-term securities in order to help maintain long-term interest rates and so halt the flow of capital to foreign countries and the resultant gold losses.

The Significance of Open-Market Operations

Although not provided for in the original organization of the Federal Reserve System, open-market operations have become the most important and effective means of monetary and credit control. They can take funds out of the market and thus raise short-term interest rates and help restrain inflationary pressures. They can also provide for easy money conditions and lowered short-term interest rates. Of course, such monetary ease will not of itself start business on the recovery road after a recession. But when used with discount policy, open-market operations are an effective way of restricting credit or making it more easily available.

In order for open-market operations to be effective, the Federal Reserve must be free to buy and sell as it sees fit. This of course could not be done during the early post-World War II period, when it was committed to buy government bonds whenever such action was necessary to maintain the price above par. Open-market operations work only when there is no obligation on the part of the Federal Reserve to buy bonds to maintain bond prices. Nevertheless, open-market operations must be carried on with the financing needs of the Treasury in mind. It would be impossible to maintain the present government debt with all of the refunding operations required without the active help of the Reserve authorities. This problem will be considered more fully in the next chapter when government actions affecting monetary and credit conditions will be considered.

The Bills-Only Controversy

The "bills-only" policy announced by the Federal Reserve in 1953 led to a great deal of controversy between Federal Reserve economists and some academic economists. This controversy abated somewhat when the Federal Reserve modified the policy in 1961. This was not an abandonment of the basic policy, however, but a modification to meet a special situation. Since the issues have not been resolved, it is desirable to look at the arguments presented for and against the "bills-only" or "bills-preferable" policy.

One of the arguments for this policy is that it minimizes the direct effects on the government securities markets and on interest rates. It does this because it operates in the broadest market having the largest volume, and so its direct effect is the smallest possible. Interest-rate patterns are still set by market forces and not by Federal Reserve purchases or sales. The whole market is affected because the volume of reserves is changed, and expectations are changed. The changes in intermediate and long-term rates are not dependent on the actions of professional traders because many institutional borrowers and investors switch their operations into different sectors of the market based on the relative favorability of rates.

During the early sixties the Federal Reserve took action to keep long-term rates at relatively low levels to encourage construction but forced short-term rates up to help solve the balance-of-payments problem. This action, called operation twist, has been criticized by some for having created problems for savings and loan associations and mutual savings banks. It kept the rates on their loans low in relationship to other rates during a period when costs were rising and they had to offer higher rates to attract savings. Thus, Federal Reserve policy had an adverse effect on some financial institutions which might not have occurred if market forces had been allowed to operate.

Another argument advanced for trading in bills only is that the market for intermediate and long-term government securities can be strong enough to meet government needs only if dealers in such securities are sure no arbitrary official action will be taken. Such action would result from Federal Reserve trading in longer-term securities. Furthermore, trading in longer-term securities could so obscure market supply and demand relationships that the Federal Reserve would be all but unable to develop a sound policy because it would have no basis for judging the market situation.

One of the major arguments against this policy is that it unnecessarily ties the hands of the Federal Reserve. Speculative excesses in parts of the market for capital funds may need correction, but the total market may not. Dealing in bills affects all sectors of the market, but not to the same extent and only with a lag. This means that the short-term market may need to be changed unduly to get the needed adjustments in longer-term markets. Another argument is that the best way to have a strong market for government securities is to have relatively stable prices for securities generally and thus to encourage investment of all types. This can best be done by dealing in all sectors of the market to maintain orderly conditions. Lastly, the "bills-only" policy does not allow market support for new Treasury financing, while such support is a regular part of new private financing.

SELECTIVE CREDIT CONTROLS

All the instruments of monetary and credit policy discussed so far work uniformly to control credit in all areas of the economy, but the Federal Reserve also has power to control credit in special fields. It has permanent power to regulate stock market credit and has had emergency grants of power to regulate consumer credit and real estate credit. These selective controls of credit in strategic areas are intended to supplement the general credit controls in those areas in which the terms of the credit, other than the interest cost, are most important. This includes such factors as the percentage of down payment required to buy goods or services and the length of time allowed for repayment.

Margin Requirements

The Federal Reserve Act enjoins the Federal Reserve authorities to restrain the undue rise of bank credit for speculation in securities, real estate, or commodities. The Federal Reserve issued several warnings against the growth of stock market credit during and immediately after World War I. Early in 1926 it began publishing current figures on loans to brokers in an effort to use publicity as a method of control. In 1929 the Board issued emphatic warnings against the further expansion of stock market credit. It also instituted a campaign to have the reserve banks insist that member banks in debt to them either repay their indebtedness or reduce their loans for carrying stocks.

Despite these attempts to curb stock market credit, it expanded greatly and was in part responsible for the extreme character of the 1929 stock market boom and subsequent crash. To avoid a repetition of this experience, Congress, first in the Banking Act of 1933 and then more fully in the Securities Exchange Act of 1934, gave the Board of Governors the power to regulate stock market credit.

This regulation is accomplished by setting the amount that holders of stocks may borrow on them, either from banks or from securities brokers and dealers. The difference between the amount of a loan and the current market value of the stock at the time the loan is made is called the *margin*. For example, if a loan of $7,500 is made against stock having a market value of $10,000, the margin is $2,500 or 25 percent. The Board's regulations apply to the minimum margin required and thus prescribe maximum loan values. They apply only at the time securities are purchased and only to credit obtained for the purpose of buying or carrying securities registered on national securities exchanges. They do not apply to loans based on stocks as collateral if the proceeds are to be used for commercial purposes.

Margin requirements for the purpose of restraining stock-market credit can greatly reduce the speculative demand for stocks in a boom period, as can be seen from the following examples. Suppose that without margin requirements $10,000 of stock could be bought for a $1,000 margin and a $9,000 loan, as was often the case before the 1929 crash. If the stock rose in price by 10 percent, the purchaser had a $1,000 profit on a $1,000 investment.[5] Under margin requirements of 50 percent, $1,000 can be used to buy $2,000 worth of stock. A similar 10 percent rise would yield a profit of $200 on the investment of $1,000. High margins greatly reduce the profit to be made out of market movements and

---

[5] Not counting the cost of the loan or brokerage commissions.

in the same manner also reduce the loss. If $1,000 is used to purchase $10,000 of stock, a 10 percent decline in the price of the stock wipes out the $1,000 put up by the purchaser. If margin requirements are 50 percent, a 10 percent decline reduces by only $200 the $2,000 of stock purchased, thus leaving $800 of the $1,000 put up by the purchaser intact. In like manner, high margins remove the pressure of forced selling that is necessary to protect a loan in a declining market when margins are small. In the example of a $10,000 purchase with a $1,000 investment by the purchaser, a 10 percent drop will wipe out all of the equity of the owner. If the purchaser cannot put up additional money, or if the bank cannot get in touch with him as the market is falling, the bank will sell the stock in order to protect its loan.

High margin requirements also restrict the amount of pyramiding which can take place in a rising market, that is, traders adding to their holdings of stock in a rising market without putting up additional money or securities. Suppose that $10,000 of stock bought on a $1,000 or 10 percent margin rises in market value to $15,000. The $5,000 increase in price under 10 percent margins would permit the purchase of $45,000 more of the stock since the holder now has a margin of $6,000, that is, his original $1,000 and the increase in market value of $5,000. This gives him a 10 percent margin on $60,000 of stock in total, the $15,000 of old stock at present prices and $45,000 of additional stock. Under a 50 percent margin, only $5,000 more of stock could be bought, since the holder now has a margin of $10,000 which allows him to hold $20,000 of stock.

The regulation of margin requirements has been effective as one of the means of preventing most of the "boom and bust" character of stock trading. It can be given a large amount of credit for this, but not exclusive credit, since stock market procedures have also been changed and many more investments are being made on the basis of analysis of the prospects of the company, rather than on short-run speculation in the hope of a quick price rise.

Consumer Credit Regulation

During World War II the Federal Reserve was given temporary powers to regulate consumer credit and did so under Regulation W of the Federal Reserve Board. That regulation prescribed minimum down payments and maximum repayment periods for installment loans. The scope of the regulation was broadened later to include a larger number of items and also charge accounts and single payment loans. These regulations under more limited scope were continued on and off for several years after the war and were reintroduced during the Korean War.

The purpose of Regulation W during the war was to discourage the buying of articles that were scarce in relationship to the demand for them. Those who argue for such regulation under more normal conditions do so because they feel that consumer credit is an important source of inflationary credit. Others feel that the restriction of the use of credit during prosperity will defer some demand for durables to a later period and so help even out the sales of durables. Many economists do not believe that there is evidence to support either of these contentions. Thus, there is some difference of opinion as to the effectiveness or desirability of consumer credit regulation. Beyond question it could be effective if made stringent enough. Some oppose it because they are opposed to any direct government intervention in the economy. Others oppose it because they believe that credit controls should be general in nature, regulating only the overall volume of credit to prevent inflation and not the volume in specific sectors of the economy. Those affected have in some cases opposed it because of the extra work involved in record keeping.

Regulation W did reduce the use of consumer credit during World War II. The reduction was greatest for commodities, such as automobiles, which were in short supply. The reduction, however, was due to the lack of goods to purchase as well as to Regulation W, and for that reason it is impossible to assess its effectiveness during this period. In 1946 and 1947 consumers had such large amounts of liquid funds that it is impossible to tell if Regulation W had much effect. In early 1949, some authorities felt that Regulation W was having a very dampening effect on consumer durable goods purchases, and the lifting of regulations led to increased sales in the latter part of that year. The reimposition of Regulation W in September, 1950, slowed down the rise in installment credit,[6] but such credit expanded in 1952 after

---

[6] R. J. Saulnier, "An Appraisal of Selective Credit Controls" in *Papers and Proceedings of the American Economic Association*, May, 1952, p. 260.

controls were removed. The price level during this period, however, was fairly stable.

The regulation of consumer credit may be a valuable tool of credit policy in periods of war or national emergency. There is, however, no agreement that it would be desirable to make it a part of the permanent powers of the Federal Reserve.

Real Estate Credit Regulation

During the Korean War, the Board was given temporary power to regulate real estate credit to restrain the building boom in a period of high defense and foreign aid expenditures involving the use of many of the same materials as needed for home building. The Board laid down the rules in Regulation X that regulated credit first for residential construction and then also for some nonresidential construction. The required amount of down payment was prescribed and in addition the maximum repayment periods.

This regulation differed from Regulation W in that as the price of the house went up, the percentage of down payment increased. This was intended to discourage the building of higher-priced homes to a greater degree than low-priced homes. The goal of reducing the number of homes built in 1951 to 850,000 from a rate close to 1,400,000 was not achieved, but building was reduced materially. There was too little experience with this type of credit regulation, however, to be sure how much of the drop was due to credit restrictions and how much to other factors, such as uncertainty in a war period. In 1952 construction levels exceeded those of 1951, but the reason for this is not entirely clear since as inflation appeared to have been arrested, the terms of the regulation were eased somewhat, especially for lower-priced homes. Certainly regulation of real estate credit can be effective if made stringent enough. It can cut demand in those fields in which down payments have been very small. It also appears to be effective in reducing building of multifamily apartments for rental. Just what it will do in other areas is not clear. At present it appears unlikely that the Federal Reserve will be given the power to regulate real estate credit except in war or emergency periods.

OTHER FEDERAL RESERVE ACTIONS IN CONTROLLING MONEY AND CREDIT

Direct action by Federal Reserve authorities also has some influence on monetary and credit policy. Banks have from time to time been advised to follow loan policies in line with the objectives of the Federal Reserve. After World War I banks were urged to sell their government securities; in 1929 pressure was put on them to decrease stock market loans; and during the early days of World War II they were directed to discourage loans for carrying large inventories of consumer goods. During the Korean War a voluntary credit restraint program was put into operation to discourage all credit for nonessential uses and to restrict other credit not related to the defense effort. During the Vietnam War a letter was sent to member banks stating the need to moderate the expansion of business loans.

To enforce such policies, the Board of Governors can take action against bank officers or directors. The Board has the power, after issuing due warning to a bank officer or director and giving him a chance to be heard, to remove him for violating banking laws or for following unsound banking practices. Every opportunity must be given the officer or director to cease and desist from his action. Every director of that officer or director's bank must be kept informed of proceedings, which, except for such notice, are kept secret.

Direct action has not been used very frequently as an instrument of credit policy. It is available, however, to supplement other regulations if need be. It can be used to help direct bank credit away from undue speculative activity into productive uses. It is especially worthwhile in emergency periods, such as during wars.

QUESTIONS

1. What were the objectives for which the Federal Reserve System was established?

2. How have these objectives been broadened over the years?

3. Briefly describe the various policies that have been followed by the Federal Reserve.

4. Describe the effect of Federal Reserve policies on interest rates. What are they designed to accomplish?

5. Discuss the possible effectiveness and desirability of a policy to stabilize the price level.

6. Discuss the problems involved in setting guides for implementing monetary policies.

7. How may the discount rate be used to carry out Federal Reserve policy?

8. Discuss the rationale of discount policy.

9. Evaluate the use of discount policy by the Federal Reserve.

10. Discuss proposals for modifying discount policy.

11. What was the original function of bank reserves? What is their function in the American banking system today?

12. How may changes in reserve requirements be used to carry out Federal Reserve policy?

13. Evaluate the changing of reserve requirements as a means of monetary control.

14. Discuss several proposals for changing the law on required reserves.

15. Discuss the process by which open-market operations affect the monetary situation.

16. Describe American experience with open-market operations in the period after World War II.

17. Evaluate open-market operations as a means of monetary control.

18. Discuss proposals for modifying open-market operations.

19. Explain the process by which margin requirements can control speculative financing of the purchase of stocks and pyramiding.

20. Explain how consumer credit was regulated under Regulation W. Discuss the effectiveness and desirability of consumer credit regulation.

21. Explain the regulation of real estate credit under Regulation X. Discuss its effectiveness.

22. Discuss direct action by Federal Reserve authorities as a method of credit control.

SUGGESTED READINGS

BURGER, ALBERT R. "The Implementation Problem of Monetary Policy." *Review*, Federal Reserve Bank of St. Louis (March, 1971), pp. 20-30.

DURO, LORRAINE E. "A Measure of Monetary Policy." *Economic Review*, Federal Reserve Bank of Cleveland (January-February, 1973), pp. 19-30.

FRIEDMAN, MILTON. *A Program for Monetary Stability*. New York: Fordham University Press, 1960.

MEIGS, A. JAMES, and WILLIAM WOLMAN. "Central Banks and the Money Supply." *Review*, Federal Reserve Bank of St. Louis (August, 1971), pp. 18-30.

"Open Market Operations in 1973." *Federal Reserve Bulletin* (May, 1974), pp. 338-350.

Reappraisal of the Federal Reserve Discount Mechanism. Report of a System Committee. Washington: Board of Governors of the Federal Reserve System, 1968.

The Federal Reserve System—Its Purposes and Functions. Washington: Board of Governors of the Federal Reserve System, 1961. Chapters 3, 7, 13, 14, 15.

"Toward More Uniform Reserve Requirements." *Business Conditions*, Federal Reserve Bank of Chicago (March, 1974), pp. 3-12.

24 | Treasury Powers Affecting the Supply of Money and Credit

The final authority over monetary and credit policy was granted to the federal government when the framers of the Constitution gave the government the right to coin money and to regulate its value. The government has always exercised the exclusive power to set the monetary standard and to provide coins, but in the past it did allow private banks to issue paper money as well as to extend credit.

Gradually, more and more of the monetary and credit powers have been taken out of private hands and concentrated in the hands of public authorities. State bank notes were taxed out of existence after the National Banking Act was passed. As part of the banking legislation enacted during the depression of the thirties, national banks were no longer allowed to issue bank notes. The power to issue paper money has been concentrated in the hands of the Treasury Department and the Federal Reserve System. Although the federal reserve banks are owned by the member banks, supervision of monetary and credit functions is in the hands of the Board of Governors appointed by the President of the United States.

When the Federal Reserve System was established in 1913, most of the power to regulate money and credit was placed in its hands. The power to change the monetary standard or its value or the basic regulations for issuing paper money Congress reserved to itself. However, as the public debt grew during World War I, during the depression of the early thirties, and during World War II, the Treasury became vitally interested in credit conditions. Policies that affect interest rates and monetary ease or stringency affect the Treasury directly, since it is the largest borrower in the nation on both a short-term and a long-term basis. Furthermore, in managing the large public debt and various trust funds placed under its jurisdiction, the Treasury has acquired the power to influence the money market materially.

Treasury powers relating to the monetary standard, to the role of gold in the monetary system, and to the issuance of coin and currency were discussed in Chapter 2. This chapter considers other Treasury powers and policies affecting monetary and credit conditions. The problems of the Treasury in managing its cash balances so as not to disrupt monetary and credit conditions are analyzed first. Budget operations are then considered, including especially the monetary and the credit effects of government surpluses and deficits and the way they are handled. Lastly, debt management is considered as it affects monetary and credit conditions. Such debt management concerns the policy regarding types of securities to issue, interest-rate patterns, maturities, refunding policies, and the like.

MANAGING THE TREASURY'S CASH BALANCES

The operations of the Treasury are carried out on a large scale involving expenditures of over $300 billion a year. It is necessary to maintain a large cash balance, especially since funds are not paid into the Treasury at an even rate throughout the year and are not paid out on a regular basis either. This makes it imperative for the Treasury to handle its cash balances in such a way that it will not create undesirable credit ease or stringency during the year. The Treasury has developed detailed procedures for handling its cash balances so as to affect bank reserves as little as possible.

A part of the Treasury funds are kept on deposit in the federal reserve banks and their branches. Some deposits are also kept in insular, territorial, and foreign depositaries to provide a convenient place for depositing funds and in a few cases to permit disbursing officers to make payments in local funds. Some funds are kept in insured domestic banks designated as "General Depositaries" in areas in which no branch of the federal reserve bank is conveniently located. The Treasury also has some cash in a cash room in Washington where currency may be obtained or Treasury checks cashed.

Treasury Tax and Loan Accounts

The primary demand accounts of the Treasury for day-to-day Treasury operations are on deposit at the Federal Reserve Banks. Most cash flows into the Treasury through Treasury Tax and Loan Accounts. All incorporated banks and trust companies are eligible to have such accounts and about 13,000 banks do. Several types of government receipts are deposited in these Treasury Tax and Loan Accounts. Employers have the option of paying withheld income, old-age insurance, and railroad retirement taxes either to federal reserve banks or to one of the special depositaries; and most employers have been making their payments to the latter.

The Treasury may also make payments of income and profits taxes eligible for deposit in Tax and Loan Accounts. Many excise taxes may also be paid either to a federal reserve bank or to a qualified depository with a Tax and Loan Account. The proceeds from a large proportion of the sales of new government securities also flow into the Tax and Loan Accounts. The proceeds from the sale of nonmarketable securities are always eligible for deposit in such accounts. Most marketable issues are also sold with the privilége of credit to these accounts. Sales of Treasury bills, however, have rarely been made eligible for credit to Tax and Loan Accounts. The Treasury can also transfer funds to its account at commercial banks, if its balances at the federal reserve banks are larger than it feels they should be.

The incentive to avoid unnecessary contraction of bank reserves is built into this system. Sums which flow into Tax and Loan Accounts are the result of the business operations of the bank, both those of its customers and its own. The Treasury draws on balances in these accounts as it actually needs the funds to cover disbursements and in this way matches the flow of funds to the Treasury and payments by the Treasury with a minimum effect on total bank reserves.

Funds which are not deposited in Tax and Loan Accounts and various classes of payments made directly to government offices may be paid directly into the Treasury accounts of the Federal Reserve Banks or through about 1100 Treasurer's general accounts at commercial banks which have been designated to provide such services. About 30 of these accounts are special collection accounts used primarily for large deposits by the Internal Revenue Service. These accounts are all "flow-through" accounts which means that balances are transferred every day to the bank's Federal Reserve Bank. Any balance in such accounts, with a few exceptions, are funds in the process of collection and transfer to the Treasury.[1]

Outlays

Almost all governmental operating expenditures are paid by checks that are collectible at any reserve bank or reserve bank branch or at the Treasury Department. Only a small part of the payments made when the Treasury retires government securities, however, are made by means of checks. When banks present securities from their portfolios, or those of correspondent banks or their customers, to their district reserve bank, they receive a direct credit to their account at this bank. Series E Savings Bonds may be redeemed by banks and a few other financial institutions, which are reimbursed in turn by the federal reserve banks from Treasury accounts without the use of a check. Most interest payments are also made without the use of checks since banks present the coupons directly to the federal reserve banks of their districts for payment.

Direct Purchase of Government Obligations

Since 1942 the Federal Reserve System has been granted authority on a temporary basis, renewed periodically as it expires,

---

[1] *Annual Report of the Secretary of the Treasury* for the fiscal year ended June 30, 1973 (Washington: U. S. Government Printing Office, 1973), pp. 282-283.

to buy and sell direct or fully guaranteed government obligations directly from or to the Treasury. This authority was used with some frequency during World War II, and it has been used from time to time since then. It is used to finance Treasury expenditures when funds are soon to be available to the Treasury. In the months in which quarterly tax payments are to be made, the Treasury often finds that it has a large volume of disbursements to make just a few days before the funds from tax payments become available after the fifteenth of the month. In such situations the Treasury sells government securities directly to the Federal Reserve Banks and buys them back as soon as funds become available. Thus, rapid short-run changes in funds available to the banking system are prevented.

The Effect on the Money Market of Handling Cash Balances

The Treasury has sought to handle its cash receipts, outlays, and balances in such a way as to avoid large changes in bank reserves. To do this, the Treasury tries to keep its balances in its accounts at the federal reserve banks relatively stable. Almost all Treasury disbursements are made by checks drawn against its deposits at the federal reserve banks. Most Treasury receipts are deposited in Tax and Loan Accounts at the commercial bank depositaries, but some are deposited directly in the Treasury accounts at the federal reserve banks. The Treasury adjusts the withdrawal of funds from its accounts at the commercial bank depositaries, or calls on these accounts as they are referred to, in such a way as to keep its balances at the federal reserve banks as stable as possible. This means that the funds shifted from depositary banks and the funds deposited in the federal reserve banks directly must closely correspond to the volume of Treasury checks that are likely to be presented to the federal reserve banks.

When the Treasury account at the reserve banks is kept at the same level, bank reserves are not changed. This is possible only if accurate forecasts are made of the daily receipts and expenditures from the Treasury account so that funds from the Tax and Loan Accounts may be shifted in the right amounts at the right time. If such forecasts and procedures for shifting balances in depositary accounts had not been worked out with a reasonable degree of success, the operations of the Treasury would cause bank reserves to fluctuate a great deal over short periods of time. Such forecasts are more difficult to make in unusual periods, such as those during the Vietnam War and the period of inflation following the end of the war, and as a result Treasury balances at the federal reserve banks were not as stable during this period as they were in earlier periods.

POWERS RELATING TO THE GOVERNMENT BUDGET AND TO SURPLUSES OR DEFICITS

The government may also influence monetary and credit conditions indirectly through the effects of taxation and expenditure programs, and especially by having a significant cash deficit or surplus. Decisions in the budget-making area rest with Congress and are usually based on the needs of the government and on political considerations without giving much weight to the monetary and credit effects. Because of the magnitude of the government budget, government income and expenditures may be one of the most important factors in determining credit conditions.

General Economic Effects of Fiscal Policy

Various programs of the federal government act in such a way as to help stabilize disposable income and, in turn, economic activity in general. Some act on a continuing basis as built-in or automatic stabilizers, others depend on specific congressional action in each case.

One of the automatic programs is social security; especially the unemployment insurance program. Under the program, payments are made to workers without jobs, thus providing part of their former incomes. This is also true of relief payments under federal and state aid programs. Not only are expenditures increased in a downturn, but social security tax collections of all types, including those for old-age pensions, decrease when fewer men are at work inasmuch as these taxes are based on payrolls.

The farm price support programs work in a similar way. When demand falls and prices drop, the Commodity Credit Corporation buys more farm products and thus helps stabilize income in the agricultural sectors. A similar effect has, to a limited degree, come out of the government program to stockpile strategic materials. Metals and other materials were bought when demand was low, thus helping to stabilize demand and income. The farm program and stockpiling program have also made a limited contribution to stability in periods of prosperity. When demand was high, commodities were sold, which helped to restrain price rises.

Of the programs that act as automatic stabilizers of disposable income, the "pay-as-you-go" progressive income tax is one of the most important. When income rises, tax receipts rise faster than income; when income falls, tax receipts drop faster. The result is to a large degree immediate under our system of tax withholding since, for the large proportion of wages subject to withholding, taxes change as soon as incomes change.

In addition to programs that affect disposable income in general, programs have been designed to stabilize or increase income in specific sectors of the economy or in particular geographical areas. Much of the agricultural program is of this type. Increased technology has made it possible to produce the needed food and fiber with far fewer workers and on less land. Government programs involving crop restriction, soil conservation, a soil bank with some land in it from many farms, and the like are designed to keep up the income level of those on the farm and in communities dependent on farm spending. Programs to aid distressed areas by giving them preferred treatment in government procurement are of a similar nature.

These programs are a regular part of our economy. In severe fluctuations, Congress can go further in stabilizing disposable income. Income tax rates have been raised in prosperity to lower disposable income and to restrain inflationary pressures, and they have been lowered in recession to increase disposable income and spending. Government expenditures have been increased in recession to increase disposable income. They could, of course, be cut in prosperity to reduce disposable income, but the needs of a growing population and wage increases for federal employees to keep up with the cost of living make this difficult. There was some attempt to cut expenditures to restrain inflation during the Vietnam War, but it did not meet with much success.

Unemployment compensation programs have been allowed to run for additional time periods so as to keep disposable income up when unemployment has lasted beyond the regular periods provided in the social security program.

To date no use has been made of formulas to guide government action, but some have been proposed. For example, one proposal would automatically cut tax rates when unemployment reached 5 million workers, another when it reached a set percentage of the labor force such as 4 or 5 percent. An alternative formula would set different tax schedules for varying economic conditions but allow the executive branch of the government to determine when each had been reached.

There are advantages and disadvantages to each course of action. Most economists agree that built-in stabilizers are desirable. Only a few believe they can do the whole job of promoting stability even in relatively minor recessions and certainly not in major recessions. Proponents of built-in stabilizers, and beyond that, of special action in each situation, feel economic developments differ enough in each period of prosperity and recession that each case should be met in the light of its own special features. Unemployment may temporarily top a set level of the labor force, for example, but the outlook may be such that inflation is a major hazard and a tax cut, therefore, would be unwise. Some also feel that in a free-enterprise economy government should interfere as little as possible and, therefore, oppose intervention under a formula plan.

Proponents of formula plans feel specific action is too slow and too uncertain as to timing. Congress is not always in session and when it is, there are so many problems that economic action does not always get immediate attention. Furthermore, the business community and consumers are faced with uncertainty since they do not know is Congress will act or in what way.

When a recession is so severe that larger deficits than those resulting from built-in stabilizers or formulas are required to promote recovery, there is seldom complete agreement on the course of action to be followed. A decision must be made changing the level of government spending or the total amount of tax receipts. Increased expenditures, or a tax cut of the same amount, would cost the same number of dollars initially, but the economic effects would not be the same. If income taxes are cut, disposable income is increased almost immediately under our system of tax withholding. This provides additional income for all sectors of the economy and an increase in demand for many types of goods. The amount of the increase in relation to the tax cut depends on the proportion of the funds that are spent by the recipients of the tax cut.

If increased expenditures are decided on, the amount of the expenditures determines the initial increase in income for the economy. But the effects of increased expenditures occur more slowly than those of a tax cut since it takes time to get programs started and to put them in full operation. The increased income arises in the first instance in those sectors of the economy in which the money is spent. Thus, the major effect initially will be on specific areas of the economy, not on the economy as a whole.

The secondary effects of spending from a tax cut or from increased government expenditures depend on what the recipients do with the income. To the extent that they spend it on current consumption, total spending is further increased in the short run. The goods for which they spend it determine the sectors of the economy that receive a boost in income. If they invest the added income and it is used for purchasing capital goods, spending is also increased, but with a time lag and in different sectors of the economy. If the money is saved and is added to idle funds available for investment, there is no secondary effect on spending.

The same general types of effects must be considered if economic activity is·to be restrained by a decrease in expenditures on the part of the government or by a tax increase. A decrease in expenditures by the government will cut expenditures by at least that amount, and the secondary effects may cut it farther. A tax increase may not cut expenditures by the amount of the cut since some taxpayers may keep up their level of spending by reducing saving out of current income or by using past savings. It could, however, cut total expenditures even more if higher taxes discouraged some types of spending that were currently taking place, such as that on home building or on consumer durable goods bought on credit. This could lead to a cut in spending that is substantially greater than the amount of money taken by the higher taxes.

A decision must be made not only on changing total tax revenues or total expenditures but also on changing the pattern of taxes or spending. For example, if the durable consumer goods field is depressed and the demand for nondurables has held up well, a cut in excise taxes on durable goods may stimulate demand more effectively in this area than a general income tax cut. Cutting income taxes in the middle and upper tax brackets may stimulate demand for durables more effectively than a general tax cut that provides a smaller amount of added disposable income to many people. But in a severe depression, either course of action may be ineffective since the outlook of consumers is so pessimistic that most of them will not make a major expenditure, especially one requiring installment financing. Another example is that of an inflationary economy in which demand for consumer durables is especially strong. An increase in excise taxes on durables would restrain such demand more than an increase in general income taxes producing the same number of dollars of total revenue.

Just as different types of tax changes have different economic effects, so do different expenditure programs. If housing is depressed, an increase in public housing expenditures will do more good than an increase in expenditures on conservation; whereas, if rural areas are depressed, the latter may do more good. If steel is depressed, an increase in major public works will provide more stimulus than will a general increase in many categories of government expenditures. If housing demand is inflationary, a decrease in expenditures on public housing will help restrain price pressures; if demand for capital equipment is well ahead of supply, a decrease in government purchases will be beneficial, and so on.

Using Fiscal Policy to Promote Long-Run Growth and Stability

Until recently the role of the government in promoting short-run stability has received more attention than its role in promoting long-run growth. If optimum growth is to be achieved, services provided by the government must also grow to meet the needs of the economy. If some areas which have the natural resources for growth cannot afford adequate services, such as education, growth would be aided by having the overall economy provide them. This raises questions about states' rights and government interference, and there is always the danger that outside funds may be used to keep people in an area which does not have the potential for satisfactory economic development. Services provided by the federal government must also keep pace with the economy. This includes federal highways and waterways. It also includes such programs as the United States Employment Service, the activities of the Department of Labor to promote labor peace and help settle strikes, and the work of the Federal Trade Commission.

The need for growing government programs in these areas, growing as the economy grows, is by and large not subject to much disagreement. Some disagreement arises over who will do it, local units, the states, or the federal government; and there is some hesitancy in paying for it. Many hold that the government contribution to growth ends with providing the needed services for an expanding economy. Beyond this they believe that the greatest contribution government can make is to provide an environment in which private investment can grow. Government programs to stimulate private investment, including aid to research, have been advocated. Some have advocated government investment programs which are greatly increased in scope and in volume of funds involved. Such programs have long been advocated by those who feel they are sound in themselves. But recently some have advocated programs of increased government investment as a means of speeding up economic growth. They would increase government investment in such fields as public housing, schools, hospitals, and power projects not only to meet needs in these fields but primarily to speed the growth rate.

Increased government investment programs can, of course, speed up the rate of growth only when it is not at optimum levels. Those who advocate an expanded government investment program on a regular basis feel this is generally true, or at least true so much of the time that the loss of goods to the private sector would not be material.

Another proposal would use the government budget to promote long-run growth only at those times when the private sector of the economy was not providing optimum growth. This proposal involves estimates of the most probable levels of expenditures by various sectors of the economy. If such estimates indicate that total demand will be in reasonable balance with supply at levels of full employment, governmental policy should be neutral; that is, government cash income and outgo should be in balance in the long run. The level of government income and outgo would be set by democratic processes to provide that level of services which the country feels is desirable in the light of social and economic developments and which it is able and willing to pay for in taxes.

One of the tools which is helpful in determining the effects of a government deficit in stimulating economic growth is the high-employment budget. It is an estimate of the surplus or deficit of the federal government at a level of gross national product which provides for high employment and economic activity, but does not lead to inflationary pressures. The most commonly used target is the President's Council of Economic Advisors' definition of the full employment level of economic activity, that is, the activity rate associated with an unemployment level of four percent. The high-employment budget estimates assume the same level of federal spending as that in the regular budget except, of course, for unemployment compensation. But receipts are based on estimates of income and profits that would prevail at the level of GNP which is estimated to exist at full employment. This type of analysis can be made not only for expenditure plans and tax rates which are currently in effect, but for different fiscal programs. When used in a period in which resources are not fully utilized it can help to determine the outline of a fiscal policy which will have a current deficit but will show a balanced budget or a pre-determined surplus at full employment. The high-employment budget is not completely accurate, for it may not show the true impact of fiscal policy on the economy because the private economy reacts with lags and also because other governmental factors besides the flow of taxes and spending affect the economy. It is also ineffective when unemployment is of a structural nature, that is, persons who are unemployed do not have the skills which are needed for jobs which are available. Government deficits in such situations will not lead to reduced unemployment but to inflationary pressures. The concept is of little value when the economy is operating at high employment levels because no allowance is made for the effects of inflation. But it is still a valuable tool for assessing the effects of fiscal policies in a period in which the economy is operating at less than full utilization of manpower and resources.

In periods in which forecasts of economic activity indicate that potential demand will exceed supply for a period of time, a government surplus would be planned to balance supply and demand. The average surplus should be just large enough to prevent inflation due to excess demand. In the inflationary economy of the early post-World War II period, a budgetary surplus helped promote stability. It also helped reduce a large public debt, so there has been little criticism of using fiscal policy in this way.

The use of government deficits to combat a long-run deficiency in demand is open to more question than the use of deficits on a short-run basis to help restore full employment or surpluses to control inflation. Many fear the problem involved in an expanding public debt. It makes debt management and monetary management more difficult. It also creates psychological problems since continual deficits for a period of years may undermine faith in the credit of the government. It can set the stage for inflation if demand picks up rapidly since the government deficits will provide the base for credit expansion. There is also a question about balancing an economy by continuous government deficits. Many would argue for developing an economic situation in which private demand balances supply at levels of full employment.

The ideal is to achieve such balance in the long run rather than use budget planning to offset inflationary or deflationary unbalances elsewhere. Budget planning is useful to achieve balance during a period in which tendencies toward long-run unbalances are being corrected either through market forces or through governmental programs.

Effects of Tax Policy

The tax policy and tax program of the federal government have a direct effect on monetary and credit conditions which may work in several ways. The level of taxes in relation to national income may affect the volume of saving and thus of the funds available for investment without credit expansion. The tax structure may also help determine whether saving is done largely by the upper-income groups, middle-income groups, or by all groups. This fact could affect the amount of funds available for different types of investment. Persons in middle-income groups may be more conservative than those with more wealth, and many tend to favor bonds or mortgages over equity investments. Persons in high tax brackets may on the other hand tend to invest in securities of state and local governments, the income from which is not subject to income taxes. Or they may invest for capital gains since the tax rate on such gains is much lower than that on regular income.

Changes in corporation tax rates may also affect the amount of funds available for short-term investment in government bonds and the balances kept in bank accounts. This is true in part because larger tax payments reduce the amount of money a corporation has available for current expenditures. Also, if tax rates are raised with little advance warning, as has been done at times in the past, a corporation may be forced to use funds it is holding for future use to meet the higher tax payments. Some concerns that are short of funds may be forced to borrow to meet the tax payments. In either case a smaller amount of credit is available for other uses than was available before.

Federal taxes on corporations may also be used to effect investment expenditures through the investment tax credit. This credit was enacted in the fall of 1962 and provided an incentive for new investment in depreciable equipment for domestic use. It allowed a 7 percent credit against income tax liabilities for expenditures on such investments with a service life of 8 or more years and partial credit for assets with a shorter life. An overall ceiling was set on the tax credit of $25,000 plus 25 percent of the remaining tax liability. By 1966 economic activity had reached inflationary levels, and Congress suspended the tax credit in November of that year. It was again put into effect in 1967 as economic activity moved at a slower pace and the permissible ceiling was increased from 25 percent to 50 percent of the tax liability in excess of $25,000. In 1969, when inflation again became a serious problem, the President asked Congress to repeal the investment tax credit.

It was reinstated again in 1971 after economic activity had declined during the recession of 1969-70. This tax helped stimulate investment in the period after 1962 and helped the economy achieve full utilization of resources. Its use on an on-again off-again basis is subject to serious question, however, because it adds an element of uncertainty based on political factors to investment decisions.

Effects of Deficit Financing

The government spending program affects not only the overall economy but also monetary and credit conditions, especially when cash disbursements exceed receipts. When spending is at a faster rate than collecting of taxes and other funds, the resulting cash deficit will affect the monetary and banking system. The effect will depend on how the deficit is financed.

Sales of Bonds to Individuals. If treasury securities are sold to individuals, business corporations, insurance companies, or any institution other than commercial banks or federal reserve banks, there is no permanent effect on bank reserves. As the securities are sold, the government may keep the funds on deposit in the Tax and Loan Accounts at the commercial banks. This does not affect bank reserves; but as the government gets ready to spend the funds, it will transfer them to its account at the federal reserve bank and so cut reserves. They are increased again, however, as soon as the funds are spent.

Temporary changes in reserves occur as the funds are shifted to the federal reserve banks. The Treasury can influence credit conditions by keeping newly borrowed funds in commercial banks or by transferring them immediately to the Federal Reserve, and by controlling the length of time that elapses between borrowing operations and the expenditure of the borrowed funds.

Sales of Bonds to Commercial Banks. When government bonds are sold to commercial banks, deposits are increased but primary reserves are not. If the bonds are sold to banks having a Treasury Tax and Loan Account, the funds are at first transferred to that account. In time, they are shifted to the Treasury account at the federal reserve bank, thus reducing bank reserves. These reserves are restored, however, as the funds are spent. The net result is that some funds which were not previously in use are now being used because of borrowing by the government. The process of credit expansion is carried on just as it is if the bank funds are used for a loan to a business. It can, of course, take place only if there are excess reserves available in the banking system, and it reduces such reserves as part of them become required reserves for a larger total of deposits. If the bank holding the government bonds sells them to the federal reserve banks, primary reserves are increased. Thus, the purchase of government bonds by the banks not only can lead to credit expansion, but it also provides a liquid asset that can be used to increase primary reserves, especially if bond prices remain stable.

Sales of Bonds to Federal Reserve Banks. Primary reserves and deposits are also increased directly when bonds are sold by the government to the federal reserve banks. Deposits are increased at the commercial banks as the funds are spent. These are primary reserves since they have been added to the commercial banking system from the Federal Reserve and were not previously withdrawn as in the other cases. Such direct sale was authorized during World War II, but it was not used to any large extent. When bank-held bonds are bought by the Federal Reserve, however, as they were between bond drives in World War II, the final effect is the same.

Effects on the Volume of Credit and on Reserves. The Treasury can thus influence the credit conditions of the country by the methods used to borrow funds to meet a deficit. If bonds are sold to nonbank investors, credit is not expanded; but when bonds are sold to bank investors, the basis for credit expansion is laid. During periods of high level of business activity and of a large demand for funds, the credit expansion process will probably take place. During depression periods, checks may not be drawn against the new deposits, since private spending is at low levels; and then the credit expansion process will not take place even though added reserves have been made available.

Just the reverse process takes place when government surpluses are used to retire bonds. As the money is raised by taxes, bank deposits are reduced by the checks made payable to the Treasury.

Primary reserves are also reduced as these funds are deposited at the federal reserve banks or kept in the Treasury. If bonds held by individuals are retired, both deposits and reserves are restored to former levels as the checks received from the government are deposited in commercial banks.

If bonds held by commercial banks are retired, reserves are again restored as the banks receive the funds from the Treasury. The assets of the bank have changed since it now has cash instead of bonds, but deposits are not restored. The bank, however, can extend credit since it now has additional cash available.

If securities held by the federal reserve banks are retired, both reserves and deposits of commercial banks are reduced. They were reduced when the funds were raised by taxes, and they are not increased as the bonds are retired since the federal reserve banks now have fewer bonds and more cash.

DEBT MANAGEMENT

Since World War II, federal debt management has become an important Treasury function affecting economic conditions in general and money markets in particular. The economy and the money markets are affected in several ways by the large government debt. Interest must be paid on the debt; and this has become one of the major items in the federal budget, amounting to almost $28 billion in the fiscal year 1974.[2] Interest payments do not, of course, transfer resources from the private to the public sector; but they do represent a transfer of funds from taxpayers in general to bondholders. When the debt is widely held, there is little or no redistribution of income by income groups. However, the taxes levied to pay the interest may have an adverse effect on the incentives of taxpayers and so affect economic activity. This could lead to less risk taking and so slow down economic growth.

A large public debt may also create problems for the monetary authorities in carrying out their policies. Such an effect depends on the way in which the Treasury manages the debt. Debt management includes determining the types of securities to sell, the interest-rate patterns to use, the types of refunding to

---

[2] *Federal Reserve Bulletin,* June, 1974, p. A35.

do, and making decisions on callable issues. Debt management is at times used in a wider sense to include budget policy, the financing of deficits, the methods used to pay off debt, and borrowing more than immediate requirements. These were discussed in the previous section, leaving the technical problems of debt management for this section. Before considering the techniques of debt management and in order to evaluate them, it is desirable to consider the objectives.

Objectives of Debt Management

One of the basic objectives of debt management has been to handle the debt in such a way as to help establish an economic climate which would encourage orderly growth and stability. This has been done in an effort to avoid inflation in boom periods, such as World War II, by encouraging saving and bond purchases by large numbers of individuals. It has also been done during periods in which inflationary pressures were strong by issuing bonds that could not be sold or transferred to a commercial bank, thus making use for credit expansion impossible.

Debt management can and has been conducted in such a way as to maintain conditions that help assure economic stability. During prosperity, the Treasury can borrow money when that becomes necessary for new financing or refinancing by selling bonds to nonbank investors so as not to add to the money supply. During depressions, the Treasury can borrow in ways that are least likely to compete with private demands for funds. This can be done by selling short-term securities so as to attract idle short-term funds and especially idle bank reserves. Thus, there will be no restriction of credit for business and individuals. Credit will be available in larger amounts to the extent that bank purchases of bonds lead to credit expansion.

Some advocate that the Treasury go further in this area and affect the supply of long-term funds so as to promote stability. If long-term bonds are issued at attractive rates, funds can be taken out of the long-term market. This action can reduce the supply of available funds for home construction, capital development, and the like and so help restrain a boom. The Treasury can also do more financing on a short-term basis when it wants to increase the amount of funds available for capital improvements. There is no agreement that the Treasury should use debt management in this way, and no serious attempt has been made to apply such a policy over a period of time. There is some evidence that the Treasury planned its financing in the early 1960's in order to maintain a relatively low level of long-term interest rates and encourage housing and capital investment.

Another objective of debt-management policy is to hold down Treasury interest costs. The influence of Treasury policies may also tend to reduce all interest rates; and lower interest rates tend to stimulate home building, the construction of business plant and equipment, commercial building, and the like. This objective and the first one may, however, conflict at times when higher interest rates may be helpful to restrain inflationary pressures.

A somewhat more restricted objective is to maintain satisfactory conditions in the government securities market. This means that investor confidence should be maintained in government securities. It also means that wide price swings should be discouraged and that buying and selling should be orderly.

More technical objectives are to issue securities of different types so as to fit the needs of various investor groups and to obtain an evenly spaced scheduling of debt maturities so as to facilitate debt retirement if funds are available, or refunding when that is necessary.

Types of Securities Issued

One of the important areas of debt management is the determination of the types of securities to issue. This involves such factors as maturity, interest rates, marketability, and eligibility for various investor groups. Of the total gross public debt of the federal government of almost $470 billion outstanding at the end of 1973, there were $361 billion in public issues and $107 billion in special issues held only by government agencies and trust funds and the Federal home loan banks. The various marketable issues of securities amounted to $270 billion, distributed as follows:

Bills	$107.8 billion
Bonds	37.8 billion
Notes	124.6 billion

There was a total of $88.2 billion of nonmarketable issues out-standing, of which $60.8 billion was in savings bonds and notes. In addition there were $2.3 billion outstanding of convertible bonds which were not marketable but were convertible into marketable Treasury notes.[3]

Varying the proportions of long-term, intermediate-term, and short-term securities and of marketable and nonmarketable issues has a pronounced effect on different sectors of the money market by increasing the supply of one type of security and reducing the supply of others. For example, in the summer of 1949, the Treasury had only a small volume of notes outstanding. This small amount of intermediate-term government borrowing increased the demand for medium-term municipal securities and thus helped local financing of public works.

Changing the maturity structure of the debt also affects monetary conditions generally and monetary policy. Shortening the debt structure by issuing a larger percentage of short-term securities results in increased liquidity in the economy, and lengthening the debt structure has the opposite effect. Issuing a larger percentage of short-term securities may make inflationary pressures harder to control. Short-term securities can be converted into cash more readily at their face value than can long-term securities, which will drop in value as interest rates rise. This gives these securities a greater near-money quality than is the case with long-term securities. Short-term securities also tend to make the government securities market less stable since they are bought to a large degree by investors who are most sensitive to small changes in interest rates. Furthermore, if too large an amount of short-term securities is issued, they will be bought by commercial banks, thus providing the basis for credit expansion. The frequent refinancing required by short-term securities also makes Federal Reserve policy harder to carry out since the almost continuous financing problems of the Treasury cannot be ignored.

The money market has also been affected in the past by restrictions on bank ownership in some bond issues. The policy of issuing bank-ineligible bonds and of shifting the debt to such bonds can restrain credit creation. When bonds are sold to nonbank

---

[3] *Federal Reserve Bulletin*, June, 1974, p. A36.

investors, credit expansion does not take place. Preventing banks from buying bonds outstanding forces them to use idle investment funds for short-term government and for other securities. Insofar as bonds other than government issues are bought, the liquidity of a bank portfolio is also reduced somewhat.

Interest-Rate Patterns

Interest-rate patterns on government bonds likewise have an effect on the money markets. The rates paid by the government on short-term borrowing affect short-term rates on other securities and on bank loans. Banks will not invest in other securities unless the rates are as good as, or better than, those on government securities, and they also demand a reasonable margin over short-term government rates to compensate for the added work and risk of commercial loans. The same is true of medium- and long-term rates.

The government, even as the largest borrower in the country, cannot set the pattern of interest rates without regard to the supply of and demand for investment funds in general. But it can exert an influence over different sectors of the money market by varying interest rates on short-term, intermediate-term, and long-term security issues. Interest rates, maturities, and types of securities issued must be geared to the needs and the desires of investors if the public debt is to be financed most expeditiously.

For example, in 1954, when business was in a minor recession, average rates of interest on various types of government securities were as follows:[4]

Bills (rates on new issues)	.953%
Certificates	.92 %
Notes	1.82 %
Bonds	2.53 %

By the end of October, 1957, when business was at boom levels, rates had increased as follows:[5]

Bills (rates on new issues)	3.591%
Certificates	3.94 %
Notes	3.99 %
Bonds	3.73 %

---

[4] *Federal Reserve Bulletin*, May, 1956, p. 477.
[5] *Federal Reserve Bulletin*, February, 1958, p. 165.

The short-term rates were increased far more during this period than were long-term rates, and also more than rates on notes. The rate on notes was well below that on bonds in 1953 but above it in 1957.

Some have advocated the funding of a large part of the short-term debt by issuing long-maturity bonds at interest rates above those presently used. This would ease the burden on the Treasury, which now has several billions of dollars of securities coming due almost each week. It would not, however, serve the economy best. Short-term government bonds have become a regular source of investment for short-term funds of banks, institutions, businesses, and wealthy individuals. The government, thus, is filling a need in financing as it has, as well as saving interest costs. Any decided change would have pronounced repercussions on the money markets.

Countercyclical Debt Management Policy

Debt management like monetary policy may be carried out in such a way as to accentuate variations in economic activity or to operate in a countercyclical fashion. Countercyclical debt policy calls for lengthening the maturity of the debt in a boom period and using any surplus of government receipts over disbursements to retire short-term debt. Such a policy raises long-term interest rates and also reduces the available supply of long-term funds for capital expansion and residential and other construction, thus dampening the boom. In a recession the debt is shortened, and borrowing is done by means of short-term securities. This causes long-term interest rates to fall and thus helps provide a stimulus for investment.

There is general agreement that debt management cannot be carried out with no regard for economic conditions. But some arguments are raised against countercyclical policy as the only or predominant influence in debt management. One argument against it is that it raises the cost of the debt since it calls for government borrowing when interest rates are highest. It may also be difficult to carry out because it may be all but impossible to sell enough bonds in a boom period to maintain the desired debt structure. This is especially true in a prosperity period which has few, if any, characteristics of a boom. The policy will not work at all when the rate of growth, even in expansion periods, is too low to achieve full utilization of resources.

Techniques of Issuing Securities

The techniques used to issue new securities and especially long-term securities have an effect on monetary and credit conditions. In a prosperity period, the Treasury has problems in selling large issues of long-term securities in competition with private investors, especially when, as in the early sixties, boom conditions do not develop. In the early part of the recovery period, bonds could be sold more easily; but the Treasury hesitates to do so and thus raise interest rates before private investment has recovered fully. To solve this dilemma, the Treasury has resorted to advance refunding, described in Chapter 22.

The Treasury has used this technique several times since 1959 with a large measure of success. Advance refunding can help coordinate the needs of debt management and the implementation of monetary policy. Since the Treasury is not in the long-term market as frequently as it would otherwise have to be, monetary policy can be carried out with less regard for the problems of Treasury financing.

Several arguments have been raised against this technique. One is that it may reduce the willingness of investors to make private long-term commitments. This is really not so much an argument against advance refunding as against any issue of long-term debt by the government in an expanding economy. Another argument is that it has raised interest costs since the new bonds have been issued at higher rates than those which still had some time to run to maturity. This issue is not clear-cut since interest rates could have been even higher with regular long-term financing.

The Treasury has also been experimenting with selling issues other than Treasury bills by means of the auction technique. This may help bring bidders into the market who would not otherwise buy government securities. It has an added advantage of placing less reliance on administrative pricing of securities and more on market forces. Some fear that this technique may raise interest costs, but others feel it could reduce them. Early in 1963 the Treasury experimented with selling several issues of bonds through investment banking syndicates. This procedure tends to broaden the market for government securities and so make debt management easier, but it is also more costly than direct sales by the government.

TRUST ACCOUNT OPERATIONS

The Treasury can also influence the money markets by the use it makes of funds in the agency and trust accounts under its supervision, such as the Federal Old-Age and Survivors Insurance Trust Fund. As of the end of 1973, investments of government accounts were almost $130 billion. About $107 billion was invested in special issues designed only for government trust funds, and over $20 billion was in issues that could be held by the general public.[6] The funds in these accounts increase significantly in prosperous years.

When the Treasury buys regular bonds in the market with these funds instead of special issues, it affects the demand for such bonds. It has also engaged in selling such bonds and shifting to special issues. As long as a substantial part of these funds is in general issues, the Treasury is in a position to influence the money markets both by buying and selling government bonds. Open-market operations are thus no longer the exclusive province of the Federal Reserve.

Both the Treasury and the Federal Reserve thus can substantially influence monetary and credit conditions. If working at cross purposes, each could offset the actions of the other. Cooperation is needed if credit is to be governed so as to serve the needs of industry, commerce, and the government in the best way.

FEDERAL FINANCING BANK

Over the years Congress has created a series of federal agencies which are wholly or partially owned by the U. S. Government. These agencies raised money directly in the credit markets and this not only led to some confusion among investors as to the nature and role of the agency and the status of its obligations, but also at times led to disruption of the debt management policies

---

[6] *Federal Reserve Bulletin*, June, 1974, p. A36.

and plans of the Treasury. Interest costs were also relatively high considering the quasi-governmental status of some of these agencies. At the end of 1973 Congress created the Federal Financing Bank which was to coordinate and consolidate the borrowing activities of some 20 federal agencies. Eligible to use the services of this bank are such agencies as the following:

Export-Import Bank
Rural Electrification Administration
Government National Mortgage Association
Amtrak
U. S. Postal Service
Small Business Administration
Tennessee Valley Authority
Student Loan Marketing Association

Some large government sponsored agencies are excluded because they are privately owned. Included are the following:

Banks for Cooperatives
Federal Intermediate Credit Banks
Federal Land Banks
Federal Home Loan Banks
Federal Home Loan Mortgage Corporation
Federal National Mortgage Association

The Federal Financing Bank operates under the general supervision of the Secretary of the Treasury and a five-member board. The Secretary of the Treasury is the chairman and the President appoints the other four members from officers or employees of the Bank or other federal agencies. The FFB can buy obligations that eligible federal agencies have issued, sold, or guaranteed. Therefore, the debt management problems of these agencies have been transferred to the new bank which has access to Treasury debt management expertise. This should help make overall debt management more effective as an instrument of Treasury policy.

QUESTIONS

1. List the various depositaries in which the Treasury keeps funds. Why is each one used?
2. Describe the Treasury Tax and Loan Accounts and the Treasurer's general accounts.

3. Explain the handling of government receipts.
4. Explain how government outlays are handled.
5. How does the direct purchase of government obligations by the Federal Reserve System aid the Treasury in handling its accounts?
6. Distinguish between built-in stabilizers, formulas, and discretionary fiscal action. Discuss the advantages and disadvantages of each.
7. What types of choices does the government face when it decides to use fiscal policy to fight a boom or recession? Discuss the factors that govern the choices of policy.
8. Evaluate the use of budgetary policy for long-run growth.
9. Discuss the effects of tax policy on monetary and credit conditions.
10. How does deficit financing affect the supply of credit when bonds are sold to individuals? To commercial banks? To federal reserve banks?
11. Discuss various objectives of debt management.
12. Discuss the effects on the money markets of varying the proportions of various types of securities issued by the government.
13. Discuss the pattern of interest rates on various types of government securities and its effect on the money market.
14. Describe and evaluate the various techniques for issuing government securities.
15. How may Treasury handling of the trust accounts under its supervision influence the money markets?
16. What is the relationship between Federal Reserve and Treasury powers in the money and credit fields?
17. Discuss the organization and operation of the Federal Financing Bank.

SUGGESTED READINGS

Committee for Economic Development, Research and Policy Committee. *The Budget and Economic Growth.* New York: Committee for Economic Development, 1959.

"Federal Fiscal Policy 1965-72." *Federal Reserve Bulletin* (June, 1973), pp. 383-402.

GAINES, TILFORD C. *Techniques of Treasury Debt Management.* New York: The Free Press of Glencoe, 1962.

"Patterns of Federal Government Outlays and Revenues, 1960-1970." *Economic Review,* Federal Reserve Bank of Cleveland (November, 1970), pp. 3-14.

Report of the Joint Treasury—Federal Reserve Study of the U. S. Government Securities Market. Washington: Board of Governors of the Federal Reserve System, 1969.

STEWART, KENNETH. "Government Debt, Money and Economic Activity." *Review,* Federal Reserve Bank of St. Louis (January, 1972), pp. 2-9.

The Federal Budget—Its Impact on the Economy—Fiscal 1974 Edition. New York: National Industrial Conference Board, 1973.

25 | Interest Rates and the Money Market

In this chapter the effect of monetary policies on interest rates and on the money markets is analyzed. Consideration is given first to the nature of the supply of loanable funds and to the factors which determine the supply of such funds. The nature of the demand for funds and the major factors that affect such demand are analyzed next. Then consideration is given to the effects of the policies of the Federal Reserve System and the Treasury on the demand for and the supply of funds and on cash balances. The final section of the chapter considers the New York money market, which is the sector of the capital market in which final adjustments between the demand for and the supply of loanable funds are made.

INTEREST RATES

The basic price that equates the demand for and the supply of loanable funds in the capital markets is the interest rate. The quoted interest rate for any type of loan is a combination of several factors. Part of it is a fee for the administrative costs of making a loan, and another part of it is a payment for the risk involved. The remainder is a payment for the use of money itself.

This payment is made because the borrower has the use of the money during the period of the loan and can employ it to his advantage. It is also in part a compensation to the lender for parting with liquidity. Instead of having money that he can use at will for investment or consumption expenditures, he now has a claim for repayment at a future date.

Quoted interest rates for different types of loans are not the same but vary depending upon the use to which the funds are to be put. The costs incurred in making short-term or long-term loans to business, short-term or long-term loans to governmental units, loans to religious and charitable institutions, and loans to consumers to buy real estate, to finance the purchase of durable goods, or to tide them over emergencies vary significantly; and these variations account for differences in quoted interest rates. The same is true of the way in which lenders assess the degree of risk involved in various types of loans. Differences in the credit rating of borrowers will lead to differences in the interest rates which are charged them. Interest rates also differ because of differences in the degree of marketability of the instruments used. For example, the bonds of the United States government are more marketable than those of a major corporation such as American Telephone and Telegraph; and both of these are more marketable than the bonds of a relatively unknown corporation sold in the over-the-counter market.

Interest rates also differ because of the differences in the maturities of the loans. Interest rates for loans of differing maturities are practically never the same; at times short-term rates are above long-term rates, and at other times the reverse is true. This is true in part because of differences in the supply of and demand for funds of various types. In other words, the market is partly segmented into submarkets for funds of varying maturities. But funds are shifted between markets even though some lag is involved, and differences in rates are due in part to expectations of lower or higher interest rates in the future. Various factors affect interest rates in different sectors of the market; however, the part of the quoted interest rate that is paid for the use of the money itself and for parting with liquidity, is determined by general supply and demand factors in the market for loanable funds.

Supply of Loanable Funds

There are two basic sources of loanable funds, savings and bank credit. The supply of savings comes from all sectors of the economy. Individuals may save part of their incomes, either as direct savings or through an indirect savings program such as that involved in purchasing whole life or endowment insurance policies or annuity contracts. Governmental units at times have funds available in excess of current expenditures, and so do non-profit institutions. Corporations may have savings available because they are not paying out all of their earnings as dividends. Depreciation allowances which are not being used currently for the purchase of new capital equipment to replace that which is wearing out may also be available for lending.

Another source of savings consists of the many pension funds, both governmental and private, in existence in this country. These funds, which are building up large reserves to meet future commitments, are available for investment.

Some savings are invested as ownership equity in businesses either directly in single proprietorships or partnerships or by buying stock in corporations. This is, however, only a small proportion of total savings; the bulk of the total volume of savings each year is available as loanable funds.

Some lending is done directly as, for example, when an individual lends money to a friend who is in business to enable him to expand his operations. As we have seen, however, one of the basic functions of financial institutions is the accumulation of savings, and most savings are made available to borrowers through such institutions.

The other basic source of loanable funds is bank credit. Banks not only are the major suppliers of credit, but they can create deposits which are the most widely used forms of money in our economy.

The supply of loanable funds can be grouped in various ways. They may be divided into short-term funds and long-term funds. The supply of funds can also be grouped by types of credit, such as business credit, consumer credit, agricultural credit, and government credit, and by the institutions supplying each type, as has been done in this book.

Factors Affecting the Supply of Loanable Funds

Many factors affect the supply of loanable funds from savings and from the extension of bank credit. Some factors primarily affect one of these types of sources, others both of them. The factors affecting each of them are considered in turn, and then attention is directed to a major factor affecting both of them.

Volume of Savings. The major determinant in the long run of the volume of savings, corporate as well as individual, is the level of national income. When income is high, savings are high; when it is low, savings are low. Important in the level of savings, too, is the pattern of income taxes, that is, both the level of the tax and the tax rates in various income brackets.

Also important from the standpoint of the individual is the stage in his life cycle. Little saving is done by young people, especially young married people with children of school age. When the children have finished school, a family usually saves money for a period of time until the wage earner retires or has his income reduced or cut off completely because of physical disability. An economy in which a substantial proportion of the families are young couples with children will have a smaller amount of savings in the aggregate than one in which older people predominate.

The volume of savings is also dependent upon the factors that affect indirect savings. The more effectively the life insurance industry promotes the sale of whole life and endowment insurance policies, the larger will be the volume of savings. The larger the demand for private pension funds in which funds are built up during working years to be used to make payments upon retirement, the larger the volume of savings. The effect of interest rates on such savings is often just the reverse of the normal effect of price on supply. As interest rates decrease, more money must be paid for insurance to provide the same type of coverage since a smaller amount of money is available from the reinvestment of earnings. Inversely, as interest rates rise, less money need be put into reserves to obtain the same objectives. The same thing is true of savings put into annuities and pension funds.

In the case of savings associated with the use of consumer credit, the effect of interest rates is felt only with quite a lag.

When, for example, a car is bought on payments over a two-year period, savings must go on for two years to repay the loan. This saving to meet monthly payments is unrelated to current changes in interest rates. There may even be an inverse effect in the case of a loan for the purchase of a house, since if interest rates drop substantially, the loan can be refinanced so that the same dollar payments provide a larger amount for repayment of principal, that is, for saving.

Volume of Bank Credit. The availability of short-term credit depends to a large extent upon the lending policies of the commercial banks of the country and upon the policies of the Federal Reserve System that affect the banks. The attitude of bankers is important, and this is influenced by such factors as present business conditions and future prospects. The volume of bank reserves is also important, and this is determined to a large extent not only by the Federal Reserve but also by governmental borrowing policies. Thus, the policies of commercial banks, the Federal Reserve, and the government are the important factors.

The availability of long-term credit of different types depends upon the policies of the many different suppliers of credit. Since commercial banks are by no means dominant in this field, credit is not expanded directly to any appreciable extent to meet long-term credit demands. Indirectly, however, their policies and those of the Federal Reserve are very important because, if funds are being supplied by the banking system for short-term needs, a larger proportion of the supply of loanable funds may be made available for long-term credit.

During the post-World War II period, the policies of the Federal Reserve and the Treasury influenced the supply of long-term funds materially. As part of the program of supporting bond prices, the Federal Reserve bought all bonds offered for sale at par or better. This meant that federal reserve credit was available for long-term investment since government bonds could be sold without fear of loss of principal to get additional funds for current lending.

Liquidity Preference. A significant factor at times in determining the available supply of loanable funds, both long-term and short-term, is the attitude of lenders regarding the future. Lenders may feel that the economic outlook is so uncertain that they are reluctant to lend their money, preferring to keep it in liquid form. This preference may be so strong that large funds lie idle as they did in the depression of the thirties. Lenders may also have a preference for liquidity because they feel that interest rates will be higher in the near future or opportunities for direct investment will be more favorable, and they will therefore hold funds idle rather than lend them at current rates. Thus, liquidity preference may hold some funds idle that would normally be available for lending.

Demand for Loanable Funds

The demand for loanable funds comes from all sectors of the economy. Business borrows to finance current operations and to buy plant and equipment. Farmers borrow to meet short-term and long-term needs. Institutions such as hospitals and schools borrow primarily to finance new buildings and equipment. Individuals borrow on a long-term basis to finance the purchase of homes and on an intermediate- and short-term basis to purchase durable goods or to tide them over emergencies. Governmental units borrow to finance public buildings, to bridge the gap between expenditures and tax receipts, and to meet budget deficits.

Factors Affecting the Demand for Loanable Funds

The factors affecting the demand for loanable funds are different for different types of borrowers. They have been considered in detail in the analysis of the various types of credit. Therefore, the only factor to be considered here will be the effect of interest rates on the major types of borrowing.

One of the biggest borrowers is the federal government, and Congress is generally little influenced in its spending program by interest-rate considerations. Short-term business borrowing for some purposes may be affected but little by minor changes in interest rates. For example, a change in interest rates is of minor significance in a decision to borrow to hold goods in inventory for 90 days longer than normal because prices are expected to advance 10 percent or more or because a major labor strike is in prospect.

A change in interest rates from 6 to 8 percent a year, for example, changes carrying costs from 1½ percent of the value of the goods to 2 percent, a negligible factor when compared with possible changes in prices, costs, and profits.

Fluctuations in long-term interest of ½ or 1 percent do, however, have an effect on long-term business borrowing. Most corporations will defer long-term borrowing when such a rise in rates has taken place but only if prospects are favorable for lower rates in the near future.

Moderate changes in interest rates have little effect upon consumer borrowing. The monthly repayments of principal are so large in relationship to the interest cost that the total effect of a small change in interest rates on the repayment schedule is minor. For example, if a $2,000 loan on a car for two years could be obtained for a 7 percent add-on, the monthly payment, excluding insurance, is about $95. If the rate is raised to 8 percent add-on, payments are increased to only about $96.50 a month, hardly enough to deter purchase of the car on credit. The effect may be somewhat greater when loans are used to buy homes; but even on a $10,000 mortgage repaid over a period of 20 years, a change in the interest rate from 7 to 7½ percent would change monthly payments less than $3.

No doubt in all fields some marginal borrowers are affected by moderate changes in interest rates. But for many types of loans the demand for credit is not very responsive to minor changes in the cost of borrowing.

Role of the Banking System and the Government

Changes in interest rates do not directly or quickly change the supply of some types of loanable funds. The demand for loanable funds of many types is likewise not directly or immediately affected by interest rates. On the other hand, both the supply of and the demand for loanable funds are affected materially by the actions of the banking system and the government. When credit is expanded through an increase in the total volume of short-term loans made by commercial banks, the supply of loanable funds is increased; and when credit is contracted, the supply of loanable funds is decreased. All actions of the Federal Reserve in setting rediscount rates, in buying securities in the open market, and in changing reserve requirements also affect the supply of loanable funds. In fact, all factors that were described in Chapter 6 as affecting the supply of purchasing media affect the supply of loanable funds in the market.

Furthermore, on the demand side government borrowing has now become a major influence and will remain so in the foreseeable future. Government surpluses or deficits make funds available in the market or take them out of the market in substantial amounts. Treasury policies regarding debt management which materially affect the supply-and-demand relationships for short-term, intermediate, and long-term funds were treated in some detail in Chapter 24.

The capital markets are thus under the influence of the Treasury and the Federal Reserve and are likely to remain so. Their policies are thus important factors in these markets. They affect the demand for funds to a limited degree, and they have important influences on the supply. In fact, their major influence is through the effects their policies have on the availability of credit of various types.

An Alternative Approach: The Demand for and Supply of Money

Some economists prefer to analyze interest rates from the viewpoint of money rather than loanable funds. This is an alternative formulation of the problem rather than an opposing viewpoint. The total supply of funds may be divided into those funds needed to meet the demands for money and those available as loanable funds. Therefore, in each approach the emphasis is put on one part of the total supply of funds, money in one case and loanable funds in the other.

The factors which determine the supply of money were considered in detail in Chapter 6 and therefore need not be reviewed here. The demand for money has also been considered to some extent in Chapters 1 to 6 and will be reviewed briefly. There are three basic motives for holding money: the transactions motive, the speculative motive, and the precautionary motive. The *transactions motive* has already been considered in some detail and refers to the need for money to meet the gap between the receipt of income and the time when payments must be made. The amount of money to be held for the transactions motive varies with the level of national income and is primarily responsive to changes in such income rather than in interest rates. The *speculative motive* refers to the desire to hold money currently in the belief or hope that more profitable investment opportunities will arise in the near future. The *precautionary motive* refers to holding cash for emergency needs. Some money is always held to meet emergencies by many businesses, institutions, and individuals. However, the amount so held varies with the confidence in the future of the economy and of the monetary unit. In a severe depression, large-scale hoarding of cash may take place. On the other hand when inflation is rampant, money is spent as soon as possible to avoid loss. If carried to the extreme, this lack of confidence in money leads to uncontrolled inflation.

The demand for money is also influenced by the existence of "near" money and the markets which exist to buy and sell such highly liquid investments. If short-term investments can be made easily and quickly and can also be converted back into cash quickly and with little or no chance of loss, there is less demand to hold money than when such investment possibilities do not exist.

The interest rate can be analyzed from either point of view, the supply of and demand for money or the supply of and demand for loanable funds. Many economists prefer to use the approach based on the supply of and demand for money since it fits more easily into their analyses of change in national income. Most short-run forecasts by analysts in the capital markets are made from the point of view of the supply of and demand for loanable funds. This approach requires an analysis of the money supply since it is a major factor in the supply of loanable funds. It also involves an analysis of the amount of money to be held in idle balances since this, too, is a factor in determining the supply of loanable funds.

The Long-Run Relationship Between Changes in Money and Interest Rates

The short-run effect of an increase in money is a decrease in interest rates, but the long-run effect may be different. If there is an increase in the money supply which was not fully anticipated, investors will probably want to make some changes in their portfolios. The holders of the increased cash will have more funds than they planned on and will try to convert some of them into securities. This will bid up the price of securities and so lower the interest rate. Since someone must hold the cash, interest rates will tend to be lowered until there is a new equilibrium between the desire to hold money and interest rates.

This process may also be viewed from the actions of the Federal Reserve in increasing the money supply. This would ordinarily be done by increased purchases of securities which will have a tendency to depress prices. These increased purchases will add to reserves in the banking system which will increase the supply of loanable funds and thus tend to reduce interest rates.

But this short-run effect is not the only effect of an increase in money supplies. If the demand for credit is such that a large part of the additional money is spent on investment, the total demand for goods and services will rise and so will national income. The same thing will happen if people spend the excess money for goods or services. Initially, inventories will be reduced and production will then increase to replenish stocks of goods. The increase in the level of production will lead to an increased demand for credit to finance it. If the increased demands for credit which result from an expansion of the money supply are greater than the supply of credit which is created, the net result, after some lag, will be pressure on interest rates and an increase in interest rates.

If the rate of increase in the money supply and the increase in total demand are faster than the rate at which output can be increased, prices will rise. This increase in prices leads to further increases in demands for credit since more funds are needed to finance the production of a given volume of goods. Wages will also rise with little lag in labor groups having a union contract calling for cost-of-living adjustments and with a lag for other groups. This raises costs and thus increases the demand for credit. The expectation of inflation also has an effect on interest rates. Borrowers are willing to pay higher rates since they expect to repay the loan with cheaper dollars, and lenders will expect higher rates in order to get the same real return as before. Interest rates also have a tendency to rise in an inflationary period since rising prices increase the cost of holding cash. Therefore, smaller cash balances will be held in relation to income; and more funds are available for spending and investing, thus reinforcing the increase in economic activity which is already in progress.

In summary, rapid increases in the money supply will cause interest rates to be lower in the short period immediately ahead than they otherwise would be. However, sustained changes in the rate of growth of the money supply which last for several months or longer will work in the opposite direction if the rate of growth is greater than the supply of money desired to be held as cash balances. The result will be an increase in the demand for goods, services, and credit and in prices. The rise in prices will be most severe when the economy is operating at capacity levels. As a result, market rates of interest will rise in response to increased credit demands and will compensate for the rise in prices.

The Record of Interest Rates

Interest rates have varied throughout our history as the supply of and demand for loanable funds has shifted. Since just before the end of the Civil War, there have been four periods of rising or relatively high long-term interest rates and three periods of low or falling interest rates on long-term loans and investments. The first period of rising interest rates was from 1864 to 1873 and was based on the rapid economic expansion of the period after the ending of the Civil War. The second period was from 1905 to 1920 and was based on large-scale prewar expansion and after 1914 on the inflation associated with World War I. The third period, from 1927 to 1933, was due to the boom from 1927 to 1929 and the unsettled conditions in the securities markets during the depression from 1929 to 1933. The last period, from 1946 to the present, is based on the rapid expansion in the period following the end of World War II.

Beginning in 1966 interest rates entered a period of unusual increases which led to the highest rates in our history. This increase in rates was due in the early part of the period to demands arising out of the Vietnam War. In the 1970's it was due to dislocations arising out of a policy of on-again, off-again price controls, increased demands for capital arising out of ecological concerns and the energy crisis, and worldwide inflation fueled in part by several periods of poor crops and greatly increased prices for crude oil put into effect by oil producing nations.

The first period of falling interest rates was from 1873 to 1905. This was a period of falling prices in which there were large-scale savings and funds made available by the redemption of the public debt. Even though the economy moved forward during this period, the supply of funds grew more rapidly than the demand for them; and interest rates fell. The same general factors were at work in the second period, 1920 to 1927, but this period was much shorter than the one after the Civil War. The third period of low interest rates was from 1933 to 1946. Low rates resulted from the actions of the government in fighting the "Great Depression" and continued when interest rates were "pegged" during World War II.

Short-term interest rates generally move up and down with the business cycle and therefore show many more periods of expansion and contraction. Both long-term and short-term interest rates tend to rise in prosperity periods in which the economy is expanding vigorously. The only major exception was during World War II when interest rates were pegged. During this period the money supply increased rapidly, and this laid the base for the postwar inflation.

THE NEW YORK MONEY MARKET

The national money market in New York City is not a definite organization, such as the New York Stock Exchange, but an intangible relationship among various participants that demand and supply funds in this market. It has been described by the Federal Reserve Bank of New York as:

> . . . the central national market in New York City where temporary surplus funds of various types of organizations (including secondary reserves of the banks) go to find income-producing employment without sacrifice of liquidity, and where short-term needs for funds are satisfied, usually at interest rates that are advantageous to the borrower. It is a place where final adjustments between the supply of funds and the demand for funds are made for the country as a whole, after much regional clearing has been effected. In general, it is an impersonal market involving the usual lender-customer relationships only

to a limited extent. The open-market borrower frequently has certain sources from which he expects to obtain part of the funds he needs fairly regularly, but he usually feels no obligation to go to any particular lender or group of lenders for his financing any longer than he considers that to be in his interest, and he gets his money from whatever source he can on the most favorable terms. Similarly, the lender in the money market ordinarily assumes no responsibility for financing the borrower any longer than suits his convenience.[1]

This market is located in the financial district on lower Manhattan in the general neighborhood of Wall Street. The Street itself is surprisingly short, running only seven blocks from Broadway's old Trinity Church to the East River less than half a mile away. In the area a few hundred yards to the north and south of this Street, which is less than a half mile square, are most of the purely financial institutions of the New York money market. On the northern boundary is the 60-story building of the Federal Reserve Bank of New York, and on the southern boundary is a 30-story building housing the Produce Exchange. The buildings in between, 40, 50, and 60 stories high, house the great stock and commodity exchanges, the head offices of the nation's largest banks, government security dealers, investment bankers, corporate and municipal bond houses, foreign exchange dealers, and many subsidiary financial specialists. This small area is probably the most intensively used land area in the world. So much steel, stone, brick, concrete, and mortar are packed on each square foot of Manhattan bedrock that engineers once feared the island might sink from the weight. So many people work here that they could not all crowd into the streets at one time.

As is to be expected in a market of final money adjustments, most credit is extended for short periods of time, some of it on a day-to-day basis. The procedure is largely impersonal since borrowers and lenders do not have a regular demand for and supply of funds but are in and out of the market so as to adjust their finances.

Sources of Funds in the New York Money Market

Many institutions and governmental units supply funds to the New York money market from time to time. Included are

---

[1] *Money Market Essays.* Federal Reserve Bank of New York, 1952, p. 1.

commercial banks, businesses, investing institutions (especially insurance companies), state and local governments, foreign central banks and commercial banks, and the federal reserve banks. Each of these is considered in turn.

Commercial Banks. Commercial banks are usually the most important source of funds in the money market. Banks throughout the country have correspondent relations with New York City banks. Many banks keep some funds on deposit with these banks, some of which have 2,000 or more correspondents. This is especially true of state banks that are not members of the Federal Reserve System, since they frequently keep part of their primary reserves with their New York City correspondent banks. Some banks also send temporarily idle funds to their New York correspondents for investment in the money market.

This concentration of funds in New York City was greater before establishment of the Federal Reserve System. Many banks then kept reserves in New York that they now must keep with their federal reserve banks as required reserves. It was expected that the establishment of the 12 regional reserve banks would end this concentration of funds in New York City, and it has decreased it considerably.

Eurodollars

In recent years, and especially since 1966, large commercial banks have raised money by borrowing from the Eurodollar market through their overseas branches. The Eurodollar market is one in which overseas branches of United States banks and banks outside the United States get funds by accepting dollars in interest-bearing time deposit accounts. These dollar deposits are lent almost anywhere in the world, usually on a short-term basis. The transfer of funds is generally made by telephone or teletype and lending between banks is done without collateral in large sums. The transfers of funds usually involve shifts of balances from one bank account in the United States to another account in the United States. Banks which handle Eurodollars are located in Europe with London as the center, but are also located in financial centers throughout the world, including such places as Lebanon, Singapore, and the Bahamas. A demand deposit in a United States bank becomes a Eurodollar when the holder of such a deposit transfers it to a foreign bank or an overseas branch of an American bank. Demand deposits in the form of dollars in United States banks arose because of the widespread use of the dollar as an international currency and the increase in dollar holdings of foreigners due to persistent balance-of-payment problems for the United States. Eurodollars are supplied by national and international corporations, banks, insurance companies, wealthy individuals, and some foreign governments and agencies. Eurodollar loan recipients are also a diverse group, but commercial banks, multinational corporations, and national corporations are heavy users.

There are several major reasons why United States banks have entered the Eurodollar market by means of their overseas branches: to finance business activity abroad, to switch Eurodollars into other currencies, to lend to other Eurodollar banks. The most important reason, and the one which has received the most publicity in the United States, is the lending of Eurodollars by overseas branches to their head banking offices in the United States. This is done to obtain funds at lower costs, to reduce reserve requirements below those on demand deposits, and to obtain funds during periods of tight money.

The first period in which this was done was in the period of credit tightness in 1966. During the second half of 1966 banks increased their liabilities to their foreign branches by about $1 billion. Such borrowing became much more significant in the 1969 period of credit stringency when borrowing of United States banks from their foreign branches increased by over $6 billion.[2] In October, 1969, the Federal Reserve Board established a 10 percent reserve requirement on net borrowings of member banks from their foreign branches to the extent that these exceeded the daily average amounts outstanding in the four weeks which ended May 28, 1969, in an attempt to moderate such borrowing. This rate was increased in 1971 to 20 percent and then reduced to 8 percent in 1973, but the reserve free base was eliminated early in 1974. In the summer of 1974, when credit was again tight, the amount of borrowing by large commercial banks from their

[2] *Economic Review*, Federal Reserve Bank of Cleveland, July, 1969, pp. 13, 14.

foreign branches approached $3.5 billion.[3] It is not likely to become as large as it was in 1969 so long as the Federal Reserve continues to require reserves against such borrowing.

Federal Funds

New York City banks lend not only funds of correspondent banks and funds made available by foreign branches but also their own funds. Day by day some of the large New York City banks and also some banks in other cities have some funds available over and above the demands of their customers and required reserves at the Federal Reserve Bank of New York. These temporarily excess reserves, or federal funds as they are called, are loaned on a day-to-day basis to banks that are temporarily short of reserves. This process involves the transfer of reserve balances on the books of the federal reserve bank from the reserve account of the lending bank to the reserve account of the borrowing bank.

The lending for a one-day period is generally done by an exchange of checks. The deal may be made by one or more telephone calls from the bank wanting to borrow funds, or it may be arranged through a federal funds broker. The lending bank draws a check on its reserve account and sends it by messenger to the borrowing bank, which exchanges it for its own cashier's check for the amount of the loan plus interest. The borrowing bank takes the first check to the federal reserve bank for immediate credit to its reserve account. This cashier's check made out to the lending bank is paid through the clearinghouse on the next day, thus effecting repayment of the loan. Many of these transactions are between New York City banks, but banks in other cities also enter the New York money market, usually as lenders but also as borrowers. In such cases, the borrowing and repayment are effected by telegraphic transfer of funds held at federal reserve banks.

The most common trading unit for federal funds is $1 million, but this is often exceeded. Trades may at times be made for

---

[3] The Federal Reserve included some 178 banks in its series of large banks. Data from *Federal Reserve Bulletin,* June, 1974, pp. 9, 24.

$250,000 or multiples thereof, but they are practically never made for less. The number of banks trading federal funds has increased since the period of credit stringency in the middle and late sixties and the volume of funds traded has gone up very significantly. In one week in the spring of 1974 gross transactions of 46 large banks, 8 in New York City and 38 outside, reached almost $23 billion.[4]

Businesses. Another major source of supply of funds is the temporarily idle funds of business concerns. Many large concerns keep all of their funds in New York City banks except those needed to meet day-to-day operating needs. Funds often accumulate that will be idle for a foreseeable period of time before they are needed for construction projects or other capital improvements. Many concerns invest these funds temporarily in the New York money market. The volume of such investing has grown materially since World War II.

Investing Institutions and Governmental Units. Another source of funds, but smaller in amount, includes the idle funds of investing institutions, especially insurance companies. Their funds are put into longer-term investments, but they may not be invested immediately upon receipt. Such institutions may hold their funds for more favorable market conditions or to buy securities of a new issue to come out shortly. In the meantime, these funds are often put to use in the money markets. From time to time state and local governments and their agencies, as well as some agencies of the federal government, supply funds to the market. Funds may be available because a bond issue was sold to finance a construction program over an extended period or because they are being accumulated to retire bonds. This source of funds, however, is minor and irregular.

Foreign Banks. Of more importance are the funds of foreign central banks and commercial banks. Since World War I, New York City has become one of the most important international financial centers. Foreign central banks frequently keep some of their funds in New York City in the form of gold especially earmarked for their account or in dollar assets of various kinds.

---

[4] *Federal Reserve Bulletin*, June, 1974, p. A7.

These dollar assets, by and large, are kept on deposit in the reserve banks. More than twenty-five years ago the Federal Reserve Bank of New York offered to use the temporarily idle funds of foreign central banks to buy banker's acceptances, which it guaranteed for a fee. The supply of banker's acceptances has been too small recently to meet such demands, and some central banks have asked that their funds be invested in Treasury bills and in other short-term government securities.

Foreign commercial banks also have correspondent relationships with New York banks or have offices in New York City. Through them they supply sizable sums to the money market, especially for loans to security dealers and for investment in short-term government securities.

Federal Reserve Banks. The last source of funds is the federal reserve banks themselves when member banks borrow from them. The Federal Reserve Bank of New York supplies funds when it buys government securities in the market either for its own account or for the System as a result of operations of the Open Market Committee. This source of funds is of special significance since changes in open-market operations by the Federal Reserve have their first effect on the supply of funds in this market.

Negotiable Certificates of Deposit

One of the major new developments in the money market in the 1960's was the greatly increased use of negotiable certificates of deposit or CD's. Many banks had issued such certificates as early as the turn of the century, but before 1960 they were rarely issued in negotiable form. A certificate of deposit is in essence a receipt issued by a bank in exchange for a deposit of funds. The bank agrees to pay the amount deposited plus interest to the bearer of the receipt on the date specified on the certificate. Because the certificate is negotiable, it can be traded in the secondary market before maturity. Funds to purchase CD's are generally supplied by business corporations, but state and local governments, foreign governments, central banks, individuals, and institutions also supply some of the funds.

Within a short time after CD's were issued in substantial amounts, a government securities dealer decided to trade in outstanding negotiable certificates of deposit. This beginning of a secondary market was followed by trading by other security dealers so that by 1969 virtually all of the nonbank dealers and many of the bank dealers in U. S. Government securities bought, sold, and maintained an, inventory in CD's.

The supply of CD's has increased substantially since February, 1961, when a large commercial bank in New York City announced that it would issue negotiable certificates of deposit on a large scale. The volume at that time was considerably less than $1 billion; and by the end of June, 1974, the volume of CD's with denominations of $100,000 and over was over $80 billion.[5]

The rates paid on CD's are usually somewhat higher than those paid on Treasury bills when market conditions are such as to permit higher rates. Maximum rates that can be paid on CD's are set by the Federal Reserve under Regulation Q. Rates that could be paid on large CD's were set at levels up to 7½ percent while they were in effect, but in 1970 rates were suspended on some single maturity CD's and in 1973 on all CD's. Rates paid on 90-day CD's at the end of July, 1974, were above 12 percent, a rate above all money market rates except the Federal Funds rate.[6]

Demand for Funds in the New York Money Market

There are also many types of demands for funds in this final money market in New York City. These are in the form of security dealer and broker loans, commercial paper, banker's acceptances, tax anticipation notes, Treasury bills and certificates, federal funds, and Eurodollars.

Security Dealer and Broker Loans. Before 1929 the most important demand for funds was from security dealers and brokers. They borrowed either on demand or on a time basis to finance the buying of securities on margin by their customers and to carry their own portfolios of securities. Most of the borrowing was on a demand or "call loan" basis; that is, the loan was repayable

---

[5] *U. S. Financial Data.* Federal Reserve Bank of St. Louis (July 24, 1974), p. 10.
[6] *Ibid.*, pp. 6-7.

through the clearinghouse on one day's notice. Such loans were referred to as "Street loans" from their use in Wall Street. As the character of the security markets has changed and as regulation has reduced the percentage of the purchase price of stock that can be borrowed, such loans have decreased in importance.

Commercial Paper. Another source of demand for funds is open-market commercial paper. The market for short-term notes of well-known concerns with strong credit ratings is relatively less important than it was in the twenties. In recent years, however, a new type of commercial paper has become more important than the notes of well-known business concerns. It is the short-term notes of several of the major finance companies, which are known as *finance company commercial paper* or simply as *finance company paper*. The volume of such paper grew rapidly in the fifties and far exceeded that of regular commercial paper. The supply of commercial paper placed through dealers, which is mostly that of nonfinancial business firms, increased much more rapidly during the 1960's than did finance-company paper. At the end of 1973 there was $41.1 billion of commercial and finance company paper outstanding, of which $13.1 billion was placed through dealers and $28.0 billion was placed directly.[7] The paper placed directly is placed by large finance companies; that sold through dealers is sold by a large number of industrial and commercial concerns.

Bankers' Acceptances. A third source of demand also involves the sale of business paper, that is, bankers' acceptances. This form of paper became important as a source of demand because it was encouraged and supported by the Federal Reserve System. Since this paper, which is used to finance exports, imports, and the storage of staple commodities, is also the unconditional obligation of the accepting bank, it has a rating as top-quality business paper. The use of such paper declined after 1929 due to the use of direct loans from banks, but it has increased in recent years as foreign trade has increased greatly.

The volume of acceptances was about $5 billion in early 1969 and had increased to about $11 billion in the summer of 1974. The most significant increase was in bankers' acceptances arising

---

[7] *Federal Reserve Bulletin, Op. Cit.,* p. A27.

from domestic transactions, most of which involved commodities in storage or transit which reached a level of about $5 billion in the summer of 1974. This shift to the use of acceptances in domestic transactions was due in large part to the very large demands for credit in this period which often exceeded the ability of a firm's bank to supply it. Interest rates on prime bankers' acceptances at the end of July, 1974, were 12 percent, a rate just slightly below that on 90-day CD's, but somewhat higher than that on prime 4-6 month commercial paper.[8]

Tax Anticipation Notes. Occasionally state and local governmental units enter the money markets for funds for a short period of time. They usually do this by selling tax anticipation notes to provide funds until tax payments are received. Much of this borrowing is done locally, but some of it is done in the New York money market.

Treasury Bills and Certificates. The most important source of demand since 1929 is the sale of Treasury bills, which usually run for 90 or 91 days. They are sold at a discount through competitive bidding in a weekly auction. These bills are offered in all parts of the country, but most of them are bought in New York City. Almost all of the trading after they are issued is done there. As early as World War I, the Treasury has also, from time to time, raised short-term funds by selling certificates of indebtedness for a fixed price, commonly for a one-year period. In addition, government instrumentalities, such as the Federal Intermediate Credit Banks, are a minor source of demand for funds from time to time.

Commercial Banks. The final source of demand is the commercial banks, primarily the large city banks. Banks that are temporarily short of required reserves borrow federal funds on a one-day basis from banks that have excess funds. They may also from time to time borrow Eurodollars from foreign banks or foreign branches of another domestic bank.

Changing Character of the New York Money Market

The character of the New York money market changes as business and economic conditions change. The whole complexion

---

[8] *Ibid.*, p. A27, and *U. S. Financial Data, Op. Cit.*, p. 6.

of the market has changed since the twenties, and especially since 1933. Both the supply of funds and the demand for funds have increased greatly. The supply went up due to the monetary and fiscal policies under the New Deal, and the demand increased because of the great increase in the volume of short-term government securities offered for sale. Business borrowing through commercial paper and banker's acceptances decreased after 1933 as banks made more direct loans on just as favorable bases as those in the money market. Their use increased again after World War II and especially in the periods of tight money after 1951. Call loans have all but disappeared as an important factor in the money markets. The role of certificates of deposit increased materially after 1960; that of Eurodollars, after 1966.

The use of federal funds has increased greatly and has in fact become the final source of funds before the federal reserve banks are resorted to. As a result, the rate on federal funds has become the most sensitive interest rate in the market. The change in this rate from a lower limit of almost zero to several percentage points above the discount rate is a signal indicating the degree of tightness in the money markets.

Relationship of Money Policy to the Money Market

As the final money market, the New York money market is affected directly or indirectly by all factors that affect the supply of and the demand for loanable funds. A demand for additional funds in St. Louis, for example, would first be met locally. If it continued, however, funds would be obtained from balances held by New York correspondent banks and by the sale of short-term governments, probably in the New York market. Similarly, excess funds of banks and businesses tend to flow to the New York market. The most important determinant of day-to-day conditions in that market is the reserve position of New York City banks. When excess reserves exist, they are made available; when reserves are low or practically nonexistent, credit is tight in this market. Conditions in the New York market and in other markets are also equalized quite rapidly. If reserves are short in New York but plentiful elsewhere, funds will flow to the money market. Likewise, if funds are available in New York, they will be loaned out and find their way into the channels of trade throughout the country. Therefore, any policy that affects the money market will affect the supply of loanable funds throughout the country.

Changes in Federal Reserve policy have a pronounced effect upon this market. In fact, the direct impact upon the economy of changes in Federal Reserve policies is often through this New York money market. Changes in reserve requirements directly affect the market for federal funds. Changing the rediscount rate affects the top rate on federal funds; and by influencing this most sensitive of all rates, it has an effect on the whole market. Open-market operations have their first impact almost entirely in the New York money market as government securities are bought and sold here. Treasury financing by means of short-term securities is also largely done in this market. Thus, Treasury policies regarding money management have an important influence. In fact, all types of changes in monetary policy influence the money market materially. Since it is a sensitive market, it does not take major changes to affect it substantially. Monetary policy has a more direct and immediate effect on the availability of funds than it would have if this final market for balancing supply and demand did not exist or was not organized so well.

QUESTIONS

1. Discuss the various types of costs involved in a rate of interest such as the quoted rate of interest on a high-grade bond.
2. Why do interest rates for different types of loans vary widely?
3. What are the basic determinants of the rate of interest?
4. What are the basic sources of loanable funds?
5. What factors affect the volume of savings? the volume of bank credit?
6. What is the relationship of liquidity preference to the supply of loanable funds?
7. What are the sources of demand for loanable funds?
8. What factors affect the demand for loanable funds?
9. What is the nature of the influence of the Federal Reserve System and the Treasury in the market for loanable funds?
10. How do short-run and long-run influences of changes in the money supply on interest rates differ? Account for these differences.
11. Define the money market.
12. What are federal funds? What is their relationship to the money market?

13. Briefly discuss each of the sources of funds in the money market.
14. Describe the development and role of negotiable certificates of deposit in the period since 1960.
15. What is the nature of the demand for funds in the money market?
16. Describe the organization and operation of the money market.
17. Discuss the major changes in the money market as it has adapted to changes in the financial structure of the economy.
18. Explain how federal reserve policies affect the money market.

SUGGESTED READINGS

"Banker's Acceptances." *Economic Review,* Federal Reserve Bank of Cleveland (July, 1970), pp. 3-11.

BOGEN, JULES I., and PAUL S. NADLER. *The Causes and Effects of Higher Interest Rates.* New York: Graduate School of Business Administration, New York University, 1960.

"Commercial Paper, 1960-1969." *Economic Review,* Federal Reserve Bank of Cleveland (May, 1970), pp. 15-26.

GIBSON, WILLIAM E. *Effects of Money on Interest Rates.* Washington: Board of Governors of the Federal Reserve System, 1968.

"Recent Activities of Foreign Branches of U. S. Banks." *Federal Reserve Bulletin* (October, 1972), pp. 857-865.

"The Eurodollar Market: The Anatomy of a Deposit and Loan Market." *Economic Review,* Federal Reserve Bank of Cleveland, Part I (March, 1970), pp. 3-19, Part II (April, 1970), pp. 3-18, Part III (May, 1970), pp. 3-14.

"The Federal Funds Market Revisited." *Economic Review,* Federal Reserve Bank of Cleveland (February, 1970), pp. 3-13.

26 | Monetary Policies and the Price Level

Monetary policies have an effect not only on interest rates but also on other phases of economic activity, especially on the level of prices, on cyclical fluctuations in economic activity, and on international financial equilibrium. This chapter is concerned with the relationship of monetary policies to price changes and the effects of such changes on the economy in general. The following chapters consider the relationship of monetary policies to the other basic areas in which they have an effect.

Any factor that changes the value of the money unit or the supply of money and credit will affect the whole economy by affecting the supply of loanable funds and interest rates and, in time, both the demand for and the supply of goods in general. The price changes that arise from changes in the monetary system are the topic for this chapter. As a background for understanding such changes, a brief examination will be made of past changes in the price level of an unusual nature, especially in the United States.

584

SOME OUTSTANDING PAST PRICE MOVEMENTS

Changes in the money supply or in the amount of metal in the money unit have influenced prices materially from time to time since the days of the earliest records of civilization.

The money standard in Babylon shortly before 2000 B.C.[1] was in terms of silver and barley. The earliest available price records show that one shekel of silver was equal to 240 measures of grain. At the time of Hammurabi, which was just before 2000 B.C., a shekel in silver was worth between 150 and 180 measures of grain, while in the twentieth century B.C. it declined to 90 measures. After the conquest of Babylonia by Persia in 539 B.C., the value of the silver shekel was recorded as between 15 and 40 measures of grain.

The greatest inflationary period in ancient history was probably initiated by Alexander the Great when he captured the large gold hoards of Persia and brought them to Greece. The effect on prices was pronounced for some years; but twenty years after the death of Alexander, a deflationary period began that lasted over fifty years.

The first recorded instances of deliberate currency debasement occurred in the Greek city states. The government debased currency by calling in all coins and issuing new ones containing less of the precious metals. This must have been a popular form of inflation, for there are many such cases in the records of Greek city states.

Roman Experience

Similar inflationary situations occurred in Roman history. Caesar Augustus brought such large quantities of precious metals from Egypt that prices rose and interest rates fell. During the Punic wars devaluation led to inflation as the heavy bronze coin was reduced in stages from one pound to one ounce. From the time of Nero, debasements were frequent. The weight of gold coins was gradually reduced, and silver coins had baser metals added to them so that they finally were only 2 percent silver.

---

[1] The material in this section draws heavily on the book by Paul Einzig *Inflation* (London: Chatto and Winders, 1952).

Few attempts were made to arrest or reverse this process of debasement of the coinage. An attempt by Aurelian to improve the coinage by adding to its metallic content was resisted so vigorously that it led to armed rebellion.

Experience in the Middle Ages and Early Modern Times

During the Middle Ages debasement of coinage was frequently used as a source of revenue for princes and kings. The rulers of France used it more than others, and records show that profit from debasement at times exceeded the total of all other revenues.

One of the outstanding examples of inflation followed the discovery of America. Gold and silver poured into Spain from Mexico and Peru; and since they were used to buy goods from other countries, they were distributed over the continent and to England. Prices rose in Spain and in most of Europe, but not in proportion to the increase in gold and silver stocks. This was due to the demands of increased trade resulting from the discovery of America and to large-scale hoarding of the precious metals.

Paper money was not used generally for domestic exchange until the end of the seventeenth century. The first outstanding example of inflation due to the issuing of an excessive amount of paper money was in France where John Law was given a charter in 1719 for a bank that could issue paper money. The note circulation of his bank amounted to almost 2,700 million livres [2] against which he had coin of 21 million livres and bullion of 27 million livres. Prices went up rapidly, but they fell just as fast when Law's bank failed; and the money supply was again restricted.

The next outstanding example of inflation is the American experience during the Revolutionary War. This is considered in the following section, which deals with American monetary experiences. Shortly after this American inflation, the government of the French Revolution issued paper currency in huge quantities. This currency, called assignats, declined to $1/2$ percent of its nominal value. This experience was so disastrous that the French financed the Napoleonic wars without inflation, but such inflation did take place in the countries that opposed Napoleon.

---

[2] The livre was the monetary unit in use at that time in France.

Inflation During World Wars I and II

The only outstanding case of inflation in the period between the Napoleonic Wars and World War I took place in the United States during the Civil War. Inflation during World War I was widespread, but it was held in check to some degree by government action. The most spectacular inflation took place in Germany when in 1923 prices soared to astronomical heights.

Greater attempts were made to control inflation during World War II, and they met with some measure of success. Runaway inflation occurred, however, especially in China and Hungary.

MAJOR AMERICAN PRICE MOVEMENTS

Prices in the United States have been affected in a pronounced way by monetary factors on several occasions. This has been especially true during major wars.

Revolutionary War

The war that brought this nation into being was financed to a large degree by inflationary means. The Second Continental Congress had no real authority to levy taxes and thus found it difficult to raise money. As a result this Congress decided to issue notes, at first for only $2 million. More and more were issued until the total rose to over $240 million, and the individual states issued $200 million more. Since the notes were crudely engraved, counterfeiting was easy; and this fact helped to swell the total of circulating media. This continental currency depreciated in value so rapidly that the expression "not worth a Continental" has become a part of the American language.

War of 1812

During the War of 1812 attempts were made to avoid the inflationary finance of the Revolutionary War. But since the war was not popular in New England, it was impossible to finance it by taxation and borrowing. Paper currency was issued in a somewhat disguised form by the issuance of bonds of small denomination bearing no interest and having no maturity date. Wholesale prices based on 1913 as 100 rose from 152 in 1812 to 221 in 1814. They declined to about the prewar level by 1816 and continued downward as depression engulfed the economy.[3]

Civil War

The Mexican War did not involve the total economy to any extent and led to no inflationary movements in prices. The Civil War, however, was financed in part through the issuance of paper money. In the early stages, Congress could not raise enough money by taxes and borrowing to finance all expenditures, and therefore it resorted to inflation by issuing United States Notes with no backing, called "greenbacks." In all, $450 million of such paper money was authorized. Even though this was but a fraction of the cost of the war, prices went up substantially. Wholesale prices on a 1913 base increased from 87 in 1860 to 189 in 1865.[4] Attempts to retire the greenbacks at the end of the war led to deflation and depression in 1866, and as a result the contraction law was repealed. Greenbacks are still a part of our money supply.

World War I

During World War I no resort was made directly to printing-press money, but inflationary policies were nevertheless followed. About one third of the cost of the war was raised by taxes and two thirds by borrowing. A substantial part of this credit was obtained from the banking system, and this added to the supply of purchasing media. Individuals were even persuaded to use Liberty Bonds as collateral for bank loans to buy other bonds. Prices rose from 98 in 1914 to 221 in 1920, and then as credit expansion was finally restricted in 1921, they dropped to 139 in 1922.[5]

World War II and Postwar Period

A much larger proportion of the cost of World War II was met by noninflationary means. Nevertheless, large sums of bonds were

---

[3] Albert Gailord Hart, Peter B. Kenen, and Alan D. Entine, *Money, Debt and Economic Activity* (4th ed.; New Jersey: Prentice-Hall, Inc., 1969), p. 273.
[4] *Ibid.*
[5] *Ibid.*

still taken up by the banking system. By the end of the war, the debt of the federal government had increased by $207 billion. Bank holdings of government bonds had increased by almost $60 billion.[6] Prices went up by only about a third during the war as they were held in check after the first year by price and wage controls, but they rose rapidly when the controls were lifted after the war. In 1948 wholesale prices had risen to 236 from a level of 110 in 1939, using 1913 as a base (100).[7]

Wholesale prices increased during the Korean War and again during the 1955-57 period of expansion in economic activity as the economy recovered from the 1954 recession. Consumer goods prices continued to move upward during practically the entire postwar period, increasing gradually even in those years in which wholesale prices remained more or less stable.

Wholesale prices again increased and consumer goods prices increased substantially during the period of escalation of the Vietnam War after mid-1965. Prices continued upward after American participation in the Vietnam War was reduced in the early seventies and especially after American participation in the war ended. Prices rose at the most rapid levels since World War I days in part to correct imbalances and adjust to increases in the money supply during periods of on-again, off-again price controls, and also because of crop failures in many parts of the world and the greatly increased costs of crude oil put into effect by petroleum producing countries. Inflation in the middle seventies was a world-wide phenomenon which was much worse in many industrial countries than it was in the United States.

ANALYSIS OF MONETARY FACTORS DETERMINING PRICES

The record of outstanding monetary changes throughout history shows that inflation usually occurred because the supply of money was increased faster than was the supply of goods. In the earliest cases this was true because large stocks of gold and silver were acquired as part of the booty of war. Later on, governments increased the money supply by cutting the metal content of existing coins and using the extra metal to issue more coins.

---

[6] Committee for Economic Development, *Flexible Monetary Policy* (New York: Committee for Economic Development, 1953), p. 25.

[7] Hart, *op. cit.*

Beginning in the eighteenth century paper money was issued in quantities, which led to higher prices. In the last half of the nineteenth century, and especially in the twentieth century, bank credit expansion was the basis for inflation, and credit contraction was the basis for deflation.

Such changes in the volume of money were probably the most important factors affecting prices. They were by no means the only influence, however. Prices did not always go up in proportion to the increases in money supply. This was especially true in connection with the increase in the money supply as gold and silver were brought to the Old World from Mexico and Peru. Trade went up at the same time, and so more money was needed to meet the demands of such commerce. Hoarding of precious metals also took place, or in other words, the rate at which the money was used in the market to buy goods was slowed down.

Equation of Exchange

Changes in the volume of money, in the rate at which money is used, and in the volume of goods being exchanged must be considered together to understand their relationship to price changes. These factors have been put into an equation, known as the *equation of exchange* or the quantity equation, which serves as a ready frame of reference for analysis: $MV = \Sigma\, pQ$.

In this equation M is the total supply of money in circulation, and V is the velocity of circulation or turnover expressed as the average number of times the money supply is used to purchase goods during the year. On the goods (right) side of the equation there is a summation of the amounts spent on all goods, which is equal to the average price of each article sold, as for example, bushels of wheat, multiplied by the quantity sold. For convenience, the right side of the equation may be written as PT with P a weighted average of all average prices, or p's, and T the sum of all the Q's. The equation then becomes $MV = PT$.

Often the equation is rewritten by adding bank credit and its velocity as separate factors, M' and V'. The equation then becomes $MV + M'V' = PT$.

This equation can aid in the understanding of factors involved in general price changes. It views two equal quantities from different points of view. The total money value of goods and services sold is seen from the point of view of the price of the goods by summing the quantities of goods multiplied by a weighted average of prices and from the point of view of the sum of the money transactions to buy such goods. These two magnitudes must of course be equal, but valuable information can be gained from a study of the factors at work on each of them.

Effect of Changes in the Factors in the Equation of Exchange

An oversimplified picture of the way in which the various factors affect prices may be obtained by varying one factor while others are assumed to remain constant. Let us begin by seeing how changes in M will affect prices. Suppose that the government debases coinage under the monetary system based on metals alone and issues two coins for each old one. The denomination of each coin remains the same, but the amount of metal is cut in half. There are now two lighter coins for each one that was formerly outstanding, for example, two $5 coins each one half the weight of each $5 coin outstanding before, and so on. If all other factors remain the same and time lags are ignored, prices must double to keep the equation in balance. The result will be the same if the government does not debase the coinage but simply duplicates each coin in existence. If twice as many coins are in existence as before and are used at the previous rate to make purchases, prices must double to keep the equation in balance.

The same principles hold for the total of M and M'. If the quantity of purchasing media is doubled and all other factors remain the same, prices must double; if it is cut in half, prices must drop to half of their former level.

The same is true of other factors in the equation. If V and V' change and other factors remain constant, prices must change in the same proportion. If T increases by 50 percent but the other factors do not change, prices must drop by a third to balance the equation, that is, to keep the product of $P \times T$ the same.

Changes in M and M' and Other Factors

This analysis is too simplified to be a satisfactory explanation of monetary phenomena in the real world. When one factor such as M changes, other factors will probably also change so that the effect on prices may not be proportionate, or a change may not occur at all. For example, the supply of money, that is, the total of M and M', may double; but the rate of use, or V and V', may be cut in half. Then the other side of the equation need not be affected at all. Or, V and V' could decrease somewhat and prices go up somewhat to again balance the situation.

So far the effect of a change in M, M', V, *or* V' has been assumed to be on P. It is possible, however, for T to be affected. If in a period of unused resources M and M' are increased and V and V' do not decrease, or at least not proportionately, T can go up to balance the PT side of the equation. The actual situation is likely to be far more complex than the situation in which a change in M, V, M', or V' leads to a proportionate change in P.

The Cash Balances Approach

An alternative way of analyzing the effect of money changes on prices is through an analysis of the cash balances held by the public. Several equations are used to explain the relationship of money to prices and trade. One of the most useful is the following: $M = KTP$. In this equation M is the money supply, T is the physical volume of trade to be transacted with money during a year, and P is the price level of the things included in T. The new factor, K, is the amount of money held in the form of cash balances, that is, cash plus bank deposits. It is expressed as the fraction representing the ratio of cash balances to the amount of transactions in a given period of time, such as a year, a quarter, or a month.

K is thus related to the velocity of the circulation of money. If the amount of cash balances held is equal to one fifth of a year's transactions, V is 5 and K is $1/5$. In other words, K and V are reciprocals of one another, that is, $K = \dfrac{I}{V}$. The cash balances equation therefore can be written $M = \dfrac{I}{V}(TP)$ or $MV = TP$.

Thus, this cash balances equation and the quantity equation are but somewhat different ways of looking at the same thing. There is an advantage, however, to using both equations as alternative approaches to the factors affecting prices. The equation of exchange focuses attention on the rate at which money is spent and the reasons for spending it at that rate. The cash balances equation puts special emphasis on the reasons for holding money as cash balances, as well as on the reasons for spending it, by stating the relationship between the money supply on one side and the demand for money to be held as cash balances and to be used in trade on the other side. It is, therefore, possible to use traditional economic supply and demand analysis to help understand what is happening to prices.

Effect of Changes in Cash Balances

One or two brief examples will show how the cash balances approach can be useful in analysis. For example, an increase in the supply of money through government deficits is likely to affect cash balances. If there is less than full employment at that time, the volume of trade will go up and there may also be an abnormal increase in cash balances. This will occur if businessmen do not feel that future prospects for a continuing volume of business at profitable levels are good and, therefore, do not spend normal amounts on replacement of inventory, repairs and maintenance, and capital expenditures. As a result, the increased government expenditures at such a time will not have the same effect on the volume of business as they would have had if the outlook for the future were more optimistic. This was the situation during the thirties when government deficits led to abnormal increases in cash balances.

If government deficits, however, increase the money supply when the expectation is for a continued increase in business at profitable levels and for inflation, as is true during a war, cash balances, or K, will not increase. They may even be reduced as businessmen rush to buy raw materials and machinery and equipment before prices advance. On the other hand, if prices are held in check by price controls as they were during World War II, and for a time in the post-Vietnam War period, cash balances, or K, will increase greatly. When price controls are lifted, these additional cash balances will be used to buy goods and services;

and prices will rise at that time. Thus, inflation has not been avoided but only repressed for a time and shifted to a period when more goods are available.

The Quantity Theory

One of the oldest, and also one of the newest, theories which attempts to explain the relationship of money to prices is the quantity theory, which holds that changes in the quantity of money are the main causal determinants of changes in the price level. All versions of this theory have relied in part at least on some form of the equation of exchange to develop their relationships. In its crudest form, the quantity theory holds that changes in the money supply lead to equal, proportionate changes in the same direction in the price level. This may have some validity in a free-enterprise economy in which institutional arrangements are such that the full-employment level of output is the norm and the level of V does not change, but such an economy does not exist today and probably never did. Professor Irving Fisher was one of the early exponents in America of a more refined quantity theory. He recognized that V and T might change at times, thus offsetting the effect of changes in the money supply on the price level. But he held that such changes took place primarily during the upswing and downswing of the business cycle and were thus cyclical in nature. At about the same stage in the next cycle he felt that V and T would have about the same level.

The experiences during the depression, which began in 1929, and the writings of J. M. Keynes convinced most economists that the quantity theory was inadequate as an explanation of general price changes. But it has come back into prominence in recent years, largely as a result of the work of Professor Milton Friedman and some of his colleagues at the University of Chicago. Friedman holds that the money supply is the major determinant of the value of output, that is, PT, rather than P alone. This means, of course, that the velocity of money or its reciprocal, the demand for cash balances, is a fairly stable, or at least a reasonably predictable, factor. Friedman also holds that M determines the level of PT, rather than the level of output determining money demand.

This version of the quantity theory is based on the premise that an outside influence which changes the prices and quantities of some assets initiates a series of adjustments in the prices and quantities of other assets in such a way that equilibrium is again established. Under a given level of income, interest rates, prices, and services received from holding real assets, spending units will want to hold a given amount of real assets and a given amount of money and other financial assets, and to buy a given amount of goods and services. This is true whether the spending units are businesses, governmental units, or individuals. Any amount of money they receive in excess of the amount they desire to hold is used to acquire real and financial assets and to buy goods and services. Changes in the rate of spending are part of the adjustment, tending to close the gap between desired and actual money balances.

Assets are generally produced in changing quantities in response to changes in demand, but changes in the money stock are in the short run largely independent of changes in the demand for money. When the Federal Reserve increases the money stock by supplying banks with additional reserves, they have more reserves than desired and, therefore, invest them or increase their volume of lending. Spending units will sell securities or borrow as long as the interest rate charged by banks is less than the yield from hiring labor and from buying and using other assets. These spending units in turn use their demand deposits to buy additional services and goods and to invest in real and financial assets; and so other spending units receive additions to money balances in excess of the desired amounts. This process leads to an increase in the rate of spending or investing to eliminate the excess. But spending or investing does not destroy the money balances; it merely passes them on to someone else. The process continues until new levels of income, prices, interest rates, and services received from holding real assets are reached and spending units desire to hold the expanded stock of money.

The demand to hold money need not be the same as it was before the money stock was expanded since the demand to hold money changes in relationship to income and wealth and changes in the price level. The same person usually wants to hold more money when his income or his real wealth is greater than when it is smaller. When the price level increases and the nominal wealth of an individual or of a corporation increases, the desire is to hold more money. When prices have not increased, but are likely to increase in the future, the demand for money will tend to decline since the cost of holding it becomes higher. Interest rates also affect the amount of money an individual or corporation desires to hold, since at higher interest rates the opportunity cost of holding money is higher. These and other factors will affect the equilibrium level of money which the community desires to hold, but changes in the money supply and the desire to hold money will affect the volume of output so as to reach the desired equilibrium levels of money, other assets, and spending.

FACTORS INFLUENCING THE MONEY SUPPLY, VELOCITY, AND THE VOLUME OF TRADE

To provide a background for understanding the types of adjustments that may occur in actual practice, some of the factors which may affect each variable in the equation will be considered.

The Money Supply

Since a detailed analysis was made in Chapter 6 of the factors affecting the supply of money, M and M', in the American monetary system, they will be reviewed only briefly here. The total currency supply is influenced by government and banking policies that determine the amount of subsidiary coinage and paper money outstanding, as well as by the demands of the public for cash. The largest part of the supply of money today is bank credit. The amount of such credit is determined by the demand for holding such credit as deposits in checking accounts and for borrowing such credit by private individuals and the government, and by the policies of the commercial banks and central bank authorities that govern its availability. The basic reasons for holding a certain level of money in checking accounts are complex. They will be considered under the factors determining V and V', since the amount of money a community decides to hold at any time determines the rate at which it will be turned over in use.

The Velocity of Money

The velocity of money is the relationship between two factors: the volume of monetary transactions; and the amount of cash balances (cash and bank deposits) that individuals, business units, institutions, and the government feel they must keep on hand to meet demands for funds and to tide them over emergencies. These factors in turn depend upon the organization of the financial system of the community and expectations concerning the future.

The organization of the financial system is an important factor in determining the needs for money and bank credit. If money can be borrowed easily, quickly, and at a reasonable cost, smaller money balances will be kept by individuals, businesses, and government. A highly developed system of savings institutions that provides safety, liquidity, and some income on savings also increases velocity since individuals will place funds in such institutions rather than hoard the money. The degree to which such funds can be kept fully invested by such institutions also affects velocity. If, for example, a savings and loan association can get a loan from a home loan bank when it has an unusual or unexpected demand for funds, it can keep its resources more fully utilized than it could if it were entirely on its own.

The mechanics of the system of money receipts and payments in a community also has an important effect on velocity. The more rapidly checks can be sent from place to place and cleared, the greater the velocity of money. The frequency of money receipts and payments affects velocity too. If income is received every thirty days and spent regularly day by day, velocity is lower than if it is received every seven days, since in the former case cash balances are higher and expenditures are the same day by day.

Velocity is also affected by the timing of receipts and disbursements. The closer they correspond, the smaller the need for cash balances and the greater is the velocity of money. This may be seen by comparing three different ways of receiving the same income for a month and paying for the same volume of purchases. In the first case, income is received daily and expenditures are made daily. This means that cash balances are at a relatively low level in relationship to purchases for a month, and the average velocity for the month is relatively high.

Assume in the second case that income is received once a month and expenditures are made daily. In this case cash balances at the beginning of the month and on the average during the month are much higher in relationship to expenditures during the month than in the first case, and velocity is much lower.

Assume that in the third case income is received once a month and that goods are bought more or less regularly during the month, but they are bought on credit, using charge accounts that are to be paid once a month. In this case, cash balances at the end of the month are the same in relationship to monthly expenditures as in the second case. Monthly expenditures in relationship to average cash balances, or velocity, however, are much higher since cash was on hand only long enough to pay the bills. If in this last case an individual received his monthly income on the 20th of the month and did not pay for his purchases until the end of the month, his average cash balances would be higher and velocity lower than if he received his income on the last of the month and paid his charge account on the same or the following day.

Business cash balances and the velocity of payments are also affected in various ways by the timing of receipts and disbursements. A business may sell for cash only and receive its income from sales more or less regularly throughout the month. If payments are made more or less regularly during the month, as would be the case, for example, for a huckster who sells fruit and vegetables that he buys and pays for daily, cash balances can be lower and average velocity will be higher than in the case of a store that pays for merchandise and most other expenditures once a month.

A business such as a wholesale establishment may sell almost all of its goods on credit. If it gives discounts to its customers for payment by the tenth of the month, it may receive most of its cash shortly after the tenth. If this business must in turn make its payments by the tenth in order to take advantage of discounts, cash balances that must be kept to make such payments will be relatively high in relationship to sales for the month and velocity will be relatively low.

Another major factor affecting velocity is the state of expectations about the future level of economic activity. Consumers will spend more freely when they feel that money income will remain stable or will increase than they will when they expect incomes to decrease. They will also spend their money more rapidly when they feel prices are likely to increase in the near future. Businessmen keep smaller sums of money on deposit to meet emergencies when they feel the future outlook is favorable than when it is doubtful or unfavorable. This is especially true when they expect the prices of the goods they have to buy to increase. They also defer expenditures on capital equipment and cut purchases for inventory when expectations are for a decline in business, and this reduces the velocity of money. Expectations regarding interest rates and the future level of security prices may make new financing more or less desirable and so increase or decrease velocity.

The Physical Volume of Trade

Not only the volume and velocity of purchasing media but also the physical volume of trade is subject to many influences, some of which lead to changes in prices. The basic volume of trade is determined by such factors as the size of the population and the labor force and its technical competence, the quantity and the quality of the natural resources and man-made capital, and the techniques of production, distribution, and administration. The extent to which resources are fully used is equally important. The volume of trade effected by means of money transactions depends upon the extent of barter and upon the number of times goods and services are exchanged for money before sale to the final consumer. This is affected by the degree of specialization in production, the degree of integration from raw materials to finished products in one concern, and the number of middlemen in the distribution process. Since T includes financial transactions, it also depends upon the volume of new securities issued and the frequency with which already existing securities are sold. The same is true of the volume of sale of durable goods, such as houses, that were produced and sold in the first instance in an earlier period.

The general price level is thus the result of the interaction of all of these factors that affect M, M', V, V', and T. Changes in the money supply can lead to changes in price, but many other factors are involved.

ANALYSIS OF CHANGES IN THE GENERAL PRICE LEVEL

On the basis of all of these factors that affect the price level, it is possible to further analyze various types of changes in the general price level.

Price Changes Initiated by a Change in Costs

The general price level can at times increase without the original impulse coming from either the money supply or its velocity. If costs are increased faster than productivity increases, as in the case of wages, businesses which have some discretion over prices will attempt to raise them in order to cover the increased costs. Such increases are likely to be effective in a period in which the demand for goods is strong in relationship to the supply. The added need for funds to meet production and distribution at higher prices usually leads to increases in the money supply and velocity. But the basic influence on prices comes from the cost side, not from increases in the money supply. It may not go up, however, if the monetary authorities restrict credit expansion, but in that case only the most efficient concerns will have enough demand to operate profitably, and as a result some resources will be unemployed.

This type of inflation has been referred to as the wage-push, or cost-push, type of inflation to distinguish it from inflation due to an increase in the money supply, which is called demand-pull inflation. In actual practice both aspects of inflation are likely to be operative at the same time since cost-push can occur only in industries in which institutional arrangements are such that labor negotiations are carried out on an industry-wide basis and in which management has a significant amount of discretion over prices. This has led some economists to ascribe this type of inflation to institutional factors rather than to a wage-push.

Inflation may also be initiated by changes in demand in particular industries which are greater in relationship to supply than overall changes in demand. The demand for nonferrous metals, for example, may be greater than demand in general, and prices may rise in this industry before they rise generally. The first raise is likely to be in the basic materials themselves, and such raises will lead to increased profits in the producing industries. Labor will press for wage increases to get its share of the total value of output, and thus labor costs will also rise. Price rises in such basic industries lead to price increases in the industries with administered prices which use their products. Wage increases in one major industry are also likely to lead to demands for similar increases in other industries and among the nonorganized workers in such industries. Thus, a process is set into motion which can lead to general changes in prices, provided the monetary authorities do not restrict credit so as to prevent it.

Price Changes Initiated by Changes in the Money Supply

The interrelationship of the factors that affect prices in actual practice is quite complex. In this topic additional consideration will be given to the adjustments that take place when the primary change is in the money supply or its velocity. In the following chapters the more complex interrelationships arising out of changes in both the money supply and goods side of the equation during business cycles will be considered.

Several types of inflation may be due to an increase in the supply or turnover of money. Inflation may be generated by an increase in the supply of purchasing power, such as was the case when the supply of metals was increased or their value was cut. In modern times such inflation is often initiated by government deficits financed by credit creation and at other times by private demands for funds. If this is done in periods of less than full employment of men and resources, the volume of trade will go up; and prices may at first be affected but slightly, if at all. As unused resources are brought into use, however, prices will be affected. Some items, such as metals, may become scarce while other resources are still in plentiful supply, and the prices of the scarce items will rise. As full use of any resource is approached, expectations of future price rises will force prices up. Attempts to buy before such price rises will also increase demand above current needs and thus force prices up. Since some costs, such as interest costs and wages set by contract, will lag, profits will rise; and this will tend to increase the demand for capital goods. Such changes will be considered more fully in the discussion of monetary factors in business cycles in Chapter 27.

After resources are fully employed, the full effect of the increased money supply will be on prices. It may be more than proportional for a time as expectations of higher prices lead to a faster rate of spending and so raise V and V'. The expansion will continue until trade and prices are in balance at the new levels of the money supply. Velocity will probably drop somewhat from those levels during the period of rising prices since the desire to trade money for goods before they go up in price has disappeared.

Even if the supply of purchasing media is increased in a period of relatively full employment of men and resources, prices may not go up proportionately. Higher prices will increase profits for a time and so lead to a demand for more capital and labor. This may lead to an increase of the labor force by inducing married women, retired workers, and similar groups to enter the labor force. Capital will also probably be utilized more fully by such devices as having two or three shifts use the same machines.

Speculative Type of Inflation

Inflation due to an increased money supply can lead to additional price pressure of the speculative type. Since prices have risen for some time, the idea becomes current that they will keep on rising. This may become self-generating for a time since instead of higher prices resulting in decreased demand, people may buy more to get goods before they go still higher. This may not happen in all sectors of the economy but may be confined to certain areas, as it was to land prices in the Florida land boom in the 1920's or to security prices in the 1928-1929 stock market boom. Such a price rise leads to an increase in V and V' since speculators try to turn over their funds as rapidly as possible and many others try to buy ahead of needs in anticipation of further price rises. Such an inflation can only lead to collapse since speculators will hold goods or securities only if they feel they are going higher. When they are no longer sure of price increases and try to liquidate, prices collapse as they did in the commodity markets in 1920 and the stock market in 1929.

A Long-Run Inflationary Bias

Since the end of the Korean War, price pressures and inflation have existed despite stringent policies of credit restraint. In fact prices continued upward in recession periods, though at a slower rate than in prosperity periods. The Federal Reserve was hampered in promoting growth and also in fighting recessions because of the need to restrain price rises. The reaction of prices during this period and other economic developments have led many to feel the economy has developed a long-run inflationary bias.

The following factors are used to varying degrees to substantiate the case for such a bias. Prices and wages tend to rise during periods of boom as is to be expected in a competitive economy. This tendency is reinforced by wage contracts that provide escalator clauses to keep wages in line with prices and by wage increases which are at times greater than increases in productivity. During recessions, prices tend to remain stable rather than to decrease. This is due to the power of major unions not only to resist pay cuts in depressions but also to get pay increases in recession years through long-run contracts calling for annual wage increases irrespective of economic conditions at the time. It is also helped along by the tendency of large corporations to rely on nonprice competition rather than cut prices. Furthermore, if prices do decline drastically in a field, government programs are likely to be used to help take excess supplies off the market. There is little doubt that prices would decline in a severe and prolonged depression. Government takes action to restore employment, however, before such a level of economic activity is reached and the downward price pressure of a depression has been lost.

The inflation resulting from these factors has been referred to as *administrative inflation*. This is to distinguish it from the type of inflation that results from demand exceeding the available supply of goods, either because demand is increasing more rapidly than supply in the early stages of a recovery period, or because demand from monetary expansion by the banking system or the government exceeds available supply.

Traditional monetary policy is not wholly effective to combat administrative inflation. If money supplies are restricted enough, prices can be kept in line; but this will lead to chronic unemployment and slow growth. It also makes it difficult for new firms and small growing firms to get credit since lending policies are likely to be conservative.

Administrative inflation calls for new tools of governmental policy if it is to be dealt with effectively. The government has taken steps to create a general awareness of the importance of price and wage restraint on the part of business, labor, and the general public. This was done in part in the Economic Reports of the President in the late 1950's. The Council of Economic Advisers in its 1962 Annual Report proposed voluntary wage-price guidelines. The general guidelines called for wage increases in industry equal to the trend rate of the overall increases in productivity. In industries in which the rate of productivity increase exceeded the overall rate, the guideline called for appropriate price reductions; if the increase was less than the overall rate for price increases, and if the rate was the same, no changes in prices. These guidelines were to be applicable in markets in which discretionary power exists over wages and prices. The guideposts were repeated and elaborated upon in subsequent reports of the Council of Economic Advisers. Between 1961 and 1965 wage and price increases were generally within the guidelines, but there were occasional departures. Some wage settlements were above the guidelines, and some industries with above-average gains in productivity did not reduce prices. The guidelines did not work after 1965 because of the increase in the general price level resulting from the policies followed to meet the increased demands due to the Vietnam War. In its report submitted in January, 1969, the Council recommended a policy for that year that would bring wage increases back at least halfway from the levels of the previous year or two to the ultimate productivity standard. This would have permitted wage increases between 4 and 5 percent, but the actual increases negotiated in most contracts in 1969 were well above these levels. Not only did the voluntary guidelines fail to work when restraint was needed most, but some question if they can ever work effectively because they have the major impact on large industries whose wage and price policies get public attention. Thus, their operation is at best uneven and at times capricious.

Several other courses of action have been proposed, but none has gained general acceptance. One proposal is to outlaw industry-wide bargaining so as to cut the power of unions to obtain wage increases of an inflationary type. Another is to outlaw escalator clauses. A related proposal is to return to one-year contracts in order to provide greater flexibility in adapting wage policies to economic conditions.

Another series of proposals would have a present or new federal agency hold public hearings on any price or wage increase that threatened price stability. After a waiting period, industry and labor would still be free to set prices and wages. It is hoped that publicity would forestall or moderate inflationary increases. Some proposals go further, calling for a public board to decide on the price and wage policy needed to maintain stability but leaving management and labor free to take final action. More drastic proposals call for price and wage controls, some in general and some only in basic industries. Another proposal is to use the tax program to discourage profits from administrative inflation. Profits above a predetermined level would be taxed at steeply progressive rates.

There is no one solution to the problem of administrative inflation, and it is not likely to be solved easily or soon. The situation became more complex and inflation more serious in the middle seventies because inflation due to crop failures and energy problems was added to administrative inflation.

QUESTIONS

1. Describe the process by which inflation took place before modern times.
2. Discuss the early periods of inflation based on the issue of paper money.
3. Discuss the basis for inflation during World Wars I and II.
4. Discuss the causes of the major periods of inflation in American history.
5. State the equation of exchange. Identify each factor in it. Why are the two sides of the equation equal?
6. Analyze the effect of changes in M, M', V, V', and T on the price level.
7. State the cash balances equation and identify each factor in it.
8. How may focusing attention on cash balances be useful in analyzing the factors affecting the price level?
9. Discuss various formulations of the quantity theory of money. Explain, step by step, how the Friedman version of the quantity theory is supposed to work.

10. Outline and discuss the major factors affecting the money supply, the velocity of money, and the physical volume of trade.
11. Explain the process by which price changes may be initiated by a general change in costs.
12. Explain the process by which a change in the money supply leads to a change in the general price level.
13. Discuss the speculative type of inflation.
14. What factors are used to support the case for a long-run inflationary bias?
15. Describe the wage-price guidelines recommended by the Council of Economic Advisers. Comment on their effectiveness.
16. Describe and evaluate other proposals for combating administrative inflation.

SUGGESTED READINGS

ANDERSEN, LEONALL C. "The State of the Monetarist Debate." *Review,* Federal Reserve Bank of St. Louis (September, 1973), pp. 2-14.

EINZIG, PAUL. *Inflation.* London: Chatto and Winders, 1952.

FISHER, IRVING. *The Purchasing Power of Money.* New York: The Macmillan Co., 1926.

FRIEDMAN, MILTON. "The Supply of Money and Changes in Prices and Output." *The Relationship of Prices to Economic Stability and Growth.* Washington: Joint Economic Committee, 1958, pp. 241-256.

GILBERT, R. ALTON. "Monetary Policy and Relative Prices in an Incomes Policy." *Review,* Federal Reserve Bank of St. Louis (November, 1971), pp. 2-7.

"Inflation." *Business Conditions,* Federal Reserve Bank of Chicago (October, 1973), pp. 3-15.

MILLER, GLENN H., JR. *The Process of Inflation.* Washington: Board of Governors of the Federal Reserve System, 1966.

SPENCER, ROGER W. "The National Plans to Curb Unemployment and Inflation." *Review,* Federal Reserve Bank of St. Louis (April, 1973), pp. 2-13.

27 | Monetary Policies and Business Fluctuations

In the two previous chapters, an analysis was made of the effect of changes in monetary policies upon interest rates and money markets and upon the price level. Because price changes and fluctuations in interest rates are strategic variables in the continually recurring cycles in business activity, the role of monetary policies in the cyclical process is analyzed more thoroughly in this chapter.

Since records have become available, and especially since business activity has been carried on almost exclusively by means of monetary or credit transactions in an economy with highly developed financial institutions, economic activity has not grown at an even rate but has fluctuated between prosperity (inflation) and recession or depression. These recurring fluctuations in economic activity have come to be known as *business cycles* even though they are not of equal intensity. They have ranged from such mild downturns as those in 1927 and 1960, of which many people were hardly aware, to the deep depression of the early thirties, in which about a third of the labor force was out of work. They are also of unequal length—from a little over a year to almost nine years.

In order to understand the role of monetary policies in such cycles, consideration is first given to the conditions under which the economy would remain in equilibrium and the role of monetary policy in maintaining such equilibrium, especially the policy relating to the long-run trend of prices. Then some of the factors that are at work in the business cycle are considered, especially those related to price level and interest rate changes. The role of monetary factors in the upswing and downturn in the cycle is emphasized.

ECONOMIC EQUILIBRIUM

To understand the nature of business cycles, it is necessary to understand the conditions under which the economy would remain in *equilibrium*, that is, all of the productive resources of the community being effectively utilized and no factors at work that would cause some of them to be in short supply or to be unused in the future. In analyzing the nature of economic equilibrium, attention is first directed to the circular nature of economic activity and the resulting circular flow of money in the economy. This is done because in a pecuniary economy such as ours, equilibrium can exist only when money flows through the economy smoothly and without interruption. The nature of equilibrium is then explored more fully. To focus attention on the nature of such equilibrium in a growing economy, consideration is first given to the nature of equilibrium in a static economy and then to the requirements for equilibrium in a growing economy.

The Circular Nature of Economic Activity

Economic activity is a circular process in which income is generated in the act of producing goods and services; this income enables the recipients to buy goods and services; their expenditures lead to production to satisfy their wants; the wants are satisfied by the production of goods; and so on in a continuous circular process. Expenditures of one individual or group are income to another individual or group.

At any given time, a nation has a structure of production and governmental facilities that is set up to produce consumer goods and services of all kinds; producer goods; governmental goods, such as military equipment; and government services, such as fire protection. Some goods and services are produced for export to the rest of the world, and other goods and services are bought from foreign countries. This structure for producing goods and services, called the *structure of production,* has been developed over a long period of time, and only a part of it is in the process of changing at any one time. Various parts of the structure are related to each other. The number and type of steel mills currently in existence, for example, are such as to provide the different types and quantities of steel needed to meet the demands of consumers, producers, and the government. Some parts of the structure of production are being changed constantly as the demand for steel changes. The amounts and types of goods being produced in any period of time in the economy are referred to as *the pattern of production of goods and services.*

In the act of producing goods and services, income is paid to the factors of production in the form of wages, interest, rent, and the distribution of profits. Money is paid to the government in the form of taxes on income, indirect taxes, payments for licenses, etc. Some money is also transferred to other agencies and to individuals in the form of gifts and grants. The remaining funds are kept by businesses, some as depreciation allowances to provide for the replacement of plant and equipment, and some as retained profits to increase the equity of the owners. This pattern of income distribution and other money receipts is referred to as *the pattern of money flow receipts,* and it has developed over a period of time as the economy has developed. Tax structures, for example, have evolved gradually; and business and consumer decisions have been adjusted to them. Wage rates are set by bargaining, which is affected by the relative strengths of business and labor bargaining units in general and in each industry, and so on. Just as in the structure of production of goods and services, only a relatively small part of the pattern of money flow receipts is changing at any one time.

The funds from the pattern of money flow receipts continue in the circular flow when they are spent on goods and services either directly by the recipients or by others to whom they have been made available. The recipients of money flow receipts include individual consumers, nonprofit institutions, businesses, and governmental units. They, in turn, decide how they will spend this money on goods and services of various types, and the proportion of it they will save. They may also make use of credit and, in this way, spend more for a period of time than the money they receive. From time to time, such debts may be paid off faster than new credit is extended. The goods and services that consumers, businesses, governments, and institutions purchase and the prices they are willing and able to pay determine what is produced in the next round.

Money kept in businesses as depreciation allowances and as retained earnings and the savings of individuals and institutions also enter the expenditure stream to complete the circular flow of money. Depreciation allowances and retained earnings may be spent by the business on plant and equipment or additional goods for inventory, and so are entered into the expenditure stream. If the business does not have an immediate need for these funds, it may make them available for investment in the money market; and the borrower will then spend them. Savings may enter the spending stream by being invested directly in real estate, equipment, or other assets; or they may be put into financial institutions and entered into the spending stream when they are spent by a borrower. The amount and type of all expenditures by the recipients of money flow receipts constitute the *pattern of expenditures* in any period of time.

The monetary and banking system is used by individuals, institutions, governments, and businesses to facilitate the transfer of money in the circular flow of activity. The operation of the banking system can create a problem in maintaining equilibrium since money may at times accumulate in the banking system rather than be spent or invested. At other times individuals, businesses, or governments may have money available for an expenditure that did not arise out of the circular flow of economic activity but which came from credit creation by the banking system.

The Nature of Equilibrium

In order to understand business fluctuations, it is helpful to see under which conditions this system of circular flow would remain in equilibrium. Equilibrium would exist if the pattern of production of goods and services, credit creation, and transfer payments gave rise to a pattern of money flow receipts that was used for a pattern of expenditures which, in turn, took the goods being produced off the market at prices that yielded a return on capital which businessmen considered adequate. Not only would these patterns have to be in balance currently, but also anticipated patterns of production, money flow receipts, and consumption would have to be in balance or adjustments would have to be taking place or be contemplated to bring them into balance in the future.

Using the Keynesian terminology, equilibrium exists when the present and expected money flow receipts from a given pattern of production are and will be used in such a way that the expected proceeds of businesses from such expenditures are just equal to the supply price of the pattern of production, that is, the price that would induce business to produce newly such a pattern of goods.

Equilibrium in a Static Economy

It is desirable to analyze the nature of this equilibrium somewhat further under static and dynamic conditions. Let us first analyze the nature of this equilibrium in a static economy in which total production remains stable and no appreciable changes are taking place in technology. Not only must aggregate money flows and plans for their expenditures balance with present and projected patterns of production, but also all of the sectors of these patterns must be in balance. This means that there must be no factors either in the current or anticipated situation leading to maladjustments in the pattern of production or in the pattern of expenditures. It means, too, that the government budget must be met without resort to credit creation.

Borrowing could go on out of current income of individuals, institutions, or businesses, but no money creation could take place because, if it did, adjustments would be in process to change the economy to the higher level of money flows. Savings could likewise not be added to cash balances but must be loaned to borrowers. No net new investment could take place, which means that equipment would be replaced as it wore out but no new equipment would be purchased. Full employment of labor and capital would have to exist, or adjustments would be in process to bring them into use. Under a system of static equilibrium, the economist's concept of no profit would hold since there would be no basis for earning any return above the payments to natural resources, labor, and capital. Such a state is, of course, impossible in our economy. It has been described to show how growth affects equilibrium and to show that problems of maintaining equilibrium would also be difficult in a static economy.

Equilibrium in a Dynamic Economy

Equilibrium in the pattern of the flow of goods, the flow of money receipts, and the flow of expenditures as described above is a static concept. But the economy is dynamic. Even in the absence of fluctuations in economic activity, there would still be the long-term trend in the economy. The trend of business activity in the United States has been generally upward even though it has been interrupted at times by severe depressions, such as that of the 1930's. This upward trend is due to such factors as increased population, a larger percentage of married women working, increased knowledge and skills of the labor force, and increased technology resulting in more and better capital equipment.

In dynamic equilibrium, an expanding pattern of production must be growing fast enough to employ fully all resources seeking employment, both labor and capital. This expanding pattern of production must give rise to a pattern of money flow receipts which, in turn, leads to a pattern of expenditures that takes all goods currently being produced off the market at a price which leads producers to produce the required expanding volume of goods. There must be no factors in the current or anticipated situation leading to maladjustments.

Credit creation could be taking place at a rate just fast enough to finance the added production due to the rising trend in economic activity. Such credit creation could be used either to meet the needs of the government or of private investment or both. Plans for such financing would have to be in balance *ex ante* and *ex post*, that is, at the planning stage and in the implementation of plans; or adjustments would be underway because of the failure of plans to work out. Equilibrium could also exist without credit creation if all economic plans were made and carried out on the basis of a decreasing price level due to the transaction of a larger volume of business with a fixed supply of purchasing media. Equilibrium could also exist with any combination of these two situations, that is, some credit creation and some decrease in the overall price level, provided the total is just equal to the value of the new goods produced and plans are made and carried out in anticipation of such a situation. In the next section the various types of monetary policies that may be followed to achieve equilibrium in the long run are analyzed further.

Monetary Policies and Dynamic Equilibrium

If the economy remained in equilibrium and if the supply of purchasing power was not increased as the supply of goods increased, the long-run price trend would be downward. Before the establishment of the Federal Reserve System, this was the underlying situation. Prices rose during war periods due to inflationary war financing, but they dropped gradually thereafter. The monetary agitation in the period from the end of the Civil War to 1896 was due in a large measure to the deflation caused by increased supplies of goods and a relatively fixed money supply. The two major exceptions were in the late 1840's and after 1896. The money supply was increased greatly in the first of these periods by the discovery of gold in California and in the second period by increased world gold production due to new discoveries of the precious metal and improved techniques for separating it from gold-bearing ores.

The provision of the Federal Reserve Act for the issuance of federal reserve notes with a backing of gold and commercial paper was designed to allow the money supply to increase along with the needs of business. The present limited use of commercial paper has rendered this automatic adjustment largely inoperative. Therefore, the size of the money supply depends to a large extent on government and Federal Reserve policy. If they keep the money supply fixed, prices will drop as the production of goods and services increases. If they allow the money supply to increase as the production of goods and services increases, long-run prices will remain about stable. If they allow the money supply to increase faster than the supply of goods and services, prices will rise.

Fixed Money Supply. A case can be made for each of these types of long-run price policies. Some persons argue that the money supply should remain fixed or at most be increased only in proportion to the increase in the labor force. In this way increases in technology would result in lower prices and so would be spread to all sectors of the economy including those on fixed incomes. This would, of course, imply more or less fixed money wages with increased real wages. Opponents of such a price policy maintain that it is unrealistic in an economy with highly organized labor groups to expect them not to press for increases in money wages. They also feel that the prices of many manufactured goods will not be adjusted downward rapidly, and as a result prices of raw materials would bear the brunt of the decline, since many of them are still set in more or less free markets.

Money Supply Related to Production. Many feel that the disadvantages of a fixed money supply so far outweigh its advantages that the money supply should be adjusted to the level of production. One group favors a monetary policy that would increase the supply of purchasing media as the volume of production goes up. This would maintain more or less stable long-run prices. It would permit money wage increases equal to increases in productivity and would lead to no serious price disparities. It would also develop confidence in the value of money, and this would help produce an economic climate which would stimulate savings and, in turn, investment, and so help promote balanced growth in economic activity.

Some persons contend, however, that a gradually rising price level is to be preferred to either of the other alternatives. This means that the money supply would be increased faster than the volume of production. The proponents of this policy argue that business is more likely to be prosperous when prices are rising and that the economy is more likely to grow at a faster rate than when prices are stable or declining. This may be true to some degree in the short run because costs lag behind increases in prices, and as a result, profits increase. Profits may increase further in money terms because inventories are increasing in value and depreciation is figured on the historical cost of fixed assets. Business may also tend to expand somewhat faster in a period of rising prices because expectations for the future are likely to be somewhat brighter if no severe deflation is foreseen. To the extent that these factors lead to an increase in capital formation and the more effective utilization of productive resources, growth is speeded up.

The gains which are made under a rising price level, however, are not made without cost to the economy. Any profits from increased prices of inventories or from costs lagging behind selling prices are at the expense of fixed income groups; so are the increased real incomes of some groups, which can keep income increases ahead of price rises. Such gains by some groups at the expense of others are not equitable whether due to rapid inflation as in wartime or to gradual inflation.

Furthermore, as prices continue to rise gradually year after year, forces are set into motion which will nullify the advantages for growth which existed at first. Unions will tend to get wage increases as fast as prices rise and even in anticipation of price rises. Speculators will bid up raw material prices, and this will reduce inventory profits. Business decisions will be made on the basis of real as well as monetary factors, so the stimulus from inventory profits and historical depreciation charges also will disappear.

It is possible that conditions may develop in which growth may actually be retarded. This could happen if powerful labor unions got wage increases which were larger than increases in productivity and this resulted in the cost-push or administrative type of inflation. If under such conditions the money supply is not increased fast enough, growth could be slowed down. An oversimplified example can clarify this process. Assume that overall productivity is increasing at the rate of two percent per year and wages are going up at a rate of five percent per year. If monetary policy is such that the price level is held to an increase of one percent per year, profits will be reduced. This will create problems for marginal firms, some of which will fail; and it will also slow down expansion by those that remain in business and continue to be prosperous but at lower profit rates. Unemployment will also be increased since some firms have failed and others are not creating new jobs. Thus, growth has been retarded rather than stimulated. Allowing prices to increase so as to maintain profits is also self-defeating. As this happens, interest rates must increase if the supply of savings is to be adequate to meet investment demands; and this

increase in interest rates also tends to slow down capital investment. Further problems may develop since it may become all
but impossible to know under which conditions dynamic equilibrium would exist. This may make the proper monetary policy
all but impossible to determine.

THE ROLE OF MONETARY POLICY IN CYCLICAL FLUCTUATIONS

As has already been shown, monetary changes are important in
the cyclical process because of their effect on interest rates. Their
influence is more pervasive than this, however. In fact, modern
business cycles could exist only in an economy with a banking
system that has the ability to expand and contract credit. In the
analysis of the factors at work in the cyclical process, expansion
will be considered first. An analysis will be made of the factors
that can initiate an upturn in economic activity and of the cumulative process which occurs after the upturn has begun. This
same type of analysis will be made for the downturn. Monetary
factors will be seen to play an important role in all stages of this
cyclical process.

Initiating Factors Leading to an Upswing

Many factors can initiate an upswing in economic activity.
First, factors arising out of changes in the patterns of production,
money flows, and consumption are considered; then actions of
the government; and last, monetary and banking changes.

General Initiating Factors. Any change in the pattern of
production, of money flows, or of consumption can be the factor
that initiates an upswing in business activity. The pattern of
production may be changed because of unusually good crops,
and this will affect other sectors of the economy. Unusually large
crops will lead to lower prices for the commodities in bountiful
supply. Many consumers already buy all of the food they need and
want so they will have money left for other goods or for saving.
If they increase expenditures on other goods, production of such
goods will be increased; and such increased production will require additional expenditures for the factors of production.

When a new consumer good, such as a television set, is introduced, consumers also adjust their expenditure patterns. The demand for the new item will lead to increased production and increased expenditures on plant and equipment to make the added production possible. Expenditures on other items or savings or both are reduced to free money for the purchase of the new good. The pattern of production will be changed to turn out the new pattern of consumer goods.

Since supply of a new product falls short of demand for a time, its price will be high enough to yield a larger profit than those in industries in which supply and demand are in approximate balance. These above-normal profits will temporarily alter the pattern of money flow receipts and are likely to lead to additional expenditures by those receiving the added money income.

New inventions in the producer-goods field may also make it possible to turn out goods at lower prices. Such inventions may make present equipment obsolete and so lead to a demand for capital goods, which would not otherwise have existed.

Increases in the rate of foreign spending may also initiate fluctuations in the domestic economy by increasing the total demand for goods. Fluctuations can also occur if the types of products demanded by foreigners are changed materially even though total expenditures remain much the same. This may happen, for example, when crop failures abroad lead to an increased demand for American farm products and a reduced demand for manufactured goods. Since the increased demand will raise the price of farm products, farmers' income will increase; and the farmers are likely to increase expenditures, especially on farm machinery.

Actions of the Government. Under present conditions, the most important initiating factors in business cycles arise from the actions of government. The effects of increased expenditures during periods of defense and war production need no further explanation. Increases in government expenditures during any period of time, even though of a smaller magnitude, initiate increases in economic activity. The same is true of changes in the methods of financing such expenditures. A shift from the payment of government expenditures through taxation to payment by borrowing or credit creation materially affects the economy by increasing the incomes of those individuals whose taxes have been cut. Government activity in regard to the public debt likewise has a pronounced economic effect. Rapid reduction of the public debt through income raised by general taxation has a deflationary effect since it cuts income available for consumer expenditures.

A change in transfer payments affects the pattern of money flow receipts and, in turn, the patterns of expenditures and production. This happens, for example, when social security taxes are raised and increased sums are paid to those receiving benefits under the social security programs.

The government can also initiate changes in economic activity by actions in the housing field. Making more money available for financing, or making financing easier to obtain, changes the patterns of money flow receipts, expenditures, and production.

Governmental bodies can also influence business conditions and thus initiate upward movements in economic activity by changing the legal rules under which business is carried on as, for example, tariff and banking legislation. The introduction of a high protective tariff after the existence of low rates causes a demand for producer goods with which to produce the items that were formerly imported. The higher prices for the domestically produced goods likewise will lead to a change in consumer expenditure patterns.

Monetary and Banking Changes. Initiating forces may also be set in motion in the monetary and banking fields. Since gold is the basis of the monetary system of the United States, a new discovery of gold increases purchasing power without a corresponding increase in the supply of goods other than gold and thus changes the pattern of consumption. Changes in monetary policies can also initiate fluctuations in the economy. If credit is made more easily available at lower rates, investment expenditures for the improvement and expansion of plant and equipment will increase. If the actions of the Federal Reserve restrict credit, the rate of business investment will be slowed down. Monetary policy also has a similar effect on the housing market, which is especially vulnerable to severe credit restriction, and it has some effect on the durable consumer goods market.

Some of these initiating factors have their original impact on business; others have their original impact upon consumers and upon their pattern of expenditures. As businessmen operating under the profit motive attempt to adjust to changes in consumer buying habits, there will also be an impact upon the pattern of production and in turn on the pattern of income distribution and money flow receipts. This, in turn, again affects the pattern of consumption.

The Cumulative Process During Expansion

After one of the initiating factors has begun an upswing, various intensifying factors may reinforce the upward movement. One of the most significant of these is the multiplier, that is, the process by which an increase in investment expenditures or government expenditures leads to a multiplied effect on national income. For example, as investment expenditures are increased, the level of national income increases, and this leads to an increase in consumption expenditures, which again in turn raises national income, which leads to more expenditures on consumption, and so on. If investment expenditures do not increase, the total effect on income will depend on the marginal propensity to consume, that is, the relationship of consumption expenditures to changes in income. Suppose the increase in investment expenditures is $5 billion and the marginal propensity to consume is .8, that is, 80 percent of the increased income is spent on consumption. This means that in the next round $4 billion is spent on consumption and $1 billion is saved, and this increases national income by $4 billion. Of this amount $3.2 billion is spent in the next round, and so on. If all other factors remained constant, this process would go on until the total change in income would be $25 billion of which $5 billion is the increase in investment expenditures and $20 billion is the increase in consumption expenditures. The situation in the real world is much more complex since many more factors are at work. Some of these are considered in the remaining portion of this discussion of the cumulative process during expansion.

As the demand for goods rises, prices will also tend to rise, especially if the supply cannot be augmented immediately. Such increases or prospective increases in prices that businessmen expect from past experience will cause them to increase their orders for goods above current demands so as to lay in a supply of goods before the price rise. This leads to an accumulation of inventories above current consumption needs on the upswing of the cycle and so reinforces the upward movement.

The increased prices and the increased volume of business, along with a lag in costs, lead to an increase in profits. This increase in profits induces businessmen to expand production facilities and, by doing so, add to the increasing income stream.

As prosperity spreads, it is also carried along by the psychological reactions of businessmen according to the process that has been described as "waves of optimism." When business is good, a businessman is led to believe that it will be still better, especially when other businessmen have the same reaction to the situation. This emotional response leads to a demand for goods greater than that which is justified by the underlying situation, especially during the period when capital goods are being produced. Increased expectations of profit also raise the potential earnings from additional capital equipment and thus intensify the demand for capital goods.

During the upswing of the cycle, it becomes comparatively easy to raise money by means of the sale of securities and in this way to obtain the necessary funds for capital expansion. Some of these securities are purchased with funds that were previously idle, and the introduction of this money into the income stream also has an inflationary effect. During the expansion period, speculation also plays a part and helps reinforce the cumulative upward movement of business. Speculators buy goods and securities in anticipation of price rises and so increase the demand for them. Such capital gains as are made are usually spent more readily than regular income and in a different pattern from that of ordinary consumer expenditures. Furthermore, when they are spent on consumer goods, money that was intended for saving is shifted to the consumption sector of the economy. If, for example, a man sells for $1,500 common stock for which he paid $1,000, he may consider the $500 capital gain as current income which he may spend on current needs or wants. The man who paid him the $1,500, however, usually takes it from savings, so that $500 intended for saving has now been shifted to consumption expenditures.

Another factor that intensifies the upswing as the demand for consumer goods increases is the derived demand for additional producer goods. The demand for producer goods increases by a larger percentage than that for consumer goods due to the operation of the accelerator principle. Since capital goods last for a relatively long period of time, only a small proportion needs to be replaced each year. For example, if capital goods last for ten years, 10 percent will be replaced each year on the average. At a time when all of the capital equipment is being utilized fully, a 10 percent increase in consumer demand may lead to a doubling of the demand for capital goods, 10 percent of the current stock for normal replacement, and another 10 percent to meet the added demand for consumer goods. The effect of such an increase in demand and of further increases is seen below.

DEMAND FOR CONSUMER GOODS	PRODUCER GOODS NEEDED TO PRODUCE THE CONSUMER GOODS	NORMAL REPLACEMENT OF PRODUCER GOODS
1,000 units	100 units	10 units
1,100 units	110 units	10 units
1,200 units	120 units	10 units

ADDED DEMANDS FOR PRODUCER GOODS TO MEET ADDED CONSUMER DEMAND	TOTAL DEMAND FOR PRODUCER GOODS	PERCENTAGE INCREASE IN DEMAND FOR PRODUCER GOODS
. . . .	10 units	. . .
10 units	20 units	100
20 units	30 units	50

In actual practice, as the upswing begins, unused plant and equipment are first brought into use. As capacity is approached, the magnified demand for producer goods is felt. At the same time equipment that is old and partially obsolete is replaced so that the firm may operate more efficiently to meet the increased demand for goods. After full employment of men and resources is approached, there is pressure on prices of capital goods as the derived demand for them continues to exert itself because of continued increases in the demand for consumer goods.

The accelerator principle also is at work during the upswing in the durable consumer goods field. It magnifies the increase in demand for new houses over the increase in demand for all houses, both old and new. The same is true of the increase in demand for new automobiles, new refrigerators, and other new durable goods.

This whole process is aided and given added impetus by the expansion of credit through the banking system. Since the additional funds needed to finance the expansion need not come from current income or saving but can be created by the banking system, there is additional purchasing power over and above that created in the production of goods. Since there are no added goods coming into the market when this purchasing power is put into the system, it leads to an inflation of the price level. Credit is used during the expansion not only by businessmen but also to an increasing degree by consumers as they become more optimistic about the future and businessmen and bankers become more liberal in granting credit.

Relationship of Monetary Factors to Intensifying Factors in the Expansion

In the final analysis, all of the intensifying factors are related to credit creation, the reduction of cash balances, or an increase in the velocity of money, or to the level of interest rates. When businessmen build up inventories in anticipation of price rises or expand production as profits increase, they either use previously idle funds or increase short-term borrowing. This borrowing has been an important source of added purchasing media in past cycles.

Speculation in commodity and security markets is also aided by credit expansion. The same has usually been true of government deficit financing during an upturn. Long-term business financing is done primarily from current savings; but in the early stages of an upturn, funds held in short-term investments are drawn into the capital markets. Some funds made available to a business from bank loans may also find their way into permanent investment in plant and equipment.

The accelerator principle would apply even if credit could not be expanded, but its effect on the economy would be far different. As demand for producer goods increased, prices could rise only if some other prices declined or if the velocity of money increased. This would lead to adjustments of a different nature from those that now take place. Also, interest rates would rise faster than they do under a system that allows credit to expand, and this would make capital expansion less profitable.

The credit that is created as a result of the various factors at work in the upswing leads to inflation since the supply of money is being expanded faster than the supply of goods. Inflation helps to intensify the upward movement in business, and also it pushes the economy further away from equilibrium. A rise in the price level reduces the *real income* of consumers, that is, the quantity of goods which can be bought with a given number of dollars of income. Some groups, such as organized labor, will succeed in getting wage increases to offset the increase in prices and so restore their real income. Other groups, such as those living on pensions or on income from bond investments, cannot increase their money income and so suffer a loss in real income. Others, such as government workers and teachers, may experience a considerable lag in getting their incomes increased and so suffer a loss in real income for a period of time during the upswing.

Reduction in real income of some groups in society is called *forced saving* since these individuals have been forced to do without their former volume of goods and services. These goods and services have been made available to those groups who received additional money from credit creation. The concept of forced saving must be considered from the viewpoint of the total economy since the individuals who have suffered a loss in real income have nothing to show for it. The level of consumption in the economy, however, has been reduced; and investment in plant, equipment, inventory, and houses has been increased through the expenditure of the new money that has been created. So in real terms, the saving of the economy has been increased.

Forced saving unbalances the pattern of money flows since some groups have more money to spend and others have less real income to spend. Unbalance is continued because the groups that have suffered a loss of real income will make every effort to get their money incomes increased so as to restore their former level of real income.

Thus, the whole nature of the expansion in business is determined by the character of the monetary system, especially its expansibility. Monetary policy is thus one of the important factors in the cycle.

Initiating Factors Leading to a Downturn

The downturn in business may be brought about by an initiating factor from outside the circular flow of economic activity, such as a decrease in government spending or a reduced availability or higher price for bank credit. Changes, however, are going on during the expansion period that tend to slow business down or even to cause a downturn. Costs tend to rise faster than do selling prices after a period of time, and the cut in profits reduces the motive for expansion. Inefficiency increases, and this in turn reduces profits.

During the expansion period, maladjustments occur in the structure of production. As business expands and the capital-goods industries expand at a much faster rate than the rest of the economy, various bottlenecks develop that cause expansion to take place at an uneven rate. Basic raw materials especially become short and increase rapidly in price. This makes it unprofitable to produce some of the goods that are needed for a balanced structure of production. It also means that cost and price relationships in other fields are unstable and will shift radically when the pressure of the demand for the basic commodities eases somewhat.

Inflation and forced saving also lead to distortions that cannot help but result in unbalance in the system. Prices of some commodities rise faster than others, and so they lead to a shift in the patterns of both consumption and production. As money incomes are increased, consumers again strive to reestablish the old relationships so that the economy is continually kept off balance. After prices have risen for some time and incomes of some groups have been increased several times to offset the price rises, serious maladjustments may occur. Those having fixed incomes and those not sharing fully in the increases in income are forced to alter materially their pattern of consumption. This may reduce demand for luxury items and durable goods to such an extent that overproduction exists in these fields and unemployment results.

Furthermore, errors of forecast made during the upswing do not show up while activity is expanding rapidly. After a while, however, it becomes apparent that all of the goods that some businessmen thought would be demanded in their field cannot be sold at prices to yield a reasonable profit, and this factor also slows down the expansion. These errors of forecast result in more production in some fields than is demanded by consumers under present income patterns. Since the economy is not perfectly competitive, production is likely to be cut rather than prices in order to correct the unbalance. As production is cut in these over-expanded fields so as to bring effective supply and demand into balance, there is a downward pressure on income working counter to the other upward pressures.

During the period of business expansion there is also an increase in interest rates because the demand for funds rises faster than the supply. This makes it less profitable to finance expansion by means of bonds and also makes capital investment less desirable. At the same time that interest rates are rising, the marginal efficiency of capital, that is, the expected rate of return which can be earned by adding units of capital equipment falls, first in a few fields and then in others. This is true because expectations of future profits are reduced as supply becomes larger in relation to demand and costs press against selling prices. The result is a decrease in the expenditures on new plant and equipment.

As the cycle develops and full employment is approached, the main effect of the accelerator is an increase in the price of capital goods. According to studies by the National Bureau of Economic Research, the maximum rate of advance in quantity in the capital goods field has often taken place during the early part of the upswing, while the maximum rate of increase in price has taken place during the last part.[1] This rapid increase in the price of capital goods during the last segment of the upswing along with reduced profit expectations makes it less desirable to expand the use of capital equipment.

Monetary Factors in the Downturn

Money factors are strategic in the forces making for a downturn. Inflation and forced saving have caused some of the basic unbalances that need to be corrected to again bring money flows and goods flow into balance. Monetary factors are also strategic

---

[1] Frederick C. Mills, *Price-Quantity Interactions in Business Cycles* (New York: National Bureau of Economic Research, Inc., 1946), pp. 41 and 79.

in determining the rate of interest, which, together with the prospect for return from capital, determines the level of investment. Rising interest rates, along with declining prospects for return from investments in producer goods, lead to a reduction in investment, which is an important factor leading to a downturn.

The Cumulative Process During Contraction

The process of income generation, decreasing profits and future expectations of smaller profits, credit contraction, and increasing pessimism intensify the downturn just as their converse did the upturn. The fall in prices now causes businessmen to buy less than is needed to meet current demands since they want to cut inventory losses. Inventories from the past prosperity period are reduced below the point where they are adequate to take care of the current volume of business so as to cut losses from future price declines. Hoarding on the part of individuals and businessmen takes funds out of the current economic stream, whereas credit creation adds funds during an upswing. In the Keynesian terminology, liquidity preference is increased during the downturn, and this intensifies the depression. Furthermore, funds that would normally be used to buy consumer goods are used to retire debts because of the fear of the future, and such payments are usually saved by the recipients so that funds which would normally go into consumption now become a part of savings. As profits are reduced and gross errors of forecast become apparent in some fields, there is liquidation of many businesses. This leads to a forced sale of assets to pay off debts and to distress prices, which further complicates the business picture and intensifies the depression.

Factors Leading to Another Upswing

In many past cycles, initiating factors arising outside the circular flow of economic activity have started business on a new upward movement. These have included such things as new inventions leading to increased business spending, new consumer goods leading to increased consumer and business spending, increased foreign purchases in the United States, and increased governmental expenditures. Even in the absence of such outside initiating forces, the economy will gradually generate the momentum for an upturn.

Excess inventories built up during the expansion period are eventually depleted sufficiently to bring them in line with the reduced level of business during the downturn, and then current consumption necessitates current production. Decreases in raw material costs, some wage costs and overhead costs, and increased efficiency make it possible to turn out goods at lower prices. These changes enable some businesses to operate at a profit again or at a rate of profit high enough to encourage expanded output even though the rate of activity in general may be low; and they also lead to some increase in demand. Horizontal maladjustments due to excess production capacity in some fields are also corrected in time. Some businesses in the overexpanded fields fail, some capital equipment wears out, and the least efficient equipment is taken out of production.

After liquidation has gone so far that only reasonably strong concerns remain and some businesses are again operating at reasonable profits, confidence returns gradually. This leads to an increase in expenditures for repairs and for some replacement of equipment. After a period of time, this replacement demand will become greater because many producer goods do not last more than a few years and have to be replaced if production is to continue. At the same time, the drive for a further reduction in costs is likely to lead to the introduction of cost-cutting devices, thus further augmenting the demand for new capital. Lower interest rates and increased profits will also lead to an increase in investment expenditures. The National Bureau studies on the business cycle have shown that orders for some new capital goods increase during the last phase of contraction.

There is also likely to be an increase in consumer expenditures after the downturn has gone for a period of time. New goods are almost always being introduced, and consumers who were saving part of their income will use it to buy such goods. Increases in population also increase the demand for food, clothing, and shelter. The drop in prices of consumer goods, which is most rapid after the contraction has been under way for a time, leads to increased sales and production of these goods during the last phase of contraction and, consequently, helps reverse the downward movement.[2] Thus, it can be seen that even in the absence of initiating factors such as increased government expenditures, increased demand from abroad, or a major innovation, the economy would gradually experience a revival and a new period of expansion.

Alternative Theoretical Formulations of the Effect of Monetary Policy on Economic Activity

The discussion of the cyclical process indicates clearly that monetary actions and fiscal policy play a significant role in the cycle. Either can act as an initiating factor leading to an upturn or a downturn; and they also have a relationship to the intensifying factors. The processes by which such actions affect economic activity were described in a general way, but were not developed in detail. These processes are receiving a great deal of study, and there is not complete agreement on how they work. Several alternative approaches will be considered first in this section. Then consideration will be given to another area of disagreement, the relationship of prices, wages, and employment.

Monetary Policy and the Level of Economic Activity

There are basically two different approaches to the relationship of monetary policy to economic activity, the one holding that the major effect works out through interest rates, the other that it works through changes in the money stock. The standard Keynesian national income analysis puts major emphasis on interest rates. Government expenditures are held to be largely autonomous, and consumer expenditures are determined by the level of income and the consumption function, that is, the relationship of consumption expenditures to income. Investment expenditures depend upon the interaction of the schedule of the marginal efficiency of capital, that is, the demand for investment of the whole economy expressed as a function of the rate of interest, and the interest rate. Different rates of interest induce different rates of investment and,

---

[2] *Ibid.*, pp. 79, 83.

in turn, different equilibrium levels of income. Therefore, the level of interest rates is one of the key variables in the economic process, and a change in interest rates leads to a change in economic activity. When Federal Reserve policy, for example, leads to lower interest rates, the equilibrium level of investment expenditures is increased; and so forces are set in motion through the multiplier and accelerator which increase the level of national income until a new equilibrium is reached at the lower interest rates. Fiscal policy is, of course, of prime significance in the Keynesian framework since government expenditures along with investment expenditures are the major dynamic determinants of the level of national income. No economist holds that the relationships in the real world are anywhere near as simple as the simplified national income model, but the significance of the rate of interest and of government spending is still basic even after many other factors are taken into consideration.

A more sophisticated approach which puts basic stress on the level of interest rates is the portfolio approach developed in the last few years. This approach also holds that changes in monetary policy lead to changes in interest rates which are basic in determining the level of economic activity. But the basic effect is through adjustments of portfolios to disequilibrium brought about by monetary policy. This starts with bank portfolios as they take steps to adjust to new levels of credit, spreads to other financial institutions, to business portfolios, and throughout the economy. The relative prices of financial assets and real assets are changed when interest rates are changed and steps are taken to adjust to the new situation. These adjustments lead to changes in spending by various sectors of the economy and to changes in the level of total economic activity. Interest rates remain the key factor in this transmission process since they influence decisions to hold money versus other financial assets as well as decisions to invest in real assets.

This approach also assigns an indirect influence to government spending as well as the direct influence of the spending itself. The indirect influence arises out of the methods used to finance the debt, that is, the relative amounts of short-term and long-term debt. For example, a shift from long-term debt to short-term debt is viewed as an expansionary move. The effect on interest rates affects portfolio decisions and spending just as is the case with monetary policy.

The alternative approach is the modern quantity theory which holds that the most significant factor affecting the economy is the effect of Federal Reserve policies on the monetary stock. Some aspects of this theory were considered in the previous chapter in the discussion of the effects of changes in the money supply on prices and so need not be covered again here. This view holds that changes in the money stock result directly and indirectly in increased expenditures on a whole spectrum of capital goods and consumer goods. The most significant factor is the relationship between income and the amount of money individuals and businesses choose to hold. When money supplies change, spending is adjusted to bring money balances to desired levels. Such adjustments affect the relative prices of goods; and such changes in prices, as well as changes in interest rates, are the transmission mechanism according to this point of view. Since someone has to hold the total money supply, changes in income occur until actual money holdings are in line with desired holdings.

According to the modern quantity theory, the role of fiscal policy is generally minor when compared with that of monetary policy. The size of the federal budget, or even of a deficit, is not of major importance. There may be some influence on total spending resulting from changes in the interest rate and in real and nominal wealth, but the relationship is not clear. When a deficit is financed by the monetary system, the effect is expansionary. This is true, however, because the money supply expands, not because of the federal deficit itself.

It is impossible at this stage to choose between these conflicting viewpoints since the evidence is not all in. In all probability both interest rates and the size of the monetary stock play a significant role in determining the level of economic activity. And the role may well be different at different times and under differing conditions. Interest rates may be more significant than the monetary stock when the economy is operating at levels of less than full employment of resources, and changes in the money stock most important in boom periods of full or overutilization of resources. This may be the explanation for the failure of most national income models of the economy to fully account for price increases in a boom period such as 1968 or 1973.

The Relationship of Prices, Wages, and Employment

Another unresolved problem is the relationship of the rate of unemployment to wages and prices. The trade-off view holds that it is impossible to have high employment without inflation and that policy makers must choose between some degree of unemployment and some degree of inflation. For example, between 1958 and 1964 the unemployment rate consistently exceeded 5 percent of the labor force; and price increases as measured by the implicit GNP price deflator were below 2 percent each year. In 1956-57 and 1966-68 the unemployment rate varied between 3.6 and 4.3 percent of the labor force, and prices increased between 3.1 and 4.1 percent.[3] This historical relationship has not been a precise one, but has held in a general way. If such relationships are plotted, the curve slopes downward from left to right and is usually shaped like a rounded "L." This curve is often called the Phillips curve after the British economist who first stressed the relationship between levels of unemployment and wages. The trade-off view holds that such relationships are stable, and that when the economy reaches a high employment range, excessive wage increases and price inflation result from expansionary fiscal policies rather than further reductions in unemployment.

Opposed to this view is the long-run equilibrium view, which holds that if proper policies are followed, inflation need not result. For illustration, assume that the economy is at the stage of a cycle in which there is significant unemployment. Monetary or fiscal action starts an upswing in activity. Spending occurs at first with the anticipation that prices will remain as they are and output and employment rise more rapidly for a time than wages or prices. But as demand increases and prices rise, real wages are reduced and workers demand higher wages and get them during periods of high employment. If inflationary monetary and fiscal policies are pursued, wages will continue to rise and inflation will result. But as wages rise, employers are no longer ready to hire workers or raise wages as rapidly as early in the upswing, and they also find it profitable to use more labor-saving equipment. If some degree of deflationary action is pursued after the upswing has lost momentum, there

---

[3] *Economic Report of the President* (Washington: U. S. Government Printing Office, 1969), p. 94.

will be some increased unemployment, but it will be temporary. As soon as a new price trend not only becomes a reality but is anticipated for the future, nominal and real wages will coincide; and unemployment will again fall. According to this view, inflationary policy is not necessary or desirable as a way of achieving high levels of employment. It is impossible to determine at the present time which view, if either, is the correct one, or if monetary and fiscal policies can be so used as to achieve long-run equilibrium. There are enough questions, however, that policy makers should be cautious about assuming any set relationship between employment and wages and the resulting level of prices.

QUESTIONS

1. Describe the circular nature of economic transactions.
2. Describe the circular flow of money in the total economy.
3. What is the relationship of funds from depreciation allowances, retained corporation earnings, and savings to the circular flow of money?
4. What is the role of the banking system in the circular flow?
5. Describe the patterns of production, of money flow receipts, and of expenditures.
6. Describe the conditions under which the economy would be in equilibrium. What is the relationship of government financing to equilibrium? What is the relationship of savings and investment to equilibrium?
7. What are the requirements for equilibrium in a dynamic economy?
8. Discuss the role of different types of monetary policies in achieving dynamic equilibrium. How are they related to economic growth?
9. Analyze the general factors that may initiate an upswing in economic activity. Show in each case why the rate of economic activity would be increased. Do the same for initiating factors arising out of the actions of government and out of monetary and banking changes.
10. Describe the various intensifying factors that may reinforce the upward movement in business. Show in each case how the rate of economic activity is speeded up.
11. Describe and discuss the relationship of monetary factors to the intensifying factors in the upswing.
12. Discuss the operation of the factors that may lead to a downturn.
13. Describe and discuss the role of monetary factors in initiating a downturn.
14. Describe the cumulative process during contraction.
15. Analyze the factors that may lead to a renewed upturn in economic activity.

16. Outline the case for interest rates as the prime factor in implementing monetary policy and also for monetary stocks. Evaluate these opposing theoretical formulations.
17. Discuss the trade-off view and the long-run equilibrium view of the relationship of unemployment rates to wages and prices.

SUGGESTED READINGS

ANDERSEN, LEONALL C. "A Monetarist View of Demand Management: The United States Experience." *Review,* Federal Reserve Bank of St. Louis (September, 1971), pp. 3-26.

BRILL, DANIEL H. *Criteria for Conduct of Monetary Policy: Implications of Research.* Washington: Board of Governors of the Federal Reserve System, 1965.

CARLSEN, KEITH M. "Monetary and Fiscal Actions in Macro-economic Models." *Review,* Federal Reserve Bank of St. Louis (January, 1974), pp. 8-18.

CLARK, J. M. *Strategic Factors in Business Cycles.* New York: National Bureau of Economic Research, Inc., 1934.

DAUTEN, CARL A., and LLOYD M. VALENTINE. *Business Fluctuations and Forecasting.* Cincinnati: South-Western Publishing Co., 1974. Parts 2 and 3.

McMILLAN, ROBERT A. "A Reexamination of the Full Employment Goal." *Economic Review,* Federal Reserve Bank of Cleveland (March-April, 1973), p. 3-18.

MITCHELL, W. C. *Business Cycles and Their Causes.* Berkeley: University of California Press, 1941.

"The Relation Between Prices and Employment: Two Views." *Review.* Federal Reserve Bank of St. Louis (March, 1969), pp. 15-21.

VON HABERLER, GOTTFRIED. *Prosperity and Depression.* Geneva: League of Nations, 1939. Chapters 9-12.

28 | Monetary Policies and International Financial Equilibrium

Of great importance in the nation's international financial relationships is the role of monetary policy. Just as monetary policy plays a strategic role in the nation's stability, growth, interest rates, and price levels, so, too, it is relied upon to relieve the pressure of imbalance in international financial relationships. No nation is a world unto itself, however; nor can a nation pursue whatever policies it desires without regard to the reactions of other nations. This is especially true of the United States with its far-flung international commitments. Since World War II the United States economy has become ever more closely bound with other nations by ties of trade, investment, communication, transportation, science, and literature.

Briefly, the nations of the world strive to achieve international financial equilibrium by maintaining a balance between their exchange of goods and services. Yet, such equilibrium has become the exception rather than the rule in the years since World War II. The imbalance in the exchange of goods and services among nations may be offset or may be aggravated by borrowing and lending, by the sale or purchase of accumulated monetary reserves, and by outright grants. Monetary policy plays a primary role in its influence on borrowing and lending among nations. It plays an indirect role in all international economic relationships. This chapter explores the special problems facing the United States in maintaining international financial equilibrium.

THE NATURE OF THE PROBLEM

Since World War II the United States has enjoyed a favorable balance of trade; that is, it has generally had more exports than imports. Yet, during this period she has engaged in a massive program of international aid to countries whose productive facilities were destroyed by the war and has shouldered the preponderance of the burden of military capability and action. She has given vast measures of assistance to developing nations of the world. One of the results of these efforts has been the large accumulations of foreign claims to United States dollars and the loss of a large amount of gold reserves.

Even with loss of gold reserves, the United States has far greater reserves than has any other nation. Too, the large accumulation of claims against United States dollars had long been considered desirable. Indeed, one of the most serious difficulties facing international trade in the early postwar period was the so-called "dollar gap." That the dollar gap has been replaced by a "dollar surplus," that is, by a large accumulation of foreign claims to United States dollars, testifies to the successful reconstruction of the war-devastated economies of Western Europe. Now the United States is but one among many vigorous trading nations, each vying eagerly for markets with which to maintain its international position. Nor has this successful reconstruction of Europe enabled the United States to scale down her international obligations. In the face of continuing international commitments and ever-increasing intensification of competition for international markets, the amount of gold loss and the buildup of international claims to United States dollars has increased markedly. It is the substantial and continuing increase in foreign claims and gold loss rather than the present level of international monetary reserves that provides serious concern.

The International Balance of Payments

In our discussion thus far we have made general reference to levels of exports and imports, to gold flows, and to changes in the claims to United States dollars. We may be more precise and understandable by directing our discussion in terms of the *international balance of payments*. A payments table is an accounting device for expressing in summary form all of our international transactions, including foreign investment, private and government grants, expenditures of United States military forces overseas, and many items in addition to purchases and sales of goods and services. In Table 28-1 the components of the United States balance of payments for 1971, 1972, and 1973 are shown.

The item "merchandise" in this table relates exclusively to the export and import of commodities and is the most important single item in the statement. The net balance between exports and imports is referred to as the *balance of trade*. It is immediately apparent from the table that we experienced a small favorable balance of trade in 1973 after large deficits in 1971 and 1972.

The Balance of Payments and External Liquidity

The financial position of the United States with respect to the rest of the world is a function of our current assets relative to our current liabilities. Our current assets are made up of gold holdings and ownership of convertible foreign currencies by our Treasury and Federal Reserve System. It is from these assets that the United States is able to meet the financial claims of the rest of the world as they are presented. The nation's current liabilities, on the other hand, reduce our external liquidity since they represent an offset to our current assets. Current liabilities are represented by both public and private liquid liabilities. In a sense, external liquidity for the nation is very much like liquidity for the business firm, that is, measured in large part by the relationship of current assets to current liabilities.

U. S. Gold Holdings. Gold is considered to be the basic medium of external liquidity because of its general acceptance among the nations of the world in settlement of international

Table 28-1

U. S. BALANCE OF PAYMENTS

(In millions of dollars)

CREDITS +, DEBITS —	1971	1972	1973
Merchandise trade balance	−2,722	−6,986	623
Exports	42,754	48,768	70,252
Imports	−45,476	−55,754	−69,629
Military transactions, net	−2,908	−3,604	−2,201
Travel and transportation, net	−2,341	−3,055	−2,710
Investment income, net	5,021	4,526	5,291
U.S. direct investments abroad	6,385	6,925	9,415
Other U.S. investments abroad	3,444	3,494	4,569
Foreign investments in the United States	−4,809	−5,893	−8,693
Other services, net	2,781	3,110	3,540
Balance on goods and services	−170	−6,009	4,543
Remittances, pensions, and other transfers	−1,604	−1,624	−1,943
Balance on goods, services, and remittances	−1,774	−7,634	2,600
U.S. Government grants (excluding military)	−2,043	−2,173	−1,933
Balance on current account	−3,817	−9,807	667
U.S. Government capital flows excluding nonscheduled repayments, net .	−2,111	−1,705	−2,938
Nonscheduled repayments of U.S. Government assets	227	137	289
U.S. Government nonliquid liabilities to other than foreign official reserve agencies	−478	238	1,111
Long-term private capital flows, net ..	−4,381	−98	127
Balance on current account and long-term capital	−10,559	−11,235	−744

SOURCE: *Federal Reserve Bulletin*, Board of Governors of the Federal Reserve System, Washington, D. C., August, 1974, p. A60.

claims. As described in Chapter 2, in the United States only the Treasury could own gold before December 31, 1974. The holding of gold by the United States Treasury rises and falls with its purchase and sales. As its supply of gold rises through purchases, the external liquidity of the nation increases. As its supply of gold falls through sales, the external liquidity decreases.

Treasury and Federal Reserve System Ownership of Convertible Foreign Currencies. External liquidity of the nation is increased as ownership of readily convertible foreign currencies by the United States Treasury and the Federal Reserve System is increased. Such foreign currencies may be used to settle obligations owed to foreign creditors. Foreign currencies owned by individuals and companies are not considered part of our external liquidity resources because they are not available to official agencies for use. Rather, they are at the disposal of their owners, and it is believed that they make no contribution to the nation's ability to meet emergency conversion demands by foreigners. U. S. residents would probably not choose to convert their claims to dollars at the very time that foreigners were attempting to do just the opposite. Like foreigners, U. S. residents would value their holdings of convertible foreign currencies more highly than dollars at such a time.

Public and Private Liquid Liabilities of Foreigners. The principal liquid claims of foreigners against the United States are deposits in our banks, ownership of government securities, and the short-term debt obligations of issuers in this country other than the federal government. An increase in such liquid liabilities to foreigners decreases the external liquidity of the United States; a decrease in such holdings increases our external liquidity.

The Balance of Payments Deficit and External Liquidity. Although Table 28-1 reveals overall deficits in 1971, 1972, and 1973, in the last analysis the balance of payments must balance. In those years of deficit the balance is established by a combination of factors that results in reduced external liquidity. These factors may include the sale of gold, the loss of claims to foreign convertible currencies, a decrease in the reserve position with the International Monetary Fund, and an increase in foreign holdings of short-term claims to U. S. dollars. During a year of surplus, external liquidity is increased.

Balance of Payments Trends Since World War II

To the extent that one year's decrease in external liquidity is offset by another year's increase, little concern is warranted. Yet, decreases in external liquidity of the United States have persisted since World War II.

The Balance of Trade. During the early postwar years, exports of the United States were almost twice as great as imports. By 1971, the export surplus had ceased to exist. The general decline in export surplus in the postwar period was due mainly to the decline in exports of autos and parts, iron and steel, and petroleum products and a shift to a net import position on finished textiles. The position of the United States has remained relatively strong as a net exporter of capital equipment. There has been a declining trend in export market shares for tractors, agricultural machinery, and office machinery. Chemicals, paper, and textile yarns have enjoyed a rise in export market shares. With respect to the import side, consumer goods have risen rapidly. Much of the increase in importation of consumer goods has been in automobiles and parts, edible animal products, and petroleum. The relationship between merchandise exports and imports from 1965 through 1973 is shown in Chart 28-1.

Private Investment. The net flow of private capital investment to foreign countries has increased greatly. As of the end of the year 1973, United States foreign investment totaled well over three times the foreign investment in the United States. Although the annual increases in net United States foreign investment create an additional balance of payments deficit, the increased inflow of earnings on such investments has become one of the strongest props in the current account of the balance of payments.

Foreign Expenditures by Government. Throughout the last decade foreign expenditures by the United States government have remained approximately stable. The composition of such

Chart 28-1

EXPORTS AND IMPORTS OF MERCHANDISE: 1965–1973

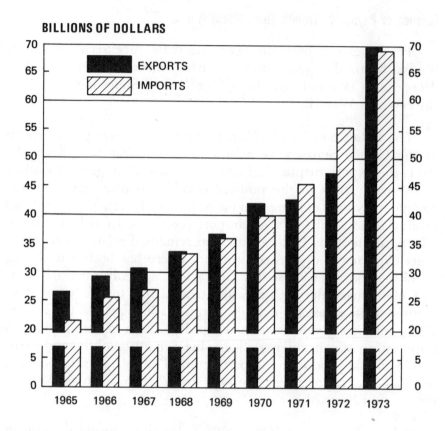

SOURCE: Dept. of Commerce, Bureau of the Census.

expenditures, the beneficiary countries, and the objectives of such expenditures, however, have changed substantially. Since the Korean War, military expenditures abroad have increased until they constituted approximately $4.6 billion annually by the end of 1973. Before the Korean War, such expenditures averaged about one half billion dollars. Military grants of aid have averaged approximately $1.5 billion annually since the Korean War. Such outlays were small in the immediate post-World War II period. Economic grants of aid, which had reached a peak of $5 billion under the Marshall Plan in 1949, have averaged about $2.2 billion annually since 1963. Economic grants of aid have been shifted from Western Europe to the underdeveloped countries of the Near East, Asia, and Latin America.

To the above expenditures should be added government loans through various agencies, including the Export-Import Bank and the Development Loan Fund. Such loans have been running at the rate of approximately $1 billion annually. Although this represents an increase in such loans, it is but a small percentage of the amounts loaned in the immediate postwar years of 1946 and 1947. It seems clear that much of the deficit in the nation's balance of payments over the years has been due to the large financial burden of expenditures for military and economic support.

The Problem of United States Balance of Payments Deficits

As we have seen, the United States balance of payments not only reflects economic trade matters but encompasses the whole of our international position. It reflects economic aid, military spending, and contributions to international political and economic institutions. And as noted in the early pages of this chapter, the symptoms of the nation's balance of payments problem are a continuing loss of gold and an increase in international claims to dollars. It is the continuation of these symptoms that offers cause for concern. Since 1958 the United States has lost approximately one half of its gold stock. Gold stocks are reduced when foreign central banks and governments convert to gold their United States bank deposits and other dollar claims. Such gold is ordinarily not removed physically from the country but becomes earmarked and held for the account of the owner in the vaults of the Federal Reserve Bank of New York. The United States gold stock as of midyear 1974 amounted to $11.6 billion, the lowest level since 1936. This gold stock still constitutes 26 percent of the monetary gold stock in the Free World.

During the period since 1958 while the nation was losing large stocks of gold, there was a spectacular increase in foreign holdings of dollar assets, mainly short-term securities and bank deposits.

Such claims increased from around $14 billion in 1958 to nearly $104 billion by midyear 1974.[1]

Economic Aid, Military Expenditures, and Investment in Foreign Countries

Most of the expenditures which led to a loss of gold had their origins during World War II when the United States assumed the economic and military leadership of the Free World. In the immediate post-World War II period, the nation's economic commitments shifted from military expenditures to that of assistance for economic reconstruction; they have now shifted back to military security and to economic aid to the developing nations of the world. The need for economic aid appears undiminished, and there seems to be little hope for reducing our international commitments for military security. Further, investments abroad by individuals and corporations of the United States have served to markedly increase foreign claims to United States dollars and to increase the deficit in the nation's current account. It is true that such investments give rise to a continuing flow of earnings; but, as noted earlier, privately owned foreign currencies are not considered part of the nation's external liquidity resources because they are not available for official use.

It is only through a large surplus in the balance of trade that the nation will be able to continue meeting its international financial commitments and its foreign investment. Until a few years ago our international commitments were borne in this way. But as the war-torn countries of the world become rehabilitated, we are encountering increased competition in foreign markets. Continuing our foreign economic aid, military expenditures, and investment in the face of declining export surpluses has resulted in a general liquidation of our financial resources, that is, our gold stock and dollar liabilities. This deterioration of our financial resources indicates the extent to which we are failing to pay for our foreign expenditures from current productive effort. Since the financial resources of the nation, as great as they continue to be, have a definite limit, it becomes obvious that the deficit must be eliminated sooner or later through an increase in the nation's export surplus, a decrease in international expenditures, or both.

---

[1] *Federal Reserve Bulletin* (Washington, D. C.: Board of Governors of the Federal Reserve System, August, 1974), p. A63.

The Requirements of International Liquidity

The solution to the nation's international financial problems is complicated by the fact that the United States dollar now plays an important role as a world currency, and thus her actions must be evaluated in terms of their impact on world trade. The phrase "requirements of international liquidity" is as impressive in substance as it is in appearance. Gold has long been the international reserve currency of the world and the basic medium of exchange in international commerce. Yet, as the volume of world trade has increased over the years, the supply of gold has failed to keep pace. Without some form of supplementary international money, the result would be international deflation. The situation may be roughly likened to the community that runs short of minor coin. Without a quick replenishment of such coin, the orderly commerce of the community would be much impaired, not to mention the difficulties the vending machine companies would have. The increasing volume of world trade requires an increase in international currency reserves.

Monetary gold stocks have increased from $35.4 billion in 1949 to approximately $45 billion as of the end of 1973. There is no prospect of especially large increases in gold production, and the International Monetary Fund has estimated the future growth of monetary gold stocks to be approximately $700 million annually. This would represent an increase in current world monetary reserves of a little less than 1.5 percent per year. The volume of international trade is expected to expand much faster, requiring an even greater reliance on supplementary monetary reserves.

It should be recognized that gold serves purposes other than as a government monetary reserve. Arts and industrial uses have increased greatly over the years as indicated by the fact that the United States consumes far more in gold than it produces. Not only have the traditional uses of gold expanded, but entirely new industrial uses have been found. For example, some of the newer spacecraft have been gold and silver plated.

In most of the nations of the world, private citizens may now hold gold. The extent of private hoarding varies with the confidence of the people in the strength of the money in which they deal. The threat of paper money inflation has invariably given rise to vast increases in private gold hoarding. To meet the

demands of people of moderate means, several foreign governments have begun to coin gold for circulation as a commodity
rather than as money. Private interests had found that conversion
of bar gold to coin brought a premium from people unable to
purchase a bar of gold.

Although the British pound sterling and the West German
mark are also used by nations as national monetary reserves, their
roles have been much less significant than that of the United
States dollar.

Chronic International Problems Become Critical

The unfavorable balance of payments problem of the United
States and the world's requirements for a growing monetary base
to meet the needs of increasing international liquidity came into
sharp focus late in the 1960's. The year-by-year growth in short-
term financial claims on the dollar resulting from our continuing
unfavorable balance of payments served foreign central banks well.
It provided them with a growing base of reserve assets. Since these
claims to United States dollars were convertible into gold at a
fixed rate, such claims were considered to be as good as gold. But
just as the annual growth of the world's monetary gold supply
was not increasing at a rapid enough rate to accommodate expanding international commerce, it was inevitable that the United
States stock of monetary gold would cease to be adequate to support the vast increase in claims against it.

Special Drawing Rights. Recognizing that the dollar could no
longer serve as a steadily increasing international money, in January, 1968, the principal nations of the world agreed to a supplementary world money—Special Drawing Rights. The Rights, sometimes referred to as "paper gold," can be created freely by the
International Monetary Fund.[2] The drawing rights are assets that

---

[2] The United Nations Monetary and Financial Conference, meeting at Bretton Woods,
New Hampshire, in the summer of 1944, proposed the establishment of the International
Monetary Fund and the International Bank for Reconstruction and Development (The
World Bank). The International Monetary Fund attempts to provide for balanced
growth of international trade and exchange stability. The "World Bank," in contrast,
promotes long-term capital loans between nations for productive purposes. Approximately 120 member nations make up the membership of these two organizations.

the participating central banks accept from one another up to specified limits. Like gold, they are claims on the world's resources and are allocated to participants in proportion to their International Monetary Fund quotas. As of mid-1974 the Special Drawing Rights could be accorded little credit in achieving the objective set out for them. The turbulent conditions in the international exchange markets prevented them from becoming accepted as an international asset. It is to be hoped that the nations of the world can ultimately come up with a new and strengthened Special Drawing Right that will be accepted as a suitable substitute for gold.

Gold. In 1968, the emphasis in international monetary circles was on national productivity as the true basis of international exchange as opposed to the historic reliance on gold. There was in fact a strong effort made to demonetize gold and to suggest that it be traded and treated as just another commodity—such as copper, tin, or soybeans. The Special Drawing Rights or paper gold created that year represented an effort to deemphasize the role of gold as an international monetary reserve asset. Also, in 1968 the central banks of the world agreed to a so-called "two-tier" gold market in which none of the governmental central banks were to buy or sell gold on the market. Official exchange rates were to continue between central banks, but since there would be no further drain of gold from the monetary stocks of central banks, there would presumably be little shifting of gold ownership among the central banks. While the official exchange rates were to prevail for gold among central banks, the price of gold was free to seek its own supply-demand level in the private markets. The United States Treasury, by terms of the agreement, could not sell gold to jewelry makers, dentists, industrial concerns, and other domestic users.

In 1971, as a result of strong inflationary pressures in the United States, our trade balance swung into deficit. Further, higher interest rates in Europe than in the United States created a torrent of capital outflows to Europe. The resulting deterioration of the dollar became so great that on August 15, 1971, the President suspended convertibility of the dollar into gold in an effort to protect our declining gold stock.

In November, 1973, the "two-tier" gold market arrangement was terminated by the central banks of six European governments and the United States. The only discernible effect of such action was to momentarily depress the price of gold in the markets of the world. Prices had risen to high speculative levels. There was little expectation that central banks would either begin to buy or sell gold.

Fixed vs. Floating International Exchange Rates. Suspension of dollar convertibility in the fall of 1971 was a monumental milepost in the deteriorating United States international monetary situation. At the same time an equally significant event was that of allowing the dollar to "float" in relation to its exchange rate with other currencies of the world. Under the previous rules of the International Monetary Fund a nation was to alter the established (or pegged) exchange ratio with other currencies only with the Fund's approval. The arguments for and against flexible exchange rates had been debated in academic circles for a dozen years as it became obvious that nations were moving steadily down the road of monetary disaster with neither the will nor desire to take corrective action until forced to do so. Under flexible exchange rates, it was contended, supply and demand would establish appropriate exchange rates between nations, and cost and price structures as well as changing monetary policy would be reflected in such supply and demand relationships.

One of the principal objections to flexibility in exchange rates is the possibility of wide swings in exchange rates in response to changes in supply and demand with a resulting uncertainty in international trade.

After only four months of floating exchange rates, this concern for international monetary stability resulted in a meeting of a group of ten representatives of central banks of leading industrial nations at the Smithsonian Institution in Washington on December 17 and 18, 1971. Out of this so-called Smithsonian Agreement came a new alignment of fixed exchange rates. Major currencies were officially revalued against the dollar and the dollar was devalued in terms of gold, bringing the price of gold to $38 per ounce. Within a very few months weaknesses in the new rate structure developed as speculative pressures caused central banks to engage in a host of defensive actions. By February 9, 1973, European exchange markets were closed because of chaotic monetary conditions. On February 12, after international consultation, the United States Treasury announced another devaluation, bringing the price of gold to $42.22 per ounce. Instead of dampening speculative activities, the second dollar devaluation caused such severe shock to confidence that the dollar again fell to its lower limit. The Smithsonian Agreement became completely inoperative by March 1, 1973, and rather than attempt to establish another realignment of fixed exchange rates the leading industrial nations decided to again let their currencies float.

Reasonable Stability Achieved

As of early 1974, the currencies of the leading countries continued to float and some stability had been achieved as the dollar again gained strength. The role of gold seems destined to increase rather than decrease as a result of the repetition of the age-old practice of governments increasing their money supply far beyond the level of productivity increases, resulting in rampant inflation. For the same reason, Special Drawing Rights, or paper gold, will probably play a lesser role as investors flee from paper money generally. The public's well justified lack of confidence in currencies generally makes it highly desirable for nations to hold gold in their reserves.

Public pressure on Congress resulted in legislation making it possible for U.S. citizens to legally buy, sell, and hold gold as of December 31, 1974, after more than forty years of prohibition against such activity. The current success of floating exchange rates is tenuous indeed. The principal weakness of floating exchange rates lies in the need for cooperation of nations in maintaining a free float. With the development of economic recession, nations are tempted to alter the rules of the game and try to adjust the rates in their favor. The term "dirty float" indicates a condition in which central banks try to have the best of both worlds by tinkering with rates otherwise established by the forces of supply and demand in international exchange.

MONETARY POLICIES AND THE BALANCE OF PAYMENTS DEFICIT

Monetary policy has long been one of the nation's important tools for economic stabilization. During periods of economic boom and inflationary pressure, monetary authorities have traditionally attempted to increase interest rates through restrictive measures on the supply of money. During periods of recession, they have attempted to lower interest rates to encourage the use of borrowed funds on the part of businessmen. It is apparent that the freedom to pursue these policies has been greatly modified by the existence of the nearly $70 billion of short-term dollar claims held by foreigners. These claims can be quickly transferred to other capital markets where interest rates may exceed those available in the United States. The Federal Reserve System is, therefore, severely restricted in its credit-ease efforts as an anti-recession measure.

Although interest rates in many foreign countries exceed those of the United States, it appears that a differential of as much as 1 or 1.5 percent between foreign rates and those of the United States is required to cause a flow of capital abroad. Aside from the withdrawal of short-term investments on the part of foreigners, there is another reason for keeping interest rates at competitive levels. When interest rates are kept low by large increases in the money supply, there may result excessive demands for loan funds, which in turn may exert an upward pressure on price levels. Such increased prices serve further to price the United States out of export markets and domestic markets as well. Actions of the Federal Reserve System must be carefully designed to retard inflationary pressures in order to maintain our balance of trade at its present level. It is necessary, therefore, to balance our domestic and international requirements.

TREASURY AND FEDERAL RESERVE FOREIGN EXCHANGE OPERATIONS

The Federal Reserve System has not limited its actions in solving the nation's balance of payments problem to its traditional tools of monetary policy. One of the activities of the System is designed to protect the dollar against the impact of occasional speculative attacks. Although international financial speculation ordinarily plays a most valuable role in the foreign exchange market by helping to correct exchange rates that are temporarily out of line, such speculation serves to aggravate the reserve position of the United States at the present time. Gold lost through a flurry of speculative activity is seldom returned to United States ownership after the speculation has run its course. On the contrary, such gold losses increase the probability of further speculation. In order to counter the impact of such speculation, the Federal Reserve System in February, 1962, began a cooperative effort with foreign central banks. The United States Treasury had begun such operations nearly a year earlier; at the present time the activities of both the Treasury and the Federal Reserve System are closely coordinated. The instructions of both organizations are carried out through the same staff members of the Federal Reserve Bank of New York.[3]

This foreign currency activity has involved the establishment of reciprocal currency arrangements with leading foreign central banks and the Bank for International Settlement in Basle, Switzerland. Under these arrangements, the Federal Reserve System borrows, or reaches agreement to borrow, on call, certain amounts of foreign currencies. Such contracts usually run for three months. At the same time, the foreign central bank acquires a similar claim on dollars for the same period of time. During the period of these contracts, each party is protected against loss in terms of its own currency from any devaluation of the other's currency. These contracts are subject to extension by agreement. A further purpose of these reciprocal contracts is to counter speculative attacks on the dollar. When the price of dollars falls relative to quotations for other currencies, Federal Reserve officials use supplies of foreign money they have borrowed to buy dollars and bid up their exchange price. The result is that short-lived speculations that would otherwise result in a loss of gold are kept under control. By the time the currency contracts expire, the Federal Reserve officials hope to have replenished their supply of foreign money in more orderly markets for resale to the contracting central bank. Although such activities do not solve the long-term

---

[3] Federal Reserve Bank of New York, *Monthly Review* (January, 1963), p. 13. See also "Treasury and Federal Reserve Foreign Exchange Operations," *Federal Reserve Bulletin* (March, 1974), pp. 191-208.

balance of payments problem, they do serve to even out the impact of sudden speculative attacks on the dollar and the losses of gold that accompany such attacks. As of February 1, 1974, agreements had been established with 14 foreign central banks and the Bank for International Settlements involving a total amount of $18,980 million. (See Table 28-2.)

Table 28-2

FEDERAL RESERVE RECIPROCAL CURRENCY ARRANGEMENTS

(In millions of dollars)

INSTITUTION	AMOUNT OF FACILITY FEBRUARY 1, 1974
Austrian National Bank	250
National Bank of Belgium	1,000
Bank of Canada	2,000
National Bank of Denmark	250
Bank of England	2,000
Bank of France	2,000
German Federal Bank	2,000
Bank of Italy	3,000
Bank of Japan	2,000
Bank of Mexico	180
Netherlands Bank	500
Bank of Norway	250
Bank of Sweden	300
Swiss National Bank	1,400
Bank for International Settlements:	
Swiss francs-dollars	600
Other authorized European currencies-dollars ..	1,250
Total	18,980

SOURCE: *Monthly Review,* Federal Reserve Bank of New York, March, 1974, p. 55.

QUESTIONS

1. Distinguish between the nation's international balance of trade and its international balance of payments.

2. Unlike the balance of trade, the balance of payments must ultimately be in a state of balance for each period. How is such balance accomplished?

3. Explain the impact on the balance of payments of United States tourists abroad; of a domestic corporation's construction of an industrial plant in France; of a foreign purchase of common stock in the United States Steel Company.

4. Describe the meaning and significance of the nation's external liquidity position.

5. Trace the changes in the United States balance of trade position since World War II.

6. Summarize the current condition of United States gold stocks. Do you observe any special problem in the future relative to these gold stocks?

7. Since banks operate successfully with but a small fraction of their total assets in the form of cash, why could not the United States government manage its international reserve position with a much smaller amount of gold than it now has on hand?

8. Describe the problem of an inadequate supply of world money (international illiquidity), and describe some of the proposals that have been offered as solutions to the problem.

9. Describe the nonmonetary uses of gold and their importance.

10. Discuss some of the limitations on monetary policy that result from the chronic deficits in the nation's international balance of payments.

11. Comment on the foreign exchange operations of the United States Treasury and the Federal Reserve System.

SUGGESTED READINGS

Business Looks at the International Monetary System. New York: The Conference Board, Inc., 1973.

HUTCHINSON, HARRY D. *Money, Banking and the United States Economy,* 2d ed. New York: Meredith Corporation, 1971. Chapter 22.

International Bank for Reconstruction and Development. Annual Reports. Washington, D.C.

International Development Association. Annual Reports. Washington, D.C.

International Finance Corporation. Annual Reports. Washington, D.C.

International Monetary Fund. Annual Reports. Washington, D.C.

KLEIN, JOHN J. *Money and the Economy,* 2d ed. New York: Harcourt Brace Jovanovich, Inc., 1970. Chapter 24.

"Treasury—Federal Reserve Foreign Exchange Operations." *Federal Reserve Bulletin* (March, 1974), pp. 191-208.

TRIFFIN, ROBERT. *Gold and the Dollar Crisis*, Rev. ed. New Haven, Connecticut: Yale University Press, 1961.

——————. *The World Money Maze*. New Haven, Connecticut: Yale University Press, 1966.

WHITTLESEY, CHARLES R., ARTHUR M. FREEDMAN, and EDWARD HERMAN. *Money and Banking*, 2d ed. New York: The Macmillan Company, 1968. Part 6.

Monetary and fiscal policies have been important factors in the economy since World War II. There has frequently been a cleavage of opinion since the end of the war as to the types of policies to follow. This led to open disagreement for a time between the Treasury and the Board of Governors of the Federal Reserve System. Even after they reached an accord, opinion was still divided at times as to the proper course to follow. In order to understand the issues involved, it is necessary to look at the financing of World War II which, in the early postwar period, gave rise to the problems that created this divergence of viewpoints.

THE PRE-WORLD WAR II MONETARY SITUATION

During the depression of the thirties, and especially after the passage in 1932 of the Glass-Steagall Act which permitted government bonds to serve as collateral for federal reserve notes, the Federal Reserve System took steps to maintain easy money conditions. Government bonds were purchased by the federal reserve banks in sufficient quantities not only to allow member banks to pay off all debts at the reserve banks but also to give them substantial excess reserves. After 1933, gold came into this country in large quantities due to the gold buying program of the Treasury. This increased reserves much faster than the banking system was able to put funds to work. As a result, in 1940 excess reserves reached almost $7 billion.[1]

MONETARY POLICY DURING WORLD WAR II

When the international situation worsened in the spring of 1939, the Federal Reserve System took steps to meet any serious disturbances in the securities markets. The Open Market Committee authorized its executive committee to make large purchases of government securities to prevent disorderly conditions in the market and to exercise an influence toward maintaining orderly conditions. When war broke out later in the year, the System purchased almost a half billion dollars of government bonds and announced that all the federal reserve banks stood ready to make advances on government securities at par to both member and nonmember banks. These actions helped to maintain an orderly market in government securities.

As our country increased the production of war material and as European countries bought large quantities of such goods here, the purchasing power of civilians expanded faster than did the supply of consumer goods, thus creating inflationary pressures. The Board of Governors helped to restrain these pressures by raising reserve requirements to the legal limits in the fall of 1941.

When the United States entered the war in December, 1941, the financing of war expenditures became the major concern of the Treasury and the Board of Governors of the Federal Reserve System. In order to accomplish this end, the Federal Reserve System had two primary objectives: (1) to maintain relative stability in the market for government securities so as to make sufficient funds available to the Treasury at low interest rates, and (2) to restrict the creation of purchasing power to the lowest amount consistent with the first objective.[2]

---

[1] Karl R. Bopp and others, *Federal Reserve Policy* (Washington, D. C.: Federal Reserve System, 1947), p. 13.

[2] *Ibid.*

To emphasize its willingness and ability to supply all the funds needed to meet the needs of the government and of private business, the following statement was issued by the Federal Reserve Board shortly after the United States entered the war:

> The financial and banking mechanism of the country is today in a stronger position to meet any emergency than ever before.
>
> The existing supply of funds and of bank reserves is fully adequate to meet all present and prospective needs of the Government and of private activity. The Federal Reserve System has powers to add to these resources to whatever extent may be required in the future.
>
> The System is prepared to use its powers to assure that an ample supply of funds is available at all times for financing the war effort and to exert its influence toward maintaining conditions in the United States Government security market that are satisfactory from the standpoint of the Government's requirements.
>
> Continuing the policy which was announced following the outbreak of war in Europe, Federal Reserve Banks stand ready to advance funds on United States Government securities at par to all banks.[3]

Interest-Rate Pattern

Another step to meet the needs of the government for funds was an agreement with the Treasury on a pattern of interest rates that would be maintained by Federal Reserve open-market operations. It was decided to stabilize rates to keep down the cost of borrowing and also to remove any incentive to wait for higher rates later instead of buying bonds when funds were available.

The pattern agreed on was much the same as that prevailing during the depressed period of the thirties. The rate was fixed at ⅜ percent on 90-day bills, ⅞ percent on certificates of indebtedness, 2 percent on 8-year to 10-year bonds, and 2½ percent on the 15-year maturities.

Having agreed on this pattern for financing the war, the Federal Reserve System took steps to maintain such a pattern. To maintain the ⅜ percent rate on bills, the federal reserve banks announced that they would purchase any quantity of such bills offered in the market at a price necessary to maintain that rate. They also agreed to give the seller an option to repurchase his bills at the same rate. This, in effect, made bills as liquid as

---

[3] *Ibid.*, pp. 18, 19.

cash and enabled the banks to invest their excess reserves at ⅜ percent. This kept excess reserves in banks at a minimum.

Rates on other securities were prevented from rising by open-market purchases of securities of all issues in amounts large enough to keep the price at par or above. To help encourage bank participation in war financing, discount rates were set at 1 percent. On advances secured by government securities that were due or callable in one year or less, a preferential rate of ½ percent was set. This was to encourage banks to invest in short-term government securities.

Shift to Longer Maturity Bonds

As the war went on, there were strong incentives for banks to purchase bonds of longer maturities. The deposits of most banks were rising due to the increased business and money supplies resulting from war production, and they invested them in what they considered to be a balanced proportion between bonds of various maturities. As they needed reserves, they tended to sell the shorter issues, and thus they increased their proportion of long-term bonds.

Nonbank investors and some banks consciously adopted a policy of carrying mostly longer-term bonds. They felt that if a pattern of rates was to be maintained through open-market operations, all maturities would be equally liquid since the investor was assured of being able to sell them at any time at par or better. This gave them the advantage of higher interest rates on the long-term bonds for funds intended for short-term investment.

There was another advantage to holding longer issues for a period of time. As they approached maturity, the price went up, due to increased demand since such bonds were now attractive to investors who had money to invest for only a short period of time. The price increased until the rate of return on them was brought into line with that on securities of shorter duration. Therefore, some institutions and individuals bought longer maturities, sold them later at a premium, and bought newly issued long-term issues. This process aptly became known as *playing the pattern of rates*.

Federal Reserve System Bond Purchases

The process of maintaining rates forced the Reserve System to buy large quantities of short-term securities. The large volume of short-term securities issued by the Treasury also led to almost continuous refunding operations. To sell all of the securities needed required either interest rates high enough to meet the demands of the market or a continuous increase in the money supply. The latter course was followed as reserves were supplied by open-market purchases, especially of short-maturity securities.

The details of this process are interesting since they show how the banking system was used to inflate the money supply. Many banks were designated as special depositaries in which the Treasury kept war-loan accounts. Such a bank could pay for new issues of government securities purchased for its own account or for the account of its customers by crediting the war-loan account rather than transferring the funds to the federal reserve bank. These accounts were made exempt from reserve requirements and were not assessed for deposit insurance in order to encourage their use to the fullest extent. After this was done, a bank no longer needed additional reserves against deposits resulting from its own purchases of government securities. When its customers bought bonds, reserves were freed as the funds were shifted out of regular deposit accounts to reserve-free war-loan accounts. These excess reserves were used by the banks to buy government securities. As the government spent its funds, deposits were shifted from war-loan accounts to regular deposit accounts requiring reserves. To get the necessary reserves, banks sold securities, especially the short-term ones. These were bought by the Federal Reserve System to maintain the pattern of rates, and thus new reserves were created and the money supply increased.

Bank Purchases of Securities

Even though it was part of the Treasury policy to sell as many bonds as possible to nonbank investors and banks were practically excluded from the last six bond drives, banks still bought large quantities of securities. During bond drives, savings institutions and other corporations sold bonds they held, and these were bought by banks. These bonds were usually sold at a premium, and the sellers then bought bonds of the new issues at par. The real result of the war-bond drives was an expansion of bank credit even though banks were excluded from the direct purchase of securities from the Treasury. As the government spent the money it raised during a bond drive, that money was deposited in the accounts of businesses and individuals. The increase in deposits increased the amount of reserves required to be held against these deposits. The banks obtained the money for the additional reserves by selling some of their government securities to the Federal Reserve. Thus, in the final analysis, the Federal Reserve supplied a large quantity of the primary reserves that made the whole operation possible.

This was a case of wartime money inflation just as definitely as the continental currency or greenback inflation, but the process was more complex and, hence, less generally understood. It is true that after the third bond drive the Federal Reserve discouraged banks from participating unnecessarily in the absorption of government securities. As long as the pattern of interest rates made expansion of bank credit profitable, however, it was not unusual that many bonds were bought by the commercial banks and the Federal Reserve System when individuals and institutions found it desirable to dispose of them at premium.

Effects of War Financing

The magnitude of war financing changed the whole character of the financial structure of the American economy. The federal debt increased from somewhat over $40 billion in 1939 to nearly $280 billion in February, 1946, a sevenfold increase. The total was so large that it exceeded the total of all other regular debts. Some idea of the magnitude may be gained from the fact that interest payments on this debt were larger than total government receipts in any peacetime year before 1941.[4]

Not only did the government become the biggest factor in the demand for funds, but also government bonds assumed a new

---

[4] Charles Cortez Abbott, *The Federal Debt* (New York: The Twentieth Century Fund, 1953), p. 3.

and often dominant importance in the investment of many institutions. Government securities were 26 percent of the assets of member banks of the Federal Reserve System in December, 1939, but they had gone up to 57 percent at the end of 1945. They were 18 percent of the assets of legal reserve life insurance companies in the earlier year and 46 percent in the latter year. The proportion of funds of the federal reserve banks in government securities increased from 14 percent to 54 percent during the same period.

Government securities also increased in importance as an investment medium for liquid assets. Financial business corporations, such as real estate companies, finance companies, and investment companies, had 29 percent of liquid assets in government securities at the end of 1939 and 56 percent at the end of 1945. The proportion of liquid assets of regular business corporations invested in government securities increased from 14 percent to 46 percent during the same period, and that of unincorporated businesses from 17 percent to 36 percent.[5]

EARLY POSTWAR MONETARY PROBLEMS AND POLICIES

It may seem in retrospect that at the end of World War II steps should have been taken to reduce the money supply or at least not to allow it to increase further. Many governmental officials were afraid to tighten credit, however, because of the fear of a major depression. It had taken the demands of all-out war to eliminate the persistent large-scale unemployment of the thirties. Now government spending was to be cut from $100 billion a year to $40 billion or even less. Predictions were common that as many as eight million would be unemployed in 1946.

The rapid reconversion from war production to consumer goods production, however, was almost as miraculous an achievement as the rapid buildup of production to meet the needs of war. Consumers had buying power and pent-up desires for goods from the wartime period and spent it on goods as fast as they were available. The government also failed to cut expenditures as fast or as far as some had predicted. As a result, there was no depression in the early postwar period.

---

[5] *Ibid.*, p. 18.

Situation in 1946 and 1947

Practically all economic controls were abandoned in 1946, however, and prices went up sharply through 1947 and until the fall of 1948. Price controls had held prices in check sufficiently so that wholesale prices rose from 79 to only 107 (1926 = 100) during the war. By early 1948, they had increased to 170.[6]

Even though economic controls were abandoned quickly, monetary policies changed slowly. This was due in part to economic uncertainty and to fears of a postwar depression. The new situation in which government bonds dominated the market also led to cautious action as both the Federal Reserve System and the Treasury Department were working out policies under these changed conditions. There was also a reluctance to do anything that might unsettle the security markets since the large volume of government securities with short maturities called for frequent large refunding operations.

The action of Congress was also on the inflationary side. Controls were abandoned, and in 1948 taxes were cut sufficiently to increase the amount of money available for consumer spending by over $5 billion.

Action was gradually taken, however, to get away from the wartime pattern of interest rates. In the summer of 1946, the preferential discount rate on advances secured by short-term government securities was discontinued. This had no immediate effect on the market since banks were not borrowing, but the action was opposed for a time by the Treasury for fear it might unsettle the market for government securities. It was the middle of 1947 before the buying of Treasury bills at a price to yield ⅜ percent was discontinued, and it was some time after that before yields on certificates of indebtedness were allowed to rise. Treasury bills were then allowed to rise in yield from ⅜ to over 1 percent, and certificates from ⅞ percent to 1¼ percent. Long-term government bonds, however, continued to be supported; but the support price was dropped to near par from levels that had been as high as 108.[7]

---

[6] E. A. Goldenwiser, *Monetary Management* (New York: McGraw-Hill Book Company, Inc., 1949), p. 75.
[7] *Ibid.*, p. 78.

Retirement of Bank-Held Debt

One of the factors that restrained credit expansion in 1946 and 1947 was the retirement of bank-held debt by the Treasury. The Victory Loan in the fall of 1945 had been oversubscribed, and this gave the government an unusually large cash balance. Furthermore, the Treasury did not need as much cash after the war as it did during the war. Treasury balances were used to retire bank-held debt, and the record shows that there was a contraction of bank credit. The effect was largely on the books, since the funds from the bond sale had not been used and were now again offset against the bonds. It did, however, reduce an inflationary potential, which would have become real if the funds had been spent. A Treasury surplus in 1947 was also used to retire bank-held debt, and this restrained inflationary pressures.

As the money supply was being cut by government action, however, it was being expanded by business borrowing. From a level of under $20 billion in 1943, bank loans rose to almost $40 billion early in 1948. The net result was that, except for the reduction of the large government deposit accounts built up to meet war needs, the volume of money after allowing for seasonal fluctuations expanded continuously until early 1948.

The Situation in 1948

By the middle of 1948, inflationary pressures were again strong. Tax reduction had increased consumer expenditures, world tension led to higher military expenditures by the government, and large sums were also appropriated for foreign aid. Since the Treasury no longer had excess cash balances and since no substantial surpluses were in sight, there was no hope for restraint from this area. The Federal Reserve System, which held over $20 billion in government securities, was technically in a position to tighten the money supply by bond sales. The policy, however, was one of attempting to hold the money supply about constant so as to avoid deflation as well as inflation.

A new situation developed, however, in the summer and fall of 1948. Insurance companies and other financial institutions sold large amounts of government bonds in order to invest in mortgages and corporate bonds at more attractive interest rates. Commercial banks bought many of these bonds, and the Federal Reserve had to buy most of the remainder of these bonds to prevent them from dropping below par. The commercial banks then sold short-term securities in order to get the funds to buy the longer-term bonds, and the Federal Reserve was also forced to buy many of these to carry out its policy of maintaining an orderly market for government securities. The Federal Reserve made every effort to sell short-term securities to keep total bank reserves from increasing materially, but this made it impossible to make bank credit tighter to reduce inflationary pressures.

To offset these conditions, Congress was asked to give the Federal Reserve additional powers. An increase in required reserves of 4 points on demand deposits and 1½ points on time deposits was authorized by a special session of Congress in the summer of 1948. This increased the maximum level to which reserve requirements could be raised on demand deposits of member banks to 30 percent for central reserve city banks, 24 percent for reserve city banks, and 18 percent for country banks. The new maximum on time deposits was 7½ percent for all member banks. This action enabled the Federal Reserve System to absorb more government bonds so as to keep the market above par and to offset the additions to bank reserves by raising reserve requirements. The Federal Reserve also asked for power to set additional reserve requirements in government bonds, but Congress refused to act upon this request.

The Federal Reserve System handled a large volume of government securities in 1947 and 1948 as it bought bonds of longer maturities and sold shorter-term obligations. Total transactions of government securities in those two years amounted to almost $80 billion, but the net change in the total portfolio was small.

Inflationary pressures abated late in 1948 as the increase in government expenditures slowed down and as private borrowing for capital expansion and especially for increasing inventories decreased. There was a minor recession in business activity in 1949, but consumer expenditures did not decrease appreciably. To ease money conditions, reserves were reduced in May and June of 1949 and again in August. This reduction in reserves freed bank funds, and the demand for government bonds on the part of banks increased. Bond prices rose, and yields on short-term securities fell. The Federal Reserve System moderated this increase by selling a part of its portfolio of securities.

Federal Reserve Action in Early 1950

As business again picked up in the early part of 1950, the Federal Reserve System acted to tighten money supplies. Insurance companies, pension funds, and personal trusts had funds available for long-term investment from extensive current savings and also as a backlog from past accumulations. To take some of these funds off the market so as to prevent overextension of private long-term financing, the Federal Reserve sold a substantial amount of long-term government bonds not eligible for bank holding, thus reducing the supply of funds in the market.

MONETARY PROBLEMS AND POLICIES FROM THE KOREAN WAR TO THE VIETNAM WAR

When the Korean War started in June of 1950, the increased demand for goods led to renewed inflationary pressures. Government deficits were not the cause of price rises in the last half of 1950, since the Treasury had an excess of cash income over cash outgo in the last half of the year of almost a billion dollars. The explanation lies in private spending. Consumers, fearing the shortages of World War II, spent large sums on various types of durable and semidurable goods. Business also spent heavily for inventories and for capital investment. The annual rate of gross private domestic investment went up over $12 billion from the second to the fourth quarter of 1950. Loans of insured commercial banks rose nearly $7.5 billion from June to December.[8] Life insurance companies also supplied long-term funds by selling government bonds and putting the funds in mortgages and corporate obligations.

Treasury-Federal Reserve Controversy

Under these conditions, reserve bank credit increased materially. The Board of Governors of the Federal Reserve System

---

[8] Abbott, *op. cit.*, pp. 92, 93.

wanted to act to restrict expansion, but it could not so long as it felt obligated to support the bond market by buying all government securities at par or better. The Treasury wanted to follow a pattern of low rates as it did in World War II; and this, of course, required price-support operations, since interest rates would have gone up in a free market as the demand for funds increased.

The controversy between the Treasury and Federal Reserve System developed into an open conflict in the summer of 1950, especially after the Reserve System had to engage in larger-scale open-market operations to assure the success of some financing at a rate the market did not find attractive. When the Secretary of the Treasury stated in a speech in January, 1951, that the Treasury had not changed its position and was not willing to allow even fractional increases in interest rates, the controversy became acute. Not only Federal Reserve officials but the press and the members of Congress entered it. Such a situation could not last long, and the President appointed a committee to study ways and means to provide the necessary restraint on private credit expansion and at the same time to maintain stability in the market for government securities. Before this committee could report, however, an agreement between the Treasury and the Federal Reserve System was announced in March, 1951.

Basis of the Opposing Viewpoints

Before looking at this agreement, it is desirable to see the basis of the opposing viewpoints. Treasury officials were interested in keeping interest rates on the debt at a low level. They favored low rates not only to keep the cost of servicing the debt at a minimum but also from a belief that low interest rates were necessary to keep investment in plant, equipment, housing, local public works, and the like at high levels. The Treasury also emphasized orderly conditions in the bond markets since stable interest rates were as important for debt management as low interest rates. The Treasury officials believed that the emergency arising out of the Korean War should be met by direct controls such as material allocation, rationing, and price controls.

Federal Reserve officials felt that in the absence of all-out war such controls were unnecessary if proper monetary and fiscal policies were followed. They believed that if the government kept cash outgo and income reasonably in balance, monetary controls would be sufficient to prevent inflation. Such a course would also prevent the building up of idle funds by consumers as was done during World War II, causing inflationary pressures when controls were taken off.

The Accord

The accord that was announced in March, 1951, was designed to check credit expansion without the use of direct controls. One direct result of the accord was the offer to exchange long-term 2½ percent bonds that were being sold to the Federal Reserve in quantities for a nonmarketable 29-year issue at 2¾ percent. Although these bonds were nonmarketable, they could be exchanged at the option of the holder into marketable 5-year 1½ percent notes. After this time government bonds were no longer bought in the market by the Federal Reserve to the same degree as before, and the price pegs were no longer rigidly adhered to. Toward the end of the year, the longest-term government bonds had dropped to below 97 in a free market.

The Federal Reserve did not stay out of the market completely but continued to buy and sell some securities so as to maintain an orderly market. As the private demand for funds increased due to a boom in residential building and in the capital markets, interest rates rose and long-term securities dropped further.

Policies from the Accord to the 1957 Recession

The Republican Administration elected in November, 1952, followed the same general line of policies reached in the accord in the spring of 1951. They decided to issue long-term government securities whenever funds were available in the market. Early in 1953 the Treasury issued 30-year bonds at 3¼ percent. As available funds were already at a low level, this helped to tighten the money markets and to raise interest rates.

The Federal Reserve also acted to restrict credit in the early part of 1953. There was much debate about the correctness of monetary policies during this period. Many felt that credit was restricted too severely and that the Federal Reserve would be forced to return to a policy of fixed interest rates. Therefore, the Federal Reserve acted in early 1953 to convince investors and dealers in government securities that it was not undertaking to peg interest rates and especially not rates on intermediate- and long-term securities. It did so by announcing in April, 1953, that until further notice open-market operations would be carried on only in the short-term area where operations would have the least market impact. Operations in other markets would be undertaken only when disorderly conditions arose and then only to the extent needed to correct such conditions. The arguments for and against this "bills only" policy were discussed in Chapter 23.

Since it was not the policy of the Federal Reserve authorities to force deflation, reserve requirements were lowered in the early summer to provide the funds needed to meet a sizable government deficit. As funds were needed for seasonal use, the Federal Reserve System bought government securities to provide such funds. When signs appeared during the summer that a business readjustment was in prospect, credit was eased still further. As business turned down somewhat in a minor recession, the Federal Reserve used all the instruments at its command to reverse the recession. The reserve banks reduced discount rates, the Board of Governors reduced member bank reserve requirements, and the Open Market Committee acted to maintain more than adequate reserves. Under this policy of "active ease," the free reserves of member banks rose materially.

This policy of active ease was followed during most of 1954. As a result, interest rates dropped to the lowest level in several years. This reduction did not prevent a slight decline in short-term business loans or consumer loans during the year, but it did help increase loans on real estate materially and, thus, activity in the home building field.

Business started to expand late in 1954 and continued upward in 1955. When it became apparent that a business boom was developing, steps were again taken to restrict credit. The Open Market Committee reduced the holdings of government securities.

Discount rates were increased in April and May and again several times later on in the year. Margin requirements on stock purchases were also raised, first to 60 percent and then to 70 percent. By the last quarter of the year, borrowing from the federal reserve banks exceeded excess reserves by $350 million.[9] As credit became more and more restricted, interest rates rose, especially short-term and intermediate-term rates.

There was little question raised about this reversal of policy from credit ease to credit restraint during most of 1955. When more price pressures developed in 1956, the Federal Reserve acted to tighten credit still further. The rediscount rate was raised again, and general tightness of credit was maintained through open-market operations.

The advance in general economic activity was slowed materially in 1956, due especially to fewer automobile sales and some decrease in residential building. For a time it appeared as if a new controversy might develop when the Secretary of the Treasury stated publicly that he felt that the last increase in the rediscount rate was not only unwise but might lead to a downturn in business. Businessmen in various lines also questioned the policy of credit restriction. The Federal Reserve made credit somewhat easier in early summer of that year through open-market operations, but it did not believe that economic conditions at the time called for a major reversal in policy. Economic activity, however, continued upward in 1956 as business capital expenditures increased to record levels. Economic activity continued to expand during the first three quarters of 1957 as business capital expenditures continued to increase and state and local government expenditures kept on increasing.

Beginning in 1956 and through 1957, wholesale prices and prices of consumer goods began to advance after having been more or less stable for several years. To hold inflationary forces in check, the Federal Reserve followed a policy of active restraint through open-market operations and also by raising the rediscount rate on several occasions. Their policies were designed to curb the price rises and speculative excesses at the top of a cycle. They were also designed to counter what the Chairman of the Board of Governors referred to as "the alarming spread of the

---

[9] *Federal Reserve Bulletin,* February, 1956, p. 101.

belief, not only in this country but also abroad, that creeping inflation under modern economic conditions was to be a chronic and unavoidable condition." [10]

The inflation during this expansion period was of a somewhat different nature from that in the early postwar period. It did not result from a demand pull in the main but was a result of a cost push and primarily a wage push. This made traditional tools of monetary policy less effective than they would have been against inflation of the more usual type. In trying to stem this type of inflation by the use of its regular monetary instruments, the Federal Reserve was forced to use more active restraint than many felt was in the best interest of the economy. Even with such restraint it was impossible to halt inflation completely, and a significant rise in prices took place. Federal Reserve policy during the whole period of expansion was marked by an independence from the policies and actions of the Treasury. It was also carried on without regard to criticism that was at times vociferous in the business community and in Congress.

In the late fall of 1957 business began to decline, and Federal Reserve policy shifted from restraining credit to making credit easier and cheaper to obtain. The policy was applied cautiously, however, since price rises continued in the early stages of the downturn.

Policies from 1958 to Mid-1965

The depression which began in 1957 was a short one, and by late spring of 1958 the economy was again moving forward. By late summer the Federal Reserve began to restrict credit expansion and continued to do so in the first half of 1959 when it appeared for a time that a real boom would develop. The economy suffered a severe setback when the longest steel strike on record began shortly after midyear. When the strike ended in November, there was a new surge of economic activity, and the economy reached new highs. In the second half of 1960, a fourth postwar recession began, but it was also short and mild. The

---

[10] In a statement by William McChesney Martin, Jr., Chairman, Board of Governors of the Federal Reserve System, before the Joint Economic Committee of Congress, February 6, 1958.

Federal Reserve relaxed pressures on the money supply early in 1960, and again in the second half of 1961. Monetary policy remained expansionary throughout the period until mid-1965.

Federal Reserve policy in the period from 1958 to 1963 was governed by the changing nature of economic developments. Inflation was no longer the major economic problem, at least not in the short run. All basic commodities were in good supply, and business and consumers had a good stock of durable goods. Excess capacity existed in many industrial fields, and labor was not fully utilized. The wholesale price level in the spring of 1965 stood at about the same level as in 1958, and consumer prices had increased only about one percent a year during this period.[11] Part of this small increase was probably spurious since the consumer price index cannot accurately measure short-run changes in the quality of goods and services.

Two major factors governed Federal Reserve policy during this period and especially after 1960. The first was the recurring deficits in the United States balance of payments, and the second was the problem of underutilization of resources and especially the problem of unemployment. The United States had a sizable deficit in its balance of payments in each year during this period. In 1960 this problem was aggravated by a substantial flow of short-term funds from the United States to foreign money centers. This outflow was due, in part at least, to lower interest rates here than abroad. Interest rates had dropped here as a result of the policy of monetary ease to combat the recession.

This situation presented a dilemma for Federal Reserve policy makers. If they continued to buy Treasury bills, they might drive short-term interest rates so low as to encourage a greater outflow of funds. But if no additional funds were provided to the banking system, the Federal Reserve could not make its maximum contribution to stimulating the domestic economy. This led the Federal Reserve in late October, 1960, to provide additional reserves to stimulate the economy by buying certificates, notes, and bonds maturing within 15 months instead of buying Treasury bills. The Federal Reserve has since that time bought and sold such securities on a number of occasions. In addition to carrying

---

[11] *Federal Reserve Bulletin,* September, 1968, p. A64.

on open-market operations in securities other than Treasury bills, the Federal Reserve began in 1961 to carry on operations in foreign securities and to develop reciprocal currency agreements with foreign central banks as described in Chapter 28. These policies slowed down the outflow of funds, but the deficit in the balance of payments had not been corrected by the end of 1965.

The second major influence on Federal Reserve policy was the problem of unemployment and underutilization of other resources, especially capital equipment in many industries. The problem was more than a cyclical one since, as industrial output increased during this period, the number of jobs declined. Increased technology was replacing men with machines at a faster rate than the economy was growing to absorb them. Monetary policy alone could not solve this problem, and the situation was complicated by the balance of payments problem. This problem cannot be solved only by stimulating growth, even though this is essential; it requires retraining and upgrading of large segments of the labor force. Therefore, the Federal Reserve kept credit relatively easy but did not flood the banking system with reserves since to do so would have led to renewed inflation. Fiscal policy was also used to expand the level of economic activity during this period. In 1962 the investment tax credit was enacted, and depreciation guidelines were liberalized to stimulate investment expenditures. In early 1964 personal and corporate income taxes were cut significantly, part of the cut becoming effective in 1964 and part in 1965. In response to expansionary monetary and fiscal policies during this period, real gross national product rose at an average rate somewhat over 5 percent per year, while prices rose only a little over one percent. Unemployment dropped gradually, but was still 4.5 percent of the labor force in 1965.[12]

THE VIETNAM WAR AND POSTWAR PERIOD

In mid-1965 the economy entered a new period of inflationary pressures due to increased military spending resulting from the escalation of the war in Vietnam. These expenditures, added to rising expenditures for plant and equipment and to increased

---

[12] *Ibid.*, p. A62.

spending for inventories, led to greatly increased demands for funds, to labor shortages, and to price increases. The Federal Reserve took steps to restrict bank credit expansion, and interest rates moved up. Since little was done to impose fiscal restraint, the burden of restraining inflation fell on monetary policy. Monetary policy became progressively tighter during the first half of 1966, and interest rates reached the highest level in forty years. Savings which normally were deposited in savings and loan associations and mutual savings banks were, to a large extent, invested directly into money market securities which paid a higher rate; as a result, the mortgage market was seriously short of funds. Residential construction was cut sharply and some unemployment developed in the construction field. This period has been referred to as the period of the "credit crunch."

There were some signs in the fall that the overheated economy was beginning to cool off, but prices continued to rise. In October, 1966, the investment tax credit was suspended to help restrict expansion of plant and equipment expenditures. Economic activity began to moderate and GNP remained about level during the first quarter of 1967 and rose little during the second quarter, and industrial production dropped somewhat. Monetary policy became progressively easier beginning in November, 1966, and fiscal policy also played a contracyclical role in 1967 when funds that had been withheld from the highway program were released. The investment tax credit was reinstated, more mortgage funds were made available through FNMA, and veterans' insurance dividend payments were speeded up. There was a very sharp recovery in economic activity in the second half of 1967. Monetary policy remained relatively easy until late in the year when a move was made to moderate restraint to help restrain price advances.

Inflationary pressures became greater in 1968 due to increased private spending but primarily to greatly increased federal government expenditures, which resulted in a deficit in excess of $25 billion in the federal budget in fiscal 1968.[13] The President asked for a surtax to be added to personal and corporate income taxes in the summer of 1967, but Congress took no action until June, 1968. At this time a 10 percent surtax was enacted and a ceiling

---

[13] *Ibid.,* p. A38.

was placed on federal government expenditures. There was a general feeling that this fiscal action would lead to a substantial reduction in economic activity, and monetary policy was eased after midyear to cushion the blow. The economy continued to expand rapidly, however, and prices continued upward. The consumer price index rose over 5 percent during 1968. Beginning in December, 1968, the Federal Reserve again moved to a policy of active restraint since it was now apparent that fiscal policy was having little, if any, restraining effect on economic activity.

Inflation continued in 1969 at an accelerated rate. Wholesale prices rose sharply in the first quarter, and the consumer price index rose at its sharpest level in years. This renewed inflation was not due primarily to federal government spending, since the budget for fiscal 1969 showed a small surplus. But business expenditures on new plant and equipment were up sharply; and private spending, in general, continued to increase rapidly. By midyear the Federal Reserve was following a policy of severe restraint on the money and credit markets, which in some respects was greater than the restraint in 1966. Interest rates rose to higher levels than in 1966 and in some cases were the highest since Civil War days. Capital spending was decreased somewhat from plans announced earlier in the year, but continued at very high levels. Credit for mortgage financing was again decreased and housing starts declined.

The economy suffered a period of recession beginning in late 1969 and continuing through almost all of 1970. This recession was to a large extent due to the restrictive credit policy followed in late 1968 and 1969 in an attempt to slow the rate of inflation. It appears in retrospect that monetary policy was too restrictive in 1966 and too easy in 1967. It should have been much more restrictive during most of 1968 when it was relaxed to partially cushion the effects of fiscal policy. As a result monetary policy had to be too restrictive in 1969 and the effects of this policy helped bring on a recession.

The recession of 1969-70 was unusually mild and recovery began near the end of 1970. To slow the decrease in economic activity and to stimulate recovery, the Federal Reserve adopted a policy of credit ease. Inflationary pressures were so strong, however, that prices continued to increase even during the recession.

The economy entered into a period of slow recovery in 1971 under the stimulus of a rapidly increasing money supply in the first half of the year. Prices moved up sharply, the consumer price index increasing by more than five percent during the year. To combat inflation, the President ordered a 90-day price freeze in mid-August and set up wage and price controls when the freeze ended. The goal was to cut price increases to an average of 2.5 percent per year while wages rose on an average by 5.5 percent. This was based on the assumption that average productivity in the economy would increase at a 3 percent rate per year. To help restrain prices, the growth rate of the money supply was cut materially after midyear.

The economy continued to have balance of payments problems which had persisted for several years. In order to correct what appeared to be a basic unbalance in the relationship of the dollar to major foreign currencies, the dollar was devalued in December of 1971 by 12 percent.

Recovery in economic activity accelerated in 1972 and by the end of the year real growth was increasing at a rapid rate. Consumer prices went up by only about 3.5 percent, the best year for price restraint since 1967. This was due in large measure to price and wage controls. Federal Reserve monetary policy was expansive in the early part of the year, but late in 1972 money growth was slowed due to renewed inflationary pressures.

These inflationary pressures continued and became greater in 1973, a year in which consumer prices increased some 9 percent. It looked early in the year as if 1973 might be a good year for the economy. American involvement in the Vietnam War ended early in the year, the dollar was devalued by 10 percent in February, and the balance-of-payments problem seemed to be on the way to solution as America again developed a surplus in its trade balance with the rest of the world. Price controls of a mandatory nature were replaced in January with more-or-less voluntary controls. The growth of Federal Reserve credit was slowed and the federal government had a surplus by the second quarter of the year.

However, economic activity increased at a rapid rate and demand in many fields was in excess of supply. Price controls also led to dislocations in many sectors of the economy, thus adding to shortages in some areas. Prices moved up so rapidly that a new

60-day price freeze was put into effect in June, and at the end of this period prices were again frozen but were allowed to be increased for the exact amount of higher costs. Provisions were made for decontrol on an industry-by-industry basis.

The price situation got worse as the year progressed for several reasons. There were poor crops in many parts of the world, which raised the prices of food products. Large amounts of wheat were sold to Russia and China and this led to rapid increases in grain prices. In October another Arab-Israeli War broke out, but it was of short duration. The Arabs, however, in order to put pressure on the United States and other countries to support their cause put an embargo on oil shipments and raised oil prices. The embargo was lifted after a time but prices were raised to several times their prewar levels. As the demand for credit remained high, the supply of credit was restricted, and investors feared continued inflation as interest rates reached unprecedented levels.

High interest rates and tighter credit would probably have led to some slowing in economic activity in 1974; but the oil crisis compounded the problem since it affected production in many industries based on petroleum products. The gasoline shortage also led to reduced automobile sales, especially of full-sized cars. High interest rates led to a major decrease in residential construction and slowed some other plans for expansion.

Price controls were removed in April, not because inflation was under control, but because of the widespread belief that controls were a failure. Prices moved up after decontrol and price pressures intensified when the midwest farm belt was hit by a severe drought. By summer, prices were increasing at a faster rate than at almost any time since World War I days and interest rates reached new historic highs. The economy suffered a decline in real growth and was in a state of recession at the end of the year. Inflationary pressures were strong in all industrial nations and prospects were for continued inflation and recession into 1975. By early 1975 there were indications that the recession would be the most severe of those in the post-World War II period. Monetary and fiscal policies could not be used to maximum effectiveness to counter recession because of the continuing problems of inflation and balance of payments.

QUESTIONS

1. Describe the monetary situation prior to World War II.

2. What were the primary objectives of the Federal Reserve System in its policies designed to aid in financing the war?

3. Describe the interest-rate pattern the Federal Reserve System and the Treasury agreed on for financing the war. How was this pattern maintained?

4. Why did many individuals and institutions carry mostly long-term bonds during the war?

5. Describe the process of playing the pattern of rates.

6. Describe the process by which bond sales led to credit creation during World War II.

7. Describe the effects of war financing on the financial structure of the American economy.

8. Describe the economic and financial situation in the immediate postwar period. What was the role of monetary policy in this period?

9. Why were inflationary pressures strong in 1948? What steps were taken to combat them?

10. What was the major cause of inflation during the Korean War?

11. Describe the Treasury-Federal Reserve controversy during this period. Discuss the opposing viewpoints. What was the nature of the accord they reached?

12. Describe the monetary policies followed during the early first part of 1953 by the Republican Administration and the policies of the Federal Reserve System.

13. Why was a policy of active ease adopted in the second half of 1953 and followed during most of 1954?

14. Describe and evaluate Federal Reserve policy during the prosperity period from late 1954 to late 1957.

15. How did Federal Reserve policy in the 1958-1963 period differ from that in 1954-1957? Why?

16. Review monetary and fiscal policy during the period from mid-1965 to the 1969-70 recession. Evaluate policy decisions during this period.

17. Describe the inflationary period of 1973-74 and discuss the factors which led to it.

SUGGESTED READINGS

Board of Governors of the Federal Reserve System. Annual reports.

BOWSHER, NORMAN N. "1973—A Year of Inflation." *Review,* Federal Reserve Bank of St. Louis (December, 1973), pp. 2-14.

Federal Reserve Bank of New York. Annual reports.

Monetary Policy and Management of the Public Debt. United States Congress, Joint Committee on the Economic Report Subcommittee on General Credit Control and Debt Management. Washington: Government Printing Office, 1952.

"1971: A Year of Reluctant Recovery." *Federal Reserve Bulletin* (January, 1972), pp. 1-14.

"1972: A Year of Accelerating Recovery." *Federal Reserve Bulletin* (January, 1973), pp. 1-11.

"Review and Outlook: 1973-74." *Economic Review,* Federal Reserve Bank of Cleveland (January, 1974), pp. 3-31.

Index